PRAISE FOR
MODEL

"Rewarding . . . highly enjoyable, perhaps unprecedented. The definitive work of the Barbizon school." —*New York Times Book Review*

"Sensational. . . . Reveals the steamy secrets of the superbabes. . . . Delivers everything." —*New York Daily News*

"Staggeringly well-researched. . . . Hideously fascinating." —*Cosmopolitan*

"A book stripping models bare has electrified fashion. . . . Lurid stories of sex, drugs, rock, and frocks." —*International Herald Tribune*

"A relentless evisceration of an industry normally swathed in more shadows and light than Cindy Crawford." —*Entertainment Weekly*

"One long, scurrilously detailed dish. . . . A chewy read." —*Harper's Bazaar*

"Modeling is a dirty business—and we can't get enough of it. . . . The book . . . names names and dishes dirt. . . . On-the-record kiss-and-tell." —*Newsweek*

"Page-turning exposé." —*Vogue*

"Sprawling . . . energetic." —*People*

"An elegantly aimed dagger to the heart of the posing profession." —*Spin*

"The first hard-hitting, serious tome about the multimillion-dollar modeling business." —*Chicago Sun-Times*

"Dishy and detailed. Not a pretty picture." —*Associated Press*

"Exhausting, exhilarating—and the reason Mr. Gross may never do lunch in fashion circles again." —*Dallas Morning News*

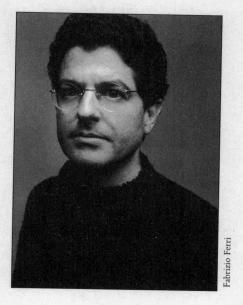

Fabrizio Ferri

About the Author

MICHAEL GROSS, a columnist for New York's *Daily News,* is the author of *Genuine Authentic: The Real Life of Ralph Lauren* and *My Generation: Fifty Years of Sex, Drugs, Rock, Revolution, Glamour, Greed, Valor, Faith, and Silicon Chips.* His articles have appeared in magazines and newspapers throughout the world, including *New York, GQ, Esquire, Travel + Leisure,* and *Vanity Fair.* He lives in New York City.

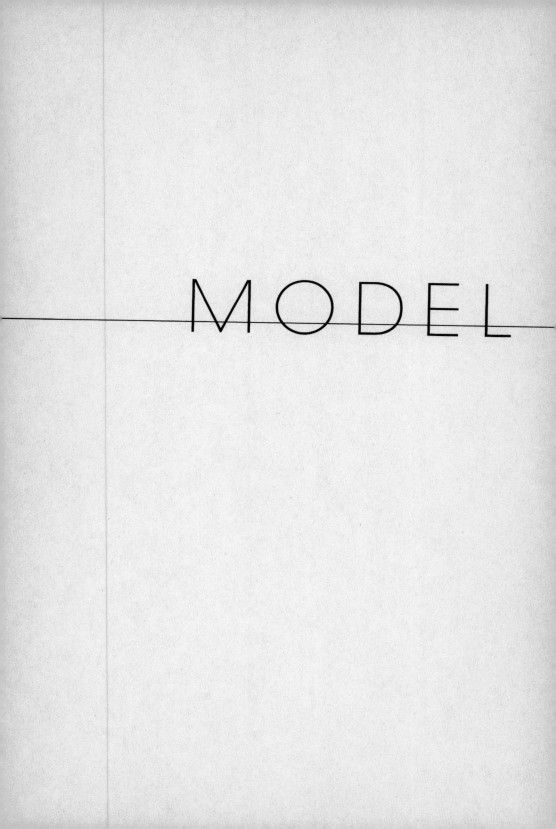

MODEL

Also by Michael Gross

Genuine Authentic: The Real Life of Ralph Lauren

My Generation: Fifty Years of Sex, Drugs, Rock, Revolution, Glamour, Greed, Valor, Faith, and Silicon Chips

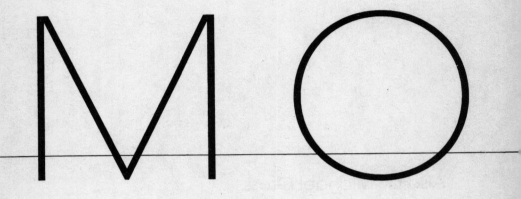

THE UGLY BUSINESS

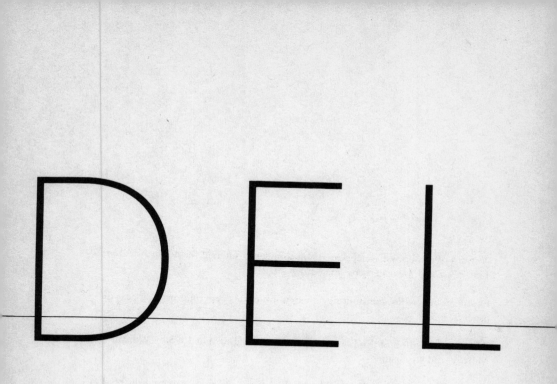

DEL

OF BEAUTIFUL WOMEN

MICHAEL GROSS

📖 Perennial

An Imprint of HarperCollins*Publishers*

Portions of this book have appeared—in somewhat different form—in *New York, Vanity Fair,* and *Manhattan, inc.* magazines.

Photographic credits, constituting an extension of this copyright page, appear on pages 523–524.

A hardcover edition of this book was previously published in 1995 by William Morrow and Company.

First Perennial edition published 2003.

Designed by Brian Mulligan

Library of Congress Cataloging-in-Publication Data is available.

ISBN 0-06-054163-6

03 04 05 06 07 RRD 10 9 8 7 6 5 4 3 2 1

This book is dedicated to
Clay Felker,
A. M. Rosenthal,
and Edward Kosner

and to Barbara Hodes, my wife, who didn't mind
when Cindy Crawford called

CONTENTS

INTRODUCTION

PART ONE
IN LOCO PARENTIS

PART TWO
BAD AND BEAUTIFUL

INTRODUCTION

MILAN, OCTOBER 1993

It is about 1 A.M. on a weekday in October 1993, and the piazzas of Milan are dead quiet. But it is the beginning of collection season, the semiannual frenzy when the women's clothing designers in the world's fashion centers—Milan, London, Paris, and New York—launch their new lines to buyers and the press. The six-week-long process begins here in Italy. So the calm is illusory.

Although all seems quiet at the door of Nepenthe, inside the exclusive club is seething. Tonight is a gathering of the clans, an annual meeting of the international royalty of fashion modeling so secret not even Italy's infamous and ubiquitous paparazzi are poised outside.

They call it Tartuffo Night. Regulars have special plastic cards that admit them to this orgy of pasta and mushrooms and champagne. The elect include modeling's kingpins, the agents who run the business, like the host, Riccardo Gay, of the eponymous Milanese agency; Ford Models co-president Joe Hunter; Elite Models chairman John Casablancas; and their counterparts from around the world. There are queens, too, like models Christy Turlington, Kate Moss, Karen Alexander, and Naomi Campbell. Orbiting around them are the lesser mortals of the model scene: There are the young agents who dream of the power wielded by Hunter, Casablancas, and Gay, the rich young Milanese boys known as *Milano per bene,* all long-haired and chic, who chauffeur models to the shows all day and to the town's discos by night. There are older men, too, sniffing the air like silver foxes on the hunt.

Their prey? The young models, seated at almost every table, whose names are as yet unknown. They don't speak the language. They don't know the ropes. They don't know Guido Dolce, who runs Italy Models, from Giorgio Sant'Ambrogio, who co-owns Fashion Model. They know nothing about the history of the business or the relentless march of ravaged casualties who preceded them. They don't know the rules, but who cares? They just changed! They look around wide-eyed at one another, wondering if they'll be the next big thing, swilling Cristal champagne with a rock star boyfriend. They know that already the cognoscenti are saying that Kate and Christy are out, and Bridget Hall, a sweet-faced Texan, and the Teutonic blond Nadja Auermann are in. They dance with the silver-haired men, wondering which one, if any, will give them *their* big break. They see the menu but not the agenda.

The music pounds, the champagne flows. There is brimstone in the air along with Poison and Obsession and Vendetta.

It is the smell of a factory that feeds on young girls.

Modeling occupies two separate parallel planes. It resembles one of Mexico's Yucatán Peninsula lagoons, where freshwater from inland and salt water from the sea meet, sharing a space, but separately. In the Yucatán, freshwater creatures swim on one level, and saltwater species frolic on the other. In the top layer of the modeling lagoon swim supermodels like Naomi and Christy. Pampered creatures, they are sent straight into the sweet waters of success, never tasting the brine of the bigger ocean. Inches away, beginners and those who will never surface swim in murkier, more dangerous waters.

It has been ever thus in the modeling world. The heights are incredibly bright and glamorous. The depths are equally dank and appalling. Only a few can reach the pyramid's point. It is crowded around the bottom. Wannabe models, lacking the looks, the will, and the sense to understand their precarious position, are junk food for modeling's predators and bottom feeders. But rarely is anyone in this business of illusions what he or she appears to be. The good can be not so. And the bad often *do* hold the keys to success—or at least know how to pick the locks.

Modeling was invented by a genuine good guy: John Robert Powers, whose name still lives on in a chain of schools and small agencies. But immediately behind him came an endless parade of unsavory others; crooks, con men, and operators have been attracted to the field right from the start. Both Harry Conover and Walter Thornton, early model agents, were arrested and ended their careers in disgrace.

Conover and Thornton were followed by a generation bent on cleaning up modeling's image. But in their wake rose a group of men like playboy-agent

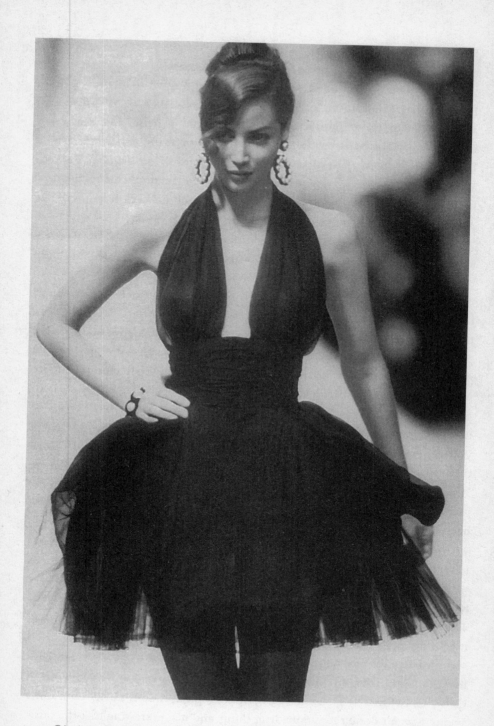

Christy Turlington modeling Chanel couture in 1991,
photographed by Charles Gerli

John Casablancas and others. "I got involved because that was where the pretty girls were," millionaire Bernie Cornfeld says.

All was not pretty. Claude Haddad, the French agent who discovered Grace Jones and Jerry Hall among others, was exposed by television's *60 Minutes* for allegedly having sex with underage girls. He closed his agency and now scouts in the former Eastern European bloc, working for many major agencies in Paris. Among them is Karins, which is run by Jean-Luc Brunel, who was alleged, on the same TV show, to have drugged and raped models. At the time he was in league with Eileen Ford, the so-called godmother of the modeling business. And Brunel isn't the only skeleton in Ford's closet.

Ford's reputation is that she cleaned up modeling and policed its standards as a benevolent despot until Elite's Casablancas came along, sleeping with young models and being generally immoral. But Ford's moral despotism eventually turned great numbers of her onetime employees and allies against her and her agency. They knew that agents have slept with models right from the beginning, that agents have slept with models at Ford, that models are the people agents meet. Meanwhile, Casablancas built the largest, strongest agency in the world, based entirely on the very quality of his character—seductive sexuality—that his detractors disdain.

Models love Casablancas. But then, models are women of twenty who like to have a good time, and he is a man who likes both good times and twenty-year-old women. And what do models know? Self-centered by professional definition, they care little about how their business works when it does. When it doesn't, they have little interest in remembering. After all, what twenty-one-year-old wants to come home and tell stories of how she *didn't* become a top model.

Top models may be the worst judges of all. The underbelly of modeling is never seen from their gilded perch. Right from the start, when a modeling pro spots a potential new star, he or she is on best behavior. Sex and fun are easy to come by in modeling. A million-dollar face is a bit more rare and valuable. The flesh and bones of beautiful women are worth a pretty penny. You never mess with quality merchandise.

"It's like, take care of her, because you don't want to scare her and have her run away back to Illinois and never model again," says supermodel Cindy Crawford. "It's true that most of the top girls haven't dealt with slimy agents, haven't done the whole drug thing, and it's interesting that the business says, unspokenly: These girls, protect. Luckily I didn't go to Milan when I was sixteen."

* * *

However bad the rest of modeling is, Milan is worse. "I don't go to Milan," says Eileen Ford. "I don't like Milan." If modeling is, as one of Ford's children once said in an unguarded moment, a business of "whores and their pimps" (a nice way to talk about your parents), then Milan is to modeling what Cheyenne was to the American West, an untamed, lawless frontier.

It was in Milan, in the mid-1970s, that wannabe models were put up in a hotel nicknamed the Fuck Palace and a residence dubbed the Principessa Clitoris. It was here, all through the early 1980s, that models flying in from around the world would be unexpectedly met at the airport by Rolls-Royces driven by playboys with a dozen roses in one hand and a big bag of cocaine in the other. It was here that excess became modeling's norm, that financial chicanery with models' money was raised to an art form, that money laundering was whispered to be common, that the Mafia and the outlawed P-2 group of power brokers were said to have their hooks into agencies, and that even reputable agents were said to have—more than once—fire-bombed their competition's offices. And it was here most notoriously, in 1984, that a wannabe model, high on coke, shot an equally strung-out playboy to death for claiming that she liked drug and sex orgies. She was in fact no stranger to orgies.

Ciao, Milano.

It is the season of the supermodel. Before coming to Nepenta that night, most of the evening's cast of characters has spent the day at the Fiera Campionaria, the ugly, sprawling convention center on the outskirts of Milan where designers show their clothes. The first show is Gianni Versace's. After the lights go down on his white marble runway, Versace plays black transvestite RuPaul's big hit "Supermodel," while Richard Avedon's photographs of model Stephanie Seymour are projected on a backdrop. Then, one after another, the actual supermodels of the universe parade down the runway to officially open the fashion season.

First is Kate Moss in a pleated short kilt, a sheer white blouse, and stockings that look like psoriasis. "Work it girl," RuPaul sings, and the models do, trying hard to make Versace's faux-punk frocks appealing. There is no question who the stars of this show are. Fashion now follows their lead.

After Kate comes Yasmin Parveneh Le Bon, who is married to Duran Duran's lead singer, Simon Le Bon. Then Veronica Webb, who has parlayed

jobs as a writer and television news personality. Eve, who
white hair in a crew cut, the better to show off the dragon tat-
her skull. Claudia Schiffer, who makes more money than any other
del—$12 million a year at last count. Christy Turlington, the prettiest girl
in the world, who can carry off even Versace's stringy, greasy hair. Helena
Christensen. Her boyfriend, Michael Hutchence, singer in the rock group
INXS, is seated right next to the editors of *Vogue* in the front row. Yasmeen
Ghauri. The smile of an angel atop—as a fashion editor might say—"the body
of death!" Naomi Campbell. Meghan Douglas. Each more beautiful than the
last. The parade lasts about thirty minutes. The twenty models alone cost Versace in excess of $100,000.

Ever since the Italians started mounting circuslike ready-to-wear fashion
shows in Milan in the late 1970s, the world's top models have arrived twice a
year, like clockwork in March and October, to earn sums of up to $15,000 an
hour, walking back and forth, back and forth, in impossibly expensive clothes
and impossible-to-maintain hairdos. The shows in Milan revolutionized the
fashion business, made designer clothes accessible to millions through the
mass media, and changed modeling as well. Every one of Milan's agencies
takes a booth at the Fiera, where models can check on their bookings, have a
smoke (all models smoke), or meet their cute young drivers between shows.
The booths reveal a lot about the agents. Top dog Riccardo Gay's space has
the names of all his top models—and there are many—printed all over the
walls. The Italy Models booth is done up in red, green, and white. Elite's has
a saddle suspended on a rail; why is anybody's guess. Beatrice Traissac's Beatrice Models booth is smaller and sparer. She doesn't approve of the other
agents in the city. "She is the hated one," a Milanese playboy hisses.

Beatrice (pronounced Beh-ah-tree-chey, although she is French), stands in
the doorway of her booth, looking darkly at the scene before her. The men
who dominate the business in Milan stay away from her in the hallway leading out of the Fiera, which the modeling folk have claimed as a minipiazza for
posing and preening. Beatrice watches as stars breeze past, lesser models hesi-
tate, groupies congregate, and her fellow agents manipulate. Scouts, called
scoots here, skittle around, sneaky as rodents hunting for stray bits of cheese,
trying to lure models to the coffee bar, where they'll tell them how bad their
agencies are and why they should change to another. It doesn't matter which
other. Models are sold back and forth for bounties. It is a thriving trade.

Ford's Joe Hunter, who doesn't have a Milan agency, works the booths
furiously, negotiating for his visiting models while simultaneously hunting for

more. Gérald Marie, the president and part owner of Elite in Paris and ex-husband of supermodel Linda Evangelista, does the same. The two are bitter rivals and seem to back away from each other like magnetic Scottie dog toys. Ford has just signed up Naomi Campbell, moments after Elite announced in a press release faxed around the world that it was firing her for unspecified bad behavior. Carol White, Campbell's London agent, defended Naomi on Sky TV, claiming she'd never seen her behave badly. If so, she was about the only person in fashion who hadn't. Though Campbell's diva routines were particularly stellar, bad behavior is the norm in modeling. That may explain why whispered slanders are the coin of the realm.

At an agency that afternoon a booker studied a photocopy of an Italian magazine article. It featured Luca Rossi, who works for Elite's Milan agency, seeming to mount and suckle the nipples of topless buxom women at the Voile Rouge beach club near St.-Tropez. A note accompanied the copy when it arrived, anonymously, at various agencies. "TRUST ELITE THE HEAD BOOKER IS A NICE GUY HE IS GOING TO TAKE CARE OF YOUR GIRLS," it said.

If you don't have anything bad to say, don't say it here. Which model has slept with every photographer in town? Which one serviced the shah of Iran? Which one, high on LSD, jumped out a window? Which ones jumped out a villa's second-story window, escaping a horny, hashish-smoking playboy? Which one disappeared on a shoot with a nonexistent Saudi Arabian magazine, ending up who knows where?

It's not just the models. Ask them, and they'll tell you about sadistic photographers like the one who makes a habit of exposing his penis while exposing his film. And playboys like the Hollywood producer who lures models to gang rapes by his friends and then ships them home suicidal. They are no worse than their agents. Which one tries to bed every model who passes through his office? Which one *doesn't?* Which one is in Milan's Mafia Bianca? Which one sells his agency over and over yet remains on the scene, a modeling monument? Which agent sells cocaine to photographers? Which ones feed it to their girls? Which one sends the stuff across the Atlantic, inside videocassettes carried by unwary friends? Spend a few weeks in model world, and you'll hear about all of them. Some of these stories are true; some not. But all are repeated as gospel.

This is a world in which lawsuits fly as frequently as the models do from city to city, agency to agency, magazine to magazine, boyfriend to boyfriend. Loyalty is nonexistent. Betrayal is everywhere. But what else do you expect from a world that caters to envy and lust? Is it any wonder, then, that back at the Fiera a booker named Alessandra exits Riccardo Gay's booth, grimacing in pain, and leans her forehead against a wall for all to see?

Standing on the sidelines, Beatrice Traissac observes, "It's like the pit in which the lions play at the zoo."

The top cats hate each other, but they need one another, too. That is why they come together at the Nepenta party. Every year a class photo is taken there of all the agents in attendance. Riccardo Gay arranges it and then sells the photos to Italian magazines. Gay never misses a chance to make a buck. The agents all cooperate and stand together in a group. "Plotting to stab the next guy in the back," one whispers as they head back to their tables.

The night wears on. A satisfied glow comes over the crowd. Naomi Campbell is moving across the dance floor without a partner. She doesn't need a partner. Everyone—apart from Elite—wants the next dance. Kate Moss and Christy Turlington are head to head, puffing on cigarettes. They will stay and drink and dance until two-thirty, and they will both look vacant and pimply at a show the next morning, but it doesn't matter. The gods of makeup and hair will be there to tend to them. But still. "I need some hair of the dog," Turlington will say at eleven that morning, quaffing a glass of champagne in Gay's Fiera booth. "It's the only thing that helps."

If they act like chosen people, it's because they are. They've been chosen by the hand of fate to have chic bones. And they've been chosen by the agents in a never-ending process that leads from one young girl to the next and the next and the next. . . .

Take Elite's John Casablancas. He is here, of course, a man in his element, beaming a satisfied, proprietary grin at his long table filled with long-legged women. His back is to the wall, so despite the presence of his mortal enemies, no one can stab *him* in the back here. Casablancas's arm is draped around the shoulder of his adoring third wife, eighteen-year-old Aline Wermelinger, a Brazilian Baptist whom he met when she entered Elite's Look of the Year model search contest. She isn't his first model, not by a long shot. His second wife was a model, too. And by his own admission, he's loved several others and bedded countless more. He is past fifty. But it shows only in his belly, which creeps out over his belt. It is doing that now as he leans back and puffs on his cigar and swigs some champagne and the kittenish Aline curls against him.

A new song starts playing on Nepenthe's dance floor. Hearing it, Casablancas starts lustily singing along. "We are the champions," the song goes. "We are the champions . . . of the world!"

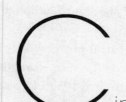indy Crawford taps her foot
and tsk–tsks impatiently. She's clocked into photographer Patrick Demarchelier's
studio twenty minutes earlier—a mere six minutes late for a 9:00 A.M. modeling
job. Crawford is prompt and expects as much from those she works with in fashion's photo factories. But Demarchelier isn't in sight. Nor are the day's editors
from British *Vogue.* Nor hair and makeup artists. Finally Demarchelier, a bearish
fellow, drifts in, but after saying hello, he drops into a chair with the *Times.* A
woman enters and gets on the phone. She's an editor, looking for several stray
bathing suits, which, she announces, will be the focus of the day's shoot. Crawford is under the impression she's been booked for a cover, and she isn't pleased.
Besides the loss of the prestigious cover, there's the fact she has been booked
under false pretenses. And bathing suit photos require . . . certain preparations.

"Somebody should have told me," Cindy mutters. "I didn't shave."

Just then the rest of the crew, including Mary Greenwell (makeup) and Sam
McKnight (hair) arrives. Crawford eyes her watch; it's nine-forty.

"What time were we supposed to be here?" Greenwell asks innocently.

"Nine," Crawford says. A pause. "I'm ready whenever you want to start."

At last the studio stirs. Demarchelier rises and begins hulking around, mut-
tering in incomprehensible French-accented English. The phones—and the
British editors—chirp. Crawford settles at a makeup table under a wall of
blown-up old *Vogue* covers. They look down as Greenwell, barefoot, circles
Cindy, smearing foundation on her face. Sarajane Hoare, *Vogue's* fashion editor, approaches. "I'm *so* glad I got you," she says with a sigh.

Though she's since been replaced in fickle fashion hearts by waifish models like Kate Moss, Beri Smithers, and Amber Valletta, Cindy Crawford (then

twenty-three) was the model of the moment that fall day in 1989. She was the *top du top des top models,* according to French *Vogue,* one of the "divine," according to Francesco Scavullo, who shot her sexy *Cosmopolitan* covers. She had the look, and the perks that came with it: her own show, *House of Style,* on MTV; appearances in lucrative Japanese soda pop commercials; sexy *Playboy, GQ,* and *Sports Illustrated* layouts; a best-selling swimsuit calendar and posters; proposals by mail from men in prison; and a Prince song, "Cindy C," written just for her. She'd been dating Richard Gere for more than a year and would soon marry him, and Hollywood had already beckoned, although only with parts for bimbos and babes.

Crawford was and is neither. And that summer she'd first proved it when she grabbed modeling's brass ring and was named the latest in a languid line of Revlon models, a series of fabulous faces dating back to 1952's Fire and Ice face, Dorian Leigh.

These are pointedly different times, and Crawford is *their* girl. She may have lost the fashion flock's ardor, but she's won the admiration of the world. "There are lots of beautiful girls," said Marco Glaviano, who photographed her swimsuit calendars. "But you need to have the brains to manage it. A lot of these girls don't use them because they've been told models are supposed to be stupid. And it's not a very stimulating business. They spend the day— poor girls—wearing lipstick and changing clothes. And look who they're with. Photographers—and I include myself—aren't noted for their intellectual attainment. And editors! Models spend their formative years with people who worry about skirt lengths. Even if they start smart, they can become stupid. Cindy's not afraid of being smart. That's a change."

Models and modeling have in fact undergone an extraordinary change since 1923, when an out-of-work actor named John Robert Powers opened the world's first agency for pretty faces in New York. Back then models earned $5 an hour. Today a day's work can ultimately reap a five- or six-figure harvest. For a mere twenty days of Crawford's work, Revlon anted up nearly $600,000 in 1989. And she probably made more based on escalators in her original three-year contract (since renewed) that govern how and how often her image is used. Add to that all she's done since—her contract renewals, her Pepsi commercials, her celebrity endorsements, her continued modeling, and her ever-rising profile—and you end up with a lucrative lifetime career.

It's a far cry from the first models, whose working lives usually ended by age thirty and left them with little except, if they were lucky, rich husbands

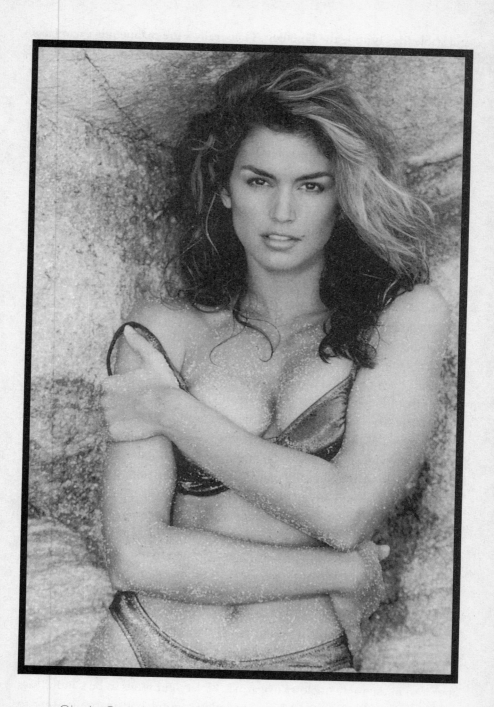

Cindy Crawford photographed by Marco Glaviano

and stable lives outside the limelight. They really were mannequins: nameless, affectless two-dimensional creatures in twin sets, pearls, and white kid gloves, whose only purpose was to draw the eye, most often in drawings made by commercial illustrators working for magazines or product manufacturers selling various goods to women. Nowadays models still sell, but they are the primary product. The "clothes hanger," as one of the greatest models of all time, Lisa Fonssagrives, often called herself, has become more important, better known, and more sought after than any mere lipstick or designer dress. She is frequently not only better paid than the people who make those things but richer than those who buy them. More and more, the tail wags the dog. The fascination with models shows no sign of abating.

So as Crawford sat around Demarchelier's studio that day, she wasn't just a model but a supermodel. The term itself wasn't new (it had first been used in the 1940s by Clyde Matthew Dessner, the owner of a small model agency), but the phenomenon was. Crawford's predecessor Dorian Leigh had led a similar jet set life, living footloose and free among the international set, making headlines and scandals almost everywhere she went. But Crawford and Claudia Schiffer, Linda Evangelista, Naomi Campbell, Christy Turlington, Stephanie Seymour, and Paulina Porizkova have become something much greater than the sum of their body parts.

They are the visual projection of the dreams of millions, the contemporary repositories of glamour, as powerful, sought after, and celebrated as the movie stars of Hollywood's heyday. The supermodels of the nineties are icons, emblems of an industrial society that is ever more accomplished in the replication and use of selling imagery. Though they exist in an apparently superficial milieu, models are metaphors for matters of cultural consequence like commerce, sexuality, and aesthetics. Through the work of the image merchants who manipulate them in photographs and advertisements (and sometimes in their real lives), today's models hawk not only clothes and cosmetics but a complex, ever-evolving psychology and social ambience, a potent commercial fiction that goes by the name lifestyle. Designers and photographers and fashion magazines create stories to sell products. Models are the stars of those stories. In the same way that young boys worship and want to be sports stars, today's adolescent girls want to be like Cindy, Claudia, and Naomi and live the life the supermodels appear to in the pages of glossy magazines. "Every girl wants to be Cindy," says model scout Trudi Tapscott. "She's not only beautiful, but smart, she went to college, she transcended the business, and she married a guy they think is the greatest. She's a symbol of the empowerment of women."

Unfortunately for the many, only the few are genetic accidents of precisely the right kind. And even then good looks, a certain height, and a photogenic arrangement of features aren't all it takes to succeed in this sometimes viciously competitive sphere. Indeed, it's not so much her looks as her out-look and her drive to succeed that made Crawford the first supermodel and then an international celebrity. She's the living proof that it takes more than a pretty face to scale modeling's Mount Everest.

"Cindy's incredibly aggressive," says her friend Mark Bozek, a fashion executive turned television producer. "She always wants to be challenged." And she constantly challenges others to meet her standards. "If I'm giving a hundred percent, I expect everyone else to," she says. So she second-guesses everyone from photographers to cabdrivers. And when, inevitably, they don't live up to expectations, she gets downright irritated. But then, this child of a broken blue-collar home will say, "I always felt I had to take care of everything myself." It's all made Crawford a candidate for an ulcer. "I internalize a lot," she said that day. "I didn't have an operation, but I take Xantac." Sitting at Crawford's side, fashion editor Hoare defends her perfectionism. "All the photographers love Cindy," Hoare says. "She's not tricky, no bad vibes, no headaches. She's so professional, so thoroughly reliable, so kind. And here bang on time."

"But some people don't appreciate my bossiness," Cindy says.

"You're *not* bossy," Hoare replies, dropping her voice in conspiracy. "Most models, when they get to Cindy's stage, become prima donnas. They treat you like shit."

McKnight looks up from a magazine. "Who's this?" he demands.

"Girls in their prime," says Hoare.

"Really?" Cindy asks.

"Yes."

"Well, I'm gonna start," Cindy says.

Cindy Crawford is unlike the demure white-bread blondes who domi-nated modeling for about thirty years before she came along. "I wouldn't have been a model ten years ago," says the olive-skinned brown-eyed brunette with the distinctive beauty mark near her mouth. "I would have been a freak."

That's not the only rule of modeling Crawford has turned on its head. Once, models would rarely pose seminude and then only if their faces were hidden. Crawford turned down star photographer Bruce Weber's request that she pose nude for designer Calvin Klein's hosiery and perfumes precisely because her face *wouldn't* be seen. When she did pose nude for a new ad campaign for Revlon's Halston perfume, the headline read CINDY IN HER HALSTON. Her careful insouciance about showing off her form has always been a part of her model's marketing arsenal. A young man arrived at Demarchelier's studio to give her a copy of *Max,* an Italian magazine with her photo—barebreasted—on the cover. "I can't believe they put a nipple on the cover," she says, delighted. Later the subject of her many nudes comes up again. "It's my choice," she says. "I'm not going to let other people's stereotypes and problems influence me. On a practical level, sometimes it's harder to say no. And when I'm fifty, I'll be so happy I did those pictures. I'll go, 'Remember when?' "

Crawford always looks out for number one in a game where she knows "no one else will." In the past such an attitude would have put a model on a collision course with her agents, but no more. "Aside from the fact that she's extremely beautiful, she is professional to a fault," said Monique Pillard, director of Elite Models, who was then Crawford's manager and coconspirator in the plot to make her famous. "It's a pleasure to deal with her in my business. You know what I mean?" Pillard cocks her head. She means that despite the changes heralded by Crawford's success, her business remains full of the self-absorbed, the self-abusive, and the self-deluding. "Modeling has changed a bit," Pillard continues. "The economy in fashion is not that great. People are watching their budgets. They can't take a chance on someone not performing—on not getting the picture. With Cindy, there's no chance. I can put my hand in the fire."

One model with Crawford's earning power can make a modeling agency. And an agency can make a lot of money. In recent years modeling has become an international business. Crawford's agency, Elite, is the world's largest, with branches all over the world, some in partnership with strong local agents, an association with the franchised John Casablancas Center modeling schools, a scouting network, and the annual Look of the Year model search, which serves as both a promotional vehicle and a recruitment system. Elite is said to have annual gross sales of about $70 million. Other major agencies include Ford Models, arguably the best known and most respected in the world, with branches in Paris, Miami, and Brazil; IMG, which is associated with sports agent Mark McCormack's International Management Group; Metropolitan, which books the world's highest-earning model of the moment, Claudia Schiffer, who reportedly grosses about $12 million a year; and Wilhelmina, which is owned by Dieter Esch, who served eight years in a German prison for negligence and fraud.

These stars of modeling—both bright and tarnished—do not quite out-shine the countless smaller agencies in cities around the world. Some, like Next in New York and Miami, Karins in Paris, and Fashion Model in Milan, are joined together in informal networks. Others, like Company in New York, Riccardo Gay in Milan, and Marilyn Gaulthier in Paris, are strong and individualistic enough to stand on their own. In the international marketplace they play the field, entering and leaving informal associations with one another and the giant mega agencies, trading models like playing cards as they globe-hop from fashion centers to shooting locations as far-flung as Bali and the Seychelles Islands. "The world really is smaller," says Kim Dawson, an ex-model who runs an agency in Dallas, Texas. "The ridges aren't as high any-more. You can be a model in one place, but you have to be in transit all the time to get into the real big game."

It is a game played on shifting sands, however. All an agency owner really owns, says Jeremy Foster-Fell, "is the right to pay rent." Even though they've sometimes tried to tie their assets down with contracts, agency owners—espe-cially small ones like Foster-Fell, who says he's "been gradually going out of the modeling business for twenty-five years"—have only the most tentative hold on their models and bookers, the key employees who field phone calls, negotiate jobs, and pass appointments on to their models. A model's primary relationship is with her booker, who is at least a temporary employment agent and at best a cross between banker, best friend, and priest. Bookers leave. Models follow. With a lethal combination of insecurity and narcissism instilled by their business, they are incredibly susceptible to the question, Why aren't *you* on the cover of *Vogue* this month? If you've got a big-name agency, though, it doesn't matter. Even if established models—an agency's prime assets—depart, new ones are knocking the door down, begging for the chance to be the next Cindy Crawford.

Agencies (as they are known, although legally they are management com-panies) earn money in several ways. Often they have to spend it first. Take a hypothetical model named Chandra, who is discovered in Omaha, Nebraska. After her parents are convinced to let her model (a process that lately some-times includes the payment of a cash "bounty"), she is given a round-trip air-plane ticket, flown into New York, and put up in a "model apartment" with a chaperone and other girls who typically sleep in bunk beds, several to a room. In her first weeks she is groomed and remade with new clothes, makeup, and a chic haircut and sent out on "go-sees" with photographers and clients. If she is bound to succeed, she may be sent to top studios, but more often she sees only those at the bottom of the fashion food chain—assistant or neophyte photographers seeking to break into the business. If Chandra is lucky, one of those photographers will shoot "test pictures" with her and give her prints for free, which she'll put in her portfolio, typically a vinyl or leather binder stamped with her agency's name.

When Chandra has enough pictures in her book, sequenced in an alluring way, she will finally be sent out to the fashion magazines. Her goal is to appear in the influential trend-setting pages of *Harper's Bazaar, Vogue, Glamour,* or *Mademoiselle.* They pay badly—as little as $100 per day—but are considered on the cutting edge of creativity. Appearing in their pages functions as a sort of endorsement and leads to more lucrative commercial work. If Chandra is unexceptional, she will end up in unfashionable magazines and catalogs but nonetheless gross about $250,000 a year. The better the face, the better the paycheck. The biggest come from national marketers—the agency's most valued clients after the star-making magazines—like Calvin Klein and Revlon. They'll pay in the millions for exclusive rights to a model. That's what Chandra wants.

The agency cashes in on both sides. If Chandra gets a $1,000 one-day job, $1,200 actually changes hands. Clients pay a 20 percent service fee. The agency also collects a commission from the model. Typically that is another 20 percent, although the model's commission can be negotiable. Stars are sometimes lured to new agencies that take no commissions from them. New models are now being asked to pay 25 percent until their careers are established. Sometimes a portion of the model's commission is paid out to what is known as the mother agent—the company that groomed or discovered the model. A mother agency can claim a piece of the action for several years. But with her agency raking in $100,000 on Chandra's $250,000 in bookings, that's a price well worth paying.

Top model agents like the Fords or John Casablancas live very well on what they take out of their businesses. To support their glitzy images, they fly the Concorde to Europe, stay at the Ritz Hotel in Paris or the Four Seasons in Milan, wear Rolex watches, and own multiple houses. Agencies have few expenses: rent, staff, and champagne. Models pay for everything else, from composites to messengers to "model" apartments. They often even pay to appear in an agency's promotional "head" book.

But back to Chandra's job. The $1,000 is just for one kind of use in one geographical market for a specified period of time. Use Chandra's picture longer, use it on a tag as well as a bag, use it in Europe as well as in America, or buy it out for all uses for all time all over the world, and a one-day job has become an annuity.

Still, that's not enough to explain why men like Esch, Cornfeld, Bob Zagury (a playboy backer of Elite), Thierry Roussel (the pharmaceutical heir and ex–husband of Christina Onassis), Carlo Cabassi (the younger brother of one of Italy's most important real estate developers), and sundry lesser-known Wall Street types, Middle Eastern businessmen, and others get into the relatively small-time modeling game.

The obvious reason is money. "The modeling world is driven by a powerful fundamental force," says Foster-Fell. "But it's rather hard to escape sex as a motive, a power to influence. Men are fascinated and envious of men who have power over women. Would he spend the same amount for a diaper company? I doubt it. Most men looking to get into this business have an ROI complex, and I'm not talking about Return on Investment. *Roi* is French for 'king.' "

It is ten-twenty, and Cindy Crawford has been transformed into what Sarajane Hoare calls a Cindy doll. Blemishes are banished. Eyelids are a dusky gray. For the finishing touch, Greenwell picks up a pot of bloodred Chanel lip gloss. She is supposed to use only Revlon products, but Crawford doesn't seem to notice. Still, though she's already appeared on two hundred magazine covers ("and counting," said Pillard), Crawford is hardly blasé. She eyes herself in the mirror. "It looks like I have no top lip," she says. "And I think the cheeks are a bit too much."

"Cindy Crawford, shut up your mouth," Greenwell says. Then she does what Crawford wants.

"I look sort of like a tart," Crawford says when she's satisfied.

"You can write that down," Greenwell tells me.

Crawford quickly agrees. "Sultry Cindy," she says. "Vixen."

Finally, around noon, the missing swimsuit surfaces. Cindy is ready to dive into work. "*Uh, Patreek,*" she says to Demarchelier in a broad French accent. "*Uh,* maybe we should *work* today?"

Finally the team piles into a location van and heads for SoHo. "Where is he going?" Crawford demands of the driver. "You're way out of your way. Take a right at Houston." To herself she adds, "This *isn't* my job." But at last it is time for her job. McKnight removes her rollers, and she sits at a mirror as he combs her hair into masses of Cindy doll curls. Crawford studies the mirror again. "I did my hair like this every day in high school," she says dreamily.

As he exits, Demarchelier leaves the van's door open. "We've got fans," Cindy warns as three young girls approach. She signs autographs. They giggle. As they leave, one cries out, "I saw her mole!"

"I come from the Midwest, and I'm just a normal girl."

Cindy Crawford was the second of three daughters born to a blue-collar family in 1966. "We never had any extras," she says. Her father worked variously in a pizza parlor, as an electrician, and as a glazier. He separated from his wife when Cindy was a freshman in high school. "We were angry," she says. Crawford had a happy childhood but admits she was driven. She was a straight A student who, in junior high, fantasized about being the first woman President. "I was rebelling against what my mother was at the time," she says. "I loved her, but I didn't respect her."

Though she'd always been pretty, she'd never worn makeup, looked at fashion magazines, or considered modeling until her junior year, when she was asked by a local clothing store to be in a fashion show. "Some people got jealous, but it was worth it," Crawford recalls. "I was still buying on layaway. We got a discount on clothes." Soon afterward a local photographer asked her to pose as the "Co-Ed of the Week" for a college newspaper and introduced her to a local makeup artist, who suggested she volunteer as a model for a hairstyling demonstration Clairol was sponsoring in Chicago. Lured by the promise of an all-expenses-paid weekend in nearby Chicago, Crawford agreed. A Clairol representative gave her the number of a local model agency.

Though its scouts arranged test photographs, they couldn't see past Cindy's mole, and she returned to De Kalb, Illinois. But one of her photos stayed in Chicago in another makeup artist's portfolio. "It was a funny-looking picture," recalls Marie Anderson, an ex–photographer's assistant who, in 1982, was just starting out as a model agent. "She had her hair up like a palm tree, a kooky dress, a parasol, and a pucker."

Anderson looked up Crawford's parents and "tried to explain Cindy wasn't average." The Crawfords weren't enthusiastic. "They thought I was a cute kid, not a model," Cindy says. She also had a summer job, working with all her friends detasseling corn for minimum wage in the seed cornfields of De Kalb Ag. "Sort of like my job now," Cindy says jokingly. "Worms, snakes, slugs, and bugs in your hair."

Still, the Crawfords decided to let Cindy take a chance. "They gave me five hundred dollars—all they could afford to lose," she says. "I paid them back with my first check." That didn't take long. A photographer down the hall from the agency shot a composite, carefully hiding Crawford's mole in shadows, and she went out looking for work. When potential clients turned her down, suggesting she have her mole removed, Anderson supported Crawford's inclination to keep it. "Someday they'll know you by that," she advised.

But at first Crawford gained renown because of other natural attributes. "I had no hips then, but I had boobs," she says, and they made her a natural for the lingerie ads that many other models refuse. Her first job was a bra ad for Marshall Field, the department store. It caused a stir among her fellow students, but Crawford didn't care. "If you knew what I was getting paid, you wouldn't be laughing," she told her tormentors. After a few weeks of driving back and forth between her two jobs, Crawford gave notice at De Kalb Ag. She was hooked. Senior year she arranged her classes so she could drive to Chicago every afternoon. "She worked her ass off—excuse the expression," Anderson says. "She was a pro from the beginning."

Six months later her agency was sold to the big New York firm Elite. Bob Frame, then a Chicago photographer, met Crawford at the party celebrating the merger. "Cindy hadn't really done much yet," he recalls. Frame used her often. "I was learning, too. We sort of grew together. But even then she knew what it was about: You're a product. You have to maintain it and sell it."

Crawford was already in demand—she'd seen ten top photographers, including Richard Avedon and Albert Watson, in her first two days in New York—but she was not yet willing to take the bait being dangled before her. She was entered in Elite's Look of the Year contest and made it to the national finals in New York. "I didn't win," she recalls. "They asked you if you'd leave high school. I wanted to graduate." And she did—as valedictorian.

For most models, postgraduate work begins in Europe, where agencies learn who will sink or swim by throwing them into a pool full of sharks. For the model it's a crash course in the real world of modeling. They are paid little, if anything, but if they're lucky and photogenic and develop a "look," they can emerge with all-important tear sheets—pages from European magazines that go into their portfolios and serve as their visual calling cards. Cindy—who already had tear sheets galore from Chicago—only lasted three weeks there. She started in Rome, where Italian *Vogue* had Demarchelier shooting the *alta moda*—or high-fashion—collections.

He wanted her to cut her long hair. She said no. He insisted. He also had her hair dyed. "I was crying," Cindy says. "I wouldn't look in a mirror for two weeks. Patrick was going, 'Oh, *bébé* doesn't like her hair. Oh, ha-ha-ha.' The only way you learn is by making mistakes." Even something as simple as going to a dinner with other models and photographers and agents after a shooting can be a mistake. At one dinner that week in Rome, Crawford recalls, "someone, an unnamed certain model, was on the table in a skirt with no underwear on, and all the models were sitting on all the men's laps. You go to one of those, and then you figure it out."

Then it was on to glamorous Paris, where "they put four girls who don't speak French in a tiny apartment and leave them alone," Cindy says. "I worked, but I had this short hair. I didn't know who I was." Then came an offer to pose for French *Elle*. "They wanted me nude, and I was like eighteen, and it was my first week in Paris—how could I say no? I felt used, because they played off my insecurities or my right to say no."

She started thinking of quitting and called her mother to see if a scholarship she'd refused could be reinstated. So when she was offered a British *Vogue* booking in Bermuda, she says, "It was perfect. I could come back." But first there were more lessons to learn. "They had me lying in the surf for two hours with a mud mask on and waves splashing over my head," she says. "I didn't know I could say no. Those same people now would be, 'Anything you want.' " She was supposed to return to New York but grabbed the first flight home instead. "I waited three hours and paid like five hundred dollars one way, but I was going home, and I didn't care."

Crawford decided to split her attention between modeling and college. She wasn't ready to decide. She enrolled as a chemical engineering major because it was an easy way for a girl to get a scholarship. She lived in a dorm at Northwestern University for one semester but spent most of her time thirty minutes south in Chicago, where she met her most important teacher.

Victor Skrebneski is the long-reigning king of Chicago fashion photography. For the next two years Crawford was his queen. "I went to obedience school," she says. "The Skrebneski School of Modeling." Even competitors are in awe of the dapper, hawk-faced Skrebneski. "Cindy and I were doing amazing photos," says Bob Frame, "but then Victor started using her, and she disappeared. Victor has a group he works with and is very loyal to. He's a really incredible teacher. His photographs are meticulous in detail, so the people in them learn how to work with themselves. If a strong girl comes around, Victor adopts her," Frame says. Unfortunately for Skrebneski, he adds, "the good ones always leave."

For two years Crawford was satisfied. She quit college and moved to Chicago. Her income shot up to $200,000 a year. "And it's cheap to live there," she says. "My rent was half what it is now, I had a car. I was only two hours from home. It was great. But slowly you start wanting more."

From the moment she first saw Crawford work in 1985 at an Azzedine Alaïa fashion show, Monique Pillard tried to lure her to New York. Now, for three months in 1986, Crawford commuted between her place in Chicago and a New York model's apartment. But she didn't move mentally until she had a falling-out with Skrebneski. To this day he won't discuss what happened. Crawford remembers precisely because it was her twentieth birthday.

"I was leaving for New York that night," she says, "and I didn't want to work that day." But two clients begged, so Cindy—ever the pro—obliged. The first client was so grateful he gave her roses and a birthday cake. At the second studio—Skrebneski's—she was asked, "Why do you have all that?"

The next day, in New York, Crawford learned she'd won a ten-day big-money job in Bali. She had to cancel a conflicting shoot with Skrebneski. "That was it," she says. "I understand his feelings. He made me. He did. But you can't make something and keep it for yourself. That was the break. Even if I didn't make it in New York, I couldn't go back to Chicago." A day later she moved into a friend's apartment in Manhattan.

She now cut another tie as well. For several years Crawford had dated a quarterback from her De Kalb high school. A friend since elementary school, he was her "grounding link" when she started modeling, she says. Even though he was in college in Arizona, he protected her from many model pitfalls. "I had blinders on and gave off 'unapproachable, don't ask me out, don't talk to me, not interested,'" she says. "But our lives totally diverged. This might sound bad, and I don't mean it to, but it's like a little kid who is finally ready to give up that security blanket. I can go to sleep by myself in the dark now."

New York wasn't always easy. Crawford's worst moment came one night in June 1988, when she returned at 1:00 A.M. from a five-week working trip and discovered things out of place in her Greenwich Village apartment. Her phone book was missing. There was fresh food in the refrigerator, but her bed wasn't fresh. Then the phone rang. "Don't be mad," said a man's voice that then started listing the contents of her drawers.

"He went on to confess," she says. "I don't know why." He'd somehow entered her apartment, made friends with her neighbors, taken an extra set of keys, and nightly made himself at home after calling to be sure the apartment was empty. Now he said he was coming over again.

Crawford threatened to leave, but he said he could always find her. "I told him I was moving," Cindy says. "He knew the address." Finally she agreed to meet him the next day in a restaurant. She sneaked out to sleep at a friend's and called the police the next morning. At the rendezvous the man was arrested, and the police discovered he had a prior armed robbery conviction. He ultimately pleaded guilty to second-degree burglary charges and was sentenced to two and a half to five years in jail.

The night after the indictment, Crawford says, "I had a mini–nervous breakdown, and then I was fine. I knew it shouldn't be a major event in my life. I wanted to tidy it up and get it taken care of. Now I live in a very secure building. I don't have a listed phone. You don't learn until you make mistakes."

Mostly life here has been good for Crawford. "She hit immediately, like a house on fire," says her friend Mark Bozek. "She was very naïve, but she got street smart quicker than anyone I've ever met. The first six months always set the pattern. I stayed friends with her because she stayed real."

When she first arrived, Crawford was often compared to a better-known model, Gia Carangi, a bisexual drug abuser who had a short but highly visible career. "I was Baby Gia, but more wholesome," Cindy says. "She was wild. Completely opposite me. She'd leave a booking in the clothes to buy cigarettes and not come back for hours." A pause. "She's not living anymore." Carangi died in 1986 of AIDS.

Crawford was never like that. "She was not your typical model," says Marco Glaviano. "She wasn't flirty. That slowed her down a little bit at the beginning, but it was good. That way you don't get burnt out." Crawford had no intention of burning out. She knew just what she wanted. Every time she saw Pillard at modeling functions, she'd shake her hand and say, "Contract, contract."

"They're not very organized," Crawford complains when, at 1:00 P.M., the British *Vogue* shoot still hasn't started. She buries herself in Italo Calvino's *The Baron in the Trees* until finally Hoare is ready to dress her. A few minutes later she emerges in a silver lamé bikini, matching fringed jacket, cowboy hat and boots, and a holster and a pair of mirrored sunglasses. "I hope I don't run into any neighbors," she says.

Instead she attracts a crowd as she clambers onto a wrought-iron fence, spreads her legs, and pulls her guns. When she disappears into the van to change, the bystanders stay glued to the spot. Drivers park their cars. A deliveryman deposits his boxes on the curb. "It's the lunch crowd." Crawford laughs.

For the third setup Demarchelier wants Crawford, who is wearing a suit sprinkled with silver sequins, mesh wrist cuffs, and a pair of red stiletto heels, to push a baby carriage up Wooster Street. As she walks there, Demarchelier drapes her shoulders with his jacket. Eyeing the crowd that trails behind her, she tells him, "I'd rather cover my ass." Crossing West Broadway, she causes actor Wallace Shawn to do a triple take. Then, turning onto Wooster Street, she stops work on a building site. Hard hats pour into the street. "How come my wife didn't look like that after she had a baby?" one of the workers mutters. Cindy stares into her pram. "I'm still looking for a baby," she says.

"I'm sure any of these guys will help you," an assistant comments.

Several rolls of film later, "My shoe's falling off," Crawford complains. "My suit's up my ass." Just then a garishly customized motorcycle roars by. Greenwall yells for the driver to stop, and Cindy mounts the bike, first behind the driver on his vinyl, chrome, and fur seat. Then she clambers around in front of him and arches her back to pose with his face inches from her assets. Tammi Terrell and Marvin Gaye sing "Heaven Must Have Sent You" on the bike's radio. The *Voguettes* are elated.

"From mother to biker chick in five seconds," Cindy says. "And I thought we were just doing a regular old studio shot!"

Once upon a time a cosmetics contract was the crowning achievement of a model's career. But by the time she signed with Revlon, Crawford was pushing the boundaries of where a paper face could go. "I'm not aware of any role models within the fashion business," Crawford says. "I look at people who are doing their own thing. They have a vision and a drive to make it happen." So does she. Violating one of modeling's premier taboos by taking off her clothes for *Playboy* proved to be one of her best career decisions. An MTV producer saw those pictures and decided that Crawford had a young male following that would fit MTV's audience profile. She wasn't prepared for the demands that hostessing *House of Style* put on her. "Basically it was a day job for me. I was called in, I'd read a few cards, and that was it," she recalls. "It evolved into so much more. Now I'm much more involved with what the show's gonna be."

MTV taught her to be comfortable in front of video and film cameras and, she believes, led directly to the first of her popular series of Pepsi commercials, her subsequent signing with the William Morris agency for nonmodeling work, and her best-selling exercise videos. "People got to see me being real, so it's demystified the glamour a lot," she said in 1994. "That lets the general public embrace you and made me more valuable to Pepsi, which wanted a beautiful all-American girl that people could relate to. Five years ago I didn't really know where everything was going. Things would come up, I would usually say, 'Well, why not?' And if there was no 'Why not?' I would do it. I kind of had my one finger in ten different pies, and I learned things I did like and things I didn't like, and thank God, I didn't make any major fumbles along the way, so things have really come together. I'm doing my thing, as opposed to coming in and putting on whatever dress they hand me and whatever face they tell me."

She earned royalties from her calendars but "gave half the money away to charity," she says. "That made it palatable for me. OK, it's really cheesy, but I also understood that it went to a different audience from *Vogue* readers." Her next project was more lucrative and less cheesy. "Instead of trying to create equity for other people, I'm trying to create it for myself," she says. "That's why the exercise video was really important for me. I was a full partner in that. It was thirty degrees, and we were shooting on the beach, but hey, if we had to do another shooting day, it was going to cost that much more out of my part of the profit. You definitely think about that when you have something invested as well." Crawford's video sold two million copies in its first month of release.

Once again she was leading the pack. Right after her exercise video came out, she heard that Claudia Schiffer's agent had started calling the company she'd made it with, feeling it out about doing one with Schiffer. "Part of me is flattered," Crawford says. "Part of me is irritated. Why am I the one who has to come up with all the good ideas?" The same goes with being on television. "At the last collections every model had a camera crew following her around! Christy, Naomi, Veronica Webb!" Cindy exclaims. "Even Claudia had *Entertainment Tonight*. The most challenging thing now is that I gotta stay one step ahead."

One way she's done that is by branching out beyond the fashion model agency system. Although the latest agency angle has it that model managers can move models beyond modeling and can handle more than models (Dieter Esch has partnered with a firm that represents athletes; Elite's Pillard recently opened a "celebrity" division), Crawford doesn't buy it. "I'm actually really happy with Elite, and I'm happy because I'm still there," she says. "Believe me, if I wasn't happy, I wouldn't be there. But I also think that modeling agencies don't always look at the big picture. For instance, Monique didn't really understand why I was doing MTV that first year. She said I should be doing catalogs and all that. And they couldn't have done the video the way William Morris did. They wouldn't have known how to put together that kind of deal. I'd have been hired for the day and gotten a small percentage, as opposed to fifty percent."

Crawford has apparently even managed to renegotiate her agency's 20 percent commission. "Elite's made enough money from me," she says. "They understand that if I do a big, big deal, I'm not gonna be paying them twenty percent for the whole five years. They also bill the client twenty percent, which my lawyer assures me is usurious, or whatever that word is, but legal. He just can't believe that. The newer you are, the harder they work for you, because they're pushing you to everybody, you're always doing these little jobs, and they advance you money. I don't need that anymore. I see myself as a president of a company that owns a product, Cindy Crawford, that everybody wants. So I'm not powerless because I own that product. When you start thinking that the agency owns it and you don't own it, then you have a problem. You have to have a pretty strong position to go in and negotiate, but it can be done. I know that if I went around shopping for agents, each one would go a percentage point less than the next, but I feel comfortable. What I'm paying now I feel is fair. I'm not paying full twenty percent on everything. But part of the agreement is that I don't talk about it."

Ever since Anita Colby, the face of the early 1940s, went west, the typical path out of modeling had run through Hollywood. For a time that seemed to be where Cindy was going. She dated a William Morris agent. Then she met Richard Gere in 1988 at a Los Angeles barbecue for Elton John, hosted by photographer Herb Ritts, who shot her *Playboy* spread. "My mom, Shirley, pushed them together," Ritts recalled the next year. "They got to talking, and it grew. He's changed her. He's a mature, intelligent guy. Anybody older, you learn if you're open to it. It's a very easy relationship. They're very sweet and good to be around."

Gere was good for Crawford in many ways, not least because his celebrity added to hers and accelerated her momentum. While she was first dating him, she could often be found reading for movie roles and taking acting classes. "I'm sort of at the pinnacle of the model Cindy Crawford," she said in 1989. "A career should get better as time goes on. So modeling is out. I'd like to show another side of myself."

But in Hollywood she was just another wannabe actress. Typically she wanted more, and with the guidance of William Morris and Gere she managed to avoid many of the pitfalls that have tripped up models turned actresses in the past. Elite brought her an offer for one film, *White Orchids,* but she turned it down because of its sex scenes. Then came a reading for *Beverly Hills Cop II.* "I had to pretend I was holding a guy by his collar, say, 'Hey, squirrel brains,' and then pull a gun out of my leather jump suit," she says. Instead she couldn't stop laughing. Luckily, "It's not my whole life to be an actress," she concluded. "And I don't know if I deserve it if I won't give up my firstborn for it."

Her independence also showed in the way she initially concealed her relationship with Gere. Though their coupling was common knowledge among fashion and film types, in public she referred to the actor only as "my friend in L.A." "I don't want to get scooped up in someone else's fame," she explained at the time, "because then it's not mine. When I started modeling, no one knew me. I wasn't someone's daughter. I have managed to be this thing that appeared out of nowhere. I've never tried to be on 'Page Six.' I wasn't in clubs and being seen. I don't go to dinner every night when I'm on a trip, and photographers don't like that. Models are supposed to be entertainment. I do my job. That validates me. My relationships are personal."

Finally, though, Crawford and Gere went public, and when they did, it was in style. Wearing a red Versace dress with a plunging décolletage at the Academy Awards in March 1990, Cindy nearly stole the show from her actor escort. It turned out that Crawford's fame gave Gere's career a boost and vice versa. At first they were cautious about appearing together in print, turning down a chance to grace the cover of *Vanity Fair*, for example. But finally they posed for a *Vogue* cover shot by matchmaker Ritts. "There was obviously no marketing move there," Cindy says. "We never really made the decision. But unless we hibernated for the rest of our lives, it would have to be public sooner than later. How has it affected my life? I don't think it really has. I get asked a lot of questions about him in interviews, that's the main thing."

There are a lot more interviews. Crawford now graces the covers of *Rolling Stone* and *People* as often as *Vogue* and *Bazaar*. "I see myself as someone who speaks to my generation," she says. But her new role wasn't always comfortable. She and Gere were plagued in particular by recurring rumors that they both are gay. Though the couple had heard the stories in various versions— including one, Crawford says, in which Herb Ritts played their beard—they at first never acknowledged or denied them. Indeed, they sometimes seemed to be playing up the controversy, as when Gere refused to answer an interviewer who asked his sexual orientation or when Crawford posed for a magazine cover with the lesbian chanteuse k. d. lang.

"I wasn't trying to make a statement; that's my statement," Crawford said of those pictures. But then, in 1994, press reports of the couple's impending divorce caused them to reconsider. On May 6, *The Times* of London carried a $30,000 full-page ad headlined A PERSONAL STATEMENT BY RICHARD GERE AND CINDY CRAWFORD.

"For some reason unknown to us, there has been an enormous amount of speculation in Europe lately concerning the state of our marriage," it began. Citing a "very crude, ignorant and libelous" article in a French magazine, *Voici*, that claimed they were splitting up because they "wanted to assume their real sexuality," Gere and Crawford wrote that despite feeling "quite foolish responding to such nonsense," they wanted to "correct the falsehoods" and "alleviate the concerns of our friends and fans." It continued:

We got married because we love each other. . . . We are heterosexual and monogamous. . . . There is not and never has been a pre-nuptial agreement. . . . Reports of a divorce are totally false. . . . We both look forward to having a family. . . . Richard is not abandoning his career. . . . We will continue to support "difficult" causes such as AIDS research . . . Tibetan independence . . . Gay and Lesbian Rights . . . irrespective of what the tabloids try to imply.

Now, that said, we do feel we have a basic right to privacy. . . . Marriage is hard enough without all this negative speculation. Thoughts and words are very powerful, so please be responsible, truthful and kind.

In response, London's *Daily Mail* made the double-negative observation that they hadn't said they weren't *bi*sexual. In the months to come, newspapers continued to question the Crawford-Gere union, delighting in detailing Cindy's and Richard's increasingly frequent and public extramarital dalliances. And finally, in December, they issued a brief statement admitting they'd separated that July. Soon, Richard's friends started saying Cindy was at fault.

It's enough to make anyone crazy. But Crawford is tough. Or at least the tough outer shell that modeling made for her is.

She calls it the Thing.

"Are you going to do the Thing tonight?" Gere would ask her when they were getting ready to go out.

She fluffs her hair and strikes a pose, and suddenly the Thing is in the room. "I'm becoming this other character, and all of a sudden—I don't know why—all of a sudden I'm brave, I'm telling jokes, I become much more theatrical . . . and then I wash it off."

Cindy Crawford laughs, and as suddenly as it appeared, the Thing slinks away.

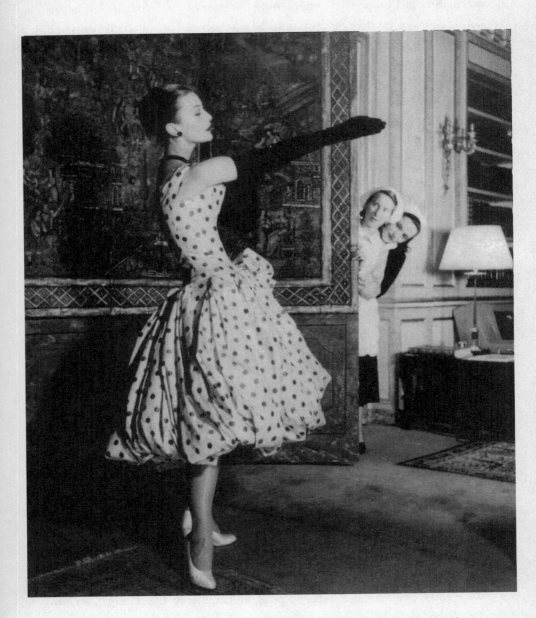

Mary Jane Russell photographed by Louise Dahl-Wolfe

PART ONE

IN LOCO PARENTIS

Who am I? I'm Polly, Polly Magoo.

But between us, I'm not sure how I can answer you.

You ask who I am.

Sometimes, I ask myself, too.

They take my picture.

Every day, they take my picture, and that makes millions of times
that they've taken my photo.

And each time they take my picture, a little bit less of me is left.

So what can I have left in the end?

I ask you. . . .

—FROM THE FILM *QUI ÊTES-VOUS, POLLY MAGOO*,
WRITTEN AND DIRECTED BY WILLIAM KLEIN

"**I**t all started with being out of a job."

John Robert Powers was a dark, handsome man but a lousy actor, as he was the first to admit. So around 1915 he took a job as a bit player and wardrobe boy with impresario Sir Herbert Beerbohm Tree, the Shakespearean actor, in his touring theater troupe. Powers's acting skills eventually won him a job as assistant business manager. When Tree closed his company, the scarcity of parts for a man with no talent became a problem.

Then, one day, a man approached Powers about posing for a photograph with silent screen star Mary Pickford. Powers showed up at the appointed time and place three days in a row. Pickford never appeared. But Powers, $30 richer, had experienced nothing less than an epiphany. He found another commercial photographer who needed a model. Although he had a long, sharp nose, thick eyebrows, and thin lips, it didn't seem to matter.

It was the Damon Runyon era, when urban fables embellished their way from the Great White Way into history. So almost every account of the birth of the John Robert Powers agency differs from the last, sharing only hyperbole and an apocryphal quality. But a sketch emerges nonetheless of how Powers invented the modeling business. By the most likely account, in about 1921, Powers showed up for a job with a photographer named Baron Adolphe de Meyer. The baron worked for fashion magazines and clothing manufacturers. He asked Powers to round up seven more men to work in an ensemble. "I got them for him and then he kept asking me to get him some more," Powers said. The job was easy because "most of my friends, like myself, were actors, and again like myself, they were what is laughingly known as 'resting.' "

These were the days when two-reel silent films were produced in a small circuit of studios stretching from South Brooklyn to Fort Lee, New Jersey. Out-of-work thespians would loiter in front of the Palace Theater in Fort Lee, hoping for work. Powers knew them all, and soon his pockets were overflowing with their phone numbers. Photographers began calling him instead of advertising for models. "I seemed to be able to get in touch with people more readily than anyone else," Powers said. "Bit by bit I seemed to be assuming the proportions of an extra's clearing house. But this was all unconscious. I didn't have the business sense to see the possibilities." Finally, though, "a great light smote me in the face. If I was becoming so useful, why couldn't I become useful to myself?"

Powers credited Alice Hathaway Burton, his wide-eyed Kewpie doll blond wife, with hatching the idea of a model agency. "There must be lots of commercial photographers looking for models," she told him. "And we know dozens of actors and actresses out of work. Why can't we find a way of bringing them together?"

So Powers "had their pictures taken, made up a catalogue containing their descriptions and measurements, and sent it to anyone in New York who might be a prospective client—commercial photographers, advertisers, department stores, artists," he recalled. "There were not more than 40 people listed in that first catalogue," which was published in 1923, "but the idea was a new one. While I had started with the idea of supplying a demand, I began to realize that I was creating one."

A lucky break with real estate helped, too. "John lived in an old brownstone over a speakeasy just off Broadway then," a friend of his remembered. "That was the humble beginning of the modeling industry. It went on like that—over the speakeasy—until Steve Hannagan, the press agent who was building up Miami Beach on a solid foundation of bathing beauty pictures, started nudging John to get away from Broadway and move his operation to Park Avenue." Hannagan had a traveling architect friend with offices on the second floor at 247 Park Avenue that he let Powers share.

Soon Powers, Alice, their three assistants, and seven French phones crowded the architect out. One wall was lined with charts—writing pads, actually—one per model, detailing jobs the agency had booked for its models, broken down into fifteen-minute intervals, and noting what accessories they needed to bring along. Powers would sit at a small table in the anteroom behind the door labeled "John Robert Powers Publications," greeting visitors

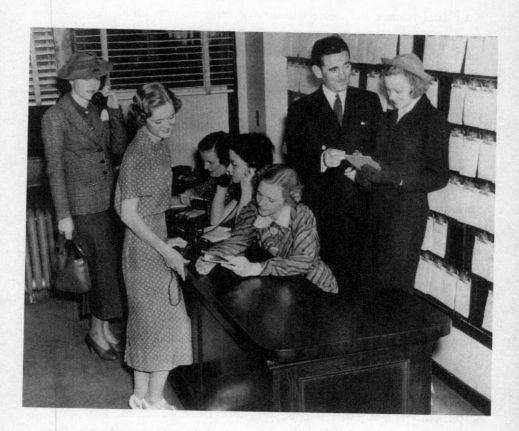

John Robert Powers in his agency
with models and bookers, 1936

himself, studying everyone who walked in with his ever more practiced eye. He called himself "the highest paid reception clerk in the city."

Charles Rainey, the aging widower of Powers's only child, an adopted daughter, lives surrounded by Powers agency mementos in the suburban ranch-style house on a corner lot in the Los Angeles suburb of Toluca Lake, where Powers lived before his death in 1977. "He did begin in 1923," Rainey says, "but he didn't get his act together until 1925." He pulls out books and columns by his father-in-law and even a couple of children's mystery novels featuring Powers Girl sleuths.

"He was a very good-looking man," Rainey continues. "As an actor he was a spear carrier. That's how he described himself." Rainey points to an oil painting on his wall, titled "Her Knight Off." It shows Powers, dressed in armor, jumping off a horse to save Alice, a damsel in distress.

Rainey hands over a yellowing booklet, the *Actor's Directory and Studio Guide of April 1925,* vol. 2, no. 2. John Robert Powers is listed as the publisher with offices at 19 West Forty-sixth Street. In an introduction he wrote, "The kind approval bestowed upon preceding issues renders it unnecessary to offer any apology for the appearance of our present number. . . . Our directory does, we think, strengthen the collusion so much to be desired among the members of the profession." What profession, he doesn't say.

From the look of Gaston DuVal, with his twirled, waxed mustache and chestful of medals, preening inside, Powers would have happily taken bookings for Prussian officers. Among the women there are flappers, dowagers, and scruffs who look as if they stepped straight off the silver screen.

By 1932 Powers's booklet had grown up into a thick hard-cover book containing about five hundred models, very similar to today's model head books. Models paid $25 a year to appear in it. Hannah Lee Sherman, a debutante in a long satin gown, is shown on page 213 in a photograph by Gabor Eder. Her height (5 feet 7 inches), weight (121 pounds), and measurements (32-27-35) are given, along with her shoe, glove, and hat sizes and her home phone number.

Rainey pulls out scrapbooks Powers kept of his clippings. They are filled with stories about his models and about the society lifestyle modeling brought him. "They lived in a fifty-two-room estate in Locust Valley on Long Island," Rainey says. "They had fifty acres. My wife grew up there. She had seven horses. He became a society person. They'd winter in Florida at the Everglades Hotel on Worth Avenue." Powers spent money like water. "John would give away the store," according to Rainey. "He wasn't ever poor. He tried to keep up." The scrapbooks show the Powerses at play at a Palm Beach dinner hosted by the Cornelius Vanderbilt Whitneys. Powers models, "gay as magpies and dressed to the hilt," traveled with him, enlivening the southern scene and not coincidentally garnering considerable publicity. Once Powers caught on, he played his hand for all it was worth.

Advertising was only a few decades old. Commercial photography was a bit younger than that. At the turn of the century a Chicago photographer named Beatrice Tonneson may have been the first to use live female models in an advertisement. Powers was in on the ground floor with a better mousetrap—a classic American success story. Illustrators like James Montgomery Flagg, J. C. Leyendecker, and Howard Chandler Christy still ruled the commercial roost and would stay key Powers clients into the 1940s. Even they had started using cameras to shoot pictures of models and draw from them, instead of from life. It took only a second to snap a picture. Previously they'd had to pay a model to sit and pose for hours. But this was their last hurrah. Magazines were starting to use photography regularly, and advertisers were following suit. The bookings started pouring in, and Powers took 10 percent of each one.

The 1929 stock market crash and the Depression that followed changed everything. Only for Powers did things change for the better. He began attracting debutantes whose families were suddenly short on cash. "I was in high school in 1929," says Betty McLauchlen Dorso, eighty-two, who became one of Powers's top models. "I wanted to be a gym teacher, a coach. But it was during the Depression, and my father, like every male in the country, lost his job." When McLauchlen was laid off from his designer's post with Cadillac, he bought his daughter a cloche and fur-collared coat and took her to be photographed by a friend who'd shot advertisements for the luxury cars. The photographer posed her on a revolving platform and sent her picture to Powers, who called the dark-haired, sophisticated beauty in for an interview.

"There was only the one agency," Dorso recalls. "I went in on a Saturday and I registered and he sent me off into the night. I didn't know anything about the business. You had to pound the pavement in those days," and stop at the agency each day to check in. "I finally found a job at Henri Bendel, modeling on the floor. It was then a wealthy women's boutique. I was paid thirty-two dollars and seventy-five cents a week, and five dollars extra for decorating the windows." She had worked there several years, supporting her whole family by showing clothes to customers, when a *Vogue* editor spotted her and asked if she would pose for a young woman photographer named Toni Frissell, who'd started working for the magazine after assisting the British photographer Cecil Beaton. Dorso began working for Frissell regularly. "Then I actually started functioning with Powers," Dorso says. "I really wanted to be a gym teacher, but I happened to have the looks that got me this lucrative life."

An important psychological divide had been crossed when Powers moved to his Park Avenue address. No longer would models—at least his models—be considered on a par with show girls. Those raffish sorts were booked out of the west side of Manhattan, the theater district, the Tenderloin. *Fashion* models came from higher-priced districts. In part because of the geographical divide, Seventh Avenue showroom models who worked the garment district as well as commercial models and runway mannequins would sit below photographic models in the model pecking order for another fifty years.

With a showman's flair, Powers even invented a symbol to differentiate his models from all the others. When a Powers girl broke the handle of the satchel in which she lugged around the tools of her trade—her pumps, her waist cinch, her war paints and brushes—Powers replaced the bag with a strong round cardboard hatbox from John Cavanagh, where he bought his headgear. The boxes sold for fifty cents apiece and became the badge of honor of the Powers model.

As the business expanded, Powers moved into larger quarters, installed direct telephone lines to *Vogue, Harper's Bazaar,* and the major catalog studios, and even hired a promotion man. "I was an unemployed actor, kicking around Broadway just like Johnny was," recalls Bob Fertig, eighty-two. "One of the guys in the crowd said he'd been to a place called Powers, and they wanted to put him to work delivering pictures. I said I could use a few bucks. There were a lot of beautiful broads around him."

Powers was looking for a label that would differentiate his beauties from the earlier Gibson Girls (the last century's ideal) and the Ziegfeld Girls of the stage. "We avoided using the word 'model,' " Fertig recalls. "Women with no means of visible support called themselves models. People thought of them as empty-headed floozies."

Finally Powers decided to call them "Long-Stemmed American Beauties," a phrase coined by illustrator Arthur William Brown. "What I seek above all else is a natural wholesomeness," Powers said. "I do not want types, nor do I want sophistication. I want girls or women who will look like what the advertisers want them to look like, and it is not an easy thing to find. Pretty girls, yes, but not models."

Though he continued booking men (including the young Fredric March, Henry Fonda, Tyrone Power, and Brian Donlevy), he would ever after be known for his Powers Girls. Over the years the agency's list included top models like Anita Colby, Helen Bennett, Kay Hernan, and Muriel Maxwell. Better known today are the models turned actresses: Jennifer Jones, Gene Tierney, Barbara Stanwyck, Lucille Ball, Joan Caulfield, Jean Arthur, Ava Gardner, Lauren Bacall, Rosalind Russell, Norma Shearer, Joan Blondell, and Paulette Goddard.

Powers Girls who didn't go Hollywood often stayed in the public eye as the wives of the millionaires who pursued them as avidly as they had the show girls of earlier generations. From the first, model agents have maintained a sideline in informal matchmaking. Bachelors were said to shop the Powers catalog for dates, just as rock stars later browsed the books from Ford and Elite. Woolworth Donahue, Marshall Hemingway, Winthrop Gardiner, Alfred Gwynne Vanderbilt, Jack Chrysler, Earl E. T. Smith, Rutherford Stuyvesant Pierrepont, Jr., Count Rodolfo Crespi of Rome, Stanley Rumbough, Jr., and Dan Topping all married Powers Girls. "Sometimes it seems to me that instead of a modeling agency, what I'm running is a matrimonial agency for millionaires," Powers boasted.

By 1935 Powers and a handful of other New York agents were running stables that contained a total of about two hundred working models, most of them women. Most of them earned about $25 per week. Some commanded $75. And a few, perhaps ten, who had signed exclusive deals with advertisers, took home as much as $100 a week.

Powers made his reputation with high-fashion models, but his business was actually much broader. "One girl would specialize in hats," says Bob Fertig. "Another did junior modeling and could adapt for cosmetics. Powers did pulp magazine pictures, too. He'd say, 'If there's a buck in it, I'll do it.' Wherever you had a pretty girl, a dog, and a baby, you had the potential for a publicity picture." Powers drew the line only at nudes and ads for underwear, depilatories, deodorants, and bathing suits, calling them "objectionables" and demanding extra pay for models who agreed to do them.

It was only a matter of time before competition sprang up. As early as 1929 Walter Thornton announced the opening of a new model agency. Claiming he'd been an orphan, a delivery truck driver, a bricklayer, a shipping clerk, a sculpture student, and an underage enlistee in the Army before beginning to model professionally, Thornton promoted himself as the perfect male type. He'd had fifteen hundred plaster casts of his head made for illustrators to use while *he* posed for photographers. As an agent he styled himself a "Merchant of Venus."

Fashion modeling had actually existed for more than three hundred years when John Robert Powers "invented" it. Women wore important clothes in paintings by artists like Van Eyck, Rembrandt, Goya, Sargent, and Whistler. The first recorded instances of models' selling fashion involved wooden dolls dressed in miniature versions of couture—or hand-sewn—clothes that were sent in the seventeenth century to wealthy dress buyers in the capitals of Europe. By the mid-eighteenth century the first fashion magazines had appeared, showing the work of royal seamstresses like Rose Bertin, a favorite at the court of Versailles. *Le Costume Français* and *Journal des Dames et des Modes* contained early fashion plates. The first known fashion photographs as such were probably taken in Paris around 1840 in Charles Reutlinger's Maison Reutlinger studios on Boulevard Montmartre. In England David Octavius Hill and Robert Adamson photographed Lady Mary Ruthven in the fashions of 1845.

The first true model came along soon thereafter. Marie Vernet started out as a salesgirl in a Paris clothes shop, Gagelin et Opigez. In 1852 she married a salesman named Charles Worth and became his house model when he opened Worth, the first "designer" couture salon, in 1858. When she approached the Austrian ambassador's wife, Pauline de Metternich, and sold her two crinolines, her husband's fortunes were assured. He went on to dress Empress Eugénie, the wife of Napoleon III. Inspired by his wife, Worth pioneered the use of live models in selling his haute couture designs.

The first photographic model of any accomplishment was the Countess of Castiglione, a Tuscan noblewoman at the court of Napoleon III. In 1856 a book of 288 photographs of her by Adolphe Braun displayed her renowned style and wardrobe. She even demurely raised her skirts to show off her shoes.

Technology made photographic modeling something more than a dilettante's avocation. The halftone process that allows photographs to be printed on the same page as type was patented in 1881 and refined throughout the proceeding decade. In 1892 *La Mode Practique* was the first to use halftones to show fashion. A few years later John Robert Powers was born in the farm town of Easton, Pennsylvania, the son of an engineer. As he grew up, worked as a newspaperboy, attended local schools, and caught the acting bug, other key figures were coming onstage as well—all over the map. Adolphe de Meyer was born in Paris in 1868 (as Adolphe Meyer Watson). Edward Steichen was born eleven years later in Luxembourg. Louise Dahl-Wolfe was born in San

Francisco in 1895. Baron George Hoyningen-Huene was born in Leningrad in 1900. The four were pioneers of fashion photography.

At first their subjects were actresses and aristocrats whose names were known to at least some of the public and who were sometimes given the clothes they wore as compensation for posing. Steichen, for example, shot a portrait of the wife of a swell named Condé Nast in 1907. Two years later Nast, an ambitious young man from Peoria, bought *Vogue* magazine. Two years after that Steichen took what he later modestly claimed were "the first serious fashion photographs ever taken."

Paul Poiret, a Parisian haute couturier, had used his wife, Denise, as his muse and model and had hired others to stage fashion shows on a barge on the Seine. In 1911 *Arts et Décoration* commissioned thirteen Steichen photographs of Poiret dresses for an article on "The Art of the Dress." His models were not great beauties. But Poiret became a patron of fashion photographers and models, and the visual quality of his *cabine*—his private group of models—improved with time.

Ten years later, when Man Ray, the American surrealist, arrived in Paris during the summer fashion shows there, he met Poiret and photographed some of his Orientalist designs. In Man Ray's autobiography, *Self Portrait,* he remembers his first meeting with Poiret's models: "They were beautiful girls . . . moving about nonchalantly in their scanty chemises, stockings and high-heeled shoes. . . . I tried to look as if I did not see anything. The girls were cool, almost forbidding. All except one black-haired, wide-eyed girl. . . . She, too, was from New York, studying singing and making her way by modeling." She agreed to pose for him and said she hoped the photos would be published in a fashion magazine. In fact, they became monuments in the history of photography: Man Ray's first "Rayographs." He stumbled upon the process when his darkroom door was accidentally opened while he was making contact prints of the American model.

Baron de Meyer, an admirer of Whistler, Sargent, and Europe's great court painters, had started working for *Vogue* in New York in 1913, earning $100 a week as the world's first full-time fashion photographer. He'd dropped his original last name when, despite his homosexuality, he married a woman reputed to be the illegitimate daughter of Britain's Edward VII. "There was always a slight air of mystery about him," said *Vogue*'s then editor, Edna Woolman Chase, who remembered him as "Von" Meyer. His first model was Gertrude Vanderbilt Whitney, the bohemian society matron. His photographs were mysterious, a bit stiff, but always extravagant.

Meanwhile, in 1913 the publisher William Randolph Hearst bought a magazine called *Bazar*—the second *a* was added in 1929—and retooled it as an elite fashion magazine. In 1918 Hearst lured De Meyer from *Vogue* with a higher salary and a promise of work in Paris. The baron's move began a fashion war between *Bazaar* and *Vogue* that has lasted the rest of the century. The next year Hearst's newspapers announced—prematurely—the demise of Nast's British *Vogue*. Chase complains in her autobiography, *Always in Vogue,* that Hearst poached her stars "with money often beyond their worth and beyond what Condé was willing to pay."

The fashion runway that supermodels now prowl likely came into being at a trade exhibition held in Chicago in 1914—the first recorded instance of a catwalk being built out into the audience to afford a good view of the clothes. *Vogue* organized its first fashion show in New York that year, too, and advertised publicly for models. "They beat our doors down," Chase said. "The following year, mannequins started to become an important factor in the American fashion scene." By 1924 French fashion designers had heard the call. Jean Patou decided to recruit in America and held the first model search, finding, among others, Dinarzade, aka Lillian Farley, and Edwina Prue, who was just seventeen. In 1931 Prue married Leo D'Erlanger, an English banker, who later saved Condé Nast from bankruptcy.

Slowly, fashionable magazines began moving away from their first models, actors like Marion Davies, dancers like Isadora Duncan (who posed for Steichen at the Parthenon in a Grecian tunic), and celebrated women like Mrs. Whitney. When *Vogue* next had a fashion show, it imported two professionals, Hebe and Dolores, from the salon of the English designer Lady Duff Gordon, who worked as Lucile. Models in houses like Lucile and Poiret were already marketing themselves with single names, but that may have been because they were considered disreputable, one step above courtesans. Their clandestine affairs with rich aristocrats were the subjects of alternately horrified and fascinated whispers in polite society.

Vera Ashby worked as head model in the Molyneux couture salon. She went by the exotic name Sumurum. "Modeling was considered very fast and loose in France," she recalled. "We were not received in society. I used to have four or five boys after me at a time. The Comte-de-this and the Vicomte-de-that. Whatever mannequin or young woman was fashionable at the time, they always wanted her." But designers still treated them in a second-class manner. "Do not speak to the girls," Poiret would say. "They are not there."

That soon changed. A whole new fashion business had sprung up between the high-priced couturiers of Paris and mere manufacturers of clothing for Everyman and -woman. It made dresses magazines could "cover." Powers was already positioned to provide models to wear the dresses. All that was missing was class, and the courtly gentlemen photographers of the era were there to provide it, even as they effected a silent coup d'état against the ruling elite of illustrators.

Edward Steichen joined *Vogue,* replacing De Meyer as chief photographer and De Meyer's florid style with something crisper. Steichen's favorite model was Marion Morehouse, who later married the poet e. e. cummings. She "was no more interested in fashion than I was," Steichen said. "But when she put on the clothes that were to be photographed, she transformed herself into a woman who really would wear . . . whatever the outfit was." Condé Nast, still smarting perhaps from the loss of De Meyer, told Steichen, "Every woman De Meyer photographs looks like a model. You make every model look like a woman."

De Meyer's career went into decline. Fired by *Bazaar*'s new editor, Carmel Snow, in 1932, De Meyer went to *Vogue* and begged for his job back. "He seemed wasted somehow and his gray hair, which had given him an elegant air, was dyed bright blue," Chase recalled. Unfortunately for the baron, he "was now known as a *Bazaar* personality. Also his work was sadly passé." Steichen had just taken the first color fashion photograph and the first photographic *Vogue* cover! Forgotten, Baron Adolphe de Meyer "wandered into the night-dark of opium and cocaine," according to a Condé Nast history of fashion photography, and ended a broken man. He died in Los Angeles in 1949.

Fashion is a vicious business. Long before De Meyer died, another baron had come on the fashion scene, ready to replace him, and this time his social position was unquestionable. George Hoyningen-Huene moved to Paris in 1923 to work at his sister's fashion house as a sketch artist. Born in 1900 in St. Petersburg, he was the grandson of an envoy to a past czar of Russia and the son of the chief equerry to the last czar. Hoyningen-Huene's mother was a product of Grosse Point, Michigan. The family fled prerevolutionary Russia for London in 1916. After World War I Hoyningen-Huene went to Paris. In 1925 he was working as a background designer for the new French edition of *Vogue* when he collaborated with Man Ray on a photo spread. After seeing it, Main Bocher, who was French *Vogue*'s editor before he became the designer

Mainbocher, decided that the baron could take fashion photographs. A modernist like Steichen and a homosexual, like many of his other contemporaries Hoyningen-Huene was far more interested in the photograph than in the girl who posed for it and considered his models "nothing more than clotheshorses." He was more polite than Cecil Beaton, who joined *Vogue* in 1926. He called models "silly cows."

Lee Miller probably would have bristled at Beaton's misogyny. A blue-eyed blonde from Poughkeepsie, New York, she ran off to Paris as a teenager to be an artist. Dragged back by to America by her father, she was saved from being hit by a car by Condé Nast and became a *Vogue* cover girl, working for Steichen. (She was horrified when his pictures of her turned up in an ad for sanitary napkins.) Returning to Paris, she modeled for Hoyningen-Huene and moved in with Man Ray, working in his darkroom. It is said that it was she who opened his darkroom door and created the first Rayograph when something ran across her foot in the dark.

Miller learned to take pictures from Man Ray. (She learned more than that, in fact. He once took her to dinner in the hotel room of a fetishist, who had a girl chained up on the floor during their meal.) She returned to New York in 1932 and became a photographer herself, moving eventually from fashion to reportage. Her photographs of the devastation of World War II were highly regarded.

Indeed, models like Miller helped Hoyningen-Huene and his brethren capture the first commercial evidence of women moving out of servitude toward freedom. Just as high fashion had once bound them in whalebone corsets, designers like Madeleine Vionnet were now freeing them in bias-cut dresses. "Was there no way to render images of women the way you saw them, in their normal surroundings, pausing for a moment in their daily activities and not posing for a photograph?" Hoyningen-Huene asked. The answer was right around the corner, just past the Great Depression.

HANNAH LEE
SHERMAN

On a small table in the entrance to Hannah Lee Stokes's house in Cooperstown, New York, there is a black-and-white photo of her by De Meijian. She wears a Mariano Fortuny jacket and dress. She still has the jacket, though it's a bit worn. On display in the house are paintings of George Washington and several other military men, including some who are her ancestors. Medals they won as far back as the Civil War hang artfully framed on her walls. There are none of Hannah Lee's medals—photographs by Edward Steichen. She was one of his favorites, but she never talks about it.

Hannah Lee has a scrapbook of her achievements as a model tucked into the bottom of a closet. In it is a clipping from an old New York *Telegram*. THAT LOVELY, ANONYMOUS GIRL OF "ADS" ADMITS SHE'S IN THE SOCIAL REGISTER, the headline says. "Unwittingly, she has pointed a trend that is now veering gay Junior Leaguers from the chiffon of boudoir and lounge to the jersey of subway and office," the *Telegram* reported. "It is the new expression; the economic, subjecting the cosmic, urge."

It was the birth of the modern woman. Stokes was an early model.

"My father's uncle was General William Tecumseh Sherman. My mother's father was General Joseph T. Bartlett. My father was a lawyer in Boston. He lost his inherited fortune because of unfortunate stock market investments. After he died, when I was five, mother brought my brothers and me to New York. She took one of those lovely and fashionable brownstone houses at 109 East Fifty-fifth Street and became an interior decorator. Her name was Bertha Bartlett Sherman. I went to Brearley and then to finishing school near Lake Geneva in Switzerland.

"I grew up during Prohibition. We went to beautiful, extravagant coming-out parties. All those robber barons wanted to spend their money. It was the end of an era. You always knew everybody. But things were changing. My friends would have fainted if someone asked them, 'What are you doing?' I was one of the first. I didn't want to be a fat sponge, sitting around. Natica Nast, Condé Nast's daughter, said I had to see her father and he'd give me something. So I hotfooted it down there, and Mr. Nast gave me an office. He said, 'You just call all your friends and get them to subscribe to *Vogue.*' I did it for a week, and I thought I would go out of my mind. I said, 'Please, your magazine is wonderful, but I can't do this.' He said I should go see Mr. Edward Steichen.

"I kept saying to Mr. Steichen, 'You don't want pictures of me, oh, please, no,' and he said, as though talking to a kid, 'Allow me to be the judge.' He took a whole roll of pictures of me, and I went home. That's that. Then he called and said, '*Vogue* wants you.' I worked exclusively for them, for Mr. Steichen or Mr. Gabor Eder. He was Hungarian. They were of the old school, proper and gentlemanly. Mr. Steichen was so nice. One day he said, 'It isn't fair you are tied down to *Vogue.*' He opened his drawer, and there were letters from different companies, Chesterfield cigarettes, Coca-Cola. He said, 'I must give them to you.'

"John Robert Powers was just a room with telephones. His head man had seen my pictures. Mother was getting a bit . . . hmm . . . she wasn't too crazy about it. She didn't want me to sign up with him. But he was a nice man. I rather liked him. We never made friends. I didn't mean not to, but we went with different crowds.

"In those days girls who came out didn't go out and get jobs. Some people had been modeling already, but they were—how to put it politely?—stage people. It was all so new. But it caught on. Mr. Powers wanted me to help him get a start. He never charged me anything. He said, 'You give glamour." He intimated that he wanted to get a little more social. He said, 'You'll draw them in.' He only had about three or four models like me. He didn't want frivolous little silly people with frizzy hair posing for ads. I took people to him. Then they all wanted to get into it.

"I was one of the finalists when Jean Patou came to America, looking for models. There were five hundred girls at first, then they got it down to fifty, and then the final five, and I was one. My mother was furious. She said I

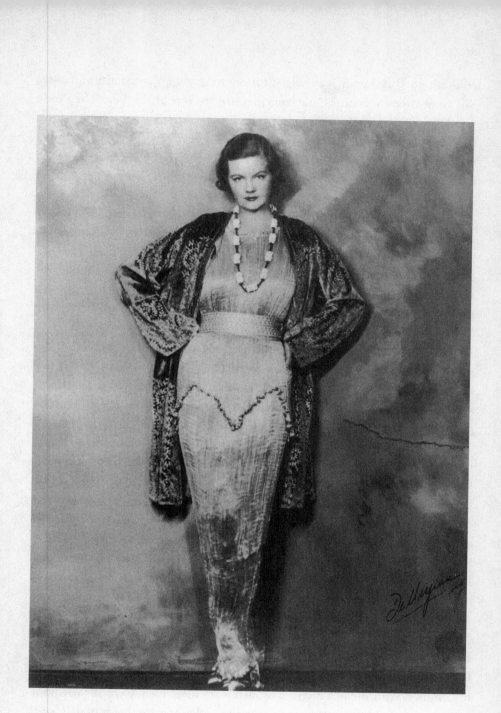

Hannah Lee Sherman wearing Mariano Fortuny,
photographed by De Meijian

couldn't go. But my uncle arranged for me to stay with an American family. We went over by boat. The arrangements were top of the line. They took good care of us, and Patou's clothes were so chic. There was a rumor that his mistress was the money behind the business. None of us ever saw her, but that was the rumor. He was always perfectly well behaved, however, and a good thing, too. I was asked to stay a year, but I came home after nine months. When we got back, we were even more popular than before.

"Our fees kept going up. At the very beginning I got double what anybody else got. It was a big fat joke, twenty, forty, one hundred dollars. And think what a five-dollar bill meant in those days! This was, after all, just after the crash. I got a thousand dollars once for something where they used my name. It was probably a big billboard. The clients would bring little gifts. Suppose they made a perfume, they'd bring you a box. Or jewelry. Good jewelry, not cheap junk.

"It was all very businesslike. We all had hatboxes. They helped a lot. You just threw everything in. Boy, to this day I can change clothes fast. Powers had a secretary who attended to things. They would call and say, 'Be at such and such a place, and you won't need special shoes. Do you have a dog?' You got paid extra if you brought your dog and your Chrysler car.

"I crashed into the general advertising field, and soon billboards appeared. One even called me 'America's Sweetheart.' I started working for everyone. Pepsodent. Vapex cold remedy. My friends told me, 'It's in all the subways.' I'd say, 'How awful!' They'd say, 'Noooo.' I'd meet cutout figures of myself in the drugstore. It was the queerest. I'd make extra money on the side doing fashion shows for Lord & Taylor, Henri Bendel, Bergdorf Goodman. That was kind of fun. And gorgeous clothes. I could get them for a song. But you didn't talk about how you got dresses. You wouldn't tell some *lemon* who'd talk about it.

"My friends were just fascinated. They would want to come with me. I wanted to do it right and not bring a bunch of pals who'd talk their lungs out. Men were fascinated, but I shoved it away immediately and got on to another subject. What did they know about it? None of the other models were my friends. They were fairly nice. I was never high hat. I just didn't have anything in common with them. The male models were nice. They were all very poor and courteous. Mother was very upset about them at the beginning. I said, 'Oh, pipe down.'

"How did people react? Sometimes I'd walk into a restaurant and people would say, 'That's the such and such girl.' I would turn scarlet! At house parties people would stick my ads in frames. I went to terribly chic dinners, and some man would always say, 'I've seen you before,' and you'd want to bop him over the head. But I met royalty and diplomats. I became a favorite of Mrs. Cornelius Vanderbilt. They had a mansion at Fifty-first Street and Fifth Avenue, and boy, did they have distinguished people there. I was always the youngest. I was just twenty. Too bad I wasn't a little older. I felt like a sap.

"I stopped modeling the day before I married in 1934. He was a state senator, and he owned a Wall Street brokerage house. I had to call John Robert Powers up and tell him. He said, 'What!' Everyone was trying to get in, and here was somebody calling up and saying, 'I'm getting out.' I could have pursued fashion, I suppose. It would have been so interesting. Instead you fall in love, get married, and move to a dinky place like Cooperstown.

"If we could all stay twenty for years and years, wouldn't it be fun?"

Harry Conover registered as a John Robert Powers model in 1935. He was twenty-four years old and, like his agent, came from the American heartland—Chicago. Like Powers, Conover was charming, too, but there the similarity ends.

Conover was a little *too* charming and definitely no gentleman.

He was born in 1911, and his parents separated soon afterward. His father was a traveling salesman, a bigamist, and a rascal. After his mother tracked her wastrel spouse down and divorced him, she sent Harry away to military school in 1923, hoping he'd become a priest. He dutifully headed for Notre Dame University but lasted only a day. He bounced from Chicago, where he worked in an uncle's biscuit factory, to New York, where he was a radio soap opera actor and a salesman at Abercrombie & Fitch, to Michigan, where he was a disc jockey, before returning to New York and a job as a tie salesman at Saks Fifth Avenue. One day he went along to provide moral support for a friend who wanted to model. The friend's fate is unknown. But John Robert Powers signed the green-eyed, wavy-haired six-foot Conover.

Conover was so smooth that Powers soon asked him to introduce new models around. "He knew he was showing himself off, too," says Powers promo man Bob Fertig. "He was a self-promoter. We got along very well." Conover was the first, but hardly the last, *rabatteur* in the world of models. The French word refers to the man who leads a hunt, beating the bushes to flush out the day's prey.

One day Conover met a willowy ash blonde in an elevator in the Chrysler Building, where Walter Thornton's agency had its offices. "You look like a model," he told her.

"Not a very successful one," she replied. She was with Thornton.

"Come with me," Conover said, leading her to the Powers office on Park Avenue. "We'll make you the most famous model in New York City."

Her name was Anita Counihan, and despite heavy legs and a thick figure, she did indeed become the first supermodel, appearing on fifteen magazine covers in a single month. The daughter of Daniel Frances "Bud" Counihan, a sportswriter and artist on the *Betty Boop* cartoon strip, Anita was from Washington, D.C. It was there one night at a Georgetown University dance that she had an encounter with a Powers model. "I suddenly found myself deserted," she recalled. "I followed the mob to the center of interest. It was a girl named Peggy Leyden. I was just as pretty as she was, but she was a model. So I decided to be a model in New York. My parents were outraged."

Not for long. While her body wasn't great, her face was so flawless that a friend of her father's, war correspondent Quentin Reynolds, nicknamed her the Face. Almost immediately it was on newsstands and billboards across the country. A Broadway bachelor proposed to her with the line "You're the only woman in the world I'd like to pay alimony to." She smoked and drank. She ground her teeth when she slept.

A year after she started with Powers, Anita recruited her sister, Francine Counihan, to join her at Powers and then, lured by RKO Pictures, left for Hollywood. As Anita Colby she appeared in a series of films. But by 1937 she was back in New York, modeling and hanging out with Francine at the newly voguish Stork Club, dancing at El Morocco, and chatting with Ernest Hemingway, just returned from covering the Spanish Civil War. "I came in with my little hat box," she recalled, "and Hemingway was talking about Spain. Well, I didn't say a thing for an hour, which was an all-time record for me."

Colby joined Conover when he opened but didn't stay around very long. "I said to myself, Colby, you better give it up while you're on top," she recalled. "A model's days are numbered." Late in 1938 she astonished her friends by getting a job as an ad salesperson at Hearst's *Harper's Bazaar*. Not only did she become a top money earner there, she also kept modeling, but only for those who'd pay her ever-increasing fee. In 1945 it hit $50 a hour. She eventually got $100.

In 1944 Colby returned to Hollywood as the ringleader and press agent for a gang of Conover models—including sister Francine—who'd traveled west in a special train car to pretty up a movie called *Cover Girl* (on which Conover served as technical adviser). The newspapers followed every step as the Cover Girl Caravan crossed the country to Beverly Hills. There "wolves" howled at their door, and Mickey Rooney turned handsprings on their lawn. Behind the scenes there was an even wilder circus. Producer Harry Cohn treated the models like galley slaves. They were benched—and virtually imprisoned—for months while Cohn searched for a star (finally ending up with Rita Hayworth). Meanwhile, Colby's astonishing success with the press—she averaged three magazine covers per cover girl—won her a new job as "Feminine Director" of the David O. Selznick studio.

As an "image consultant" for stars like Ingrid Bergman, Katharine Hepburn, and Jennifer Jones, Colby made the cover of *Time* magazine. Later she worked for Paramount Pictures; opened a public relations firm; bought and sold the Women's News Service; wrote "Anita Says," a syndicated newspaper column, and several books; and appeared on the *Today* show in its early years (with the young Barbara Walters as her scriptwriter). Over the years Colby turned down marriage proposals from Clark Gable and James Stewart ("I'd rather be lonely than sorry," she'd say), but finally married businessman Palen Flagler at age fifty-six. She lived out her days on Long Island's North Shore and died in 1992.

When Conover brought Colby to the Powers agency, it was prospering. Although the country was still mired in the Depression, the advertising business was going strong. So, too, fashion: A British edition of *Vogue* was first published in 1916, and a French edition was added four years later.

In 1930 George Hoyningen-Huene picked up a handsome young man in a Paris café. He began seeing him regularly and using him as a model. Horst Paul Albert Bohrmann (later known as Horst P. Horst) was the second son of a bourgeois hardware store owner and his eccentric wife. He grew up in a small German town, studied architecture at Walter Gropius's Bauhaus, and toyed with the nascent naturist movement with a nudist girlfriend. Though a local artist once painted him as St. Sebastian, nude and tied to a post, Horst found his countrymen provincial. "That's why I went to Paris," he says. "I wanted to find out what there is, you know? I wanted to get somewhere."

Horst took an unpaid internship with the architect Le Corbusier in Paris, but the work bored him. He preferred wandering the city. After their chance encounter in the café, Horst accepted a weekend in a château with the dapper, difficult Hoyningen-Huene, who soon set the younger man up in a servant's room above his own apartment.

When they met, Horst had never heard of Hoyningen-Huene's employer, *Vogue*. But the handsome and muscular Horst was soon assisting Hoyningen-

Huene and even posing for him bare-chested in a photo that wasn't seen for many years. "You didn't *dare* publish it," Horst says. Indeed, there was much that fashion photographers couldn't publish then. *Vogue*'s owner, Condé Nast, even dictated the kind of camera his photographers used. Yet when Hoyningen-Huene introduced his protégé to Dr. Mehemed Agha, *Vogue*'s art director, in 1931, the fact that Horst had never taken a picture didn't keep him from a job as a French *Vogue* photographer.

In 1935 the temperamental Hoyningen-Huene turned a restaurant table over on Dr. Agha after the art director told him he was badly behaved. Hoyningen-Huene decamped for *Harper's Bazaar.* Horst was his logical successor as *Vogue*'s chief lensman. Summoned to New York, almost immediately fired ("You are not Steichen!" Condé Nast thundered), then rehired in Paris, Horst spent the years before the Second World War photographing the famous, the wellborn, and the beautiful.

There weren't many models yet in Paris. "In those days we had no hairdressers, makeup people or modeling agencies," Horst says. "Girls just turned up or somebody knew somebody. I have no idea what they were paid, but it was very little." Horst worked with the best, including Marion Morehouse, Lee Miller, Betty McLauchlen, and Muriel Maxwell. Princess Natasha Paley, an aristocratic Russian who married the couturier Lucien Lelong, was one of his favorites. So was another Russian, Ludmilla, who lived on a barge on the Seine River. Horst met her when she delivered some sweaters to his studio, and he talked her into modeling. "At first," Horst recalls, "Mr. Nast said she wouldn't be right; she wasn't elegant. She was a Russian girl, and her nose was too short and thick. Later he nearly wanted to marry her." The couturier Elsa Schiaparelli fell for Lud, too, and demanded to use her exclusively. Years later Horst tried to find her again and learned she'd run off with a lion tamer.

Horst first photographed Lisa Fonssagrives in 1934. He came to consider her the most professional model he'd ever met. Born Lisa Bernstone in Uddevalla, Sweden, in 1911, she was sent to a cooking school by parents who thought she should be well trained to become a housewife. She had other ideas. She went to Paris, danced in minor ballet companies, and in 1935 married another dancer, Fernand Fonssagrives. "I couldn't take my eyes away from her," remembers Fonssagrives, eighty-four, now a sculptor in Little Rock, Arkansas.

One day, in an elevator as Lisa was coming home from a dance lesson, a man asked her to model some hats. "I was terribly shy but flattered," she later said. Fernand took the resulting pictures to *Vogue,* and another photo session was arranged, this time with Horst. "I had never seen a fashion magazine," she said. "I made all my own clothes. I arrived so frightened with my hair long and wild and completely unmanageable. . . . I had no idea what to do with myself." At her first shootings with him, Horst recalled, she trembled from set fright. But finally she put her dancer's skills to work on the photo sets. "The movements I chose in modeling were arrested dance movements. My training gave me terrific control. It was 'still-dancing,' really," she said.

Horst says she started visiting the Louvre, studying statues and portraits to learn how to sit, stand, fold her hands, and smile. "I would imagine what kind of woman would wear the gown," she said, "and assume different characters. I would look at the cut of the dress and try different poses to see how it fell best, how the light would enhance it. . . . I was terribly serious about being responsible and even studied photography to learn what the problems might be. I would stand before the camera on a set and concentrate my energy until I could sense it radiate into the lens and feel when the photographer had the picture."

Fonssagrives liked Horst and Hoyningen-Huene particularly. Despite his imperiousness, she thought Hoyningen-Huene considerate because he used a stand-in while setting up his lights and then had the model led onto his set as if she were part of "some mystic ritual." Hoyningen-Huene ruled his studio with an iron hand. "No one was allowed on the set in those days," Fonssagrives recalled. "Not even an editor." (By the time that changed, Hoyningen-Huene, "bored with it all," had moved to Los Angeles. He died there in 1968.)

Between jobs Lisa and Fernand traveled. He had a Brownie box camera and took pictures of her dancing, skiing, canoeing, and sunbathing in the nude. When he hurt his back in an accident, he started selling his pictures to magazines. "A lot of money started coming in," he says. Everyone wanted Lisa. In 1937 Erwin Blumenfeld shot her hanging from the girders of the Eiffel Tower. Jean Moral photographed her parachuting from an airplane. Horst shot nudes of her and, in 1938, helped her husband get work with fashion magazines.

The couple moved to America when war broke out. Fernand started shooting for *Town & Country*. Lisa signed with Powers, but she was so popular she found she could work without an agency and handled her bookings from her husband's studio. "A lot of top models didn't have agents," says Dorian Leigh, who started modeling around the same time. "It was a small world, and photographers knew where you lived and called you."

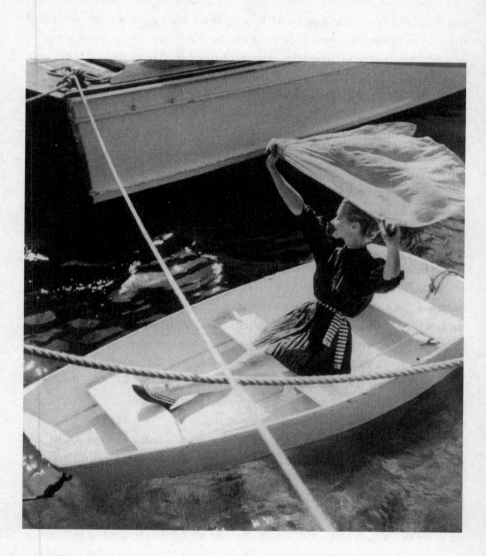

Lisa Fonssagrives afloat, photographed by Louise Dahl-Wolfe

* * *

A model of Fonssagrives's stature might be able to live without an agent, but most models could not. In 1937 a reporter who came calling described the Powers agency in New York as "a madhouse." There were five secretaries answering seventeen telephones. Powers claimed he'd interviewed half a million model hopefuls in his fourteen years in business. His success had changed the social status of models. Elsa Maxwell, the society hostess, said that while she might give a party without debutantes, she wouldn't dream of having one without inviting a few Powers Girls. He'd also raised their pay. While starting models were still taking home $5 for every ninety minutes' work, top Powers Girls were earning as much as $300 a week.

Unfortunately for Powers, success had made him a busy man—too busy to deal personally with all his many models. Conover, for one, began to feel that Powers was inaccessible. Here he was doing his agent's job, and what was he getting for it? "I saw there was more money at the top," he said. Conover began thinking of opening his own agency. Anita Colby agreed to switch if he opened. So did Phyllis Brown, who'd started modeling while on a summer vacation from college. Brown's boyfriend, a tanned blond Yale law student named Gerald Ford, was a Powers model, too. He ended up sharing an apartment with Conover and agreed to invest. Conover and Ford scraped together $1,000 to pay a month's rent and a security deposit on an office near Grand Central Station. There wasn't enough money to pay for telephones, so Conover "installed" toy phones in the office, pretending to talk into them to demonstrate how busy his agency was.

Brown helped recruit models, who arranged to leave Powers a few at a time, so as not to set off alarms. She also engaged in a bit of petty theft that won the Conover agency ten fresh faces. She'd been working for an illustrator for *Cosmopolitan* magazine, and one of her jobs was to serve as a judge in a *Cosmo* Girl contest. Though the contestant lists were secret, Brown made off with the names and addresses of the best-looking entrants and gave them to Conover. "Of course, I eventually got caught," Brown told Conover's daughter, Carole, in *Cover Girls,* her memoir of her father's life. "As I recall, Jerry and I went off for an extended skiing vacation to avoid my being drawn and quartered."

Brown and Ford modeled for Conover for the next three years as the agency grew from one room to four. After America entered World War II, Ford enlisted in the Navy. Conover didn't follow his friend. "Harry was turned down for flat feet," his second wife, Candy Jones, said later. "Harry bought out Jerry's interest. . . . Not for as much as he asked for but he was satisfied. He was going into politics. I remember Harry coming back from Washington after the war saying 'Jerry's going places.' " Indeed, in 1974, Ford became President of the United States.

At first Conover operated much as Powers did. He even published a model book just like Powers's directory, titled *Who Is She?* Unlike Powers, Conover favored well-scrubbed collegiate types, preppies and campus queens. He derided the high-fashion Powers Girls as "Adenoid Annies, rattling bundles of skin and bones." He liked his women healthy and round. "Frankly, I made up my mind long ago that life was too short for me to kowtow to these Melba-Toast prima donnas whose waspish figures are matched by equally waspish temperaments," he wrote.

He called his finds Conover Coeds, then Cover Girls. But Conover's greatest gimmick was the way he renamed his models. "A good, startling name establishes an identity and personality that increases her calling power," he said. "Most women are natural actresses, and a change in name is like putting on a masquerade costume; it lets her blossom."

Marion Sorenson, a former Watermelon Queen, arrived at Conover's office in 1944. Now she joined a different food group. Conover pulled out the list of names he kept tucked into his desk blotter and dubbed her Chili Williams. She soon lived up to her new moniker. In 1944 Mura Moran, the wife of an illustrator, arrived at her husband's studio and found him having a hot time with Chili. Both denied any wrongdoing in subsequent press accounts. And there were many. New York's columnists loved Conover's kooky Cover Girls.

The very first Cover Girl with a startling name blossomed not from Conover's agency but from a proletarian beer promotion. It was 1939 in Paramus, New Jersey, and Bob Wechsler, a junior account executive at the Einson Freeman advertising agency, was after the Rheingold beer account. His bait was provided by Paul Hesse, a California-based photographer. Hesse had pictures of an athletic young woman he'd spotted playing tennis. Wechsler gave them to Philip Liebmann, Rheingold's ad manager and the son of Alfred Liebmann, its president. The pictures inspired Liebmann to hire Wechsler and Einson Freeman to start work on what was to become one of the longest-running advertising campaigns in history, Miss Rheingold.

Jinx Falkenburg was in the right place at the right time. She was nineteen when one of Hesse's first pictures of her ended up on the cover of the *Saturday Evening Post*. Hesse kept shooting her and introduced her to Anita

Colby—who'd gone west to try to break into movies—and they became fast friends. Colby urged Jinx to come back to New York, offering to support her until she could live on her own. Jinx refused.

Late in 1938 a shipping line in San Francisco hired Jinx for a shoot in Hawaii. The photographer was Edward Steichen on his last commercial assignment. They shot for six weeks in the sand and surf. On the last night Jinx and another model were sitting in the outdoor dining room of their hotel with Steichen and the ad executives. They had a five o'clock flight the next morning, so the men suggested they go to bed early. Jinx and the other model went to their room on a low floor of the hotel. It had a veranda that looked over the glass and steel roof of the dining room. Miffed at being sent off to bed, the giggling teenagers decided to creep out onto the roof and shock the men still at the table by waving down at them.

Unfortunately the roof wasn't as sturdy as it looked. Jinx crashed through the glass, hit her head on a steel beam, and landed, unconscious, on the table where she'd been eating minutes before. Luckily she suffered only a few cuts, bruises, and a minor concussion. But a few months later she doubled over in pain at a tennis match, and it was discovered that one of her kidneys had been dislodged. During her monthlong convalescence, Hesse sent her photographs to Bob Wechsler. Instead of being "the end [of my modeling career], it was the beginning," she says. "It gave me the incentive to get better. It sounded like a wonderful adventure."

Her doctor approved, and Jinx and her mother flew to Palm Beach, where the photographs were to be taken. Jinx was to be featured in all of Rheingold's advertising and display materials. The pay was $1,000 for two weeks' work—"a huge sum for me in those days," she says. The team arrived in Palm Beach on a rainy day—January 21, 1939—Jinx's twenty-first birthday. Hesse gave her the day off, and she went off to visit some old friends. Returning to the hotel, she found her mother and Hesse talking to Philip Liebmann. In introduction, she got to hear Liebmann rant, "She works for me now, just as if she's a secretary at the brewery! She is not to leave the hotel or her room without my permission; she belongs to the brewery!"

"But Jinx is like a flower," her mother sputtered. "She needs to be outdoors!"

Hesse piped up to say how dependable Jinx was.

"I could feel this terrible tension created by all these rules and regulations," Jinx remembers. "I was so upset. I'd never experienced anything like this before." She was so upset, in fact, that she had to be taken to the hospital.

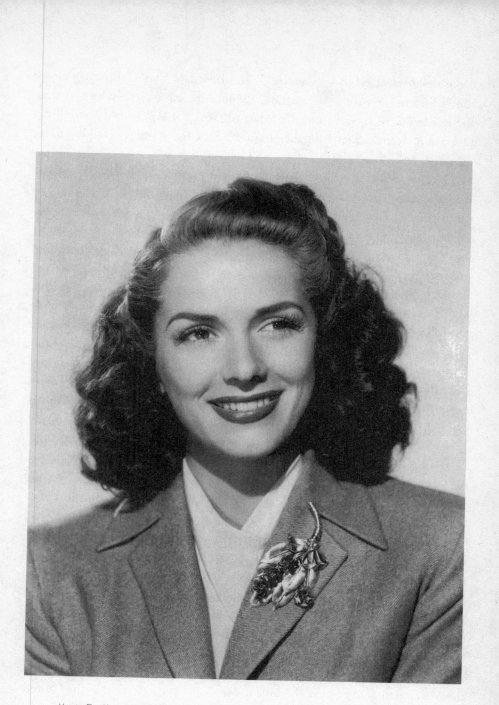

Jinx Falkenburg in a Hollywood publicity photograph

Now she'd never be Miss Rheingold! But two days later Liebmann's father showed up in her room. All was fine, he said. She was to take whatever time she needed to recuperate and then start to work for Rheingold beer. Philip Liebmann, twenty-eight, had taken himself a little too seriously. Daddy had set him straight.

The pictures Hesse took were immensely popular. "Rheingold was the springboard to success for the rest of my life," Jinx says. Within a year Al Jolson gave her a part in a Broadway show, *Life* magazine did a cover story naming her 1941's Girl of the Year, and Columbia Pictures offered her a contract without a screen test. Finally, in 1945, she took Anita Colby's advice, moved to New York, and joined the Conover agency. But her modeling career was almost over. Falkenburg had met broadcaster and newspaper columnist Tex McCrary in 1941, when he interviewed her about her role as a cowgirl in Jolson's *Hold On to Your Hats.* The war separated them, but they stayed in touch. In 1945 NBC offered Tex and Jinx a radio show of their own. Falkenburg quit Conover and became cohost of the immensely popular *Tex & Jinx Show* and coauthor with her new husband of a column for the New York *Herald Tribune.*

In the second year of the Miss Rheingold campaign, Einson Freeman printed a book of twenty-six Miss Rheingold aspirants, all personally approved by Philip Liebmann and all, like Jinx, well scrubbed and WASPish. In 1942 Rheingold opened the voting to the beer-drinking public, and for the next decade Miss Rheingold ads saturated America's Northeast. Cartoons about the contest appeared every year in *The New Yorker.* One showed a bartender fleeing a burning restaurant carrying the Miss Rheingold ballot box. *The New Yorker* wasn't the only American institution to take notice of Miss Rheingold. Howard Hughes owned the apartment right over Paul Hesse's studio and frequently offered the winners screen tests and contracts with his Hollywood studio. Some Miss Rheingold contestants went on to fame in Hollywood without Hughes's help. Tippi Hedren was a runner-up one year, as was Mary Ann Mobley. Grace Kelly was actually rejected by Rheingold in 1948. She was thought to be "too thin."

By 1951 Rheingold's share of its market had risen to 49 percent. That year the Miss Rheingold contest "became the second-largest election in the United States," Wechsler says. "We actually counted twenty-five million ballots."

The background of Rheingold's beauties was always 100 percent European—Irish, Scandinavian, German—mirroring the ethnic backgrounds of the residents of the area where the beer was sold. Irish contestants would win the votes of the Irish and so on. But starting in the late fifties and early sixties,

Hispanics, blacks, and Asians settled in the New York area and began putting pressure on Rheingold to select contestants who represented them. Liebmann refused and instead, in 1958, began a separate campaign targeted to African Americans featuring Ella Fitzgerald and Jackie Robinson. The pressure kept up, nonetheless, to include black and Hispanic nominees. In a final act of stubbornness, Liebmann stopped the contest altogether. Nat King Cole replaced Miss Rheingold on the point-of-sale displays, and at that point, one salesman says, Rheingold became "the black man's beer." The brewery soon lost its share of the market and was finally sold.

The same year Rheingold chose Jinx Falkenburg, Harry Conover got hitched. Ruined in the Depression, Gloria Dalton's father, a banker, started urging his seventeen-year-old daughter to model and got her in to see Conover, who took her on. Within a year Conover married her, moved her into his penthouse apartment on Gramercy Park, and made her stop working. In rapid succession she gave birth to two daughters.

On the professional front, Conover was relentlessly pursuing Powers. He employed five bookers in 1940 in an office decked out with discarded benches from Central Park and with murals depicting park scenes, including a balloon seller whose wares were emblazoned with top model names. Conover's private office was a portrait in masculinity: oak walls, mahogany desk, and leather furniture. Bob Fertig joined that year as Conover's head of promotion. "I'm the only living person who worked for both Powers and Conover," he boasts. "Harry had a completely new approach. At that time fashion people discovered different activity groups, career girls, college girls. A new panorama of talent was needed. John Robert Powers never had the windblown outdoor girl."

Powers never reacted publicly to the new threat from Conover. "He was very phlegmatic," says Fertig. "It was 'Hey, Harry, good luck.' We'd go out and drink after work. If you're making money, you don't care. Later on a sour note invaded the relationship when Powers models started going to Conover." In private "John simply wouldn't talk about Harry Conover," says his son-in-law, Charles Rainey.

Modeling's pioneer was starting to lose his grip. He'd spread himself too thin. His wife, Alice, had begun teaching charm courses at the first in what eventually grew into a nationwide chain of John Robert Powers Schools. She charged $200 for a ten-week course covering such matters as grooming, diction, and coiffure. Powers was the first person to realize that charm schools associated with modeling agencies could make money from the hopes of the many young women who would never be models but wanted to be.

"John knew you couldn't teach it," says Rainey. "You were a model or you weren't." But the power of the Powers Girl was not to be denied. "Girls from all over the country want fashion advice and all that bullshit," says Bob Fertig. "The idea was, you couldn't register everyone [who arrived on an agency's doorstep] because the working models felt threatened." So you signed them up for a course. "To make money," Fertig says flatly.

In 1941 Powers published his first book, *The Powers Girls,* which was part autobiography, part model manual, and in large part advertisement. Many more books followed. In 1943 Powers added a seven-week $25 correspondence course, including "practical hints about what men really do and don't like." He had a radio show and wrote a regular syndicated newspaper column, "Secrets of Charm." And he would stop and do a promotion at the drop of a newspaper column item. Servicemen were always going out with Powers Girls. Warner Brothers announced plans to do a movie on them. Released in 1943, it was a flop.

Powers soared away on the ether of publicity. His girls were always going to dances with servicemen on furlough, and photographers were always along. "Could the Hotel Pierre's sleeping beauty (who took an overdose of sleeping pills and is still unconscious) be Mary Rogers, Powers Model?" Walter Winchell asked in his gossip column in 1940. POWERS HAND MODEL ARRIVES, said a Cincinnati *Post* headline in 1941. The Ashland, Kentucky, *Independent* watched as twenty-one models visiting a Marine camp found "convenient seats on the shoulders of members of the Quantico Rifle Team while they try out the 'devil dog' weapons."

With so much going on, it wasn't easy to tell from the outside that the competition was gaining on Powers. But the business had changed dramatically, and "he did not want to be that competitive," says Barbara Tyler, an executive vice-president of Robie Enterprises, which today owns the Powers name. "Everybody was out to make a buck. He wanted to make people feel good about themselves." But by 1946, one Powers model relates, it became an effort to get her earnings out of the agency. "He was a bad businessman," admits Tyler, who taught at a Powers school in the fifties. "He wasn't advised well. And he was too nice."

Powers kept on selling his name until the very end. He launched a line of Powers cosmetics (including John Robert Powers Privilege, a $5 poultice "bursting with super oils, moisturizers, soothing agents and beauty vitamins"), opened an accessory products company, and briefly sold clothes labeled "John Robert Powers Model." But his days in the actual model business were just about over. After franchising his schools and selling the rest of the company off in bits and pieces, Powers simply dropped out of the agency business, shutting his doors and moving to Beverly Hills in 1952. In a promotional film from the 1950s a nameless narrator tells how Powers "transcended flesh peddling to become an educator" and stressed that most of his students "want no part of modeling." At first Powers refused to sell the right to open model agencies bearing his name, but multimillionaire Richard Robie finally bought that, too, in 1974. Today the Powers name is on schools and agencies in many different countries.

Powers lived for another twenty-five years after his move to California, and he died at age eighty-four in 1977. Why did he quit? "I think he just got old and he got tired," says son-in-law Charles Rainey.

The year 1945 was a heady one for Harry Conover. He created a Cover Girl line of cosmetics for Borden, Inc. And his agency became the city's biggest, with 750 models. Everyone wanted a piece of the action, and not just on the magazine page. Advertisers asked for girls to take out on the town. Usually they were told no. But when a Navy admiral, a pilot, and a couple of generals called and offered $100 each for six girls for a private dinner at the Stork Club, certain models were told of the offer and allowed to decide for themselves. And private dates, though rare, could be arranged. "If a guy was married, a trusted friend would take her out," Fertig says. "There's all kinds of ways of skinning the kitty."

A new breed of playboy appeared on the scene, the model hound. Harry Conover, Jr., remembers Bobby and Ted Kennedy hanging around his father's agency. Says Fertig: "I used to sit with new girls and say, 'Now that you've arrived from Upper Japoop, Indiana, and you're in New York and at the top, you're gonna meet a lot of weird guys. Wolves. They're going to call you up." Like Huntington Hartford, the dissolute A&P supermarket heir. "He used to come up," Fertig says. "He had all that money. He would date girls. It was hard to control, so we tried to head it off at the pass. We told them, it's OK to participate in the life, but don't get a reputation as a party girl."

Conover didn't play by Fertig's rules. He left Gloria to deal with the kids while he went out with a different model every night. "There was an interest here and there," admits Fertig. "Where you have a concentration of women, you're going to have a problem." When the Women's Army Corps sent a group of officers for charm training, Conover fell for a lieutenant. Then he chased a model named Jiggs Butler. In 1944 he spotted an aspiring twenty-year-old in his office and named her Lassie Newland. "He went off the beam with Lassie," says Fertig. "We'da been out of business, fer chrissakes, if it hit the papers."

Lassie and Harry spent weekends at the Cinnabar Dude Ranch in Peeks-kill, New York. "She rode western saddle," Fertig says meaningfully. "She was an oversexed broad, to be sure." She told friends they were getting married and bought herself a dress. By April 1946 Gloria Conover, twenty-four, was in Reno. Proclaiming that Harry was still her best friend, she sued him for divorce on the ground of mental cruelty. She revealed they'd been separated for almost a year.

June brought the surprise announcement that Harry was going to marry not Lassie but Candy Jones, twenty-three, another blond Cover Girl. Candy was discovered at the Miss America contest in 1941. She was sixteen years old, the daughter of a movie theater ticket taker and car salesman who called his daughter Doll. After spurting eight inches in high school, Candy, whose name was then Jessica Wilcox, won a Miss Atlantic City contest and was hostess of that year's beauty pageant. Afterward she approached John Robert Powers, who'd judged the contest for several years. "You'll be hearing from me," he promised her.

"This is the beginning of the end, Jessica," her irate mother said. "This is the start of your downfall."

That fall Jessica got a telegram from Powers, offering her a cigarette adver-tisement. With her mother's grudging permission, she arrived in New York only to discover that there was no ad. "You have wrinkles in your neck," Powers told her, before offering to enroll her in his charm school. When she threatened to report him to the Miss Atlantic City contest organizers, he agreed to let her sit in his model room and see if any work turned up. Two weeks later, having earned a mere $10, she went to Conover's agency to look up a friend's sister. "You could model, you know," the receptionist told her, sending her in to see Conover.

"I'm Jessica Wilcox," she said.

"You're Candy Johnson," he replied. "And your rate is $5 an hour."

By 1943, thanks to her good looks and his aggressive promotion—includ-ing candy-striped outfits and calling cards—Candy Jones (the name was shortened because she couldn't remember the longer one) was a top model, winning eleven covers in a single month. Conover later said he'd had only

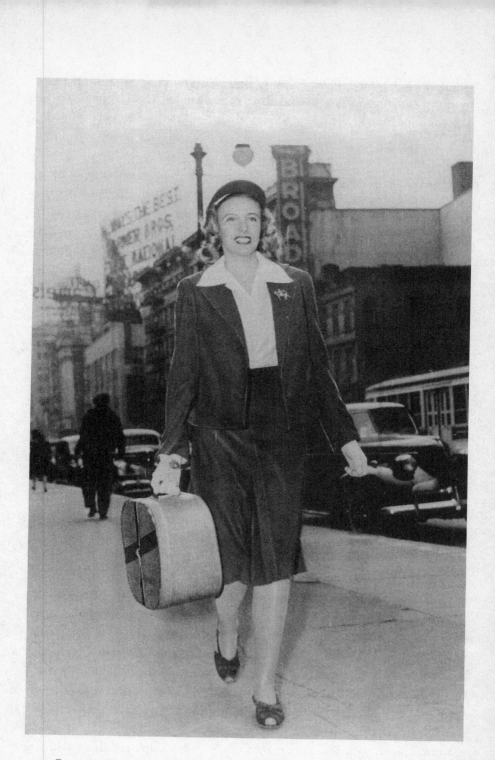

Candy Jones carries a Harry Conover Agency hatbox
in New York, 1942

one date with her before he proposed long distance while she was on a promotional trip for Cover Girl cosmetics in Portland, Oregon. Their engagement announcement included the news that they planned to start a Tex and Jinx–like radio show after their honeymoon. "They began to see a commercial potential in marrying their two names," says Bob Fertig.

After the announcement a public relations man from Canada called, asking Harry to judge a July 4 Miss Canada contest in Hamilton, Ontario. "Are you thinking what I'm thinking?" Conover asked Fertig. With the contest organizers paying for everything, Harry and Candy flew off to Canada to get married and judge the contest together. Speakers were set up outside their church for the benefit of the overflow crowd. The next day they were married again in an Iroquois ceremony, feathers and all.

"Do you love me now?" Candy asked as they returned to their hotel.

"As much as I can," Harry answered, "but don't pin me down. Nothing is forever." Conover fell asleep on her that night and didn't consummate the marriage for some time. "I don't want to break in a virgin," he complained.

Candy knew she was in trouble but was determined to make the best of things. "I wanted to be held and caressed," she said. "Harry didn't like that and soon, I didn't care one way or another."

Meanwhile, intrepid tabloid news hounds had sniffed out Lassie Newland, nursing her wounds at the dude ranch. She told them she'd left Harry because he was an introvert who cared only about business. "Right in my own office we have the very thing that every man looks for, works for, fights for and dies for," Conover said, just before he was excommunicated by the Catholic Church in New Jersey.

It wasn't the best of times for modeling. A dress manufacturer named Samuel Chapman and oleomargarine heir Minot Frazier Jelke III both were arrested for procuring in 1952—and the women arrested with them called themselves "models." The resulting scandal "threw the whole modeling business back twenty years in public esteem," according to Harry Conover. A bright light had been cast on the murky underworld of modeling. "When I first came to Seventh Avenue, house models doubled as escorts for out-of-town buyers," says designer Bill Blass, who arrived in the garment center as a sketcher in the early 1940s. "The assumption was true. Those girls really did put out, Christ, with the gross manufacturers who employed them. Most of the models were kept, and some turned a trick or two."

Within a week of the arrest, a bill was introduced in the City Council to regulate model agencies, and two models appeared at the entrance of the Criminal Courts Building carrying placards that read THERE ARE 5,000 LEGITIMATE MODELS IN NEW YORK CITY. DON'T BELIEVE SENSATIONAL NEWSPAPER HEADLINES! Prostitutes were said to be carrying hatboxes as part of their pose. Models carrying hatboxes were being spit at on the street. The hatbox fad ended.

It was also the beginning of the end of the Conover agency. Harry still lived high. In 1955 he and Candy shared a ritzy six-room apartment at 1199 Park Avenue. But as anyone in the modeling business knows, appearances can deceive. Conover's weight had risen over two hundred pounds, he'd grown a little mustache, and his psoriasis was spreading. He rarely saw his children from his first marriage. And his relationship with Candy wasn't much better. He made her pay for her three births and two abortions out of her own earnings. Candy's mother moved in with them. "He seemed to tolerate Grandmother; she had an incredible hatred for my father," says Harry, Jr. "My pop psychology guess is that she felt he took her little girl and turned her into a wicked, wanton Cover Girl in lipstick." Harry started spending his nights and the agency's money in restaurants and bars, entertaining employees and friends. When he *was* home, he frequently shuttered himself in the bathroom.

"Our relationship became one of simply sharing living space," said Candy. "I didn't much care that he almost never made a sexual advance towards me. In fact, I was relieved." He initiated sex only when drunk. He referred to his wife's ample bosom as "revolting." Sometimes he hid friends in his bedroom closet when he tried to seduce her. Her mother figured he was cheating. But Candy felt he just wanted to be revered and preferred the company of dependent pals to that of an increasingly independent woman. "I detested our marriage," Candy said. Although she adored their children, "I didn't care whether Harry Conover even existed."

Not only was he never at home, he was rarely in the office. Neither was Candy. She'd formally quit the agency after the marriage and set herself up next door at the Conover School for Career Girls, a supposedly separate operation that actually fed Conover's agency. Harry bragged that he wouldn't make a deal without consulting Candy first. Indeed she was taking over the business as he became ever more scarce. "He liked hanging out at all the watering holes, the Stork and Toots Shor's," says Harry, Jr. "It kept him in the columns."

In his absence Candy stepped out front. "The main source of income was Candy, sitting at that desk at the school, talking to mom and a girl," says Fertig. "Depending on her sense of what kind of money they had, she'd decide what to charge them. She always tried to get money up front. She liked cash because it was untraceable. I remember Harry laughing when she was away, saying she'd stash hundred-dollar bills in books and they'd flutter all over the living room."

In spring 1958 Conover disappeared. "I was eleven," says Harry, Jr. "I'd just come home from Trinity. He said, 'I've been a bad boy,' slung his laundry bag over his shoulder, and that was the last time I saw him as a father." He registered under a pseudonym at the Plaza Hotel, took up with an eighteen-year-old model named Astride, and started giving nightly parties. "I never thought of him as being with a girl," Candy said. "I assumed he was sitting talking in the same restaurant, telling the same old story to some man in the agency." She didn't even blink when he had a friend sneak into the office and take furniture to fill up the new apartment he'd rented. But when her absent husband started signing checks, Candy used her power of attorney to close his bank accounts. He screamed. She gave him money. He went on a car-buying spree. Finally he even spent $125,000 of Candy's. "He cleaned out the accounts, and he did it swiftly, too," says son Harry. When Candy discovered she'd bottomed out at $36, she started talking divorce and headed to Mexico.

Just after she returned, in May 1959, the district attorney seized Conover's books, and his license was revoked after a lawsuit was filed alleging that he and Candy had stolen fees belonging to child models. His remaining models immediately started demanding the money he owed to them. "It wasn't easy being a Conover that day," says Harry, Jr.

Outside court the next day Candy's lawyer revealed to the world that she'd divorced her husband in Mexico six weeks earlier. "I left her no alternative," Harry said. "I just got tired of Candy. We were married fourteen years. The very nature of our business—fourteen years is a lifetime." He admitted he was responsible for the agency mess and allowed that Candy had stepped in to run things in his absence. "The story goes back seven years when I wanted to sell the agency after suffering a heart attack," he said. "It was for reasons of health that I walked out nine months ago." He estimated that he owed about $25,000. Candy said Harry owed her alone $100,000. She had to wear a wig to avoid process servers.

The Conover affair ended anticlimactically. In 1960 all charges against Harry were dropped when it was proved he hadn't stolen the money. But he had mismanaged the agency—and his family. Several of his children died young, and at least one more has disappeared, according to daughter Carole,

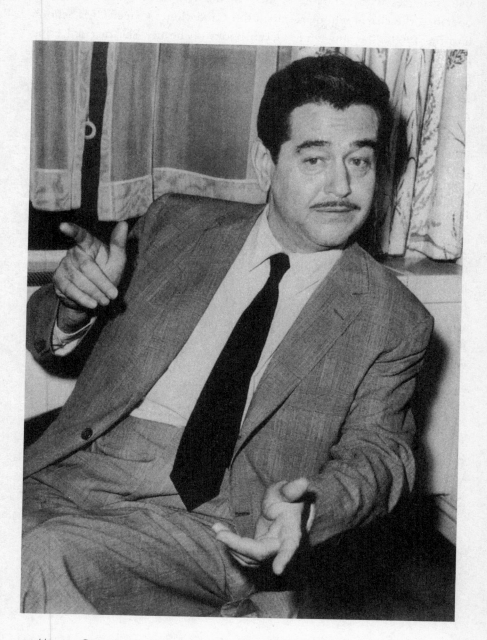

Harry Conover on the day his divorce from Candy Jones
was revealed, May 1959

who struggles with her father's ghost to this day. Candy Jones continued operating the charm school, renamed the Candy Jones Career Girls School, into the 1960s. She also wrote eleven books on beauty. She married Long John Nebel in 1972 and became cohost of his late-night radio talk show. She hosted the show alone from his death in 1978 until just before she died in 1990. An obscure book written about her before she died, *The Control of Candy Jones,* tells a chilling story about her life after modeling.

After she married Nebel, Candy Jones started having insomnia, suffering mood swings, and showing two distinct personalities. Her husband, an amateur hypnotist, put her under his spell, and it emerged, the book alleges, that she'd been recruited, drugged, brainwashed, used, and sexually abused as a pawn of the Central Intelligence Agency.

The book is based on transcripts of unscientific question-and-answer sessions with Nebel and later with a professional hypnotist. It carries an endorsement from Candy herself. But it is also laden with pseudonyms, "could haves," "must have beens," and "possiblys." Regardless, Harry Conover, Jr., believes it. "There was clearly a double life going on," he says. "It's not just Candy Jones, model. It's Candy Jones, superpatriot. Candy Jones, chump. And if she hadn't been a model and gone on USO tours and gotten to know generals personally, none of this stuff would have happened."

And Harry, Sr.? Despite his legal vindication, Conover was ruined. Unable to find a job, he went to his mother for support, kept on hanging out in nightclubs, and traveled to California, where he tried to set up a chain of Harry Conover Charm Schools. "We'd give Harry a bottle of Wild Turkey and prop him up on a sofa to meet people," says Nina Blanchard, a Los Angeles agent who worked at a school. "He was double-selling franchises. He was an old con man who ran out of gimmicks."

Finally, in 1964, Candy had him arrested for nonpayment of alimony and child support, and he was put in jail, where he suffered his second heart attack. Out of prison the next year, he had another heart attack and died, aged fifty-three. An autopsy found he was suffering from cirrhosis and toxic blood.

No models attended his funeral.

FRANCINE COUNIHAN

Anita Colby's sister, Francine Counihan Okie, was a lady, dignified and proper. She offered a drink before a lunch of deviled egg and rolled slices of ham. She wore a nautical print dress, gold, red, and blue against white, and a gold necklace, bracelet, and ring. Her gray hair was worn off her face. Her husband, Jack Okie, an OSS operative during World War II and an international businessman afterward, puttered in and out of their house in Rhode Island. A swimming pool shimmered beyond a set of floor-to-ceiling glass doors. Although she was being treated for the cancer that would claim her life in October 1994, that spring she gave no sign that she was suffering. Like most of the models of her time, even approaching her death, she wore her charm and beauty like an impenetrable suit of armor.

In a small room upstairs in her home is a chest of drawers covered with decoupage—cutout and lacquered photographs and magazine pages—that are all that remain now of her thirteen years as a model with John Robert Powers and Harry Conover. There is a photograph from a *Life* magazine article naming Counihan one of America's ten best-dressed models, a Chesterfield ad drawn by Bradshaw Crandall, another showing Counihan with a cigarette dangling in her lips, a photo from *Town & Country*, a shampoo ad, a Louise Dahl-Wolfe photo, a *Mademoiselle* cover, a photograph from the Stork Club. On the walls are photographs and paintings, several by her sister, whom she called Colby and admired greatly. She nonetheless pointed out that she modeled for far longer and implied that she probably made more money than her more famous sister. "Oh"—she seemed to sigh—"but that was a hundred years ago.

"We lived in Washington, D.C., when we were young. Colby designed, she drew, she'd design our clothes, and my mother was very capable of sewing, and she'd make the things that Colby would design. Sometimes I wasn't as crazy about the outfits that she had in mind, but she'd say, 'You must.' I'd say, 'People turn around and look at me all the time.' And she'd say, 'The day they stop looking, you start to worry.' Colby was always in the future, you know. She might be here, but she was always thinking of someplace else. Woodward and Lothrop is a department store in Washington, and she modeled there, and she got a taste of wanting to be a model. Colby wanted to work. I didn't. I thought, 'Oh, I'm never going to work, I'm having a wonderful life tea dancing and all that kind of thing.'

"Colby started in '34 with Walter Thornton. There was an ad in the paper, and my mother went over with her. The minute they saw her they said, 'This is it.' She would walk into a room and everybody else could go home. And she was bright, very very bright. Then she went on a job—the first job she had—and Harry Conover was with her on the job. And he said, 'What are you doing at that agency? That's an awful agency.' Then she went with Powers. Thornton was nothing. Powers had everyone. You didn't go anyplace else but Powers. A week later she was on everything. I mean, they had her on magazines and billboards and everything.

"Colby started me in '35. Conover said, 'Have her come with you on one of the jobs and I'll talk to her.' I was eighteen, and Colby was nineteen. Conover said, 'You're crazy if you don't start modeling. There's so much money in it.' Well, in those days it was five dollars for an hour and a half. So I went to Powers. He was very interested in people, and he was interested in you being successful. He was a great morale builder. I went into everything. Fashion shows; Sears, Roebuck; *Vogue; Harper's Bazaar;* all the catalogs. I went to Canada, and I went to Arizona—any place that there was money.

"My parents had moved back to New York. Quentin Reynolds was working at the *Evening World* with my father. He became the war correspondent, and he was very famous. And he decided that we should meet certain people in New York. And so the whole world was at our feet. It was 'Twenty-one,' Stork Club, El Morocco, tea dancing at the Plaza Hotel. We were always more popular than the girls that drank because they sometimes got sick. Then we had their dates along with ours.

"My mother would never allow us to go anyplace unless we were chaperoned. She would say, 'You have a date tomorrow night? Well, then you get one for your sister or you can't go.' Why we did it, I don't know, but we'd try to get the worst date for the other one. Isn't that awful?

"One weekend Quentin Reynolds gave us his house in Westchester. He was renting from Heywood Broun at the time. My mother was the chaperon. And there was Harry Conover, Harry Ubhiroff, another model, Colby, myself,

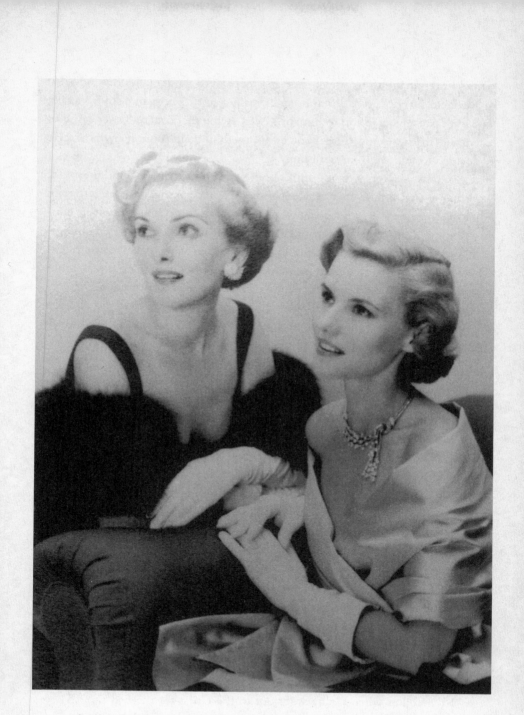

Anita Colby *(left)* and her sister, Francine Counihan,
photographed by John Rawlings

and I'm trying to think of who else, but there were about eight of us. And that weekend Harry said to my mother, 'I really want to start an agency.' I said, 'Don't pay any attention to him; he's been saying that over and over.' And so we said, that weekend, 'Either you do it or let's not talk about it anymore.' He decided to, and we went with him.

"In those days they didn't think about your health. They figured they were paying you, and this was a very expensive job, and that was it. I used to faint maybe three or four times a day, wearing fur coats in studios without air conditioning. In the cold weather they'd say, 'Meet us at the pier,' and you'd get in bathing suits and jump in the East River when it was below zero. But as you became more important, you could say, 'I'm not going to do that, I'm not going to do this, and I'm not going to do underwear. That would not be correct.' I had children. And so I didn't want my pictures all over the place in negligees and nightgowns and all that. That was a no-no for me. And today they're nude in *Vogue!*

"We always dressed to the nines when we worked. We were never late; we were always on time. And if they said, 'Bring the jewelry,' we brought the jewelry, and if they said, 'Dress as though you're going to a black-tie dinner,' we had to bring that kind of dress.

"Colby was more glamorous than I was. I thought glamour was fine, but I wanted the money. She was doing a lot of *Vogue* and a lot of *Harper's*. I was more commercial, and she was more high-fashion. I made a lot of money. See, for me, being a model wasn't as important as the money. I had a seven-room apartment in New York, I had two children in private school. I got married in 1936 for the first time. But after our daughter was born, about eight months later in 1941, we separated. I was separated for about eight years.

"Colby would see somebody who was very attractive, and he'd be attracted to her, and that would last about two weeks. She wanted somebody that was going to take the lead, you know. But in no time at all they were her little puppy dogs. And I think she always said, 'Getting married is not difficult; staying married is difficult.' And I think she always felt, 'If I marry, it must be for life.' She was very Catholic. She finally married Palen Flagler when she was fifty-six.

"I remember when Colby went out to the Coast for the first time. They were doing *Mary of Scotland* with Katharine Hepburn, and the director used some unattractive language, and Colby walked off the set. And she was *not* a big star. But we were brought up a certain way. I had very strict rules and regulations. Photographers could not be in the dressing room. When I look back over it, it's a wonder they ever put up with me.

"We did *Cover Girl* in 1943. There was Jinx Falkenburg, Colby, me, fifteen of us all together. *Cover Girl* was produced by Harry Cohn. Oh, he was a monster. He decided to put us all in one house together where he could see that nobody could get out. So we stayed in Marion Davies's home in California. He only let us out to go shopping.

"Colby and I were friends of Cary Grant and [his then wife, the heiress] Barbara Hutton. And they would give a dinner party and invite us. Cohn would say, 'I don't want any of the girls to go. And if they do go, I want a guest list.' Remember, he was not that accepted in society out there. Barbara Hutton didn't have to give a guest list to Harry Cohn. Finally he decided that Colby could go, but nobody else could. Cohn put policemen at the gate so that we couldn't go. He said it was because of the reputation of the picture.

"I was incensed. I said to the other girls, 'We can go. We'll go two at a time as though we're going shopping, and when we get back'—we had to be back at a certain time—'we'll each say we're Anita Colby,' because she was allowed to do whatever she wanted to do. So they each said, 'I'm Anita Colby,' when they came back. 'But Anita Colby just went in.' 'How dare she use my name!' And the next one, and the next one. All of a sudden I come along, and the guard says, 'I have at least six Colbys up there right now.' So I say, 'I think that's disgusting for somebody to use my name. Wait till Mr. Cohn hears about this.' Colby came in after us, and they wouldn't let her in. They called Cohn. Cohn got out of bed and came over, and it was Anita Colby.

"Finally I said to him, 'This is ridiculous. My mother and father weren't this strict. And I'm not staying here.' Then all the girls decided to get out, and Cohn was in a rage. He said, 'She's the troublemaker.' I said, 'Yes, I certainly am, and I plan to do it for the length of time I'm here, if you don't release me.' He was a most repulsive man. So arrogant. He was paying us, I think, a hundred dollars a week. And everybody could have made that in no time at all. For a month it was fine, but seven months?

"I got married again in 1949 after a trip to Europe with Colby. We sailed on the *Queen Elizabeth* with Rita Hayworth, a maharaja, the Churchills. I met my husband on that trip. Dior and all of them wanted me to model for them over there, and he wouldn't allow it. He said they had very bad reputations.

"I stayed with Harry Conover until I quit. He was smart, he really was. But then he got into some trouble, I don't know how, and when I left the agency, a lot of money was owed to me, a couple of thousand dollars. Harry said, 'Bring your books in.' But my husband was successful, and he just felt, 'Why go through all that? Forget it.' "

$25 AN HOUR

"The only magazines I read were *Ladies' Home Journal* and *Good Housekeeping,* and those only intermittently. My dear, I was an intellect!"

It was 1944, and for Elizabeth Dorian Leigh Parker, becoming a model was an act of prefeminist rebellion. A degree in mechanical engineering from New York University had helped the young woman win a job as a tool designer, fighting World War II at home at Eastern Aircraft, a defense plant in New Jersey. She was the only woman in a room with eighty men; more than a living, breathing Rosie the Riveter, she was their group leader. But the men made twice what she did. Refused a raise, she quit, only to learn that under wartime regulations she wouldn't be able to work anywhere else—at least not as an engineer.

So Dorian got a job as a promotional copywriter at Republic Pictures in Manhattan, where a co-worker soon had an idea: Dorian was pretty enough; why didn't she try modeling?

"As far as I was concerned," she says, "all of the models in the magazines looked Chinese and terribly sophisticated. I didn't wear makeup. I was sure that was not me." But she agreed to try, and one lunchtime she joined the crowd in Harry Conover's waiting room.

"What's your name?" a man suddenly demanded. "You want to be a model?"

"I don't know," she said. "I don't know if I'm the type."

"I'll tell you if you're the type," Harry Conover snapped. "How old are you?"

"I'm going to be twenty-four in April," she answered.

"Don't tell anybody that!!" said Conover. "You're nineteen, and that's over the hill. Can you go to see some people this afternoon?"

She had to go back to Republic, but the next day Parker appeared as instructed at the studio of Louise Dahl-Wolfe. A woman barked, "Go home, come back tomorrow, and don't change your eyebrows!" Dorian thought the woman was crazy. How could you change your eyebrows? But she returned, and the barking woman, an eccentric editor named Diana Vreeland, put her on the cover of *Harper's Bazaar*'s June 1944 issue. "So I was a model," Dorian says, "but I was ashamed about it. At parties a guy would say, 'And what do you do, little girl?' I'd say, 'I'm in advertising.' I was such a snob."

Dorian soon found herself at the center of an image revolution. The only job requirement was that she look right for the times. No questions asked. "I feel like a fool," Vreeland said a year later. "Somebody just told me that you have two children. I thought you were seventeen years old!!"

"There's so much water under the bridge. You'll never, never be able to tell all of it," says Dorian, the most influential, the most larger-than-life photographic model in the seventy-year history of the business. She uses her real last name, Parker, these days and admits to being seventy-four years old. Careworn, with soft brown hair and sad periwinkle blue eyes, Dorian has lost her looks but not her bite.

She started two modeling agencies (including the first ever in France), but she's ended up "the poorest entrepreneur in the world," she says, tooling around in a Ford Escort with smashed windows and sixty-six thousand miles on the odometer. Though her sister, model Suzy Parker, once joked that Dorian's autobiography, *The Girl Who Had Everything,* should have been called "The Girl Who Had Every*one,*" she's ended up alone. And although she was one of the most loved models of her time, her memories are laced with bitterness and hurt, and her relationships are roiled with mixed feelings. Dorian's former agent and business associate Eileen Ford calls her "a pathological liar." Her sister, Suzy, is happiest when she doesn't call at all.

"Dorian was ahead of her time," says model Carmen Dell'Orefice. "She did things her own way. But in a social context she was outrageous beyond being. Everyone knows she screwed the Eastern and Western worlds. We all felt people took advantage of Dorian. It was shocking and possibly embarrassing to Suzy, who lived a different way."

Dorian Leigh was born on a farm in San Antonio, in either 1917 (according to Suzy) or 1920 (according to Dorian). Raised by strict parents who approved of neither smoke nor drink, she finished high school at fifteen and went to Randolph-Macon College in Virginia. She was engaged to three men there when she married a fourth. "To me it didn't mean anything," she says.

Thrown out of Randolph-Macon for cohabiting with her husband, she stayed with him long enough to have two children, then left him and moved to Metuchen, New Jersey, to live with her parents while she earned her degree at NYU. She worked at Bell Labs, the Brooklyn Navy Yard, and Eastern Aircraft. But she was still something of an innocent when she arrived on the fashion scene.

"I was commuting to New Jersey," she recalls. "No matter how many dates I had a night, and I usually had a dinner date and a late date, I would then go to Penn Station and get home. The next morning I would drive to the station in Trenton and leave my car there and take the seven fifty-one A.M. back to New York." She truncated her name to Dorian Leigh for her parents' sake. "My mother and father thought modeling was so low-class that I shouldn't use the last name Parker."

One of her first jobs was with Horst P. Horst, who'd left Paris one step ahead of the Nazis, resettled in New York, and joined the American Army. He was still in uniform the first time he shot Dorian. "I was madly in love with him, I really was," she says. "And that was when I found out what a homosexual was, because the advertising woman who had booked me for this job said, 'My dear, it's a lost cause.' I said, 'Well, he's not married!' And she said, 'Yes, he is, to a photographer named George Hoyningen-Huene.' "

Dorian believes she was the first working model to shoot with an eager young Richard Avedon, then a bespectacled newcomer at *Bazaar*. "He got the clothes at Henri Bendel because he said he'd booked Dorian Leigh, and all the time he was taking pictures of me in his little Merchant Marine uniform, he was saying, 'You're a famous model.' "

In fact, she wasn't yet, but she was about to be.

It was one of those rare moments in history when everything was made over. World War II brought both bad and good. In America the fashion industry was hit with staff reductions, fabric restrictions, price controls, and the loss of communication with Paris, still thought to be the source of all style. But this set the stage for the emergence of the American sportswear industry after the war. Centered in New York City's Seventh Avenue garment district, a native fashion business rose to the occasion and rewrote the rules of getting dressed for a generation of optimistic victors.

The new mood and new fashions were reflected in profound changes at the major fashion magazines. For models and photographers, those changes opened up new worlds of possibilities. Carmel Snow had left *Vogue,* where she worked under Edna Chase, and joined a moribund *Bazaar* in 1932. Her first act was to make the émigré Alexey Brodovitch her art director. Severe money troubles had already caused Condé Nast to lose control of his magazines to bankers in 1929. Now Snow's defection set the abstemious publisher reeling—literally. It is said he got drunk for only the second time in his life. "The crown princess had abandoned him. Everything was based on her," says Alexander Liberman, who became *Vogue*'s art director and later the editorial director of all the Condé Nast magazines.

Brodovitch and Snow created "a remarkable magazine" for Hearst, according to Liberman. "It had more style and class than *Vogue,* which was extremely conservative. In many ways, I had to follow." Brodovitch published Henri Cartier-Bresson, Man Ray, André Kertesz, Bill Brandt, and Brassaï and ran articles and stories by the greatest writers of the time. *Vogue* fought back, banning the work of the defectors, poaching illustrator Christian "Bébé" Berard and, later, fashion editors like Nicolas de Gunzburg and Babs Simpson. But until S. I. Newhouse bought Condé Nast in 1959, "it was not a healthy situation," Liberman says. "Control was in distant hands, and there was very little money." Liberman was also saddled with Edna Woolman Chase, the aging pioneer who held on to *Vogue*'s editorship until 1952.

Meanwhile, Snow and Brodovitch used Hearst's financial vigor to their advantage, snapping up new talents. For the next quarter century *Bazaar* was considered the leading fashion magazine. It never beat *Vogue*'s advertising revenues and only rarely sold more copies, but its stunning, disturbing Brodovitch layouts set a high new standard and redefined the genre.

A Hungarian sports photographer named Martin Munkacsi moved to New York and began to take snapshotlike blurry-action pictures for *Bazaar.* Soon Toni Frissell started doing similar work for *Vogue.* A debutante and sportswoman, she rose to prominence when Cecil Beaton, whom she'd assisted, was dismissed from *Vogue* after penning anti-Semitic remarks in a drawing. She, too, switched to *Bazaar* during the war, only to quit fashion photography in 1958, after Brodovitch's successor dared to look through her viewfinder. Skirmishes between magazines and photographers over creative control have always been in fashion.

In 1935 a Leica camera with a 1/1000-of-a-second shutter speed was introduced and allowed outdoor location fashion photographs for the first time. Kodachrome film arrived that same year. In 1937 Diana Vreeland's arrival as a fashion editor at *Bazaar* brought another kind of color. A grand grotesque with Roman coin features, Kabuki makeup, and enormous style, Vreeland enlivened fashion for fifty years. She later wrote a famous column, "Why Don't You . . . ," in which she dispensed advice like "Have a furry elk-lined trunk for the back of your car?"

In fact, that elk-lined world was gone. As American arms and soldiers headed to Europe in the early 1940s, fashionable Gypsies, White Russians, and French aristocrats were flitting in the other direction. They'd played by rules of their own until Hitler forced them to play by his. In 1939 many of them opted for safe haven in America. Horst P. Horst left Paris. *Vogue* closed its doors there the following year, when the Nazis took control of the city. Erwin Blumenfeld, a *Vogue* photographer, was put in a concentration camp but escaped and arrived in New York in 1941.

Liberman, who'd been art director of an influential magazine in Paris called *Vu,* joined *Vogue* in 1941, as did Norman Parkinson, a spindly, mustachioed British dandy. Both Irving Penn, who'd assisted Brodovitch, and Richard Avedon, who later studied under him, took their first photographs in 1944. George Hoyningen-Huene had grown old. He quit *Bazaar* the next year.

During World War II some illustrators—perhaps sensing that their day had passed—joined with catalog photographers to form their own model agency, the Society of Models. "They didn't want to pay advertising rates," says Dorian Leigh. "They all grumbled about that." Natálie Nickerson—an incredibly long-necked young woman—joined the Society of Models in 1945. Within months she was working regularly for Frissell, Hoyningen-Huene, and Dahl-Wolfe, and *Vogue*'s Irving Penn and John Rawlings. She also worked for fashion stores like Henri Bendel, Saks, Russeks, and Arnold Constable. She called herself Natálie. Just Natálie.

The Society of Models was a mess, as the preamble to its 1946 model catalog attests:

> *After rather a tempestuous beginning, the Society of Models, Inc. is at last coming into its own. We have suffered through the growing pains of a new organization and now feel that we can proudly hold up our heads and present to you our models. . . . It is the purpose of this bureau to eliminate the friction that has existed in the past between models and the users of models. . . . We shall in fairness to our clients start our new talent at our basic rate. . . . [W]e do not increase our models [sic] rates without prior notification of the clients who have been using*

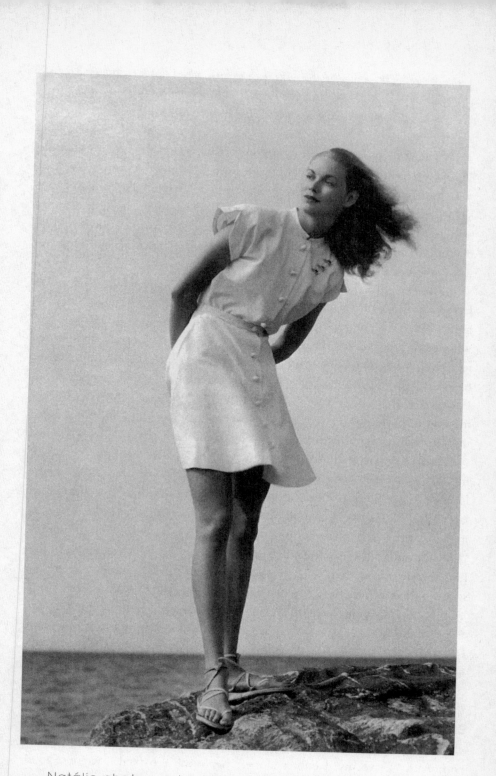

Natálie photographed by her husband, Wingate Paine

the services of these models. . . . We have recently added two more cubicle offices
for casting and bookkeeping . . . to eliminate the noise and confusion which per-
vades at our booking desk with its ever busy buzzing of telephones. . . .

If Natálie's experience was in any way indicative, the anonymous author had reason to be defensive. "They were sweet, dear, ineffective people," she says. Some of Natálie's clients suggested she switch to Powers. Though Grace Kelly briefly modeled for the agency before becoming an actress and a princess, not long afterward the Society of Models failed. "Why would a model join an agency that's going to sell her for less?" asks Eileen Ford, who was a stylist at Arnold Constable.

Powers charged more, but "they were worse," Natálie recalls. "They collected our money for us, and I had thousands owed to me. I couldn't pay my rent." When she confronted Powers, he didn't know her name. "His secretary whispered it into his ear. That started things going in my brain." She decided to take over her own billing and printed invoices, which she asked her clients to sign. "When I got the checks, I would make out a check for ten percent to Powers for their commission." But Natálie's pique only increased with her income. "They didn't understand the business they were in," she says. "There was a great big vacuum that needed to be filled."

Dorian Leigh was thinking along the same lines after a couple of years of modeling. She was a huge success, earning as much as anyone. "I just never looked back," she says. "I went from twenty-five dollars an hour to thirty dollars an hour." Gene Loyd, an illustrator and art director, used to love watching her work. "When Dorian posed, it was like a jolt of electricity," he says. "She put out both feet in infallible positions, then she set her knees, then her hips, then her waist, then her arms and hands, and at the last minute an expression would come across her face. If a photographer didn't wait for that, she'd look at him with such anger!" Emerick Bronson, who started shooting for *Vogue* in the late 1940s, had a similar reaction. "When I pointed a camera at Dorian, I felt like seven five-thousand-watt lamps had been lit and were looking at me," he says.

Despite her star power, Dorian decided against going to Hollywood, even though Diana Vreeland, who'd discovered Lauren Bacall and sent her to director Howard Hawks in 1943, gave her the same push. Leonard Lyons chimed in in his show business column, even calling Dorian's mother for comment. "Leave my daughter alone," her mother barked. "We're a good middle-class family and we're quite happy the way we are."

Dorian got a different message: "Go. I'm taking the children."

Twice Dorian was summoned by Howard Hughes, the billionaire who had produced *Hell's Angels* (1930) and *The Front Page* (1931) and gone on to control RKO Studios. Their meetings did not go well. "I thought he was the rudest man in the whole world!" Dorian says. She wasn't the type to take direction, as Harry Conover was about to find out. By 1946 her clients were complaining that they couldn't get the bookers at Conover on the phone. "My clients weren't interested in his other models. I was working for *Harper's Bazaar* and *Vogue,* and his models were doing cheesecake. Candy later said he was really running a call girl service, getting dates for airmen!" He even tried to get Dorian to go out with Pappy Boynton, the World War II flying ace. She told him that unless he put in separate phone lines for his top models, she would leave.

"You can't exist without me," he told her.

"Honey, I could stand in Grand Central Station and my clients would find me," she snapped back.

She was right. Dorian had hit the top quickly. "*Vogue,* you know, that's the mark of success, when you're editorialized at fifteen dollars an hour," she says sarcastically of the relatively meager wages paid to models then, as now, by top fashion magazines. "We'd pay nasty little rates because we made stars of them," admits Babs Simpson, a fashion editor during World War II.

Dorian and a friend at Conover, a tall, glacial blonde named Bijou Barrington, took a suite at the Elysée Hotel. They slept there at night when they had early bookings or late dates, and by day Barrington's sister-in-law took their appointments. They were soon joined by other Conover models and a second phone girl. The business wasn't very well organized at first, but, says Dorian, it *was* a legal modeling agency. She called it the Fashion Bureau. Within a matter of months four more agencies joined her in taking on Powers and Conover. "I started a revolution," Dorian says. She certainly lived in a revolutionary manner, setting a swashbuckling style in model agentry that still lives today—although mostly in male agents.

Just after the Fashion Bureau opened, Dorian's parents and her children moved to Florida, and she took her own apartment on Lexington Avenue, between Ninety-third and Ninety-fourth streets. She shared the address with Henry Drawant, a friend of a *Vogue* editor, Leo Lerman, whom she knew from high school. They introduced her to their friend Truman Capote. She says Capote used her as the basis for Holly Golightly, the unforgettable character in *Breakfast at Tiffany's.* "I took all my phone calls in a candy store across the street,

not a saloon," she says, "and it was a private house, and it had never been made
into apartments, so when I wasn't there, Truman and Henry and Leo would
come up to my apartment because I had a Siamese cat named Posy."

She surely lived a Golightly life. "I came home one morning about dawn,
and Leo Lerman was coming out of my landlord's apartment on the ground
floor. They'd had a big dinner the night before with Truman. I got out of the
taxi, and Leo was going to take it, and he said, 'Oh, profligate one!' I rushed
upstairs, got the dictionary, and looked up 'profligate.' Then I knew that what
was so funny was *him* coming out at the same hour I was arriving."

"Profligate" was understatement. "Many shall be nameless," she warns, but
she admits to many more. "There were very few that she missed," says her
friend Gene Loyd. There was a fling with calypso king Harry Belafonte.
Another with her exercise instructor, Nicholas Kounovsky, who trained New
York's elite for years. She met the drummer Buddy Rich at a party thrown by
photographer Milton Greene. "We had this two-day marriage," Dorian says.
"We go through a ceremony, and then he tells me, 'My wife in California is
going to use this against me to get a bigger settlement!' "

Then came Irving Penn. Born in New Jersey in 1917, Penn began study-
ing design with Alexey Brodovitch at age eighteen and became his unpaid
assistant at *Bazaar* in 1937. Three years later he was made art director at Saks
Fifth Avenue, but in 1941 he left for Mexico to try his hand at being an artist.
Two years later, back in New York, he went to work as an idea man for
Alexander Liberman at *Vogue*. When photographers balked at executing
Penn's ideas for covers, he began photographing them himself. He met
Dorian some months later.

"He took hat pictures in a car in front of the synagogue on Park Avenue,"
she recalls. "Here I am, thinking he's a young know-nothing. I'm telling him
the best angles because he had just started with *Vogue*. He thought that was
adorable of me, telling him how he should be doing it." They soon went to
bed together, though she judged him "a neurotic lay. Afterward he'd drink
bottled water. Sex dehydrated him."

One of Penn's best-known photographs is a 1946 group portrait of *Vogue*'s
photographers, including Serge Balkan, Beaton, Blumenfeld, Horst, Con-
stantin Joffe, George Platt Lynes, Rawlings, and Penn himself. Tucked in
among them is Dorian Leigh. Penn inscribed a copy of the photograph to
"Dorian, the beautiful muse of all these strange men." On the same wall in
her home are two more Penn pictures from 1946. On one Penn wrote, "To
beautiful Dorian, with admiration, gratitude and a heart."

"Well, of course, Irving at that point was in love with me," she says with a coquettish grin. She also says Penn "was just terribly . . . self-involved. Terribly, terribly important to himself. He acted as though we should be posing for him for the pure joy of being tortured. He was a still life photographer. And that's how he wanted people to be."

In his famous portraits he wanted personality. Fashion pictures were different. "I don't think the girl's personality should ever intrude," Penn said. Who she was as a real person "was not of any significance." Not only did Penn objectify his models, but he was also obsessively meticulous about posing them. When he wanted a picture of a model blowing the perfect smoke ring, Mary Jane Russell smoked several packs of cigarettes nonstop. Penn could also be painfully insecure. Says Dorian: "He used to go into a little cubicle in the back of the studio and call Alex Liberman and say, 'Alex, I can't do it, I'm sorry.' "

Penn could turn cruel, too. "He would look through the camera, and he'd say, 'Do something else,' " Dorian remembers. "He reduced Jennifer Jones to ashes, hysterically sobbing and crying. He never took one picture; he just kept saying, 'Do something else. Perhaps you don't want to work today, Miss Jones? Perhaps you don't feel like having your photograph taken?' He did it, he told me, because she lied to him when he said, 'I understand that you were a model, Miss Jones?' She said, 'Never.' She was lying. She *was* a Seventh Avenue model, and it made him mad."

Dorian made him happy. He included her in a 1947 group portrait of the twelve most photographed models of the time. "It was an extraordinary sitting," recalls *Vogue* editor Cathy di Montezemolo. "There was almost no noise in the studio. The atmosphere was almost reverent."

"They represent an omnibus of beauty, current replacement of Gibson and Ziegfeld girl legends," the caption in *Vogue* read. "These twelve share a look of nonadolescence, a look gained not so much from being beautiful as becoming so. And they've gone on to be a magazine editor, an actress, newspaper columnist, a singer and a designer, and some are even mothers! All to prove that beauty may very well be as beauty does." Seven of the dozen, including Betty McLauchlen Dorso (who also produced the photograph in her role as Condé Nast's studio manager), weren't working models any longer. But one who worked long afterward was Lisa Fonssagrives. "That was the first time that Penn met her," Dorian says tartly. "And I was his lady friend." Eileen Ford claims to have been there, too. "It was *coup de foudre,*" she says. "That was that."

Two years later *Time* magazine chose Fonssagrives as the subject of a cover story on the burgeoning model business. Dorian says she suggested Fonssa-

grives to *Time* because she was still embarrassed to be known as a model. But
Gillis MacGil, a model who worked with her that week, remembers things a
little differently. "Dorian almost killed Lisa," she says. "The tension was *so*
acute. Dorian was like a 1930s movie star. Remember how they were portrayed? Dorian behaved that way."

"Do illusions sell refrigerators?" *Time* asked in the headline of its story,
which described Fonssagrives as the "highest-paid, highest-praised high-
fashion model in the business." The piece followed Lisa through a typical day
in her life, as she sped at 70 mph from her cottage in Muttontown on Long
Island in her red-upholstered Studebaker convertible. She picked up her
bookings and went to a fitting, her hairdresser, and two sittings. "She responds
instantly to the photographer's every direction, almost before it is spoken,"
Time burbled. "Her body (bust and hips 34 in.) is so supple that she can pull
in her normally 23-inch waist to 18 inches. She has the gift of mimicry every
good model needs, and a keen fashion sense."

Lisa's fairy-tale life was marred only by her marriage. Her husband, dancer
turned photographer Fernand Fonssagrives, had opened a studio on Madison
Avenue and briefly, at least, had some success, moving back and forth among
Vogue, Town & Country, and *Harper's Bazaar.* But commercial photography
soon lost its appeal for him. "You were no longer the initiator," he says. "Layouts began to be sent," and photographers had to execute them exactly.

When the couple's daughter, Mia, contracted rheumatic fever on a trip to
Europe in 1950, the family extended a vacation into a convalescent stay of
three months. Fonssagrives closed his studio. "I was finished, and Lisa thought
her career was over," he says. "She panicked and wanted a divorce. She felt I'd
never get back on my feet." She'd worked with Penn extensively, and Fonssagrives believes he'd asked to marry her. "I understood her anxiety," Fonssagrives says. "When she became a top model, she got caught in the world of
the in crowd. I didn't. I wasn't interested. She didn't want to give it up."
Immediately after marrying Penn, she was back in *Vogue* and had another ten
years. "Both Penn and Avedon were very prestigious and money-oriented. I
had no interest in moneymaking," says Fernand Fonssagrives.

He retired to Spain and became a highly regarded sculptor. Lisa married
Penn, six years her junior, on her return to America. "She respected him, and
he loved her," says her first husband. "Her moment of fear was quickly gone.
We remained friends. We had our wonderful daughter, and we were intelligent enough not to make her life tragic." Lisa started taking photographs her-

self but gave it up when she became pregnant with her son, Tom, in 1952, and turned her darkroom into a nursery.

She kept modeling through the 1950s and had one of the longest careers in the history of the profession. "She had incredible genes, and you can go on looking good if you do the right things," says her daughter, Mia Solow. "She was also Irving's muse. She saw things that he was then inspired by." At the end of the 1950s she started designing clothes and, like her first husband, sculpting. "By the 1960s she was finished modeling," says Solow. "Sculpture was her passion." She was still with Penn in their sylvan house in the middle of Long Island when she died in 1992. "If I lived it over again, I would not change a thing," she told an interviewer late in her life.

Lisa and Irving Penn's marriage was one of the great love stories in fashion photography. But before Fonssagrives, Penn had had one other important attachment to a mannequin. Her name was Jean Patchett, and her agent describes her as the Babe Ruth of the new agency in town, Ford Models. "She was a big, big deal," says Jerry Ford. "The first girl we started. The first big star." Jerry took her test photographs himself. "I didn't do that for very long," he says. "There were just the two of us then," says his wife, Eileen.

Patchett and Mr. Penn—as he was henceforth known—were together late in 1948 on his one and only location trip to Peru, where he took one of his most famous photographs, of Patchett sitting in a café, shoes kicked off, chewing moodily on a string of pearls. Dorian Leigh believes that Penn and Patchett were lovers. So does photographer Francesco Scavullo, who shot Patchett's first professional tests. "The pictures they did were so wonderful they could have suggested that to people," Jerry Ford allows. Patchett won't address the question directly. Dorian, she says, "is either jealous or unhappy with her life to have to say things like that." And Penn always claimed to dislike models. "To photograph them is enough," he said. But clearly there were some models he disliked less than others, and the prim and proper Patchett was one.

"When I started to work . . . ideal women were remote, with European overtones. They were beyond my experience," Penn once said. "So at first I photographed simple uncultivated girls—the girls I went to school with. They seemed right for America in the postwar period. . . . The models I used were people, and I would have a favorite model with whom I might have more real emotional involvement, which sometimes meant I saw more in the ground glass than was there, and photographed with more objective power than I was going to get back. I was a young man with no knowledge of style, but I knew when an image had guts."

Unfortunately for Penn, his images sometimes overdosed on guts. Though he shot the autumn Paris collections for *Vogue* in 1950 (". . . the showings were at night, black-tie, no mob of paparazzi, no loud music," he said. "Just little gold chairs . . . very civilized. Then the girls came out, and they were so snotty to the audience. It was wonderful . . ."), by mid-decade his work for *Vogue* had dwindled. Readers complained that his photographs "burned on the pages." Alexander Liberman later wrote of the "violence" in his work. Penn continued shooting portraits for the magazine, but he no longer received many fashion assignments, and he began doing advertising, still lifes, and photo-essays in lieu of fashion pictures. Though he still takes graphic beauty and fashion pictures for *Vogue* and has engaged in an ongoing photographic collaboration with the Paris-based avant-garde designer Issey Miyake, by 1955 Penn had moved beyond fashion.

Just as Penn was meeting Patchett, Dorian Leigh linked up with Roger Mehle, a naval commander (who was divorced from the woman who later became the gossip columnist Aileen "Suzy" Mehle). Dorian was two months pregnant when she and Mehle were married that August. She hired a bus to take all her models to the wedding. Her teenage sister, Suzy, and Suzy's new best friend, Carmen Dell'Orefice, both with the Fashion Bureau, were her bridesmaids. Suffering from morning sickness in a new home in faraway Connecticut, Dorian soon closed the Fashion Bureau, took back her kids from her mother, and made a stab at settling down. "I was never a businesswoman, never," she sighs today. "I just had marvelous ideas."

Jean Patchett comes from Preston, Maryland, a little town on the Eastern Shore, population 395. Today she lives in a prestigious community in the California desert, smack on the fairway of a golf course, with Louis Auer, a onetime investment banker, her husband of forty-plus years. Glass animals are everywhere, and the walls are hung with trophies of Pancho Patchett's modeling years, photographs by Louise Dahl-Wolfe, Rawlings, and Blumenfeld and two walls covered with nothing but *Vogue* covers. The prominent beauty mark on her lip is featured in almost every one of them. Long before Cindy Crawford, Patchett made a mountain of money on a mole. Though Patchett still has the thin frame and fine-boned face of her photographs, the mole is gone now. "It got icky," she says, and she had it removed.

After she spent a stint in secretarial school, Patchett's parents sent her to college, but she wasn't prepared. Her roommate looked at her one day and said, "You're so unhappy, why don't you go to New York and be a model? Just get up and go look in the mirror!"

Her parents weren't pleased, but Patchett prevailed. She headed off to New York in February 1948, moved into a Methodist home for girls for $13.50 a week, and signed with Harry Conover. She paid for her own test pictures and then "traipsed the streets," she says. Her first job was with *Mademoiselle.* She thinks she was paid $12.50 an hour. "Whatever bookings I got at Conover I had to get myself. You just went from studio to studio to drop off your test pictures. He had five hundred girls. I don't think he paid attention to any of them."

In March 1948, while working for the *Ladies' Home Journal,* she met Natálie, who said, "You ought to get out of Conover and go with Eileen Ford."

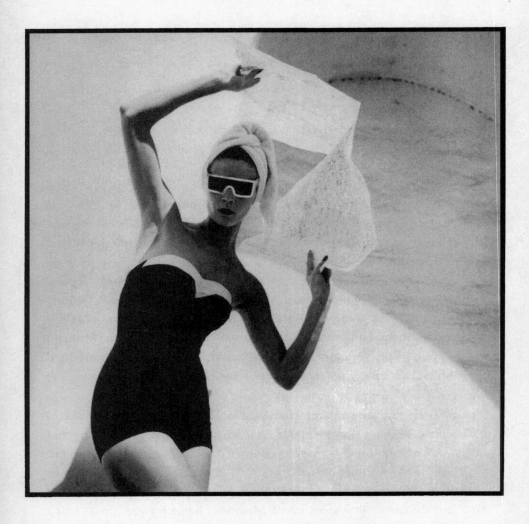

Jean Patchett photographed by Louise Dahl-Wolfe

Patchett recalls, "I went to Second Avenue, to a red door in a walk-up, and I go into this room, and there's Eileen Ford sitting at a card table, in an ice-cream chair, with about six phones on the card table, two phones on her shoulders, and talking away into a third, and I came in the door, and I said, 'I'm Jean Patchett.' "

Ford turned in her chair. "You're as big as a horse," she bellowed.

Patchett, who weighed about 127 pounds, burst into tears.

"I lost weight. Eileen made appointments. I was working—immediately! White gloves, my dear. I dressed every morning to go to work in white gloves. My first cover on *Vogue* was September. The next one was October, on *Glamour*. The following November I moved into the Allerton House. When I was living at the Allerton House, Barbara Mullen was living there, too. Some cover had just come out on the stand, and I was just full of myself. Barbara and I were having a whiskey sour, and she said, 'Look, just get off that high horse! Who in the hell do you think you are anyway?' I didn't realize I was being such an obnoxious woman. That just brought me right down, and after that I think I became very modest about the whole thing and realized that really, it was nothing more than a tabloid on the newsstands that's going to last for about a week and it's going to go to the trash heap! And I just never let it go to my head again.

"I went to Cuba with *Life* magazine. My *Life* cover was January first of 1949. After my trip to Cuba I went to South America with Penn.

"I'd done only one sitting with Penn in New York. I didn't even know who he was. We get to Lima, and we're there for five days, and we don't take a picture. We had thirteen outfits to do for *Vogue Patterns,* and I was getting kind of nervous because I thought maybe my face was turning green or something. I thought he didn't like me. We'd get up at five-thirty in the morning for the mist, and he'd look in his little Rolleiflex, and nothing would happen. He just couldn't take a picture. Finally, we went to this café one day, and I had on this lovely hat and cocktail dress, and there's a young man sitting there, and I'm sitting with a glass of wine, and I kind of just said, 'Oh, the hell with it,' and I kicked off my shoe and sat back. I thought, 'Nothing's going to happen.' I'm sitting there eating my pearls, and he said, 'Stop!' And it was the most horrible sound I ever heard in my life, because what he wanted me to do was not to be pose-y. He wanted me to do things that I would do if I was sitting talking to a young man, and that was the whole secret, and it just went from there. It's interesting today to look back on it. We really made history. To have five pictures of yourself hanging in the Museum of Modern Art! I didn't know that I was going to be doing that!

"As we kept working, he'd tell me little stories. In New York he would get me in front of the white paper, and he would said, 'OK, it's intermission at the theater, and your young man has gone out to get you an orangeade, and it's been an awfully long time, and you're standing there, and you're waiting for him, and you can't find him.' So my neck would get longer and longer, looking for my young man! There was always a story behind every picture.

"I didn't belong to Penn. I belonged to *Vogue*. You couldn't work for *Harper's* and *Vogue* at the same time when I was working. If you went to work for *Harper's*, you couldn't work for *Vogue* anymore! I did work for Dick [Avedon], but I don't know, I always felt inadequate. He jumped around too much for me. Penn was a serene person and quiet, always chasing the bluebird. We'd take five hundred pictures on one outfit. It would be a whole day. We had thirteen outfits in Lima, and we took thirty-two hundred pictures! I don't think he ever took a model anywhere after that.

"I knew nothing about Dorian. [Penn and I] were very fond of each other. We had a very good time together. I didn't even realize that he had been seeing Dorian. When we were in Lima, I think he was seeing Lisa; he was getting letters from Lisa. We were in the elevator one day, and I said, 'Oh, you've got a wonderful long letter,' and he said, 'Yes, from my tailor!'

"The only time [I met Dorian] was when I first started at *Vogue* in May [1948]. I was working for [fashion editor] Bettina Ballard, who I adored. She loved me because I called her Miss Ballard, and I'd always say 'Yes, ma'am' and 'No, ma'am' to her. We didn't have cubicles in that dressing room, and Dorian was out on the set, being photographed, and she came back in, and she said, 'That dress is mine. Take it off!' Here, I'm really a meek person, and I'd heard of Dorian Leigh and she kind of scared me! Luckily Mrs. Ballard walked in right behind her, and she said, 'Now, Jean, we're ready to take you onto the set.'

"I did not mix business with pleasure. I never dated any photographers, ever, like Billy Helburn or whatever. Oh, Billy was a naughty boy! God! But he adored me, and I adored him, and I never had any trouble with him. But he would do such awful things—burps and wheezes in the studio—and I'd say, 'Bill Helburn, if you don't stop that, I'm out of here!' He'd try to sneak in the dressing room when we all had no clothes on. I always had a petticoat on, a slip. He never had a chance!

"I was twenty-one years old. I was dating a lot of guys. Young Gussie Pabst from Milwaukee, the Pabst Brewing Company. Tim Ireland. Jimmy Magin from the fuse box family. I met my husband, Louie, even before I went with Eileen and Jerry. He was working at Macy's on their training program. Then he went to the New York Trust Company and was an executive vice-president. We saw each other for three years, and we became very good friends. If I wanted to go to 'Twenty-one' for dinner, I'd call him up, and I'd pay our way. I was going on trips to Paris with *Vogue*. I went with Mrs. Ballard and Norman Parkinson and actually began to realize that the person I was missing was Louie Auer!

"After we were married, I gave all my money, all my checks, to Louie, and he gave me back five hundred dollars a month to pay the maid, the rent, my taxis. I would bring home checks for fifteen hundred dollars a week or more. I think the best I ever made was fifty thousand dollars a year. But that's nothing today.

"I didn't travel much after that. We were married when I went to do the collections in '53. I went to Spain with Louise Dahl-Wolfe, and he came over. Our first child arrived in '59, and Amy arrived in '62, and I worked, but I found that I couldn't really be three people. It was impossible, to be the wife, the mother, and the career gal. I don't know how women do it, I swear!

"The last photograph that I took was in '68, and it was one of my favorites of all time. But I'm so glad I didn't live in that era because I don't think I would have made it. Or in today's world, either. The new *Vogue* is out, this little girl is on the cover, the skirt's up to here. Who, at the age of forty, is going to wear that? I just think that things are not as elegant as they used to be."

T he woman who made Jean Patchett cry, and then made her one of the world's top models, was born Eileen Otte in 1922. She grew up on the North Shore of Long Island, went to Barnard College in New York City, and worked briefly as a model. She joined Harry Conover's agency "because I was a real live college girl and *Mademoiselle* was publishing a college issue," Ford says. "I made five dollars an hour, which my father thought was highly suspicious. I was on the cover of the Columbia Minerva Knitting Book, and you want to know why? I was the only person in the agency with a pair of white ice skates."

That was as good as it got for Eileen Otte, model. She graduated from Barnard in 1943, met a photographer named Elliot Clark, and told him she could handle his books and correspondence—even though she couldn't do long division and her father's office staff had typed her college papers. Nonetheless, she got the job. Among other tasks she booked his models.

The next summer she met her future husband, Jerry Ford. Although he shared a name with Harry Conover's onetime partner, future President Gerald Ford, Eileen's catch was born Gerard, the New Orleans–raised son of a riverboat pilot. A Notre Dame football player, he'd dropped out of college to attend officers' school at Columbia, where he was training to become one of World War II's ninety-day wonders. In November 1944 the couple eloped to San Francisco, where Jerry waited to ship out with the Navy.

Returning to New York while her new husband "was floating around on a ship," as she puts it, the newlywed got a job as a stylist at the studio that shot the Sears, Roebuck catalogs. "I coordinated, numbered, packed, and shipped clothes to Arizona," she recalls. "Then I spent twenty-five cents on an eraser,

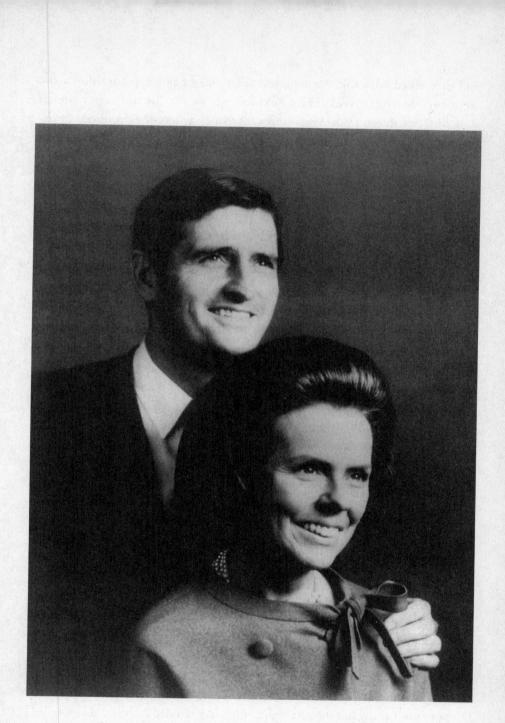

Jerry and Eileen Ford, the moral exemplars
of modeling, in July 1969

and they asked who told me to spend the money. I put a quarter down and went back to Great Neck." Her next job was as a stylist and copywriter at Arnold Constable, a Fifth Avenue specialty store, where she produced newspaper ads and catalogs and met more models. Then she went to work for the *Tobe Report,* a fashion industry newsletter. "I was notably unsuccessful there." She laughs.

Jerry Ford came home from the service in March 1946. The couple planned to move to South Bend, Indiana, that September so he could finish school. Then, in June, Eileen learned she was pregnant. Suddenly everything changed. Eileen Ford denies it, but Dorian Leigh recalls being questioned closely by the young stylist at a studio one day. Ford wanted to know how Dorian planned to compete with Powers and Conover. Dorian said that top models needed secretaries, not agencies.

Ford had also been talking to Natálie. "She booked me for a shoot at Arnold Constable, and we became friends," the model recalls. Before Jerry came home, Natálie sometimes had an extra bed put in her room at the Barbizon, and Eileen would sleep over. "I told her I wanted to open an agency, that nothing was being done right," Natálie says. "Models were treated as though they worked for the agencies, not as if the agencies worked for them. There was no career planning, no individual advice on makeup, hair, clothes, or anything else. We talked about things that had happened to me, because I was out there, and how it could be done better. It was first come, first served with no control. Models could be handled with more attention paid to who they worked for. This was a whole new concept that broke the monopoly of Powers and Conover."

That summer, while Jerry Ford studied accounting at Columbia, Eileen's conversations with Natálie led to an offer. "As I couldn't get a job doing anything else," Ford says, "I took a job as a private secretary for Natálie and Inga Lindgren, a Swedish model." They each paid her $65 a month to take their bookings. Though she wasn't yet licensed and legal, Eileen Ford became a model agent that fall.

"Our plan was to gradually evolve," says Natálie, who agreed to become Ford's *rabatteuse.* "I was influenced very much by the fact that Bijou and Dorian didn't really get the established girls. We needed to prove that we had a lot to offer that models didn't know they were missing. I realized that for any new operation to be successful, they had to have at least one top girl, and I was the model of the moment. It was decided I would be a silent partner because I could be more effective as a happy model with Eileen, which I was. We were not exactly open and straightforward about it, but on the other hand, we were benefiting the industry tremendously."

Soon Ford was taking bookings for eight models. Eileen's father gave her and Jerry an apartment in his credit and collection company's building on Lexington Avenue and a tiny space on the ground floor to set up shop. There was a garden out back, and Eileen put phones there and started taking bookings. "Conover and Powers went crazy trying to get the police after her" for running a clandestine agency, Dorian Leigh recalls. Eventually Ford got a license.

Jamie, the first of the Ford's four children, was born in March 1947. When Eileen went into the hospital, Jerry Ford took over the business. And when he got a close look at it, he saw there might be a future in it. "I find all this very glamorous," he says. "I'm not from New York. I thought models were the most incredible things in the world."

"And they are," Eileen adds quickly. Still, she was reluctant. "Nothing could have interested me less," she says, scowling.

Jerry prevailed. "Eileen was very good at it," he says. "Avedon booked Eunice Sherman one day and took her to Long Island and ran over an hour. He stopped at a filling station to call Eileen, and she tore him apart. 'No more models if you can't get them back on time!' " Another time Eileen sent a model to meet Louise Dahl-Wolfe, who wasn't there. "When I make an appointment, I expect you to be there!" Ford thundered at the eminent photographer. Says Ford's husband: "The amazing thing is, they put up with it."

Everyone agreed that Eileen was awfully good at agentry. "I used to think, even if this woman loses her address book, she'll still be in business," says Natálie. To this day Ford can reel off models' phone numbers from the 1940s. "I was very good at recommending models," Eileen admits. "Let's say the Wool Bureau called and needed someone who could wear Norell well. I knew who could. And I'm fanatic about getting people to the right place at the right time." If she was sometimes blunt and hard, as with Patchett, it was necessary if she was going to succeed against two powerful men like Powers and Conover. She was a woman in business. There were precious few precedents in the world at large. And none, except in London, where Lucie Clayton had reigned for years, in the modeling business. Jerry played the feminine role, good cop to her bad one. "When Jerry came in, he added a soft kind of quality to the operation," Natálie says.

Through a photographer the Fords met Sherman Billingsley, who owned the Stork Club, the famous supper club. The meeting proved a bonanza.

"Billingsley loved to have models in his club," Jerry says. He'd signed a deal with CBS to broadcast a Stork Club talk show six nights a week with Chrysler as sponsor, and he offered the Fords carte blanche. "Bring as many people as you want—no check," Billingsley said, "but you have to sit in the background of my show." They went about twice a week and became part of the set written up regularly by columnists like Dorothy Kilgallen, Tex McCrary, and Walter Winchell. One night Winchell took them to a boxing match in a limousine. "Can you imagine, kids in their twenties in limos?" Eileen asks unbelievingly.

The Fords were in the right place at the right time. There was money again and energy and optimism. The Fashion Group, the nonprofit society of women in fashion—designers, writers, editors, and manufacturers—had begun mounting large shows. Then, just after the war, an energetic young publicity woman named Eleanor Lambert began aggressively promoting Seventh Avenue's less expensive ready-to-wear clothing. American sportswear designers like Claire McCardell, Anne Klein (at Junior Sophisticates), and Bill Blass (at Ann Miller) thrived in this new environment, despite fresh competition from a revived French fashion industry. With wartime restrictions on fabric lifted, Christian Dior launched his voluminous New Look in Paris in 1947, sending a reviving charge through the international world of style. The Fords were in a bull market for female flesh.

On October 9, 1947, Natálie and the Fords formalized their relationship with a letter confirming that they had "been operating as partners . . . in carrying on the business of a Modelling Agency" for over a year. They agreed that Ford's salary would be paid by the business and that they would share all profits and losses equally. "That wasn't much," says Jerry Ford. "It's a miracle we survived." A month later the Fords sold their 1941 automobile for $900 and used the proceeds to move into their own space, a third-floor walk-up between a funeral parlor and a cigar store. Patchett arrived shortly thereafter.

Meanwhile, others were having the same bright idea. Stewart Cowley, a theatrical agent before the war, got out of the Army Air Force around the same time Jerry Ford left the Navy. After a brief stint as a production assistant on a Broadway play, he and a friend, an actor and model named Russell Hoyt, decided to open an agency together in February 1947. "We were new; we had a different angle," says Cowley. "Conover was never available. He was too busy screwing his models." Though she denies ever meeting him, Cowley claims he sat down with Natálie and offered her and several other top models 2 percent of the agency each in exchange for being its "nucleus."

"We were driving in a taxi, and I could see adding machines going in her head," he says. "We had a big meeting, and everyone showed up but Natálie. She wanted fifty percent, and she knew who to do it with—a little nooch named Eileen Ford. We went ahead without her and started as Russell-Stewart, and a few weeks later Eileen started, and they came running from Powers and Conover." Cowley tried specializing in photographic models, but "Eileen got the better of me," he says. Instead he booked runway and showroom models who quit the Seventh Avenue companies where they worked for meager salaries of about $75 a week. Cowley sold them back to their ex-employers for considerably more—$15 an hour.

Bill Blass remembers those days well. "Each house had five or six girls," he says. "The models would go to the Colony for lunch and dance all night at El Morocco. Betty Bacall was a house model at David Crystal. She replaced Dusty Anderson and Lucille Ball, who were both house models, too. It was her first job before the war. She worked for us by day and as a theater usher by night. The other girls? It gave them pretty clothes until they hooked up with a man." Blass's favorites also included mannish Toni Hollingsworth ("the first model who'd parade around without clothes; she never wore a bra and she had great bosoms, big ones") and Wendy Russell ("the first mannequin who ever dragged a sable coat down a runway"). He booked them all through Stewart Cowley. "He was the best-looking guy," Blass says. "He must've fucked every one of those girls."

Cowley scouted new talent at the Miss Rheingold contest, among other places. "There were lines around the block," he recalls. "They were the supermodels of their day. God, I almost married three Rheingold girls. My brother did marry one." The Cowley brothers weren't the only model lovers mixing business and pleasure. The A&P playboy Huntington Hartford had decided to stop hanging out at Powers and Conover and opened an agency of his own in 1947.

Today it is difficult to imagine Huntington Hartford, eighty-three, running anything at all. He spends his days in bed in a run-down town house on the edge of Manhattan's midtown business district. Only a bronze bust of a handsome, younger Hartford, placed in a niche in the elegant curving stairway, gives a hint of what he once was.

There is a shuttered, makeshift bedroom on the parlor floor. A television set buzzes at the foot of a bed. Hartford lies amid piles of books, newspapers, and dirty laundry on stained blue-and-white-striped sheets that are pinned to his mattress. Barely covered by a ratty orange plaid blanket, he wears once-stylish boxy eyeglasses, boxer shorts printed with red dots, and an M. C. Escher T-shirt. It, too, is covered with stains. His long white hair reaches his shoulders. His nails have grown into claws. He has trouble moving, and his eyes constantly wander behind the thick lenses. A wastepaper basket next to the bed is filled with empty candy wrappers. Inexplicably, short lengths of cut-up soda straws are scattered on his bedside table.

"There really isn't much to tell," Hartford begins vaguely. "I got interested because I was interested in Hollywood, and I figured top models could become actresses. It didn't work out because Eileen Ford had the inside track with the inside people in the fashion business and got all the best models. I hired people to run it. I don't remember anything about it. It wasn't important in my life."

George Huntington Hartford's grandfather had left him 10 percent of the A&P supermarkets. Hartford also inherited his father's share when his mother died in 1946. His fortune totaled about $500 million. After studying at Harvard, Hartford got married and divorced, fathered an illegitimate son, and worked as an A&P clerk and as a tabloid reporter (who went to assignments in a limousine) before he joined the Coast Guard in 1942. His first venture after the war was the Hartford agency.

Hartford was friendly with Steve Elliot, a fashion photographer married to a top model named Georgia Hamilton. He would go to Elliot's studio and watch him work. He liked the idea of work that involved pretty girls. "What was he trying to do?" Elliot asked. "He just wanted to be somebody, a John Powers, Harry Conover, as though that were something." Hartford thought that by guiding young women, he might find direction in his own life. He decided to open offices in New York and Los Angeles, hoping to use his models to lever himself into the movie business. "His family felt he couldn't take care of himself and got my father to take care of things," says Clay Deering Dilworth, daughter of William Deering, who was installed as the Hartford agency's director.

His money gave Hartford a gimmick that changed modeling forever, a scheme that made his agency—briefly—the city's strongest. He financed his models' paychecks through what came to be called the voucher system. It is still in use. At every model booking the client—be it a magazine, photographer, studio, or ad agency—is obligated to sign a voucher attesting to the hours the model worked and the agreed-upon rate. Each Friday Hartford's agency made good on the vouchers, subtracting only a commission, at that

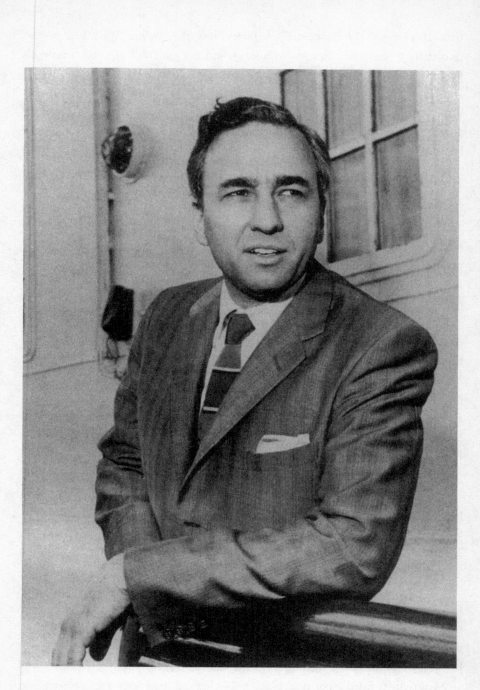

Huntington Hartford arrives in New York on the SS *Liberté* in November 1957

time 10 percent. "Unheard of!" exclaims Stewart Cowley. "We'd wait a year, two years to get paid; then the model would get paid. All of a sudden here's Hunt. Models went there because they got paid right away."

It took a lot of money to get the voucher system up and running, but that wasn't Hartford's problem. His problem was his reputation. He was a rake, or at least a rake manqué. "He was very unsuccessful in his attempts to be the lover of the modeling business," Jerry Ford says. That didn't stop him from trying. Hartford denies making passes at his lasses. "I could get dates," he says. "I had no problems finding girls." But Polly Ferguson Knaster, a fashion editor Deering hired to run the agency with him, remembers, "When a mother said, 'I'm sending my daughter,' I stood at the elevator. I knew where to look if a model was late. Hunt would be talking to her. I was not Hunt's favorite person." She finally made a rule barring Hartford from the agency. "It took me nine months to find people willing to deal with the Hartford agency because of his reputation. He was in the news. Photographs were taken."

While he owned the agency, Hartford also opened an artist's retreat, produced several films, financed Broadway plays, bought a theater, and provided fodder for a lot of gossip columns. Later, after selling half his A&P shares, he developed the Paradise Island resort in the Bahamas and opened a supper club/disco, a magazine, a parking garage, an institute to study handwriting, and a private modern art museum. He lost money on just about all of it.

He did succeed, however, in scaring the daylights out of Eileen and Jerry Ford. Despite his reputation, the voucher system took hold. "He had the power to kill us," says Jerry Ford. Models "wanted to come with us but couldn't afford to. We eventually got them, but not until we were in a position to finance vouchers. He had no idea how many of our models were thinking of going to him." Hartford soon tried to buy the Fords out. But in 1949 two Ford family friends mortgaged their houses and lent them $50,000 to start a voucher system.

"A generation of mothers and girls owe Eileen Ford a debt," says Carmen Dell'Orefice. "People took advantage of young women. You'd do the jobs and never get paid. She put a price on young womanhood and got a lot of young women college educations. She opened a doorway and defined a profession. But Jerry is actually the unsung hero. He figured out how to get backers."

Meanwhile, Ford's partner, Natálie Nickerson, had met a photographer named Wingate Paine in March 1947. They'd gotten involved and had begun working together all the time. Paine was wealthy and willful. Blind in one eye from a lacrosse accident at Yale, he'd talked his way into the Marine Corps and ended up a captain. On reemerging, he decided not to resurrect his interrupted business career and took up fashion photography instead. Now Natálie's efforts promoting the Fords were augmented by his. Their first success was beating back the Hartford challenge.

Voucher system in place, Jerry says, "We were very hot, and the word was all over town." His innovation co-opted, Hartford's agency puttered along for about a dozen years, ending up concentrating on male models. Finally, in 1959, he offered to buy Ford again, for $1 million. When Hartford promised the Fords they could retain total control, Eileen agreed to meet him. "I have to ask you a couple of questions," Hartford said. "If I want to go out with a girl and she says no, will you drop her?" Ford said no.

"If I want a girl to be with the agency, will you hire her?" No again.

"This won't work out," he decided.

Soon thereafter Hartford's lawyer approached the Fords and asked if they would buy *him* out. According to Lisa Gubernick, Hartford's biographer, the abrupt change of heart came only after the New York City Department of Consumer Affairs had begun investigating the agency. "They felt it was a toy," confirms Don Stogo, an agent who later worked with refugees from Hartford. "The city couldn't prove anything, but they gave him a lot of trouble, and he decided to give it up. It had degenerated anyway. A lot of models left because of all the innuendo. He was a playboy, let's face it, pre–Hugh Hefner. I heard he took a minor over the state line into California." Models were interviewed by city officials and asked if Hartford had ever propositioned them. "The girls started laughing and responded, 'Of course,' " Gubernick reported.

The Fords absorbed the Hartford agency. It had been losing money for years and was carrying $750,000 in debts on its books by that time. In exchange for assuming its debts, the Fords got one of the best stables of male models in the city. One of Hartford's close associates joked, "Hunt's lost a million dollars in this business, and he's never gotten laid." Hartford himself is hazy on the details.

"Ask Eileen Ford," he says. "She'll remember."

By 1948 the Fords were already well established. That year they signed up Dorian Leigh. "Dorian was *the* star," says Eileen Ford. "She could swell her chest to fill the clothes," says Jerry. "She knew how to breathe," says Eileen. She also knew how to bargain. Two years earlier, just before her parents left for Florida, Dorian had come home one day to find her kid sister, Suzy, crying at the kitchen table. "She thought she was a monster," Dorian recalls. "Imagine, that was the real teenybopper period; my mother made her wear pigtails with red hair and freckles. And she was taller than her whole class. I said, 'No, you're beautiful, and I'll prove it to you.' "

"Please take some pictures of my baby sister," Dorian begged all the photographers she knew. They happened to be the best. Suzy tested with Penn, Rawlings, and Karen Radkai. "I hid in the dressing room, because she said she didn't want me there," Dorian says. "She was marvelous. She moved, she did everything naturally, just like I did. Karen was carried away." That summer Suzy Parker joined the Fashion Bureau. "*I* couldn't use the last name Parker, but then, when Suzy started, it was OK, because I had made a lot of money and I was established," Dorian says.

Irving Penn, for one, was horrified. "Mrs. Parker, do not let this delicious creature ever model," he told the girls' mother. "Do you want her to turn out like Dorian?" Mrs. Parker patted Penn's cheek.

Suzy didn't get off to as fast a start as Dorian had. "She'd be in her room sobbing," Dorian recalls. "She felt photographers were comparing her to me. She was bigger and taller, and they made a big thing out of not photographing her full length. It was very morale-beating. I'd say, 'Go back to school,' and she'd say no and cry herself to sleep."

Suzy worked with Richard Avedon that summer of 1948. "In came this girl, who looked utterly unlike the usual model type, wearing one of the most rebellious expressions I've ever seen on anybody. She positively glowered," he recalled. "She was taller than any model then working and I only photographed her to oblige Dorian."

Though she was tall, Suzy was still a child, as was her best friend, Carmen Dell'Orefice. Born in 1931, Carmen was the daughter of a Hungarian dancer and an Italian violinist. Her parents were continually breaking up and reconciling, so Carmen grew up with relatives and in foster homes. When she was seven, Carmen moved in with her mother, who worked as a building superintendent. In 1942 they moved into a fourth-floor walk-up apartment under the elevated train tracks on Manhattan's Third Avenue. Carmen caught rheumatic fever and was in bed for a year. Healthy again in 1945, she was approached by the wife of photographer Herman Landshoff as she rode the Fifty-seventh Street bus to a ballet class. "I'd always been the ugly duckling of my crowd," Carmen says. "I was the tallest, the skinniest, and I had braces on my teeth. The boys couldn't stand me. I always beat them at running, jumping, throwing a ball." Maybe that was why her mother agreed to let her pose for test pictures on Jones Beach.

"I was a big flop," Carmen says. "The magazine sent my mother a letter saying I was charming and well brought up but, unfortunately, totally unphotogenic." A godfather with connections "came to the rescue," she adds. "He introduced me to *Vogue*." A few weeks later the fourteen-year-old's image was spread across seven pages of the magazine, and she signed an exclusive contract with Condé Nast for $7.50 an hour.

Carmen had no agency at first. *Vogue* sent runners to her mother's apartment when they needed her because she had no telephone. "Then *Vogue* let me have the message that Powers was trying to reach me," she says. When she visited the agency, Powers had full-length photographs of her on the wall behind his desk. She joined up.

Carmen was just a skinny kid in love with a neighborhood grocer's son when *Vogue* first used her in 1946. She was so undernourished her dresses had to be pinned down the back to make them fit. Tissues filled out her bust when she worked with Horst and Cecil Beaton. These gentlemen—and homosexual—photographers "devirginized me, if you will," she says. "They were a difficult act to follow. I was very spoiled. They showed me what manhood was about, really. I was madly in love."

That summer Irving Penn booked her. When she arrived, he took a look at the frail child and immediately consigned her to a cot outside his office cubicle. He insisted she sleep while he and Dorian Leigh, whom he was also shooting that day, repaired within. "I was so impatient," Carmen recalls today, sitting in her Park Avenue apartment, surrounded by Norman Parkinson's photographs of her and personalized Salvador Dali prints that she earned posing for the surrealist artist. At sixty-three she is as sexy as she has ever been. "I didn't feel I needed a nap before standing in front of a camera," she says. "His office had a partition that didn't reach the ceiling. I listened to billing and cooing and moaning and groaning, and then Dorian came out. I didn't know Penn was in love with her. I wasn't astute, but I knew something wonderful was going on."

Dorian adopted Carmen, who, to this day, calls her Big Momma. "Dorian was the rage!" Carmen exclaims. "She was very solicitous. She asked Penn, 'What is this child doing here?' I had such a crush on him. Dorian perceived this and was darling with me about it." Carmen and her mother, both accomplished seamstresses, were soon making clothes for Dorian, and when she opened the Fashion Bureau, Carmen left Powers and signed up. "It was winter," she recalls, "and I go there, wearing what I owned, a chic trench coat my mother bought me for Easter, not a winter coat. No boots. Needless to say, I walked out with Dorian's coat."

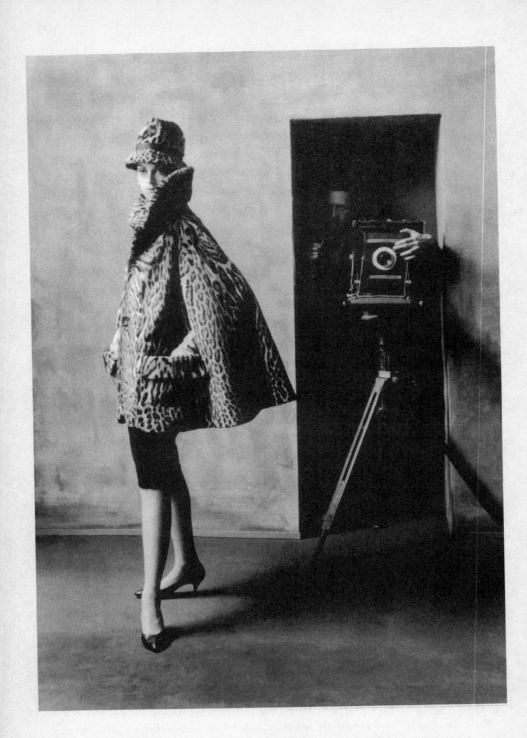

Carmen Dell'Orefice photographed by Melvin Sokolsky
(standing behind the camera)

Carmen roller-skated everywhere she went. A bus was five cents, and she didn't have it. Dorian gave her taxi fare. "I took it home for my mother to buy food with," Carmen says. "Or else Suzy and I would go to the movies instead of my bookings. That's the worst thing I've ever done." Perhaps. The pair were, in fact, model troublemakers for years. In 1954, for example, they attended the opening of the Fontainebleau Hotel in Miami, on assignment for *Vogue* with photographer Roger Prigent. "There was a big fountain in the lobby," Prigent remembers, "and they put bubble soap in it." Then, at dinner in a seafood restaurant, Suzy and Carmen begged Prigent to buy them a shark from a display tank. "Like a fool, I did," he says. The next morning the manager called in a panic. The shark was in the Fontainebleau's swimming pool.

In 1947, with Dorian's help, Carmen won a raise from *Vogue* to $10 an hour and the right to shoot ads for $25 an hour. She appeared on her first *Vogue* cover that October, at age fifteen. That year, too, a doctor working for Condé Nast prescribed shots to force her into puberty. Soon afterward Mr. John, a milliner, gave a party to introduce her to eligible bachelors. Her mother insisted on a personal interview before she let Carmen out of her sight with a man. Pat di Cicco, who later married Gloria Vanderbilt, took her to El Morocco on her first real date. Igor Cassini, who wrote a gossip column under the nom de plume Cholly Knickerbocker, introduced her to a friend of his, a grandfatherly fellow who offered her a Park Avenue apartment. Her mother told Joseph P. Kennedy sorry, no. Carmen was seventeen going on thirty-five.

When Dorian got married and closed the Fashion Bureau that year, most of her models, including Carmen Dell'Orefice and Barbara Brown, joined Huntington Hartford's agency, the only one then on the voucher system. "Hartford used the agency to look at all the girls," Carmen says. "By then I was pretty insightful about what goes on, and it was hard earned. I'd heard about Hunt's reputation. Bill Deering assured me it was a totally professional operation."

Suzy went to Walter Thornton, who set her price at $15 an hour. Dorian urged her sister to switch to Hartford. He pegged Suzy's price at $25 an hour. Dorian still wasn't satisfied. She wanted $40 an hour for Suzy. "That's when Dorian entered our lives," says Eileen Ford. Dorian called Ford and said, "Take Suzy, sight unseen," Eileen recalls. "Can you imagine how we felt?" They arranged to meet at a restaurant, Mario's Villa d'Este, and once Ford saw Suzy Parker, she recovered from her shock and agreed to take Suzy on one condition: that Dorian join the Fords, too. "I always said, that was the best bargain Eileen ever got in her life," Dorian says. "She didn't realize what she was getting. She just thought she was getting my kid sister. Suzy put them on the map."

"I grew up with talk about mink coats," says Richard Avedon. "Should we buy fifteen or four? Short or long?" He was born in 1923 and grew up in New York and Cedarhurst, on Long Island, the son of Jacob Israel Avedon, who owned Avedon's Blouse Shop in Harlem and then Avedon's Fifth Avenue, a specialty store at Thirty-ninth Street, with his brother Sam. Gertrude Lawrence appeared in its ad in *Vogue*. Sonia Delaunay designed its scarves. Their houses were always full of copies of *Harper's Bazaar* and *Vogue*. When Sam Avedon lost all his money in bad investments, Jacob went to work as an insurance salesman and then as a buyer at the Tailored Woman, a top women's fashion store. He ended up with another Avedon's Fifth Avenue, in Woonsocket, Rhode Island.

Dick had a Kodak Brownie box camera as a boy. But he'd taken his first pictures without a camera. After his father taught him the principles of photography, he tried them out by taping a negative of his younger sister, Louise, to his shoulder and sitting in the sun as her image burned into his skin. Louise was also his first model. He took her to Central Park and posed her, copying photographs by Munkacsi and Frissell. Her later mental illness and death in a hospital at age forty-two are Avedon's Rosebud, the source of his focus on the thin line between high style and deathly rictus. In Avedon's photos there's barely a difference between a laugh and a scream.

"Louise's beauty was the event of our family and the destruction of her life," he said in an interview with *Egoïste,* which published his work in the late 1980s. "She was the prototype of what I considered beautiful in my early years as a fashion photographer. All my first models . . . Dorian Leigh, Elise Daniels, Carmen . . . were all memories of my sister. . . . Beauty can be as isolating as genius, or deformity. I have always been aware of a relationship between madness and beauty." Fifty years later his photograph of model Stephanie Seymour baring her carefully shaved pubic patch in a sheer dress evoked the same attractive madness.

After dropping out of high school, Avedon joined the Merchant Marine in 1942 and was assigned to the photo department. "I learned the techniques of photography," he says. "I did hundreds and hundreds of ID photos." Pictures he took for a service magazine caught Alexey Brodovitch's attention. Brodovitch brought the young man after a year of study to Carmel Snow, who started him at *Junior Bazaar,* an ambitious new section that briefly turned

into an influential magazine for teenagers. "He used to scout the streets looking for new models," remembers photographer Lillian Bassman. "At the
beginning he used teenage models. Then he got the chance to work on
Harper's Bazaar, and of course he had to use older models. They were crazy
about him. He was a jazzy little character."

"There were no young photographers before me," Avedon says. "I was the
first. Now there are only young photographers. I had to be hidden from
Louise Dahl-Wolfe. When she saw my first two pictures, she lost her memory
and was found stumbling down Fifth Avenue."

But Avedon was actually stumbling until 1948, when he shot the couture
collections in Paris with model Elise Daniels, who didn't so much pose as act.
The palpable anxiety she betrays in Avedon's portrait of her wearing a tulle
turban in a restaurant brought something new—subtext—to fashion photography. By 1949 Avedon was king at *Harper's Bazaar.* That June Avedon asked
Dorian Leigh to go with him to Paris. "I didn't pay much attention to Dick
until he asked me to go to Paris," she says. Dorian's daughter Young had been
born that spring, and they'd moved to Bucks County, Pennsylvania. But she
wanted to get back in harness and had started working with Milton Greene
and Carmel Snow's niece Nancy White, an editor at *Good Housekeeping.*
Though her love affair with Irving Penn was over, she was working with him,
too. In fact, they'd just completed a series for *Vogue,* of Dorian dressed in the
fashions of different periods. When Penn heard that Dorian had been asked to
Paris by Avedon, he "was furious, absolutely furious" and was convinced that
Dorian had told Avedon about their recent session. Though they did become
friends, Penn and Avedon were always also competitors.

"In that period, we could maintain a close working relationship with our
models," Avedon wrote in *Portfolio,* a brief-lived graphic arts quarterly
Brodovitch designed in 1950. He and Penn "rarely encroached" on each
other's turf, Avedon added, "so that when Penn was working with Dorian
Leigh for *Vogue,* I wouldn't use her: there are no photographs of Jean Patchett or Lisa Fonssagrives by me and none of Dovima by Penn." Avedon later
compared his relationship with his models to that of a choreographer with his
ballerinas. Sometimes the closeness turned comic. "Suzy Parker used to go
through the top drawer of my desk, spying for messages, seeing if I was using
anyone else," the photographer revealed. "I knew that she did that, and I
would leave chicken wings in the drawer for her. She loved chicken wings."

Avedon had originally already booked another model, Mary Jane Russell,
for the Paris trip. A Sarah Lawrence College graduate, Russell had worked for

a photographer booking models until one day in 1948 an editor asked to book *her.* "I'll be straight with you," Eileen Ford said when Russell called to ask if the agency would represent her. "You're too tiny. Nothing's going to fit you." Jerry Ford convinced his wife to take Russell on. Jerry sent her to Diana Vreeland, who sent her to Lillian Bassman, Dahl-Wolfe, Frissell, and Avedon. All four booked her immediately, and she started posing for *Bazaar, Ladies' Home Journal,* and *Vogue.* She was among the first to break down the wall between the dueling magazines.

Early in 1949 Mary Jane had been asked to go to Paris with Avedon. "I got my passport, I got my ticket," she says. But one day a letter from Avedon arrived by messenger. It said that he'd decided Russell's small size would be too limiting. She quickly discovered he was going to take Dorian to Paris instead. "I think Dick had a crush on Dorian," says Russell. "I thought my heart would break."

Says Mary Jane's husband, retired advertising executive Edward Russell: "She'd spent night after night working. She colored her hair because Dick wanted something different. The whole enterprise was a lust to do better. Then this letter arrives. Dorian, other than a bigger chest, was the same size as Mary Jane."

Avedon met Dorian when her airplane landed in Paris. "We got in the taxi, and they sliced peaches into glasses and poured champagne on it, and when we got to the Hôtel San Régis," where all the photographers and models stayed, "we had the suite at the right of the glass door, a sunken bathtub full of flowers. It was just marvelous," Dorian says. On that trip she was smuggled through the streets swathed with sheets so no one could see what *Bazaar* was photographing.

Avedon took one of his best photographs on that trip, of Dorian, wearing a tiara and laughing hysterically, at Le Pré Catalan restaurant in the Bois du Boulogne. "When I saw that, I thought it was Princess Margaret bombed out of her mind; I didn't know it was you!" Suzy told Dorian. *Bazaar* wouldn't publish it, deeming it, quite rightly, unflattering. "It was in the Metropolitan Museum," Dorian says proudly. "Still is."

She was the first jet set model, cavorting with what would have been the *Vanity Fair* set had *Vanity Fair* still been in existence. "It was so marvelous," she says, "everyone was young and we were all starting—Byron Janis, Lenny Bernstein, Adolph Green, Betty Comden—all of them were friends of Dick's, and I was, to them, a prize, because here was this model who is talking to us and knows what she's saying. They thought models were empty-headed."

Dorian started working for everyone. One garment center client told her, "You're the thing I admire most, a lady who looks like a whore." When another potential client called her in the country and asked what she'd done lately, Dorian picked up the latest issue of *Vogue* and counted forty-nine pictures of herself. She soon began shooting Revlon's first national ads with Richard Avedon, including images that are remembered to this day for the lipsticks and nail polishes called Cherries in the Snow, Ultraviolet, and Fire and Ice.

Although she was paid a mere $250 for her famous Fire and Ice ad, Dorian claims she was making $300,000 a year. "Everybody was making forty dollars, I was getting sixty dollars an hour," she says. "I used to imagine the clients were behind the camera, whispering to the photographer, 'A dollar a minute, a dollar a minute.' I also did something that Eileen said would ruin me: lingerie. And then, of course, I got a hundred twenty dollars. I also went to Europe twice a year, and they paid me a lot of money to come and work freelance for them."

Meanwhile, her sister, Suzy Parker, had married her high school boyfriend secretly, just before she graduated from high school at age seventeen, in 1950. "Mother came upstairs and found them in bed and had hysterics," says Dorian. "Suzy said they were married, and they were." Although her parents wanted her to stay in the South and go to college, Suzy and her husband moved to Bucks County near Dorian and Roger Mehle. But Suzy's marriage was already in trouble. As it deteriorated, she was becoming a top "editorial," or magazine, model. Diana Vreeland called her "an intelligent American beauty who is interested in independence and making money." Her income shot up to $100,000 a year.

When Avedon approached the Parker girls that spring to shoot the all-important fall collections with him in July, they jumped at the chance. Dorian went to Italy first with photographer Genevieve Naylor. She met designer Emilio Pucci on that trip. He and a friend took their clothes off, cornered her, and tried to rape her. Escaping to Paris, she hooked up with Suzy, and they fell in with the era's gang of hot young Frenchmen, including the actor Christian Marquand, director Roger Vadim, magazine director Daniel Filippachi, and journalist Pierre "Pitou" De La Salle of *Paris Match*. Suzy fell for Pitou and almost immediately "retired" and moved to Paris. "She couldn't afford to just be a model, because they didn't pay enough money in Paris," says Dorian. So Suzy got an MG sports car, an apartment on the Left Bank, a camera from her friends Sam Shaw and Robert Capa, and an "apprenticeship" with Henri

Cartier-Bresson. She started taking pictures herself and eventually worked for *Elle* and French *Vogue* and signed up with the Magnum photo agency, although one of its members later admitted, "We never managed to sell a single picture of hers." Suzy shot a portrait of the handsome expatriate and best-selling writer Irwin Shaw. Dorian had an affair with him before returning to New York.

It was a season of failing marriages. Dorian was about to leave Mehle. Suzy was off to Mexico for a divorce. Richard Avedon had split up with his first wife, too. Unlike Penn and the many photographers who followed them into fashion, Avedon was never known to pursue sexual relationships with models. Early on Avedon told Dorian Leigh that Suzy Parker intimidated him. "He was scared of me, too," Dorian recalls. "One day he said, 'It takes a lot of courage to photograph beautiful women.' " That's why he used a nobody named Dorcas "Doe" Nowell as his model at first. He'd met her in 1945, and they married soon thereafter. "Doe had an androgynous look," says Lillian Bassman. "Dick, like all of us, has always been fascinated by androgynous sex and theatricality. When they walked down the beach in dungarees, they looked like two little boys." But in 1948, while Avedon was shooting Elise Daniels in Paris, "Doe was doing summer stock and she met somebody else," says a friend of the couple's.

"You can't fuck and photograph at the same time," Avedon told writer Anthony Haden-Guest in 1993. "Taking fashion pictures of models is not a matter of arousement. It's hard work." Asked for recollections of models he's worked with, Avedon demurs. "I have no thoughts about models," he says. "I have no interest in models. I've had great friends who were models—Suzy, Dorian, Penelope Tree, Anjelica Huston, China Machado, and now Stephanie Seymour—but these are interesting, feeling women, with good hearts, minds, and, only coincidentally, good bodies. I'd be interested in them no matter what they looked like."

By 1950 he'd fallen in love with Evelyn Franklin, the nonmodel wife of photographer Milton Greene. They were introduced at one of Avedon's regular Sunday get-togethers by Lillian Bassman and her husband, the photographer and artist Paul Himmel, who'd shared summer houses with Dick and Doe on Fire Island. "In the period when Evelyn was leaving Milton and going to Dick, she used to come to my apartment on Lexington Avenue," Dorian Leigh remembers. Avedon married Evelyn in 1951, and although they live apart, they remain married today.

Dorian wasn't so lucky. Appearing as a model in a Broadway play, she took a leave of absence and returned to Paris in 1953 to see Suzy. "She was living with Pitou," Dorian says, "and writing very strange letters. I was worried about her, because I never liked Pitou, and I had heard too many stories." While there, Dorian went to a nightclub, the White Elephant, with Robert Balkany, a wealthy playboy, but slipped off long enough to make a date with the Marquis de Portago, who was known as Fon. Although he was married (to the former Carroll McDaniel, now the very social widow of Milton Petrie), Portago began an affair with Dorian. He was a race car driver, handsome, rich, and very charming. When she appeared on the cover of *Look* magazine that June, he noticed a quote: "I'd rather have a baby than a mink coat."

"I think I can take care of both," said Fon, who soon impregnated her.

"I never stopped to think, never," says Dorian, who aborted the pregnancy, but not the affair with Fon, who'd promised to get a divorce and marry her. Late in 1954 she won a Mexican divorce from Roger Mehle and then married Portago. Unfortunately he was still married. Fon, who promised to divorce Carroll, promptly got Dorian pregnant again and headed back to Paris. Worried about her sister, Suzy set up a lunch for Dorian with designer Coco Chanel, who'd become a close friend. "Chanel said I was throwing my life away on an idiot," Dorian reports. "She told me to find a rich husband. But the millionaires were all my friends because I wasn't interested in their money."

Early in 1955 Dorian asked Eileen Ford to keep her busy with assignments while she waited for Fon's return. He bounced in and out of her house in Bucks County but was mostly tied to his family's purse strings. When Dorian heard that Carroll and Fon had reconciled, she headed back to Paris. "He was living in his flat in Avenue Foch, which was next to his mother's flat, and he gave me a key to the garden," Dorian says. "I had to sneak in, and I just suddenly thought, 'I'm out of my mind. How can I ever make things right?' "

Pregnant again, she tried to kill herself. The doctor who pumped her stomach and sewed up her wrists offered to end this pregnancy, too, but she refused. Fon reappeared and stayed with her until the baby was born. They named him Kim. "Two days after the baby was born I flew to New York to do a series of photographs," says Dorian.

Suzy met her plane. Suzy's irresponsibility about money had caught up with her. The Internal Revenue Service was after her for back taxes, and she'd returned home to put her financial house in order. Before she left Paris, Pitou and Coco Chanel had both cynically urged her to marry a rich man, but she'd refused. Pitou had even tried to "sell" Suzy earlier that summer in the south of France when a playboy made him an indecent proposal. "He was a South American son-of-a with a yacht," recalls Carmen. "He saw Suzy and Pitou and said, 'How much for a weekend?' The Cunt De La Salle named a price. That's the kind of guy he was. He was very appealing, very sexual, but it was all very self-centered, uncaring, unloving, unconstructive."

The designer Oleg Cassini knew Pitou De La Salle well. "I kept warning Suzy," he says. "She told me he was Dostoyevsky in the making. He never worked a day in his life. He wrote the same chapter for years." Nonetheless, that August Suzy married De La Salle, and they took up residence together in an East Fifty-seventh Street penthouse. At Pitou's request, she kept their marriage secret. And despite the high profile the Parker sisters had assumed, news of Dorian's suicide attempt and her out-of-wedlock child didn't leak out, either.

Dorian's on-again, off-again affair with Portago continued, although by now he was also seeing Linda Christian, the actress who'd been married to Tyrone Power. Fon told her his divorce from Carroll would soon be final. Dorian's heart soared. Then he crashed his race car in Mexico in May 1957 and died. Eileen Ford, who'd become a masterful crisis manager for her models, helped the grieving Dorian gather her children and retreat to Paris, where she remained for the next twenty years.

Meanwhile, Suzy went to Hollywood. Her first film appearance was a cameo in *Funny Face,* a 1957 movie starring Audrey Hepburn, as an existentialist turned model, and Fred Astaire, in a role based on Avedon. Avedon, a consultant on the film, suggested Parker play a model in the fashion sequences. Many of the pictures Astaire "takes" in the film were first shot by Avedon of Suzy. By the time the film was released, Suzy was making another movie in California, with Cary Grant, at Audrey Hepburn's suggestion. Unfortunately Suzy was dreadful in it. "You saw on the screen a terrified girl who didn't know the setup," Avedon said. Horst, who hated working with her because she couldn't hold a pose, said, "In the movie she stood still. It is exactly what I always wanted her to do for me."

Dorian, meanwhile, was hiding out in Paris, trying to keep Fon's child a secret and furious at her paramour for "marrying" her in Mexico even though he was still married to Carroll de Portago. Then Suzy revealed Kim's existence in an interview with the Hollywood gossip Louella Parsons. "Suzy just didn't approve of me," Dorian says. "Cary Grant said to her, 'You must not let yourself be associated with this scandal.' So she gave an interview saying that we were 'estranged,' because she didn't approve of my having a child out of wedlock. But anyway, that's how Mother and Daddy found out about Kim. They read it in the newspaper."

The next time the Parkers made the papers, it was far more serious. On June 6, 1958, Dorian, pregnant again, was in the American Hospital in Paris, trying not to have a miscarriage, when her doctor came in with the Paris *Herald Tribune*. A story on the front page said that her father had been killed when his car was hit by a train in Florida. Suzy, a passenger, had been thrown through the windshield and was in the hospital with two broken arms. That caused another scandal. Suzy had signed into the hospital as Mrs. Pierre De La Salle. "And he denied it!" Dorian recalls. "He thought it was embarrassing to be married." Within months Pitou returned to Paris as Suzy, even more famous and determined to conquer Hollywood, headed west again.

Their agent, Eileen Ford, wasn't pleased at that. "They throw you into a pond out there and let you sink or swim," Ford said. "Our world, fashion, is a very gentle one. We may be a bunch of cats, but we wouldn't slit your throat."

SUZY PARKER

"**I** want you to meet my wife, the mute," the actor Bradford Dillman says when he introduces his wife, Suzy, at parties. Once she starts talking, it's hard to get her to stop, and, as with her sister, Dorian, it's sometimes hard to know where truth ends and invention begins. "I embellish," admits Suzy Parker Dillman, sixty-one. "The Kirkpatricks—that's my mother's family—will make every story a little bit better, a little bit bigger. I've said a *lot* of stupid things."

Those days are pretty much over now, gone with her modeling career. But Richard Avedon still pops his head in every once in a while, driving up from L.A. in a limo to eat the chocolate chip cookies Suzy bakes in the kitchen of the large white hacienda-style house she, Dillman, and their children share in the hills above Santa Barbara, California. She's a plumpish housewife with frosted blond hair, a sunburn from a sailing vacation, and a Chrysler Le Baron in the driveway. But it has a "vanity" license plate that reads "FAKOKTA"— Yiddish for "dizzy."

"**I** was an afterthought. My mother thought I was menopause until she was five months pregnant, and for the next three months she didn't talk to my father. All my mother had ever wanted was a son. Fortunately for me, she didn't let Daddy name me Billie Jo. Billie Jo Parker. She named me after three friends: Cecelia, Rena, and Ann. Dorian laid them out that way so my initials would spell CRAP. I had no idea what the word meant! Daddy never called me Cecelia because he hated the name, so he always called me Susie. Later on, when I was working as a photographer for French *Vogue,* they said, 'S-u-s-i-e, how pretentious!' So they spelled it S-u-z-y, and then I came back to the

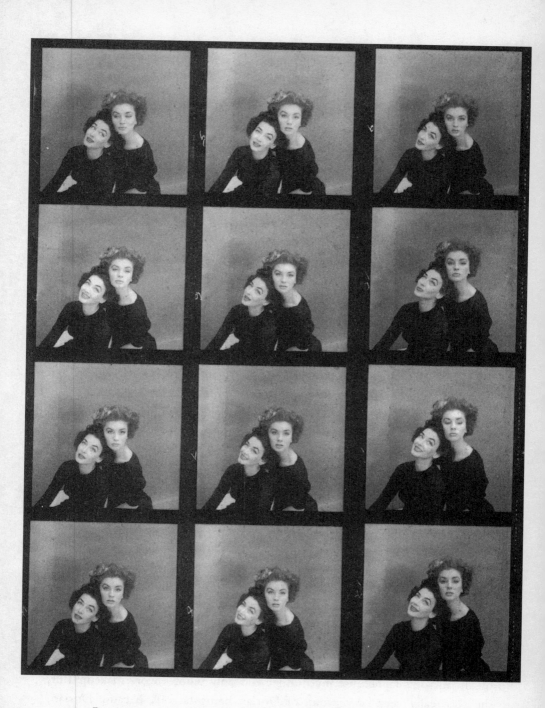

Dorian Leigh *(left)* and Suzy Parker photographed
by Richard Avedon in Paris, 1950

United States, and they said, 'S-u-z-y, how pretentious!' And I said, 'Oh, to heck with it.'

"My father was so disappointed in what Dorian had done. She was the oldest and the brightest, and every book he gave her would say, 'To Dorian, with merit.' She had wasted her life on what he thought was an inferior way to make a living. And then, of course, hers was the first divorce in the whole of our family, and I'm talking about sixty first cousins—that's how big our family was.

"Dorian had me come to the studio, and I'd have long braids, and she'd wrap them around my head. She'd do my hair and my makeup. I was so hapless. I was a tomboy from Dorian's point of view. I don't think she ever learned how to ride a two-wheeler bicycle. There's absolutely nothing that she does physically—except for that one important thing! She wanted to help me realize that I was attractive because I didn't think so. Dorian had friends who were photographers, and she really kind of crammed me down their throats. She created a monster.

"Models were all teeny tiny. I was always tall, so I photographed as if I were older. I was this height already when I was thirteen, so I could start modeling early. The other models all hated me. I drank milk shakes and ate tuna salad sandwiches. Also, my sister was a successful model and had her own agency.

"Dorian lived in a hotel, and her bedroom, the entire wall, floor to ceiling, was photographs of herself! It struck me as the funniest thing I had ever seen in my whole life. Modeling was something I kept a secret. None of my classmates in Florida knew anything about it. I would commute from Florida for the summer and stay with Dorian. She had a house on Lexington Avenue, a brownstone, and if my parents had had any idea of what was going on! I mean, it was just unbelievable. She was going out with Dizzy Gillespie, who was the sweetest man in the whole world. He used to wear a big clock around his neck and he'd let me wear that. Harry Belafonte. I mean, there were legions. She was up to no good! I didn't approve of her. I think Dorian thinks of me as a prude.

"Dorian and I were both extremely successful and very well known, but we'd still have to wash our face on the airplane or the train for when we'd get off in Jacksonville, because my mother said only whores wore makeup. But she was really very, very proud of Dorian being famous, because Dorian looked a lot like my mother.

"We met the Fords at a restaurant, some dump on Lexington Avenue. Dorian walked in first, heading for the Fords' table, and I was behind her, and according to Eileen, she and Jerry said, 'Oh, my God!' I was very tall, I had carrot red hair, but they saw the possibilities of my being a model. No question. And that's how I started—big time. The people who would use me—and I worked an awful lot—were usually the people who made the sleaziest, worst-looking clothes you've ever seen in your life, and I'd do ten ads in an hour. I hated that part. The joy was working for *Harper's Bazaar* or *Vogue* because of the quality of the clothes and the photographers, but they paid nothing. They paid twelve dollars and fifty cents, I think.

"I married in 1950. We were both underage, so we drove to Georgia, and I'll never forget, I was wearing a bikini bathing suit with a raincoat over it. He was part Cherokee, and he sat behind me in school, and he copied all my work, and he drove Harley-Davidson motorcycles, and he was very good-looking, and it was just a sheer disaster. Basically I was making a lot of money and supporting us. And then that marriage fell apart. We simply married too young.

"Going to Paris the first time was just unbelievable. I'll never forget that Dick met us at Orly Airport, and he had especially ordered one of those taxicabs that has the top that rolls back, so I got to stand up and see Paris! A lot of things I did or said to Dick, like the time in the train station, he incorporated into *Funny Face*.

"Every night Dorian would go out with a different guy, and every night she'd lock me in and I'd have my supper in my room at the Hôtel St. Régis. The first time I went to Paris by myself, she told these three different guys, the worst three leches in France, to look after her little sister. I've got to tell you, I fought my way out of more cars! Once I had to walk all the way back at night to my hotel!

"I met Pitou at a party Jacques Fath gave outside Paris for all the New York buyers on that first trip. Dorian got up to go the ladies' room, and even though she is extremely nearsighted, she could always, even in the darkest room, walk out with the handsomest man. She comes back with this smirk on her face and these two guys, that famous actor Christian Marquand and Pitou. She had picked them up somehow, and they were dressed in a very odd way. I later found out why. Only one of them had an evening suit, so one wore the pants and the other wore the jacket. The sad part is that many years later, after nine years of a disastrous relationship, I found out that it was Christian who wanted to take me to dinner. Isn't that weird? I went out with the wrong guy. I thought Pitou looked like Ashley in *Gone With the Wind*. I came back to America, went to Mexico, and got a divorce.

"Modeling was always only a way to make money, never any more than that. The only joy I ever got out of modeling was working with Dick Avedon. He was into movement and action, and I never stop talking and moving. I was always in the middle of something, usually talking. What drove Horst crazy was what made Dick happy; he wanted me talking or laughing. I was meant for strobe. But one thing that stuck in my mind constantly was my father's attitude. 'I want you to do something with your mind.' He had been so disappointed that Dorian had not used her great intellect, so I started doing photography. Bob Kaplan at Magnum sent me as a joke to be Cartier-Bresson's assistant. Cartier-Bresson needed me like a hole in the head! A tall redheaded model dragging along behind him!

"The Fords would send me money. They treated models like the idiots we are, and they would withhold enough money for the moronic models to pay their taxes. I left before the taxes were paid and started borrowing on that money, because I wasn't making any money as a photographer. I finally did some photographs for *Elle* and for *Ladies' Home Journal,* and then I got a contract with French *Vogue,* but it was very little money. Every time I'd get broke, I'd model for French magazines. I was making enough to make ends meet and support Pitou.

"Was he a ne'er-do-well? Absolutely. And very pretentious, too—with a title. We registered as Count and Countess De La Salle at the ski lodge. He had been so unfaithful to me, and I didn't know it! I spent all my money on Pitou. Talk about a gorilla on your back. His mother supported him, and then I supported him, and he was very expensive! He was the most pretentious son of a bitch you've ever met. He had his shirts made by an English shirtmaker, and since we were living in Paris, they had to be sent back to London to be washed because of the quality of the water.

"You know what my daughter Georgia said when she finally met her father? She was sixteen years old. She said, 'Mom, I can understand when you married Pitou you were very young, but nine years!' I was going to hang in there and make it happen. I was very much in love, or thought I was; it was an obsession. I was going to make this person into a wonderful human being. And I think that's how most of these models get into trouble, where they marry someone who has to be totally dependent on them. That silly power trip, wanting to be totally in charge, marrying beneath themselves intellectually.

"When I'd left [for Paris], I owed possibly sixty thousand dollars in back taxes. It was more than that when I got back to the United States. A nightmare! I came back to pay it off. Jerry Ford, that sweet angel, paid it up front and never charged me interest because had it been allowed to keep running, it would have quadrupled. So I worked like a maniac, any job that would pay my hourly fee, and I would only receive about twenty percent.

"I was the best. I was very strong. I could work six days a week, from six in the morning to nine at night, do a lot of quick changes, hit the marks, have an idea when the photographer was looking through the camera, a pretty good idea of how I was framed. If I'm charging somebody X dollars for an hour's work, I'm going to be on time, my hair's going to be done, my makeup's going to be done.

"Dorian became jealous. She has this younger sister who's very famous, who's on the cover of all these magazines, and men are paying attention to her. I'm grateful to Dorian for what she did, but I can also understand why she turned against me when she did, and that was because of that age difference. Here she was still modeling, and she was in her forties. Now, that's very unusual. And here I am in my heyday, and then what really put the lid on the whole thing was that I got into movies.

"I felt it was important that Kim be recognized, that Kim be known as Fon Portago's son, so when Louella Parsons called, I said, 'Yes, my sister, Dorian, had a baby with Fon Portago.' I thought that was very important from Kim's point of view because who else was going to believe it? I'm the one who took ol' Fon to lunch in New York City, and I said, 'You have to recognize him as your son! What if something happened?'

"One of the breaks between Dorian and me was, here she had this illegitimate child, that was bad enough, but damn it, when she's in Switzerland having the illegitimate child, she's writing my parents and telling them she's in a tuberculosis sanitarium. So when I go home to spend Christmas with my parents, I've got to listen to these sob stories about poor Dorian dying of tuberculosis. Plus she dumped her children on my mother! I wanted to kill her.

"We're as different as night and day. Dorian has a very intellectual approach to things. I'm more practical. She sows her oats and never looks back, and when she does look back, she writes her script the way she wants to write it. She's like a child, like the hub of a wheel, and she sees the world revolving around her.

"One time Dick played a terrible trick on us. We were photographing suits. Dick had decided to put us against white paper, and he had a whole stack of lemon meringue pies on one side of the set, and he had us throw pies at each other, and at the very beginning we said, 'Oh, no, we can't do that,' but then we really got into it. He understood the competitive thing between us, the opposite thing between us, he understood Dorian's possible anger at me, he understood my jealousy of Dorian being the sophisticated woman, and he put it all together with the lemon meringue pies.

"In 1958 I got a letter from my mother. My father had angina, and I came home to be with my daddy, and that's when the train hit him. It was a Saturday afternoon, and we were actually on our way to see my mother, who'd just had a mastectomy. This was like a really bad soap opera. We hit that train head-on. My father died. Our car was thrown up in the air, turned around in the air, and came down on the other side of the train facing in the opposite direction.

"Dorian came back from France for that. She was pregnant. When I was in the train accident, the one thought that went through my head was, if I survive, I want to have children. There was a lot of damage done. I lost my daddy, and he adored me. I was in the hospital for three months. I had broken arms, broken shoulders. I had glass in my eyes and my ears, glass everywhere, but I didn't have a scratch, except for one little scab on my forehead.

"That was a bad time. Pitou was cutting up. That's when I found out about him and the drugs. He wanted me to find out; that's why he started being less cautious, leaving things around. He was worried that he'd lost his meal ticket. I had terrible dreams, the car accident all over again every night. I was in a very bad frame of mind, and I took an overdose of pills. I was saved by my lawyer, Paul O'Dwyer, who hushed it up and kept it out of the papers. The next thing I knew, Dick showed up and said, 'Get your clothes, Evey and I are going to Round Hill, Jamaica, and you're coming with us.'

"I said, 'Can Pitou come?' This is how stupid I was. Anyway, Dick handed me this phone number of a psychiatrist, and he said, 'I'll be very ashamed of you if you don't call this man.' So one day I was walking around New York City, and I went by the public library, and I dialed the number, and the doctor said, 'Well, finally!' Wonderful Viennese accent. And he proceeded to cut me off from Pitou. He went at it like crazy. He convinced me that I was being selfish in keeping Pitou from having a career, so I sent Pitou back to Paris, with an allowance. At Christmastime I said, 'I want to go to Paris and be with Pitou.' The doctor said, 'All right, but just promise me one thing: Don't get pregnant!' Course, guess what I do? I used to wonder if he wasn't using me as a test case, to see how dumb you could be!

"Pitou left me! He didn't want to be a father. I had already hired a nanny, and the housekeeper was in this apartment that I had rented in Paris, and they knew that Pitou had moved out. He was gone, history. He moved in with a

Romanian tank heiress who had more money than I did. Pitou was having affairs all over the place. I was just so dumb. It was so obvious he was having an affair with this woman, and I thought he was in Algeria for *Paris Match*. All my friends were seeing him in restaurants, and they didn't want to say anything to me because the French are very superstitious. I was nine months pregnant, and I wasn't even allowed to see any bad movies. It didn't hit the fan until I was in the hospital giving birth to Georgia.

"Dick took a picture of me with the astronauts in about 1962—John Glenn, Alan Shepard, and Gus Grissom, the one who died. I pretended I was the editor of *Harper's Bazaar*, and it was a Hearst publication, so I used my Hertz rent-a-car card as proof that I was with Hertz magazines, and I was actually allowed in! This was before anyone had photographed them, before anyone had seen the missile, and they didn't want to put on their suits, and I talked them into it. Dick knew what he was doing. He had a plan in his head, and I was going along with it only because of the fun of working with him. He has a tic in his cheek that starts going when he's really serious about something, and he's so nearsighted, when he looks at contact prints, he squints. I loved all his different mannerisms, clicking his fingers, pacing around his studio.

"He couldn't stand advertising people looking over his shoulder. We did photographs for *Harper's*, for Mrs. Snow's niece Nancy White, who was a devout Catholic. I remember she had a screaming fit over bikini bathing suit pictures, not only because my navel was showing—at that time you couldn't show the navel—but also because I was wearing a religious medal, St. George and the Dragon. I have known a lot of fashion editors who are dragons! Anyway, she didn't want to publish any of them, and Dick said, 'OK, then I quit.' They finally had to back down and publish it. She didn't like any of our pictures. She thought they were a disaster, and so did most people at the time. It's always been that way with Dick. What he does today, they'll be copying ten years from now.

"I would do the Revlon ads with Dick. I never had a contract. What Mr. Revson offered me was such peanuts I told him to go take a flying jump. But I always ended up doing retakes for all these other models. Revson got so mad that he said, 'You will not use Suzy Parker.' So they gave me these weird names like Bubbles Macao, and we'd be doing it in the middle of the night, the ninth retake after eight other models.

"The greatest thing that happened to me is that Bradford Dillman and I made a film together in 1960 and became best buddies. We were the dearest, best friends in the whole world. The most I can hope for my children is that they marry someone with whom they've had a working relationship and become best friends before they become lovers. I married a good man. I've never loved a man as much as Bradford. He's been a marvelous parent. We've raised six kids together.

"I was still doing Revlon ads, I was still doing Hertz, Pabst beer, but it was lousy stuff. I didn't retire until '63, and that's because I was pregnant. But my work was dwindling off. I would still do things with Dick, but that was it. I totally stopped in 1965. That's a long career.

"It was a job, that's all. You know, my friend Coco Chanel said it. Fashion is a joke. It isn't an art, because if it were an art, it would be permanent, and it isn't. It's something that changes constantly. I was just lucky. Sheer luck. I was lucky to have been born with cheekbones."

The trouble really started on Labor Day weekend, 1954, when James Courtney Punderford, Jr., started seeing double. In November he went into the hospital, dying of brain cancer. So his wife, Ford model Barbara Mullen, worked every day from 9:00 A.M. until 4:30 P.M. to pay their bills and then spent another six hours at his bedside. Mullen was lonelier than she'd ever been in her twenty-seven years. Ironically, she looked better on film than she ever had before. "I was very much in demand," she says dryly. "During the day it was marvelous. The one place that I found freedom and relief was in front of the camera."

When she learned Jim would never recover, Mullen called the Ford agency and was bundled off to the duplex Park Avenue apartment Eileen and Jerry Ford shared with their two children, Jamie and Billy. Ford called Tom Rees, a doctor (who was married to a Ford model and performed plastic surgery on many more), "and got some sleeping pills and gave me some swift drinks, because that was the solution in those days," Mullen says. She stayed two nights and then checked into the Allerton House.

Then, one bad night in March, she called the Fords again, and Jerry answered the phone. Eileen was in Florida with the kids, he told her, but he would come pick her up. After all, personal service was one of the prides of the Ford agency. A few years before, *Life* magazine had run photographs of Eileen sewing Barbara's gown before a party and soaking another model's feet under the headline FAMILY-STYLE MODEL AGENCY. The Fords provided diets, dermatologists, and hairdressers and urged their models to improve themselves by studying culture, speech, dancing, acting, and languages. There was no hanky-panky at Ford, nor would there ever be. They wouldn't even let their

girls hawk deodorant, let alone lingerie. Jerry Ford could be counted on to
take good care of a model in trouble. He came and got her that night, and they
talked about unhappiness. "And of course we had a drink, and then we had
another drink, and he said, 'Come back to the apartment,' and we had
another drink," Mullen says. "And that's how it began."

She was a New York City girl, raised by a single mother and relatives in
Illinois and Texas. She wanted to go to college, but money was scarce, so she
ended up a beautician. "I hated it," she says. "I couldn't stand all those dirty
heads and fingernails, and as I was very thin, somebody suggested that I should
go see John Robert Powers."

Powers sent the seventeen-year-old to Bergdorf Goodman. Its in-house
couturier needed a showroom model, $35 a week. Bergdorf models were kept
hidden in a special room, but one day in 1947 a *Vogue* editor sneaked up the
back elevator. "We've been trying to contact you for a very long time, but they
would never give us your name," she told Barbara. It seemed there was a dress
that had been made on Mullen, and none of *Vogue*'s models could get into it.

She shot the picture, and the magazine wanted her again and again. *Vogue*'s
staffers suggested she call Ford Models. "They were very insistent," Mullen
recalls, so she went to the agency. Eileen Ford was away, but Jerry agreed to
take her bookings. "You're the new model my husband has taken on?" Eileen
Ford said as she eyed the girl a month later. "You have a terrible profile, and
you must never show it." Thus Mullen was admitted to the most select company in modeling.

Eileen Ford had already assumed the mantle of godmother of modeling. A
tiny, pretty, but tightly wound woman, she was a know-it-all with an answer
for everything, eight answers at once if need be. She was typically photographed, furrow-browed and talking, with two phones draped over her
shoulders, another to her ear, and a fourth being handed to her by her dutiful
and handsome husband, Jerry. At her meeting with Mullen she decreed that
the model would charge $25 an hour to start. "You'll either make it or you
won't," Ford told her.

That annoyed Mullen. "I don't think Eileen did it deliberately," she says.
"It just didn't register that people would be hurt. I think that's what turned a
lot of people off about her. She was young, she was pretty, she seemed very
happy, but she was always barking at Jerry. He was always smiling and looking
handsome, and there they sat, side by side, and took the bookings. They were
a fabulous team."

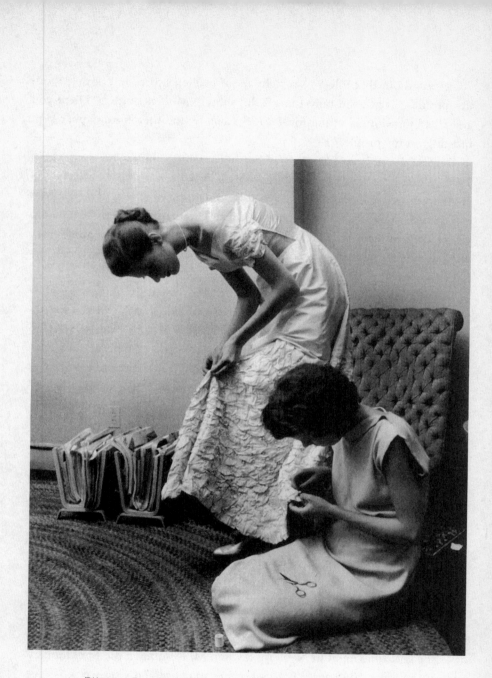

Eileen Ford sews Barbara Mullen's hem in 1948

It turned out that Eileen was right about Mullen's price but wrong about her profile. "That's the only thing I did show!" Mullen laughs. "There you are! I had just done a sitting for *Town & Country,* and the photographer kept insisting on my profile."

Jim Punderford was from a good but not wealthy family. They married in 1949. While he struggled to establish himself after the war, she shot to the top as a photographic model. Mullen was also something of a party girl. "Barbara and I used to go on location trips together," remembers Ruth Neumann, who started at Ford in 1950. "She was a very fast liver. We'd get home from work at five and go out again at nine. We were young and beautiful, and nothing ever showed."

In 1951 Mullen went on a trip to Montego Bay, Jamaica, with a young photographer, Frank Scavullo. A fashion-obsessed city kid, Scavullo started sweeping studios when he was sixteen and became Horst P. Horst's assistant. Soon he got a job with *Seventeen* magazine, and that led to little advertising jobs. Scavullo fell in love with his models indiscriminately. "You never knew who was coming out of Francesco Scavullo's room, a male model or a female model," he says. "I didn't refuse. I was a horny little Italian. Didn't matter to me!"

In Jamaica Barbara Mullen dressed in men's clothes every night, smoked cigars, and danced with a lady fashion editor to scandalize the vacationers at their hotel. She also mesmerized Scavullo, who photographed it all. "I was very much in love with her," he says. "We were gonna get married. She said she fell in love with me, and then in the middle of the trip, we were sailing and she said, 'Just kidding. I wanted to see how far a faggot would go.' I smashed her. I beat her up. She said she was committing suicide. I gave her pills." Mullen remembers it a little differently. "I told him to cut that out, that blue eye shadow, and he did! He combed his bangs back, and he looked normal!"

On the surface Mullen was a perfect Ford model, the soul of propriety. But "we were the kind of ladies who, when we were turned loose, didn't always behave like perfect ladies—and said we didn't remember anything the next day," she says. One night in New York, when Mullen joined the Ford models' table at the Stork Club, Jerry Ford asked her to dance and whispered, "I love you." She thought he was being silly. "I was Jerry's pet, the only model he'd taken on without consulting his wife," she says. But she thought he was good-looking, danced very well, and "he always laughed at my jokes," she adds.

By then laughs were few and far between. "I had quite deliberately become a recluse," Mullen says. "Jim had been virtually dead from the day he walked into the hospital; he just had a very strong heart. I really was in an extremely weak condition when Jerry came to pick me up that night. And after about the third scotch on an empty stomach, that was it." They made love, but when Ford called the next day, Mullen begged, "Don't call me." The secret affair continued nonetheless, even after Eileen Ford returned to New York. Mullen and the other models had discussed the Ford marriage before, and they all thought Eileen was as tough on her husband as she was on the models. "Very frequently to my young eyes she publicly humiliated him by bossing him around in the agency in front of all these beautiful women," Mullen says.

Jim Punderford died in July. Complicating matters considerably was the fact that Eileen Ford was pregnant. Mullen's nerves were shot. The reckless affair had begun to scare her. She demanded her lover tell his wife what was going on. "And I think he did, so give credit where credit is due." Never was Eileen Ford's steel better displayed. "I hope you will stay with the agency," she told Mullen.

For two weeks the model didn't hear another word. "I was quite frankly in a terrible shape," she says, "but I got the eyeliner on, and I went to work." Jerry Ford started taking flying lessons. "I can spend most of my time in the air where nobody can get me," he told Mullen. Then one day, in fall 1955, there was a knock on the door of Mullen's apartment. "It was Eileen's father and her brother, who came into my apartment and pushed the curtains aside as if they thought they'd find somebody there," she recalls. "They were look-ing for Jerry. They asked me what my intentions were. I said I'd go along with whatever decision Jerry made. I mean, it was really ghastly."

Finally Ford reached his decision. What happened between him and Eileen isn't known, but they seemed to refer to the incident years afterward in an interview. "Once Jerry was really mad at me," she said. "He told me I had to mend my ways or we'd be divorced."

"I told her she was too bossy," Jerry added.

"So . . ." said Eileen, offering him a placating smile, "so I mended my ways. That's why I'm so docile now." But was she really? "If Jerry Ford left me," she'd said earlier in the same interview, "I'd kill him."

Ford told Mullen they were through, and then they all tried to act as if nothing had happened. "I would call up and get my bookings, but I was so unhappy," Mullen says. "I was told not to talk to either of them. I was mourn-ing the loss of my husband, and I was mourning the loss of a good friend and lover, all at the same time."

Finally she wanted out. "I had the feeling that people were avoiding me socially in New York. I didn't really know what was happening. I was on the skids. I just thought it would be smart of me to leave. It was not a very comfortable situation for me, and it must have been terribly painful for Eileen. Never again have I gone anywhere near a married man! So I wanted to be in the middle of nowhere for a year. It was January 1956, and a friend of mine at United States Lines got me a cabin on a nice ship to Europe." Jerry gave her a Cartier passport case as a going-away present.

For nine months she worked all over Europe. When she came home, she was still a Ford model, but "My reception was rather cool, I thought, and then I heard a few things, and I changed agencies." Years later Mullen heard "some not very nice things" about the denouement of her career: "There was a rumor in the air that Eileen was not doing me much good."

The word was certainly out. Yet curiously it stayed within the small circle of friends that then constituted the modeling business. In that web of magazines and ad agency types, photographers and models, Eileen Ford's dominion over modeling was already absolute. On the spot where John Robert Powers planted a long-stemmed rose, Eileen Ford had erected a fortress of propriety and moral rectitude that was to stand for fifty years. Today neither of the Fords will talk about Barbara Mullen. But when the subject comes up, Eileen Ford's eyes still grow red, and her hands start to tremble.

The agency Barbara Mullen joined in October 1956 was called Plaza Five. Its founding, in June 1953, had been another sort of betrayal to Eileen Ford, one that, unlike her husband's, she had to face time and again. "It was the biggest news in the business: Models dared to leave Eileen and open an agency!" says Dorian Leigh. "And it was an immediate, immediate success!"

The Fords' only real competition at the time was Fan Krainin. An imported-rug dealer turned sales promotion agent and the sister of a photographer, Ewing (né Irving) Krainin, who ran a big studio on Fifth Avenue, she started the Frances Gill Agency with a $5,000 investment at his suggestion in 1951. "We made the name up out of nowhere," says Ewing Krainin, who ended up marrying a Gill model.

Gill booked an important handful of top magazine models, most memorably Evelyn Tripp and Betsy Pickering. Pickering was at Sarah Lawrence College late in 1953, when Edith Raymond, the editor of *Mademoiselle,* sent her to photographer Mark Shaw, who in turn sent her to see Frances Gill. Her father wasn't pleased. "It was not considered the most reputable profession" the year after the Jelke case broke, she recalls.

Pickering worked regularly for nine years, beginning at $25 an hour and ending at $65, grossing, she estimates, $1.5 million. She remembers that Fan (who now assumed the name Frances Gill), a sister named Edith, and brother Ewing all were involved in the agency. Gill was tiny, feminine, and always decked out in exotic jewelry. "There was money there," Pickering says. "She was very well brought up. She'd never say; she'd suggest. No one ever knew where she lived. She was so elegant and so dear. She was a mother to everyone."

Frances Gill also booked runway models. Gillis MacGil was one. Born into a Jewish immigrant family in New York, MacGil worked in the stock room at Bergdorf Goodman as a girl and was fascinated by the store's models. She moved to Nettie Rosenstein's dress company, where she was one of ten house models earning $75 a week, showing clothes in Rosenstein's showroom and at trunk shows all over America. Before long MacGil was photographed for *Vogue* by Alan and Diane Arbus. In 1950 she heard that an agent named Frances Gill wanted to meet her. Gill, who'd instituted a voucher system backed by her family's money, recruited MacGil with the promise that she'd send the model to *Harper's Bazaar*. "I tagged along behind her," says MacGil's friend Barbara Brown. They both soon decided they'd made the right decision. "I felt comfortable," says Brown. "Frances didn't try to rule your life the way Eileen did."

MacGil and Brown both loved fashion shows and often did them together. There was a constant round of collection openings on Seventh Avenue. "You never had a chance to put your clothes on," MacGil says. "You raced up and down the back stairs at Five Fifty, Five Thirty, and Four Ninety-eight Seventh Avenue in your raincoat." But despite the increase in bookings, Frances Gill kept her business small. "She never wanted an empire," says Betsy Pickering.

A few blocks away Jerry and Eileen Ford argued about that issue. "I wanted to grow," says Jerry. "We were the first boutique agency, but I thought it was crazy to stay small. The fact is, boutiques either grow or die. I wanted to get as many good models as I could." Eileen wanted only high-fashion models. The girls who worked with Avedon and Penn and *Bazaar* and *Vogue* didn't walk runways or pose for Pepsodent. Eileen even turned down Grace Kelly, whom she thought too "commercial."

"But the truth is, everyone in this business including *Vogue* and *Bazaar* and Avedon and Penn, *everyone* is commercial," Jerry says. Still, they did it Eileen's way. "And Eileen was right," her husband says.

Just as the attentions of *Vogue* or *Bazaar* could make a model, they could also make an agency. Polly Knaster, who'd previously worked for Huntington

Hartford, took over the management of *Vogue*'s studio in 1949, booking all the models for seven Condé Nast magazines. When the studio closed in 1952, because the magazines could no longer afford to keep stables of exclusive photographers, Knaster moved to *Vogue* as its models editor.

"I saw anybody, but I warned them to be prepared to be told they had no potential," she says. "When I had somebody right, I'd work on their books, I'd make appointments. It was fun to groom a model so she'd be used, collaborating with the agent. When tests came through well, I'd show them to Babs Simpson, and she'd try them." Knaster would push to get new models on one of *Vogue*'s then twice-monthly covers. "And when a new girl got on, she was made."

"We'd use them a lot," agrees fashion editor Babs Simpson. "And we'd ask them, please, not to work for the *Bazaar*." Adds another *Vogue* fashion editor, Catherine di Montezemolo: "I would have lunches and meetings with Eileen to find out about new girls. She would send them to both magazines to feel them out. Then, if we really wanted a girl, we'd have to guarantee a certain number of pages in order to get her."

Once a model was wanted, she was treated like a rare gem, and many of them came to believe that's what they were. Retired Ford mannequin Ruth Neumann calls her generation of models the Untouchables. "We looked like we couldn't say 'shit,' " she explains. "We were snotty, cold. You couldn't speak to us."

Though it wasn't the only game in town, the Ford agency epitomized that look with its icy blondes, gaunt brunettes, and snooty society types. It all came down to Eileen's taste in women. "I have to like the girl," she said. "Unless I'm sold on her, I can't sell her. I don't want to sound corny, but she has to be somebody I would like to have over to dinner." It helped if a model was haughty and a little bland. "A model shouldn't have a particular nationality, since she's selling to everybody," Ford said. And models had to be hardworking. When a Ford model went to the Riviera and came back a little spoiled, Ford dismissed her with a telegram. "I adore you, but I can't afford you," it said. "There's no room for playgirls in this picture," she explained. "We just can't afford them. The people footing the bills aren't fooling. They're looking for a girl who's trying to make money with her face."

Natálie Nickerson stopped modeling the day she married Wingate Paine in 1949 and went into business with him, running his studio and acting as his agent. "By that time Eileen didn't need much recruiting," she says. "Everybody wanted to be with them. There was no competition. We saw each other socially." When a good model appeared in Wingate's studio, the Paines told her about Ford.

"But then," says Natálie, "I disagreed on some things. There was too much controlling, control of clients, control of models. People were being told that models were busy when they weren't, so Eileen could bring newer girls along, and maybe dissipate their strength!" By 1952 Natálie thought Ford was abusing her position.

There was also the matter of money. "We gave her half of everything," says Eileen. Adds Jerry: "But that wasn't much." Between 1946 and 1952 Natálie says she never received more than $20,000 from Ford. She got regular financial statements, and she never questioned the Fords about what she considered overly lavish entertainment expenses. But then came "expenses I considered personal," she says, declining to elaborate. "Rightly or wrongly I felt cheated and betrayed, and in my mind everything between us had changed." Stewart Cowley says he told Natálie that the Fords were using her money to light cigarettes in Paris with $100 bills.

Toward the end of that year the Fords suddenly asked the Paines to buy them out and take over the agency, but by December Eileen had changed her mind. "On behalf of my clients, Gerard and Eileen O. Ford, notice of termination and dissolution of partnership is herewith given you, effective December 31, 1952," said the letter Ford's attorney sent to Natálie on December 29. Her attorney advised her to sue but warned that any settlement would likely keep her out of the model business.

With her husband's grudging blessing, Natálie opened her own agency in 1953 with two top Ford models—Sandy Brown and Dovima—and five telephones. "I couldn't think of a name for the agency, and I wasn't going to use my own name," Natálie says. "I wanted to be very behind the scenes and not publicized and I never was, incidentally. I sent out notices that Dovima would be at Plaza five-five-eight-nine-three or whatever it was, and the same for Sandy Brown, and that's where the Plaza Five came from. I had given Dovima twenty-five percent to come with me, because I, like Eileen, needed a top model, a big name."

Dovima was that. After Dorian Leigh and before Suzy Parker, she was Richard Avedon's favorite, but she was more. Dovima was the quintessential 1950s high-fashion model and in that, arguably, the apotheosis of all models. "Dovima was simpleminded and uneducated, [but] an absolutely incredible person," says Dorian Leigh.

Dorothy Virginia Margaret Juba was born in the Bronx in 1927, half Polish, half Irish, the daughter of Patrolman Stanley Juba of the Fourteenth Precinct. She grew up in a two-story brick apartment building in Jackson Heights. The students at the Blessed Sacrament Elementary School called her Skinny Dottie Pigtails. "*We* called her Doe," says her mother, Margaret Juba. She had brown hair and large, luminous blue eyes that helped her win beauty contests as a child. Her picture appeared in the *Patrolman's Benevolent Association Bulletin.*

At age ten Doe developed rheumatic fever, and she spent the next seven years at home in bed. Tutored at home, she'd talk on the phone with her visiting teacher's other bedridden young patients. Doe dreamed of being a ballerina and developed into a talented artist. At twelve she started signing her drawings and paintings with the first two letters of each of her names: Do-vi-ma.

Doe Juba was finally declared well at age eighteen. She got a job selling candy at Schrafft's on Fifth Avenue, went to art school, and even saw John Robert Powers; but modeling didn't pan out. "I never thought I was a beautiful woman," she once said. "As a child I was a gangly, skinny thing and I had this ugly front tooth that I broke when I was playing dress-up in my mother's clothes."

In 1948 she married Jack Golden, an orphan who worked at a bank and lived upstairs from the Jubas with cousins. He moved downstairs into her bedroom. Six months later Doe was laid off by the advertising agency where she'd gotten a job as an artist. She was waiting by an elevator at 480 Lexington Avenue to meet a girlfriend for lunch when someone grabbed her arm and said, "Come with me." Within minutes she had a new hairdo and was earning $17.50 posing for *Glamour* magazine.

"I was an instant success," she said later. "They sent me to Eileen Ford." The very next day she had a booking with Irving Penn to model an off-shoulder gown for *Vogue.* Penn asked her to smile. She gave him an enigmatic look to hide her cracked, discolored front tooth. Penn asked her name. "Dovima," she replied.

"She was the super-sophisticated model in a sophisticated time, definitely not the girl next door," Jerry Ford once said, summing up her visual appeal. But Dovima *was* the girl next door at heart. "It always seemed like I was watching a movie," she said of her model years, "and I'm in the movie, only it really isn't me."

In the early scenes of that movie she bought an $18,000 brick house in Jackson Heights and was earning modeling's top rate, $30 an hour. "After my initial discovery, *Vogue* began booking me every day and I found myself beginning to think of *me* as a model," she said. "I was a prima ballerina one day, then an adagio dancer, a movie queen, a clown, a forlorn waif. I was anything that could be portrayed with a look, a gesture, a stance, a mood and the right costume. The more the photographer demanded, the more I was willing to give. . . . I found ways to change my hairdo in three minutes . . . and sometimes when we worked on location, I had to change outfits in taxis, or behind a tree. Once, I changed in a telephone booth."

"Just look at that waist!" Diana Vreeland cried the first time she saw Dovima. In August 1950 she went to Paris with Vreeland and Avedon for *Harper's Bazaar.* An innocent abroad, she used the bidet in her hotel room as a flower pot. When she arrived in Egypt for another shoot with Avedon, she was asked how she liked Africa. "Africa?" she asked. "Who said anything about Africa? This is Egypt." Told Egypt *was* in Africa, she responded, "I should have charged double rate!" Years later Richard Avedon told model Lauren Hutton about that trip. "They were going on a camel trip across the desert," Hutton says. "Dick had told everyone to bring just one small bag, but Dovima had this huge trunk, so he thought she was bringing a lot of clothes, and he said, 'What are you doing, bringing all those clothes?' And she said, 'Those aren't clothes, those are my books!' And he thought, 'I can't take books from a girl!' But it turned out to be all comic books—a gigantic steamer trunk of comic books."

Dovima never lost that innocence, friends say, even as the money started pouring in ($5,000 her first year; $15,000 her second; $30,000 by 1954) and she grew more accustomed to her new, sophisticated world. By 1953 she had worked with almost every star of photography. But she'd grown unhappy with Eileen Ford. Natálie's offer of a partnership in a new agency was hard to refuse. Jerry Ford recalls that Paine sweetened the pot by offering Jack Golden a job.

Eileen's response was instantaneous, says Natálie. "She refused to give Wingate any models. Nobody could exist without Ford models at that time. I called everybody and said, 'Look, I'm not asking you to do this for Wingate, but who's gonna be next? You? Should she be allowed to have the power to shut down a studio?' I'm sure a lot of people called her and said, 'You can't do this, Eileen.' And there was never another problem."

Ultimately Plaza Five benefited the Fords. In 1954 Dovima raised her rate to $50, and other top models followed suit, Ford's included. "Dovima had trouble being on time," says Natálie, "but when she arrived late at a studio, she would be so remorseful that she was usually forgiven. I'm not sure this would have been tolerated from any other model."

Avedon played a large part in her career. Traveling to Paris, London, Rome, Egypt, and Mexico, "we became like mental Siamese twins, with me knowing what he wanted before he explained it," Dovima said. "He asked me to do extraordinary things, but I always knew I was going to be part of a great picture."

In 1955 the duo collaborated on what may be the best-known fashion photograph of all time, "Dovima and the Elephants." She estimated they took a thousand pictures in an hour that day. "By the time I finished, I thought of the elephants as friends working with me in complete synchronization, all of us gently swaying back and forth," she once recalled. Avedon instructed her to be aloof and so above it all that it would seem as if the pachyderms weren't there. He later called that photo "her peak of elegance and power."

She was Avedon's fashion doll. She would do whatever he wanted, all the while looking like an unruffled swan. Off the set she tried to live the same story. "I began to [have] the idea that I was a photograph . . . a plastic image," she said. "I could only be myself behind a camera." By 1955 Jack Golden had quit his job at the bank. He joined her that year, at her expense, in Paris. He got drunk, as he often did at home, and threw up in the wastebasket in front of a reporter as Dovima stood by patiently waiting to clean up the mess. "If I didn't have my husband, what would it all be worth?" she asked another interviewer. "I think my husband is the only boy I ever met who told me I was beautiful."

Dovima raised her rate to $60 an hour and cut her working hours down to four a day. In 1957 she appeared in *Funny Face* as a model named Marion. Back in New York, she signed up to study at Lee Strasberg's Actors Studio. There was a whole new world opening up for models on television, and Dovima was determined to be part of it. She appeared on *The Phil Silvers Show* and Joe Franklin's *Down Memory Lane* and made personal appearances for NBC, divorced Golden, and married again, to Alan Murray, an Immigration and Naturalization Service officer. She gave him her money, just as she had given it to Golden. They lived in a nine-room apartment on Seventh Avenue and went out almost every night. A daughter, Allison, was born in 1958. Dovima was getting older, but nonetheless, at the end of that year she raised her rate to $75 an hour.

"She had married her second husband, who I felt was not a very nice person," says Natálie Paine. "He told her that she had to raise her rate, much against our wishes. She was booked every minute, and she raised her rate, and she stopped working. Then she wanted to get involved in the agency. Her

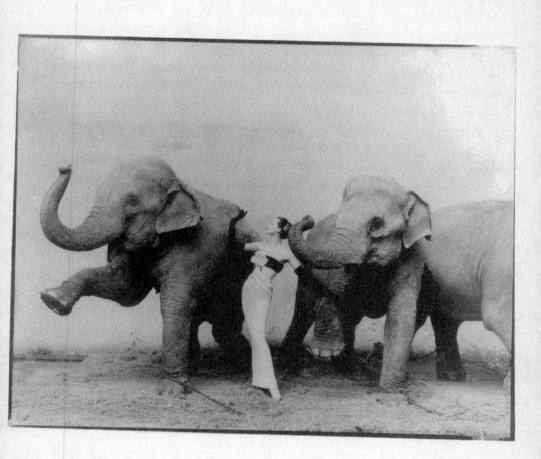

Dovima and the elephants photographed by Richard Avedon
at the Cirque d'Hiver in Paris, 1955

husband said she should. She was absolutely his puppet, or so it seemed to me. So she started announcing to the world that she owned a part of Plaza Five—which indeed she did—without ever discussing it with me. My lawyer had a meeting with her, where she demanded that she have the same salary that I do, and *I mean,* it was not rational. I ended up buying her out, which was very unfortunate, because she could have grown into that business. She was wonderful with girls; she could have worked with makeup and hairstyles. There was a lot she could have done."

Dovima always called her life a Cinderella story, so it is hardly surprising that she planned a happy ending. "I didn't want to wait until the camera turned cruel," she said. Although she didn't stop posing entirely until 1962, she later told an interviewer that the moment of decision came atop a wrought-iron ladder at Avedon's studio in 1959. She was dressed in hot pink, holding a huge letter *A* that was to be incorporated into the *Bazaar* logo on the cover she and Dick were shooting. Teetering high off the ground, she recalled a friend's telling her to quit while she was at the top of her profession. "This is my last shoot," she told a startled Avedon. He cracked open a bottle of Dom Pérignon.

Dovima immediately set out to prove that she was more than a comic book–reading model. She appeared with Johnny Carson, on Broadway in *Seidman and Son* with Sam Levene, and as a newspaper columnist, replacing the vacationing Dorothy Kilgallen. Her private life wasn't so successful. Her second marriage ended. Her luck in love stayed bad. "Sadly she could only be with men who beat her," says Carmen Dell'Orefice. "I'd find her on my doorstep black and blue, and I'd take her in and she'd live with me. . . . Religion served her very well. She had great faith. But she had no education, and she never picked it up. And so she had no self-esteem."

Soon Dovima was broke. A downward spiral began. In 1960 she filed a $500,000 slander lawsuit against Eileen Ford. She alleged that Ford had accused her of writing a letter to the government, "to try and stop foreign girls from coming here, so they wouldn't compete with her." The suit sank without a trace. Finally, lured by television, she moved to Los Angeles. Murray called the FBI and accused his ex of kidnapping her own daughter. He then got a divorce in Mexico. Dovima never saw Allison again.

"The Hollywood bug had bitten her," says her brother Stanley. In the next few years she appeared on *Dr. Kildare, The Man from U.N.C.L.E., My Favorite Martian, Bewitched, The Danny Kaye Show, Kraft Suspense Theater,* and *The Art Linkletter Show.* But she was also bouncing from man to man. "Anyone stuck it in her," says Carmen. "I'd say, '*Please,* Dosie, I'll find you a guy.' "

* * *

There were no model agents on the European continent after World War II. In France, fashion's heart, employment agencies had been declared illegal, as it was considered improper for anyone to take a portion of someone else's earnings. Such arrangements smacked of prostitution. Models in the Paris couture houses took their own bookings, just as Lisa Fonssagrives had done twenty years before.

When Dorian Leigh emigrated to Paris in the mid-1950s with her son, Kim, she booked her own work, too, and was typically paid on the spot by either photographers or clients. Studying French employment laws, she decided it would be legal to open an agency if she took fees only from clients and not from models. With the encouragement of Hervé Mille (the director of *Paris Match*—France's equivalent to *Life* magazine—and the monthly women's magazine *Marie Claire*) and his brother, Gérard, a society decorator, she financed a start-up with her own modeling earnings.

The Milles were socialites and collectors of wealthy and famous friends. After the war the two bachelor brothers had moved into a house together on the rue de Varenne on the Left Bank and created a salon that attracted Coco Chanel, Juliette Greco, Jean Cocteau, the Rothschilds, Marlon Brando, and Suzy Parker, whom Mille introduced to Chanel. Hervé Mille also arranged for several French magazines—his own, as well as *Elle* and *Marie France*—to hire Dorian as their *collaborateur,* or formal associate. "All the magazines kept saying they couldn't get top models, they only got dropouts from New York who wouldn't accept being paid so little money," Dorian recalls. "I promised them American models, and they promised to use me exclusively, and so the French government gave me a working permit." Leigh opened her little office just down the street from the Élysées Palace in fall 1957.

Until then the stars of Paris fashion had been the exotic creatures of the couture *cabines.* Among the most famous were Bettina Graziani and Sophie Malga. Sophie worked at Jacques Fath and Christian Dior and was to marry film producer Anatole Litvak. Bettina, born Simone Micheline Bodin, a freckle-faced rail worker's daughter from Brittany, was renamed and re-created by Fath, who told her, "We already have a Simone; you look to me like a Bettina."

Although they sometimes posed for pictures, Sophie, Bettina, and the rest of the couture *cabine* models (many of whom used exotic single names like

Praline, Victoire, and Alla) lived in a world totally apart from that of American photo models like Dorian. "We hired them full-time for a small wage," remembers Percy Savage, who worked for Lanvin couture as a textile designer in the fifties. "They had great bodies and knew how to walk. They weren't necessarily photogenic, although if they were, we let them do photos. They didn't belong to agencies. They were above all that."

Savage was great friends with Christian Dior, who opened his couture house in 1947. "Dior found his girls in bordellos," according to Savage. "He went practically every night. He was gay; but he loved that life, and the girls became models *and* clients. They knew men with money. They'd go to Cannes, Monte Carlo, and Deauville for dirty weekends. They had to have their suit from Chanel, their cocktail ensemble from Dior, their evening dress from Fath. Then they'd marry an English duke and need still more clothes."

By attempting to open an agency and change the way models worked in Paris, Dorian Leigh established herself as a maverick, and she quickly met a maverick's fate. "The police kept dropping in all the time because they said I had a *bureau de placement clandestine,*" she says. Early in 1958 she was summoned to a tribunal, found guilty, and fined a hundred francs. "I went by myself. I didn't even have a lawyer!" Dorian laughs. "I didn't know it was important." The court told her to find another formula if she wanted to stay in business. "I wanted to start a real agency, and then I went to the Fords, who were very interested," Dorian says. She and the Fords agreed that she would represent their models in Europe and scout for them there.

The Fords visited Europe for the first time in 1957, traveling to Rome, Paris, and London, checking out the modeling scene in each city. "We'd dealt with European models before," Jerry says. "In the late fifties any girl from Europe would make it. People wanted to see what they looked like, and in fairness, they came because *Life* or *Vogue* was there and the editors saw people and would tell us, or Dorian would tell us." Bettina and Sophie had come to New York with Jacques Fath on his personal appearance tour a few years before. When Eileen got Sophie a job modeling in a Seventh Avenue show, the designer called her, screaming. "She'd come to a fitting without underwear," Ford remembers, and the designer "just about died."

The Fords' arrival in Europe changed modeling forever. Not long before, *Life*'s Sally Kirkland, who often shot fashion spreads in Europe, had introduced the couple to Anne Gunning, a London model. In England models were accepted into society in the 1950s. Their aristocratic mien fitted Britain's class system, and models often married politicians and wellborn men.

Bronwen Pugh married Lord Astor. The German industrialist Baron Hein-rich von Thyssen-Bornemizsa married Nina Dyer in 1954 and Scottish model Fiona Campbell-Walter in 1955. Dyer went on to wed Prince Sadrudin Aga Khan in 1957 (but their marriage was dissolved in 1962, and three years later she was found dead of a sedative overdose). Anne Cumming-Bell became the duchess of Rutland, Jean Dawnay the Princess Galitzine, and Gunning was to marry the statesman Anthony Nutting and later be made Lady Nutting. With her connections, it was easy for Gunning to get the Fords a room at the ultraexclusive Connaught Hotel.

Then, Jerry Ford recalls, "some British newspaper did an article saying that a millionaire American agent was coming to seek English models." Before they'd even arrived, the Connaught's switchboard was swamped with calls, and its lobby was filled with model aspirants. Gunning headed the Fords off at the pass and put them up at her apartment in Belgravia, but an impression had been made.

Moving on to Paris, the Fords stayed in a terraced suite at the Hôtel Cril-lon (for $40 a night) and discovered another treasure trove of models at Dorian Leigh's agency. "Dorian *was* Paris," says Jerry. "There was nobody else, and she was, of course, courted by every roué in Paris, and she loved it and kept them for herself and didn't let them meet any girls. But we met some very nice models, and we became the only importer in the United States. It was easy. Models were dying to come to America because they were paid ten cents an hour there and a dollar an hour here."

The key question wasn't whether Dorian's business was viable, but if it could be made legal. Finally, Hervé Mille's boss, Jean Prouvost, a textile mil-lionaire turned publisher, came to the rescue. After Leigh received another summons to court in 1959, Prouvost suggested that Mille hire his lawyer, Robert Badinter, to defend her. Backed by the powerful magazines, they eventually won the case and changed the laws. "We established that model agencies were different," Leigh says. Later she opened branches of her agency in London and Hamburg, Germany.

Until that time most of Ford's models had come from within fifty miles of New York City. "We didn't go looking," says Jerry. "They came to us. Then came a flood of girls from California." Leigh went looking for models all over Europe, and the Fords followed suit. "Eileen started traveling in Germany, because Otte is a German name, and she is very proud that she's half Ger-man," Dorian recalls. "She became friends with photographers in Switzerland and Germany."

Today Eileen Ford won't discuss the trips on which she laid the tracks for the Ford agency's model railroad from Germany and Scandinavia. "I'm not going to write a manual for every person who wants an agency," she snaps. "We just went around. It wasn't hard." Anna-Karen Bjork, Ford's first Scandinavian discovery, was working in a drugstore when she won a magazine's modeling contest in 1960. Ford was a judge. From then on, Ford traveled from Stockholm to Göteborg to Malmö to Copenhagen, meeting photographers, agents, and magazine editors, panning for golden-haired lovelies in dreary cities young girls couldn't wait to leave.

In agreeing to "trade" models with Dorian, Ford had created modeling's first career development plan. "Eileen would ship girls who weren't working to Dorian for a year and bring in Europeans to replace them," says Rose Bruner, a booker. "It took a while to get rolling, but when those girls came back, they were *hot*."

In 1958 *The New York Times* estimated that the eight biggest agencies in New York had combined bookings of $5 million. Top models were earning as much as $3,500 a week. Flush with success, the Fords, whom the *Times* credited with putting modeling on a "business basis," had moved from Park Avenue into a town house around the corner after their third child, Katie, was born. In their role as the moral exemplars of modeling, they had their underage models and European imports live there with them. Just back from a trip to Europe, Jerry Ford told the *Times* that the "underfed, indoor, super sophisticated fashion model is fading out of the picture" and the American look was everywhere he went. But in fact, it was the American model who was on the wane—at least in the lofty editorial realm where the Fords operated.

"When I first started, the names were Petersen and Hollingsworth," says Ford's secretary, Naomi, Rose Bruner's sister. "Then all of a sudden it was Monique LeFevbre and Anne de Zogheb. We had a girl with an American name. One day I came in, and she was Caroline di Napoli. I asked, 'Who's this?' and they said she'd gone back to her real name because it had become fashionable to be a European model." Once, when the Fords went to Europe, Eileen asked Rose Bruner to stay at her house and chaperon the immigrant models. "One of them was fifteen years old," Bruner recalls. "The most precocious human being I ever met. She never came home until three A.M., and I had to be with her every night or I was in *a lot* of trouble."

Trouble was all around, even in those more innocent days. "There were hangers-on who wanted to date models, but also a lot of models who wanted to date men," Bruner says. "You screened people. Eileen did it. There could have been ulterior motives. It could've been somebody with a lot of money, but they weren't 'bad.' They had good qualifications."

Bobby and Charlie Evans, for example. The two sons of a dentist ran Evan-Picone, a Seventh Avenue sportswear company. Bobby had been a child actor. Beginning at age eleven, in 1941, he performed on hundreds of radio and television shows before founding the rag trade firm with his brother and Joseph Picone in 1951. In 1957 Bob Evans returned to acting; in the sixties he became a movie producer and eventually rose to become head of worldwide production at Paramount Pictures. He made *Barefoot in the Park; Rosemary's Baby; Goodbye, Columbus; Love Story; Chinatown;* and the *Godfather* films. In 1980 Evans was convicted on a misdemeanor charge of possession of cocaine. But in the late 1950s the Evans brothers were best known as men-around-the-garment-business—or, as some would have it, the varmint business.

The Evans brothers both had a taste for pretty girls. Charlie married the sister of a Ford model. When Bobby subsequently broke up with a girl friend, Charlie's wife called Rose Bruner for a Ford head sheet—a poster showing all of the agency's models—and they went over it, hunting for a girl for Bob to date. "Things like that happened all the time," Bruner says. "We had a guy who was a vice-president at an ad agency who spent half the day outside the agency watching models. He'd call and describe the girls to us for go-sees. That's how desperate he was to go out with a model." Eileen Ford tried to set Bobby up with the model named Anne de Zogheb, who married Paul Anka in 1963. "Eileen was devastated when Anne chose Anka over Bobby," booker Jane Halleran says. Ford loved playing matchmaker. "Eileen wanted all her girls to marry rich husbands," says April Ducksbury, a London agent. "Then she'd have social friends who were loyal and faithful to her, because not only had they been her models but she found them a husband."

Oleg Cassini was another fan of models, but hardly a contender for husband-hood. Half Italian and half Russian, he was a hereditary count who later became Jacqueline Kennedy's official dressmaker while she was in the White House. Earlier he had opened a couture salon in Rome after starting his career sketching for Jean Patou in Paris. Cassini used local society girls as his models. In 1936 he came to America, passing through Seventh Avenue en route to California, where he designed costumes at Paramount, married the actress Gene Tierney, and served in the Army before going to work as a designer in New York. Cassini got his models from Paris or discovered them himself. He was invited to Eileen Ford's once, but never again. "I was too European, too playboyish," he says. "She told her models, 'He's dangerous.' " Cassini was unabashed in his pursuit of women. "I told the girls I was like a doctor, examining them from all points of view," he says. "A lot of beautiful women marry their doctors. And you could give them clothes to wear, so it was good advertising."

In the middle fifties models joined the jet set. "They became part of the movement," says Cassini. "All the playboys, Rubirosa, Agnelli, were operating the same way. It was de rigueur. You couldn't arrive in St. Moritz without a beautiful woman. So there was a chase. You had to book your girl for the season. When I'd go to Austria to ski, I always brought two girls with me. Power in life is not money. He who controls women is the most powerful."

The problem was the Fords expected their girls to behave. "Ford was a family, a school," according to Cassini. "Her girls had to go out with college guys like her husband. They had the same ties, suits. But girls from Europe wanted more spicy food. They fought against the rigid puritanism of the agents. Particularly Swedish girls. You'd often see them in black parts of the city the agents said were dangerous. Sometimes it excited a girl to violate a commandment."

Something about modeling seemed to attract women who attracted trouble. "So many tragic lives" is all Richard Avedon will say about the models of his formative years in fashion. "They're not very bright, you know," Bill Blass says of the models he's known. "They have the worst taste in men. Muriel Maxwell, my God, was on welfare before she died. Tragedy after tragedy. They ended up penniless and destroyed." On the pages of magazines models presented images of perfection. But the real girl behind the controlled image on the page was often a total mess. Nancy Berg was, and proud of it, too. "I want to live my life grandly," she pronounced to the New York *Journal-American* in 1955. "Grandly?" She laughs, rereading that clipping today in a network television studio where she works as a makeup artist. "I did it druggedly and drunkenly. I did *anything* I could get."

Berg was born in Kenosha, Wisconsin, in 1931. At age three she posed for her first photograph. "It was the first time I got any attention or affection from my mother, and that made me think, 'This is what I have to do with the rest of my life,' " she said. Her long-separated parents divorced when she was eleven. "My mother beat the shit out of me every day with belts, shoes, boiling coffee," she says. "I said, 'This isn't going to happen anymore,' and I left." At fifteen she tossed a suitcase out her bedroom window and ran away from home.

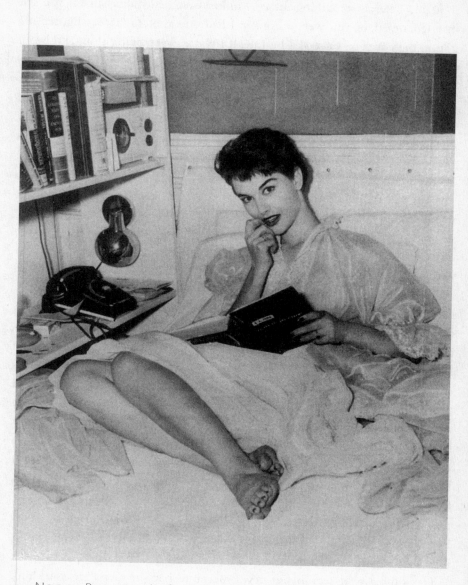

Nancy Berg reads C. G. Jung on the set of her TV show
Count Sheep in 1955

"People had said I was pretty," Berg relates. "I looked in the mirror and thought, 'There's something there.' I didn't have many alternatives. You got married, typed, or you were a hooker. I had one asset, my face. I figured if I got on the cover of *Vogue,* I'd be OK. If I was a sweet, pretty thing, I'd be all right in my mother's eyes."

With $50 in her pocket, she headed for Florida, rented a room from a family in Fort Lauderdale, and got work as a trick water skier and as a model at Burdine's. From there she bounced to Chicago, where she met her first boyfriend, the broadcaster Dave Garroway, who later was the host of NBC's *Today* show. When he moved to New York early in 1951, she followed and checked into the Plaza Hotel.

Berg had tremendous energy. Unfortunately it came from an elixir Garroway introduced her to—"a red liquid called the Doctor," Berg recalls. "It was pure speed. One sip, and I could conquer the world. With a little Doctor or a vodka, I had the courage to make it. I was just a scared little five-year-old with a birth certificate that said I was twenty-five." Berg appeared on her first *Vogue* cover six months after hitting New York. "It was such an easy living," she says. "But after the first few years, the first few covers, and no response from my mother, I got really bored. It's not intellectually stimulating or spiritually nourishing work. You're an object, a thing."

She was earning $40,000 a year, but she didn't hold on to it. "Brilliant advisers" in the investment business ended up with a lot of her earnings. She went out every night, tossing back vodka tonics, sometimes smoking cigars and dancing barefoot in nightclubs. "I'd go to the theater with a critic like Richard Watts or Harold Clurman, he'd go write his review, and I'd meet Leonard Lyons at Sardi's, go to El Morocco, meet a date, dance till dawn, go home, take a bath, some more speed, and go to work," she says. "I didn't sleep for ten years." Ironically, in 1955, she starred in a television show, *Count Sheep,* that aired at one each weeknight. Designed to help insomniacs, it followed Berg through a bedtime routine that found her cuddling a little dog, changing into a nightie, and then signing off, yawning and counting.

Her suitors were legion, but never special to her, she says. "Do you think anybody went out with me for my mind? Everybody wanted a trophy, the girl of the moment. I was invited to parties by people I barely knew. I went out with Sinatra, Jack Kennedy, Aly Khan, Yul Brynner, George Peppard, Orson Welles, James Michener, William Saroyan, Clifford Odets, both Cassinis. I almost married Efrem Zimbalist. Then there were those social freaks, Claude Cartier, Reinaldo Herrera, Peter Salm. I didn't get fucked because I kept moving. I was very angry. I was in analysis all the time. Thank God for acting. It was an acceptable way to vent."

Her strangest suitor was undoubtedly Roy Cohn, the bulldog attorney and closeted homosexual who made his name as counsel to Senator Joseph McCarthy and the Senate's permanent subcommittee on investigations during the Red Hunt of the early fifties. She would have Cohn meet her at the Russian Tea Room, and she would show up in a red dress. Once, in a jazz club, Cohn asked for a telephone and called someone to order that the singer they were listening to be investigated. Berg picked up her dessert—cherries jubilee, of course—and dumped it on Cohn's head.

Berg finally married at twenty-six and was divorced three years later, just after she had a baby. She married again, to a diet doctor "who had these wonderful pills," she says. "I was never so thin." But two weeks after their wedding Berg says he beat her *and* her young daughter, and she left him. All along she kept working. While the models Berg knew and lunched with saved their money and had families, she kept playing and paying. "I blew my money on externals," she says. "A high profile is very costly to maintain. I thought you had to do all that. That's how you survived."

Finally she even lost the face that had served her so well. She'd married again in the mid-sixties, to a man with four children of his own. One day one of his sons got high and violent on LSD. "He meant to hit his father, but he slugged me," Berg says. She lost four molars, chipped fourteen more teeth, and had extensive plastic surgery. "All I was was a face," she says. "All of a sudden I had no assets. I really started to drink then." Her analyst treated her with more drugs, "a rainbow of downers, Thorazine, Stelazine, and lithium at the same time," Berg says. Finally she hit bottom and joined Alcoholics Anonymous. Another divorce followed. "My husband didn't like me sober," she says.

Berg was hardly alone in her substance abuse. Drinking and pill taking were epidemic in the modeling world. This was the fast lane after all. "A lot of Ford girls went to a Park Avenue doctor who gave us appetite suppressants—nice name, huh?" Berg says. Drinking was the drug of choice, though. "They were terrible, terrible drunks," Berg says, pointing as an example to Brooklynite Annemarie Margot Elfreda "Sunny" Harnett, an ash-blond Ford star of the era. One newspaper said she epitomized "the clean-living code adopted by the successful model of 1955." But after she separated from her record executive husband, she grew depressed. Around that time she ran into Gene Loyd, the illustrator and editor, on the street. She put her head on his shoulder and burst into tears. "Wasn't it fun once?" she asked.

Harnett dropped from sight after that. "So bright and so beautiful," adds Betsy Pickering. "She got fat, had a mastectomy, and her mind went." Jerry Ford believes her husband had her hospitalized. "Did she lose her mind?" he says. "I don't know." What is known is that in May 1987, although she was only sixty-three, Harnett was confined to a long-term geriatric care facility when a fire broke out in the room she shared with two other women, twenty years her senior. One of them was killed instantly. Harnett suffered second- and third-degree burns over 40 percent of her body. Moved to the burn unit at New York Hospital, she died a few days later, anonymous and unmourned. "It's a very scary world when all you are is a face," says Nancy Berg.

Berg calls modeling "a world built on sand." The sands also shifted beneath Carmen Dell'Orefice. *Vogue* lost interest in her once she reached puberty and her figure developed. Unhappy at this turn of events, she quit the Hartford agency in 1950 and went shopping for a new agent. Eileen Ford turned her down. For the next decade Carmen did catalog work and posed seminude for Vanity Fair, the lingerie company, for fees that reached $300 an hour.

She moved in with Bill Miles, a man she describes as "a hanger-on" to a social group she met at playboy Peter Salm's Long Island beach house. It was called the Port of Missing Men. Carmen's first weekend there, the men in the house left her alone. But in secret they'd made a bet on who would bed her first. Miles, whose mother owned a Madison Avenue restaurant, won. "He was one of the golden boys of the time," Carmen says. "He was stunning. He'd been kept by a woman who died. Her husband hired him to run a farm in Oyster Bay so she could have her lover." He picked up Carmen's checks at the agency every week. When she heard that, a horrified Sunny Harnett demanded Carmen get her own bank account. Instead Carmen made a deal with Miles to give her $50 a week to put in a savings account. "I was afraid he'd leave if I disturbed the status quo," she says. "It's all to do with an early lack of self-esteem."

In 1953 Carmen finally joined Ford and had a comeback as an editorial model. As her marriage crumbled following the birth of a daughter, she began traveling to the collections in Paris, where she worked with Richard Avedon and Lillian Bassman for *Bazaar*. In 1958 she met a photographer named Richard Heimann on a shoot. Six months later she married the photographer, who was younger than she. She retired. He left her. At age thirty-two, in 1963, she went back to work. She married again, to a wealthy young architect, Richard Kaplan. By 1966 she'd quit modeling again and called herself the

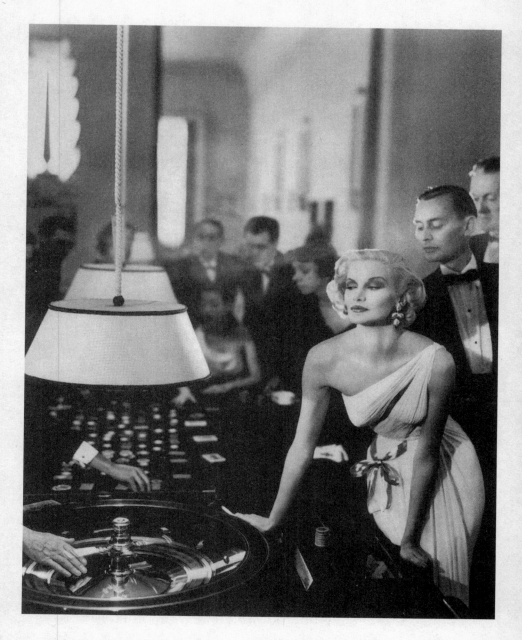

Sunny Harnett photographed by Richard Avedon in the
casino at Le Touquet, France, 1954

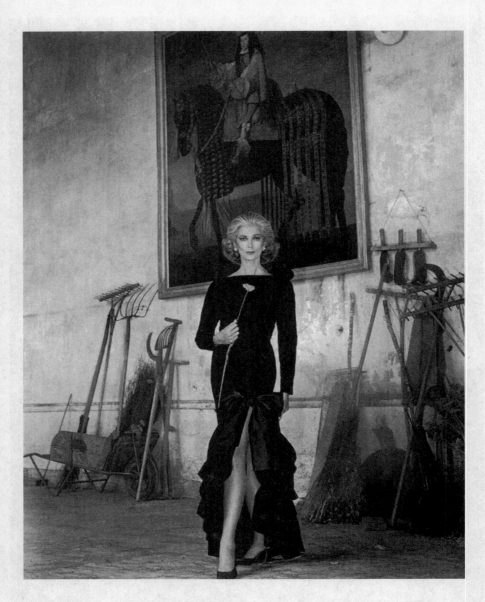

Carmen Dell'Orefice photographed by Norman Parkinson

"matron" of their triplex Park Avenue penthouse in New York and a beach house on Long Island's east end. After "nine wonderful years" together she broke up with Kaplan in the mid-1970s. Carmen was forty-three and desperate. She had a breakdown. But she'd have the last laugh. She went back to work in 1978, did nudes in 1982 at age fifty-one, and is still working today.

"I had a lot of fun," Carmen says. "I did the best I could. My career is atypical." But her bad luck with men was not. "A lot of [models] were lonely," says Rose Bruner. "They started at sixteen, seventeen. They never really learned those skills. They weren't good at getting out and mingling. It was frightening for them. That's why we did it for them."

Of all the agencies that came into being after World War II, only one still exists, the Fords. Today Huntington Hartford is a ruined recluse, Dorian Leigh is dismissed as a cranky born-again Christian, and Frances Gill is dead. In the early sixties Ford co-founder Natálie Paine grew . . . vague. "I developed a devastating chronic fatigue which changed my life," she says. "I was often bedridden. It was just not possible, and it broke my heart." Today she is involved with medical research into the disorder that disrupted her life. After buying Plaza Five from her, Stewart Cowley briefly challenged Ford, but he ended up a limousine driver.

Only Eileen and Ford go on. But their eventual triumph was by no means clear. It was a time of great cultural transition. John F. Kennedy was America's vital new President; astronauts and cosmonauts were riding rockets into the new frontier, and the Beatles were barnstorming Europe. It was only natural that upheaval would hit modeling, too. For the next few years bookers, models, and modeling executives hopped to and fro like fleas in the fur of the fashion business. No one paid attention to the passing of modeling's aristocracy. "*Our* era was finished," says Ruth Neumann. "The Untouchables were not anymore."

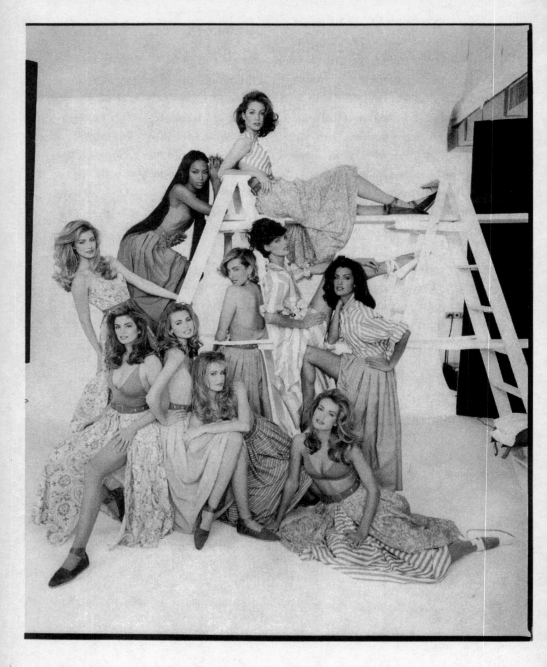

The Supermodels of 1992 photographed by Patrick Demarchelier. *Clockwise from bottom left:* Cindy Crawford, Elaine Irwin, Naomi Campbell, Christy Turlington, Linda Evangelista, Yasmeen Ghauri, Karen Mulder, Claudia Schiffer, Niki Taylor, and Tatjana Patitz *(under the ladder)*

PART TWO

BAD AND BEAUTIFUL

Polly Magoo, you have become for the civilized world a symbol of
elegance and sophistication.
But I have the impression that all this is only a game.
You're acting.
Your life as a model is a masquerade.
You act it out and others help you to act it.
The Fairy Godmother tapped you with her magic wand, but if
midnight sounds, your coach, will it turn to a pumpkin,
your footmen to lizards?

—FROM THE FILM *QUI ÊTES-VOUS, POLLY MAGOO,*
WRITTEN AND DIRECTED BY WILLIAM KLEIN

CELIA HAMMOND

Her blond hair still seems Sassooned, her lips bee-stung, her lilting accent naggingly familiar, neither totally passé nor fully present. Celia Hammond, fifty-two, is still the British Dolly Bird incarnate, *Darling* and *Georgy Girl* rolled up in one, the embodiment of London circa 1964, the Beatles and the Stones, Carnaby Street and Mary Quant, fab and gear.

At nineteen, in 1961, Hammond was a contract model with editor Jocelyn Stevens's pacesetting *Queen* magazine, working with Norman Parkinson, the last of England's gentlemen photographers. Then she had a romance with Terence Donovan, one of the Terrible Trio (with David Bailey and Brian Duffy) who changed fashion photography as radically as Penn and Avedon had when *they'd* seized fashion photography's crown and scepter in the late 1940s. All three photographers came from the rough and raffish East End of London, a working-class neighborhood not known for its refined tastes. Indeed, refinement was the first thing that went out the window when the East End boys and their girls hit it big.

Suddenly there was pop, and models were its princesses.

It was a time when models no longer lay down with lords and rose up ladies of the manor. Suddenly a model was au courant only if she was coupled with a top photographer, although a pop star wasn't a bad catch either. Patti Boyd snared the ultimate prize when she married Beatle George Harrison. Jean Shrimpton had famously tempestuous relationships with David Bailey and the actor Terence Stamp. After Donovan, Hammond hooked up with Stamp and comic actor Dudley Moore, before ending up with a genuine guitar hero, Jeff Beck, who played with the Yardbirds before founding his own group.

Hammond and Beck met in summer 1968. A few months later she bought a five-hundred-year-old cottage set in ten acres of woodlands in Kent and announced her retirement from London night life, if not the modeling scene. "It simply bores me to death," she said then. "I realized last year that I earned an awful lot of money but I didn't have anything to show for it." She was looking, she said, for peace of mind.

Today, thin in a thick Irish sweater, Hammond looks more like a stable girl than a pop princess. She runs the Celia Hammond Animal Trust, a registered charity in Sussex, England, that rescues, neuters, and finds homes for stray pets. At night she drives a tiny car between building sites, saving abandoned cats. Though it might make a glamorous fashion photograph—a model in an evening gown, clutching a crying kitten—there is nothing romantic about Hammond's life. She has little money and operates constantly on the edge of ruin. Ten years ago, after sixteen years with Beck, she was traded in for a younger model. So she is alone, except for the dozens of cats she keeps. But they may be a better breed than those with which she used to play.

"I was born in Indonesia. My father was a tea taster. We went to Australia when I was one year old, and then my mother and I came back. I was left with aunties and uncles, and I was in boarding school. I had a series of jobs that had nothing to do with fashion whatsoever. I was very overweight. Somebody must have seen something under the fat and said, 'Why don't you be a model?' I said, 'I couldn't possibly.' But I went to a few agents. They said, 'No, no, no, it's absolutely out of the question. You couldn't possibly do it.' Finally the Lucie Clayton agency took me on. I stayed with Clayton all the way through.

"Jean Shrimpton and I started Clayton's course the same week. Bailey discovered her, took her right under his wing, and she was right at the top, on the cover of *Vogue* immediately. It took me a long time to get there. I'd go around to all the fashion houses and do their collections. Commercial, the low end of the market. Really hard work, six or eight shows a day. I did that for about a year.

"What used to happen was Norman Parkinson would come a couple of times a year and go around to all the agencies and see if he liked the look of anybody. He called them his cattle markets. The agency said, 'We haven't got anything for you this time.' He said, 'I'll have a look anyway.' And we were lined up upstairs, and he came down and said, 'There's a star up there.' And they said, 'Who?' And he said, 'Celia Hammond,' and they said, 'It couldn't possibly be.' I weighed about ten and a half stone. I don't know what that is

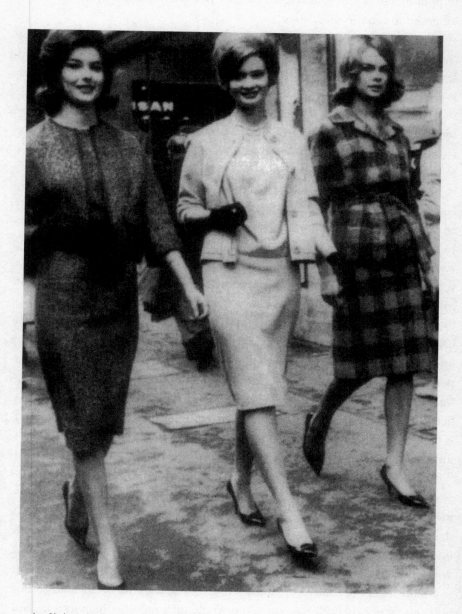

Left to right: Fiona Laidlaw-Thompson, Celia Hammond, and Jean Shrimpton on the day of their graduation from the Lucie Clayton School in London, 1960

in pounds, but it's very heavy. And totally not looking the way models were supposed to look in those days.

"Within about a fortnight I was to be at the Paris collections. I didn't eat anything for that period, three weeks I think it was. They still had to send seamstresses to open the back of the clothes and find a way to hold it together at the back and then sew it back together for the shows the next day.

"That was for *Queen* magazine. They put me under contract, and Parkinson and I worked together. When I first started going abroad with Parkinson, I was so green and useless. I was twenty-one going on sixteen, because that's how you were in the fifties. You didn't grow up very fast.

"Models have got it pretty easy these days. I've done one or two shoots lately recalling the sixties. They say, 'Oh, don't worry about your makeup or anything, just turn up. If your hair's bad, it doesn't matter; we've got people.' In the actual sixties, when you turned up for a job, you had to have a bag about three feet deep. My left arm was longer than my right arm for about a year after I stopped. You had to carry about six or eight pairs of shoes, your rollers, different pairs of scarves, gloves, jewelry, accessories. You used to have to do a different hairstyle for every photograph. All your own makeup. You had to do everything yourself.

"We were a pretty good bargain, really. What I'd like to know is, at what point did the girls become worth ten thousand dollars a day? I was modeling only because there wasn't anything else I could have done. I've got no qualifications of any sort. I wanted to end up with a bit of security for myself, I wanted to earn enough to buy a house, because obviously a model can't do it indefinitely.

"I worked with Parkinson for a couple of years. And then, once my contract expired in the early sixties, I started getting other offers. I started working with Terry Donovan, I started working for Bailey and doing *Vogue,* and that was the beginning of the end of Parkinson. I still did the odd thing with him, but it was never the same. He couldn't handle it when I got involved with Terry. He liked working with a raw canvas. He sort of takes that person over and makes her into something. And your getting involved with somebody else is not part of his picture. You would pick up other mannerisms, and then he would stop using you.

"Bailey and Terry were very sexually oriented. That's how they worked. They would just tell you to, you know, fuck the camera or something. That's what their message was, sex and raunchiness. You've only got to look at their pictures to see what was going on.

"Donovan was enormously sexy and attractive. He was married when I met him. But he was so good-looking. He was thin and with this curly, black Irish hair and piercing eyes. It was a real cliquey set, Donovan, Duffy, and Bailey, a lot of the young people, editors, models, advertising people, music people, all just a big, great club. We kept ourselves very much to ourselves. We used to go to the same parties, the same restaurants. We'd meet up almost every night. It was far more than just a working relationship. It was a life, yeah.

"There was a rebellion against the sort of morality and the sickness of it all. It was very austere in the fifties. When I started working with Parkinson, I was living at home. I used to go out, come back at night, and I could see my mother's cigarette, that red cigarette end, burning in the hall, no matter what time I came in. My mother was so terribly strict she did drive me away. Oh, she cried. It was dreadful.

"It was exciting to be able to do what we wanted to do. The new music and the clothes and the sexual revolution. Of course, money was no object in those days, so we used to fly across the world for one picture. Drugs weren't really that much a part of it, in our lot anyway. But it was very wild. I mean, everybody was very promiscuous. You would have a boyfriend for a few months or weeks, whatever. Then you know he'd be gone, and it was somebody else.

"The work was very hard, but modeling in those days, once you were at the top, you were almost unassailable. If you were in the top half dozen girls, then you would be there for six, seven, eight years. Everybody wanted you— someone that people recognized—and they would always rather have you than take a chance on a new girl who might actually look better or even be better.

"There was not a lot of money then. I think the photographers were paid a lot better than we were. And quite rightly so. I had a jeep, a flat in West Hampstead, and I had a small house; but I never had a lot of money. It was laughable. In those days we used to earn the same sort of money as a professional person, as a doctor or a dentist or something. Not these fabulous amounts like ten thousand dollars a day. Nobody's worth that.

"The animal rescue work started in London while I was still working. There was a boarded-up house that had a mother cat in it that I'd gone past on the bus. I'd seen this cat up in the windows. And I thought, 'Well, that can't be right.' I came back later with a friend, and we broke into the house and found this cat up in a room with the door shut and three dead kittens. She'd been boarded up in there. And so I took her, and then it just . . . it was like a revelation, that this sort of dreadful thing must be happening all over London, this wouldn't be an isolated incident.

"I started a rescue service for animals in emergency situations like building sites and at the docks and train stations. At first I was just doing it myself, funding everything myself. It just got to the point where I couldn't finance it any longer. I didn't have any money left. So now it's a public charity. And the reason that the charity has taken off now is largely because of what I did then. A lot of people from the sixties are now in positions of great power and influence.

"I carried on modeling for two or three years while I was doing the rescue work. But I just couldn't combine the two. Having to get up early in the morning looking like a million dollars after not having been to bed till three or four A.M., you know, scrabbling around a building site rescuing animals. There was just one job too many. And then finally I just said, 'That's it. Pull down the curtain. I want to get on with what I really want to do.' I don't regret modeling for one minute. It was totally superficial, but it was a whole lot of fun.

"By that time I had bought a house in the country, a small house, so I moved down there with all the animals, and Jeff came to live with me. And he stayed there for about seven or eight years, and then he bought a house in Sussex and we moved all the animals over there. And I carried on doing the rescue work for, you know, twenty years or whatever, but eventually Jeff just couldn't stand it anymore.

"The animals broke us up actually. We both had our crosses to bear. He had my animals, I had his blondes. He had several. He met a blonde that got to him, and she was twenty years younger than me. All middle-aged men do it. I'm glad it happened while I still could handle it.

"People think, 'Oh, the poor bitch, she hasn't got a man; she's got no children; she's put everything into a child substitute.' That isn't true, but I suppose some people might think it could be. I could have gone on modeling perhaps for another four or five years. But it just wasn't terribly important to me. To actually love what I did, I'd have to have been a really rather extraordinary person. An enormous egotist. I mean, to love standing on a piece of paper in a funny way? You'd have to be so self-obsessed."

It was a sunny afternoon in 1958 in Windsor Great Park near London, where Britain's royals played polo. A short dark man with swept-back hair approached a pouty, snub-nosed sixteen-year-old in a gray silk dress. "You know, you really should model," he said.

Introducing himself as Colonel Voynovitch, he invited the girl and her date into the exclusive royal enclosure. She didn't say a word, so impressed was she as she spotted the queen mother and met the queen's dressmaker, Norman Hartnell. Had Jean Shrimpton not been born with eyebrows arched in permanent wonder, they certainly would have stood up at all that. So it was quite easy for Voynovitch to lure her to his Aston Martin, where he softly stroked her bare, coltish legs and cooed that he wanted to photograph her for a women's magazine. Not only that, he said, but he'd pay her £5 for an afternoon's work.

A sheltered convent school graduate, Shrimpton was a bit appalled by the stranger's behavior; but his connections were obvious, and modeling sounded better than anything Langham Secretarial College at London's Marble Arch had to offer. So she gave him her number and said he should call and ask her parents' permission.

A few days later Voynovitch appeared at Rose Hill Farm in Buckinghamshire, where Shrimpton had grown up in rural isolation, a horse-crazed daughter of an ex–Royal Air Force corporal turned pig breeder. After meeting her parents, the colonel drove her to his country home, where he stroked her legs a little more and offered her a bath, strawberries, and champagne. "Why don't you take your bra off?" he asked her. "You're not a virgin, are you?" He made a circle with two of his fingers and pushed another through it, in and out, in and out.

As the shooting progressed, so did his clumsy ardor. "I just want to touch your breasts," he said. She let him. After all, she'd come this far. But although she considered herself a "retarded sixteen-year-old," she had the sense never to see him again. But she'd tasted forbidden fruit, and wanted more. Being a secretary suddenly seemed a bleak fate, indeed. Still, it was a year before a way out appeared.

Again a male stranger intervened. At lunch break every day when the weather was good, Jean and a friend would buy sandwiches and go to Hyde Park to eat. One day just before final exams an American movie director named Cy Endfield hailed them as they crossed the street on their way back to school. He said he wanted to cast Jean in a film he was making. Tossing a business card at her, he jumped in his car and screeched away. Sadly Endfield's producer didn't agree with his assessment of Shrimpton's star quality. The director then insisted she should become a model. He even knew the name of a school where she could learn how.

It was called Lucie Clayton.

Sylvia Gollidge, a gangling brown-eyed beauty from Blackpool, came to London in 1926 and got a job as a model for 10 shillings (about $2.50) a day at a dress shop called Bantall's. On her first day at work the sixteen-year-old stood perfectly still, expecting the shop's customers to gravitate toward her. She didn't keep her job long. Vowing to better herself, she traveled to Paris, where she decided that the way to be a model was to look angry, arrogant, and condescending. Armed with this new knowledge, she returned to London, got another job, and was soon so successful that she insured her long blond hair for £1,000.

Years later she told Leslie Kark how she decided to open a modeling school and agency. "One or two of her friends, all of whom were thin giantesses like Gollidge, asked her to show them how to model," Kark says. "She thought, 'Well, I can make more money by showing them than by modeling.' " So, in September 1928, Gollidge opened the Lucie Clayton Modeling School, teaching charm, the art of the curtsy, and how to walk a runway. She changed her name because "she just liked the name Lucie," says Kark, who bought her business in 1950. "And Clayton was solid business, you know, earthy." Within months Gollidge had an agency, first booking only fashion show mannequins but soon adding photo models.

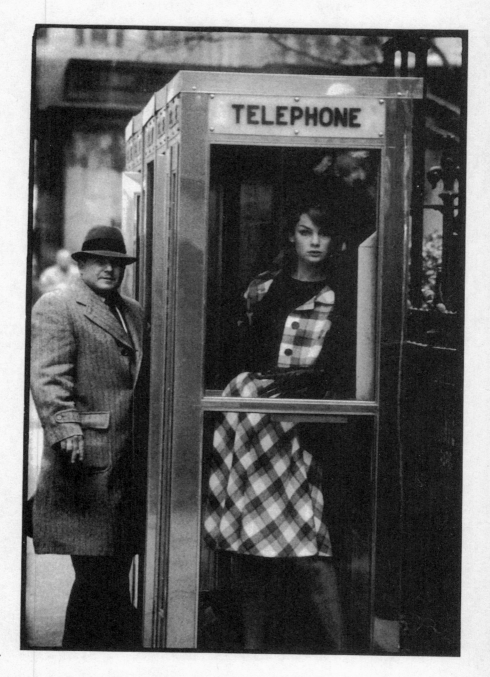

Jean Shrimpton photographed by David Bailey in a New York
City phone booth, January 1961

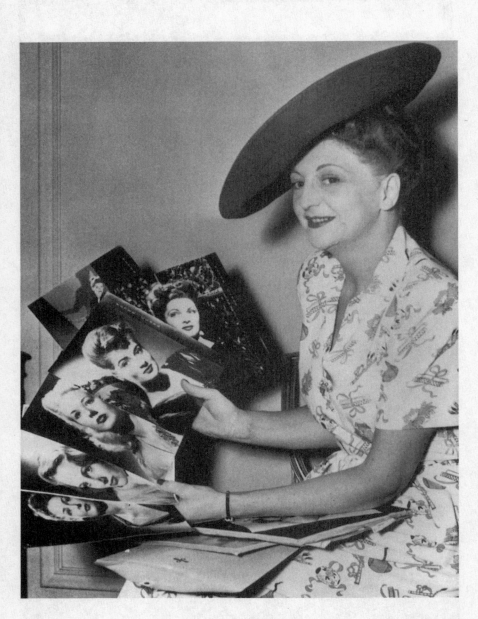

Lucie Clayton, Great Britain's first model agent, in 1946

Lucie Clayton was to modeling in London what Powers was in New York: the person who pulled the profession out of the gutter. "She made it about as respectable as opera singing," says Kark. "But I don't think careful fathers wanted their daughters to be opera singers *or* models." Clayton understood that good publicity could change that. During the Depression Hollywood mogul Sam Goldwyn came to London with a troupe of Goldwyn Girls on a publicity trip. Intrigued by the coverage the troupe engendered, Clayton "went to the depressed valleys of Wales," according to Kark, "found girls six feet tall, took them to London and trained them, and took them to Hollywood," along with trunks full of British fashions. She got British clothing manufacturers to finance the trip.

Leslie Kark had been a writer and barrister before joining the RAF during the war. In 1949 he covered a fashion show for a magazine he was editing and had an idea he thought might be profitable. As London's few model agencies were "fairly, let's say, inefficient," he recalls, he published a catalog called *Model*. He only made £500 on the project.

Fortunately for him Lucie Clayton decided to retire to Australia and offered to sell her school and agency to Kark. He bought the operation for £2,200 (less than $1,000), "and I thought I'd been robbed," he says. Before sailing off into the sunset, Clayton confided that she made most of her money selling coffee to her students.

But there was no lack of world-class photography in London. Cecil Beaton had operated there for years. John Rawlings opened a studio for *Vogue* in 1936. Norman Parkinson joined the magazine in 1941. He was born Ronald William Parkinson Smith in 1913 and learned his trade at Speaight & Son, a past-its-prime society portrait studio on Bond Street, where he apprenticed for two years after school. Parkinson opened his own studio on Dover Street near Piccadilly Circus in 1934 with a partner, Norman Kibblewhite. They called their firm Norman Parkinson and he took that name when they parted company soon thereafter. Friends called him Parks.

Parkinson began his career photographing debutantes, who didn't always pay their bills. He was running low on funds by 1937, when the editor of the British edition of *Harper's Bazaar,* first published in 1929, saw his work and hired him. For *Bazaar,* Parkinson shot portraits of the famous: the Sitwells, the American couturier Charles James, and Rose Kennedy, then the wife of America's ambassador to Britain. But fashion photography was the magazine's focus. He tried his hand at it and liked it a lot.

That didn't mean he was content to take pictures like everyone else. Photographers then showed women "standing in scintillating salons with their knees bolted," Parkinson said. "I never knew any girls with bolted knees. I only knew girls that jumped and ran. So I just started to photograph these girls. Everyone said, 'How bold!' " In 1939 he shot model Pamela Minchin leaping off a breakwater on the Isle of Wight in one of the first modern fashion photographs.

In 1943 he married one of his favorite models, Wenda Rogerson, who'd been discovered by Beaton. She, Barbara Goalen, Anne Gunning, Carmen Dell'Orefice, and Enid Boulting appeared in most of the photographs he took for *Vogue* in the 1950s, both in quintessential English locales like Hyde Park Corner and on unprecedented location shoots in exotic spots around the world. Once, photographing Wenda in the rubble of the demolished New York Ritz Hotel, both the photographer and his Mainbocher-clad model were briefly arrested.

At six feet five inches, topped by a Kashmiri bridal cap on a balding head, Parkinson dressed for excess in caftans and gold jewelry or a decades-old vanilla bespoke suit made for him by the British tailor Tommy Nutter. His eccentricities extended to his hobbies, listed in *Who's Who* as "pig farming, sun worshipping, bird watching, breeding Creole racehorses." He dabbled in them all on the Caribbean island of Tobago, where he and Wenda moved in 1963. Later Parkinson set up a sausage factory there and began marketing its products as "the famous Porkinson banger."

By the time of his death in 1990 Parkinson was best known as the portraitist of choice of the British royal family. But long before he attained that privileged position, a new photographic royalty had emerged in London. Its source was the studio of John French. Born six years before Parks, French originally wanted to be a painter. But commerce called. He picked up a camera and opened a studio in 1948. At first he worked for England's *Harper's Bazaar*, but he soon became a pioneer in daily newspaper fashion photography, beginning on the *Daily Express*. French dressed his models in pearls, stud earrings, and white gloves, called them all darling, and treated them like Dresden china dolls, never touching them but giving them directions in a high-pitched, languid voice. Until his death in 1966 French was renowned for never loading his own camera, clicking its shutter, or setting the lights he was famous for. Among the assistants who did all that for him were Richard Dormer, who soon became the chief photographer of British *Bazaar*, David Bailey, and Terence Donovan.

The son of an East End truck driver, Donovan began shooting photographs at age eleven, studied lithography, and then went to work on Fleet Street, the center of London's thriving newspaper business, making the wooden blocks that were then used to print photographs on newsprint. But what he really wanted was to be a fashion photographer. "I don't know why or anything," Donovan says. "It wasn't for the women oddly enough. I just liked doing it. We were fashion photographers."

After a stint as a military photographer in the army Donovan joined John French as an assistant in the late fifties. "He was the most important fashion photographer in this country at the time, an extraordinary man. Couldn't actually open the lid of his camera. He was a marvelous sort of queen. He got married to a girl because somebody made her pregnant, and he thought morally he ought to help her. At that stage in England all fashion photographers were gay." Heterosexuals were "unheard of apart from Norman Parkinson," according to Donovan. Gay gentlemen dominated the field because "nobody else knew how many bangles to put on. I was an East End bloke. I remember thinking, 'I'll never be able to do that; I just don't know how many jewels to put on.' And then suddenly you realized that you didn't have to know. All you had to do was make a strong picture of a girl. I was earning eight dollars a week, and so I borrowed ten thousand dollars off of a bloke who thought I had something going, and we were off and running! I paid him back in a year."

The sadness and poverty that had enveloped England ever since the war began were finally lifting. "It was a spectacularly exciting time because everything was possible," Donovan says. "A cheese sandwich never tastes so good as when you've just come off of a terrible situation like a war. Everything had an absolute crystal sharpness and clarity. The world was open. You did what you liked; you went anywhere. We were really the first people to think in a much looser way."

David Bailey joined John French as his second assistant soon after Donovan departed. Born in 1938, the son of a tailor, Bailey grew up hoping to be an ornithologist. "But for a cockney in the East of London to look at birds through binoculars was very suspect," Bailey said. "In my father's eyes, I had to be queer as a coot." He nonetheless took pictures of birds and processed them in his mother's cellar, an old air-raid shelter. At sixteen his ambition changed. He put down his camera and picked up a trumpet. His new ideal was Chet Baker. "You had two ways of getting out in the Fifties," he once said. "You were either a boxer or a jazz musician." He started collecting modern jazz records and was intrigued by the cover photographs shot by William Claxton (who later photographed and married Peggy Moffitt, Rudi Gernreich's topless swimsuit model). To pay for his records, Bailey sold shoes and carpets, worked as a messenger, and cleaned windows before he was drafted into the Royal Air Force in 1956.

Bailey served in Malaya and Singapore, where "cameras were cheap," he said. "I bought a £60 camera for £20 and that was it." After shooting a roll of film, he would pawn the camera to pay for processing, reclaim it on the next pay day, and start all over again. On his return to England he took a job sweeping floors at an ad agency and wrote to eight fashion photographers asking for work. "I didn't even know what a strobe was," he's said. But John French hired him anyway, probably because he liked the way Bailey looked. "Six months later, everyone thought we were having an affair," Bailey recalled, "but in fact, although we were fond of each other, we never got it together."

Dressed in Cuban-heeled boots and a leather jacket, the tough but pretty Bailey reminded the effete French of the scruffy young photographer hero in Colin MacInnes's 1959 novel *Absolute Beginners,* which chronicled the alluring new street culture of working-class England. In fact, young rebels were rising everywhere, from the Left Bank in Paris, where the existentialists reigned, to Greenwich Village in New York, where beat was growing out of bop. Author MacInnes and the Teddy boys, mods, and rockers he depicted were the earliest British contribution to a cultural movement that was sweeping the Western world. Fashion, ever alert to the newest and the now-est, quickly picked up the beat. The marketing of international youth culture soon became a British specialty.

Designer Mary Quant and her future husband, Alexander Plunket Greene, had opened Bazaar, a boutique on the King's Road, in Chelsea, in 1955. By 1960 Quant was designing for the shop. She is often credited with inventing the miniskirt. In fact, it started on the streets. But without doubt Bazaar was the launching pad that put the mini—and the whole youth-driven sixties look—into orbit. When Quant came to America in 1959, she was the advance guard of what was, five years later, after the Beatles, deemed the British Invasion. Following in her footsteps came more designers who ignored the directives emanating from the Paris couture and instead took their lead from London's kids.

For his part, David Bailey had no intention of getting into fashion. "It was just a way of breaking into photography," he explained. "I didn't really mind what I did. In fact, my first portfolio didn't have any fashion in it." But dur-

ing his eleven months working for French, Bailey began to be published in
Woman's Own magazine and, every Thursday, on the fashion page of the *Daily
Express,* where French's work had often appeared. Bailey had become a fash-
ion photographer in spite of himself. Late in 1959 he signed on to shoot for
Vogue's front-of-the-book "shophound" pages.

If he hadn't already discovered the perks of fashion photography, he did
then. "The only reason I ever did fashion was because of girls," he admitted
in 1989. "It was the gates of heaven. But I only wanted to photograph girls I
liked. I had to have some sense of being with them or it wasn't interesting."
And it was particularly interesting when they went to bed with him. "A
model doesn't have to sleep with a photographer, but it helps," Bailey said.

Photographers everywhere had already begun evolving the language of
fashion photography, seeking a new reality and naturalism within its artificial
confines. But by 1960 British magazines were leading the way. *Queen,* recently
purchased by a brilliant editor named Jocelyn Stevens, was using Parkinson
and Antony Armstrong-Jones, who soon married Princess Margaret and
became Lord Snowdon. Meanwhile, *Man About Town,* a men's fashion trade
magazine also being revived by new owners, took on England's new angry
young men, Donovan, Bailey, and their third musketeer, Brian Duffy.

A graduate of London's prestigious St. Martin's School of Art, Duffy had
spent the fifties in the antiques business, before becoming a fashion designer.
He started taking pictures in 1959 and immediately became part of the "new
group of violently heterosexual butch boys," he said. "We didn't just treat
models as clothes horses. We emphasized the fact that there were women
inside the clothes. They started to look real."

While the Terribles were learning their trade, Jean Shrimpton was doing
the same at Lucie Clayton's modeling school. "I was as green as a spring
salad," she remembered, when she took the train to London for her first day
there. She was seated next to Celia Hammond in class. For four weeks they
and their classmates learned to sit, stand, walk, paint their faces, and do their
hair. They also learned tricks of the trade, like what a model was still expected
to carry to sittings in the early sixties: stockings in various shades; jewelry;
strapless, flattening, and bust-enhancing bras; a waist cincher; slips; shoes;
gloves; hair ribbons, hairpieces, and hairstyling tools; makeup and brushes;
rubber bands and bobby pins.

On graduation day the top graduates of the class, including Hammond and
Shrimpton, were photographed for the *Evening News* striding happily down

Bond Street. The next day, armed with a new photographic composite and a list of thirty photographers, Shrimpton started her career. But she lacked both a look and confidence. In fact, by late 1960 she'd run through all her money as well as loans from her mother and from Lucie Clayton.

Finally the awkward, saucer-eyed Shrimpton was booked for a *Vogue Patterns* sitting after another model failed to turn up. Those pictures in hand, she climbed another rung on the ladder and got a job with John French. Late in 1960 Shrimpton was working with Brian Duffy in a London studio when a gorgeous black-eyed man in jeans introduced himself. David Bailey had left John French's employ only three months before. But he was already acting superior toward "new" models.

"Come back in six months," he told Shrimpton, she has recalled.

"God, Duffy, I wouldn't mind a slice of that one," Bailey once remembered saying after she left.

"Forget it," Duffy replied. "She's too posh for you. You'd never get your leg across that one." Bailey bet he would bed her, and three months later, he's claimed, they were shacking up.

Shrimpton has remembered what followed their first meeting somewhat differently. She recalls working with Duffy again, on a Kellogg's cereal ad shot on the roof of *Vogue*'s offices on London's Hanover Square. Bailey popped onto the set, supposedly to see if her eyes were as blue as advertised. "He rather fancied me," she thought. He later agreed that he'd found the girl of his dreams in Shrimpton.

He was twenty-three. Shrimpton was eighteen. There was only one roadblock to commencing a relationship. Bailey had just married a typist. So Shrimpton held out for a month as their uncommon courtship commenced. Finally she succumbed, and they made love for the first time in a park up the road from Shrimpton's parents' house. The experience was "quite awful," she recalled. "I was miserable. . . . But our lives seemed to be inexorably entwined. I was becoming his model. . . ."

Later Shrimpton was called Trilby to Bailey's sulky Svengali. "Bailey created the Jean Shrimpton look," she admitted. "I owe everything that I am as a model to David Bailey." She was a gawky urchin, the image of innocence lost sometime in about the last ten seconds. And in creating and propagating that look, she and Bailey became the archetypes of a new breed of fashion photographers and models. By letting the heat of their sexual relationship into their pictures, by letting their models seem touchable, indeed, by merely admitting the possibility of a sexual relationship between model and photographer, they transformed themselves into fashion's first real celebrities outside fashion. Things were never the same again.

A new generation was taking over the world of style, not only in London but all over the world. Suffering in part from the supremacy of *Harper's Bazaar,* Condé Nast's company, owned by British financiers for decades and then sold to a British tabloid publisher, had been losing half a million dollars a year. In 1959 it was sold to S. I. Newhouse, an American newspaper publisher. Shortly thereafter he bought the oldest magazine publisher in America, Street and Smith. Newhouse folded its *Charm* magazine into Nast's *Glamour* to cut costs and competition but decided to continue publishing its *Mademoiselle,* which had a different audience.

In 1962 Alexander Liberman was promoted from art director of *Vogue* to editorial director of all the Condé Nast magazines, and one of his first moves was to lure Diana Vreeland away from *Bazaar.* Hired as *Vogue's* fashion editor for "a very large salary, an endless expense account . . . and Europe whenever I wanted to go," she recalled, Vreeland rose to editor in chief in January 1963, replacing Edna Chase's stodgy successor, Jessica Daves, who fought against Vreeland's innovations until the bitter end of her career.

"Boy, was I in the greatest seat at the greatest hour of the greatest time," Vreeland said. "The year of the jet, the Pill. A completely different social world was being created." Although the Terrible Trio was in the lead, a new generation of photographers was coming into its own all over the world, most of them dancing to what Bailey called the sexual rhythm of snapping 35 mm camera shutters. Helmut Newton, a German who started working on Australian *Vogue,* settled in Paris in 1962 and began taking provocative and unsettling pictures for *Queen* and British *Vogue.* Jeanloup Sieff was flying in from France, where he'd begun working for *Elle* in 1955. Americans like Sol Leiter, Art Kane, Jerry Schatzberg, Bill King, and Bert Stern were part of the movement, too. But the center of all the heat and light was London, and Bailey, Duffy, Donovan, and their models were the brightest of the city's bright young things. The Terribles worked together (sometimes even secretly shooting one another's assignments) and played together as well, at night spots like Hélène Cordet's Saddle Room, where Shrimpton learned to do the twist, and at the Ad Lib, the center of pop society.

"There was always something happening after the day's work was done," Shrimpton has written. "None of the photographers went home to their wives." When Shrimpton's parents objected to her carrying on with a married man, she moved out and was taken in by photographer Eric Swain and *his* wife. Soon, though, Bailey, Shrimpton, and his twenty finches and budgerigars moved into a flat of their own on London's Primrose Hill. Her father stopped speaking to her for a year, but that wasn't the last shock the Shrimptons had to endure. Not long after Jean started seeing Bailey, her mother walked into her younger daughter Chrissie's bedroom and found *her* boyfriend, Rolling Stones singer Mick Jagger, sleeping there.

For young Terry Donovan, moving into an apartment of his own was one of the great moments of his life. "Nobody *ever* had a flat," he says. "The only shagging that took place was up against a wall!" Now, suddenly, not only did he have a place to shag (cockney slang for having sex), but he had an endless supply of beautiful women who were eager to shag along with him. Fashion photography "*was* a good way of getting a crumpet," Donovan recalls, laughing. "I mean, Bailey and I shagged ourselves absolutely senseless in those days. It was fun, but it wasn't the kind of vicious scoring thing. It was like being a chocoholic in a chocolate factory. I mean, everywhere you went there were fucking women strobing past!"

Harry King, a hairdresser who began his career in London in the late sixties, recalls working on one of his first jobs with Brian Duffy, shooting the Paris collections for the *Sunday Telegraph Colour Magazine*. "*Vogue* and *Bazaar* had the luxury of getting clothes right away," King says. "We had to wait all night. Duffy kept taking [the model] in back, fucking her. Every time a dress arrived, he'd be pulling up his pants and she'd need her hair done again."

Donovan insists that despite their promiscuous image, all the Terrible Trio *really* cared about was taking pictures. "We were photographic nutcases," he says. "We would walk the streets of Paris for eight hours, talking about f-stops. I used to do four assignments a day. Work, work, work. We were out every day, year after year, here, America, Paris, Rome, photographing."

In 1961 British *Vogue* had asked Bailey to shoot a regular feature called "Young Idea." The idea was to pair a model with brash new British celebrities like David Frost, Dudley Moore and his partner, Peter Cook, and the hot young haircutter Vidal Sassoon. *Vogue*'s fashion editor, Lady Clare Rendlesham, wanted to use a French model, Nicole de la Margé, who'd become the visual spirit of *Elle* magazine in Paris, but Bailey insisted on his new girlfriend, and he prevailed. After it was published, *Vogue* asked Shrimpton and Bailey to take the "Young Idea" to New York early in 1962. Bailey's photos of Shrimpton on a city street corner, in a Harlem market, and in a telephone booth are among his most memorable images.

"England has arrived!" declaimed Diana Vreeland when Bailey and Shrimpton turned up at her *Vogue* office. They'd both gotten soaked with rain while trying to hail a taxi, and Shrimpton's makeup had run all over her face; but Vreeland nonetheless declared them "adorable." Said Shrimpton: "We both knew we had it made."

Inevitably they began attracting attention. In 1963 Bailey's wife filed for divorce. Shrimpton was named as the other woman. "Which, of course, I was," she said. That didn't bother her. What did bother her was the nickname the tabloids gave her: The Shrimp. "Shrimps are horrible pink things that get their heads pulled off," she said.

The pressures of being the most beautiful of the beautiful began to take their toll. Charming off the set, Bailey could be brutal on it. He hated fashion editors and stylists, rarely let them on his sets, and sometimes reduced them to tears. He did the same to Shrimpton. "Sexless ratbag!" he screamed at her. "You should never have come down from the treetops." Years later he proudly admitted that he was awful to everyone. "I pioneered badness. I did diabolical things. Awful. Terrible. I had this compulsion to push forward all the time. . . . I was trying to create a mood and see the whole image and I had to cope with these women with no visual sense, getting hysterical about some amusin' little seam."

Bailey, at least, had something to aim for. At twenty-one Shrimpton was as good as she was ever going to get and was bored. Although Bailey encouraged her to work with other photographers—at least with those he approved of—she started to feel that their relationship was limiting her career.

Nonetheless, early in 1964 Bailey and Shrimpton announced their engagement. The wedding was to be held after another trip to New York. But feeling she needed time to herself, Shrimpton flew ahead alone. When Bailey arrived two weeks later, Shrimpton found herself avoiding him. Then a peripheral member of their crowd, the movie star Terence Stamp, turned up in New York. Discovering she was attracted not only to him but also to a *Bazaar* photographer she was working with, named Mel Sokolsky, *and* to Sokolsky's partner, Jordan Kalfus, who was then living with their assistant, Ali MacGraw (who later became a model, a movie star, and Mrs. Steve McQueen), Shrimpton decided to break up with Bailey. So when Stamp asked her to visit him on a film set in Los Angeles, she said, "shabby or not, I was going." Within days she was madly in love, informed Eileen Ford she was "booking out," and moved in with Stamp in L.A.

Bailey was "moody and upset," but he quickly recovered and got involved with Sue Murray, an eighteen-year-old green-eyed blonde, whom he photographed for the cover of British *Vogue* six times in the next six months. Murray, he said, "is much more mysterious than Jean Shrimpton."

Shrimpton's relationship with Stamp soured within a few months, but nonetheless, in fall 1964 she agreed to accompany him to New York, where he was set to star in a Broadway version of the film *Alfie.* There was always work in America for Shrimpton. Revlon, Max Factor, and Pond's all were using her, and Eileen Ford called to say that Richard Avedon wanted to book her for a shoot with Steve McQueen. Working with Avedon was one of the model's few remaining ambitions.

But as 1965 rolled in, Shrimpton was "bloody miserable" with Stamp. "I was withdrawn, more silent than usual. I couldn't be bothered to make myself up, I never washed my hair unless I was working, and I had become very thin. . . . I did not want to model. I did not want to do anything much."

In mid-1966 Shrimpton agreed to costar in *Privilege,* a satirical film about a pop star. "I was terrible," she later admitted. Though he lingered a bit longer, Stamp was moving out of the picture. (He later described their breakup as "terrifyingly chilly" in *Double Feature,* his autobiography.) Shrimpton hardly missed a step, signing a three-year £70,000 contract with Yardley of London (which, despite its trendy name, was an American company). It required her to model and tour the States twice a year, making personal appearances. When Jordan Kalfus and Mel Sokolsky turned up as the team making the first Yardley commercial, Shrimpton began an affair with Kalfus and moved to New York with him.

Jerry Ford thinks *Privilege* hurt Shrimpton's career. "All her clients felt she'd gotten too famous and was a distraction from their ads," he says. But she modeled for another half dozen years, eventually earning $120 an hour. She kept touring for Yardley and shooting with Bailey, Penn, and Avedon. But her personal life was a mess that took years to clean up. She spent the seventies bouncing from man to man, taking up photography, opening shops selling antiques and souvenirs, becoming something of a recluse ("I dread exposure," she told an interviewer), and undergoing Jungian analysis, before finally marrying photographer Michael Cox (who was married when their affair began) in 1979 and buying The Abbey, a hotel in Penzance.

"I wasn't involved in my own life," she told the London *Sunday Times* in the early nineties. To another interviewer she said, "I had a case of arrested development until I was 25. I just traveled on other people's ambition, but I've got a steely enough streak that enabled me to survive."

Asked what she thought was important in life, Shrimpton replied, "Nothing."

It seems clear that Jean Shrimpton's career had already peaked in 1965, when Richard Avedon shot the April issue of *Harper's Bazaar* and put her on its cover in a spacesuit, and *Newsweek* magazine followed by putting the twenty-two-year-old on a cover in May, describing her as the "template from which the face of Western beauty will be cast until further notice." Shrimpton's face "somehow symbolizes the emergence of London," the news-magazine said, "as a new world tastemaker in pop culture."

Ironically, the moment coincided with the high-water mark of British influence. By 1965 both Beatlemania and Anglophilia were epidemic in the United States. Quant, Stamp, James Bond, Peter O'Toole, the Dave Clark Five, the Animals, the Stones, Petula Clark, Dusty Springfield, and countless more followed. In America alone, the "youthquake" market was estimated to command spending power of $25 billion a year.

In 1966 *Time* magazine "discovered" the new British culture and named it Swinging London. It was one year after Bailey announced that he wanted a new career as a movie director. In line with that desire, he'd decided to marry a twenty-one-year-old French actress he'd photographed named Catherine Deneuve. As a good-bye of sorts to pop fashion and society, Bailey collected and published three dozen of his portraits in a set called *Box of Pinups*. Journalist Frances Wyndham, who wrote the accompanying notes, said that the pictures—of the likes of Shrimpton, Hammond, Sue Murray, the Beatles, the Stones, and their managers—"are illustrations of a certain movement that is possibly over now."

The last nail in Swinging London's coffin, says Terence Donovan, was director Michelangelo Antonioni's brilliant (but pretentious) thriller *Blow-Up*, released in 1966 and starring David Hemmings as a vacuous, sex-crazed London fashion photographer. "*Blow-Up* was in fact an amalgam of my life, Bailey's life, and a few other people's lives," Donovan says. "That film kind of crystallized everybody's idea of these free young English fashion photographers. I was the first photographer in England ever to drive a Rolls-Royce, and suddenly the Rolls-Royce was in the film! An irritating experience. I never saw the film for twenty years." But millions of other people did, and a significant fraction of them, watching Hemmings have group sex on crumpled no-seam paper in his studio, decided to become fashion photographers.

* * *

Suddenly it was chic to prowl the streets carrying a 35 mm camera. So it was probably inevitable that more and more modeling agencies emerged in London. One of the strangest and most influential opened early in 1967. English Boy was the first model agency based on street fashion and street looks. Its credibility came from its connection to its rebellious times. Its models wore long hair and love beads, not twin sets and pearls. If they appeared threatening to the denizens of the world of *haute* fashion, all the better.

The agency was the creation of Sir Mark Palmer, a twenty-four-year-old fifth baronet whose typical dress was a wide-brimmed green hat, a wide-lapelled green velvet jacket, a satin tie, blue plaid trousers, and elfin green shoes with turned-up toes. As a page to Queen Elizabeth Sir Mark had once borne her train at the opening of Parliament. Educated at Eton, he dropped out of Oxford in the early sixties. Palmer disdained the world of privilege he came from. "I had what's called a country upbringing and it was never my scene," he said. "I was waiting for a scene that suited me."

Palmer was part of a set that included the Honorable Tara Browne, an heir to the Guinness brewing fortune and best friend of Brian Jones of the Rolling Stones; antiques dealer Christopher Gibb, the nephew of the governor of Rhodesia; Lord Gormanston, an Irish viscount; and the Honorable Julian Ormsby-Gore, son of Lord Harlech, who'd been Britain's ambassador to America during the Kennedy administration. In fall 1966 they all were photographed at a party for *Gentlemen's Quarterly,* which called them evidence that "the peacock mood of young London today is not confined to the sons of working-class blokes what shop on Carnaby Street."

Drugs were also part of the new mood. In 1966 LSD became the drug of choice in the world inhabited by Palmer, Browne, and their friends in the Rolling Stones. Brian Jones, in particular, was entranced by the hallucinogen. When the Stones recorded their trippy, acid-inspired album *Their Satanic Majesties Request* that year, Jones spent many of the sessions curled on the studio floor, tripping his brains out.

That December Tara Browne was killed in a car crash after he ran a red light, apparently under the influence of drugs. John Lennon of the Beatles later wrote a song, "A Day in the Life," about the incident. "He blew his mind out in a car," Lennon crooned. "He didn't notice that the lights had changed." In a peculiar twist of fate Mick Jagger's girlfriend Chrissie Shrimpton attempted suicide that same day, after learning that Jagger was two-timing her with the pop singer Marianne Faithfull.

Two months later Browne's friend Sir Mark Palmer inherited £12,000 on his twenty-fifth birthday and used some of it to open English Boy Ltd. in a small white room above an iconoclastic boutique called Quorum, near the King's Road on Radnor Walk in trendy Chelsea. Annoyed that magazines were photographing, but not paying, the style-setting longhairs on London's streets, Palmer and company had decided to cash in. "They wanted models like us," says one English Boy. "We didn't follow fashions; we set them."

Despite its name, the agency's books listed ten women, four babies, and several dogs. The women made most of the money, but the two dozen long-haired, foppish male models were English Boy's calling card. When a photograph of a dozen of them ran in the British press, it was the biggest scandal since the Beatles had returned their MBE honors the year before. Palmer was unfazed. "The English Boys are not just models, but model people," he said, "models for other people to model themselves on. By our appearance we are indicating our way of life, the way we think, the way we feel. This is our way of getting under the public skin, turning them on to what we believe and like. Our appearance is indicative of our inner scene. It's an outward manifestation of an inner grace."

It was quite a lark. When Brian Jones and his girlfriend Anita Pallenberg signed up in March 1967, Palmer announced it would cost 100 guineas an hour to photograph them. But Pallenberg "never turned up" for jobs, says the English Boy. "She was too beautiful to get out of bed." That August Christine Keeler, the centerpiece of the 1963 Profumo sex scandal, which had brought down Britain's government, signed on as one of English Boy's girls. Mick Jagger and Marianne Faithfull followed a month later. When Pallenberg left Brian Jones for his band mate Keith Richard, Jones hooked up with another English Boy model, Suki Poitier. Remarkably she'd survived the car crash that killed Tara Browne.

Until then Chelsea had been a little village "with a butcher and a baker," model Ingrid Boulting recalls. "But it was being taken over by far-out clothing stores. God, the clothes we would wear were wild! Work wasn't work. The focus was transition and transformation and letting go of old values and pushing for new meaning. It was a fun attempt at something different."

Within eighteen months, however, Palmer "decided that a flat and the hustling in the gray world that goes with it were really not my scene," he said,

and dropped out once again to seek New Age enlightenment. He began traveling the British countryside with a tribe of like-minded souls in a hippie caravan of horses and carts, fueled with soft drugs and what Palmer called "holy
lunacy." He remained on the road until 1977, when he married Catherine
Tennant, the daughter of Lord Glenconner and the younger sister of Colin
Tennant, owner of the Caribbean island of Mustique, and settled down to
work as a horse trader in England's countryside, where he remains to this day.

After Palmer left, control of the agency passed to Quorum's owner, Alice
Pollack, and her partner, the youthquake designer Ossie Clark. They fired
their chief booker, Jose Fonseca, and in 1968 she and a friend, April Ducksbury, a photographer's assistant, opened a new agency, Models One, snatching
models Marisa Berenson, Ingrid Boulting, and Sue Murray from English Boy.

They had plenty of competition. As the sixties began, there were about
twenty agencies in London. By the end of the decade, says Lucie Clayton's
Kark, there were five dozen. Initially Lucie Clayton had an advantage over
them all: a direct line to Ford in New York. "If a girl wanted to go to America, we'd call and say, 'Here she comes,'" Wynne Gordine-Dalley, Jean
Shrimpton's booker at Lucie Clayton, recalls. "We handled each other's girls
as they came and went. Eileen and Jerry would come and visit. It was all nice
and social. We'd talk shop, have dinner at the Karks' home." Kark recalls that
Ford liked Clayton "because I didn't want ten percent."

Unfortunately the trade with America was a one-way street. "It was very
much girls leaving London," says Gordine-Dalley. "Who were we to force a
girl who'd seen an opportunity? That was our philosophy. We were kind of
dumb, letting all those beauties slip away. Nobody would allow that to happen now."

Then London sank into an economic decline that lasted for almost a
decade and drove longtime agents like Peter Hope Lumley out of business.
Though London's financial district, known as the City, recovered in the 1980s,
under Margaret Thatcher, the lowercased city's fashions and trends were subsequently easily dismissed as clothes for kids and successive waves of glitter,
glam, punk, and new romantic rock stars. London was considered of secondary
importance to fashion until a youthquake revival hit in the early 1990s. Lucie
Clayton stopped booking models in 1979 and concentrated instead on its
charm, secretarial, and nanny schools. "I decided it wasn't our milieu," says
Leslie Kark. "It was becoming sleazy. And we weren't doing so well. There
were lots of competitors, and they were very much more sharp and clever and

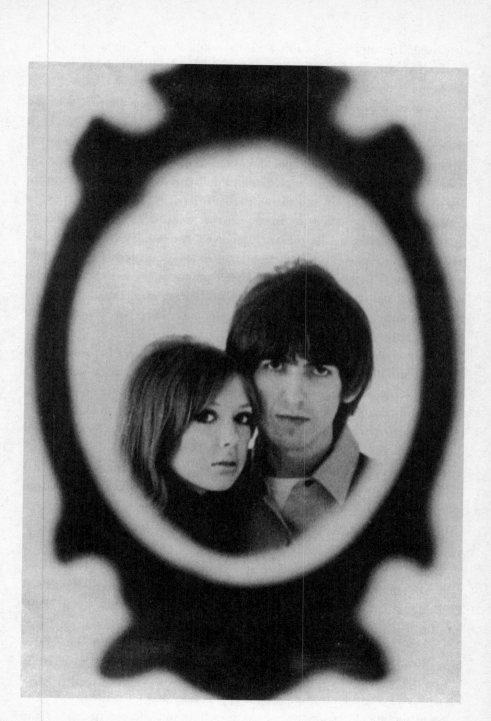

Patti Boyd with her husband, Beatle George Harrison

successful. The more impressionable girls would leave. There was simply no loyalty. The bitchery between the agents was horrifying. The dislike between the agencies was so great."

One who held out was Cherry Marshall. A model just after the war, she opened her agency and school in 1954. Two years later she made headlines when she took six of her models to Moscow for three weeks to show off British fashion. Her best-known discoveries included Paulene Stone, who later married the actor Laurence Harvey and the restaurateur Peter Morton; actress Suzy Kendall; and, most famously, Patti Boyd.

While still in school, Patti Boyd went to work at Elizabeth Arden. "I thought I wanted to be a beautician," she says. "And while I was there, somebody came from one of the Fleet Street magazines and suggested that I should try modeling." Early in her career she met photographer Eric Swain, "who sort of took me under his wing." Swain was friends with David Bailey and Jean Shrimpton, "so the four of us would, you know, hang. We were definitely what was happening."

Boyd was with Bailey the day her agent phoned and sent her to a casting call with film director Richard Lester. She'd worked with Lester before on a commercial for potato chips and assumed she was up for another one. "I heard later from my agent that it was a Beatles film and I was horrified, because, I mean, I wasn't terribly ambitious to be a model, and here I was, being pushed into a film!"

She arrived, as requested, at Waterloo Station and boarded a chartered train. "It drew out of the station and stopped at a very small, deserted station, where the Beatles hopped on!" Boyd exclaims. At the end of the day's filming, in which Boyd played a schoolgirl who encounters the pop group, guitarist George Harrison asked her out. "I said I couldn't because I had a boyfriend," she recalls, and instead, asked Harrison if he wanted to join her, Swain, and their gang. "He was horrified at this idea and said no!" she says. A week later Boyd was recalled for another day's shooting. "How's your wonderful boyfriend?" Harrison asked her.

"Of course, by this time I'd realized he wasn't quite so wonderful," Boyd says. "I was trying to extricate myself from his influence, and I was actually quite excited by the fact that George had asked me out and was rather keen. I'd realized I might be missing a great opportunity, and I accepted."

Soon she and Harrison were a couple. "I wasn't allowed on any of the tours, because the security was so rigid, and they were very worried that the Beatles would be harmed, and on occasion it was actually pretty dangerous for them," Boyd says. "So bringing girls along was totally out of the question." But when the band was in London, she joined their life of screenings, parties, and dinners with the rich and famous.

Boyd married her Beatle boyfriend in 1965 and went into semiretirement. "George was from the North of England, a very sort of traditional working-class boy, and he felt his wife should be at home," she says. "So I'd mess around at home, trying to teach myself how to cook." Though she'd left Cherry Marshall, Boyd still took the odd modeling job, booked through Beatles manager Brian Epstein's office. "I'd do special things," she says. "But quite honestly we were staying up very late at night and to try and carry on modeling would have been very difficult, so I had to really make a choice."

Boyd eventually left both modeling and Harrison and married guitarist Eric Clapton, who wrote his song "Layla" for her, before they, too, broke up.

Lesley Hornby, the daughter of a carpenter, was born in 1949 in Neasden, England, a tidy suburb of London. At fifteen she met Nigel John Davies, ten years her senior, at the hairdresser's salon where she made herself useful on Saturdays in exchange for pocket money to buy clothes. He'd worked variously in betting parlors and nightclubs, as an amateur boxer, a clerk, a porno film salesman, an interior decorator, an *antiquaire,* and a hairdresser at Vidal Sassoon (where he called himself Mr. Christian). Everything about him was dashing, from the name he'd most recently assumed, Justin de Villeneuve, to the red Triumph Spitfire he drove when he came to pick up his brother, who worked with Lesley and dubbed her Sticks, which eventually metamorphosed to Twig and then Twiggy. Justin thought she was "breathtaking" despite the fact that she "sounded like a demented parrot." When they started seeing each other, his wife left him—and took back the Triumph, which was hers. Twiggy soon made up for the loss.

"It just happened," she later said. Justin had the idea that Twiggy should model. But when she was snubbed on a visit to *Queen,* the pair went back to an earlier plan to open a boutique and stock it with trousers Twiggy sewed from antique fabrics. Then, despite the fact that she was too short at five feet six inches and too thin at ninety-one pounds, measuring 31-22-32, a friend of Justin's offered Twiggy a job modeling for a magazine. The editor sent her to Leonard's posh hair salon on Upper Grosvenor Street for a haircut. Intrigued by the girl's looks, Leonard said he'd give her some pictures in exchange for modeling a hairstyle he'd just invented. It took eight hours of snipping and coloring to get her elfin cap of hair just right. But when Leonard was through,

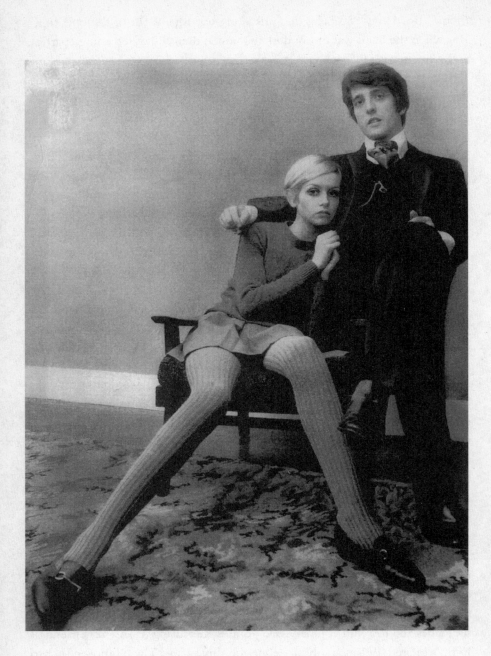

Twiggy and her Svengali, Justin de Villeneuve,
photographed by Philip Townshend

"she looked like Bambi," De Villeneuve said later. "I knew then that she really was going to make it."

Deirdre McSharry, a fashion writer for the *Daily Express,* saw pictures of her at Mr. Leonard's salon. "They phoned me that night and asked where they could find her," the photographer, Barry Lategan, recalls. A few days later McSharry published a full-page story dubbing Twiggy "The Face of '66 . . . the Cockney kid with the face to launch a thousand shapes."

Eager to cash in, de Villeneuve decided that Twiggy should join Lucie Clayton, then still the top agency in London. But in her autobiography, *Twiggy,* she says that her father nixed that idea and demanded that Justin manage her career or that she give it up. It didn't matter. Her phone number was listed. Her mother took the requests for bookings. There were lots of them.

Not everyone wanted her. The Terrible Trio, for example. "The new look of the sixties is the woman, and the Twig ain't a woman," said Brian Duffy. But her career momentum was building fast. Though she was, in effect, working outside the fashion/model system, it couldn't help taking notice. Diana Vreeland saw her in *Elle* and booked her for *Vogue.* A British clothing company signed her to create a Twiggy fashion collection. Her body was cast for shopwindow mannequins, and the Ford Motor Company even lent her one of its first Mustangs. All over Britain teenage girls started copying her hairdo and makeup style—three sets of false lashes on top, drawn-on lashes, quickly dubbed Twigs, below—and grown-ups went on starvation diets, trying to mimic her emaciated looks. "It was dreadful," says Gillian Bobroff, a British model of the sixties. "She started a trend, and you had to be just the same. I had my hair cut and started killing myself, taking a million slimming pills. I never ate. I had bulimia. It was a nightmare, trying to keep up."

Twiggy's appeal was as enormous as it was initially inexplicable. "Within a year she was on her way," says Lategan. "She started being a phenomenon." She wasn't a model like any model before her; she was a marketing miracle, the first of a new breed. Flying by the seat of his pants, de Villeneuve had created a monster. She was the first model to achieve genuine international celebrity. "That was the beginning of marketing models that agencies all do now," says Patti Boyd.

Twiggy finally did sign with several agencies. Dorian Leigh, who represented her in Paris, arranged for her and Justin to meet Barbara Stone of Stewart Models. Jerry Ford insists Leigh promised Twiggy to him. In fact, she became the object of a heated competition. "Justin was playing us off against each other," Stone says. "The decision was his." But Twiggy apparently had some say in the matter. "Eileen desperately wanted Twiggy," says Dorian, "but I couldn't make her do it. Twiggy said, 'She scares me shitless!' "

Accompanied by de Villeneuve and a street peddler turned bodyguard named Teddy "the Monk" Adams, Twiggy arrived at New York's John F. Kennedy Airport on a Monday afternoon in March 1967 and walked straight into a riotous press conference. Asked what effect his protégée would have on America, de Villeneuve, dressed in a double-breasted blue suit, green shirt, and flimsy pink neckerchief, declared, "She'll have the same effect as the Beatles. She's sort of the miniqueen of the new social aristocracy." Asked if her figure was the look of the future, Twiggy giggled and asked, "It's not really what you call a figure, is it?"

Bert Stern, who had made a deal to film Twiggy's every move for an ABC-TV documentary, hired a helicopter to fly her to Manhattan, installed her in a brand-new East Side apartment, and tossed a studio party in her honor that was attended by the likes of Andy Warhol acolyte Edie Sedgwick, art collectors Ethel and Robert Scull, and electric-dress designer Tiger Morse. On the streets, wherever Twiggy went, *The New Yorker* reported in a hundred page story on her trip to America, "a yelping, shrieking, thrashing crowd" was sure to follow. When *Newsweek* put Twiggy on its cover a few weeks into her trip ("four straight limbs in search of a woman's body, a mini-bosom trapped in perpetual puberty, the frail torso of the teen-age choirboy . . . a fallen angel . . . the first child star in the history of high fashion," the magazine rhapsodized), she raised her rate to $240 an hour. But when *Vogue* called to book her for a shoot with Richard Avedon, he got her for $100 a day. "Twiggy, even though she's so very big, has been something of a joke," de Villeneuve said in a rare moment of modesty. "Avedon can change that."

For his part Avedon was impressed. "Women move in certain ways that convey an air of the time they live in, and Twiggy, when she's in front of lights, is bringing her generation in front of the camera," the photographer said. "I think what's involved is the stripping away of certain affectations about what is beautiful. Twiggy is made for that." *Vogue*'s Mrs. Vreeland agreed. "This little girl is not a Cockney phenomenon," she said. "For us, at *Vogue,* she represents beauty, not Twiggery. We love her silky throat, her naturalness, her inner serenity." To Avedon, Vreeland was somewhat less poetic, worrying about her outward faults instead of her inner beauty. "Ask her to pull in behind," Vreeland commanded in a memo to her photographer, "and you will have a glorious girl and not an ill-fed adolescent."

Back in London, though, the bloom was off the rose. By 1968 the Twiggy fashion collection had fizzled. "You're a has-been," the manufacturer told her. De Villeneuve briefly tried his hand at photography and became successful quite fast. But he and Twiggy were never accepted by the fashion establishment they'd disdained. "Twiggy didn't sort of play or go out with all of us," says Patti Boyd, who modeled with her and became close to the couple. "They were very much apart from the rest of the people I knew."

They were also growing apart from each other. Although they announced their engagement in July 1968, mere hours after de Villeneuve had divorced his first wife, they never married or even lived together. Patti Boyd thought their problem was simple. "He treated her like a child," she says.

De Villeneuve ran Twiggy's businesses (which included a Twiggy stocking line, a hairdressing salon, a film-processing shop, a knitting magazine, an agency for singers, and a King's Road boutique), made all the decisions, and split all the profits with her. There was little for her to do. "We began to get bored," he later related. "It became fake because Twiggy didn't really like what she was doing. . . . And so Twiggy virtually retired at nineteen. If she'd continued modeling, she'd have completely burned herself out."

In 1971 Twiggy emerged from retirement to star in Ken Russell's film *The Boyfriend* and in several forgettable movies. She gained twenty pounds, got her own flat, and broke up with her Svengali. Later she married an American actor, Michael Whitney, and had a child. The couple separated in 1983; Whitney, an alcoholic, collapsed and died of a heart attack several months later, while Twiggy was appearing on Broadway in a musical, *My One and Only*.

In 1986, back in England, de Villeneuve published a book in which he claimed that he'd first bedded Twiggy when she was fifteen and then cheated on her constantly. "I could never write anything like that," she complained at the time. But sometimes her anger slipped out in public. In 1980 she'd told *Newsweek* that she was considering changing her name back to Lesley. "Twiggy's a ridiculous name, absolutely silly," she snapped. "To tell you the truth, I can't stand the sound of it anymore." But time had a healing effect. By 1993, when another skinny British model, Kate Moss, revived the Twiggy look, the original—now calling herself Twiggy Lawson and dividing her time between England and Los Angeles—was even modeling again. But more happily this time. "I used to be a thing," she said. "I am a person now."

VERUSCHKA

S tanding at the end of a car on the Paris metro is a towering woman. She is tall enough to be a fashion model, but too poor, too rough. Her clothes are ratty; her boots, scuffed and worn. She is covered with paint; it is all over her outfit and her worker's hands. It is even splattered in her mousy brown hair.

She was, in fact, the biggest model of her time—in more ways than one. Veruschka, at six feet one inch, was not only the tallest model ever to make it to the top of the fashion scene but also the highest born.

Hiding behind the pseudonym was the Countess Vera von Lehndorff, daughter of Heinrich, Count von Lehndorff-Steinort, an East Prussian landowner whose family lived in a castle on a twenty-eight-thousand acre lake called Mauersee. It was close to Rastenburg, a subterranean Nazi command post from which Hitler commanded troops as they moved on Moscow.

Hitler's foreign minister, Joachim von Ribbentrop, requisitioned Lehndorff's castle and moved in to be near his beloved Führer. The castle also served as headquarters for the German Army's *Oberkommando* or high command. Heinrich von Lehndorff, a first lieutenant in the German Army reserve, was part of the military conspiracy to assassinate Hitler. When the Gestapo foiled the plan, Lehndorff was arrested and, along with several other military leaders, was executed on September 4, 1944. His family was arrested, and his properties were seized.

Nineteen years later his second daughter, Vera, an art student, was discovered by a fashion photographer and entered the world of designer dresses and glossy magazines. "She looked like a deer, awkward and yet so graceful," says Dorian

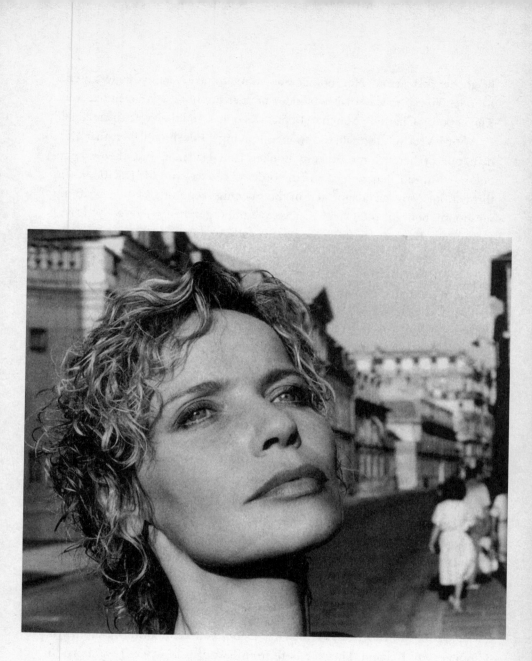

Veruschka photographed by Helmut Newton

Leigh, her first agent. "Her mother wanted me to take Vera's younger sister as a model. The sister was smaller, blonder, prettier, but not magnificent like Vera. The next day Charlotte March took pictures of her, and they were incredible!"

At first Vera was too tall, too strange-looking. "Eileen said, 'Get that German out of here,' " recalls Ford booker Jane Halleran. But then strange became beautiful, fantasy became the order of the day, and the rule book was thrown out. Veruschka appeared in the opening scene of *Blow-Up,* writhing sensuously beneath the David Baileyesque photographer portrayed by David Hemmings. By the time she retired in the early seventies, she had appeared on the cover of *Vogue* eleven times.

When fantasy fell out of fashion, Veruschka traded in the art of appearance for the related art of disappearance. Though she still sometimes models, her focus has stayed on her artistic visions. Returning to Germany, she began a long collaboration with a German artist, Holger Trülzsch, fusing photography and painting. Using Veruschka's naked body as a canvas, they spent hours transforming her first into animals and then into reincarnations of movie stars like Marilyn Monroe and Rita Hayworth. As their work progressed, the transformations became more radical. Instead of remaking Veruschka's appearance, they caused her to disappear into statues, stones, forests, the walls of old buildings and decaying, derelict factories, and, finally, an Italian rag warehouse.

"The earlier artifice, that of the fashion model, was to simulate an ideal form of oneself—to enhance an already existing, very high order of natural beauty," the critic Susan Sontag writes of these eerie works. "Here, the artifice is to simulate what is *not* the beautiful woman. . . . The person disappears, but beauty does not disappear (any more than does Veruschka's iconic status). It remains embedded in the image, like a more or less invisible ghost. What these images illustrate is an indomitable career of beauty—though made ugly, *still* remaining beautiful—as well as an escape from beauty."

"I was born in 1939. My father was Count von Lehndorff. My mother is Countess von Kalnein. They are both from East Prussia, where I was born in the Mauersee swamps. That was part of Germany, but it is all Polish now.

"My father was executed, and we—my sisters and my mother—were sent to a prison called Zeithainhof. We didn't know where we were at the time because we were taken there one night by the Gestapo. It was not exactly a concentration camp, but it was a kind of a camp where all the children of those men were sent. To Hitler we were the worst of the German race, the ones who betrayed him. We were supposed to be sent to Siberia and be disappeared. Two or three weeks before the war ended, we got out because my mother had a connection. I was four years old.

"We grew up like Gypsies in West Germany because we'd lost everything. We stayed where we could, with friends who had a house. Then they moved. We were moving every year. I was in thirteen schools altogether.

"When I was eighteen, I was in art school in Hamburg. Then I went to paint in Italy in 1962, 1963. I was in Florence, and one day on the street this man I didn't know asked me if I would be interested to do pictures. The Italian collections were being shown in the Palazzo Pitti and the Palazzo Strozzi, and he brought me there to all the couturiers. I was very shy. Do you remember Nico, the singer from the Velvet Underground? She was also modeling once in a while, and I remember her laughing her head off when she saw me. I don't know why. I got very ashamed.

"Anyhow, there I started to do my first pictures for the Italian magazines. I immediately imitated the models I had seen in the Palazzo Strozzi because I didn't really know how to do it. I did all this kind of posing, you know? I still have pictures of that. It's very funny.

"While I was there, I met Denise Sarrault. She was very famous at that time inside the fashion world. She looked like Garbo. Helmut Newton had done quite a lot of beautiful pictures of her. She was working for Dior doing all the shows, and once in a while she did pictures with Jeanloup Sieff. She said to me, 'I love your face, and I think you could be a very good model. You should come to Paris.'

"Before that a Polish friend of my mother had come to visit her in Germany. I don't know how it happened, but he said that he knew the biggest model agency in Paris, Dorian Leigh. I was a little bit interested, but not really that much at that time, because I was studying painting. But he offered to try and arrange a meeting. He said, 'She comes to Berlin. Why don't you meet her there?' So I went to Berlin and met Dorian in a hotel.

"She said, 'Yeah, maybe we try with you, but you are quite tall, and I don't know. We'll see. You come to Paris.' So I went to Paris, but I never worked there. I was too tall. Everything was too short on me, of course. They said women's knees are ugly, so they pulled on my skirts all the time. And I had this very baby face and was at the same time sophisticated because of my length, so it was very difficult. My face belonged in *Elle,* but my body was *Vogue,* so nothing worked.

"After a year in Paris I met Eileen Ford. She saw me at Dorian's in Paris when she came for the collections. She said, 'Oh, you would be great for the

States because you are tall and blond, and that's what we like. You should come over to New York.'

"But then, when I got here, Eileen was really completely rotten. She said she had never seen me. She didn't know me! In Paris she'd said it was good I was a blonde. Here, she said, I should be dark, and she sent me to the most expensive hairdresser. All the money I brought over with me was gone—into hair! Then she said, 'Never take a taxi because you will make no money here, so just walk and you'll lose weight because you're too fat.' I was *never* fat. She sent me to a lawyer to do my working visa. After I went there three times, he said, 'Listen, it's too sad to see you always coming here. I must tell you that Eileen said, "Don't make a visa for her." ' But she didn't want him to tell me! She was such a bitch. Every Friday she said to the booking girls, 'Throw her out.' And they always said, 'Oh, come on, let her have a nice weekend at least.' It went on like that for a while.

"Finally I went back to Europe in 1964 and made a little more training in Italy. And there, I said to myself, You have to think of something, because I now knew exactly how it should *not* be done. You shouldn't just go to a photographer and show your book. Hundreds of girls do that. You have to do something so they will not forget you, so they will say, 'That girl was really something different.' I had no doubts about myself. I knew I had something which was interesting and I wanted to work with that. So I said, 'OK, now we have to find a way to make sure that others see it too.'

"So I thought, I'm also going to be a whole new person. And I'm going to have fun. I'm just going to invent a new person; I'm going to be Veruschka. Veruschka was a nickname I had when I was a child. It means 'little Vera.' And as I was always too tall, I thought it would be nice to say that I'm little Vera. And it was also nice to have a Russian name because I came from the East.

"I decided this person has to be all in black. At that time everybody wasn't wearing black. So I bought myself a cheap copy of a Givenchy coat—very narrow and just a little bit flared on the bottom, quite short, just covering the knee—a black velvet hat, and very soft black suede boots, which at that time people didn't have. You could really walk like an animal in them. I thought I had to have this very beautiful walk. When I come in, it should be really very animallike.

"So when I came back, I went right away to see Barbara Stone. I said to her, 'You must tell all the photographers about this girl coming from the East, somewhere near Russia. Never be too clear from where exactly. She wants to travel to the States, and she wants to meet you because she likes your photographs. She's very interested in photography. She's really quite extraordinary. You should see her.' So of course they always said yes, because they were interested in another kind of girl.

"I would arrive and say, 'Hello, how are you?' And they would say, 'Can we see some pictures?' And I said, 'Pictures? I don't take my pictures around with me. For what? I know how I look. I want to know what *you* do.' And then of course they got interested. I remember Penn saying, 'Would you mind going over to *Vogue*?' He made the call.

"My first trip to *Vogue* was very funny. I had seen Vreeland at *Bazaar* already, and she had made remarks. 'Oh, you have wonderful legs,' or, 'Your bone structure is wonderful,' or something. But then at *Vogue* she said, 'Who is that girl? Put her name right on the wall. Veruschka,' she said, 'Veruschka, you're going to hear from me.'

"Vreeland was after me all the time. So I called her and I said, 'Listen, I would love to do a story about jewelry on the beach.' And she said, 'Take everything and go,' and she would publish the whole thing. I could call up and say, 'I would love to do this or that,' and she said, 'Wonderful!' or often, 'Maybe not,' but anyway you could talk. We were then becoming teams. Like with Giorgio [Sant'Angelo, a stylist who later became a designer]. We were together a lot and did many trips together. Working together and going on trips together, that was the fun we had. We started to work in the studio just on our own, overnight. We invented things, just working with fabrics, and a lot of pictures were done like that. And that was only possible with Vreeland.

"So I was working very well as Veruschka. People liked me. Then I started seeing [photographer Franco] Rubartelli. I met him in Rome. He was married to a beautiful blond Swiss girl. We were a little bit the same type, only she had much more beautiful hair. He'd done his first pictures for American *Vogue* with her, black and white with a wide angle from down below, and she was doing all kinds of strange movements. And I noticed that and I liked that, and when I met him in Rome, we did some pictures like that, and then we became very friendly. *Vogue* had wanted to finish his contract; but then they saw the pictures we did, and they renewed his contract.

"*Vogue* wanted me to work with other photographers then. So I went on the famous trip to Japan with Avedon. It was [*Vogue* fashion editor] Polly Mellen's first trip when she started there. But I'd really wanted to work with somebody who wanted to work with me all the time. So I was working a lot with Rubartelli, which Dick didn't like very much, because Rubartelli was very jealous and always called me up, even in the studio. So that was a prob-lem—this couple thing.

"That was just before *Blow-Up*. *Blow-Up* made me very famous. Antonioni had seen me in London, working with [photographer] David Montgomery. I admired Antonioni as a director very much. He came one night when I was doing some pictures, and he stayed, quietly, for a very long time and then said good-bye and left. Then, when I came back from Japan, there was this phone call from Antonioni saying, 'I would like to have you for my film.' I was very happy. But everybody else—especially Rubartelli—was very upset. He said, 'No, don't do it, don't do it.' But I was strong. I said, 'I'll do it.'

"When I did *Blow-Up*, I remember smoking pot. That was a big thing. At that time it wasn't so normal to smoke. And after the film it became the big thing. Everybody smoked.

"After *Blow-Up* I was not so strong with Rubartelli anymore. I got a lot of offers, and I refused them because Franco was just so jealous about it. I was very inexperienced. I'd never lived with a man before Rubartelli, and I thought, OK, men are like that. They are just so jealous. I thought it was awful, but I took it for a while. But then I couldn't anymore, and I said, 'No, it's impossible.'

"We were together five years, until the beginning of the seventies. I was already separated with him, but we did, in the time of separation, a film together called *Stop Veruschka*. I was very upset because I didn't want my name on the title, because everybody would think it was my story. But he did it any-how. He put all his own money in, and it was kind of a disaster. The film came out, it wasn't a success, and he had so much debts that I think he had to leave Rome. He went to Venezuela, and he became a producer there, but I never heard of him anymore.

"The first stone face I did was on the terrace in Rome where I stayed with Franco. I was alone, I was depressed, and I said to myself, 'What's to become of me? I've become so many things already. I've done so many different women.' I had already painted myself as animals and plants. Now, I thought, I would like to disappear into something and become like a stone. And I saw the beautiful structure of the stone of the terrace. And so I went back, got the colors, and with a mirror imitated all this on my face. And Rubartelli came, and he saw this and he photographed it. Then I did it in a much better way for the film *Stop Veruschka*. I had a rubber scalp put on and stones around me, and I was lying on the stones and the camera went over stones, over stones, stones and stones—and then one stone opened its eyes and looked at you.

"Then I disappeared, too, in about 1971. My last pictures never came out. Dick Avedon decided to do the whole Paris collection only with me. So we went to Paris with Ara Gallant, who was doing the hair, and Serge Lutens, a very good makeup man. For hours he did this powdery makeup, and then Ara did my hair very white in front and very long. We didn't like the look. We wanted to change it. We would have maybe done something else—worked with wigs or whatever. We were experimenting. But then Alex Liberman and Grace Mirabella [who had just replaced Diana Vreeland as editor of *Vogue*] looked at the pictures, and they were very unhappy, too. They didn't like this look. Grace Mirabella liked a certain look, the hair always to the shoulder and very fresh and very bourgeois. And she wanted me to be that. I felt that they wanted to change my personality into something more salable. She said, 'People have to identify with you.' I said, 'No. You have to take another girl for that.' So they actually did ask another girl. And I never did any modeling again for a long time.

"Of course I was a model, but I didn't see myself as typical. Maybe I'm a frustrated actress. I did it more like a big theater play. With accessories and clothes, you invent; you become a person who is very sexy or very Garbo or whatever. I never liked to be one thing. It was very natural for me to do it that way. Otherwise I couldn't have been in that business so long, just putting on clothes, being detached from it, making money, and going home.

"When I traveled with Giorgio [Sant'Angelo], we would even cut up clothes if we didn't like them. The designers were all happy because the pictures looked great. Now all this changed completely. You always had to see the dress. This whole thing didn't work at all with my way of working. I had always refused commercial work. They wanted to do Veruschka Vodka, but they would have been very upset later, seeing me painted like walls. For me, no million dollars is worth giving up my freedom of expression. I called Diana Vreeland about that contract. I already had decided to say no, but I wanted her advice. She said, 'Veruschka, be very, very, very difficult and then say no.' I loved that.

"I went to Germany from 1971 until about 1976. The outside world was not anymore interested in what I wanted to do as a model, so I was clearly saying, 'OK, that's it. Now I do other things.' It was very natural to go into other things. I started working on body painting with Holger Trülzsch. I had a house, and I stayed there with Holger, and we did the body painting, which made me disappear. I was working against my model career. Then we started doing the dress paintings. It was a parody on modeling. I would paint myself as a man. I did this thing in *Playboy* [in 1973] where I was painted like vulgar gangster men.

"When Holger and I found the rag warehouse in Italy [where they did a stunning series of photographs in 1988], we didn't think that it had to do with clothes. We just saw it as a visually interesting place, but it happened to have thousands and thousands of old dresses all piled up, which were related to my life. I don't want to make it such a psychological thing, but there's always a link with my background, my history. The warehouse looks very beautiful in our pictures, but if you really look close, thinking of the camps, where they tied up clothes, too, it is actually quite scary. So this is beauty with a monster sitting, hiding behind it. That's serious."

"**I** longed to grow up to be the best butcher in the world," Gertrude Behmenburg said about herself in 1943. Instead the four-year-old grew up to be Wilhelmina, America's greatest model of the 1960s. She might have been happier—and lived longer—had she kept to her original dream.

When she died of cancer in March 1980, Wilhelmina was remembered as a great success—the last star of the couture era in modeling, the top money-making face of her time. She'd appeared on 255 magazine covers, including a record 28 covers of American *Vogue*. And in her second career as co-owner and president of Wilhelmina Models, she'd won one last magazine cover four months before she died; her photo illustrated an article about the rancorous competition that had made modeling, *Fortune* said, "more lucrative than at any time in its history."

In her ten years of posing and a baker's dozen more years as an agency head, Wilhelmina saw her trade change from a polite cottage industry filled with ladylike creatures who looked as if they never went to the bathroom to a $50-million-a-year business seething with enmity and greed and—apparently, at least—running on a current of money, drugs, and promiscuous sex.

Wilhelmina changed, too. She started out a willful beauty, master of herself and her course in life. But she ended up a secret victim, known as the head of the world's second-largest model agency; a caring mother to models who could always come to her for advice; and a pacesetter who promoted blacks in the face of her industry's indifference and racism—not as the battered wife of an abusive alcoholic; a mother who couldn't protect her own children; a picture of superficial perfection whose daughter believes she chose to kill herself with cigarettes instead of facing, and fixing, her horribly imperfect life.

Wilhelmina was born in May 1939 in Culemborg, Holland, the daughter of a German butcher and a Dutch seamstress. Growing up in Oldenburg, Germany, she dreamed of a career as a nurse, a teacher, or an international spy. But on V-E Day she and her four-year-old brother were skipping down the street to get their day's allotment of food rations when a group of drunken Canadian soldiers passed by, shooting their pistols in wild celebration. One of their bullets killed Wilhelmina's brother. She determined that day somehow to make up the loss to her grieving mother, Klasina.

"She lived her life for other people," says her daughter, Melissa. "The only thing she ever did for herself was become a model."

In 1954 Wilhelm Behmenburg moved his family to a one-and-a-half-room apartment on Chicago's North Side, where he'd opened another butcher shop. Daughter Gertrude entered high school not knowing a word of English, but she picked it up quickly from television, a part-time job in a five-and-ten-cent store, and the fashion magazines that "became my favorite reading material," she said. "I even went to secondhand stores to buy all the old issues. . . . I read them cover to cover, devouring every word and every picture of my new idols, the beautiful models who reached so glamorously from the pages—out to *me*."

In 1956 she accompanied a friend to a modeling school for an interview. The friend was too short. Gertrude, on the other hand, was tall enough and had the looks: widely spaced, hypnotic eyes and a full, sensuous mouth. "My head began to spin," she recalled. Promising to repay him from her five-and-dime earnings, she borrowed the tuition from her father for an intensive modeling course. That May Sabie Models Unlimited presented her with a certificate stating she'd completed its professional modeling course "in creditable manner."

Now Gertrude Behmenburg no longer existed. Gertrude just wouldn't do, Behmenburg was too long and awkward to remember, and her middle name, Wilhelmina, was too foreign. In her place stood Winnie Hart, model. In 1957 "Winnie" began her career at beauty pageants. She was named Miss Lincolnwood Army Reserve Training Center on Armed Forces Day in May. In July she was off to Long Beach, California, to compete in the Miss Universe pageant. She had small modeling jobs, too, and she took an after-school job as a designer–secretary–house model with Scintilla, a local lingerie company, to augment her earnings.

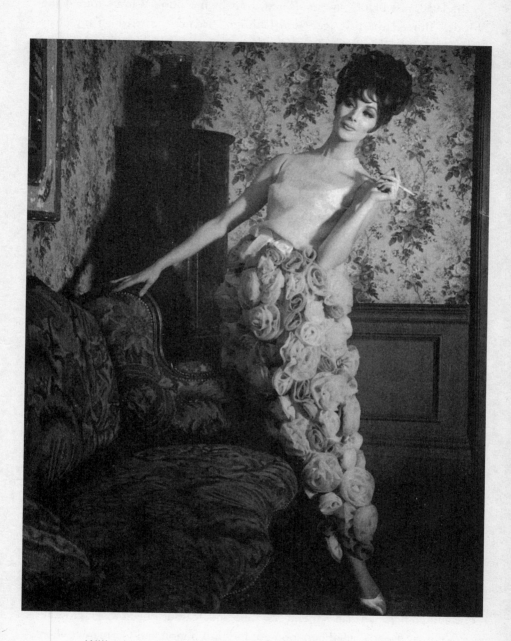

Wilhelmina photographed in Valentino couture

In 1958, just before she graduated from high school, Winnie joined the Models Bureau, the first agency in Chicago. "I damn near fell off my chair when she walked in," recalls her booker, Jovanna Papadakis. The chestnut-haired beauty was already fighting the weight problems that plagued her throughout her career. Her Models Bureau composite gives her height as five feet nine inches, her weight as 132 pounds, and her measurements as 37-24-36. "A hundred thirty-two?" Papadakis laughs. "I've got news for you: We lied even then." Winnie weighed 159. Nonetheless, the agent thought she resembled Suzy Parker and immediately called Victor Skrebneski, then, as now, the king of Chicago fashion photography.

Skrebneski, who'd started working for the Marshall Field & Company department store in 1948, had just lost his favorite model and girlfriend Mary van Nuys to the greener pastures of New York (where she later met and married literary agent Irving "Swifty" Lazar). When Winnie arrived at his coach house studio, Skrebneski took her under his wing. He even taught her how to back-comb her hair. "We spent many hours on that," he says.

In 1959 Winnie's picture started appearing in Scintilla's mail-order catalog, and sales boomed. Impressed, her boss sent her picture to the International Trade Show in Chicago, and she was named its Miss West Berlin. "I had to speak to the girls at the trade fair," says Shirley Hamilton, then a booker at another Chicago agency, Patricia Stevens. She took Winnie downstairs to a coffee shop and told her to order whatever she wanted. "Enjoy it," she said. "You're not going to have anything like it until you lose thirty pounds."

Hamilton asked her why she called herself Winnie, then declared, "From now on you will be Wilhelmina." Within six months all her advisers believed she was ready to go to New York. Early in 1960 Hamilton called Eileen Ford and set up an appointment. Skrebneski accompanied her. Ford told her that she couldn't be a model "with those hips" but that if she lost twenty pounds, she could go to Paris and try to start with Dorian Leigh. So Wilhelmina flew to Europe, "sort of saying to myself, as an excuse in case nothing happened, that I was visiting relatives," she said. She ended up staying a year and working nearly every day. "I put her on a diet, and she lost a lot of weight, and everyone adored her," Dorian remembers. "She said, 'I want Eileen to eat crow.' "

Willie, as friends called her, soon got jobs in London and Germany (where her native language came in handy). She also took her first location trip, to Gardaja, Algeria, where she was to pose in the Sahara in clothes by the couturier Madame Grès. The resulting pictures earned Willie her very first cover, for L'Officiel magazine. In fall 1961 she returned to New York, moved into a small apartment on East Eighty-fourth Street, and "took the city by storm," says Papadakis. Wilhelmina appeared on twenty-nine more covers and was booked weeks, even months, in advance. She paid off the mortgage on her parents' house, bought them a car, and made plans to send them to Europe.

It was a great time to be a model. The five top agencies in New York (Ford, Plaza Five, Stewart, Frances Gill, and Paul Wagner) claimed to book $7.5 million annually for print work alone. Beginners earned $40 an hour; top models, $60, less 10 percent commission to the agents. Even a junior category model, like Colleen Corby, could earn $45,000 a year at seventeen. Television residuals were a new and as yet unenumerated factor. "Some of us were earning seven hundred dollars before ten A.M. on the morning shows," says Gillis MacGil, who'd kept working after opening her Mannequin agency for runway and showroom models.

By 1964 Wilhelmina had "risen to the top of the heap of the 405 girls who work under contract to the city's top five agencies," the New York *Journal-American* reported in a series called "Private Lives of High Fashion Models." Jerry Ford called her the outstanding model of the early 1960s. "Her look was the look of the time," he said. Although she was to earn $100,000 a year, she was plagued with insecurity. "It's hard enough to become a successful model," Wilhelmina said later. "But it's twice as hard to stay successful. You can be out so fast if you don't deliver."

Wilhelmina delivered. For the next five years she went around the world, from South America to India to Hong Kong to Lapland. She drove herself hard, never taking vacations and often working twelve-hour days, lugging her fifteen-pound mailman's bag full of model's tricks, sometimes working from 7:00 A.M. to midnight. "She was the salt of the earth," says hairstylist Kenneth Battelle. "She was a model before she was a person, a doll and happy to be that."

"She was so sweet and generous to me," remembers photographer Neal Barr. "She and Iris Bianchi and Tilly Tizani would do anything for you. You could book them for an hour. Wilhelmina would arrive in her limousine, makeup totally on, open her bag full of hairpieces on foam things, ask what you wanted, be on the set within fifteen minutes, do the shot, jump back in her limousine, and be gone."

Barr remembers that most of the models when he started his career in the early sixties were "totally emaciated, veins sticking out, faces literally stenciled on." But Wilhelmina was different; she was a very big girl. "I was on continuous diets," she recalled. "I'm not fat as far as real life is concerned, but I certainly was when it came to modeling. I ate twice a week. In between, it was cigarettes and black coffee. On Wednesday, I had a little bowl of soup so I wouldn't get too sick or a little piece of cheese on a cracker. On Sunday, I'd have a small filet mignon, without salt or any sauce. I was running on nervous energy as well as determination." Still, she had to keep her figure under wraps, often wearing both a regular girdle and a chest girdle to flatten her bust.

In Paris a colleague introduced Willie to diet pills. No one cared what a model put into herself, as long as she performed. "I found myself walking along the Champs-Élysées with the cars coming towards me, but my body had no reaction whatsoever," she said. Finally she developed something she called the Hummingbird Diet and alternated it with binges.

Wilhelmina dated many men in her first years in New York. Early on "she was very involved with a tall dark actor," Jovanna Papadakis remembers. "I didn't care for him. She was making a lot of money, and he was using her." Wilhelmina knew that. "They take you out because they want to be seen with a beautiful woman," she said of New York's playboys. "It's easy here to be used as a display doll. But as a model, it's important to be seen at nightclubs and restaurants."

Then, in 1964, she met Bruce Cooper. Born in Ballard, Washington, Cooper later told reporters that he'd grown up in Shawnee, Oklahoma, served four years in the Navy, and entered show business as a San Francisco disc jockey. He later became an associate producer on *The Tonight Show,* where he booked guests and wrote questions for Johnny Carson. When Willie was nominated as one of the ten best-coiffed women in America, Cooper booked her for an appearance on the show. She forgot to plug the hair products she was meant to claim she used (although, in fact, she didn't), so afterward she was nearly hysterical. Cooper took her out for a martini. "I was fascinated at how fast she could change hairpieces," he later said.

They started dating, but Willie still played the field. "I was involved with a rich old man," she said, "who showered me with gifts—including a huge bouquet every day." He also provided her with a limousine. Cooper fought back. "Once in a while, I got a perfect rose from Bruce," Willie said. "It made me mad, but I never knew why. Sometimes I was actually rude to him."

Late in 1964 Cooper gave her a huge marquise-cut diamond ring, and they got married on the Las Vegas Strip in February 1965, with *The Tonight Show*'s Doc Severinson and Ed McMahon in attendance. In what their daughter, Melissa, later took as a sign of the pretense that characterized their relationship, their wedding photographs were staged after the actual event.

Handsome and fast-talking, Cooper presented a compelling facade. But behind it, says Melissa, there was turmoil. Bruce Cooper was a paradigm of the bad choices many models make in men. "We were all virgin princesses, and we all married creeps," ex-model Sunny Griffin observes. "Nice guys thought we were stuck on ourselves."

Cooper beat Wilhelmina. "A couple times she came to bookings with black eyes," remembers Kenneth Battelle. "There were products you could cover black eyes with. She had all that. But she never talked about it. It was a more disciplined time. You wouldn't spew your personal life out to anybody."

Indeed, Wilhelmina's problems with Bruce remained a secret for years. But after both her parents died, Melissa Cooper looked into her father's past and discovered its tragic dimensions. "Bruce's mother was most likely a prostitute," Melissa says. "She lied to him about who his real father was. He had seven fathers and a lot of uncles, and every night there was another man. She started him hating women. He was a misogynist in every sense."

After siring three children by his first wife, Cooper was divorced and married a neighbor. That marriage ended some time after he stabbed his second wife's first husband. Charged with attempted murder, he was briefly institutionalized. "Bruce left all that behind when he came east," Melissa says. Resettled in New York, he married his third wife, Bobbie, who was a house model at Hattie Carnegie and had come to Eileen Ford seeking more work. "He wouldn't give her any money," Eileen remembers. "Bruce Cooper was a brutal man." Adds Jerry: "He had creep written all over him." Soon, Bobbie was out and Willie was in.

The Coopers and their two poodles moved into a big apartment on Central Park. A zebraskin rug adorned Bruce's den. He'd left *The Tonight Show* and planned to become a manager of opera singers. She continued modeling for two years after their marriage. Now her dress size—12—was accommodated, not criticized. When a sample didn't fit her, stylists ripped open the back and underarm seams and pinned in matching linings to hide their work. Even the English admitted her importance. "Wilhelmina," the *Daily Express* declared in 1967, "puts the Shrimp and Twiggy in the shade."

But after seven years her bookings suddenly started dropping off. "She thought she was over the hill," remembers Fran Rothschild, a neighbor and a garment center bookkeeper. Then Irving Penn told Wilhelmina that Eileen Ford had said Willie was unavailable on a day when she was actually free. "Eileen took work away from her to give it to her new girls," Rothschild says Willie concluded.

Eileen had a *lot* of new girls. On their twentieth anniversary Jerry Ford told *The New York Times* that the agency was billing $100,000 a week. That money helped the Fords buy a new computer system, the first in the model business. They needed it. In 1967 they claimed their 175 female and 75 male models controlled 70 percent of the bookings in New York and 30 percent in the world. Ford's stars included *Harper's Bazaar* cover girl Dorothea McGowan, Agneta Darin, Babette of Switzerland, Dolores Hawkins, Dolores Ericson, who'd just appeared on the cover of jazz trumpeter Herb Alpert's *Whipped Cream and Other Delights,* and *Vogue*'s newest favorite, Lauren Hutton.

Another Ford star was Sunny Griffin, who'd replaced Wilhelmina as the agency's top model and was earning six figures a year. She'd come to New York from Baltimore in spring 1962 and joined Ford. Two years later, having hardly ever worked, Griffin was told the agency was cleaning out deadwood. "And you're it," Ford said. Griffin begged to be sent to Dorian Leigh in Paris instead. Nine months later Ford cabled her to come home immediately. A catalog studio wanted to put her under contract. Griffin also got a contract with Kayser-Roth, an underwear manufacturer. At first Ford told the company it was still the agency's policy to turn down underwear work, a holdover from the era of "objectionables." "They asked Eileen what it would take," Griffin remembers. "She said five hundred dollars an hour and five thousand dollars a year. They said yes. From then on, Ford models did lingerie."

By 1967 Griffin was part of the Ford family. "We'd go out to Quogue every weekend" to the Ford's huge beach house, she says. "If you were married, you were invited with your husband. Eileen cooked Friday night dinner, big pots of mussels. At Eileen's you always got enough to eat." Griffin remembers a family scene. The Fords' eldest daughter, Jamie, had gotten married and moved away, but the other three children were always there. "Katie and Lacey had to curtsy when they came in the room until they were sixteen," Griffin remembers. "Billy Ford lived on the fourth floor with all the Swedish models, having a good time, fucking them. Eileen was blind to it, but she finally figured it out," and young Billy had to give up his roommates.

Griffin thought Ford both eccentric and psychic. Griffin remembers, "She never looked at you, but the next day she'd tell you how many buttons you had buttoned. One day, when I first started, she grabbed me and started plucking my eyebrows. She scared me to death, but she was right. She was a great model agent. And she was a mother tiger to her models. One time a photographer exposed himself to Dorothea McGowan. He never worked again. Ford was that powerful."

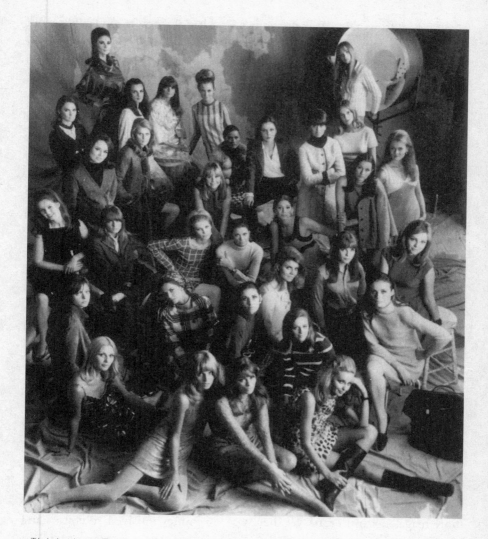

Thirty-two Ford models photographed by Ormond Gigli. *Top:* Wilhelmina; *left to right, second row from top:* Barbara Janssen, Tilly Tizani, Iris Bianchi, Sondra Paul, Melissa Congdon *(in front of light); third row:* Sondra Peterson, Hellevi Keko, Holly Forsman, Maria Gudy, Donna Mitchell, Diane Conlon, Agneta Frieberg, Dolores Hawkins, Agneta Darin; *fourth row:* Victoria Hilbert, Editha Dussler, Ann Turkel, Veronica Hamel, Renata Beck; *fifth row:* Babette, Margo McKendry, Astrid Schiller, Heather Hewitt, Helaine Carlin, Pia Christensen; *on floor:* Anne Larson, Heidi Wiedeck, Astrid Herrene, Sunny Griffin *(in stripes),* Samantha Jones *(in spots),* Ericha Stech *(sitting on stool)*

So it was no wonder Wilhelmina felt Ford had the power to take her work away and give it to models like Griffin. Says Jerry Ford: "It's a very familiar song. When a photographer uses a model a lot and then doesn't and then bumps into her, he doesn't say, 'You're too old.' He says, 'God, I've been trying to get you.' "

Regardless, Wilhelmina and Bruce decided to form an agency of their own. Cooper was "the engine," says their daughter, Melissa. "He had great ideas. She made them happen." But Willie deferred to Bruce. "He's the big boss," she said. They asked Rothschild to handle the numbers. "I knew nothing, except she was my friend," Rothschild says. "She gave me her diary, so I could learn how she worked. No one kept records like she did." With seed money of $200,000, they incorporated Wilhelmina Models on April 18, 1967.

When Wilhelmina opened on Madison Avenue that July, its namesake was the only model. "Everyone called and said, 'Thank God, now I can get her,' " Rothschild says. Willie's earnings—$17,000 in the first month alone, at the new star rate of $120 an hour—kept the agency afloat as she scouted for more talent. Other Ford models soon came. Dovima came, too. By 1967 she'd decided that "the producer and the casting couch life wasn't for me," she said. She returned to New York and joined Wilhelmina, where she was put to work interviewing aspiring models and helping Willie with the seminars she held on makeup and fashion flair.

But had Dovima really given up the casting couch routine? "Bruce was stuffing her," Carmen Dell'Orefice says flatly. "Everyone knew he was a monster, but we protected Willie. We loved her."

By 1969 European models booked half of Ford's business. There were more magazines in Europe, yet there was less money involved, so editors and photographers were more willing to take chances on new faces. And in a fashion world hooked on novelty, European models were something new. "They're green grass," said Jerry Ford, "and they know what they're doing when they arrive here."

New York was their mecca for a simple reason. "That's where the money is," Wilhelmina explained. So one of her first moves after opening her doors was to plan a trip to Europe to see the agents there. By the mid-sixties there were a lot to choose from. In Paris two competitors to Dorian Leigh had sprung up almost immediately.

Diane Gérald, Dorian Leigh's former assistant, had gone to work at a rental service called Paris Planning. Before long she and its owner, François Lano,

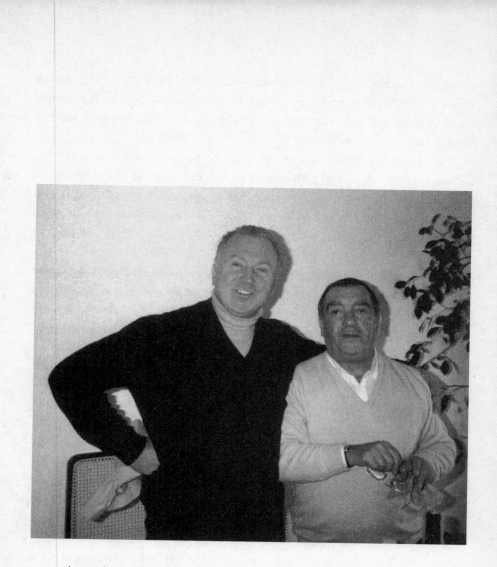

Agent and *rabatteur* Jacques de Nointel *(left)* and
François-Lano of the Paris Planning agency

turned it into a model agency, opening their doors on the rue Tronchet in October 1959. Leigh replaced Gérald with another young Frenchwoman named Catherine Harlé. But then she, too, left, announcing *she* was starting an agency, too.

Leigh had taken fees only from her clients—the magazines, advertisers, and fashion houses. "She asked fifty francs a month for the right to call anytime," Lano says. He decided to charge his models a commission as well. "I said, 'I'm not interested in this just to have groovy people around me. If I do this, I do it for money,' " he recalls.

Harlé opened shop in the Paris suburb of Levallois. Her first star was Nicole de la Margé. Discovered by an editor of *Jardin des Modes* magazine while working for a Paris dress wholesaler, the girlish Margé, mousy without makeup, was the quintessential French model of her era. "The age of the aloof model was over," she once said. "I was the anti-Suzy Parker—the girl next door could look like me." Moving to *Elle,* she became the girlfriend of art director and photographer Peter Knapp and the magazine's visual image, appearing on about 150 covers before quitting the business in the late sixties. After marrying a journalist for *Paris Match,* she died in a car crash in the early seventies.

Dorian hadn't been resting as all this agency opening was going on. In 1960 she'd met Paul Harker, a wealthy businessman who co-owned Mirabelle, one of London's leading restaurants, and Annabel, a private club. He offered to finance an agency in London. But Leigh loved life a little too much, and that eventually proved her undoing. "Dorian was a very big drinker," says Stéphane Lanson, then a male model with Harlé. When she wasn't drinking, she was usually with a man. Photographer Brian Duffy, for instance. He was one of six men Leigh slept with late in 1960, when she decided to have another child, following the collapse of a brief marriage to her gynecologist. That same year Leigh was evicted from her apartment in Paris when her landlord discovered she was running her business there. The Fords came to her rescue with a $16,000 loan for key money on a new place.

In 1963 Dorian hooked up with Iddo Ben-Gurion, a distant relative of Israeli leader David Ben-Gurion. "He arrived in my agency, looking glorious, of course, and said he'd written a book and named one of the main characters after me," Leigh remembers. "He announced he was going to make me famous and we were going to get married. Eventually I got worn down by his salesmanship." Leigh introduced Iddo to the Fords when they came to Paris in spring 1964, and they adored him. The couple's wedding caused Dorian's

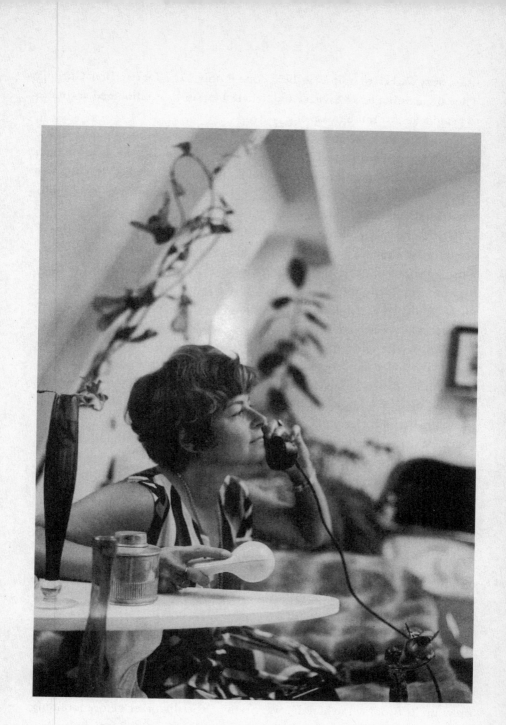

Catherine Harlé in her Paris agency in 1965

sister, Suzy Parker, to quip that she'd done it only to be Dorian Ben-Gurion. They honeymooned in Switzerland, where Dorian kept numbered accounts to avoid taxes, en route to Israel.

Over the course of the next two years Dorian Leigh's agency died. "Her business was failing," says Eileen Ford. She'd already lost the London and Hamburg offices. The Fords hoped Iddo would add stability. But models weren't being paid. "Dorian wasn't on top of her business," says Jerry Ford. "The competition was outstripping her."

Then Iddo Ben-Gurion disappeared. Dorian says, "I discovered that I owed a lot of money to models because Iddo was jogging to the agency every morning and picking up the mail. He'd opened a numbered account in Germany and was depositing all the checks. I went to the bank in Germany and proved to the bank that none of my signatures or the models' signatures were true. He had even taken out a Diners Club card and signed my name."

Leigh says she called Eileen Ford in New York and told her what had happened. She added her suspicion that Iddo was on drugs. (Several years later Ben-Gurion died of an overdose.) But the Fords didn't believe her. "He was a good guy to my knowledge," says Eileen. "Iddo was the most wonderful man in the world," Jerry adds.

Months later Leigh heard what happened after her call to the Fords. "The minute you called about Iddo, Eileen picked up the phone and called François Lano at Paris Planning and said, 'Would you like to work with me?' " Leigh was told.

"We had to do something," says Jerry. "Dorian was not in the game. We knew she felt she owned us and we shouldn't talk to anyone else. That was the beginning of the fallout. We told Dorian we had to work with someone else. We felt badly about it. But we never proposed we not work together. There was no question who our favorite was. We wanted to help Dorian."

Bobby Freedman, a businessman-around-town and friend of both Dorian and the Fords, intervened. Freedman was best friends with Bernie Cornfeld. "Bernie said, 'Why don't I back you?' " says Dorian. Cornfeld was part of the new postwar jet set, one of the rich businessmen who hopped from continent to continent, living the good life. Born in Istanbul, Turkey, in 1927, Cornfeld grew up in Brooklyn, where he was briefly a social worker before founding Investors Overseas Services in 1958. A onetime socialist and flamboyant salesman, Cornfeld claimed he created IOS, which grew into a $2.5 billion banking, mutual fund, insurance, and investment trust empire in the go-go sixties, to "convert the proletariat to the leisure classes painlessly."

In 1969 Cornfeld took IOS public, but he lost control of the company in 1970, after its share value had dropped from a high of $25 to about $1. He resigned from its board the following year, after turning control of the company over to financier Robert Vesco, who, he claimed, "walked off with the cash box." In 1973 Cornfeld was arrested for fraud and jailed in Switzerland for almost a year, but he was later acquitted. Vesco, charged by the Securities and Exchange Commission with siphoning more than $200 million from IOS, remains a fugitive.

In the 1960s Cornfeld was still riding high. "I was friendly with Eileen and Jerry Ford," he says. "They had absolutely stunning women, and every time I was in town, they would organize a party and let the girls know these were people they should be marrying, or if not marrying, then fucking." One weekend Jerry Ford asked him to look over their company. "It was our dream at that moment to get Dorian and François together," Ford says. "I'd tried to buy Paris Planning, but I had no money. Bernie said he'd invest, but he wanted us to merge with Dorian."

Cornfeld looked at Ford's books, "and the bottom line was only fifty thousand dollars," he says. "They lived off the agency. So I put together a plan for them to buy an agency in each key area of Europe. I was going to finance the acquisition and arrange to have it go public."

The deal fell apart, Cornfeld says, after Eileen Ford was rude to a girl Bobby Freedman was seeing. "She wanted to be a model," Cornfeld says, "so Bobby arranged for her to meet Eileen. Eileen kept her waiting a couple hours and then said her mouth wasn't right, her nose wasn't right, she'd never be a model. Eileen's not a bad gal, but the girl left her office devastated and in tears."

Cornfeld then met Dovima. After two years at Wilhelmina, she was ready to move on. Just months after joining the Coopers, she'd written a proposal seeking backers for her own business. "The time has arrived for the Dovima Agency to appear," it said. In fact, it hadn't, but Dovima kept trying and finally she opened Talent Management International for Cornfeld.

TMI, as it was known, never really had a chance. It did respectably. But with Cornfeld's legal problems mounting, he shut it down. Thus Dovima's career ended. Soon she was a salesgirl at an Ohrbach's clothing store. After contracting pneumonia, she moved to Florida in 1974 to be near her parents and took a job in a dress shop. "I have put away my false eyelashes," she said.

Finally, she found happiness when she met West C. Hollingworth, a bartender in a restaurant on the Intercoastal Waterway where she worked as a hostess. "She finally met somebody who loved her," says her model colleague Ruth Neumann. "She didn't care that she was waiting tables." She married Hollingworth in 1983. The next year she got another hostess job in Fort Lauderdale's Two Guys Pizzeria. But somehow, Dovima couldn't avoid a tragic script. Hollingworth died in 1986, and soon afterwards she discovered she had breast cancer and had a mastectomy. For the next four years she remained in Fort Lauderdale, alone, scared, and often "drunk as a skunk," says model Nancy Berg. Dovima died in 1990. In a show of loyalty that still brings a catch to Eileen Ford's throat, Dovima named her ex-agent her estate administrator.

"I went to open her safe-deposit box," says Ford. "She only had a hundred dollars in it."

The next intrigue in the European model war paired Paris Planning's François Lano and his rival, Dorian Leigh, who conspired to gang up on the Fords. "Jerry had offered to work exclusively with François, and François was stupid enough to believe it!" Leigh says. "They told every agency that. I said to François, 'Eileen won't let you get big. She should pay us! We find them, we train them, and we never hear from them again.' Eileen was double-dealing everybody. She was running every agency in France and Italy!"

Once the Paris agents started talking, they agreed to take action. "We formed an association of model agents in Paris," Leigh says. "I felt we should all work together and get proper payment from New York for the girls we were finding and developing."

On Lincoln's Birthday 1966 Leigh and Lano flew to New York to present an ultimatum. The luncheon meeting went badly. Lano and Leigh took the position that they shouldn't pay commissions because they trained Ford's young models. "But they wanted *us* to pay," says Jerry Ford, "and we wouldn't."

"It was awful," says Leigh. "Looking me in the face, Jerry said to François, 'Why work with Dorian? We'll pay you to work with us. We'll destroy her.' François said, 'Dorian, we made a deal, but since they don't want you, I'll make my own deal with the Fords.' By offering François exclusivity and money, she broke off our very tenuous relationship."

Says Lano: "It was impossible to stop working with Eileen." Nonetheless, Dorian was about to.

Every couture season in Paris the Fords paid for Dorian to throw a party. But when Eileen called from Rome in 1967 to make the arrangements, she couldn't get Leigh on the phone. Eileen told Jerry something was wrong. He told her she was being ridiculous. If she didn't get through from Rome, certainly she'd talk to Dorian in Paris. But a few days later, when Eileen arrived at the Hôtel St. Régis, she still hadn't made contact. So when Hiro, a *Bazaar* photographer, suggested they go to the party together, Eileen reluctantly agreed. The fete was in a photographer's studio. "Dorian was at the door," Ford says. "She'd had a sip or two. She said, 'What are you doing here?' I said, 'Do you want me to leave?'"

"You can leave by the door or I can throw you down the stairs" was Leigh's acid reply. A few days later the entire exchange was printed in a New York gossip column. The Fords still blame Leigh for the item. The twenty-year love affair between the mothers of modeling was at an end.

The Fords soon began working with a new agency, Models International, formed by the husbands of two European models, Simone d'Aillencourt and Christa Fiedler. Dorian had booked them both and believes their spouses "saw how much money they made and thought, Why should Dorian get ten percent of it?" she says.

Now, cut off from the Fords *and* from two of her top earners, Dorian was flying from New York to Paris when Jacques Chambrun introduced himself. He was a literary agent, representing Somerset Maugham and Grace Metalious, the writer of *Peyton Place,* among others. He also owned *16* magazine in New York. "He had been a priest," Leigh deadpans, "and he was very interested in models, and he said, 'I understand that you're having financial difficulties.' I gave parties twice a year, and I traveled to find models, and I said to Jacques, 'I really can't afford to travel anymore to find models.' He said, 'I'd be glad to go with you and pay for it.' So we went to Copenhagen and then to Sweden, and he paid for it all. In the course of that, I met a Swedish girl, a nurse, and asked her to come to Paris to model. Jacques fell madly in love with her, and she moved into his house on Avenue Foch, and she went to New York, worked with Eileen. In the meantime, Jacques would pay for the receptions that I gave. I gave parties at his house on Avenue Foch for Elizabeth Taylor and the Maharani of Baroda. I cooked cassoulet for a hundred forty people."

But Dorian's parties at Chambrun's *hôtel particulier* were known for more than her cooking. Nude girls cavorted in the basement pool, visible through an underwater window in his bar. "I thought, He gets his kicks because he's so unattractive that he just likes to watch beautiful young girls and men having a wonderful time," Leigh says. "And he liked to feel that I was his friend."

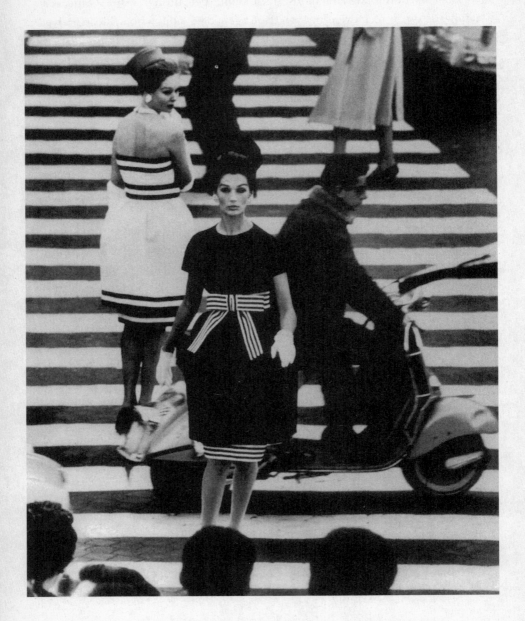

Simone d'Aillencourt *(foreground)* and Nina Devos
photographed by William Klein in Rome in 1960

She asked him to lend her $16,000 to pay her outstanding debt to the Fords. Chambrun had his lawyer draw up papers. But then the lawyer called Leigh, "in shock," she says, and told her Chambrun was *buying* her agency for $16,000. Dorian called off the deal. Then Chambrun called her. "You'll still invite me to your parties?" he asked.

By 1970 Leigh's business was nearing insolvency when, with impeccable timing, Bernie Cornfeld turned up again. "I remember sitting at the lunch table with Dorian and Bernie," says Jérôme Bonnouvrier, who went to work for his aunt Catherine Harlé in 1967. "He looked at her like a prostitute. He pulled out a pack of five-hundred-French-franc notes and told her he wouldn't do business with her, but he'd help her. Dorian threw the money back at him."

Leigh soon lost her apartment and was forced to sell all her belongings. "She'd entertained all of Paris, and suddenly no one was around," says Bonnouvrier. Finally Dorian Leigh closed, "merging" with Catherine Harlé to save face and celebrating with a party at Jacques Chambrun's house, featuring naked girls in the swimming pool.

"That's when my darling friends got together and said, 'You've been cooking for your friends for years, you might as well do it for a living,' " Leigh recalls. With investments of $1,000 each from several photographers, she opened a restaurant in Fontainebleau, outside Paris, the next summer, and spent the next four years there. She was well rid of the modeling business. "I could no longer ask a beautiful girl to be a model," she says. "I couldn't say it would be a wonderful life."

LAUREN HUTTON

I'm like, almost a grown-up,"
Lauren Hutton says from the vantage of age fifty-one. She's en route to New
Guinea to make a network television show on its natives, among the last
primitives in the world. Although she's spent a quarter century in the Western world's most sophisticated set, Hutton's interests have always been native,
as evidenced by the tableful of ethnic jewelry, the tusks, skulls, and skeletons
that surround her in her loft apartment in Manhattan's trendy NoHo district.

Raised in the Florida swamps, the gap-toothed Hutton is as strong as she is
striking. Her resilience has served her well. After a ten-year career as one of
America's top models, she made history in late 1973, when she signed the first
exclusive modeling contract in the cosmetics business, agreeing to pose only
for Revlon's Ultima brand in exchange for $400,000 to be paid over two
years. The number sounds small today, but back then, it was groundbreaking.
Richard Avedon, who often photographed her, explained Hutton's appeal in
1974, when she appeared on the cover of *Newsweek*. She's "the link between
the dream and the drugstore," he said.

Once she signed her contract, Hutton headed to Hollywood, where she
appeared in films like *Paper Lion; The Gambler; Welcome to L.A.; Gator; Zorro, the
Gay Blade;* and *American Gigolo.* Her association with Revlon ended in 1984.
Then Hutton was rediscovered in the late eighties. An appearance in an ad for
Barneys New York revived her career and led to a new three-year seven-figure
deal with Revlon. In her wake two entire generations of models aged thirty
to fifty returned to the scene. "Suddenly," she says with a happy laugh, "I'm
an everyday working model again." And earning a lot more money than she
did the first time around.

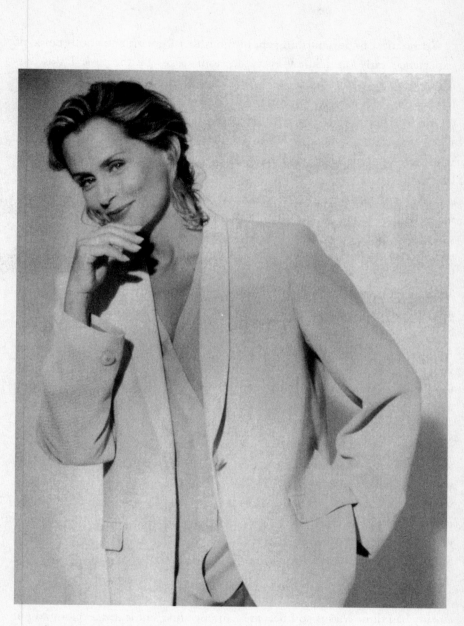

Lauren Hutton photographed by Luca Babini in 1994

* * *

"The most important thing about me is that I got an enormous range of experience early on. I knew every economic class by the time I was ten. Mother worked from the time I was born—November 17, 1943. My father left before Mother knew she was pregnant. I was the pregnantee. In my earliest life I lived in Charleston, with my godparents, who were millionaires back when that meant something. Then I was in Miami with an aunt and uncle who were solid middle-middle-class, comfortable and full of love and joy, and that saved me.

"My aunt Gaga was my caretaker. But I remember that Mother was a major fashion freak. She had crocodile shoes, and she got her hair combed out every day. She was basically raised to marry a rich man. When I was six, mother married Jack Hall, who was an Ozark Mountains Texas-type guy. Hall had some money, and Mother had an inheritance, and the next thing I knew, I was taken off by my mother and this complete total stranger to a mountain in the middle of nowhere in Missouri, where they invested in a development business; but it went bust, and we ended up in a swamp that became part of Tampa. My stepfather got a job as a milkman and worked his way up, but we were seriously poor for a very long time. We ran cottage industries to keep food on the table. We had a nursery in the backyard, and I raised fishing worms. I had a serious live wriggler business.

"When I was a teenager, I thought I was ugly, tall, and gawky. A lot changed the summer after high school. Boys discovered me. I had sort of turned beautiful or something. But I recently met my class president, and he said, 'Mary, you weren't ugly, you were beautiful, but you had ideas. You terrified us.' I went to the University of South Florida for a year. Then I fell in love with an older man; he was thirty-eight. I think it was because I hadn't known my father. He came to New York, and I followed him. I thought New York was the center of the world. People came down from there and drove very fast through the swamp and sprayed you with mud. Those were New Yorkers.

"I got a job as a bunny in the Playboy Club. It was just opening. They already had three Marys, so I became Laurence first, but it was too long to put on the bunny tag, so I remembered the great Bacall and that's when I became Lauren. I was too young to be a night bunny, so I was a day bunny. I spent the whole day in the dark. After about four months I knew that I had to get out of there. I ended up in New Orleans.

"I wanted to go back to school. Sophie Newcomb was there, and they accepted me. I looked around for a job. Al Hirt, the trumpet player, had just released 'Java,' and he'd bought a club there. The day it opened I got a job there. I was going to school by day, and by night I would put on a gold wig and be a Grecian goddess at Al Hirt's. I learned more on Bourbon Street than I did at Sophie Newcomb. Practical information. I found out all kinds of things. The police took graft. The mayor and the Mafia would sit at the same table. I served them! It was also a thrilling time. I got about four hours of sleep a night for about a year and a half. After that it got to me. I had a sort of physical collapse. So I ran away.

"I went back down to Florida, rented a house on the beach with the little money I'd saved, and slept and slept and fed seagulls for two or three months. Then I saw an article about Africa. All the game was disappearing. I decided to catch a tramp steamer there. I borrowed two hundred dollars from my mother, and I took a cheap flight to New York. I landed at Kennedy at like six A.M. I got in a taxi, and I couldn't remember a single place except Tiffany's. I had never seen that movie, but that to me was the heart of New York. So he let me off at that corner at seven-thirty in the morning on a Sunday, and there was no one around. I started crying. I didn't know what to do, and then I finally remembered a girl at the Playboy Club, and I called information, and sure enough, she was there, and she had this great boyfriend named Arnie and he was just a lifesaver.

"Somehow I found out that the tramp steamer I thought I was taking to Africa wasn't leaving for quite a while. And to tell you the truth, unconsciously, I knew New York was my beanstalk and I was Jack with my three beans, my two hundred dollars. I understood what money was. I'd seen my mother's life changed radically because of losing it. I understood very well it brought you freedom. But I had no role models. I couldn't imagine the life I wanted.

"I had to get a job, but I didn't want to cocktail waitress again because it was really debilitating. Arnie showed me how to look in the paper for a job. He pointed to an ad and said, 'You can do this. You look like a model.' Now I'd been told that all my life, but Arnie knew what he was talking about, so I went to Christian Dior. They were about to turn me down when I said the magic words 'I'll work for anything.' So they gave me fifty dollars a week, which was way below the minimum wage. But I got the job. I found an apartment downtown with two other girls. I lived on twenty-five-cent chicken pot pies. My money went for bus fare and dry-cleaning my one dress once a week on the weekend.

"One day I was walking by Washington Square Apartments. I remembered that a girl who had been in the Playboy Club used to live there. I rang the doorbell, and she was there. Now, for the five or six months that I had been in New York, I had been hearing constantly, as soon as people found out I was single, 'Oh, you should meet ——!' So one of the first things this ex-bunny said to me was 'You should meet Bob Williamson!' I didn't think twice about that because I'd heard it so much. Then she took me to *the* hipster joint downtown. It was called Duke's Cube.

"I had not had a single date in New York. I wouldn't go on dates because I knew I was easy. I'd lived with the first man I slept with, so I was afraid to even go on a date. I was looking for heart and brains and a lot of information. So I'd been interviewing boyfriends over tea at Chock Full o'Nuts. We always went Dutch. I must have interviewed about forty guys! I didn't like anybody. So we wandered into this little restaurant, and Bob Williamson was there. He knew a lot about a tremendous number of things I was interested in. Everything that I liked the sound of, he seemed to have read every book written on the subject—from Ezra Pound to Harry James to William Burroughs to LSD to anything about Africa. He even knew about bugs and snakes, and I had a bug collection and used to raise snakes. So we started to date. One day we were sitting at the outside table at Duke's Cube and he said, 'You're not really going to Africa.' I thought, No, I don't want to leave this guy. I'm *not* going to Africa.

"'Round about that same time Christian Dior tried to force me into signing a three-year contract starting at fifty dollars a week and going to one hundred fifteen dollars the third year. When I told Williamson, he said, 'That's ridiculous. You should be a photography model. They make fifty dollars an hour, for God's sake!'

"I was afraid not to sign this Dior contract because I was desperately afraid of losing my secure job. But I got the idea from Williamson that he would disrespect anyone who was so lame that they would sign it, and I blew them off. I'd met Gillis MacGil, who ran Mannequin, and she would call me when there were little jobs, and I started doing showroom modeling once every two weeks to make enough money to go on go-sees, and try and get a book together. I got the names of two or three photographers. One guy did catalog stuff and took some pictures of me. The other guy was a wonderful man named Carl Shiraishi, and for three weekends we just shot pictures, and he basically made my book.

"Finally I went to Frances Gill, Plaza Five, and Stewart, and they all turned me down; but they would always tell me why, and I would try to fix everything. I had been doing this for a while, and I figured it was time to go to Eileen, and she basically told me the same things everyone else had. I was on my way out of her office, desperate, because that was the last agency there was and I'd saved the best for last, when I saw a picture of some kids on the wall, and I said, 'Oh, is your son in college? I just left college.' She looked up. She was already on the phone, but she said, 'Where'd you go?' And I said, 'Sophie Newcomb.' I was burning with shame. I was being pushy or obvious, all these horrible things you're taught never to do down South, but I did it, and she said, 'Sophie Newcomb!' I sat right down. She accepted me because I'd gone there. I guess she thought it meant there was more to me than met the eye.

"I was on what they called the junior board to see if I would last or not. My booker would make appointments, three or four a day, and then I would make another six. It was dizzying. I would get little nibbles. A little job here, a little job there. I also did a lot of fittings, because I had a perfect size eight body. And finally, at month seven, I was doing a fitting for Cathy di Montezemolo, and she looked at me funny one day and said, 'Come on up to *Vogue*.' I told my booker that she wanted me. My booker went crazy. I had to go to *Vogue* one afternoon like three days later and try on the clothes for the real models that couldn't come. There were three fitting models. We weren't humans; we were just bodies.

"We were in this huge red room with windows all along one side, window seats, and a shiny black lacquer desk. And there at the desk at the end of the room, with these little white gloves on and this hairdo and this nose and these burning eyes, was this raptor, an empress raptor. I've always loved raptors and snakes, and there she was. Diana Vreeland. I had not heard much about her. But I could tell she was some sort of serious cheese.

"Along one side was a couch, and on that couch were maybe eight editors. Gloria Schiff, Babs Simpson, Cathy di Montezemolo, Polly Mellen, Nicky de Gunzburg with his Cartier lighters. We were just scurrying around. Nobody ever noticed models. So I tried on some things, and she was playing these games. She'd say these horrible things you've never heard before and hang some of these editors out with the wash, and they'd all say, 'How divine,' and she'd say, 'But not really.'

"Finally, after we'd been there about an hour or so, I just stopped. I sat on this window seat, and I completely forgot myself. I thought I was hidden by the racks and these other girls were marching around. Vreeland was in the

middle of a sentence, talking about the dress. 'It's too poor, it's simply too—
You!' I remember this glove, this long finger on the glove, pointing to me in
the middle of a sentence. I said, 'Me?' And she said, 'Yes, you have quite a *presence!*' I didn't quite know what that meant. But I said, 'Boy, so do you.'

"She made a face and went right back into the middle of her sentence. But
as we were all filing out, she said, 'You, come back.' I was alone with her. She
said, 'So, what do you do? How long have you been doing it? Have you a
book?' I said, 'Yes, I do.' She opened it up, and she stopped over pictures that
Eileen had hated, that were taken by a wonderful photographer named Lee
Kraft, and she said, 'I'm sending you to Dick Avedon tomorrow.' I said, 'Oh,
but I don't think so. I've seen him several times.' And she gave me this funny
smile-smirk and said, 'I think he will. You're working with him tomorrow!' It
was an eight-page spread, still some of the best pictures ever taken of me, leaping in the air.

"I became Dick's great model after all the big couture girls died. Being
with Dick was like being with another kid in the playground. *Vogue* would
put out these huge tables with two hundred pairs of shoes and another table
just piled with jewelry. *Vogue* was a huge, serious operation, but the studio was
a wonderland of make-believe. Dick and I would plow through all these
things and dress me up and tell each other stories. He would demonstrate little things past girls did with his own body, and he cross-pollinated all the girls.
He would show me a foot movement of Shrimpton's, and I'd do it my way.
He'd show Twiggy something of Veruschka's. And I've since seen Stephanie
Seymour in a pose that I discovered.

"What was funny was that *Bazaar* and *Vogue* worked together. Dick Avedon and Hiro shared a studio on Fifty-eighth Street, just around the corner
from Bloomingdale's, and *Bazaar* was on one side with Hiro, and Dick was on
the other side for *Vogue,* and they had a common reception room. In those
days the editors lived and died for fashion, and they would grab you physically
if you tried to talk to a model from *Bazaar.* It was all this huge drama and fits,
yelling and screaming and carrying on. It was high fashion. It was fabulous.
There was even a fan club of fashion students outside. We didn't know it then,
but Steven Meisel was the head cheerleader.

"Once I was in *Vogue,* that was that. I was off the junior board. The same
month I came out on my first *Vogue* cover, November 1966, I had a *Mademoiselle* cover, which was a first. What did Ford have to do with it? All Ford did
was take me on. They were a billing and booking service. And they charged
ten percent, but it was well worth it.

"I was twenty-two by then, so I was late getting started. I learned in the dressing rooms from the giant Germans. I would be sitting with Astrid Herrene, Brigitta Klercker, or Brigitte Bauer, or Veruschka, and I would watch them. We didn't have makeup men. Those girls were all artists at doing makeup. I was constantly inventing and reinventing myself in makeup. I learned the hard way. If they had makeup men, they were leftovers from the fifties. They'd do a job, you'd think you looked horrible. Then you'd wait for the ad to come out, and you wouldn't be in it!

"I was continually awestruck. I was constantly seeing things that I had never seen before, like that red room. But I never lost my goal. I was in it for the money. I always tried to remember that, and I always tried to remember, when money started rolling in, that most people made in a month what I made in a week. Now, of course, I make it in a minute.

"I had six jobs every day. Six photographers, six sets of hair and makeup, and ten suits from the ad agency who just wanted to see the models. Ten, twenty different people, five of whom were touching you. It's a big mental strain. I remember this one photographer, one of the most extraordinary lames I've ever met. He didn't know what he was doing. To make his pictures printable, barely, I had to tell him how to move his lights. I did the whole thing according to what I had been taught by the greats, but without telling him, of course, because photographers had this attitude. The worse they were, the less you could suggest to them. You had to do it without them knowing. I became a master at making them think it was their idea. So after going through all these hoops so we could get the picture, I remember him sitting behind his big eight-by-ten camera, saying, 'No wonder Penn is Penn! He gets to work with models like you!' He really was indignant, this guy. I never saw him again, and neither did anyone else.

"I had done five, six *Vogue* covers before I did catalogs. I had to learn. It took me months. They would cut the dresses apart on you and straight-pin them back on you, stuffed with toilet paper. They had giant eight-by-ten cameras, and you had to stand there with your face alive, but not moving for twenty minutes, in a walking position! If you moved anything, the dress would fall apart.

"*Vogue* models were making around five hundred, six hundred dollars a week, maybe they'd get a four-hundred-dollar booking for some ad that was snobby enough for them, and they'd go out and buy an eight-hundred-dollar dress! I remember giving lectures in the dressing room about saving your money, about making money, about taxes. They hadn't heard about taxes. We were in a fifty-three percent tax bracket. Before I bought any-thing, I would think to myself; 'Ten percent to the agency, fifty-three per-cent to the government.'

"I worked solid for the first year, and at the end of the year Williamson said, 'OK, guess what? I think it's time to go to Africa.' And that's what we did. Bob gave me great advice. There's so much stress and strain, and you can be gasping for air so hard in this business that if you don't just take off and for-get it completely and rest and sleep, you lose your real face, you lose your spirit, you lose everything. Your smiles become fake. You're so tired you have nothing to smile about. After the first two or three years I got to the position where I would be two months on, two months off. Bob was wonderful about making sure that happened. And for about sixteen years, every year we went to Africa, we went to South America, we went to Asia. I don't think I would have made it without him.

"I worked steadily for ten years. I started when I was twenty-two, and I signed my Revlon contract in 1974, when I was thirty-two. That was when Catfish Hunter came around. He signed a three-point-seven-five-million-dollar contract with the Yankees, and that started me thinking. I asked Williamson how to do it. Most of these things were my ideas, but I didn't know how to go about setting them in motion. Williamson set them all up. He knew nothing about the modeling business, but he's extremely intelligent and had enormous common sense.

"Williamson told me to call Eileen and have her tell all my photogra-phers—Dick, Penn, everybody—that I wouldn't work for the day rate any-more. I wanted a contract. Dick got it instantly. He thought it was a great idea. He decided I should try for an exclusive contract, so I'd work only for Revlon *and* I'd get more money. So he started talking to Revlon and became a coconspirator in this. We did tests together that we showed [Revlon owner] Charles Revson. Revson hated me. Revlon used me my first year in the busi-ness but never again for ten years, even though I was the biggest star around. I had the gap in my teeth; I was short and sort of funny-faced. I wasn't a Revlon swan.

"Dick was very smart politically. He told Revson he had an idea, he wanted to give Ultima Two its own look, but he wanted a free hand. We did tests together, and he showed them to Revson, and Revson didn't recognize me. He said, 'Who is that?' Dick said, 'Lauren.' I got a contract for three years. It was designed by Bob Williamson, and it became the basis of every contract that followed.

"For the next eight years I worked for Revlon twenty days a year. Otherwise I was off making movies and traveling. I didn't really care about modeling anymore. I was making five movies a year and making much more money than I had modeling. But the movies I was making weren't the movies I was watching. And except for a handful, they became less and less enjoyable, and I learned less and less making them. So I was creatively unfulfilled. And I rarely modeled anymore. The jobs dried up after I hit forty. Finally I stopped looking at fashion magazines altogether. They hurt my feelings. I was getting older and older, and the girls were getting younger and younger.

"Then two things happened at once. I was in Yugoslavia making my last movie when Jerry Ford called about the Barneys ad and I said no. He called five times, and I kept saying no. He insisted, and Steven Meisel took the pictures. I'd been spending a lot of time alone. One Sunday I was sitting in an Indian restaurant, reading the *Times,* and there was this full-page ad of this beautiful woman—not a girl—and I didn't recognize that it was me. Then I did, and I felt like I'd been punched in the heart. Meisel was the first photographer I'd worked with in years who didn't try to shoot me as if I were a young girl. After that I got stopped by women on the street who said, 'Thank you, we've been invisible for a decade.'

"Then my leg got broken in an accident, and for four months I was in bed, and I was on crutches for five months after that. Everything stopped. I was by myself—no radio, no TV—in a fishing cottage in Montauk, Long Island. I dreamed, I thought, and I read. Bob would come on weekends and bring groceries. I realized that my life had gone out of control, and I hadn't liked it in a long time. The distractions in New York are limitless, and for years I'd gone out every night and never faced myself. My best movie, *American Gigolo,* was made when I was thirty-eight, and I started to study acting at thirty-nine. The parts were getting worse and worse while I was getting better and better. My creative energy was eating me alive.

"By your mid-40s, if you haven't resolved your childhood problems, quiet desperation takes over, and in my case it wasn't so quiet. Nothing was ever cemented down for me. My life had had too many extremes. I had made Bob responsible for so much of my life I no longer felt I owned it. We drifted in different directions. So I sat down and decided to face myself. I changed a lot.

"The Barneys ads had made me understand that it wasn't just me who'd been hurt by fashion ads. I understood it was a historical, societal problem and that if I quit movies and went full tilt back into modeling, I could be of use *and* keep the wolf from the door. Until then nobody was interested in us. This was a historical fact for hundreds of years: As soon as they were out of eggs, women were out of business. Those pictures showed you could be good-looking and sexually attractive after forty. I finally understood that it wasn't just me who'd become invisible in the eighties. It was my whole generation, and none of us liked it very much, and we did not want to go quiet into that good night.

"Ever since the feminist revolt women have gone into every profession except what may be the most important one. They'd had absolutely no control over the physical image of women. Most photographers only shoot girls, and when they see a woman, they don't know what to do. So I started calling every editor I knew. British and German *Vogue* got it first and did wonderful stories about me and that idea. After that there was no stopping us. I spent the next two years talking and working. I found you *could* change your life. It's a tall order, but it can be done. I also met Luca Babini, a wonderful Italian photographer who liked women, and we fell in love.

"I've never been prouder of anything in my life than I have been of these last three years. Models are the physical mirror of femininity. They *should* come in all sizes, shapes, and ages, and now they do. If my two careers mean anything, it's that. I found a way not just to get what I wanted out of it—to educate myself and see the world—but also to be of use to everybody else. I think maybe I helped make what seemed to be the most superficial profession into one that's important."

$120 AN HOUR

"The sixties were about person-alities," Diana Vreeland wrote in her autobiography, *D. V.* "It was the first time when mannequins *became* personalities . . . these girls invented *themselves*. Naturally, as an editor, I was there to help them along."

Richard Avedon had just finished photographing and editing the entire April 1965 issue of *Bazaar*—with Jean Shrimpton on the cover—by himself and, after twenty years, was renegotiating his contract. "I felt they should treat me well, and they were very rough about it," he says. Nonetheless, he shook hands with Hearst on a new ten-year deal.

"Your contract should be ending," Vreeland said when she called him that night. He said he'd just made a new deal. She countered, "Will you at least hear what we have to say?" Two days later Avedon met with Alexander Liberman. Condé Nast's president, Iva Patcévitch, flew in from Europe to clinch the deal, and within days Avedon signed and collected an unprecedented million-dollar advance. "Then I vomited for about two weeks without stopping," he says. "I learned everything at *Bazaar,* and now I was going to 'the enemy camp.' "

The loss of Avedon marked the end of *Bazaar*'s creative preeminence. Under Vreeland, *Vogue* rose inexorably and "took first place," Alexander Liberman says. Within months fashion stylist Polly Mellen joined *Vogue,* too, and found herself at the red-hot center of the decade. Exotic was the new norm. *Vogue* became home to Edie and Andy, Courrèges and the Kinks. Irving Penn shot faucets dripping Harry Winston diamonds. Bert Stern shot Marilyn Monroe in the nude. Where just a moment before, "clothes were totally structured, you wore a hat and gloves and smoked, and it was all about gesture," says Polly Mellen. Suddenly fashion loosened up. "The flower children, the new culture, were coming forward," she adds. "It was all parties, drugs, and madness, and the girls who chose to be part of it were the girls who were booked. Everything became more eccentric, more strange."

Exotic-looking society girls like Ingrid Boulting, Penelope Tree, and Marisa Berenson became stars of the moment, thanks to another Vreeland innovation: She published their names in the magazine. Berenson, the daughter of a diplomat and granddaughter of the couturier Elsa Schiaparelli, was born in New York and raised in Europe. She started modeling in 1964 as "a young, up-and-coming debutante" studying decorating in London, she says. Her first photographs were taken by David Bailey for British *Vogue.* "From then on I worked for *Vogue* practically every day of my life," Berenson says. "My career literally took off." She worked with every great photographer of her time, including Avedon, Newton, Stern, Jimmy Moore, Sokolsky, Beaton, and Henry Clarke. "I was a cover girl," she says. "I was lucky. I didn't find myself beautiful. I was a baby, the child of *Vogue.*" Berenson modeled until 1970, when she met Luchino Visconti, who cast her in his film *Death in Venice* and launched her on a new career as an actress.

Filmmaker Roy Boulting's daughter, Ingrid, left her broken home at sixteen for London and became a reluctant model with English Boy. She was rediscovered by Polly Mellen just after her arrival at *Vogue.* Boulting was visiting the magazine with Marisa Berenson's sister, Berry, a photographer, when Mellen saw her and screamed down a corridor, "*You!*" The next day Boulting was shooting pre-Raphaelite photographs with Richard Avedon.

"It was so bizarre," she says. "Those shots had such impact that everyone wanted to work with me." She escaped to Belgium to act in a play, but Eileen Ford followed and begged her to come back. She posed for several years more, but her heart wasn't in it. "I'd sit there and stare at these beautiful girls and think, What am I doing here?" she says. "I made a commitment to Ford to be available more, but I could only take so much. My heart wasn't in it. I wasn't money-oriented. Eileen would have parties, and there'd be producers. I went to a couple, but they were lonely experiences. There was no intimacy. And I had the feeling I was invited for reasons other than my presence." Finally Boulting quit and returned to her first love, acting.

The daughter of Ronald Tree, a British multimillionaire, and Marietta Peabody, the daughter of an Episcopal bishop, Penelope Tree was bred for great things. Her mother was a patrician activist who became the first woman delegate to the United Nations. Her half sister, Frances FitzGerald, became a

Pulitzer Prize–winning author for reporting on the war in Vietnam. A lank-haired five-foot-ten exotic with wide, painted eyes, Penelope first modeled at age thirteen for Diane Arbus. Her father told Arbus he'd sue her if she ever published the picture. At fifteen she was shot again by Guy Bourdin. This time Ronald Tree let the picture run in *Mademoiselle*.

At seventeen in 1967 Tree was "discovered" again by Diana Vreeland, who sent her to Richard Avedon. "She was gawky, hunched over, with stringy hair, absolutely not a beauty at all," said Polly Mellen. "She looked like a gangly little urchin" in a black bell-bottomed outfit. Mellen was ready to toss her out of the studio, but Avedon saw something. "She's perfect," he said. "Don't touch her."

Back in London, Bailey was ready for a new adventure. He thought Tree looked like "an Egyptian Jiminy Cricket." She soon moved into his house on Primrose Hill, where she entertained her lover by painting one room black and another purple, installing a UFO detector, and bringing home Black Panthers and a Tibetan monk. Their life between location trips was a nonstop party. "The house was full of hippies, looking at the ceiling and saying '*Great!*'" Bailey later recalled. "I'd be getting into my Rolls and there would be three of them in the back smoking joints that I had paid for and calling me a capitalist pig!"

The new decade was dark for Bailey. The floors of his house were covered with the droppings of his many dogs, and his sixty parrots gave him a disease called psittacosis. A homeless party guest moved in and lived there for two weeks before anyone noticed. Bailey spent his time watching television, eating apples, and drinking cans of Coke, tossing the empties over his shoulder onto the carpet. He and Tree broke up after seven years, in 1974. She dropped out of fashion and eventually made her way to Sydney, Australia, where she still lives. Bailey later said that although he found her fantastic, he "never quite came to terms with photographing her because Avedon got to her first."

Avedon was by this time disenchanted with the superficial world of fashion. "The necessities of fashion magazines were no longer mine, no longer interesting," he said. "The sixties saved me, in a sense, for a while. I was able to do something not completely embarrassing, sometimes quite successful. . . . Vreeland and I developed together an image of a new kind of woman. The sixties was like the twenties in its flamboyance, and in its extraordinary clothing."

That flamboyance flowered in the new disco culture. In 1961 Oleg and Igor Cassini were among a group of swells who founded Le Club, a private restaurant and discotheque. "The Stork and El Morocco disappeared," says Oleg. "Playboys disappeared. That time passed. The models became celebrities.

Model agents and photographers became the important guys. Going out with them was more important than dancing all night long with some schmuck. Le Club was the link between the world that existed and the galloping future."

Like the Terrible Trio in London, American photographers were riding the new waves of fashion. A native of Forest Hills, Queens, Jerry Schatzberg started his career in his family's fur business, but after a brief stint as a baby photographer he got a job as an assistant to fashion photographer Bill Helburn in 1954.

Helburn was a rake, "a great charmer," Schatzberg says. "He had a lot of women. If we went on locations trips with three or four models, Bill would have one and I'd be with the others, talking, sometimes flirting." Sunny Griffin remembers Helburn's romantic approach well. "He'd walk into the dressing room, pat you on the back, and get your bra undone," she says. "I never knew how he did it. When front-close bras came in," she adds, laughing, "*he* was undone!"

In 1956 Schatzberg moved into Manhattan, started working for *Glamour,* and rented a studio on Park Avenue South. In 1958 Alexander Liberman moved him to *Vogue.* He liked to work with model Anne Saint Marie. She was a sensitive, artistic California girl, separated from her first husband. Schatzberg fell in love with her but kept his distance. "I was in awe," he says. "If we had an affair, it was through the camera. Anytime I needed a favor, Anne worked for me. When I worked for *Vogue,* I'd save the worst clothes for her because she'd make them look like the best."

Even if Schatzberg had wanted more, that soon became impossible. Saint Marie got involved with another photographer named Tom Palumbo. Born in Italy, Palumbo had come to America after the war, studied art, and then become assistant to *Bazaar* photographer James Abbey, Jr. Palumbo started shooting and brought his work to Edward Steichen, who'd ended up as the curator of photography at Museum of Modern Art. Steichen sent Palumbo to Alexey Brodovitch, who put him to work for *Bazaar.*

When he met Saint Marie, she was fresh to New York, still living in Eileen and Jerry Ford's town house. When Palumbo got an assignment to shoot California fashion, she was one of the models. A romance started on that trip, although "it wasn't consummated because she was in the middle of a divorce and I was married also, to a model named Kate Johnson," Palumbo says.

By 1960 they were both free, and they got married. Saint Marie had become a top model by then. After the couple had a son, Saint Marie tried to quit but found she couldn't. She started seeing a psychiatrist, who prescribed

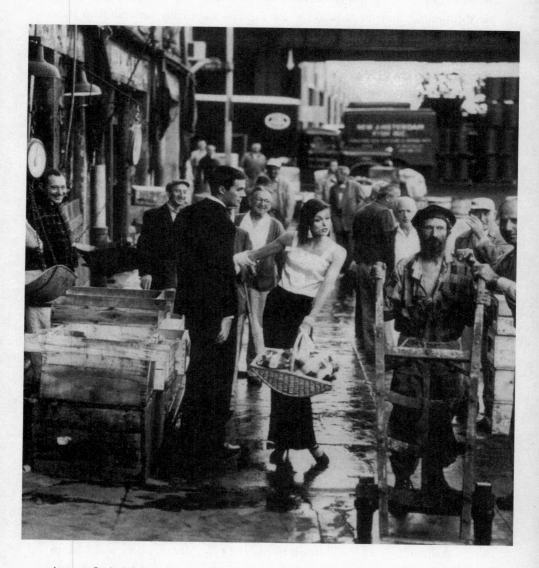
Anne Saint Marie photographed by Jerry Schatzberg in 1958

a barbiturate to put her to sleep at night and amphetamines to wake her up in the morning. She also drank. And she and Palumbo fought enough that people throughout their little world knew it. "He was totally unfaithful to her, chasing the likes of me," says model Nancy Berg.

While he doesn't deny that his eye might have roved ("Nancy Berg was there, too," he says), Palumbo insists that he and Saint Marie were very much in love. "We used to fight like hell and love like hell," he says. "We were two immature kids. The marriage got strained." And the strain showed. "He'd go and come back; she'd go and come back," remembers Dorian Leigh. "He was dreadful to her. If a woman did it, it would be called ball-breaking. He criticized her in front of people. He'd say, 'Here's the great beauty!' She was hysterical, in a *Streetcar Named Desire* kind of way. Everyone wanted to protect her."

"She was crazy," says photographer Roger Prigent. "She lived in a world of fantasy, completely dedicated to work, centered on modeling. She would beg to retake photographs. All those girls started to drink because of the pressure. It was too much too soon. They should have been salesgirls at Woolworth's, and they made in one hour what the average girl made in a week."

Finally, in 1961, at Eileen Ford's suggestion Palumbo and Saint Marie saw a marriage counselor, who suggested they separate. Palumbo moved into his studio and didn't see his wife again for three years. "Every now and then I got a call," he says. "I didn't always know where she was. She had my son. All I know is that she wound up in the hospital."

In Palumbo's absence, Jerry Schatzberg became Saint Marie's confidant. "Tom was a prick," Schatzberg says. But Palumbo wasn't her only problem. She was getting older and couldn't bear it. "It became an obsession to her," according to Schatzberg. "When you're on top, you're a queen. Then they don't need you anymore. She was taking pills, having a constant nervous breakdown. She'd say *Seventeen* magazine was going to use her. She was an absolute mess."

Finally, broke and broken, Saint Marie was hospitalized. Photographer Karen Radkai took up a collection to pay her bills. Her recovery was slow. In 1964 Saint Marie and Palumbo got back together. Rumors flew that she had died, and neither of them tried to stop them. "She *had* died," Palumbo says. "She died as their invention. She died as model. But we created another life for sixteen years. It was a pact we had." Saint Marie finally did die—of lung cancer—in 1986.

Meanwhile, Jerry Schatzberg's career had taken off. He fell in with London's Terrible Trio when he went to Europe for *Glamour* and *Esquire* and photographed the Beatles in London. "I was absolutely astounded," he says. "There were all these men in the airport with long hair. Duffy took me to the Ad Lib. Bailey told me about the Rolling Stones. I introduced him to Catherine Deneuve."

Back in New York, Schatzberg hosted the Terribles whenever they came to town, throwing parties in his studio, where Mick Jagger, Andy Warhol, and Baby Jane Holzer mixed with models and photographers, glorying in their status as the new pop aristocracy. Schatzberg also frequented Le Club, growing friendly with its manager, Olivier Coquelin. Coquelin invited him to invest in a new club called Ondine. Within six months Richard Burton's ex-wife, Sybil, and her boyfriend, Jordan Christopher, opened Arthur. Francesco Scavullo backed a club called Daisy. A photographer named Steve Horn was involved with another, the Sanctuary. New York's first disco age was in full swing.

"They were wild times," says booker Jane Halleran. "The models were very much a part of it. They were stars. But we were all so stoned it's hard to think of stories. It was so heady. It was one big dance. We would go to Le Club and Arthur, and then to the airport and Paris and Castel, and then to the airport and London and the Ad Lib, and then back to New York."

Constance Stumin, a teenager from Ohio, joined Ford in 1966 and found herself in the deep end of modeling's pool. On one of her first go-sees an advertising man invited her out for dinner and then back to his apartment. "He came out of his bedroom in red satin underwear and popped an amy [an amyl nitrate Spansule] under my nose," she recalls. "He put *Lord of the Flies* on the TV and asked me to lie on the bed. I didn't know how to behave. Finally I asked him for money for a cab. He threw my shoes over the balcony." Dressing quickly as the executive sniffed more poppers, Stumin grabbed a pair of his ruby cuff links and bolted. "I sold the cuff links and paid the rent," she says. A year later she was tossed out of the Ford agency "for lewd dancing at Le Club," she says. "Eileen was furious and said I'd never work in this town again."

As the fashion and music worlds blended, the drugs of the sixties infiltrated fashion. The alcohol and pills that did in Anne Saint Marie gave way to even more dangerous highs, and models, young outriders on the cutting edge, tried them all. In October 1969, in upstate New York, a model named Eva Gshopf fell out of a tree and died. "There's no question she was on everything," Eileen Ford says. Then, in February 1971, a German model named Agneta Frieberg, apparently high on LSD, jumped out a hotel window in Paris and died as well. French authorities asked Ford if the girl could have been involved with a revolutionary group. "I don't think she ever thought that deeply," Ford replied.

Drug taking wasn't limited to models. "I was taking lots of uppers, staying up most of the night," Schatzberg says. "I didn't know pills were a drug. They kept you functioning." In 1969 Schatzberg made his first film, based on the life of Anne Saint Marie. Faye Dunaway, whom he dated, starred as a model named Lou in *Puzzle of a Downfall Child*. "I really always loved that character," Dunaway later said. "She spent all her life trying to get to the place where it would be wonderful, and she got to that place and she hates it. It was the underbelly of the American dream . . . all the beauty and the glamour."

Schatzberg dropped out of fashion in one piece. Others weren't so lucky. Bert Stern, inspired by Irving Penn, started taking pictures in 1953. By 1959 he was shooting for *Glamour*, Condé Nast's farm team for future *Vogue* photographers. Bob Richardson, a Long Island native, graduated from art school around the same time and became a window designer for Bloomingdale's. Then he started taking pictures and eventually became assistant to Carmen Dell'Orefice's husband, Richard Heimann. Early on Richardson photographed a model named Nena von Schlebrugge (who was briefly married to LSD guru Timothy Leary and later had a daughter, actress Uma Thurman), lying on a couch crying while talking on the phone to her psychiatrist. The photos that resulted led to better work.

Both Stern and Richardson were girl-crazy. "Women were everything to me," Stern says. "You did anything to get over them or under them and get the picture. I wasn't booking models to sleep with them, but I did find women the best thing there was. And let's be honest, everything went in the sixties." Richardson felt the same way. "I hated fashion," he says, "but I liked photographing women."

The two were driven and ambitious. For ten years Stern lived his dreams and photographed them. He was shooting the best models, earning as much as $500,000 a year, and spending it all. "*Blow-Up* was a simple photographer," Stern says. "I became a thing." He owned a town house, an eleven-room condominium with a swimming pool, a schoolhouse he converted into a studio where thirty-eight employees toiled, and a second, secret studio where he could hide from them. "Work was fun," he says. "Fun was work. I'd rent a yacht and go off and shoot pictures."

Richardson chose a different, confrontational path. "I only had time for ideas," he says. "I became too involved in creating a style. My trouble was, I didn't want to be famous. Anyone can become famous. I wanted to be great." That led to constant arguments with the editors he worked for and a reputation that scared off advertising clients. "I always cause a scandal wherever I go," he says boastfully. "My photographs were so weird. I fought with all the editors I worked with. They were so old-fashioned and out of step." Then he met a kindred spirit.

Donna Mitchell grew up in northern Manhattan and began modeling when she was fifteen. When she expressed the desire to do photo work, she was sent to Eileen Ford, who told her she was too short, needed a nose job, and should probably have her back teeth extracted in order to emphasize her jaw-line. "We're talking fifteen and a half!" Mitchell remembers. "I fled in tears."

By 1964 Mitchell had appeared in *Brides* and *Ladies' Home Journal*. A year later she met Melvin Sokolsky. "I picked models people thought were odd," Sokolsky says. "I saw this incredible face at a shoot with six girls, and I put a one hundred-fifty millimeter lens on my camera and started to pan, watching her. She had a Madonna's face with inner intelligence, and she was clocking everything around her." Sokolsky sent her to editor Gwen Randolph at *Bazaar,* where she showed up in a ratty raccoon coat held closed with a safety pin. "You're putting me on," Randolph told the photographer. But he insisted, and soon they went to Paris to shoot the collections. "Donna could take the gestures of the street and turn them into the highest form of elegance," Sokolsky raves. "She had the knowledge of the world in her little face."

Sokolsky, too, had a vision, and Mitchell played right into it. "My models were more than props," he says. "I drew from who they were, how they gestured, what they feared." He wanted to chronicle his times. "I was systematically breaking down the social decorum of gesture," he says, "from women who sat on the couch with their purses to women who sat on the floor. It was about class. Poor people live six to a bedroom. That brings an intimacy to the fore that rich people are afraid to address." Sokolsky consciously played against the then-prevailing stiff couture style in *Bazaar.* He shot Mitchell sitting with her legs spread. "It was the gesture of the time," he says. "Louise Dahl-Wolfe called me a vulgarian." *Bazaar*'s editor Nancy White accused him of "saying 'fuck you' in sign language," he adds.

By the early seventies Sokolsky had had enough. "I was so busy making money I trapped myself. Some photographers can keep taking the same picture over and over, but if you're shooting people flying over Paris in bubbles or in burnt-out buildings, like I was, it gets harder and harder to come up with something new. Finally I was sick and tired of being told how to take pictures, and I just backed away. I saw what was coming. I saw the freedom being taken away by retards and monkeys. I didn't want to face it." He retired from fash-

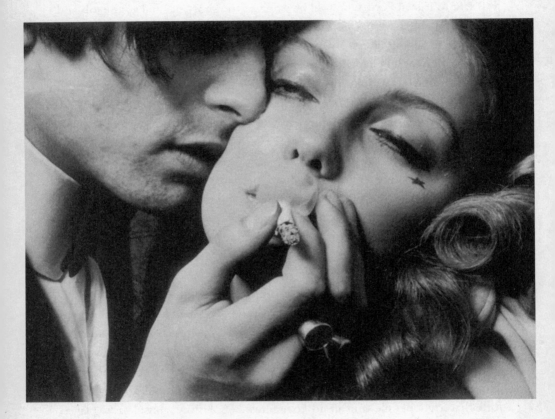

Donna Mitchell photographed by Bob Richardson
in the late 1960s

ion photography and with his partner, Jordan Kalfus, Jean Shrimpton's ex, formed a company to make TV commercials.

Donna Mitchell moved on, too. "I made it clear I wanted to work for photographers, not magazines," she said. "I'd turn down a booking unless it was with a photographer I wanted to work for. It wasn't about just having my photograph taken. I liked to develop ideas, as opposed to being someone who jobbed in. That was my greatest pleasure. My ambition was to do the best photograph with each photographer." She began a long collaboration with Bob Richardson, whose ambitions and ideas coincided with hers.

Richardson first saw Mitchell in one of Sokolsky's *Bazaar* photos. He asked to book her and was told that Nancy White didn't like her. "They said she looked drugged and beaten," Richardson recalls. "I thought she looked like a fallen angel. We became a team and caused one scandal after another. Everyone else was doing frozen little images like Avedon's. I was doing nudity, sex, and violence. We ignored the editors because they were just in the way. One time in Paris we locked an editor into the dressing room because she just wouldn't shut up. It was my way or no way. I was way ahead of them, and I knew they'd never catch up. It was not my job to educate them. I didn't have time for that." In 1966, fleeing the restrictive atmosphere in America, Richardson left *Bazaar,* and he and Mitchell went to Europe. But the fuel that was driving them, as well as Bert Stern, soon caused all their careers to crash.

In the late 1950s a new breed of physician had appeared on New York's East Side, the Doctors Feelgood. The most famous were Max Jacobson and Robert Freymann. Jacobson had fled Germany in 1936 and set up a practice in New York. By the fifties he'd become the city's top celebrity doctor, known for giving energizing "miracle tissue regenerator" shots that were actually laced with amphetamines. His patients included Eddie Fisher, Truman Capote, Emilio Pucci, Tennessee Williams, Cecil B. De Mille, and John and Jacqueline Kennedy, who started taking his shots during JFK's presidential campaign in 1960. By 1961 they were so addicted to his "vitamins" that they chartered an Air France jet to fly Jacobson to Paris, where Kennedy was meeting with Soviet leader Nikita Khrushchev. Jacobson was so involved with Kennedy that he was included in the family pictures in *John F. Kennedy: A Family Album* by photographer Mark Shaw. After Shaw died in 1969 of acute and chronic amphetamine poisoning while under Jacobson's care, the government raided the doctor's office. Six years later his license to practice medicine was revoked after he had been found guilty of fraud and forty-eight counts of unprofessional conduct. While Freymann's case was not as well publicized, he, too, was suspected of improperly dispensing amphetamines in the early seventies. Never formally charged, he eventually retired and died in the late eighties.

But in the sixties Freymann's and Jacobson's patients were still flying high on the good doctors' magic "vitamin" shots. Bob Richardson was already familiar with drugs. He was getting stoned with a model one day when she offered him his first vitamin shot. He soon became one of Jacobson's star patients. "I was a drug addict," he admits. "It forced my mind to go faster. Jacobson taught me how to mainline and gave me a set of works."

Both Mitchell and Richardson continued working separately after 1969. But they found their reputations preceded them wherever they went. "I was young and naïve," says Mitchell. "You could say stupid; that would be even more appropriate. I started taking amphetamine pills because I was always tired and depressed and my personal life was very sick and disturbed. I was very wrapped up in the world of fashion and photography, and when you're that caught up in it, you lose track of what's real. To be a really good model, you have to be extremely self-involved. There's also a strong element of masochism in it: the loss of self to another. I was very lucky to get out of it."

Meanwhile, Bob Richardson got married, had a son, left his wife, and took up with a model turned actress, Anjelica Huston. But he was finding inspiration harder to come by. "I stopped showing up, or if I did, I'd be really stoned," he says. "From working for everyone I went to working for no one. You had to be very special and understanding to work with me." After several brief comebacks fizzled, he moved to California and drifted for ten years. "I was dead," he says. "Everyone thought I was dead, which was what I wanted them to think. It's how you keep a legend going."

Bert Stern's experience was similar. His secretary introduced him to Dr. Robert Freymann. At first he believed that Freymann's shots were just vitamins. "Then I began to figure out there was something else in them," Stern says. "That spike gave me the energy to shoot all day and all night. It was chemical and magical."

In 1969 Stern's wife, ballerina Allegra Kent, left him after warning he was killing himself. "The American dream became a nightmare," Stern says. "The sixties ended. I wasn't going to stay on the high wire without her. It was all done for her in a sense. I just stopped. I had to get my head back together. I had to get my life back together."

The new atmosphere had its good points. Alongside the breakdown of standards of professionalism and behavior came a breakdown of the strict rules defining beauty. Wilhelmina needed to differentiate her agency. So when she opened her doors, she began promoting buxom models like herself, calling them a reflection of the national trend toward freedom and honesty that had recently seen women abandon bras and girdles. "Women snicker at the elongated, ironing board figures seen in the glossy magazines," Bruce Cooper told a reporter. "The concave-chested gal will never entirely disappear, but her influence is negligible." Eileen Ford disagreed. "I still say that models should be thin," she insisted, although she admitted that "today's models are more individual in their looks."

Despite the industry's resistance, Wilhelmina took on a number of what were then called "Negro models." It was another way to differentiate herself from Ford's White House, but it also seemed to stem from a real belief in equality. Asked in 1969 if they represented a trend, Willie snapped, "No, because Negroes aren't temporary. We're all people, we live in the same country. Black *is* beautiful." Nonetheless, when her first black model, Naomi Sims, started in 1967, "she couldn't get a booking," Willie said. "Photographers didn't want to use her unless it was for the Negro market."

After graduating from high school in Pittsburgh in 1966, Sims moved to New York to continue her education, paying her way by working as a model for fashion illustrators. A year later she was stopped on the street by a photographer's agent, who gave her the names of three photographers and urged her to go see them. Within days she was working for Gösta Peterson, an innovative photographer whose wife, Pat, was the fashion editor of *The New York Times Magazine* and its biannual supplement, *Fashions of the Times.* Soon Sims got her big break when one of Peterson's photos of her appeared on the cover of *Fashions of the Times.*

Sure they would sign her up instantly, Sims called the Fords. She was annoyed when Eileen wouldn't see her personally and instead, sent her to Sunny Harnett, who'd quit modeling and become a Ford assistant. Sims was thunderstruck when Harnett delivered the verdict: "Ford already has too many models of your type." The new agent in town, Wilhelmina Cooper, saw Sims personally but, like Ford, was unwilling to represent her. Taking matters into her own hands, Sims decided to send her *Times* cover to every ad agency in New York and asked Willie if she'd allow her agency's phone number to be printed on an accompanying card. Willie agreed. A few days later a telegram appeared under the door of Sims's apartment. "CANNOT REACH YOU BY TELEPHONE. URGENT YOU CALL US," it said. Sure she'd done something wrong, Sims did not reply, and two days later another telegram arrived. And then another. This one said, "WE HAVE MANY BOOKINGS FOR YOU."

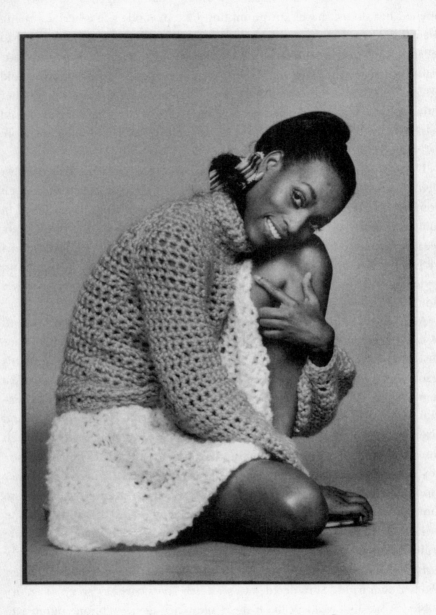

Naomi Sims photographed by Neal Barr
for *Ladies' Home Journal*

The long dark night of the "Negro" model was over. Racism was still very much in fashion, but the first cracks had already appeared in its lily-white facade. "For years, the Negro model was trapped between the unyielding images of a redcap lugging a suitcase and a mammy in a kerchief flipping a flapjack," the New York *Post* reported in a 1955 story that estimated there were 250 black models then working in New York. Most of them were part-timers, moonlighting from steadier jobs. But some were earning as much as $35 an hour, posing for "Negro market" magazines and advertisers. The Grace Del Marco Model Agency, specialists in the field, had opened. Eleanor Lambert, the fashion publicist, had used black models in her fashion shows for more than a decade.

In 1956 China Machado, a dark-skinned Eurasian beauty, got a job as a temporary replacement house model at Givenchy in Paris. Two years later she branched out into free-lance work, modeling in Italy at the Pitti Palace in Florence, where she appeared in the debut show of a young *alta moda* designer named Valentino. In Paris she was in collections for Dior and Cardin, where she was spotted by Oleg Cassini.

Cassini had used black models in his fashion shows since the middle fifties. "I was the first," he says, "but I get very little credit. I picked the girls myself and used them at shows for out-of-town buyers and press. It cost me a lot of accounts in the South. It was still the time of fashion apartheid."

After seeing Machado work in January 1958, he invited her to New York. Hours after her arrival Diana Vreeland booked her to appear in a Fashion Group show. Richard Avedon was in the audience and photographed her almost every day for the next three months. But when he wanted to take her to Paris for *Bazaar* in January 1959 as the first nonwhite model ever to shoot the collections, the magazine's publisher balked. Avedon insisted, threatening to quit his job, and the publisher capitulated. Machado continued modeling until 1962, when *Bazaar*'s Nancy White gave her a job as senior fashion editor.

In 1961 the Seventh Avenue designer Pauline Trigère had hired a Grace DeMarco model, Beverly Valdes, twenty-three, as the first full-time black house model in the garment center. In 1964 a second all-black agency, American Models, was launched. In 1968, a third, aptly named Black Beauties, opened its doors. Its director, Betty Foray, was white, but her models didn't care. "What black people want now is a passageway to economic opportunity and they know very well that the only way is through white conduits," the agency's publicist told *The New York Times*.

By decade's end Naomi Sims had left Wilhelmina for Ford and was earn-
ing $1,000 a week. Diana Vreeland had her shot by Irving Penn for *Vogue*.
The *Ladies' Home Journal* even put her on its cover, the first time a black
model had so appeared on a national magazine. And now Sims wasn't alone.
When asked whence she hailed, part-black, part-Irish, part-French, and part-
Mexican Donyale Luna answered, "I'm from the moon, darling." But in fact,
she was born Peggy Anne Donyale Aragonea Pegeon Freeman in Detroit.
The feline looks and wild behavior of this first black high-fashion model
made her a sensation in London and Paris. Although she was the first black
model on the cover of British *Vogue* (shot by David Bailey) and appeared in
Fellini Satyricon in 1970, her career was short. "She took a lot of drugs and
never paid her bills," says a designer she modeled for. By the mid-seventies
Luna had disappeared from the scene. She died in a clinic in Rome in 1979.
She was just thirty-three years old.

Katiti Kironde II also had a moment in the sun when she became the first
black model to appear on the cover of a major fashion publication—*Glamour*—in August 1968. The timing was not coincidental. A few months earlier
the Reverend Martin Luther King, Jr., had been gunned down in Memphis,
Tennessee, and race riots broke out all over America. "The death of King
shook everybody a bit and woke them up to the fact that something had to
be done," Jerry Ford told *Newsday*. He added that the Fords had increased the
number of black models on its rolls by a factor of 25 percent. But when *The
New York Times* counted the number of black models on Ford's head sheet
three months later, there were only six.

Nowhere were there more opportunities than on fashion runways, where
the black models' carriage, grace, and bearing proved nothing short of revolutionary. Bethann Hardison, a self-described "spiffy little fashion girl from
Brooklyn," arrived in New York's garment center in 1968, after a short stint as
a guard at a prison. While holding down an assortment of garment center jobs,
Hardison signed up with Gillis MacGil's Mannequin agency. Some designers
wouldn't use her. "Bill Blass, who is the Clark Gable of this business, made me
aware of why designers said no," she says. "He let me know I was barking up a
tough tree. He told me his clients wouldn't understand." But her greatest
moment came on November 28, 1973, when five American designers—Anne
Klein, Halston, Stephen Burrows, Blass, and Oscar de la Renta—joined five
French couturiers in mounting a show to raise funds for the restoration of the
Palace of Versailles outside Paris. The French used elaborate backdrops and
props. The Americans used a bare stage and thirty black models.

Paris designers, put to shame by the Americans' simple showmanship and fashion flair, embraced the black models and put them to work. Their rates rose from $50 an hour to $100. Finally, in 1974, Beverly Johnson, a champion swimmer from Buffalo, New York, became the first black model to appear on the cover of American *Vogue*. It was the August issue, traditionally not a big seller, but it *was* a cover. The last lily-white fortress had been breached. By 1975 every major American designer was using black models.

Four years after she opened her doors, Wilhelmina was booking a hundred men and women who together billed $3 million annually. The Coopers traveled constantly all over America, giving interviews everywhere they went. Willie judged Miss U.S.A. and Miss Universe contests and headed to Europe three times a year to see the fashion shows and new girls gathered by agents who worked with her.

Meanwhile, more new agencies were opening and closing like tropical hibiscus. In 1968 Rusty Zeddis, Ford's top booker, left to open Fashion & Film with another agent and a businessman backer. "Eileen went crazy," says Gillis MacGil. "How could Rusty do such a thing?" Ford sued Zeddis for stealing business secrets but soon dropped the case. "There are no secrets," Zeddis explains. "You pick up the phone and book models. What's the big deal?"

When Frances Gill died in summer, 1970, her agency ended up in the hands of Attley Craig, her cousin and bookkeeper. A year later Craig, too, passed away. Two of the agency's bookers approached model Ellen Harth at the funeral and asked her to take over the operation, she says. Harth was close to Judith Hinman, a Mannequin model married to Jeremy Foster-Fell, an importer of English sports cars, French boats, and watches. Today Harth, Hinman (who is now Judith Williams), and Foster-Fell all seem to despise one another. And each one takes credit for coming up with the idea that the two models should take over the agency from Attley Craig. What is beyond dispute is that they bought the remains of the Frances Gill agency for a dollar and renamed it Foster-Ellen.

Within a year Harth and Hinman, once the closest of friends, grew to distrust each other. Hinman says Harth, who got upset when Hinman got pregnant, began plotting to spirit their models away. Harth says the Foster-Fells secretly gained control of 51 percent of the company's stock while she was in Germany nursing her ailing mother. "I talked to the models and two bookers," Harth says, "and I left and started the Ellen Harth Agency in the same building." Hinman says she learned what had happened when she came back to work after giving birth. The Foster-Fells struck back, reporting Harth to New York City's Department of Consumer Affairs, claiming she was "morally unfit" to run an agency, Harth says. "They ruled in my favor," Harth adds angrily. "I think it's all over, and then they slap me with a lawsuit."

But the legal action went nowhere. "It just fizzled, and I gave it up," Hinman admits.

Harth has been in business ever since, first on her own and then as a division of Elite Models. "I'm here, and they aren't," she says with some satisfaction. Judith Foster-Fell started over. "I opened Foster-Fell Models in another building," she says. "Jeremy was snooping around, admiring what I was achieving. He wanted the agency. Ever since then he's been a model hound. We built a house in Southampton, Long Island, and invited a model to come out there with us. We had dinner one night. I put the baby to sleep and went to bed. In the middle of the night I heard the baby crying, and who comes running out of the forest, covered with dirt? Jeremy and my model!"

Jeremy Foster-Fell has managed to eke out a living on the fringes of modeling ever since. Some would call what he does pimping. But Foster-Fell calls it "the voluntary system." He learned how it worked from Judith, who'd taken full advantage of the sexual freedom of the times. After divorcing her abusive hometown sweetheart in 1963, Hinman had played the field for eight years, sleeping with both men and women. She is one of the rare few in fashion who will admit to bisexuality in a world where it is far more often practiced than admitted to. "I am not homosexual, but I can certainly be drawn to a woman, and I did enjoy making love to two or three women," she says. "It's quite typical in the model business. We get so hyped up and feel so good about ourselves, and we see our own images across the dressing room, all these beautiful bodies. One can't resist that."

Hinman also had affairs with club owner Olivier Coquelin and a Moroccan army general. Then, when she and Jeremy were running Foster-Fell together, another Moroccan official she'd met through her general often called her. "He'd say, 'I need models for the king and the prince,' " she says. "I didn't want to know what for, but I offered them names, and they paid them and flew them over there, and as far as I know, the girls had a great time."

"Men constantly seek attractive women for physical purposes," Foster-Fell says. "Among moneyed men and the most attractive women, that has to be multiplied by a factor of ten. Every guy I know, the minute he hears I own an agency, he brightens up. They get phone numbers; they give presents; they give money. I've never shipped a girl off. But I knew guys who'd invite girls and pay up to twenty thousand dollars for a weekend. I've invited girls to such things. I once flew five girls to the tropics. They were paid full rate and told that guys would take a shot at them and they wouldn't get a second booking. Two of them were pissed because nobody tried, one was pissed because somebody did, and the fifth, I heard later, stayed the course and still sees the fellow. This is the real world. Any agent who says it doesn't happen is lying. You only cross the line when you take a booking for money with the knowledge that sexual favors are required." It's not pimping, Foster-Fell concludes, because pimps take an 80 percent cut and model agents only take 10 percent.

In 1978, while divorcing Judith, Jeremy Foster-Fell opened Beaumont Models. "He took my bookers and paid them twice what I was paying," Judith says. "He told me, 'Ellen showed me how to do it.' " Beaumont went bust in 1982, when its backer, Juan Zavala, was charged with stealing $2.6 million from Barclays Bank and the Small Business Administration, jumped $500,000 bail, and disappeared. Foster-Fell and his second wife, Barbara, also a model, then started an agency called L'Image. It was financed by Ed Feldman, a model's husband and financial consultant who'd previously worked with Bernie Cornfeld's IOS. Feldman, who still lends money to model agencies, freely admits that their relationship ended after he put Foster-Fell in the hospital by beating him with a mallet.

Foster-Fell took a well-deserved vacation in Vancouver after that, but a year later he was back in New York and the agency business. Married to yet another model, he found yet another backer and bought the Foster-Fell name back from his first wife. Judith retired to the country "and never looked back," she says. Jeremy took the company public—and then got fired. Four days later he was back in business, in partnership with Dick Robie, who owned John Robert Powers. That relationship ended in a lawsuit. Today Foster-Fell is on his fifth model wife and is still running Foster-Fell out of a dingy office in an unglamorous neighborhood.

Back at the top of the business, Stewart Cowley and Barbara Stone had turned Stewart Models into a powerhouse. With Twiggy and the Ford rejects Veruschka and Marisa Berenson in their stable, the agency became what Stewart Cowley had always wanted. "Eileen's bailiwick was Europe," Stone says. "I'd done pretty good with her slop, her inability to spot good models. But I had to find more. So I turned toward the United States."

Lucy Angle had wanted to be a model from the moment she heard that George Harrison of the Beatles had married Patti Boyd. In January 1967

Angle celebrated her sixteenth birthday by moving to New York. By that December she'd appeared on the covers of *Seventeen* and *Bazaar,* but she worked mostly for *Glamour* and *Mademoiselle.* "They were proponents of the all-American thing that took over fashion in the seventies," Angle says. Stewart's models were in the forefront of that look.

Cheryl Tiegs also arrived at Stewart in 1966. A farmer's daughter from Minnesota, she'd spent a year in a trailer park in Wichita, Kansas, before her family moved to Alhambra, California, when she was five. Her father worked as a mechanic while studying to become a mortician. At a high school dinner she listened to a model agent give a speech and then joined his Pasadena agency. For four years she modeled part-time, posing for illustrations, department stores, and beach movies, earning little or nothing. Then she joined the Nina Blanchard Agency in Los Angeles.

Modeling was a tiny business in L.A. in the sixties. Walter Thornton was the first agent to open there, and his license passed to one Dorothy Prebble, who had a modeling school. Mary Webb Davis ran that school for a while, then took over its offices and Prebble's few models. Her office door was later immortalized on television's *77 Sunset Strip,* even though its actual address was 8532 Sunset Boulevard. Davis opened her agency there in 1947.

Nina Blanchard was married to a New York television producer, and when his show went off the air, Blanchard and her husband bought a Midas muffler franchise in Phoenix. "I know how to split a manifold," she says, "but I'll tell you, you live in Phoenix a year and you'll want to come back to your phony friends." After a series of jobs in L.A. charm schools Blanchard decided to set up on her own in June 1961.

She had one real model, Peggy Moffitt, and about a dozen pretenders. "I sent out a brochure and started getting calls. I knew ten of my thirteen girls couldn't move, so I said they were all booked." It being L.A., people decided she had to be the most exclusive agent in town.

Tiegs came to the attention of New York editors and agents in 1964, after she appeared in a Cole of California swimsuit ad in *Seventeen* magazine. Julie Britt, an editor at *Glamour,* booked her sight unseen for a shooting in St. Thomas. For the next four years Tiegs worked for *Glamour* and *'Teen,* winning covers and disproving the notion that a model had to live in New York to be successful. She'd gone from beach to big time.

Finally, in 1966, Bob MacLeod, the publisher of *'Teen,* convinced her to join Stewart Models. A former publisher of *Harper's Bazaar,* MacLeod had battled with the Fords over model rates; he'd almost opened a Hearst model agency

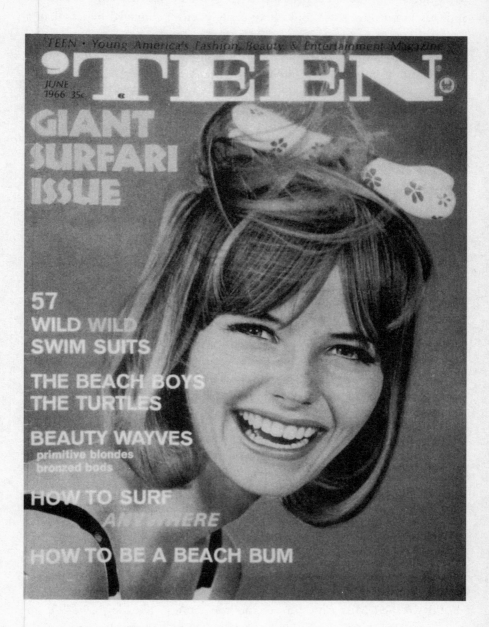

Cheryl Tiegs on her first magazine cover in 1966

to compete with them. He believed Tiegs would be lost on Ford's head sheet and was so sensitive she "could have easily been discouraged by less than a large amount of personal attention," he says.

Her image was goody-goody California blond—healthy, if a little vapid; enthusiastic, if not terribly interesting. She promoted that image with a vengeance. "I would show up on time, and I would work late if people asked me to, and I would care for the people that I worked with," Tiegs says. "I don't mean to be saying this to puff myself up. I hope it doesn't sound like that. But if they believed in [their product], then I was going to get on the bandwagon and help them out with it. That's what we were all there for. And I worked closely with people like Cover Girl for many years and had long-term relationships and cared about them and their families."

By 1967 Tiegs was one of the country's top junior models. She had seventy covers on her résumé and earned as much as $3,000 a week. That year, she moved in with an advertising executive named Stan Dragoti, whom she married in 1970. She also appeared for the first time in *Sports Illustrated*'s annual swimsuit issue, working for an editor named Jule Campbell.

Campbell came from *Glamour* magazine, where she'd been the accessories editor, under model turned editor Betty McLauchlen Dorso. Campbell joined *SI* in 1959 and put together its first swimwear spread in 1964 as an accompaniment for a travel story on a Mexican resort. Campbell didn't like New York models. "They were skinny, skinny, skinny," she says. "I wanted girls with meat on 'em, so I never booked top models. I discovered my own. I looked for girls who led a *sportif* life."

By 1968 Stewart Models was challenging Ford's preeminence. "We were the best in the world for a while there," Stewart Cowley says. Though Stone had attracted a group of top models, including Tiegs, Susan Dey, Randi Oakes, Sigourney Weaver, and Lois Chiles, television was the key to his agency's ascendance. Cowley had moved aggressively into the commercial business and opened a talent division to get its models into television and movies. More important, though, while Stone ran the agency, Cowley put together the first successful model search promotion since the Miss Rheingold contest.

"I'd watched Miss America get top, top ratings," Cowley says. "I'd go down to Atlantic City to interview the contestants. They all wanted to be models, but they were a bunch of bimbos. So I thought, what if we had a show with girls who really could be top models?" Cowley's first Model of the Year contest aired live in prime time in 1967 on CBS. It was known as Stewart's Folly, he says, until it won a huge audience share. In 1968 the winner was a

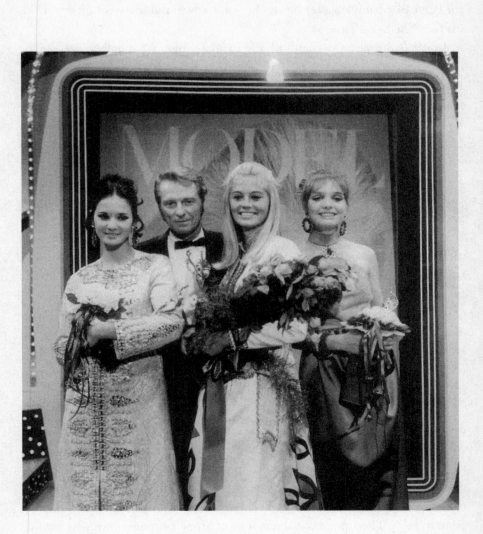

Stewart Cowley of Stewart Models with his Model of the Year, Cybill Shepherd *(second from right)*, and runners-up in 1967

recent high school graduate named Cybill Shepherd, who quickly became one of Stewart's top models. For the next two years it seemed that Shepherd and Tiegs had a lock on *Glamour*'s cover. Then, in 1970, Shepherd met director Peter Bogdanovich after he saw her on a cover, and she went off to star in his film *The Last Picture Show.*

In 1969 Stewart International Productions, Inc., went public, selling its stock on the open market and offering to buy European agencies like Paris Planning. (Ford tried to go public, too, "but the market fell apart and, happily for us, we didn't," says Jerry Ford.) Within a year Stewart's billings and earnings had gotten clobbered by the shaky economy. He also had legal problems. CBS had dropped its option to air a third Model of the Year pageant when it was sued by a man in Miami who claimed Cowley had stolen his contest idea. Although Stewart Models remained in operation until 1982, from then on Cowley's attentions were so diverted, and he was involved in so much litigation, that he came to be known in the business as Suin' Stew.

Barbara Stone was frustrated. "We were number two," she says, "I wanted to knock Eileen Ford's block off, but there was not the money to make the last thrust and really spend to almost buy girls in Europe and set them up in apartments here. Another factor was that I had a husband and a life. The Fords never had dinner without three or four models and photographers. They didn't have a life." And there was another, internal problem at Stewart Models. "I just couldn't stand Stew Cowley anymore," Stone says. He was obsessed with his lawsuits. "I can't blame him," she adds. "He worked very hard to pull that contest off."

Then Cowley had a heart attack. Stone went to the hospital and, with his doctor's permission, she says, offered to buy the agency from him. "Her contract was up," Cowley says. "She demanded the presidency and a lot more money." Cowley was already angry with her. "She liked girls like Veruschka, who did prestige work," he says. "The catalog girls were money machines, and she said she couldn't stand them." Two of them had left and gone to Ford. Then there was the matter of Stone's expenses. Models would stay with Stone and her husband. "I got a bill every Monday for several hundred dollars for rooms, dinners," Cowley says. "I was paying Barbara Stone's rent!" So when she issued her ultimatum in the hospital, Cowley says, "We let her go."

When she told him she was starting her own agency, Cowley sued to stop her. Her contract had a restrictive covenant, barring her from competing for two years and calling for arbitration to settle disputes. At the end of a summer of negotiations Stone won the right to open in exchange for her agreement not to steal any Stewart models for a year. "I thought that was the kiss of death," Stone says, "but I stubbornly opened anyway," and exactly one year later ten of her models jumped over from Stewart to the new Stone Models.

Despite the high-powered models who joined her, Stone soon went out of business. Her first year operating without models had hurt her, and she never really recovered. "I had a huge apartment," she says. "Dick and my son hated girls living there, walking around in bra and panties. I'd throw parties for four hundred people. But I couldn't do anything creative without a million dollars, and everyone who wanted to inject money wanted to inject the models, if you get what I mean. I got out before I went berserk. I was too easily hurt, I think. I didn't have the hard skin Eileen Ford had."

The final blow was delivered by Cheryl Tiegs. After three years of semi-retirement, reading and playing tennis in L.A. while Stan Dragoti entered the movie business, Tiegs returned to modeling in 1972. "I'd gotten thin and fit and looked older," Tiegs says. "I went into high fashion. I just started accepting more jobs and realized that it was fun after all."

Julie Britt had gone to work at *Harper's Bazaar,* and Tiegs started working there. In July 1971 Hearst hired James Brady, then the publisher of *Women's Wear Daily,* and installed him over Nancy White as *Bazaar*'s publisher and editorial director. "Nancy saw the handwriting on the wall and resigned within a month," says Brady. He dubbed his *Bazaar* "the thinking woman's fashion magazine," brought in new editors and topical writers, and squeezed out art directors Ruth Ansel and Bea Feitler, both of whom ended up at Condé Nast, as did their replacement, Rochelle Udell. Brady even hired a Richard Nixon look-alike to pose in an early fashion layout and ran a photo of Faye Dunaway with unshaved armpits. "He was a daily journalist," says an ex-Hearst editor. "He was not visually astute."

"The magazine had leprosy," says another editor of that time. "No one wanted to come near it. It was too weird. The turmoil in the country was present in all the pages." Hearst's powers were appalled. "It was fun on the one hand and ominous on the other," Brady says. "As we were number two in a two-horse race, I thought I had a license to change." But sixteen months after he started, Brady was fired by letter. It said a new team—headed by Anthony Mazzola, a Hearst art director—would be taking over.

Mazzola remade *Bazaar* as a celebrity fashion magazine. He favored saccharine blond models, Hollywood starlets, and themed issues like "Forty and Fabulous" or "The World's 10 Most Beautiful Women" (staffers called them

"The Old Bag Issue" and the "Ten Most Available"). The models Mazzola favored were given featured treatment, and Tiegs was one of the first.

Soon she had contracts with Cover Girl and Virginia Slims cigarettes. Everything was fine until the mid-seventies, when Tiegs and Stone had what both refer to without elaboration as "a personal difference." Tiegs was in Rome, modeling the collections, when she joined Ford. "I just walked up to Eileen and talked to her," she says. "It was as easy as that." Then she adds cryptically, "It didn't come as any surprise that [Stone] shut down."

After Tiegs left, "I lost the heart one needed to continue" is all Stone will say. "A few months before she closed, Barbara and her husband came to see me about merging Stone and Mannequin," says Gillis MacGil. "But I discovered she was less than truthful about her financial condition. She was out of business two weeks later." Stone called the Fords and gave them a day to buy her out. The next morning she met with one of Ford's attorneys, the closeted homosexual Roy Cohn, who'd become a power in New York in the days since he started his career as a pit bull lawyer for Senator Joseph McCarthy. "He was the most disgusting human being that ever existed," Stone says. "He had frogs on his desk and looked like he'd come out from under a rock himself. It was a boring meeting, so I wandered around and came to a hall into a connecting town house and there was this boytoy in bed wearing satin underpants." When Ford agreed to take over and pay off her models, Stone left the business, never to return.

All through the sixties one modeling agency stayed apart from the pack. Paul Wagner, a handsome blond onetime male model, opened the Paul Wagner Agency in the Brill Building in 1957. "You wouldn't say he was a nelly, but he was flamboyant, a mad queen who knew how to run a business," says Dan Deely, a booker who later worked for him. The same year he opened, Wagner met a teenager, Zoltan Rendessy, who was known as Zoli. "I had a lover," Wagner says. "I came home one night and found the two of them flying around my apartment like naked wood nymphs."

Zoli had come to America from his native Györ, Hungary, as a refugee of World War II. He was the child of an Hungarian Army captain who was estranged from his wife, a dance instructor. She, Zoli, and his older sister, Livia, left their hometown a few hours before Russian troops took it over in 1945. "They hid the three of us among the luggage in the back of a bus," Livia Rendessy Oliver recalls. Zoli was raised in Austria and London, attended boarding schools, and he and his mother followed Livia to Alabama, where she'd settled with an American husband, in 1956. Soon, though, their mother got a job in New York and brought Zoli there. He was fifteen years old and "a rebellious young man," says his sister. "He wanted the good life, and my mother, who'd gotten a job in a cafeteria, couldn't give it to him. He probably didn't want to tell my mother what he needed."

The night he met Zoli, Wagner ordered him and their mutual lover out of his apartment. But when they met again soon afterward, Wagner says, "Zoli and I seemed to have bonded." They went to New Orleans together, returned to New York, and moved in together. Wagner needed help in his agency, so he gave the young man a job.

Wagner booked only women until 1964, when he went to England, saw what was happening there, and signed up a bunch of long-haired men on his return. "Everyone thought, 'This man's crazy,' " Wagner reports. "But in less than six months all the stores got mod clothes and wanted long-haired male models. In less than a year I controlled ninety percent of the men's photographic work in New York. The Fords laughed. Barbara Stone laughed. While they laughed, I was making money."

He started to operate in a grand manner. Wagner's office had red flocked wallpaper, a French desk, and a gold cigarette lighter in the shape of an angel that played music each time it was flicked. "The staff bought him a Persian lamb coat, and he bought a white Afghan hound to go with it," remembers Vickie Pribble, who joined him after leaving Ford. "He'd play records and sing and dance. The girls were so elegant, always swathed in fur. One of them came in with nothing underneath and would flash us. Sinatra was dating all those girls. I think that's where the fur coats came from."

Zoli and Wagner were part of the social avant-garde. In January 1966 Zoli was arrested along with about thirty friends when police raided a marijuana party in his East Fifty-fifth Street penthouse apartment. "Smelling marijuana fumes, the patrolmen searched and found—in addition to a rug, a bed and a blaring hi-fi set, the only furniture in the apartment—several marijuana cigarettes, 15 pep pills and some loose marijuana," *The New York Times* reported the next day. "They were on cloud nine and did they stink!" one of the arresting officers announced when the happy crowd of girls with Sassoon haircuts and boys with beatnik goatees was brought in to be booked for disorderly conduct. Zoli was charged with maintaining a premises for the use of narcotics.

By the late sixties Wagner wanted to be a singer more than an agent and began absenting himself from the agency as he started his new career. "Every time I tried to step away to work in Vegas or whatever, I was pulled back by some trauma," he says. "I was tired of it. Next thing I was off to Europe. I was away a long time." In his absence Wagner put Zoli and another executive in charge of his two divisions, booking models like Richard Roundtree, Pam Huntington, Christina Paolozzi, Geraldine Frank, and Cheyenne. But soon Wagner's employees grew disenchanted. Dan Deely, who'd worked in the men's division, left for Wilhelmina in 1968 to open a men's board there.

Zoli had grown close to a former Wagner model, Bennie Chavez, who'd become a stockbroker. In 1970 Zoli and Chavez decided to open their own agency. "He took half my male models," says Wagner, who sold what remained of his agency, and, after failing as a singer, moved to Los Angeles, where he's been a makeup artist in a department store ever since.

That October Zoli announced his arrival with a poster shot by Richard Avedon of the agency's twenty models, all in the nude. "It opened doors," Zoli deadpanned. He started trading men with François Lano in Paris and claimed $100,000 in bookings his first year. "It was OK, but it was not enough," says Vickie Pribble, who'd joined the agency.

In 1972 Chavez and Zoli decided to expand and bought a town house. They installed the agency on the lower two floors and lived upstairs, each on a separate floor, with a shared living floor in between. The agency's new home became a social center. "There was never a dull moment," says Bennie Chavez. Their parties attracted Jack Nicholson, Warren Beatty, Al Pacino, Dustin Hoffman, David Bowie, Mick and Bianca Jagger, Sue Mengers, Robert Altman, Lauren Hutton, Woody Allen, and David Geffen. "At one point, Genevieve Waite chased Mick Jagger up the stairs," Bob Colacello wrote about one party. "Her hair was soaking wet and his jacket had tomato juice all over it."

"All those guys were there for girls," says one of Zoli's bookers. "It was voluntary, but the girls would fall at their feet, of course. It was all about who was gonna get who. The girls were into it. Going to bed with lots of people was what sophisticated people were doing. It was the beginning of the days of cocaine, champagne, and airplanes. Gays really came to the forefront. You had straight men trying to make people think they were gay. It became fashionable for girls to be gay. Everything was wide open, fun, and accepting." And Zoli and his fashionable cabal were in the lead.

By 1975 Zoli had earned the sobriquet Svengali of the Strange. Bruce Cooper called the agency Zoli's zoo. But Cooper may have been a little jealous; Zoli's weirdos were bringing in several million dollars in bookings a year.

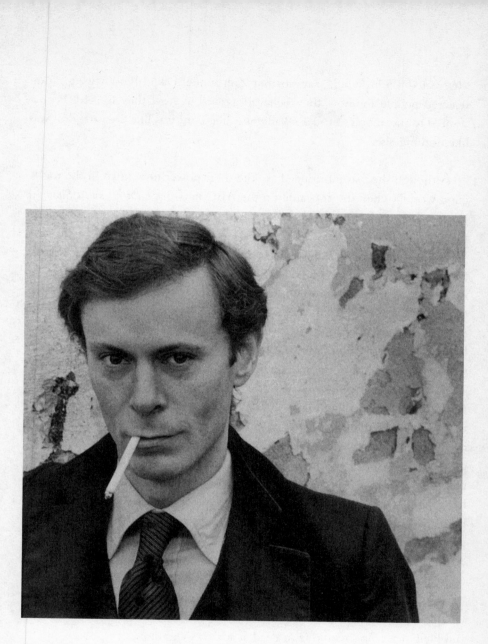

Zoli in the 1970s

"It created a whirlwind," says former Zoli model David Rosenzweig. "Zoli selected people for how they behaved as well as how they looked. People wanted to meet Zoli's models. Willie was like Ford was like Stewart. Zoli was like nothing else."

Although she was introduced as "the most powerful woman in the modeling world" when she appeared on the ABC network's *Dick Cavett Show* in January 1971, Eileen Ford was obviously not invulnerable to the upheavals of the age.

The first guest on the show was Carolyn Kenmore, a model who'd written an autobiography. She told of being pressured by men for sex because "so many models are promiscuous." Ford was the next guest, but she never got to talk about her book, *Secrets of the Model's World*. Wearing a long blood-colored dress that covered her to the neck, a knotted strand of pearls, and her hair in a bun that was almost as tight as her expression, she looked like a Victorian scold as she came onto the set, sputtering at Kenmore.

"At the risk of being rude, it's a lot of hogwash," she said of the model's tale. "I'm really . . . I'm enraged. If I had to run a business in which girls went to some filthy little office and some little pig of a guy tried to proposition them, how could I go home at night and face my children? I represent 125 girls, none of whom . . . I'm sorry. I'm not sore. I'm outraged. It doesn't happen at the Ford Agency and it needn't happen in our business. . . . It doesn't happen with *professional* models. In the first place, they cost too much by the hour. You can get a lot of girls to do a lot of things for a lot less than you can get a model."

Hoots of derision rose from the audience, leaving Ford with her mouth open and a finger in midair. Kenmore protested, saying a Ford model had sent her to just such a man. Ford said she "eliminated" and "censored" such "mangy types," sending her models only to the likes of Avedon, Penn, and Bill Helburn, who "would faint dead at such a suggestion."

"Oh, come on, Eileen," Kenmore spit back. "That's ridiculous. They're all men." The audience burst into applause.

The confrontation continued as Cavett asked questions. Can a model survive without Eileen Ford? "Lots of models are not with us," Ford said. "We get a lot more of the cream of the work."

"You have such a controlled voice when you're angry," Cavett said a bit later.

"I'm not angry now," Ford replied.

"But it sounds exactly like it did when you were," Cavett replied, breaking for a commercial.

A moment later the writer Gwen Davis joined the group on Cavett's stage. "It's a really warm kind of communication going on here," she observed.

"I guess there is a certain tension in the air," Cavett admitted.

"In the air, in the green room, on-stage." Davis laughed. Looking at Ford, she said it frightened her that "this lovely lady . . . would go to Europe and pick up four or five faces like broodmares, only not for breeding purposes. . . . It's a great deal like pimping, except the girls don't get to have any fun. . . . It's a very sad premise that a girl should be put on display to make other ladies feel that they can never look that good, but must try. But enough about the flesh business."

Stroking her neck, Ford replied, "I never worry about fat people worrying about thin people—"

"That's very constructive," Davis interrupted.

"—because slender people bury the dead," Ford concluded.

Later Charlotte Curtis, the women's page editor of *The New York Times,* joined the panel. "Models are used as agents of sales," she said, "and I think to use humans in this way is unfortunate."

Ford was ready with a reply. "I just have to ask you this, Miss Curtis, and as you're a client of mine, I realize I'm treading on very thin ice and all of you have rapier wits and I'm sort of a square. I understand all that. But why do you have models in *The New York Times* if you think they're exploiting women?"

"Our job is to report the news," Curtis replied weakly, drawing derisive laughs from the crowd. "When we report Seventh Avenue, we photograph the clothes as they are shown." Attempting to rally, she concluded that fashion is like war. "We must report atrocities, if you will."

The single-minded extravagance Diana Vreeland championed was out of fashion. "She was going too far," says an editor who worked for her. She was "too flamboyant, too over-the-top. You were beginning to feel restraint. It was time to move on, and she couldn't make the change." Alex Liberman decided Vreeland had to go.

Called back from a sitting in California, Vreeland's assistant, Grace Mirabella, was handed the daunting task of updating *Vogue* for an era of antifashion and women's liberation. After brief stints at Macy's and Saks Fifth Avenue, Mirabella had arrived at *Vogue* in 1951 and risen from a job checking store credits for captions to become Vreeland's assistant. As the sixties ended,

Mirabella had seen Liberman grow irritated with Vreeland. The clothes Vreeland showed often didn't even exist in stores. "She wasn't interested in deadlines," says Mirabella. "And women weren't buying fashion magazines. Circulation was plummeting. *Vogue* had nothing to do with anything going on in the world—zero—it was all icing and no content."

A new age had dawned. Polly Mellen sums up the change at *Vogue:* "I went home one day, and the next, Diana's red office, the leopard rug, her Rigaud candles, her scent, her being were gone. The walls were beige."

Mirabella and Liberman retooled the magazine for the new, natural-look working woman. "My *Vogue* was more accessible," Mirabella says. "I have a conviction. Women aren't inanimate objects you hang clothes on. You don't have to make fools of them." The wisdom of Liberman's choice is spelled out in circulation numbers. Until her time *Vogue* had held only a slight lead on *Bazaar.* Under Mirabella, circulation rose from 400,000 in 1971 to 1,245,000 in 1987.

Richard Avedon stayed on, but a little sadly. "The period Diana was there was the last time I could express myself honestly in fashion photography," he says. The exotic models were gone, replaced by wholesome Lauren Hutton and healthy Patti Hansen. "It went from complicated and intelligent beauty to the girl next door who'd moved away," Avedon says. "It was the beginning of fashion at its lowest common denominator, the pandering to mass appeal."

APOLLONIA VAN RAVENSTEIN * LOUISE DESPOINTES * GUNILLA LINDBLAD * SHELLEY SMITH

The era of Vreelandian extravagance was over. The revolution she'd led broadened the audience for fashion and fashion pictures exponentially, but now the market for creativity was shrinking. What had been primarily an artistic exchange became an overtly commercial one. Magazines and advertisers were worrying about selling dresses now, not about creating great photographs for a fashion elite. So as the sixties ended, fashion photography changed once again. In Europe photographers like Jeanloup Sieff, Guy Bourdin, and Helmut Newton, who'd all started before *Blow-Up* and survived it, were in their heyday, shooting dark pictures as unforgiving as they were unforgettable, full of the violence and sex, the Thanatos and Eros, that suffused life in the late sixties and early seventies. But these individualistic, often uncontrollable photographers were edged, imperceptibly, out to the fringes by a new breed of compliant lensmen who only pushed the pay envelope.

New photographers—especially Mike Reinhardt, Gilles Bensimon, Patrick Demarchelier, Alex Chatelain, John Stember, and Arthur Elgort— were emerging in Paris as the leaders of what became known as the French Mob, specialists in 35 mm street photography, happy snaps that simply denied society's downbeat mood. Though none of them alone was as influential as Avedon, Dahl-Wolfe, or Penn, together their impact was tremendous. New model agencies soon sprang up to serve them. Sympathetic gay men like François Lano and motherly figures like Eileen Ford, Dorian

Leigh, Catherine Harlé, and Wilhelmina found themselves losing models to heterosexual male agents.

There was more work, so there were more models, but as their numbers increased, they lost the singularity that made the swans of couture seem so fascinating and irreplaceable. And the new models weren't liberated women, either, even though they earned more, traveled more, and lived more freely. The genie of sex was out of the bottle. Models were touchable now. And the new breed of photographers and agents liked to have a feel for the merchandise. The good news was that "because they were interested in girls, their pictures were warmer," says onetime photographer's agent Jacques de Nointel. But more than ever, models were paper faces, commodities to be bought and sold until the next face came along. If they were infantilized before, they now stood to be traumatized as well.

As the seventies began, the center of photographic gravity shifted to Europe, where it was easier for aspirants to break into the business. They poured into Paris from all over the world, all with different stories told in a babble of languages. Shelley Smith came from America, Apollonia van Ravenstein from the Netherlands, Gunilla Lindblad from Sweden, Louise Despointes from the Caribbean. But despite their wildly varying looks and outlooks, they had one thing in common: They were citizens of the new Nation of Fashion.

SMITH: "I grew up in a not great family, not a lot of self-esteem, and so for me to go into modeling was great, because I considered myself a real ugly duckling. I went to an all-girls' school in Orange, New Jersey. I never had a date; I never dated until I was in college. I wore braces. I was tall and skinny."

RAVENSTEIN: "My brother Theo always looked at the magazines, back home, which was in the south of Holland. I think it was probably 1968, and we saw pictures of Twiggy and Jean Shrimpton. I was almost fifteen, and we were trying to find a way to get out of Holland and go into the world, so he said, 'Plo'—which is my nickname; Plonja is my middle name—'you can do it,' and I said, 'Well, all right.' He made an appointment with the agent in Amsterdam, and the following week I was in Spain for a Dutch pattern magazine."

DESPOINTES: "I came from Martinique. I was from a very protected and privileged family. My father had plantations. Then I took a secret trip to New York. We were staying in the French Embassy in Washington, and two of us, me and another young girl, got on a Greyhound bus, totally petrified, and

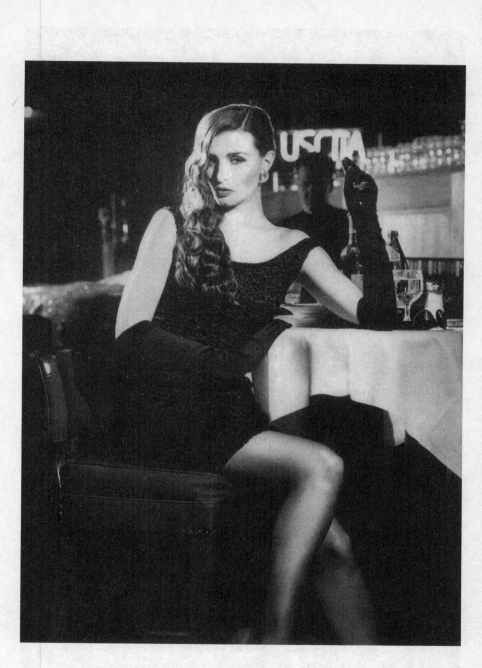

Apollonia van Ravenstein photographed by Bob McNamara

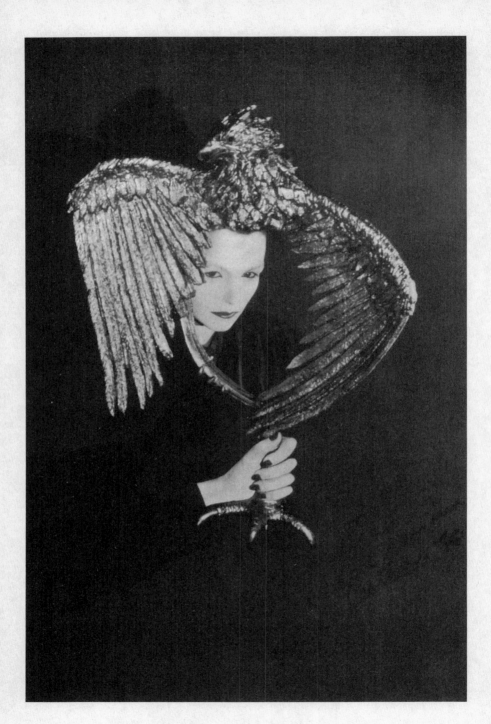

Louise Despointes photographed by Serge Lutens
for Christian Dior

came to New York. It was 1969. I was eighteen and a half. We were walking down the street, and Jerry Ford and some TV guy spotted me and said, 'Are you looking for the Ford agency?' I thought, Let's go see what this is, and the minute we walked in it was 'Go in that room! Get undressed! Pluck your eyebrows!' I was fascinated.

"I joined Ford, but I was always in battles with Eileen. Now she's the lady I respect the most. People hate Eileen because she wanted women to survive in a cutthroat business. But then we clashed right away. I had a strong mind, and I thought she was a dictator. She told me, 'Do as I say!' I said, 'No, I'm me!' I wanted to do interesting work. I didn't want to blend in. She hated that."

LINDBLAD: "I came to Paris in 1968. I was started by a woman in my town in Sweden named Kerstin Heintz. She was very respectable. She discovered many girls. She had me working for many Swedish magazines. She found me jobs, and she knew somebody in Paris who came to Sweden and he saw my book. I had a couple of tear sheets and some prints, and he liked what he saw. So he sent me to Paris, and I came to Paris Planning in 1968. It was during the student strikes. I thought it was very exciting. You had to walk to work, you'd arrive in a studio, and there was no electricity, nobody came! But I had a booking, so I said, 'I'd better be there,' and nobody else came, so I walked back home!

"The editors in France, most of them are horrible women. They're jealous of the models. They all treat you like shit. They did it to all the new girls, American or Swedish. So you were not at all treated with respect here. In America I think they're much nicer to you."

DESPOINTES: "We all went to Max's Kansas City. Everyone was there. I had no idea what was what. Then I met my chance, [photographer] Guy Bourdin. His girlfriend was a stylist. She thought I was refreshing. Guy took me back to Paris to do the collections for French *Vogue,* telling them I was a top model in New York when I'd never worked, except with [photographer] Arthur Elgort for *American Girl,* an awful kids' magazine. We were all starting, trying to make it.

"When I got to French *Vogue,* they knew something was fishy. They told me I had to have an agent. I went to Paris Planning because it was the only agency I knew. There was a sweet boy there named Patrick Demarchelier. He liked to test little girls. He said, 'I'll give her a break.' So they booked a test and said, 'Good-bye, get out.' I said, 'I can't go. I'm working.' The booker

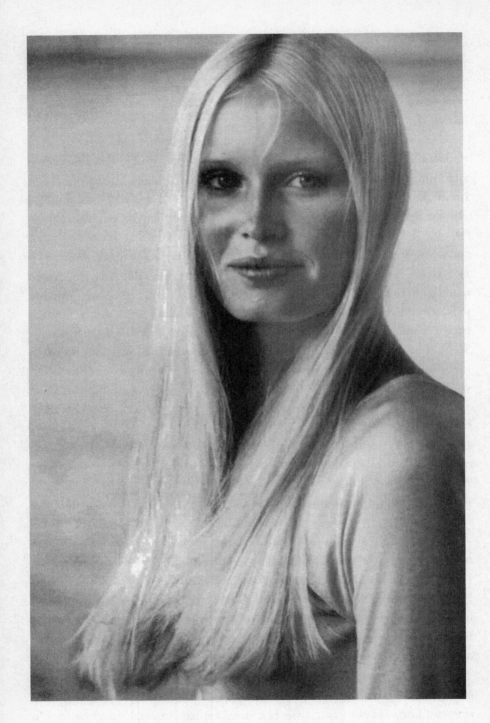

Gunilla Lindblad photographed by her husband,
Jean-Pierre Zachariasen

said, 'For who?' 'Guy Bourdin for French *Vogue.*' I thought she would fall off her chair. Then François Lano came out, saying, 'Ahhh, Louise,' and I had a contract and champagne right away."

SMITH: "I was working on the college board of Lord & Taylor department store in New York City, and Diana Vreeland came in and discovered me. She said, 'You are beautiful, and you owe it to the world to smile!' She put her finger into my face and said, 'Come to my office.' The model editor, Sarah Slavin, sent me to photographers and to Barbara Stone. It was still the era of false eyelashes and stuff like that. I remember my first big picture for *Vogue.* My eyelash was on totally wrong. I knew nothing about this, and I came into Stewart after I did the shooting, and Barbara Stone looked at me and said, 'I hope you weren't photographed looking like that!' It was so much easier later on when Way Bandy and all those wonderful people started to do makeup.

"I remember going on tests. There were always come-ons from the photographers, just about every one of them. There was never somebody who just wanted to take pictures. There was always a power play. If you wanted to get a copy of your picture, you had to come over at six and they wanted to have a drink with you. You just wanted to wash your hands and get your picture and go. It was very intimidating."

RAVENSTEIN: "I left Holland after a month and went to Milan. You're thrown into this arena, thinking people love you for who you are. There was some emotional disappointment and a lot of learning about human nature. I didn't really feel that people cared about what I was like. They had to love to be with me because I was a gorgeous young woman, and tall and beautiful, and a lot of fun. But I did feel an emptiness inside, and a certain sadness, because there was such untruth, it was such a fake. It's very overwhelming and terribly exciting, and it can be profoundly empty at the same time. I didn't understand people, I didn't understand what they were after, the promises they made."

DESPOINTES: "Guy Bourdin trained me. He was like a father to me. He was a peasant from Normandy, so like a fox, he could see everything. He had a mind of his own. He made me have my own opinions. He sent me to museums to see paintings. At our first job he had a ballet barre, up off the ground, and I had to climb up on it in high heels. I had to do it a hundred fifty times for one shot. He wanted to see what I had in my belly. He called me Shirley MacLaine. He'd say, 'Shirley MacLaine would not do that. She

The cover of *Harper's Bazaar* featuring the text:

HARPER'S
BAZAAR

GOOD NEWS ISSUE
YOUR EASY
GUIDE
TO SUPER
HEALTH
& BEAUTY

☐ 22 pages of expert advice

the new
you!

5 new cuts for problem hair
The perfect-figure diet
Clothes that work best for you

☐ Special section
PETITE BAZAAR
Terrific fashion for 5'4" & under

Your complete guide
DIVORCE & REMARRIAGE
For better or for worse

EXTRA! 88 HOT LOOKS

Shelley Smith photographed by Bill King for the cover
of *Harper's Bazaar*

would stand on this bar until she died because she had to be the best.' He liked perfection. You could think he was a sadist, but he wasn't. People say it was misogyny, but it wasn't. He was not nasty to people he cared for, but there were very few. He would make me walk through glass, but I understood that was his work, his vision.

"For the first two years Guy forbade me to work with others. I was booked by [photographer] Sarah Moon for *Elle,* and I told Guy and he locked me in the studio. My booker called, and he answered with a handkerchief over the phone and pretended he was shooting. I was banned from *Elle.* But there was always something happening with Guy. It was always '*get the picture.*' I was lucky. I worked with exceptional people. Most of them have disappeared."

SMITH: "I graduated from college in 1971. I went to Europe, and I was going to go in the Peace Corps; but an editor at *Elle* saw me on the street and sent me to Suzy Parker's sister. I thought it would probably be a good thing to do and easier than the Peace Corps, and I'd love to stay in Paris. So I waltzed over to Dorian Leigh and hooked up with her.

"She was not a good person to be a model agent or a caretaker of women. She would have dinner parties and invite you to meet men. If you told her you were hungry and you wanted money, she'd be having dinner with somebody rich, and she'd bring you along. A model can always get a free meal at the best restaurants, if you can suffer through these insufferable dinners! You didn't even have to go dancing with them afterwards. They were ugly, boring people who wanted pretty girls at their table. But I didn't want to eat dinner with these creepy guys.

"I think Dorian wanted everybody to live the life that she lived as a model, but if you're really a good agent, like Eileen Ford, you want the model to stay at your house and go to bed at night so you'll look great for the job. I went to Dorian in tears, and I said, 'I cannot pay my rent,' and she said, 'Darling, have a drink,' and she popped a bottle of champagne and said, 'This will soothe you.' Dorian drank, and she lived like a princess, and it was on our money.

"You would go in once a week, Friday from one to three, and you'd be standing in line to get your money, and there'd be this long wait. There were all these models from Sweden or America. I was one of the only ones who spoke French because I had studied it in school, and I wasn't going to let them screw me, so for weeks at a time I'd go in there and do all the translating and say, 'I need my money.' Finally you'd get a check, but it would be a *cheque barré,* and you could not cash it unless you were a French citizen. To this day Dorian has a ton of money of mine. I think she screwed everybody around her and brought everything down on herself."

RAVENSTEIN: "I was in Milan three months. Then Auro Varani [who printed composites for models] and a male model named Georges and me, we went from Milan to Paris in winter in a sports car. There was a lot of talk about me. I was with Simone [d'Aillencourt at Models International] for a short amount of time, but it was very difficult to get your money. I used to go stand on the table and demand my money. That experience was so bad that I decided to go to Morocco with this Dutch friend. So we took the boat to Casablanca, and we took buses and hitchhiked around. A Dutch photographer who worked for *Marie Claire* was there, and being Dutch girls, we visited her house in Marrakech. She was doing an issue for the London *Sunday Times* on henna. I had henna in my hair, on the inside of my hands with a rabbit motif, my feet, my forehead, my breasts, and we did beautiful pictures, and that put me right back into the business again after maybe five months. Back in Paris, I joined François Lano, and I was with him forever. I met a photographer Jean-François Jonvelle and I moved in with him. All you did was meet photographers. Who else could I get to meet? I never went to the supermarket!"

DESPOINTES: "Finally I started to feel very locked in with Guy Bourdin. I wanted to do something else. I wanted to catch Helmut Newton. I'd met Serge Lutens, and I wanted to breeze. I worked for [Newton's wife, photographer] Alice Springs for Jean-Louis David and I made myself up the way I knew Helmut would like, and he saw me in the mirror and he booked me. I was small, but I was strong, and I stood up to him, and he liked that and he didn't like that, so we battled a lot. Guy had a tendency, once you were out of his circle, you were out. So when I saw him again, I was dirty, because I was working with other people.

"Helmut was German and very straight. His fantasies were only in his pictures, not in his private life at all. Then he had a heart attack. He started to feel bad in Mexico. We were on a trip with another model named Emanuelle Dano. Later his wife told me we put him through hell. We threw knives at dinner. We took drugs. We got shot at. We had fun. Hey, we were girls in the sixties.

"Emanuelle was my girlfriend for a while. We went together. It was a big love story. But I only knew her for four months. She was murdered by her upper-class French boyfriend. One of her eyes was plucked out, her legs were broken, and she was burned with cigarettes. Her death was really unnecessary. She called me that night to go out, but I was married, and my husband put pressure on me. Two days later she was found in her apartment. Her father was a government minister, so it was totally covered up. I went to the funeral. It was 'Emanuelle has gone back to God,' like nothing had happened!

"Models started to feel badly treated when the hooligans came in. François Lano might have been a wild kid, he liked to party a lot, but he was not a vicious person. This was a new crowd. Men who dreamed about this world. All these guys came in and used drugs and sex to get girls. The important photographers had removed themselves. How many girls could Guy, Helmut, and Serge use? The new photographers had to create their own models. But they couldn't compete with genius. They brought in mediocrity. It became a game of money and power in 1973, 1974. Instead of getting their power through genius, they got it through girls. A top model is like a diamond to them, power in their hands. They went out with every new model in town. This macho thing is pretty French. To exist, you have to have every girl. It became a nuisance, so boring, so fake."

SMITH: "The photographers were hitting on everybody. Mike Reinhardt always had a model girl, but I thought he was pretty nice about it. Patrick Demarchelier was always pretty classy, too. Alex Chatelain was always saying, 'I'm too fat, but would you go out with me anyway?' That's why I have such great things to say about Arthur Elgort, because he would never hit on me. He just didn't think that he could! Artie Elgort got his start in Paris just hanging out with the models. He was this little schleppy kind of guy, and he'd stand by Paris Planning and take pictures as models came out."

LINDBLAD: "I was happy. I was making money. I was doing catalogs, I was working for magazines, and finally after about two years, in early 1970, I decided to go to New York. Of course, it was all planned between François Lano and Eileen Ford. He was working with Eileen. He had also started to work with Wilhelmina; but I had met Eileen before, and I decided to work with Eileen. And that's when it started.

"I had an appointment with *Vogue* and Jean-Pierre [Zachariasen] had an appointment with *Glamour* in the same building on the same floor. It was the time of Diana Vreeland, of course, and I had my appointment with Sarah

Slavin, and she came out and said, 'You have your book?' Jean Pierre had this enormous book, too, so she said, 'Oh, you're a photographer. Can I have your book?' He said, 'Oh, no, I didn't come here to see you! I'm going to *Glamour.*' So finally I said, 'Jean Pierre, give her your book.' She took the two books, and I was called in, and there was Mrs. Vreeland. She was so scary-looking in her bright red wool. She came and took me in her arms and said, 'I could eat you!' Three days later we had fifteen pages together.

"A couple of months later we had this trip to Fiji. Before leaving, Jean-Pierre was called into the offices of Diana Vreeland, and she said, 'Jean-Pierre, you're going to Fiji now, and you're going to have all these dresses. I want close-ups. I want to feel the clothes. I want to feel the texture. I don't give a damn about the landscape!' It was twenty pages, no makeup artist, no hairdresser, no assistant to the editor. It was just Jean Pierre, me, and the editor, and the editor was like sixty-five years old. She didn't do anything. She was not at all interested in fashion. She preferred to look at the birds. And there we were, and the first thing Jean-Pierre did was he stepped on his light meter!"

SMITH: "I wasn't in Paris that long. Maybe a year. I would go to Milan. Milan was a very lonely place for models. All the models stayed at the same hotel, the Arena. We would hang out with each other, but it was a very lonely place, because I didn't do any of those dinners [that Italian playboys and agents arranged almost nightly]. I guess there's a part of me that just didn't quite fit into that. But Milan was great because you got paid cash. You'd love Milan and Germany because there, sitting in your little letter box at your hotel, was cash!

"I met Eileen Ford through Paris Planning, and she said, 'I'd love to have you.' So I didn't go back with Barbara Stone because I'd always heard that Eileen was the best agent. She's very eccentric and up and down, but I tell you one thing, Eileen was so loyal to her models. She knew something that most agents don't know. If you support the talent, you can get anything you want from anybody else. When I came from Europe, I'd had all my stuff sent back via shipping cargo. She drove me three hours to the Pan Am place to get my stuff. Unless somebody was really late all the time or really messed up on the job, she supported you."

LINDBLAD: "We moved back to Paris in the end of '72. We'd been crossing the ocean quite a few times. We had a son then; that's why we came back. That's when Elite opened. I did not know John Casablancas before. I'd been very happy with Paris Planning before, so when we moved back here, I went to Paris Planning. John had already approached me, but I wasn't so sure. He went to Jean-Pierre, and Jean-Pierre told me. I did not like that. If he would have come straight to me, I probably would have been charmed and said, 'Sure, OK, let's try.' But finally Paris Planning made such a mess of things that I went to John. I would say out of twelve girls, there were four girls who were really, really top. Me, John's girlfriend, and a few others. He raised all our prices."

DESPOINTES: "Everything changed in 1976. By then I was only working with Serge Lutens. I was his muse. We laughed and worked and spoke about other things than fashion. We went out and were wild, and we scared everyone. I always had a black veil on. We set the studio on fire and shot pictures of Nero and Pompeii. We were children in a bubble without reality and created our own world and [our client] Dior paid the bill. It was a good laugh.

"Around that time John Casablancas proposed to me in a nightclub to come with Elite. He was with Patrick Demarchelier. But when everyone went to him in the early seventies, I stood by François Lano. Then John Casablancas started a war with Paris Planning and François Lano brought [agent] Gérald Marie in. François was gay. He couldn't take girls to bed. He needed someone like Gérald to balance things out. Gérald has changed now; he's gained class. But at that time he was a little prick. I couldn't stand the guy. I left Paris Planning because of him and went to an agency called FAM. Finally I quit in 1979 and opened my own agency called City. I was a model who had managed her own career, and I didn't sell out."

RAVENSTEIN: "I came to America in March 1973. In Rome I'd met Eileen Ford and someone from Stewart, and I preferred Stewart and I went with them. Then I went to Wilhelmina for a couple of months, and then I found Zoli. I was so attracted to him as a friend, and he stayed a great friend for the rest of my life. The American agents would all go to a dinner for Zoli in Rome. It was the only time you could get them together without fighting.

"I loved America. I never really looked at the culture too much; I just lived within it. I was so excited about the city, about the people, about the work, about the music, about life. I became very friendly with Andy Warhol. I got a cover for *Interview* magazine, and I was the model of the minute or the year or whatever.

"The bad stuff was always from drugs, but at that time it wasn't ugly, it wasn't looked at so bad. It was just, you had a good time and you felt really good. It hadn't turned negative. It was a very mind-enlarging, exciting time for me, some acid trips here and there. I don't really feel that it touched me in a negative way. I did yoga to balance myself, to find myself. But it can become pretty ugly, and it did."

LINDBLAD: "Sometimes when you were booked on trips, they booked three girls, one serious like me and two others who would enjoy some fun. I was there to work and nothing else, so it was a difficult situation because you would have the photographer and the models and the hairdressers all sniffing coke. They were in their own world, and I felt very much left out. I didn't like the scene at all because I wasn't into drugs.

"I think the sanest people in all this business are the models. The photographers and the editors and the agents are much more bizarre than the models. If you think that the girls are taken away from their homes, they come to a new country, they get so much money! For me, coming to France was weird. I didn't speak French. I was warned about the French men. I was scared. I did not get involved. I was doing my job. I didn't need all this. It's not my cup of tea. My friends were not going crazy. It was the generation after me, five or six years later.

"Turning thirty, that was the hardest part. I was really at the peak of my career. I was not really prepared to do something else. Suddenly I realized it's not going to be like this the rest of my life. My whole way of seeing things changed. Finally I knew I had to quit one day. The work started to slow down in '86, '87. I still wanted to die with my boots on, but finally it sort of ended by itself because we decided to move back to Paris and open a shop in '89. After that, I worked very little, because in France they don't like older girls. It was not hard quitting."

SMITH: "The crazy disco years were definitely going on when I was in the business. There was a lot of snorting and stuff going on. I was always a little bit on the outskirts. I talked dirty. That was my kick because I was never allowed to use four-letter words growing up.

"I didn't do drugs, but I saw them, and I kind of felt out of it in a way. I remember Bill King. He had this studio on lower Fifth Avenue, and he had a studio on one side, and on the other side he had an office or another room, and if he really liked you, he'd invite you to the office, and I know now it was to do drugs, and he invited me in there, and I realized that it was to do drugs, but I just didn't want to do it.

"A very famous model—I can't name this person, it's too destructive—was in the men's room of a disco, shooting nude pictures of various modes of sexual contact with a bunch of men. I had a really good friend who was a lawyer, and the pictures came to him. Well, what happened was that Bill King had taken the pictures, and Bill King's assistant stole the pictures, and Bill King went to this friend of mine who was an attorney to try to recoup them, because it was obviously potentially scandalous.

"Bill got a real kick out of pictures of people going wild. He'd spray water, and he'd put a fan on full force, and every picture was wildly energetic, and he got his kicks almost out of exhausting you. It wasn't the picture; it was watching you get exhausted. It all had some strange overtones. I think the drugs were a way to control the models.

"Bill was gay like crazy. There was some pathology there with women, but I have to say that I never did that stuff with him and he was always wonderful with me. I have half a dozen *Bazaar* covers with him, and he was terrific.

"But I was pretty bored with modeling. Your mind never really had to be there. It's probably better not to be too smart if you're a model. You're going to get tired of it a lot faster. Or you get to be too independent, and you have your own ideas about things and want to make your own image rather than accept what's dealt to you. So at the end of the seventies I came out to L.A. to do a television series called *The Associates*. I kept doing television series that didn't last. Then I had a tragedy in my life. Four and half years ago I got pregnant, but about a week before he was due, I had an ultrasound scan, and the doctor said there was something terribly wrong. I was rushed to the hospital, and gave birth to my son by cesarean, and he had an extremely rare genetic disease, and he survived only for three days. He wasn't here very long, but he just absolutely turned my life around. I was in therapy, and the therapist kept saying to me, 'You should be a therapist,' and I went back to school and I started studying psychology.

"Originally I wanted to work with people who had losses. But my husband and I started trying to get pregnant right away, and I began experiencing infertility, which was shocking to me, because a year earlier I had gotten pregnant right off the bat. I started to think that I could help people who were infertile. I woke up one night and said 'egg donors.' And that expanded into a surrogacy program, which I run with my husband. I get calls from Australia, Germany, from people who want me to help them get babies! Now I have the greatest job in the world!

"So much opportunity ended in so much tragedy in modeling. I think the world has to build these images of beautiful people. We fantasize that if you look perfect on the outside, your life must run perfectly on the inside. But I always saw beauty as a mask and a trap. I mean, I see this now. I certainly didn't see this when I was twenty. You're revered and rewarded for being beautiful on the outside, and nobody wants to know too much more than that. And when that beauty starts to fade, where do you go with your life?"

$1,500 A DAY

Jeanette Christjansen had just been named Miss Denmark when she came to Paris on a visit at Christmas 1967 and met a long-haired Danish photographer named Gunnar Larsen. He had a bad reputation. He took lousy photographs. But he had a great eye for girls. So when Jeanette went back to Denmark, Larsen sent her a letter, a thousand francs, and an invitation to work in Paris early the next year, shooting couture press photographs. He put her up in the Hôtel d'Argout, a tiny little place near the open markets at Les Halles.

Also at the D'Argout that week was a public relations man who worked for Trabeco, a nearby architecture firm. He'd just left his wife, and he was staying at the hotel while he looked for a new apartment. A news junkie, he would watch the broadcast every night in the reception area. And every night Larsen would stalk by with the blond, booted, miniskirted Christjansen in tow. "I fell in love at first instant," she says of the night she first set eyes on John Casablancas.

He wasn't uninterested. But as he puts it, he couldn't just walk up to Larsen and say, "Excuse me, sir, could you leave?"

Finally, one night at two, the hotel doorman told Casablancas that the blonde wasn't Larsen's girlfriend; she was his model. "I'm going to call her in the morning," the love-struck Casablancas decided. "But she has asked for a taxi to the airport in the morning," the doorman warned him. Rushing to his room, John dialed Jeanette's room and woke her up. He was a salesman at heart. He could talk for hours if he had to to get what he wanted. Minutes later Jeanette was dressing for a rendezvous at the restaurant Au Pied de Cochon. She decided Casablancas was devastatingly handsome and extremely well educated. He also spoke several languages. He was quite a catch. The trick was to catch him.

Casablancas was a child of once-wealthy refugees from the Spanish Civil War. His grandfather, who'd owned textile factories outside Barcelona, was a tinkerer who'd invented the Casablancas high draft system—a modern method for transforming cotton balls into thread—and owned the patent. "We would have been a very, very rich family had not the Civil War brought down everything," Casablancas says. Wealthy antifascists, the Casablancas family was disenfranchised by that conflict pitting fascists against anticapitalists. John's future father and his mother, who'd briefly been a model in Barcelona, were on a beach holiday when that city was overtaken by anarchists. Grabbing their eldest and then only son, Fernando, they crossed into France just before Spain's borders were closed.

Their factories were ruined, but luckily they had investments outside Spain, and as they moved about the world, seeking safe haven, they opened new plants in Manchester, Lille, and Bombay. Next stop was Rio de Janeiro, where John's sister, Sylvia, was born. Then came New York, where John joined the family in December 1942. Home was a large house in Forest Hills, Queens, but John was a jet set kid. He received holy communion in Mexico City and grew up resort hopping from Lake Placid to Palm Beach. Finally his family moved to the Riviera. John describes them as "nomads."

"My life was a dream," he says. "I always think of those people who say there's life after life and that if you're very good in one life, you get a marvelous life in the next turn. I must have been so perfect the life before."

At eight John was sent to Le Rosey, the exclusive Swiss school where the children of kings and princes of industry are educated. Among his classmates were Egon von Fürstenberg; Alfredo Beracasa, scion of Venezuelan bankers and industrialists; Alan Clore, the son of one of England's richest men; and Alain Kittler, whose family owned a textile design business, Anatolie St. Fiacre.

Though he was raised as a member of the elite, "we were poor by all the standards," Casablancas says of himself and Kittler, who became his best friend and later his business partner. "Our parents were very regular people with very average fortunes. My father spent money for the last fifteen years of his life without making any money. He was not productive, and he continued living like a king. Which I think was exactly the right thing. He earned his money. Why shouldn't he spend it?"

By the time John was finishing school, his sister, Sylvia, had become a star of international society. For five years in the late fifties and early sixties she was

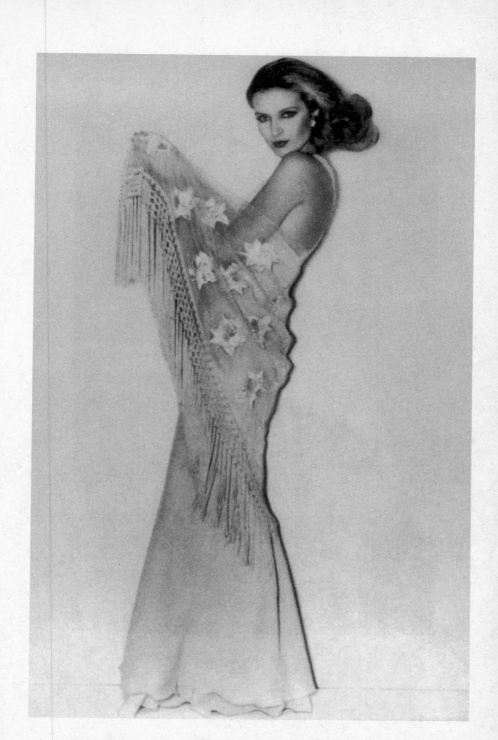

Jeanette Christjansen strikes a pose for Gianpaolo Barbieri

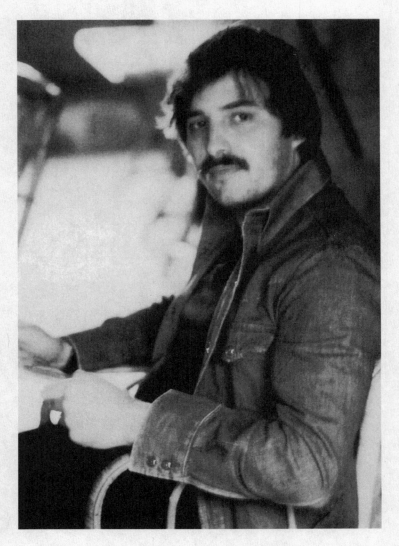

John Casablancas as a young wolf in the 1970s

the Aga Khan's girlfriend. "Together with the princess Soraya, Sylvia was the number one jet set person in Europe," John says. "On the front page of every magazine and every newspaper. She had a knack for scandal. She was very beautiful and very explosive. The press decided that we were Mexican because my sister had a Mexican passport. So she was the Mexican heiress. And I remember a big article that said my father owned as many oil wells as he owned cattle heads. And we said, 'That's the first time they write the truth; he has not any of either.'"

After Le Rosey, John attended several universities. "I used to fight with my father," he says. "When I fought, I went to work. If I made peace, I went to college." He transferred to a law school in Spain. "Then I would take my car and take off for two months and come back just before exam time and study day and night, drinking coffee," he says. "Typical kind of thing that students do." In between, he worked for Merrill Lynch in Cannes, Brussels, and Paris; for a PR company; and then, at age nineteen, for a real estate company in Barcelona, where he sold real estate to English investors with undeclared income.

Then he was offered a job in Brazil. A Le Rosey schoolmate's mother had inherited a Coca-Cola franchise in the country's northeast and thought her Brazilian managers were stealing. "At the age of twenty I went to Bahia, to become marketing manager for Coca-Cola," Casablancas says. "I had no marketing knowledge, but I could be trusted. So I was there for three and a half years. Now I was a typical European, used to a lot of dating, a lot of fun with the girls. And here I am, in Bahia, which was very, very far from any civilization. The only girls were prostitutes or society girls surrounded with chaperones and impossible to date unless you were marrying them." So he called his girlfriend in France and invited her to join him in Bahia. But her father laid down the law: not unless they got married. "So I said, 'OK, fine,'" John says. "So I married her. And you know, it was too early."

According to Casablancas, he left Brazil because of "a *Dona Flor and Her Two Husbands* very comedy-tragedy type of circumstance within the Coca-Cola factories." Luckily his wife's family helped him find a PR job in Paris. "I start working there, and of course, the moment I get back to Paris, my marriage starts falling apart because I've got in me still so much desire to party," he says. "I'm not mature enough to settle down. The only thing that tempered this was that I didn't have any money."

He left his wife and met Jeanette. But after their late date she went back to Denmark. "She was supposed to call me, and I was supposed to call her; but we didn't, and about three months later, walking in the streets of Paris, again just by chance, I bumped into her," Casablancas says. She'd returned to Paris to work with Larsen. She started dating Casablancas, who'd moved into an apartment on the rue de Seine with Alain Kittler. "I didn't want to get married at nineteen, and I didn't worry that he wasn't divorced," Christjansen says. But six months later his wife got pregnant. "I wanted to leave him, but he said he had no intention of going back to her," Jeanette says. "He wasn't exactly sorry. I either had to accept it or leave. I thought I'd stick it out and see what happens."

Though John had dated "four or five models" before Jeanette, he says, "the idea that I would be involved with their world never came to my mind." But he was looking for a career, and somehow the one he found, selling glue and construction materials, just wasn't as appealing as their friend Larsen's suggestion that he open a model agency. Casablancas had learned a bit about modeling from Jeanette. Though she'd quickly become one of Catherine Harlé's top earners, she had problems with the agency. "I didn't think they were taking good care of me," she says. "They were an old-time agency with thousands of girls, sending me on go-sees right and left. I did garbage jobs. Then John got his idea."

In 1969 Casablancas took an office in the American Chamber of Commerce's building on Avenue George V and opened a small agency with a handful of shareholders, Gunnar Larsen among them. "It was a decision of sheer ignorance," he says. "I knew nothing. But my thinking was not to do this because there's a lot of pretty girls. That's a rich man's thinking. I was a poor guy." He named his business Élysées 3—after his new telephone number and in homage to New York's Plaza Five.

Though it was years before Casablancas made his presence felt on an international level, modeling was never the same. No longer would the business be run exclusively by the women and homosexual men like François Lano. With Casablancas, a new generation entered modeling. Raised on the new values of sex, drugs, and rock and roll, they were the children of *Blow-Up,* and their arrival on the scene was explosive.

"I brought a very different eye to modeling," Casablancas says. "In those days it was a feminine activity. I was really the first total heterosexual agent in Paris. I knew a lot of models, I had met a few photographers, and I had been around, you know. I went into this with one premise: finding beautiful girls and marketing them. Getting girls was the easy part. By the time we opened the agency, I had a pretty good impression of what was missing in modeling. I did my homework. Every model I ever spoke to complained about their agency. Little did I know that models always complained. Had I known that, maybe I would not have gone into the business."

While John was setting up Élysées 3, Jeanette kept modeling, flying to Hamburg, Munich, and Milan on jobs. In the latter city she was represented by Riccardo Gay (pronounced *guy*). Gay started his career as a journalist at Milan's newspaper *Corriere della Sera* and, in the mid-sixties, became the model scout at a new magazine called *Amica*. Modeling was a new business in Milan. Colette Gambier, a friend of Catherine Harlé's, had opened the first agency there in 1962. Four years later Giorgio Piazzi, who'd modeled in London and New York, opened shop, too, starting out booking his friends on a public telephone in a bar in Milan's Brera district. He called his company Fashion Model. The next year the competition heightened. Gay's sister, Lucetta, who worked at Giorgio Piazzi's Fashion Model, is said to have made off with a client list. "I started an agency for fun with my sister," Gay says. "I was the first in Europe to use vouchers. This was quite a big shock."

Colette Gambier knew Gay from his days at *Amica*. "Before he had his agency, he went to nightclubs," she says. "When I booked models to *Amica*, Riccardo would take them out and show them off. He'd thought a long time about this. I had no time for nightclubs. I never presented girls to men. Then the times changed. The girls preferred Riccardo. He was worldly; he introduced them to princes; he took the girls for weekends in castles. He immediately knew how to profit from his position. I called him a matrimonial agent and not a model agent. And he would say bad things about me. It was a war, and he quickly won it."

Gay started booking models from Paris, Jeanette Christjansen among them. She was flying to Milan when two Frenchmen tried to pick her up on the airplane. One was photographer Patrick Demarchelier; the other, his agent, Jacques de Nointel. De Nointel made his living on the fringes of modeling. "He is a hunting dog," says a photographer who knows him well. "He steals girls from one agency and presents them to another." He tried it with Christa Fiedler, among many others. "He was always between the agencies, trying to tell one model to go to the other agency and being paid for that," she says.

Now Christjansen was in his sights. "I said, 'Hey, you're so beautiful, how come you're not working with magazines?' " de Nointel recalls. "She said, 'I'm with an agency that doesn't give me magazines, but my boyfriend is opening an agency.' And I said, 'Your boyfriend, I hope he's gay, because have you ever heard of an alcoholic opening a bar?' And she says, 'I want you to meet this guy.' So John came to see me."

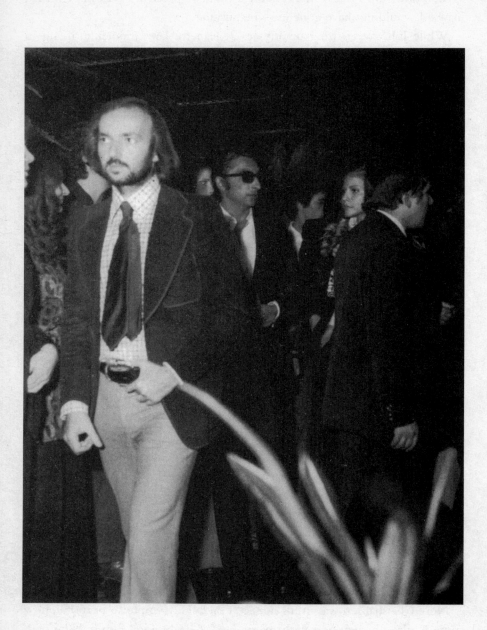

Riccardo Gay on the prowl in the 1970s

Casablancas was intrigued by de Nointel. "I don't think there was anybody who understood the business and who lived it as intensely as Jacques," he says. "He was a rep, and he had every good photographer in Paris." Among them were Demarchelier, Gilles Ben Simon (as he was then known), Alex Chatelain, Jean-Pierre Zachariasen, and Arthur Elgort. Another was Mike Reinhardt, the grandson of Max Reinhardt, the German filmmaker. In the early sixties Mike was a lawyer, married to a German model named Bernadette, who'd been discovered by Eileen Ford and placed with Dorian Leigh. In 1965 Jerry Ford suggested Reinhardt go to work for Leigh, "straightening out her tangled affairs," Ford says. "We agreed to pay her fifteen hundred dollars per month to pay Mike."

With his salary guaranteed by the Fords, Reinhardt arrived at Leigh's agency. "Dorian was obviously erratic and drinking," he says. "I was between a rock and a hard place. I really loved Dorian, but she resented any intervention. So I ended up a booker and a sort of pseudoaccountant." He stayed two years. "All these incredible girls around me!" he exclaims. "I was blown away. I met a model, fell in love, and had an affair with her. The situation destroyed my marriage." But though he'd lost a wife, he'd gained an agent in Jacques de Nointel, who met him at Dorian's and convinced him he could be a photographer.

John Casablancas listened to de Nointel also. "He started telling me about the industry," Casablancas says. "And everything he told me was true, but I didn't believe a word. He said he didn't think there was room for one more agency; it would end up a big catalog agency like Paris Planning and Models International. He felt that what was needed was an agency that concentrated on stars. He described what Elite was going to be all about. But I didn't listen to him. I did Élysées 3 instead."

Casablancas introduced his agency with a double-page spread in *Passport,* an annual publication for models. The ad promised models "a new concept of cooperation . . . cash payments . . . free preparation of dossier, financing of composites, free juridical service, permanent door-to-door bookings." For clients, Élysées 3 offered "efficiency in booking . . . precision of tariff . . . always on schedule . . . open Saturday."

De Nointel predicted Élysées 3 would die within a year. "John had a lot of ideas, but the first year he knew nothing," de Nointel says. "He learned from his mistakes." De Nointel tried to help out. He sent Casablancas to his friend Stewart Cowley's agency, for example, but Barbara Stone didn't want to work with him. Neither did the Fords. "He was a friend of Mike's, and I thought he was a nice young guy, and we wanted to work with him," says Jerry Ford. "But he took a long time getting a handle on things. We told him very frankly that we wanted to do business with him but we wouldn't until he was established."

De Nointel quickly saw what Casablancas brought to the model trade. "John introduced sex," he says. "Don Juan, Casanova, their whole life put together is not equal to one year of John! John can look at a girl, and in five minutes the girl takes her underwear off. I could tell stories! He's a hell of a successful man. He introduced the truth against the lies of the good mommy Eileen. I was going out with a girl, and Eileen said, 'Don't spend the weekend with Jacques. I have to introduce you to somebody.' And she introduced her to a millionaire, and she married him. It was a better deal than going out with a jerk like me! But *still*!"

Casablancas's first move was to fly to Copenhagen for its ready-to-wear shows with Gunnar Larsen. He went from stand to stand at the trade fair, introducing himself to models and, by the end of his visit, had a dozen girls ready to return to Paris with him. Among them were several stars from Copenhagen Models, one of the largest agencies in Scandinavia. Its owner, Trice Tomsen, then an ally of Eileen Ford's, woke up one morning and over coffee and Danish pastries, saw a photograph by Larsen in the newspaper, showing the girls and Casablancas over a caption that said they were going to Paris to join Élysées 3. Furious, Tomsen got them all back, but "she was so pissed off with me she didn't even want to hear my name for two years," Casablancas says, laughing.

Until his arrival Scandinavia had been Eileen Ford's personal fiefdom. "There were one or two agents in Göteborg [Sweden] who would keep girls for Eileen," says Monique Corey, who worked on Ford's new faces board. "Eileen would bring them home and get them ready like fruit on a window until they were ripe enough. She went to Scandinavia every three months to pick up blondes. She had the market cornered. The clients all wanted that look." Casablancas was poaching on her turf.

Back in Paris, Casablancas took over de Nointel's photographer's agency. Championed by *Dépêche Mode,* his French Mob photographers stood in opposition to the generation that immediately preceded them: Helmut Newton, Jeanloup Sieff, Barry Lategan, and Just Jaeckin. "We called them the tele-photo brigade. They threw everything out of focus in the background," says Lategan, whose carefully lit, controlled photographs for British *Vogue* were at the opposite end of the spectrum. Steve Hiett, a British photographer who moved to Paris at the time, also disdained the French Mob's approach. "Everyone was shooting long lens, the same time of the day, the same blond girl," he says. "It was all interchangeable." But the new wave of photographers were well trained. Jacques Malignon, Bensimon, and Demarchelier all had worked for older photographers like Just Jaeckin, who shot fashion in the late sixties before turning to film. "They learned the basics of technique with us," he says. "Then they left and said they'd do the same work for less money. It was a disaster for us."

The new photographers had disasters, too. In those days they kept their samples in huge wood-covered portfolios. In July 1970 Casablancas dumped the books into his Porsche Carrera, drove to Germany, and spent four days pitching the photographers to advertising agencies there. He got back to Paris at 2:00 A.M. "I was so exhausted, I didn't want to carry the books," he remembers. "Each one weighed about thirty pounds! So I shut them in the car, and someone with a knife cut open the top and stole them. I was hoping I'd get them back. They had no value. But I didn't get them. I never had the guts to tell the photographers, so I just resigned and sold the business for twenty thousand francs. Elgort never forgave me."

The buyer was Patrick Demarchelier's half brother, Gérald Dearing, who worked for the photo agency. "John quickly found out he couldn't mix photographers and models," Dearing says. Despite the offhand manner in which he disposed of them, most of the photographers stayed friends with Casablancas. The French Mob was a tight little mutual-support group. "In the beginning, when Mike Reinhardt was still a director of Dorian, all of the top models would do tests with him," recalls de Nointel. "Mike would call Patrick, and say, 'Patrick, I can't do this light, come and help me.' "

"I was hanging around with the young assistants," says Reinhardt. "Newton and Bourdin were the big guys. We were just starting. There was Pierre Houlès, my best friend, Jean-Pierre Zachariasen, Patrick, Duc, who was Bourdin's assistant. Alex was just back from New York. A couple of us had apprenticed with New York photographers. We'd assist each other when we did tests. Duc went with me on my first job. I was separated, living in a hotel, barely scraping by. I got a trip to Algeria from a magazine. Then it started rather quickly."

Photography was *almost* everything to Reinhardt. Models were the rest. "After Bernadette left me, two weeks later the other girl leaves, and I'm left with my pants down and nobody," Reinhardt says. For a while he played the field. "There's a mercenary thing going on," he says. "Even with girlfriends, there was a commercial side to the relationship. We used each other. The male psyche always wants to be the exception. I always said, 'Would you be with me if I was the garbage man?' But it's convenient. You travel together; you have the same sense of humor. It's a given that you end up with a model. I was unfortunately neurotic enough to fall in love, but I couldn't be completely faithful." Not when there were models around who would sleep with a young, sympathetic, and attractive photographer in exchange for work.

Patrick Demarchelier had a model girlfriend, too, of course—an American named Bonnie Lysohir, whose brother assisted Arthur Elgort. Of all the photographers, Demarchelier was the closest to Casablancas. Everybody loved Demarchelier. Some suggest that his gravel mumble was the key to his success. Nobody could understand a word he was saying. He also had an appealing modesty. "Now young photographers want to be like Avedon," he says. "When I was young, I didn't have a goal like that. You didn't project yourself."

Born in Normandy in 1944, Demarchelier worked in a photo shop, learning to print and retouch photos, before he moved in 1964 to Paris. There he worked in a lab, and then for a head shot photographer who gave him a list of model schools in Paris. Patrick started offering them his services. One, conveniently located next door to Paris Planning, set him up with a little studio, where he tested thirty girls a month, helping them pull their portfolios together. After a year he won a job assisting Hans Feurer. Then he hooked up with de Nointel and started shooting on his own for *Marie France* and *Elle*. Unlike his peers, he didn't settle down with any model for long.

"Those guys wanted to get married," he says. "I had a lot of girlfriends. I loved the girls, yeah, it was true." Demarchelier's girlfriends were "all tops," says Gérald Dearing. "He had a good nose for girls. He always found them before the others did. He was a tremendous asset to John."

Alex Chatelain wasn't as lucky in love as Demarchelier and Reinhardt. A struggling painter in New York, Chatelain shared an apartment with a friend who worked for *Vogue*. "We were both like rabbits," he says, "going out model fucking. That's basically how I got into the business." Through a model, he got jobs assisting *Bazaar*'s Jimmy Moore, Roger Prigent, and then Hiro, who'd just begun shooting on his own after assisting Richard Avedon. Chatelain ended up printing Avedon's pictures for $60 a week. "I slept on the couch at the studio, and they never knew it," he claims.

In 1967 Chatelain won a grant and went to Paris. He met Reinhardt and Demarchelier at a party Dorian Leigh hosted at Jacques Chambrun's house. "We'd run into each other at the lab," Chatelain says. "Eileen Ford would come and take everyone to Coupole for dinner." They all made fun of Ford behind her back. "She was patronizing, always quoting from the Bible, holier than thou," according to Chatelain. "American photographers accepted her as an institution. We could see through her behavior. We refused to let her control everything. She'd say, 'Sit next to me,' at Coupole, and I'd fart to the utter joy of my friends."

After Guy Bourdin fought with French *Vogue* and left, Alex Chatelain won a job there, "so I was the one they all looked up to," he says. But Reinhardt was the ringleader. "Everyone congregated around Mike," Chatelain adds. "There was always a box full of grass in his refrigerator. He cooked marvelously, had great taste and a beautiful place full of sun and light and pretty girls. Then came the revolution of May 1968. We'd meet at Mike's house on Avenue President Kennedy and piss on the police from the roof."

But it wasn't all fun and games for Casablancas and his crew. A group of French legislators, some of whom had models as girlfriends, responded to their frequent complaints just as Casablancas had to his girlfriend Jeanette's. Their response was a new law governing model agencies. Henceforth models in France would be considered salaried workers, and agents would be required to insure that they were over eighteen years old and held valid working permits. Not only that, but the agents, as employers, would have to pay a *charge sociale* similar to America's Social Security tax, which effectively doubled the cost of hiring a model. After taxes, commissions, and social charges were deducted, a FF10,000 job would net a model only FF2,000.

"John arrived at that time," says François Lano. "He was really unlucky." And to make matters worse, almost immediately, Élysées 3 was hit with a major defection. The bookers all left and took most of the models with them to Models International. Panicked, Casablancas called his sympathetic friend Riccardo Gay, who promptly dispatched one of his best multilingual bookers, Brigitte Grosjean, to Élysées 3.

Thanks to Gay, Casablancas hung on. "I went through so much shit, and I never complained," he says. "Every time I had a good model, she was stolen away from me. Eileen Ford contributed to that." She and Jerry arrived at Élysées 3 in a chauffeured car one day, looked the place over, and agreed to start trading models with the new company in exchange for a 3 percent commission. But Casablancas says they were double-dealing him. "They would meet my models in my agency and advise them to go to Paris Planning and Models International," he charges. "Everyone was playing marionettes with everyone else. They wanted to see if they could muzzle me."

In fall 1970 Élysées 3 ran out of money and briefly closed its doors. John's father reluctantly came to the rescue with $100,000. "John's father wasn't so happy about him doing an agency," Christjansen says. "He would have liked him to do other things." But John was committed. "He could have gone into his father's factories and been much richer than he is today," Christjansen says. "In a way he chose the hard way."

He hired a booker named Tichka from Models International and reopened, but his problems weren't over. In a letter to Eileen Ford he announced a series of changes that he hoped would prove that "our growing pains now over . . . we have become an attractive agency to do business with." Unfortunately he quickly lost the money that had been lent to him. "My father was panicky."

By mid-1971 John knew he needed more help and turned to his older sibling. *Life* magazine had closed its Paris office, where Fernando Casablancas worked, so John asked him to take over the business side of Élysées 3. They were macho siblings with look-alike Zapata mustaches, but Fernando may have thought his little brother was a bit of a flake. Not only was John mixing business and pleasure by day, but he was also losing money gambling at night. "I did have a serious gambling problem," John admits. "But if anybody could have complained about it, it was Jeanette, because I borrowed money from her." He also borrowed from Bob Zagury, a playboy, backgammon player, and onetime lover of Brigitte Bardot, nicknamed Concrete Cock by women who knew him.

Finally, in October 1971, Casablancas decided to do exactly what Jacques de Nointel had suggested two years before. He announced his intentions in a letter to Eileen Ford that month. Because of the different requirements of "beginner, average and good models as opposed to top models . . . who need no more promotion but do demand constant attention," he wrote, "Élysées 3 will continue to grow and consolidate its position under Fernando's management. . . . I will be opening a completely separate operation in new offices. . . . Elite Model Management will represent 10–20 top models." It was the birth announcement of the most important model agency since Ford.

"Before, it was divine, joyful," says Auro Varani, an Italian lawyer who came to London in 1961 and went to work with Peter Marlowe, the printer who invented model composite cards. "There were very few agencies, and the people who ran them were cultivated and refined. It was like an elite. François Lano had culture to die. Catherine Harlé made me read books. Dorian Leigh wasn't much of a businesswoman, but goddamn, she was fun, and she had more guts than anyone I know. Then, all of a sudden, other people, straight boys, realized there was an enormous potential to go to bed with dream girls. You saw the sprouting of so-called model agents who are nothing but glorified pimps. John Casablancas started it. Before him, it was not a job a straight man would do. He was divine, handsome, enormously charming. But all the acolytes of John can't kiss his shoes. He was the pioneer. He opened a new frontier, and then everyone wanted it. It became a nasty business. A few manipulative people realized beautiful girls could be fucked in every way. The society became venal. All that mattered was money. I'm not cynical or bitter. I *hate* these people."

The turbulence at Élysées 3 mirrored the chaotic state of modeling throughout Europe following the passage of the new law governing French agencies. In 1969 Colette Gambier hired Maximiliano Patrini and his partner, Athos Contarini (whose girlfriend was a Ford/Paris Planning model named Ula Bomser), to run her agency in Milan. Four months later, back in Paris and pregnant, Gambier learned that Max and Athos were about to leave with all her models and open an agency of their own, 21 International, backed by a clothing manufacturer from Bologna. She flew to Milan, where she learned that not only had the pair decamped with her models, but they had also upset her landlord so much that he wouldn't renew her lease. Gambier reopened in another office and hired Natasha Gumkevitch, an ex-model, and a friend of hers from Paris named Beatrice Traissac, to run it for her.

Max and Athos didn't last long. "It was the up-and-coming agency," says Ula Bomser. "Athos wanted to make a lot of money very fast, which he basically did by gambling. Most of the money I made went into his pocket. Athos had a very destructive streak, Max was heavily on drugs and I suppose so was Athos, and the whole thing just fell apart." Adds Veruschka, who was dating Patrini at the time: "Maximiliano couldn't really deal with this fashion world. He would come to my hotel room and throw knives into the closets. He finally left, he couldn't stand it anymore." Late in 1970 Athos put 21 up for sale.

Meanwhile, in Paris Simone d'Aillencourt and Christa Fiedler had turned Models International into a powerhouse with the help of the Fords. But John Casablancas was scary new competition. "John was strong because he represented the photographers," d'Aillencourt says. "They were all going out together, taking the girls out. It was a thing I couldn't get into." She and her partners needed a new gimmick to stay on top, so when they heard that Max and Athos were selling, they approached the Fords about buying 21 together.

"We didn't want to offend anyone else in Paris and Milan," Jerry says. But Eileen went to dinner in Paris with Simone and her husband, filmmaker José Benazeraf, to discuss it.

Over the meal she was stricken with food poisoning. "I was lying on the floor, saying I wanted to go to the hospital," says Eileen. Jerry adds: "José refused to call her a taxi. He was demanding a commitment about Milan." Finally Eileen struggled downstairs and hailed a taxi. Another alliance had ended. The Fords began working with Élysées 3, and Models International turned to Wilhelmina. But its troubles had only begun. Things had soured between Christa and Simone, in part because Simone's husband "made dirty movies and he tried to hire girls from the agency for them," Fiedler says. Then Fiedler disappeared, leaving her husband, photographer Claude Marant, their child, and their agency, to run off with a younger man she'd met on a Club Med vacation. "He was a friend of mine," François Lano remembers, chuckling. "She followed him into the desert in a long dress, like Dietrich in *Morocco*." A booker named Stéphane Lanson took over when Fiedler departed. But soon François Lano offered Lanson a job at Paris Planning. He was the next one out Models International's revolving door. "And most of the girls followed me, a whole stable of girls," he says.

At Paris Planning Lanson was put in charge of women models, but because of the new law, Lano says, French clients started balking at the prices being charged for models. "Nobody wanted to declare or pay taxes," Lano says, "so a parallel market began to exist. We were obliged to offer representation outside of France because the social security charges were so expensive." In order to avoid the new taxes, bookings had to be taken and jobs paid for outside France.

Tired of fighting her losing battle with Riccardo Gay, Colette Gambier sold her agency to Lano, who changed its name to Talents and opened branches in Germany. Lano also inherited Gambier's friends Natasha and Beatrice and her enemy Riccardo Gay. Lano believes that Gay "gave orders" to shut Talents down. "We did our best for the agency," Beatrice says, "but we always had this big, big, big competition with Riccardo Gay and Fashion Model. A lot of unfair situations were happening in Milan. The models were chased and escorted, and François Lano was going forth and back, and finally he got a little bit tired and sold the agency to Riccardo Gay."

Though he lost his agency in Milan, Lano made some important connections there. In 1969 he flew to Switzerland, to meet with a businessman who helped him form a company where money could be processed out of sight of

French taxmen. Such "black money" systems are common in Europe, where avoiding taxes is a way of life. Model agents are extremely unwilling to discuss these systems, even as they insist they are totally legal. "As babies, the first thing the French learn is how to avoid taxes," says Sebastien Sed, another composite printer, who became a key German agent.

Lano put Jean-Pierre Dollé in charge of the Swiss billing system. He'd been an eighteen-year-old singer when he met Lano in a nightclub in the 1950s, and in 1961 he went to work at Paris Planning. Now the duo met Jean-Marie de Gueldre, who was married to a model. A lawyer for Formula One racers, de Gueldre was familiar with the intricacies of cross-border commerce. "Lano and Dollé asked, 'How can we compete?' " de Gueldre recalls. His solution was to set up a Swiss company called Models S.A. But after a few months it became clear that Lano would still have tax liability if the company were in his name, so he "let it go to Swiss people," de Gueldre says.

Models S.A. allowed Paris Planning's clients to save the taxes and social charges the new French law mandated and to limit their liability to Switzerland's maximum 23 percent tax. "Dollé would bring the money back to Paris and pay the models in cash," says Servane Cherouat, a Paris Planning booker.

Most models accepted de Gueldre's explanation of why Swiss invoicing benefited them. Louise Despointes was not one of them. "Only dishonest people won with this law," she says. "They pretend they have a model agency in Fribourg. They put out a fake head sheet, fake vouchers, and pretend the billings went through there, except there is not one telephone or one booker there."

Funny business wasn't confined to the tax end of the modeling business. In the late sixties Pucci Albanese was in the lingerie business in Milan, and like Riccardo Gay at *Amica,* he booked models through Paris agencies. "Pucci and Riccardo were like brothers," says Stephane Lanson. Albanese invested in Gay's agency when it opened, and they stayed close, but Albanese hated Milan ("a fucking stink city," he says) and moved to Rome in 1968. He opened an agency and soon expanded into Bologna, Florence, Munich, Frankfurt, Hamburg, and Barcelona. "GiGi and Oleg Cassini were my closest friends," he says. "Roman Polanski was always in the agency." But then, in 1972, he was shut down by the Number One scandal.

Albanese and his friends all frequented a disco in Rome called Number One, partly owned by Paolo Vassallo, the latest boyfriend of Bettina, the Paris couture mannequin. Vassallo was arrested the day before Valentine's Day after police found two ounces of cocaine and raw opium hidden in his club's bathroom and his car. Three days later the actress (and ex-Ford model) Elsa Martinelli was arrested as she returned home just before dawn by three policemen disguised as hippies. She was questioned in the case, as were Albanese and a producer (and friend of Albanese's and Riccardo Gay's) named Pier Luigi Torri, who lived in a treasure-filled Roman palazzo. Vassallo charged that an envious Torri had planted the drugs, a charge the producer denied. Several months later Torri was arrested for his role in the affair on his yacht in Monte Carlo's harbor.

Albanese confirms that he was arrested, too, and held in custody for three months, for possession of marijuana. He is obscure on other details of what happened, however. "It was a political scandal," he says. "It was a stupid time; politics were very fucked up. They held me because I knew too much and they didn't want me to talk to anybody." Three years later, Albanese says, the charges against him were dropped. "But after what happened, I didn't want anything to do with the agency," he says. "I sold it to the employees, who unfortunately didn't have the power and personality to keep it going."

Torri was arrested again in London in 1977 and charged with forging $1.6 million in drafts on a "ghost" bank that couldn't honor them. "He was strongly suspected by the Italian police of having very close ties to the Mafia," London's *Daily Mail* later reported. "He had jumped bail in Rome, had been sentenced to five years' imprisonment in his absence for criminally libeling a judge and he had fled to London." Torri escaped from London's Central Court four months after his arrest there but was recaptured two years later by the FBI in New York and finally convicted and jailed in London after a trial filled with tales of a paper empire of companies stretching from Liberia to the Falkland Islands.

Ever since then the assumption has been that the Mafia is in the Italian modeling business. The same is assumed about many Italian businesses, but that did nothing to diffuse suspicions. Milan's agents "didn't look happily on competition in those days," says Ulla Bomser, who'd retired and opened the Top Floor agency in Rome with her boyfriend, Athos Contarini. "It was a very big fight all the time," says Simone d'Aillencourt, who'd bought 21 International from Contarini and renamed it World. The police were constantly rounding up her models and sending them out of Italy. "One time everybody was laughing because Riccardo made a mistake and the police went to the hotel where all of *his* girls were," says d'Aillencourt. Neither World nor Models International lasted much longer, after someone tossed a fire bomb into the World Models offices in Milan.

Pucci Albanese dismisses the speculation about the bombing as paranoia. "I don't think agencies were involved," he says. "Fifty yards away there was a police post. Maybe they put it in the wrong window. I know the character of Riccardo Gay. He cannot hurt one fly. He would never jeopardize his life and career and family for such nonsense." Giuliana Ducret, a booker at World, says she knows "exactly who did it" but won't name names. "It was competition," she says, laughing. "It was like a bad joke. But it was intimidating in a funny way."

Back in Paris after her desert romance Christa Fiedler met Robert Silberstein, a Parisian real estate developer, who offered to back her in her own agency in 1972. "I didn't really like him," Fiedler says. "But you know, the way to impress me was to open a Louis Vuitton wallet filled with five-hundred-franc bills. And so I became partners with him, but not with him, because he could not be involved in a partnership on the papers."

Briefly Christa Models had its moments of glory. Fiedler had worked with Wilhelmina toward the end of her career, and now they began trading girls. "Wilhelmina came to Paris, and we went to La Coupole with a couple of her models," says Jacques Silberstein, Robert's son, who worked with Christa. Among them was Lorraine Bracco, a teenager from Long Island, who'd started with Wilhelmina in eighth grade and was just beginning to work full-time. "Willie said, 'Jacques, she has the most beautiful body in my agency,' " Silberstein remembers. He agreed. "I spoke barely English; she spoke barely French," he says. But they fell in love and spent several years together.

Bracco became a top model before moving on to Hollywood, where she won acclaim as one of the rare working models who managed a smooth transition between still and motion-picture stardom. And before she left Paris, she also played a small but key role in launching the career of Christa's biggest star and one of the top editorial models of the late seventies.

Born to Byelorussian parents in Brooklyn in 1955, Janice Dickinson moved to Hollywood, Florida, as an infant. In the early seventies she enrolled in a John Robert Powers school "to learn how to put my makeup on," she says. Her little sister, Debbie, who also became a model, says Janice always wanted to model. Because of her dark skin and exotic looks, their father called her Nile Princess.

In 1972 the Powers school brought Janice to a modeling convention in New York. At these biannual gatherings, which still take place, charm and model school students compete for trophies and the attentions of agents who use the cattle calls as one-stop mannequin-shopping marts. "The babes walk up and down the runway, and whoever wins, wins," Dickinson says. "I won. I knew how to work it." The judges who agreed included such fashion experts as hairdresser turned disco star Monte Rock III, crooner Tom Jones, and Telly "Kojak" Savalas.

"I just wanted to go to New York for the weekend," Dickinson says. "I skipped some of the boring lectures and sneaked out to go to the ballet and to the Metropolitan Museum of Art." After graduating from high school, Dickinson returned to New York with a boyfriend who played piano in B. B. King's band. Only then, she says, did she decide to model. "I picked up the phone book and found out who the agencies were." But she hadn't made it to any of them yet when she met Sue Charney, a booker from the Fords, on a Second Avenue bus.

"I got this woman, Sue Charney's card," Dickinson continues. "I'm smart. I followed the card to Ford, East Fifty-ninth Street, knocked on the door, and showed my portfolio. I had seven bad pictures in it. Eileen Ford, from across the room, said, 'No. Get that girl outta here. She'll never make it.' " Charney says, "Eileen looked at her through the door and said, 'Sue Charney, you're blind. Look at that mouth. She'll never work.' "

Dispirited, Dickinson took off for Las Vegas, where she worked as a cigarette girl and married her boyfriend before returning, "more secure," to New York six months later. Eileen Ford was in Europe, so Charney put Dickinson on the test board. "Get rid of her," Ford snapped upon her return. "I don't want her."

French photographers Jacques Malignon and Patrice Casanova both were at Wilhelmina the day she washed up there. "Patrice and I saw she was wild, exuberant, explosive," Malignon says. "A photographer knows the moment he takes a picture. But she was too ethnic for New York. I remember we called two or three agencies in Paris and said we had this big potential model."

They didn't pull their punches with Dickinson. "They were nice guys," she says. "They told me I definitely had it, but I was going to have problems in New York because people in New York in those days couldn't identify with my exotic, big lips, small eyes, I don't know what you call it, my Lolita sexy, sexy look." For a while she stayed in New York, doing the rounds of go-sees. "I was trying to get in the front door," she reports. "Wilhelmina said, 'Oh, darling'—smoking two packs of Marlboros at once—'you really have it. You just have to hang in there.' I had about twelve bad photographs. Then I met Lorraine Bracco and Jacques Silberstein in Wilhelmina's office, and they took one look at a Casanova photograph, and Bracco said, 'That's the one. She gets the ticket.' That's how it happened. I owe it all to Lorraine."

Dickinson arrived in Paris in January 1975 and, in essence, set off a revolution. She was the first of modeling's bad girls, and she did nothing to hide it. "Janice was excessive right from the beginning," says Jacques Silberstein. "She made photographers feel like they were her great friends, she was a great beauty, and she had no problem taking off her clothes. French people are uptight. She made us feel comfortable. She was an instant success."

Dickinson says her every move was planned. "I had to strategically ask all the girls and sniff things out; it took me about two weeks," she says. "All the agencies were on strike against French *Vogue,* because of the tariff rate at the time. I could have cared less. My purpose was to work as a model, become a star, and go back and make the big bucks. So I walked into the French *Vogue* studio, and I saw Guy Bourdin. He was my favorite photographer in the world, and he liked me. He asked me if I was a Pisces. I was Aquarius, so I passed, and he promised me that in the next few days we'd be taking pictures. Then I went over to *Elle,* to Peter Knapp's studio, and asked him for some food. I didn't know it was him. I told him that I was real jealous of his photographs, because he was the great photographer at the time. We did about seven *Elle* covers in eight weeks. Then I traveled. I went to New Guinea."

In June Debbie Dickinson joined her sister in Paris. Jacques Silberstein's brother, Dominique, picked her up at the airport. Paris took to the two antic Americans. But Janice wasn't satisfied with Christa and soon left for Paris Planning. "I thought I could get handled with better attention and more professionalism," she says. "Paris Planning was the only agency. There was Elite, but John Casablancas had seen my photographs. Patrice Casanova had showed him one night coming out of Castel, and he just said, 'No, I don't like her.' So I had a vendetta against Casablancas. I thought he was a jerk-off for not recognizing my true gloriousness in all its rare form."

Janice also made a change in her domestic situation. "I went back to New York," she says. "I was faithful to my husband the whole entire time. I get back, and I caught him with a black chick. So I said, 'See ya,' got divorced, and went back to Paris."

Jerry Hall's mother had always wanted to model but her husband wouldn't let her, so she transferred her ambition to her eldest daughter. "I was always very tall and skinny, and I used to get very depressed about it, and my mother would say, 'Look at Twiggy. *She's* skinny,' " Hall recalls. "She sort of planted the seed."

Jerry was fourteen, but she looked a lot older when she started prowling the halls of the Dallas Apparel Mart, looking for work as a showroom model. Kim Dawson, the biggest agent in Dallas, told the youngster she was too tall (six feet plus) to make a living doing showroom work and suggested she go to Europe. "I had a car accident where they gave me some insurance money, eight hundred dollars," Hall twangs, Texas-style. "I was fifteen, and I went off to Paris with a backpack and a sleeping bag."

Her mother, obviously a liberal parent, suggested she start her trip on the Riviera. Hall decided she'd be discovered there. "I don't know what I had in mind," she admits. "I'd been watching all those Hollywood movies! So I went down to St.-Tropez, and by then I had practically no money, because I'd bought this pink crocheted bikini for the beach, and it was my first day there, and a man put this phone number in my bikini bottom, and said, 'Would you like to be a model?' "

His name was Claude Mohammed Haddad. The son of a Tunisian carpenter, he arrived in Paris in 1956. He says he worked in a factory but somehow always dated beautiful women who became models. Others say he ran a temporary employment agency. In 1972 he was at a nightclub, the White Elephant, when Stéphane Lanson of Paris Planning approached him and asked if he was interested in modeling. "He was handsome, dark, beautiful," Lanson says. But he was also uninterested. "I said no, but after we met, we became good friends, and he told me he wanted to open an agency," Haddad recalls. "So I started to think maybe I should manage the girls." Soon Lanson quit Paris Planning and, with Haddad, opened Euro-Planning/Stéphane Lanson.

Then came Jerry Hall. "It's really luck, big, big luck," Haddad says. "Truly coincidental. I was in St.-Tropez the first year of this business. I meet a tall girl, completely clumsy. It was Jerry Hall in a pink bikini. And a few weeks after she saw me, she was in Paris. We sent her to see clients, and she became very successful."

It turned out that Haddad had an exceptional eye for potential models. "I went to New York," he says. "I found Grace Jones, the black girl, in an elevator. She was coming down from an agency. She looked so angry. She said, 'They don't like black people in this country.' I said, 'Come to Paris.' "

He also recruited girls on the streets of Paris. Linda Morand had been a successful model with Ford from 1966 until 1968, when she met a viscount at the nightclub Régine's and quit to get married and travel. Divorced in 1972, Morand decided to return to modeling. She remembers walking on the Left Bank when "this swarthy character comes up to me and hands me a card."

The name and address of Euro-Planning were printed on the front. On the back was a handwritten addendum promising "85% cash every Friday."

After hours Haddad entertained his and Lanson's finds. "He was going out all night long with the girls!" Lanson says. "And I'm at Euro-Planning at eight A.M. with all the magazines calling, 'Where is she, where is she?' Or they were arriving with eyes red. And one day I told Claude, 'You can't do that!' He said, 'Well, I'll still do it,' and every night he was in the nightclubs making dinner with twenty girls."

Through Jerry Hall, Haddad hooked into the only group of fashion folk as influential as Casablancas and the French Mob of photographers. It was the circle of omnisexual renegades that surrounded a Puerto Rican illustrator from New York named Antonio Lopez. Lopez died of AIDS in 1987, but his longtime partner, Juan Ramos, recalls his lifetime love affair with fashion and fashion models. As a student at New York's Fashion Institute of Technology in 1960, "Antonio knew all the models in the magazines by name," Ramos says. "Anne Saint Marie, Carmen, and China were his favorites."

Every Saturday Antonio organized fashion illustration classes, picking up kids who were willing to pose on the streets of Greenwich Village, where he lived. "He couldn't afford top models," Ramos says, "so out of need he started creating his own." After school Antonio got a job at *Women's Wear Daily,* the fashion trade newspaper, and then jumped to *The New York Times,* but his taste in models didn't change. "He was never interested in the girl next door," Ramos says. "Healthy wasn't his thing. He wanted exotic, weird, a little fucked up. They all had their stories. Antonio loved that. He'd listen to their problems for hours on end. Most of them ended up living with us."

They would make copies of clothes they saw in magazines, dress each other up, and go out to Cheetah, Electric Circus, and Trudi Heller's. Finally, in the mid-sixties, Antonio began working with established photo models. But he always kept a couple of crazies around, such as Donna Jordan and Jane Forth, before they became Andy Warhol superstars, and Cheyenne, "always in trouble, very drugged out," Ramos says. "Antonio loved her, of course." And after cutting sixteen-year-old Donna Mitchell's picture out of magazines for months, he managed to book her, too. "She wasn't goody-goody," Ramos says approvingly. "She was neighborhood.

"We lived a crazy life," says Ramos. "We were night people. We ate breakfast at noon and started work at six. Everyone would hang out, and we'd work through the night." On Sundays dressed in python boots and flowing scarves, they'd promenade at the Bethesda Fountain in Central Park. They found more models there. "Antonio was like an employment agency," says Ramos. "We didn't care if they had bad skin, as long as they could stand still."

In 1969 Antonio's troupe moved en masse to Paris, where he started drawing for *Elle, Vingt Ans,* and Italy's *L'Uomo Vogue.* They fell in with designer Karl Lagerfeld, who was then designing for the Chloé label, and followed him to St.-Tropez every summer, where he'd rent a house and fill it with models. Antonio and Juan knew and disdained the French Mob photographers. "Those guys weren't taken seriously," Ramos says. "They were out to fuck girls. They weren't doing things in fashion. We were friends with Guy Bourdin and Helmut and June Newton."

Soon Antonio found a Paris clubhouse, a disco called Club Sept, where he and all his friends could play. "It was a little tiny gay bar when we got there," says Ramos. "They enlarged it for us. We'd bring records from New York, black music. We were transporters of culture." Antonio's entourage grew to include Ingo Thouret, a male model from Germany, Jay Johnson and Tom Cashin, two handsome Americans, the black runway models Pat Cleveland and Toukie Smith (who was designer Willie Smith's sister), and Pablo Picasso's daughter, Paloma.

Like Antonio, Cleveland went to FIT. She became a model when a *Vogue* editor's assistant spotted her on the subway. "I was only fourteen," she says. "This assistant followed me. My girlfriend said, 'You better run. There's a dyke chasing you.' I said, 'What's a dyke?' So I talked to her, and she said she loved the way I dressed and gave me her card, and I went up there. I was a designer, and they said they loved my designs. They photographed me in my creations, and I started modeling a bit. My mom helped me send pictures around, and *Ebony* responded. I modeled with Ebony's fashion shows that went around America. I did ninety-nine shows."

Modeling was so much fun Cleveland gave up on designing. But she didn't have an easy time at first. "I kept meeting these agents who weren't agents," she says. "I met a lot of playboys, sort of bad personalities, and I made some money, but I was going the wrong way. I had to get rid of them. I think my agent did porn movies. They tried to get me to smoke dope and everything."

Hanging out in clubs like Cheetah in plastic dresses studded with feathers, Cleveland met a friend of Eileen Ford's. Moving to Ford, she returned to *Vogue*, where an illustrator named Manning Obregon decided he wanted to draw her and sent her to see Diana Vreeland. "I did a pirouette into Diana Vreeland's office, and she said, 'Stand like a tree with your feet rooted in the ground!'" Cleveland recalls. She sent me to Irving Penn, and he taught me to use my eyes."

In 1967 Cleveland switched agencies. "Eileen Ford was a snob and a bit prejudiced," Cleveland says. "She wanted me to have my nose done. She didn't like black girls. I was sitting in the agency, watching beautiful black girls come in day after day, and she didn't take any of them, and I finally went to her and said, 'I am leaving.' "

Wilhelmina had just opened, and Cleveland signed up. She modeled by day and partied every night. "That's part of what makes you a good model, when you live the life and wear the clothes," she says. "I'd drive around in Rolls-Royces, and I thought that was pretty hot." Cleveland became part of the group that surrounded Stephen Burrows. "There were fashion gang wars," she says. "It was right out of *West Side Story*. You'd be in one group or another. Stephen Burrows's group, or Antonio's group, or Warhol's group. Donna Jordan, my girlfriend from school, was hanging around with Andy. All these groups would show up dressed to kill, and they wouldn't socialize together. My group said Donna was a show-off. I went over and danced with Donna. Donna would kick her legs up and show her underwear. *Nobody* did that. People were taking drugs. I wasn't used to this—yet."

Jordan introduced Cleveland to Antonio. "And oh, boy, the world stood still," she says. "But I was working with Manning, doing the collections. Then they took him off the job, and there was Antonio. Great God! This is as high as you can go in fashion. He asked me to come to Europe, and I packed my bag. This rag doll, no tits, was on her way to Europe."

Her first stop was Milan, but she soon left to join Antonio and his group in Paris. "I went to stay with Antonio in an apartment on rue Bonaparte he lent to his friends," Cleveland says. "No agency. I met Helmut Newton, Guy Bourdin, Hans Feurer. But I was turning down covers because Antonio and Karl Lagerfeld were taking my life away. We worked together in St.-Tropez. I'd go to lunch on the beach in diamond collars, bracelets, rings, high-heeled shoes and a G-string."

Meanwhile, Club Sept had been discovered. "You saw everyone there," says male model Ingo Thouret. "Yves Saint Laurent, Giorgio Armani, Grace Jones. It was one big saloon of flirting. Everything was possible, and nobody had to say, 'Are you straight?' or, 'Are you gay?' " Antonio was in the middle of it all. "He would find somebody he liked and make them," Thouret continues. "He became the number one unpaid model scout in Europe. If Antonio called a designer or an agency and said, 'You've got to see this one,' people did."

Antonio was always having affairs with his finds. He was seeing a male model when he met Jerry Hall ("this giant girl in a trashy outfit and huge

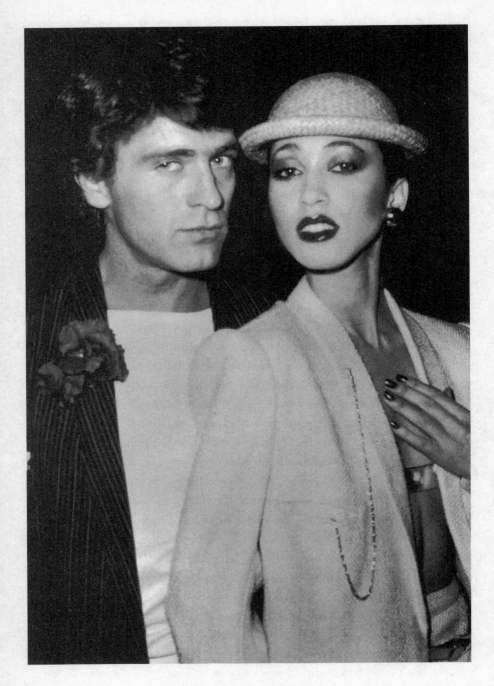

Ingo Thouret *(left)* and Pat Cleveland photographed
by Rose Hartman

cork heels," says Ramos) at Club Sept, and she became his lover. "Antonio was with women and men," says Ramos. "He liked Jerry's *Hee-Haw* quality." They all lived together in the bohemian St.-Germain district. "Jerry's room was called the Corral," says Ramos. "She knew every comic book in the room, and if you touched one, you were in trouble. She wore a new pair of panties every day and then tossed it in that room." Antonio gave Hall a crash course in fabulousness. "He had all these fantastic books on fashion and glamorous Hollywood movie stars, and I used to study all those books and look in a full-length mirror and copy all the poses," she says.

Ultimately Hall was replaced in Antonio's affections. No one was exactly monogamous. "Pat Cleveland and Antonio used to disappear for days and lock themselves up with some boy they'd found," says Ramos. "Pat was a bit of a nympho, and Antonio was, too." Once, in Venice, Antonio and Juan gave Karl Lagerfeld a birthday party at Harry's Bar. "Pat stripped naked on the tables," showing everyone the heart she'd shaved into her pubic hair, Ramos recalls. Harry's waiters scurried about, he continues, "pulling down the shades."

Cleveland says she never had steady boyfriends. "I was married to my career. I had fun with the boys, and I stayed out of trouble. But finally I got real tired, and I had to go off by myself. I cut off my hair, put on my backpack, and went to Egypt dressed as a boy. That's the kind of stuff you have to do." Cleveland ended up moving to London, where she partied with the gay crowd and went out with Mick Jagger. While she was there, she met Zoli, and she joined up with him and returned to America, ending up in Los Angeles, where she tried acting and kept playing. "I had some nice boyfriends," she says. "Jack, Warren, Ryan. All of them. Look, I grew up with the Pill. You took one, and you could have fun. So it was love 'em and leave 'em even when they tried to attach themselves to you. I'm very independent. I like to make my own scene. I don't want to be anybody's shadow."

Meanwhile, back in Paris, Claude Haddad was finding more models. Gaby Wagner, who now runs the Zoom agency in Paris, joined Euro-Planning for several months, "until he stole so much money from me, I ran away," she says. Though Haddad denies financial irregularities ("Elite don't pay any commission," he says. "I am white; they are black"), Wagner wasn't the only one who felt ripped off. "Claude used people, and Antonio used him," says Paul Caranicas, an artist who was part of their set. "We found out what a slime he was a few months later when he wouldn't pay Jerry." Haddad "never told me how much money I was making, and he never paid me," Hall confirms. "I'd get the cover of some magazine. an ad for some gasoline company, and he would just give me a hundred francs when I would cry."

The agency wasn't entirely useless. "I met Helmut Newton through them," she says. "We bought all these leather clothes and whips and chains, and I was throwing my hair and cracking a whip for *Photo* magazine, and at the end of the day I started to cry. Helmut said, 'Why are you crying?' And I said, 'I think this is pornography.' And he said, 'No, this is art!' And I said, 'But I really want to do fashion,' and he said, 'OK, if that's what you want,' and about a week later he booked me to do the cover of French *Vogue,* and I worked with him quite steadily for years." Within two years Hall was a star. "At one point I was on the cover of every magazine in Paris," she says. "I was taking Paris by storm."

Thus Antonio's set became celebrities, so it was inevitable that rumors would start flying around them. One of the most durable concerned the shah of Iran, who was said to have a procurer in Paris who would offer models money, furs, and jewels to fly to Iran for weekends of sex and Pahlavi. Jerry Hall is said to have gotten a fur that way. "It's very exciting, but it's not true," says Hall, who has heard the story. "I bought it with cash. I saved up my money in a shoe box, and a whole gang of friends went with me to Revillon. A lot of girls were very jealous about that fur coat. And people did say, 'Who bought that for you?' I think that's where that story came from."

In 1974 Hall met Eileen and Jerry Ford in Paris, "and they invited me to come and live with them in New York," she says. "I was working a lot with American *Vogue* and Richard Avedon and Irving Penn and Scavullo." She also worked with Bryan Ferry, the lead singer of Roxy Music, who booked her to pose for his band's fourth album cover and then moved her into his house on London's Hanover Square. Despite her problems with Claude Haddad, Hall stayed with Euro-Planning until 1977. "I left them because I did this Opium perfume contract for eight years for the entire world, and they only gave me a thousand dollars!" she says. "Claude was very bitter when I left. He said, 'I made you a star. Then you left me!'"

He wasn't the only man she left. She soon abandoned Bryan Ferry for Mick Jagger. By that time modeling had lost its allure for her. "Paris was so exciting," Hall says. "They weren't trying to sell clothes. It was more artistic; it was entertaining; you were creating something. When I went to New York, I started doing all this catalog stuff, making really good money, working every day, but you had to be there exactly on time, and they didn't like you to chat; you had to hurry up and get on the set, and then you had to do sixteen pic-

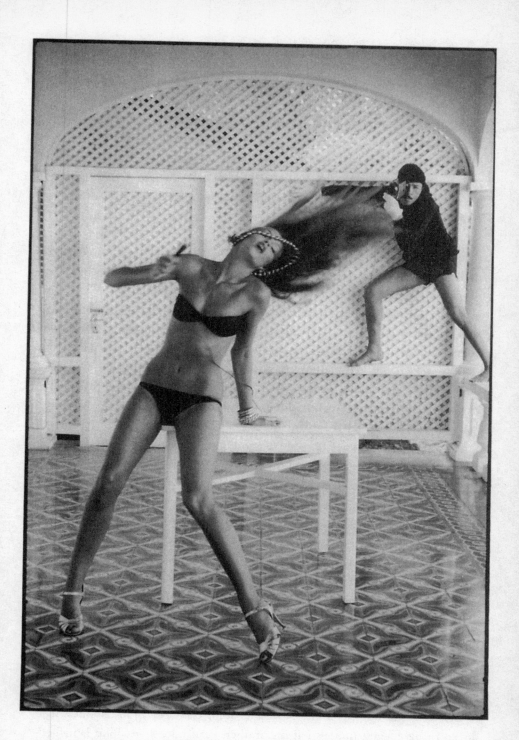

Jerry Hall and Antonio Lopez photographed
by Norman Parkinson

tures. You couldn't do anything different; you couldn't do anything artistic; you couldn't make the skirt look better. Somehow it was sort of killing. I just got very, very bored."

By 1975 Antonio and his crew had abandoned Paris, too. Though they returned often, they shifted their base back to New York, where "the gay scene blossomed and attracted Antonio back," Ramos says. "Also, the attitude was changing in Paris. Lagerfeld was getting into his eighteenth-century phase. Everything was about money and houses and socialites. It got boring and heavy. There was no more room for us."

Paris was no longer a place for artists. "It was a new age," says Jérôme Bonnouvrier. "Agencies managed by playboys were new." In 1972, suffering from throat cancer, Catherine Harlé went into semiretirement and turned her business over to her nephew Bonnouvrier and his mother. Tichka moved from Models International to Paris Planning to Euro-Planning to New York. Stéphane Lanson quit Euro-Planning, too, and formed his own agency in 1974.

Claude Haddad's reputation was starting to catch up to him. "He was serious bad from the start," says an American model who often went out with him and his friends, pretending she didn't speak French. "They were greasy, like pimps, hustling, it was gross," she says.

Refugees from his agency, Euro-Planning, turned up at Christa before it closed. "They said the guy would take money from his pocket and pay them cash," Jacques Silberstein recalls. "He tried to brainwash them as if he was the guru Claude. He had an incredible apartment, girls all around like a harem. Swedish girls. They were quite naïve. They were good meat for the hunters." Finally Stéphane Lanson couldn't take it anymore. "When I realized Claude Haddad was behind me purely to go with the girls, I told him, 'It's the girls or me,'" Lanson says. "He told me, 'It's the girls.' I said good-bye, we went to court, I sold him the name Euro-Planning, and I took back Stéphane Lanson."

Lanson's agency survived only three years. "I'm an artist," he says. "I'm not good for accounting. I owned Stéphane Lanson one hundred percent because after Haddad, I didn't want anybody else but me! But you have to support girls before they make you money, and I was giving too much away. I went bankrupt in 1977."

Élysées 3 slid out of business, too, after John Casablancas and about a half dozen of his biggest models left his brother, Fernando, there. John launched Elite Models with "some of the best models of the time," says Jeanette Christjansen. He signed up most of the French Mob's women, plus British photographer Clive Arrowsmith's girlfriend, Ann Schaufuss; Barry Lategan's wife, Lynn Kohlman; François Lamy's wife, Ingmarie Johanssen; and Paris Planning's Emanuelle Dano. But Casablancas soon realized that his all-star concept had a fatal flaw. "We didn't want it to grow at first," says Jeanette. "After a while he realized he had to create the stars of tomorrow." But he couldn't easily bring in new girls to replace his original dozen when their careers began to fade. "I was a little bit their prisoner," he says. "Elite was a private club."

Money wasn't Casablancas's only problem. Two of his original Elite models died before the agency got on its feet. Paula Brenken killed herself jumping out a window. And it was Casablancas who discovered the body of Louise Despointes's ex-girlfriend Emanuelle Dano. "We had a booking for her; we called her for two days," he recalls. He finally went to her home. "She'd been partying," he says. "She was a girl who was always excessive. She was really, really living it, drinking tequila from the bottle, whatever. It was a whole bunch of people, and apparently they played some games which became rough, because she had traces of some very wild games. I think they were fooling around in a car, and she jumped or was thrown out, and that's how she died. And then they brought her back to her apartment." Casablancas says he knows who was with her but won't reveal their names. "It was obviously not anybody who *tried* to kill her," he says. "It just went bad, and they were not interested in an inquiry that would reveal that the daughter of a *ministre d'état* was living this way."

Despite—or perhaps because of—incidents like that, Elite became the hot model shop in town. "The clients loved it," says Casablancas. "They always love the little guys. This is why I always expect my clients to betray me now. There is this irresistible attraction towards the new thing. I say this without bitterness. It's what fashion is about." The girls talked up the service they were getting from John and Christine Lindgren, a booker who'd come with him from Élysées 3. More models followed.

In the wake of Casablancas, a new breed of agent rushed into the model trade. Claude Haddad was one. But the most successful by far has been Gérald Marie. At least, that's what he calls himself now. In the beginning he used an aristocratic name, Gérald Marie de Castelbajac. "I didn't want to work under my name at the time," he (sort of) explains. "I didn't know what was possible, and at the time everybody was working under a different name. Maybe I was stupid or crazy enough to say I was going to work and invent myself another personality, another system. I didn't have anything in common with myself, so I worked with that a little bit and I dropped it."

Though some people who have worked with him believe he was an orphan, Marie has said he is the son of a hospital administrator. He apparently grew up near Marseilles and entered show business as a go-go dancer on local television, or at least that's what he told one of his many model lovers who marveled at his bedroom acrobatics. Marie says that as a student he promoted ballroom dance concerts. "It worked quite well, and through that I started to meet a lot of girls because they followed the bands, and some of them happened to be models," he says. He fell in with an older woman, and she offered him a modeling agency. They called it Modeling. "She proposed to me that I work with her," Marie says. "I didn't know a thing, frankly. But I knew how to look at a girl, how to talk to her. I think François Lano heard about me. He was in the middle of a kind of war with John Casablancas, and he proposed that I work with him."

François Lano didn't like what was happening in modeling. "The work was different, more aggressive and much more money-looking," he says. Casablancas denies it, but Lano says Elite made special commission deals to lure his stars away. "John was the first to do that," Lano says. "'Come with me, you will pay nothing.' If the girl was not interested, he would say to the boyfriend, 'Arrange something for me, and I'll give you some money.' It's not dishonest, but it wasn't right." An American photographer who worked in Europe adds that Casablancas paid bounties to photographers who steered models to him. Casablancas also slept with the girls. "John Casablancas was giving new services." Jérôme Bonnouvrier smirks. "Lano had to do something."

Casablancas says his success was also a concern for the Fords. "I'm a not bad-looking guy who is having a lot of success with personal relationships with the models, so I'm a nuisance in the sense that they send models to Paris Planning and to other agencies and they end up with me. It's a small agency; we're very prestigious; we're demanding higher prices. We've already begun to have all the characteristics of what Elite is about. Eileen and Jerry, who had slammed the door in my face at the time of Élysées 3, now came and said, 'It's embarrassing for us. You've got ten of our girls, and we don't have a relationship with you.' I said, 'All you've got to do is give me the girls yourselves.' So we started a relationship. It was a big deal for me. I was a young guy, and these were the kings of the business."

The European agents all felt like pawns of the Fords. In Paris "Eileen enjoyed the game of divide and conquer," says Bonnouvrier. "It kept the situation under control. She was here every two months. It was an obsession. But she made a major mistake. Suddenly she turned from Lano to her new toy, Elite."

A solution came to hand when Gérald Marie called Lano, who offered him a job. "I liked the way he was," Lano says. "He was pushing. He was attracted by beauty. He knew how to speak about girls and make you want to buy them. When I took him, it was not against John. I needed fresh blood in managing. But when I came back to the agency and told everyone I'd made a deal for Gérald, *everybody* immediately said, 'If Gérald comes, we'll leave.' I told Gérald, 'I'm sorry.'"

Instead Lano hired Fabienne Martin, a German-speaking student who'd gone to school with one of Dorian Leigh's daughters. She created a new department called Covers "for top girls, because of Elite," she says. Her stars were Susan Moncur, Louise Despointes, and another favorite of Newton and Bourdin's, Wallis Franken. "Fabienne was like John the Baptist," says Steve Hiett. "She was the first to promote soulful, poetic-type girls." But the times weren't ready for her approach.

"The scene became totally different," says photographer Guy Le Baube, who started shooting fashion in 1970. "Before, the girls were older, more mature; they wore glasses and read books. Some of them had Ph.D.'s. The level of conversation was much higher. Now people who have nothing to say make pictures. They are like monkeys, greedy for success. So they imitate success; they look like success, without having it. Fake emotions are their hallmark. Modeling brings the worst out in you if you don't have the background to elevate it." And the new models were looking for flash, not the careful, creative guidance Fabienne Martin was offering. "I tried to do my best," she says, "but I wasn't that strong. There were some wonderful girls there, but it was nothing compared to Elite."

Then Marie called Lano again and said he was shutting Modeling because Elite had snatched two of his top earners, Lena Kansbod and Anna Anderson. This time Lano hired him. A quarter of Paris Planning's girls weren't working. "I posed this as a challenge," Lano says. "He worked like a dog. He worked all day alone, calling photographers, protecting the models. Each time he took a new girl, he would drop another one who was not doing well. He said, 'Try another agency because I don't know how to manage you.' He built completely his own department. Then I gave him charge of all the women's division."

Lano was an excellent teacher, and Marie was a quick study. A street fighter by temperament, he learned to charm but didn't make it a habit. "François was too much of a gentleman for the concert that was playing at the time," Marie says. "When a model said she was leaving, he would take her to lunch, offer her a ring or pearls to say good-bye. François was a different generation. My goal was to catch Elite."

Rough around the edges, Marie was a road show John Casablancas. "François probably fancied him," says Sebastien Sed. "He went for Gérald like a guy would go for a fourteen-year-old girl." Marie soon earned the nickname Chevalier de Longue Queue, or Knight of the Long Tail, a not-so-subtle reference to his sexual prowess. "He was the stud," says Jacques Silberstein.

By all accounts, Marie changed his women as often as the sheets on his bed. "That's why François took him," says Jérôme Bonnouvrier. "For what he is. He's funny, but he's a pimp who fucks the girls." He doesn't deny it.

"I'm not an angel," he says. "But I'm very picky about the women I date, and I don't work by quantity. We are men in the business of women. We love women, and I think we're just acting normally. The woman at a model agency is using another kind of charm, playing mommy, sister, confidante."

For what? "Money," Marie says.

Huntsville, Alabama–born Beth Boldt, an aspiring model at Zoli, met Marie on one of his first scouting trips to America. "He tried to go to bed with me," she says. "That's why I joined Christa. Jacques and Dominique were cuter. I figured, if push came to shove, I'd rather do it with them."

Other models who met Marie in his early days at Paris Planning say there was nothing particularly sinister or sexist about him. "He was the cock of the court," says Gaby Wagner, "handling the board, all the booking, reorganizing the agency. He was bad since the beginning! I never had a problem with him, but of course, he wanted to screw me." He would tell new models that they would get editorial work if they slept with him. "I'd just go, 'Fuck you,' " Wagner says.

Another model, who asks to be called Aquamarine, says she greatly preferred Marie to Casablancas, who also made himself available to her. "There was a sweetness about Gérald," she says. "I'd liken him to a lion cub. He was young; he was fun; he was like a kid in a candy store, awed at finding himself in the position to sleep with all these girls." Marie says he's never offered career advancement in exchange for sex, but he struck Aquamarine as "somebody you could fuck for work," she says. "He'd been very helpful to the girls he slept with. It was the only time I ever compromised myself, but it didn't seem so serious. I liked him." Their interlude lasted a few weeks. "He kept asking me to marry him, but I thought we didn't have a lot in common. I never loved him, and he never loved me. And funny thing, I don't think he got me any work."

"He was an episode in everybody's life," says another of Marie's model lovers with a sigh. "His persistence amused me. He is relentless to the point of being humorous and I had nothing better to do for the day. There's a hundred thousand guys like that in Paris. They're nurturing, madly in love, and then they're out of your life as fast as they got into it. A brief encounter of the most odd kind."

John Casablancas had an active sex life, too. Often he played with Riccardo Gay, his Italian collaborator. Gay was known as Il Rabbino, the Rabbi, and he was that and more to Casablancas. "Oh, we had the best times," Casablancas says. "We did every crazy thing in the world with the girls and with drinking. I admit I was not a saint. I was a young European guy. I loved to go out, to eat, to drink. I've never, ever touched drugs in my life. But everything else, yes."

They both had steady girlfriends, but that didn't stop them. Their garter belt parties are the stuff of modeling legend. "We would be sharing an apartment, and while one of us was sleeping, the other one would push a couple of girls into the room," Casablancas recalls. "We'd have the girls take their clothes off and peekaboo. You have to remember that we were very young."

Stories about Casablancas's free-and-easy lifestyle soon spread through the modeling business. He'd pop into the agency and buy dinner for whoever was around. "Right off the plane he'd buy lingerie and cocktail dresses on the Champs-Élysées, dress 'em up, and take 'em out," says model Debbie Dickinson. But the same behavior that attracted models to him disturbed agents of the old school. Once, at a dinner in Paris, the Fords watched in disbelief as a fifteen-year-old who'd lived with them before joining Elite lit John's cigar for him. "I was a couple times shocked when I saw him with very young girls," says Jerry Ford. "I can't recall people we sent to him with whom he became involved, but I remember a lot of people he sent to us who he'd had."

Casablancas's girlfriend, Jeanette Christjansen, was more forgiving. She'd heard all the rumors, but she didn't believe them. "I never was jealous," she says. "I could not have lived with John for seventeen years if I'd been jealous. He might have been fucking around, but I never knew. I trusted him very much. He was always home when I called. I knew how badly he wanted to make it, and I wanted to help him."

So was he screwing around with young models? "As in everything, there's a little bit of truth and there's a little bit of lie," he says. "Did I ever sleep with any of the models? Yes, I did. Were they young? When you say young girls, it usually implies sixteen-year-olds. That's absolutely not true. The average age of starting models in those days was more like eighteen. Had there ever been any young girls? Of course, there had been. You know, I know sixteen-year-old girls that are going on fifty."

John Casablancas positioned himself as a child of 1968, a rebel, an outsider. "Therefore, certain people had automatic sympathy for me, others had automatic antipathy," he says. Right from the start he had problems with American agencies. "They were sucking our blood," Casablancas says. "They wouldn't let a European agent scout outside of New York. You had to go through them. I spent twenty thousand dollars on four trips to New York. I saw a hundred twenty girls, out of which I wanted fifty. I got five. In the meantime, New York agents came ten times to Paris, it cost me fifty dinners, and they took away our six top-grossing girls."

That year in Capri one of his bookers, Francesca Magugliani, sat in on an all-night conversation between Gay and Casablancas about opening an agency in New York. Casablancas was furious with the Fords. "Their philosophy was to reign through division," he says. "They would go into a city and promise the same girl to five agencies. And everybody was kissing their asses. I felt this was unbearable."

"They were playing backgammon," Francesca recalls, "and John said, 'I'm going to open in New York.' Riccardo said, 'It's not that easy.' It went on and on. They got really heated up, both of them. Riccardo had a good idea. He wanted all the agencies in Europe to form a conglomerate. Each agency would have a percentage of the stock in a holding company according to turnover so there would be no more jealousy; it would all go into the same pot."

Casablancas tried to put that plan into action in summer 1976. "It was the time of the film *The French Connection,*" he says. "I called for a meeting of SAM [the French syndicate of modeling agencies, a trade group] and proposed that five of us join forces, buy a building on the Avenue Foch, make every floor an agency, everyone independent, paying rent to the cooperative, and then go to New York and open an agency there called the French Connection. I said, 'Let's do our own scouting. America is enormous, and let's get our own girls.' It didn't happen because the fear of Eileen and Wilhelmina was so great, rumors started spreading, and they all chickened out."

In fall 1976 Casablancas and François Lano revived the idea and discussed merging Elite and Paris Planning into a new entity, Elite Planning. "We were mostly interested in Gérald Marie," says Alain Kittler, who'd begun as Elite's backer and quickly turned into a full partner. "Dollé and Lano had the shares, but they were already the old regime."

Lano agreed, but then, says Casablancas, he tried to exempt Marie from the deal. "Gérald wasn't the owner, but he was the heart of the agency," Casablancas says. "I hated his guts. But I said that he had to be in the deal, so François finally accepted. I came to the States to look into the possibility of doing this agency, and the day I arrived I got a phone call from Eileen Ford. She always used to call me at eight o'clock in the morning. She knows I hate being woken up early. She says to me, 'Gérald was in the Bahamas, and he gave us a little phone call and told us that you were coming to look at the possibility of opening an agency, and I just wanted to tell you his message: The deal's off.' " Because of what she'd learned about his plans, Ford added, Bruce and Wilhelmina Cooper would be joining them at a dinner they had planned for Casablancas that night at '21.'

At the dinner "they all started accusing me of opening this agency," Casablancas says. He shot back that Eileen Ford was trying to "screw up my scouting" in Scandinavia, "and if she's going to do that, I'm going to come to America. I don't want to come to America. But I will not take this shit any longer from Eileen." The dinner degenerated into a shouting match. Wilhelmina threatened to destroy Casablancas. "She took off on him in a way that embarrassed us," confirms Jerry Ford. "We told him we had no intention of opening in Europe, but that if he opened here, we'd be sure none of our models went to him in Paris again."

Then came the rumor that the Fords were setting up one of their models, a Swede named Karin Mossberg, in a Paris agency. Mossberg insists she opened alone, "just me," financed with her savings and aided by all the friends she'd met as a model. "People trusted me," she says. "I went to Sweden to the agencies. I picked six girls, and I started in my living room." Mossberg says she booked no Ford models for a year, but to this day the competition thinks she did. "Eileen put all her girls in Karins," says Jérôme Bonnouvrier. Adds German agent Dorothy Parker: "Everyone knew it was Ford's agency, financed by Ford, totally Ford, with Ford models."

"We really tried to talk her out of it," Eileen Ford insists. "We were working with Elite. It just rocked the boat."

Regardless, Casablancas decided he "was going to watch Eileen," he says. "I had a spy in New York who found out when she was going to Scandinavia." He followed just behind her and learned "that she was selling her new stallion, Karin Mossberg, who was opening an agency in Paris. She did exactly what she'd promised not to do at that dinner. She said I was a playboy, that all I wanted to do was date girls, that I introduced them to disgusting—one day it was Arabs, the next day it was Jews from New York. Every place I went it was someone different, Lebanese, Iranians. She denied it, but she was asking people to work with Karin and not with me. This was stabbing me in the heart. So I said, 'OK, fuck this.' I had a meeting with my partners and asked them to put up money to open in New York."

"We had to do it very quickly," says Alain Kittler. "Secrecy had to be absolute. We wanted some kind of blitzkrieg operation." They gathered $20,000 in seed money and a $300,000 credit line. "From that moment on I was devious," Casablancas says, not without a touch of pride. Early in 1977 he set up trips to New York as he always had, arranging to meet models at Wilhelmina and Ford. He was giving the Americans a taste of their own medicine. The only agent he confided in was Stewart Cowley. "John told me he was opening here," Cowley recalls. "He said he wasn't going to fuck around with me, but he was going to kill Eileen and Wilhelmina." He even briefly considered opening in Cowley's offices, but there wasn't enough room.

"I was told by my attorneys that I couldn't solicit people," Casablancas explains, "so I came to New York, visiting and pretending everything was fine, and in the meantime I was looking for offices and I had my friend [photographer] Alain Walch, spreading the rumor and giving me information. Alain made a report on every single booker in New York." He singled out Monique Pillard. "He said she is probably the best booker in town, but she has a vile mouth," Casablancas remembers. "She still laughs about that."

The daughter of hairdressers from Nice, Pillard met Eileen Ford in the late sixties in the Revlon beauty salon that Pillard ran in midtown Manhattan. Impressed with her energy, Ford offered her a job as a booker. Pillard says of Ford, "She's a tough cookie, a very shrewd businesswoman. I'm still thankful for the things she taught me."

But as the rumors spread that Casablancas was coming, Ford got suspicious. "I was getting too strong, so she tried to put the fear in me," Pillard says. "She made me feel small, like an object on a table. She had me in her office every day, telling me no one liked me. She'd beaten me so regularly and mercilessly I had no confidence. Then, when she heard John was coming, she told me to take the summer off with full pay. I didn't understand. Later on I realized she wanted me out of the way."

"She was flouncing around the office, never at her desk, fighting with Rusty, making speeches about 'What I have to do,' " Jerry Ford recalls. "We suspected she was going with John."

In February Casablancas sent a telegram to Eileen Ford, asking her to set up go-sees for him in early March. He signed it, "Love John." Elite Model Management Corporation was incorporated on March 22. A month later comptroller Jo Zagami and Pillard both gave notice to Ford. At the same time Casablancas sent a telex, fessing up to what he was doing.

"When we closed our deal with Monique Pillard, we went to Rumpel-mayer's because I was staying at the St. Moritz," Casablancas recalls. "Who comes behind? There was Roy Cohn with [Ford executive] Joey Hunter. They were obviously waiting for us. I thought Monique was going to die!"

"Eileen and Jerry wanted [Cohn] for that suit," says Richard Talmadge, the lawyer who handled most of Ford's other legal affairs. "He said he could stop Casablancas from opening in New York. I disagreed."

"Paranoia was rampant," says Gillis MacGil, the owner of Mannequin. And now, with characters like Cohn thrown into the mix, "it was starting to get exciting," says Gara Morse, who was then a young booker at Wilhelmina. "We'd started hearing stirrings, but the Coopers felt safe. They thought John was only hitting Ford." Still, they sent memos to the staff, warning them to keep close tabs on their models.

Then, the first week in May, Wilhelmina's Maarit Halinen became the first model to join Elite New York. "Wilhelmina was not doing a great job with her." Casablancas sneers. "She was becoming a catalog queen."

A week later—three weeks before Elite's offices even opened—the Fords sued Casablancas for $7.5 million for violating the "fiduciary trust" they felt he owed them. "We were really hurt emotionally," says Eileen Ford. Adds Jerry: "We were under siege. We had to do something."

"The lawsuit was the mistake of [Eileen Ford's] life," says Alain Kittler. "From one day to the other we were known; people thought we were rich and powerful when we were neither, because we were attacked for seven million dollars. So we made the breakthrough in two months, but I tell you it was a gamble." By July Elite was the talk of the town. That month journalist Anthony Haden-Guest published a story in *New York* magazine called "Model Wars." In the most famous passage he described how Eileen Ford had sent Pillard and Zagami Bibles with passages about Judas Iscariot ("And as they sat and did eat, Jesus said, 'Verily I say unto you, One of you which eateth with me shall betray me." Mark 14:18) underlined in red ink.

Ford confirms that she sent Pillard a Bible. "I'd do it all over again, too," she says.

Haden-Guest quoted Janice Dickinson boasting about running around Elite's offices in the nude; described the arrival of immigration men at Elite's offices, looking to deport Casablancas (who was an American citizen) and chief booker Christine Lindgren (whose papers were in order), and took readers into a summit conference at Bruce and Wilhelmina Cooper's house, where François Lano, Gérald Marie "de Castelbajac," and several other agents and photographers held a "council of war" to plot against Casablancas.

Aftershocks continued for months. Wilhelmina filed suit against Elite, too, for $4 million. Ford and Willie were allied against Casablancas; they declared war on two fronts: in the courts and in fashion industry gossip. "They tried to demonize John," says Alain Kittler, "but people were amused or excited. After all, he wasn't doing anything abnormal."

In Haden-Guest's article Bruce Cooper bluntly called Casablancas a pimp. "I didn't expect the violence," says Casablancas. "It was a constant climate of terror. [Eileen] told people that we had orgies every Thursday in the agency. I wasn't living a life of orgies. I had some parties that were, by American standards, very wild. You go to a wedding in America, and people just get silently drunk at their tables and throw up in the toilet. You go to a wedding in France, and usually someone will stand on a table and lift their skirt up or do something a little bit sexual, because that's the nature of that society. My nature was more French. But I mean, it was a nightmare."

The Americans decided—and still believe—that any Frenchman with a camera was working for Casablancas. "What do you do when a bunch of photographers tell your models to leave you?" Eileen Ford asks. Monique Pillard says Ford called photographers and told them they'd have no more Ford models if they ever booked girls from Elite. "When I arrived in New York, she'd invite me to dinner parties," says Patrick Demarchelier. "She never talked to me after John came to New York." Adds Jacques Malignon: "Willie told me she'd send me back to my country because I was involved with John. Everyone thought there was a connection, and John very smartly didn't deny it."

When *Fortune* magazine did a story on the model war, a reporter told Alex Chatelain that Ford had accused him of owning a piece of Elite. "I got mad and arranged a lunch with the Fords," he says. "She started crying, asking why I didn't book her girls. I told her, 'Get modern.' John's girls were different."

Model Barbara Minty became one of John's girls. Gunilla Lindblad joined immediately, too. Ford sent a letter to her. "She said, 'We believed you were part of this family, and we feel very betrayed and hurt that you gave us not a word of explanation,' which was true," says her photographer husband, Jean-Pierre Zachariasen. "We should have been courteous. We hadn't been correct. But Eileen had made some huge mistakes, too. When we had our son, for instance, she said, 'What a disaster! I have a doctor. Get rid of it right away!' Like, go to the loo and then go back to work!" Casablancas was different. "John loved the girls," Zachariasen says. "He saw that the girls had talent and that they were personalities, and he decided he would give them a status. Eileen did not love the girls. For Eileen, they were cattle."

On June 29, 1977, the Fords' request for a preliminary injunction against Elite was denied. Ford's lawyer, Roy Cohn, was on the attack when he deposed Casablancas a year later, accusing him of lying and then, late in the day, bringing up Elite's association with two Swiss companies, Fashions and Models and Sococom-Inmod, that billed and paid models for work outside France. "Isn't it a fact that these arrangements . . . were done for the purpose of evading French tax laws?" Cohn demanded. Twisting and turning, Casablancas insisted that wasn't true. Though he admitted that models were paid outside France, he claimed he knew very little about the process.

"You are just not going to give me a direct answer, are you?" Cohn said.

"I'm giving you the answer I know," Casablancas replied.

Elite fought back in a document submitted to the court in August, in which its lawyer, Ira Levinson, charged that New York's existing agencies were engaged in a monopolistic conspiracy to fix prices and commissions. Levinson was referring to actions taken by several agents in the early seventies, when they changed their corporate names (removing the word "agency"), returned their employment agency licenses to New York City's Department of Consumer Affairs, asserted that they were managers and not employment agents, and raised commissions. In 1972 the department subpoenaed Ford's records, and the following year it scheduled a hearing to investigate Wilhelmina. "The principals of the major modeling agencies . . . agreed among themselves to raise commissions," Levinson charged, claiming to have interviewed a witness who was present at the agents' meeting where the decision was made. (Stewart Cowley confirms that the agents did make the move in concert. "No such conversation ever took place," insists Jerry Ford.)

The legal actions went on for several years. But after the Fords lost their case against Pillard in arbitration in 1979, they dropped the other actions, for reasons they won't explain. Even without a legal resolution, it was already clear

that Elite was the model war winner. Stars were banging down its doors, bringing with them bookings that paid the rent, the legal fees, and champagne bills.

"Eileen controlled the industry, and then she didn't anymore," says
Monique Pillard. "They'd ask me, 'Who's your PR?' I'd say, 'Eileen Ford.'
Models kept leaving, one after another." What really lured them? Money was
part of it, certainly. And so was John's knack for promotion and publicity. In
January 1978 he bound all his models' composite cards into an oversize folder
with detachable wall posters. It was a sensation. He'd already removed prices
from all his promotional materials—making all rates negotiable—and
announced he'd increased the day rate for stars to $1,500.

Meanwhile, Jerry Ford was working to win models "reuse" payments for
photographs, a more important change in the long run. "Rates were going up
anyway," he says. "It just came a little faster. The increased traffic between
Paris and New York widened the market for top-notch models [and] created
the world-class superstars. John would take credit for that. We felt we were
laying the basis for that all along. There's no question that they created a great
agency, but we're still here. We replaced the models who were purloined and
slugged it out as well as we knew how."

Harry Conover, Jr., jokes that John Casablancas is his father's reincarnation.
But Casablancas is more: He invented a new way of marketing models. "He
was a ruthless womanizer, and the girls loved it," says *Vogue* fashion editor
Polly Mellen. "He took a sleepy backwater business run by a dowager empress
and turned it into Hollywood," says photographer Peter Strongwater. "He
was the first to use sexy pictures, naked bodies," says booker Monique Corey.
"You'd never seen that before." "He made the girls known," says Maarit
Halinen. "People started to get interested. They wanted to know, 'Who is this
guy?' Everyone was talking."

Casablancas boasts, "I said to models, 'I'm going to sell you like women,
I'm going to bring out the sex appeal and sensuality, *and* we're going to make
more money.' " The difference was simple, he says. "Ford was a prude, and I
was not."

JANICE DICKINSON *
MIKE REINHARDT *
CHRISTIE BRINKLEY

They are older now. Janice Dickinson's toughness is no longer tomboyish. Mike Reinhardt *is* still boyish, but he's gone gray. Christie Brinkley is no longer a lithe *Sports Illustrated* bathing suit girl. But in the mid-seventies they were the prettiest of the pretty, the fastest in the fast lane.

The daughter of a television producer, Christie Brinkley started high and rose higher. In the early eighties she was probably the world's top model, earning $350,000 a year working for Chanel, Cover Girl, MasterCard ("You're so chic . . ."), and Water Pik. Her boyfriend was champagne heir Olivier Chandon. They met at Studio 54. The celebrity club's co-owner Steve Rubell introduced them. When *People* magazine wrote them up, Christie said her only problem with Chandon was his hobby: driving race cars. That hobby killed him not long afterward, when he raced off a track in Florida and crashed into a canal.

Brinkley met singer Billy Joel on St.-Barthélemy in 1983. Just divorced, he was also on the rebound. Though they were something of an odd couple, the squat singer-songwriter from Long Island and the ultimate California blonde made beautiful music together. She licensed her name for a line of sportswear, appeared in calendars, on posters, and in his "Uptown Girl" video. They married in 1985, had a daughter, Alexa Ray, nine months later, and moved into a huge ocean mansion in Amagansett. Christie fumbled as a television personality but won ribbons riding cutting horses. Then, in 1994, in the space of a few short weeks, she almost died in a helicopter and announced her split from Joel and her engagement to Colorado-based real estate developer Rick Taubman (whom she went on to marry that Christmas). What happened? "I was searching for honesty," she said.

At the same time Janice Dickinson was giving birth to her second child, a daughter she almost named Diva, presumably after herself. She was certainly the most operatic character ever to grace a fashion page. Janice claimed that Savannah Dickinson, as the child was finally named, is the daughter of actor Sylvester Stallone, and even he took credit, but then DNA tests proved him wrong. A tattooed California biker later told reporters that he was the father. Then Dickinson revealed she was pregnant again and again said Stallone was the father. She miscarried and next hooked up with the publisher of *Vogue*.

This was all nothing new. Dickinson wasn't always at the center of a storm; she *was* the storm from her first photo sessions in 1974 until she entered a drug rehabilitation clinic in 1982. "Totally, totally, totally nuts," says Polly Mellen. "Big, big, big heart. *Incredible* body. And all that noise? *Hoo-hah,* forget it!" Her affair with Mike Reinhardt was legendary, and its aftermath provocative.

Dickinson took to taking her clothes off wherever she could. Once she did it in a Roman fountain. "We were coming back to the Grand Hotel after dinner, and she was having a fight with Mike," remembers Lizette Kattan, an editor of Italian *Harper's Bazaar.* "At a certain point she took her clothes off and went swimming in the fountain, completely naked. Mike was out of his mind because he didn't know how to stop her. She really stopped the traffic. Then the police came, and they finally had to send somebody to the hotel to get a towel to wrap her up."

Then there was the time designer Calvin Klein took a planeload of top models to Japan. "Janice, Iman, Debbie, Apollonia, Kelly Emberg, Jeff Aquilon, Nancy Donahue, you name it, everybody of that era was on one plane," recalls model Tara Shannon. "We met at Calvin's, and they handed out sheets that said, 'If you get drunk or have drugs, see ya. We don't want to have nothing to do with you.'" So on the plane the models took everything they were carrying. "Quaaludes, coke, pot, everything," Shannon says. "That was a pretty wild flight, man. I have a picture of Janice opening her shirt right in the middle of the plane."

Nowadays, it is Dickinson taking the pictures. After Reinhardt, she moved to Italy in 1985 and had a romance with a rich young Italian. In 1988 she moved to Los Angeles, married Simon Field, a music video producer, and had her first child. Today, at thirty-nine, working as a photographer, she is still larger than life and louder than that.

One dark, one light, Dickinson and Brinkley were the two poles of modeling at the turn of the eighties. But they had two things in common: They

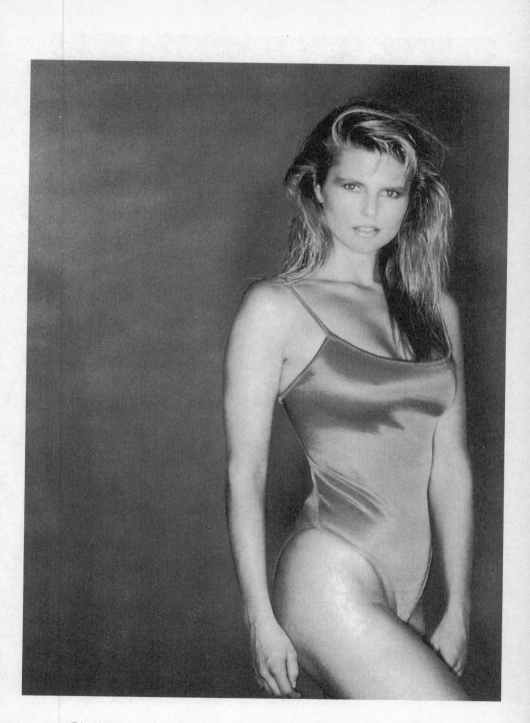

Christie Brinkley photographed by Patrick Demarchelier

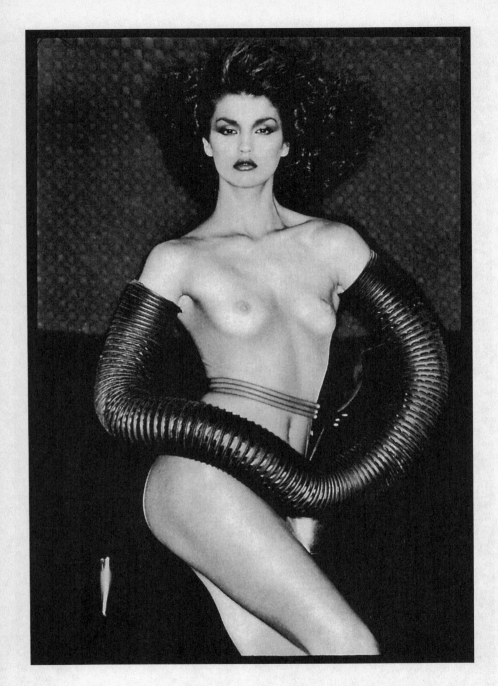

Janice Dickinson photographed by Marco Glaviano

were both among the first stars at Elite Models, and they both slept with Mike Reinhardt.

Sitting in his sunlit studio atop Carnegie Hall, Reinhardt, fifty-six, gives a rueful smile, shakes his curly graying head, and asks his current wife, Tammi, how many models preceded her in his life. "We're all three years and three months apart in age," she replies. "Minty is forty-two, Janice is thirty-nine," and that's not to mention Bernadette, Lisa Cooper, Renata, and Ely. Reinhardt jealously protected his women. "I introduced Janice to Mike, and I never worked with her again because he was so jealous and insecure," says colleague Alex Chatelain. "Anytime I worked with any of his squeezes, he made sure they didn't show up. But I really like him a lot."

Reinhardt's fashion career stalled in the eighties. People said he'd burned out after too many models, too many drugs, too many late nights at the club he opened on Long Island. In fact, he was shooting cigarette and liquor ads, he says. But when he broke up with his last wife, he admits, he went on a bender. It wasn't until the late eighties that he pulled out of his tailspin, stopped smoking marijuana for the first time in a quarter century, met Tammi, and started shooting fashion again. In 1994 he even signed a long-term contract with *Elle* magazine.

Two souvenirs of his heyday hang on the wall of Reinhardt's apartment. One is a drawing of Reinhardt, Patrice Casanova, and a North Beach Leather model, all passed out on a bed at 3:00 A.M. The other is a picture Mike shot in a mirror of himself, Christie Brinkley, and his best friend and next-door neighbor Pierre Houlès, sitting at a shoeshine stand. The trio are laughing and smiling. They wouldn't be for long.

CHRISTIE BRINKLEY: "I grew up in California. I used to make my own magazines. I'd cut pictures out and put them together my way. I remember seeing Cybill Shepherd and Susan Dey and knowing their names. But I was really sort of more into the art direction aspect of it. I wanted to be an artist. I was for sure going to go to Paris, live in a garret, and paint. I moved to Paris to study art when I was eighteen and I fell in love with Jean François Allaux, a very well-respected political cartoonist; but he got drafted. We had this military service kind of relationship until he was out of the army.

"I lived in a *chambre de bain* with no telephone or bathrooms. It was so charming. The toilet was two flights down; the telephone was about a block and a half away. I had a little dog, and he had distemper. So I went to the phone to call the vet, and this guy, Errol Sawyer, this kind of loud, crazy black

American photographer, said, 'Oh, there you are! I spotted you one day at the telephone office, and I was hoping I would see you again because I've got a job, and the clients are looking for a girl just like you. Would you be interested? This is my address. I don't have a telephone, but if you could just drop by.' I was like, 'Yeah, right.' I said, 'No, I don't think so, but thank you, I'm flattered, good-bye.' But I took his address, and I put it in my pocket.

"A couple days later I bumped into a friend, a French girl who knew what was going on in Paris, and she was talking about lines that different guys were coming up with. I happened to have the same jacket on with the piece of paper in it, and I found the paper and said, 'Listen to this one, a photographer, looking for a girl just like me.' She said, 'I've seen that name in magazines. He's for real!'

"I'd spent my last penny on vet bills. I was broke. I worked as an illustrator, but I didn't have a working permit, so I was grossly underpaid. But I was determined to make it on my own, and I thought maybe I should swing by this guy's place. If he really is legitimate, then I can do one job and see what it's like. And I went by, and he said, 'Can you run home and put on something nice?' I had this dreamy Cacharel dress, and I put that on, and I pulled this knit cap over my head, and he took me to a park and took some pictures, and then he took them to Johnny Casablancas, and he said, 'Bring her in.' I was really scared. I thought, 'I'm not model material.' "

JOHN CASABLANCAS: "Errol Sawyer was a scout on our payroll. He saw Christie in a post office, brought her to the agency. It was kind of funny because another agency was trying to get her, Élysées 3, my brother, and he was kind of pissed off because she came to us. It was one of the rare times we competed for a new model."

BRINKLEY: "I didn't know Errol was a scout. He just took those pictures, and then he took me out another day. I think he said the job had fallen through.

"I was very big, athletic, let's face it, on the fat side. But my spirit of adventure said, 'See what it's like.' So I went in, and Mike Reinhardt was there, and a bunch of other photographers, and they all said, 'Oh, where'd you hide her? I want to use her. A job in Morocco, a glamorous ski trip.' I'm thinking, 'Morocco? Ski trip? This is incredible!' But the first job I did was the cover of *Parents* magazine. I'm thinking, 'Modeling, beautiful clothes,' and they hand me this yellow bikini, and I was absolutely scared to death to walk out of the dressing room.

"I was very reluctant in the beginning. I didn't call myself a model. I still considered that I was a struggling artist. I did a couple jobs, and then I got a check, and then I packed up and I left town. The agency was pretty upset, but I think that the fact that I had suddenly appeared on the scene, done a few jobs, created a minor buzz, and disappeared was good. The agency said, 'She's booked, She's unavailable,' and people thought, 'Wow, she's working a lot. We've got to have her!' Because when I returned, there were jobs all over the place. I would go to jobs in Germany, where I would have a room with a bath, which was quite a luxury, and all the great rolls and bread that they'd bring up in the morning.

"In the meantime, Mike Reinhardt went back to New York and told Eileen Ford about me. And right away Eileen started calling, and so did Nina Blanchard. They were all anxious to get me back to America. But I just kept saying, 'I love Paris.' Basically I was waiting for Jean François to get out of the army. He and his artist friends didn't really approve of this job. So I was being very low-key about it. I was very reluctant to really grasp it as a job. It was better-paying than waitressing. I wasn't making the money back then that I made once I got to America, but I thought it was an exorbitant amount, and I was trying to spend it as foolishly as I possibly could. I would buy plane tickets for friends, and we'd go off places. I was also eating better.

"I came back to L.A. to see my family. Nina Blanchard took me to lunch at Chasen's. We're sitting there, and somebody comes over to the table and says, 'Nina, where have you been hiding her? I want to book her for our commercial.' It was for Yucca Dew shampoo in Arizona. Five minutes later somebody else comes over. Noxzema. A few minutes later somebody else comes over. Max Factor perfume. I also met Eileen Ford on that trip. She was in Palm Springs, vacationing with her family, and she asked me to come over to her house and bring my book. I remember her saying, 'This is dreadful, lose this, lose that,' pulling things out. I was so nervous because she was a legend. So I went back to Paris, Jean François got out of the army, and we decided to go to New York for two months. We knew that he'd get work, too.

"We really started enjoying the energy, and Jean François was working and I was working and two months became years. One of the earlier jobs I did was for a hair salon's window. They were pushing shoulder-length frizzy hairdos. I thought modeling meant that you get a new look, so I was really into it, but they chopped off my hair and permed it and I looked like Bozo the Clown. It was fine for that picture, but the next day it wasn't even hairlike. So I bought a bunch of berets. I was wearing one when I met Jule Campbell of *Sports Illus-*

trated. She said that beret was the reason she liked me, because I looked like I had so much attitude, and she booked me for a *Sports Illustrated* trip to Cancun. I had no idea that *Sports Illustrated* was becoming prestigious. But with those pictures and the *Glamour* covers, I never had to knock on doors or do go-sees. I never really became part of the modeling world either. The second my work was over, I'd be out the door, I'd come home, and Jean François and I would be painting or sculpting."

MIKE REINHARDT: "I was with Barbara Minty four years. I lived over Carnegie Hall and used it as a studio, too. The first time I saw Janice was before she went to Paris. I was leaving on a trip, I was preoccupied, and she never let me forget that."

JANICE DICKINSON: "Mike was so incredibly rude. He was a total narcissist. He would just stare at himself in the mirror. I remember saying, 'Excuse me, I've been sitting here for about ten minutes, will you have a look at my book?' He goes, 'Not today,' and then he walks away. I was hurt and I thought to myself, What a rude prick. I'll get him someday."

REINHARDT: "She couldn't get a photographer to test her, and one night she was walking in the rain, and she met a man who obviously took a fancy to her and gave her a ticket to Paris."

DICKINSON: "Isn't that typical, Mike trying to make me look like an old whore? Mike fantasizes that he was the man who gave me the ticket. He never gave me anything. I gave him all his French *Vogue* covers. They were all my ideas."

REINHARDT: "When Janice came back to New York, she came to see me again. I was shooting, but I kept her here. She showed me her book. I pointed my camera at her and fell in love. Our relationship started through the camera. She was incredible."

DICKINSON: "I was very selective. I knew that if [I got involved with a photographer], my name would get out. I went on trips with Patrick Demarchelier and Alex Chatelain. I worked with Stember and Pierre Houlès and Jean-Paul Goude, and you can ask them, I touched no one's feet. It just didn't go down. They're all a bunch of pussies anyway.

"I avoided Mike for a couple of bookings. He was after me when I was married, and I don't cheat when I'm married. He used to call me from all parts of the world, and I just said, 'Forget it,' and put the phone down. Finally he had a French *Vogue* booking for me. I said, 'Airplane tickets? What's the money? OK, I'll take it.' So we did a couple French *Vogue* shoots, and then we went back to New York, and I guess the relationship began. He finally had somebody who understood photography.

"I was working all over the place, France, Italy, England, Germany, Japan, Paris. I was still with Wilhelmina. I was rockin' and movin'. I was a star. I was booking anywhere that the larger digits came in, and I controlled it, honey, they didn't control me. I brought a lot to everything, and Mike took all my money. I was naïve enough to give it to him. He started smoking a lot of pot, and he started to get nuts because he wasn't the star, I was the star. He wasn't like that in the beginning. He changed."

REINHARDT: "I'd been a big grass smoker. I started in Paris, and it became the love of my life. I was smoking morning to night. Eventually it affected my work. I got repetitive. I'd smoke just to stay even. I went out with Lisa Taylor around that time, but I don't remember when. See how much pot I smoked? But when I was with Minty, I stopped. I was vegetarian, doing transcendental meditation for three or four years. Janice was also clean at the beginning, but slowly it dilapidated [sic]."

DICKINSON: "Let's get it straight. I did my share of drugs. What's the big deal? There were times when it was appropriate, like after work, sometimes during work. I mean, it was the disco era. It was the fast lane. Every playboy, every shah of Iran, every movie star, every rock'n'roll star, they all wanted me. But it was just really a lonely time for me."

REINHARDT: "Janice brought an unfortunate vibration to my life. Things started getting crazy. Nobody would mistake Janice for sane. We're both crazy. In hindsight we were a bad combination, but we had good work energy. You fall in love with a model, and then you work with her. She would do anything, and I thought it was really great. When I see her now, I think, How could I? but I adored everything she did. Now I think it's very bad to work with your girlfriend. You know each other too well. But we helped each other. We worked. And we fought like cats and dogs when we were working.

"Nothing could be done without much ado. We were noisy. Other people thought we were obnoxious, but I thought we were great. One night in Paris we were having dinner with Alex Chatelain, and Janice got on the table and mooned somebody.

"Janice had a boyfriend before me, a French model humper. She was mad at him because when she left Paris, he had an affair with Debbie [her sister]. We were in Paris for French *Vogue,* and we decided to get this guy. She called him and said, 'I'm in Paris, and I'm *dying* for you.' We were in town, but she said she was working at the airport, staying at the Sofitel, and leaving for Germany the next morning. Would he drive out there with four dozen oysters, some sea urchins, and champagne because that gets her really horny? She said, 'Get a room and I'll be there at six.' She called him every half hour and said the shoot was still going on. Then at midnight she called one last time and said, 'You're an asshole. Fuck you!' "

DICKINSON: "That's not true. That's not true. I'm gonna sue him for that. Did he name names? I'll sue him for that. That's libel against my sister. I don't appreciate that. And it was Mike who was doing the mooning, OK? Mike was the mooner."

CASABLANCAS: "Mike was just on a power trip, smoking joints all the time, crazed with all kinds of things. He was a nightmare to deal with."

MONIQUE PILLARD: "Janice was brilliant. She made Mike, let's face it."

REINHARDT: "I didn't know that we defined our moment. I wish I had, but I was too involved with drugs. I looked down on the business. I didn't realize what I had."

BRINKLEY: "Then came the model wars. I was with Elite and Ford simultaneously. Then John wanted me back with him in New York. I agreed with his philosophy, and I felt I had to be faithful, and it made sense to me, so I went into the Fords and I said, 'Please don't take this personally, but I have to help him out.' I can't say that they were pleased, but they were very gracious. Eileen and Jerry said something like 'We think you're making a big mistake. We can do a lot more for you in your career, and when you come to realize that, we'll welcome you with open arms.' To me, it wasn't that big of a deal."

CASABLANCAS: "I will always remember that Christie asked me, 'Am I the first model who will join Elite?' There was Maarit, but I said, 'Yes, you are,' and she said, 'Then I'm coming.' She hated Eileen's guts. Eileen represented everything that she didn't like: big business, American hypocrisy. She was really the young wife of a French idealist. She was becoming a big star, but she was very, very, very sweet. Our relationship continued in that way as long as she was married."

DICKINSON: "I left Wilhelmina to go to Ford. I don't remember when. I was working every day, every night, in a different studio, with a different photographer, in a different country. Willie wasn't a good negotiator. Eileen was a better negotiator. I always threw [what had happened between us] in her face. I said, 'Listen, you don't know what you're talking about. You didn't want me anyway.' Jerry always backed me up. But Eileen's a money-maker. She'd yes me to death. I was hot.

"Then John came to me on bended knee and asked me if I wanted to go with Elite. I said, 'Yeah, how much? What's in it for me? I'll go with you if you bring Monique Pillard, my booker, and you give me the commission that you get from the client, plus you pay me my percent.'

"What do you think model agents are? Pimps. Meat market. But John Casablancas made no money off me. And I was the only model in his agency that he hadn't slept with. He was sleeping with all of them, twosomes, threesomes. But he had to take my orders, and he had to kiss my ass. I was making a pretty good living. And Mike had nothing to do with this, OK? I made all my own decisions."

CASABLANCAS: "Mike Reinhardt, who was my friend, could not tell Janice to change agencies, because he would have been held responsible for it. He explained to me. He couldn't do anything because ninety-nine percent of the models he booked were with Ford. But Janice probably started to become a little bit obnoxious. Instead of being smart and saying, 'She's trying to be obnoxious,' Ford got rid of her. This was like a present from God, you know. So I took Janice, but I said, 'I don't want to lose my health on you. Not only don't I want to take a commission for you, I'm going to return to you the twenty percent the client gives me [on these conditions]. I don't want to hear your name; I never want to see you in the agency; I never want to talk to you. You're going to get the best financial deal in the world, but I don't want to see your face or hear from you or from Mike.' They were obnoxious. For a while this was the deal."

BRINKLEY: "I like business to be business, and I like things to be above-board, and I got wind that certain models were having to pay less commission than me, that there were deals being made. I'm sure he had a deal with Janice, and I didn't like that. I'd heard all the stuff about young models, too, but I wasn't going to be swayed by gossip. But when I was told by a model that Janice had this deal, I didn't like it."

DICKINSON: "Mike was antagonistic, a Nazi. He wouldn't let me take trips, because he was a jealous photographer. He hated Patrick; he hated Alex; he hated Albert Watson; he hated Avedon. He was so jealous that I was working for Avedon and Penn it used to make him green. He used to call up the studios, and torture me and make me cry. I'd say, 'Just shut the fuck up, man. I'm working for these masters, and you're just this little thirty-five-millimeter jealous B list photographer.' I'd hang up, and he'd make a scene. I'd switched agencies, and he'd get Casablancas in on it and make havoc for me. He always pitted me against my agents. Any opportunity I had to get out of his studio, I took it."

REINHARDT: "There was no cocaine in the relationship until the very end. We went on a binge for a few months. But that whole last year, 1979, was pretty drug-ridden. We had a breakup in May. She heard from a male model that I'd screwed his girlfriend. I don't really remember. I think it was true. I was in Paris, Janice was here, and she flipped out and told me to fuck off and went off with some model, and I think she stopped taking coke. We reconciled. That Christmas Pierre Houlès, Christie, Janice, and I went to St. Moritz. I had to go to Paris afterwards, and when I got back to New York, she was gone. It broke my heart. I was devastated, but I deserved it."

BRINKLEY: "Most of the time that I was friends with Mike, he was going out with Janice. And then they had their meltdown. My marriage broke up around 1980. I got a divorce, and I moved to California. No sooner did I get there than I got a job in New York, and I came back and met Pierre Houlès. I went back to California, and we kept talking. Pierre was very knowledgeable about the business. He had wonderful ideas. Gilles Bensimon and Mike Reinhardt used to call him for advice. Pierre was the least well known, but amongst that group he was probably the most respected. And so I learned from him. Pierre would give me advice about agents, but I really went more on just a gut instinct."

DICKINSON: "I was young, you know, and I left Mike because he was sleeping with half the models in the head sheet. He was a pig. Girls that I was shooting with told me, and it really hurt my feelings. I'm a street kid, and I should have been tough; but I really thought I kinda dug this guy for a minute. And it's just not very nice, it's not very discreet when other models come up to you and sort of flaunt in your face: 'Nyaa, I slept with your boyfriend.' But this is high school shit. I don't want to talk about it."

BRINKLEY: "Unbeknownst to me, Pierre had another girlfriend, Valerie. But I, being the type that passionately throws myself into things, gave up my apartment in California and went back to New York and Paris. Pierre and I had a very rough relationship. He was trying to appear like somebody who didn't have another girlfriend. I moved in with him in Paris, and I think Valerie must have been in Carnegie Hall, because I still had my apartment in New York. Anyway, Pierre had come up with this idea for *Elle,* a special issue, just me, but it wasn't going to be obvious that it was just me. I was to have wigs made, contact lenses, and we were going to start out at a heavier weight and then show a complete metamorphosis. We started it, and that's when I found out about Valerie. I was heartbroken. So I went back to New York, devastated beyond belief. And Mike picked me up at the airport. He was really my best friend at the time. We had a lot of fun. He's a good guy."

REINHARDT: "Pierre and I became estranged because of Christie. She and I were really good friends. She'd just broken up with Pierre, and she came to my house, distraught. Pierre called and said, 'Kick her out immediately.' I said, 'That's ridiculous.' I was with Ely at the time, but she'd gone on a trip, and Christie and I were alone in the country, and I was pissed at Pierre for demanding I throw her out. It just happened, and it lasted three weeks. But it felt incestuous. It wasn't right."

BRINKLEY: "It wasn't like we ever admitted to being anything more than friends because that's what we were. But we had a little affair. That was that. And we both realized we'd made a mistake. Valerie and I spent a weekend together talking about Pierre. Once you know the truth, things get resolved."

REINHARDT: "Christie and I are still friends, but Pierre didn't speak to me for two years. I was in Paris for *Bazaar*, and I ran into Pierre and Patrick Demarchelier. Patrick said, 'Don't you think it's enough?' It was Saturday. We decided to have lunch on Monday. But Pierre was found dead on the street on Sunday. He was jogging, and he had an aneurysm."

CASABLANCAS: "This sweet little girl suddenly starts having marital problems. Then she gets caught in a love triangle with the two most obnoxious power players in the business. They're best friends, and they're competing with each other, and they're trying to show her how strong they are by bullying the agent, us. She's going through—I don't know exactly what—success, which destroys so many models. My ex-wife hated Mike with such a passion because she saw what he did to me. I would come home, I would be in tears. Pierre and Mike were playing mind games with me, telling me that I was going to lose Christie if I didn't do this. So I would do this, and they'd say that was not good enough. They were in agreement. It was the most bizarre relationship. They were competing for Christie, speaking bad about each other to her, but at the same time they were best friends and agreeing on what they had to do with me. It was a totally destructive thing. It was such a shitty period."

BRINKLEY: "John wanted to do posters with his top girls. So he had it set up. Mike Reinhardt was shooting it, and the picture came back, and I didn't like it; but John put the poster out without my approval, and we took him to court. Mike and I sued John Casablancas, and quite honestly I was amazed that we ended up winning our lawsuit. I called up the Fords and said, 'You were right, and I want to come back.' But I had a little problem with the guy that worked at Ford's, Joey Hunter. I had only met him four times in my entire career. But he said some things about me that were not nice, and I didn't really want to go to that agency when he was there. So I went to Zoli for a few minutes."

CASABLANCAS: "I was in Hamburg on a business trip, and I stayed two and a half hours on the telephone over this, and I came to the point where I couldn't take it anymore. I broke down, and I said to Pierre, 'You can take Christie and you can stick her up your ass.' It was bizarre. She went from being a loyal, faithful wife to becoming the mistress of two guys that had other girlfriends. This is how crazy she got.

"I get this letter from both of them, Christie and Valerie: that they're both going to Zoli. It was extraordinary, the mind games that these guys played. I mean, I have to take my hat off to Mike and Pierre. Pierre was a madman. May he rest in peace. But when he died and Patrick and Mike were lamenting him, I said, 'I'm not going to miss this guy one day.' He hated everything; he was Mr. Critique. He used people, but at the same time he pretended he didn't. End of story.

"So this is the story of Christie. She went to Ford [in May 1980] and started going out with Olivier Chandon, and she went from being a model to being a celebrity. And everything following the scenario I had laid out for her. Christie will always be a mystery to me because in thirty years I have never seen such a change in personality. It was not an evolution; it was a complete flip-flop. She went from the sweetest, not-money-interested, not-VIP-hungry to this. . . . I don't think it was only Mike and Pierre. She must have had something in her. Also, you know, drugs. I believe that Christie probably never did drugs except during that period, which could explain why she changed. I don't know that for a fact. But the only way that I can explain certain things is that she probably did."

BRINKLEY: "I have never been strung out on drugs. I was aware that I was hanging around a lot of crazy people and a lot of crazy things were going on, but I really have to say that is not my style. I was always aware of not wanting to go to the bathroom. If you went to the bathroom, it looked suspicious.

"I don't believe I was ever manipulated. I've always made my decisions from the gut. When Mike and Pierre started talking about things, it was far too political and beyond what I needed to know. It really goes back to never really feeling that this was the business I was going to stay in. Still, to this day I've always kept different things going on the side.

"I think it all started happening after the third time I was in *Sports Illustrated*. Things just kept on happening, and I kept going along with it. I was getting a lot of fan mail asking for beauty advice, and so I came up with the idea of a newsletter answering the most commonly asked questions, and then I decided to do a book and went to Simon and Schuster and sold the idea. *Sports Illustrated* asked me to be their first calendar girl, and it was so wildly successful, that I took it the next step and thought, If they're making all this money off my image, why not produce it myself? So I was the first model to produce my own calendar. And I did that for the next few years."

DICKINSON: "I didn't think a lot in those days. If I had to do it all over again, I would change some things. I was working all those hours, and the agents don't give a crap. They get these poor young girls wrapped around their fingers. I couldn't handle the pace."

REINHARDT: "Cocaine destroyed Janice. Coke was never my drug although I was around it and I did it, and once I got arrested in Milan with a sizable amount for personal consumption in my pocket. I was shooting the collections for *Harper's Bazaar.* It was the best thing that happened to me. I'd never understood why anyone wanted to put that shit in their nose; but I did it, and before you know it, it creeps up on you. I could have very easily fallen into it. It was just at that point when I got busted."

DICKINSON: "I took drugs like everybody else. You take a young girl. Most of these playboys only want to get in their pants, so they dangle coke in front of their nose, and inevitably, boom, the pants come off. I would do a couple lines, and then I'd just split. 'Free blow? Why not! Later . . .' And I was not ripping my clothes off and running around either. I mean, this comes out of like fag hairdressers' mouths and then [people] believe it. Show me Polaroids; show me tapes. I wanna see 'em. Show 'em to me, and then I'll gladly come clean, but I never did that once. I'm a Catholic girl.

"Get it straight. I was the top, the number one model, top, top, top. I was offered *Flashdance,* but why would I want to do anything else? I sang at Studio 54 [in February 1982 because its owner] Mark Fleischman wanted to have an event, and he didn't know what to do. I said, 'Why don't we help people? Alvin Ailey has no money; the company is about to close. I'll sing.' I knew a few tunes, I was hanging out with rockers. To make a long story short, I sang two songs. I bombed completely. The next day the press said, 'Nice try, but stick to modeling.'

"Right after that I just had it, so I went into rehab at St. Mary's in Minneapolis. It was the show and everything else. I went to clean out for a month, detox, and then go back to work. It was just to recharge my batteries."

PILLARD: "I really loved that girl. She was every agent's dream, a huge money-maker. She had an enormous drug problem, but she got herself fixed up. I was her partner in rehab. I'd forbid her to have a boyfriend without my approval. I was the only one who could control her. She'd say, 'OK, agent.' I brought her to every studio to show everyone what was happening. Then she became a bad girl again. But I had moved off the booking table, and I wasn't handling her day to day anymore. She wanted to be handled by me, and I said, 'I can't do it.' I was a little bit more than a booker by then. Things weren't said, but I was more or less the director of the Elite division. With Janice, it was twenty-four-hour service, not nine to seven. She became pretty bad and blamed it on the fact that she couldn't talk to me. Finally there were no more bookings. Nobody wanted to take a chance. Would she show up? Would she be abusive? I told her, 'You threw your career to the dogs.'

"One day Joe Hunter calls and says, 'Send Janice Dickinson's book to Ford.' It was no longer a loss because Janice had ruined her name. It goddamn broke my heart, and I promised myself I'd never let that happen again."

DICKINSON: "I'm still exuberant. I'm still an extrovert. I won't be challenged. If someone challenges me, then I'll back them into a corner. Talk to me about fashion; talk to me about concept; talk to me about lighting; talk to me about makeup; talk to me about Yves Saint Laurent, about opening the show for Azzedine Alaïa for seven straight years, about being Gianni Versace's favorite model. I mean, everybody wanted me: Valentino, Calvin Klein, Halston, Blass, Beene. Let's talk about the greats, not the darkness and the evilness and the bullshit about model agents.

"I represented hope for the ethnic girls, Spanish, Italian, Portuguese, anyone with a darker image. They looked at me and knew that they, too, could be as beautiful as a blonde. Let me tell you something, no blonde ever had more fun than me. I am the queen of fun. I had a ball. I was young; I was rich; I was beautiful; I was intelligent. I leveraged my modeling to learn how to take photographs.

"I don't want to come off sounding so cocky, but I used to help a lot of people, too. I would help all these young models with their makeup, and show 'em how to walk, and tell them what to do, and give them money, and blah, blah, blah, blah, blah. No one tells you stories like that. They don't tell you that if there was a job for five hundred dollars, I said, 'Charge six fifty,' and they paid it. When it got to be eight hundred, a thousand, two thousand, twenty-five hundred, I was the one who set 'em up, so all those models can kiss my ass."

$2,500 A DAY

Afew nights before Elite opened in New York, Zoli Rendessy tossed one of his famous all-star parties. Apollonia von Ravenstein came with Ara Gallant, the hairdresser who counted Jack and Warren and Anjelica among his very best friends. Apollonia and Ara were a couple of the moment, but that didn't mean they slept together. Indeed, after Zoli's party Gallant headed off alone to the Anvil, a bar near New York City's downtown docks, where the entertainment consisted of men fist-fucking other men. "I love the Anvil," Gallant said. "Of course, it would be extremely embarrassing to be caught fucking there."

Embarrassment may have been the last taboo, but discretion was out of fashion.

"Me with four men?" says a Wilhelmina model of the era. *"Sure."*

With uncanny synchronicity, Studio 54 had opened a few weeks before Elite, and it quickly became a symbol of the revival of recession-plagued New York. It was also a symbol of the prevailing social ethic of libertinism, dissolution, and the quest for easy gratification. Drugs—especially cocaine and the soporific Quaalude—were given away like candy by the club's co-owner Steve Rubell and consumed by all and sundry. Semipublic sex took place regularly in the club's balcony and basement.

The rules of acceptable conduct had changed. The exotic and unspeakable had become the new norm. The models, agents, and photographers who joined the dancing sea of celebrities were central figures in a new society— the first, perhaps, since the fall of Rome to declare so openly and in such numbers that sin was in. They all believed they were special, and Studio's exclusionary door policy reinforced that notion. Above morals, above ethics, and especially above those kept waiting outside, Studio's denizens were modern Olympians, inhabiting a special world of notoriety. And the wages of their sins were astonishing. Each new excrescence brought them more celebrity, more reverence, and more money to fuel their shenanigans.

The addiction to pleasure was international, and models were in the vanguard of the pleasure seekers. Thanks to John Casablancas, models had become rootless mercenaries, traveling the world in search of bigger bucks. In the late seventies no one earned more than Cheryl Tiegs, whose day rate hit $2,000 in 1977. Although many assumed that her husband, Stan Dragoti, was running her career, Tiegs insists she was in charge. "I pretty much did it myself, for better or for worse. I certainly made mistakes along the way. But I was very much a long-term thinker."

Tiegs downplays the importance of her January 1978 appearance—in a fishnet bathing suit that bared her full breasts—in *Sports Illustrated*'s annual swimsuit issue. "It's a sweet little picture, that's it," she says. But in fact, it was a major coup, adding the powerful appeal of the pinup picture to modeling's arsenal of promotional gimmicks.

"It was our last day of shooting on the Amazon River," recalls *SI*'s Jule Campbell. While Walter Iooss, Jr., was shooting a young Brazilian model, "Cheryl was waiting in the boat, getting impatient because we weren't using her," Campbell recalls. "I told Walter to get a picture of her and send her back to the hotel. She got in the water, but she was annoyed, and she was just standing there to get it over with." Back in New York, Campbell decided against using the picture but showed it to her editors just in case they liked it.

They did. And the response was overwhelming. The magazine's swimsuit extravaganza had always been the second best-selling issue of the year, just behind its Super Bowl special. "That year I beat the Super Bowl," Campbell says. "They had posters of the photograph in Times Square the next day, and we had to sue to stop it. We got letters from outraged mothers, librarians, priests telling me I was going straight to hell. We never turned back. And Cheryl's career took off after that."

Two months later Tiegs appeared for the second time on the cover of *Time* and was featured in its competitor, *Newsweek,* the very same week. "Where else could I go from there?" she asks. "It was time to move on." In rapid succession she posed in a pink bikini on a poster that knocked Farrah Fawcett-Majors off the walls of the rooms of several million adolescent American boys, announced a deal to write a book on beauty, and signed what was reported to be a $2 million contract to appear on ABC-TV.

"My whole world turned upside down, and I certainly noticed the difference," she says. "Whatever I did was recorded on the cover of the New York *Post*. I wasn't in as much control as I would have liked. I didn't know how to stop it. The media kind of threw me for a loop."

Tiegs won't talk about what happened next. Indeed, she answers questions about the next three years of her life with stony silence. But just as her career hit the stratosphere, her marriage to Dragoti ran aground, and she became the first victim of the new, heightened interest in models. In 1978 the New York *Post* and its competitor the *Daily News* were locked in tabloid combat. Gossip items were part of the ammunition they used in their war, the more scurrilous the better. Tiegs got caught in the crossfire.

That December Tiegs was reportedly spotted necking with tennis player Vitas Gerulaitis at a birthday party for Steve Rubell at Studio 54. Not long thereafter she flew to Kenya with photographer Peter Beard to narrate an *American Sportsman Special* documentary based on Beard's book about African wildlife, *The End of the Game.* Five months later, en route to the Cannes Film Festival, Dragoti was arrested at the airport in Frankfurt, Germany, with about an ounce of cocaine, wrapped in aluminum foil, taped to his back and thirty more grams of the stuff in his suitcase. In July, after he was fined almost $55,000 and given a suspended sentence of twenty-one months in jail, Dragoti said he'd started sniffing the stuff after he learned that Beard and Tiegs had begun having an affair in Kenya. "I was very depressed," he said, "and needed something to take away the pain."

Peter Beard had been involved with models for twenty years before he met Cheryl Tiegs. In 1958 the Yale student and photography buff was a patient in New York's Hospital for Special Surgery when Suzy Parker was wheeled into the next room following the train crash that killed her father. "Seeing her and the various people who came in to see her was my first entrée to the world of what Diana Vreeland called the beautiful people," Beard says.

Out of college in the early sixties, he began taking fashion and beauty photographs for *Vogue*. Alex Liberman sent Dorothea McGowan to him for one of those sittings. Beard says, "I hate clichés, but she had star quality. It's a certain inner light that emanates from some people. Dorothea couldn't take a bad picture. A photographer is basically a parasite on his subject matter."

Beard remained with McGowan for several years, until he went off on a shoot with Veruschka and a German model, Astrid Herrene. "Dorothea got totally bent out of shape because Astrid and I were having a bit too much fun together, so to speak," says Beard, who subsequently married and divorced socialite Minnie Cushing and dated Jacqueline Kennedy's sister, Lee Radziwill.

After a while, Beard says, he came to hate fashion, "a horrible, shitty little industry governed by phonies. *Harper's Bazaar* was by far the better magazine. *Vogue* had all the money and the boredom and a very confused collection of social-climbing people who were ruining the creative process. They ruined Bert Stern; they ruined William Klein with their lack of vision. All the great photographs were put on a shelf."

In 1975 Beard went to the Sudan, where he discovered Iman Mohamed Abdulmajid, the daughter of a diplomat and a gynecologist. She was a student at the University of Nairobi when Beard spotted her on the street with Kamante, the majordomo of Isak Dinesen, the author of *Out of Africa*. "Iman was dead anxious to get out of Africa," he says. That October Beard brought her to Wilhelmina and called a press conference to introduce his discovery to the fashion world. He claimed he'd met her on Kenya's northern frontier "because it's not very interesting to meet somebody on Standard Street in a disgusting tourist town like Nairobi," he says. The reporters at the press conference embellished Iman's tale further. *Newsweek* called her "a Somali tribeswoman . . . part of a nomad family in the East African bush."

"They made up a lot of lies that we didn't think of," Beard recalls gleefully. He and Iman were never an item, although "everyone thought we were," he continues. "It was just mutual admiration. Everyone immediately realized the delicacy, strength, and poise of this African woman. She hadn't forgotten how to walk. She'd not been spoiled by the galloping rot." Though she had a hard time at first ("The Black Panthers were after her," Beard says), Iman soon became one of the top models of her time. She was once reputedly paid $100,000 for appearing in a single fashion show.

Iman married basketball star Spencer Haywood in 1978. One year later, while playing for the Los Angeles Lakers, he became a cocaine casualty. Though he later said that his wife never knew his full involvement with drugs, as a glamorous couple in L.A., he recalled, they went to parties where silver plates of cocaine were served like hors d'oeuvres. But Iman's world was at least as drenched in drugs as Haywood's. "I shot doubles with Iman and Janice Dickinson," says one photographer, "Janice would come here, and if I was out of coke, she wouldn't do the shot. Everyone got so fucked up Iman couldn't get into a pair of pull-on pants."

In the mid-eighties Iman and Haywood divorced, and she turned to acting. She is probably now best known as a tireless crusader for her native Somalia,

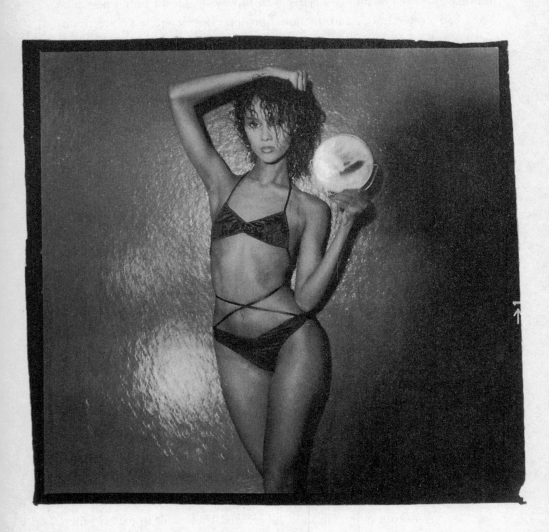

Iman photographed by Anthony Barboza

and as the wife of glam rocker David Bowie, whom she married in 1992. That same year she lost custody of her daughter, Zulekha, to Haywood, who, ten years after kicking drugs, now renovates housing for low-income inner-city families.

In fall 1979 Cheryl Tiegs signed the largest cosmetics contract ever written with Cover Girl, which reportedly agreed to pay her $1.5 million over five years. The following summer she signed another major contract with Sears, to create her own line of clothing. The ongoing soap opera in her personal life was apparently no problem for the Middle-American catalog house. It was announced that Dragoti would shoot her commercials, and Beard was slated to photograph her print ads.

Dragoti was seen out and about with Zoli's Jan McGill and Ford's Lisa Taylor before he finally sued Tiegs for divorce at the end of 1980. It became final the next May, and Tiegs immediately married Beard in Montauk, Long Island, where they took up residence. In spring 1982 they split up. He went to Kenya. She went out with—if the tabloids were to be believed—hockey's Ron Duguay, tanning's George Hamilton, *Superman*'s Christopher Reeve, and an unidentified man she was spotted passionately kissing on the street. By the end of 1983 Tiegs was seeing her future third husband, actor Gregory Peck's son Tony, a boy-about-town ten years her junior.

What happened? Peter Beard can't say. Their 1984 divorce agreement—signed after reports of extramarital affairs, changed locks, clothes thrown out windows, and bitter disputes over Beard's Montauk property—forbids either of them to talk about the other. Jerry Ford says Beard was the problem. "I like Cheryl a lot, and Peter was a real shit to her," he says. "He let everyone know that he thought she was the stupidest woman in the world. He's a little crazy. His is not an everyday kind of brain."

Others say drugs were the problem. "Cheryl was doing coke before anyone," says a magazine editor who knew her well. "She was heavy on it. At the wedding in Montauk they handed out silver vials." Then there are those who say Tiegs was attracted to danger. "Women just go crazy over Peter," says model Bitten Knudsen. "He's very rustic. They want this adventurer. It's a turn-on to try and tame this wild man."

Tiegs addresses the subject of the turn of the eighties carefully. The tabloid stories "hurt a lot, because a lot of it was not true," she says. "A lot of it was true, but I didn't wish it to be published. Even if it were true, it's none of their business." Was she promiscuous or a coke user? "I wasn't, but to even deny it gives it credibility," she says. "What can one say if somebody calls you an elephant? You know you're not an elephant, but if they're going to see you that way, that's their problem. There were times that I stayed up too late, but that was, maybe, the worst of it." Sears didn't care, she continues. "So I was out at a disco, what could they say? I wasn't home needlepointing, but that was none of their business, as long as I did my job. And I certainly never did anything that would ruin my reputation. I've read in the tabloids I've had an affair with Muhammad Ali; I've read I was up in a spaceship with aliens; I've read all kinds of things. That doesn't make it true."

Today she is happy and healthy, a mother and wife, who also happens to design and manufacture a vast range of products like eyeglasses, fine jewelry, watches, socks, hosiery, and shoes aimed at the people she says she understands best, Middle Americans. Sitting on the back porch of her house overlooking the Pacific Ocean in California, looking back at her heyday, she says she has no regrets. "A world opened up [to me] during that period of time," she says. "It was a period of my life when I let go and lived for the moment. If I hadn't, I think I'd be sorry. It was a big leap in a career, in my life, that I took very quickly, almost too fast, but that's the way it happened."

Surviving the recession at the start of the seventies, Wilhelmina became the hottest shop in town, working with several agents in each European city, holding its own model conventions, and signing up models like Patti Hansen, a Staten Island teenager who'd been discovered at a hot dog stand, Shaun Casey (who became an Estée Lauder contract face), Pam Dawber, who went on to television fame as Mork's Mindy, Juli Foster, who was discovered waitressing, and Gia Carangi, a Philadelphia teenager whose wild ways and sultry looks made her a favorite of photographers from Francesco Scavullo to Chris von Wangenheim, who specialized in pictures that captured the madness of the disco era.

With the money those stars earned (variously estimated at $5 million in 1977 and $11 million in 1978), Willie and Bruce Cooper bought a two-story Tudor mansion with swimming pool, tennis court, and several outbuildings in Cos Cob, Connecticut, expanded their theatrical division (which represented models in television and film), and, in 1978, opened Wilhelmina West, an office in Los Angeles, in an attempt to hold on to models like Dawber, Jessica Lange, and Connie Sellecca when they went Hollywood.

"They were mature and adult and sophisticated and larger than life," says Kay Mitchell, who started out as the agency's receptionist and rose to head the women's division in 1975. "They were a very, very glamorous couple. Bruce helped Willie see what she could do. She was the voice. He wrote the script."

Despite the pretty facade, Willie's life was in turmoil. "Willie had a problem, the husband," says Dan Deely, who opened Wilhelmina's men's division when he left Paul Wagner in 1968. "He drank at lunch and got in the way. He wasn't interested in anything for very long, and he really had nothing to do. He'd write fluffy promotional pieces about the dreamworld of Wilhelmina and how you, too, can become a model. She was the presence, and I think that drove him crazy."

Bill Weinberg came to Wilhelmina from Ford in 1970. A commercial agent and troubleshooter, he specialized in the kind of subfashion model who brought home the bacon but never saw the cover of *Vogue*. Eileen Ford looked down on his kind of model, but within two years of his arrival in 1966, Weinberg's division was bringing in $500,000 a year. Weinberg enjoyed watching the Fords work. "Eileen was the artist, and Jerry was the mechanic," he says. "People were afraid of her, and then Jerry would pacify them, so bridges were never burned."

But working for Ford took its toll. "She really ran her ship with a reign of terror," Weinberg says. "No one wanted to take Eileen on. I'd see her sit at a desk near the main board with people on each side of her who were there for different purposes. She'd be screaming at the person on her left and simultaneously charming to the person on her right. To turn it on and off like that is kind of amazing."

After the Coopers approached Weinberg in 1970, Jerry Ford called him into his office one day and demanded he sign a contract. When he told Weinberg the document was not negotiable, the executive declined to sign it and asked, "Have I quit or did you fire me?" Two weeks later he got his answer in a letter from Ford dismissing him for breach of fiduciary trust.

As his job evolved at Wilhelmina, Weinberg acquired a small share of the agency and took over many of what had been Bruce Cooper's duties. "Bringing me in solved a problem, but it diminished Bruce's role," says Weinberg. "He'd come in, go through the mail, pinch a couple of fannies, make a few jokes, corral a couple of models, go to lunch for a few hours, and come back with a snootful." Willie started disappearing from the agency for days at a time "because she'd been roughed up," Weinberg says. "A couple of times [Cooper] stood up and raved at Wilhelmina when people were around. When he got that way, there was no cooling him off."

Melissa Cooper was eight years old when her brother, Jason, was born in 1974. A few days later the Coopers released a photograph of Willie and her newborn son. "They had to airbrush it," Melissa says. "Bruce was with another woman when Jason was born." When he came back, he gave Willie a black eye.

Melissa describes the world Jason came into at Cos Cob as something out of a bad movie. "There were parties every Sunday," she says. "Food, booze, mounds of coke, people wasted all over. I never wanted to do cocaine because I'd seen how people acted. Nobody did anything in moderation. I saw sex in the open all the time, since I was little. It was my house. I always investigated. You couldn't shock me as a child."

Sometimes Jason and Melissa joined in the celebrations. "Jason doesn't remember this, but he got drunk when he was two and fell into the pool." Melissa knew to stay away from the substances her parents provided because she'd overdosed on her mother's amphetamines when she was three. "I thought it was candy," she says.

At first Cooper's drinking was somewhat controlled. "In 1974 he was a charismatic, charming man," says John Warren, who arrived from Ohio to join the agency as a model that year, becoming Pam Dawber's boyfriend and a friend of all the Coopers. "Bruce had been around; he'd seen things; he was very bright. But he was also a master of self-sabotage. Being in her shadow was more than he could deal with. He hated being Mr. Wilhelmina." Bruce's drinking escalated along with the couple's fortunes. "He never had a hangover; he never threw up," says his daughter. "That was Bruce's curse. If not for the drinking, he would have been so accomplished. He was incredible, articulate, but he couldn't see anything through."

By the late seventies Melissa and Jason had learned to stay out of their father's way. Sometimes Melissa ran off into the woods. As Cooper's drinking escalated and his behavior grew violent, Willie took to locking the children in a wing of the house. "There were bolts on both sides of the doors," says Melissa. "He'd go on six-day binges, get totally looped, and mix up his wives and his children. We were all whores." Just like his mother.

But Wilhelmina was a stand-by-your-man woman. So when there were disagreements in the agency, they were always between Fran Rothschild and Bill Weinberg on one side and Bruce on the other, with Wilhelmina behind him. "It made for bad blood," says Dan Deely. "From 1978 to 1980 it escalated and escalated and never really ended."

Finally Cooper's exploits got to Wilhelmina. They'd met an aspiring model at a convention, and Bruce fell head over heels in love with her.

"Nobody could understand it," says John Warren. "He had me meet her. I told him he was putting me in a strange situation." Cooper also brought her to the agency to see the head of new models, Kay Mitchell, who considered herself Bruce's protégée. When she refused to sign the girl up, Cooper went over her head to Weinberg. "I didn't want to accept her either," Weinberg says. "Bruce got somewhat insistent; but I knew he was having an affair with her, and I felt it would be unhealthy."

Cooper set the girl up in an apartment at 300 East Thirty-fourth Street, a building full of models. Then he announced to Wilhelmina that he was leaving her, packed his car, and drove to New York. "He got to Manhattan and called [the girl] from a phone booth," John Warren recalls. "And she said, 'I can't see you. I'm entertaining.' " Cooper checked into a hotel, thought things through, and "went back to Willie on hands and knees," Warren says. She said she'd take him back if he promised to stop drinking and never see the girl again.

There was only one bright spot in Wilhelmina's otherwise dismal existence. She'd formed a bond with one of her neighbors in Connecticut, a tall, striking Dutch-Austrian investment banker named Edward "Edo" von Saher, who commuted to New York with her. "We were aware of Edo, and we were glad," says Dan Deely. "We didn't talk about it."

"I was a very good friend of hers," von Saher says. "She was a very good friend of mine." Their families were close, and von Saher became Willie's adviser and confidant. "It was a very sad situation," he says. "Her life was the business. Her husband was the business. She had nobody to talk to. Everybody needs a friend. If people can't have friends, then something's wrong. Bruce had a lot of good points, but he was sick. Willie stayed with him because of the children. She was breaking her butt, keeping things going, keeping the facade up. In spite of what was going on around her, she still got things done. Fran and Bill played an important part. The agency continued to be very profitable. As long as she was well, she could deal with it. But then she got a cough, and it wouldn't go away."

For weeks in the fall of 1979 Willie ignored it. After all, she'd been a chain smoker since she started modeling. Finally, von Saher made her see a doctor, who diagnosed pneumonia. It seemed to clear up, but then Willie relapsed and had exploratory surgery in January. Only then did her doctors discover she was suffering from inoperable lung cancer.

"Bruce was unglued," says John Warren, who was with him that night. "His wife had crushed him, but by dying, she'd destroy his identity." Warren commuted to Cos Cob and took care of Melissa and Jason for the next six weeks. "Bruce wasn't capable," he says. "He'd get drunk and threaten to burn down the house." Finally Warren took to doubling Cooper's drinks so he would pass out sooner.

Early in February agency lawyer Charles Haydon drew up a codicil to Wilhelmina's will. It put two thirds of her shares in Wilhelmina in trust for Jason and Melissa. "If Bruce could have voted their shares, he would've had a majority," Haydon explains. "Willie was concerned about Bruce's habits. He was shacking up with models all over the country. He put it on their credit card. That's how she found out. Everyone was concerned about the children. Bruce was completely off the wall." Haydon's wife and von Saher were named trustees for the children.

Willie died on the morning of March 1, 1980. She was forty years old. Cooper didn't learn about the change in his wife's will until after her funeral, when the Cooper family and about two dozen friends went back to Cos Cob. "We were all sitting on a screened porch, and [artist and Wilhelmina investor] Jan de Ruth took a walk with Bruce," Weinberg says. "When he came back, he was berserk, purple."

"Fucking cunt!" Cooper screamed. "I can't believe she did this. Any of you who knew about this, I'll get you! And if you think I'm going to that memorial service, you're out of your minds!"

Wilhelmina was buried on a cold, clear morning. That night scores of models attended the memorial service, along with Cooper, who'd been convinced to appear, Norman Mailer, Calvin Klein, Jerry Ford, and John Casablancas. Riverside Chapel was so packed that the crowd overflowed into two adjoining rooms. But even as they remembered Wilhelmina, nobody could forget there was a model war going on. "I heard people were outside, trying to poach models," says Dan Deely.

In the weeks after Wilhelmina's death, fear gripped her agency. Cooper would arrive at the offices drunk and cursing. "I was glad Willie wasn't around to see it," Rothschild says. He wanted to fire her and Weinberg. "Bruce made a stand to run the company," Deely says. "We prepared for the worst. If Bruce stayed, the company would be down the tubes within months."

In July, after months of acrimony, an agreement was signed. Bruce resigned as an officer and director of Wilhelmina and sold his and his children's shares back to the corporation in exchange for $16,666 a month plus interest for two years. He was also guaranteed a salary of $45,000 a year for two years, $20,000 a year for nine years after that, and full employee benefits, and he was given the right to open Wilhelmina schools outside of a few major urban areas. Dorothy Haydon and von Saher resigned as trustees, and a bank was appointed in their stead. Weinberg and Rothschild took over the agency, and soon afterward Kay Mitchell quit, she says, "because obviously I was not going to be queen of the hop."

Wilhelmina's gross estate totaled $830,000. Cooper eventually got his hands on most of it. "The trustees at the bank didn't do a damn thing," von Saher says. "I thought I safeguarded the children's money, but the law at times provides ways of piercing a trust." With the proceeds of the sale of Jason's and Melissa's stock, Cooper bought three condominiums on a hundred acres in Colorado and moved there with the children. "He tried to be a good dad, but he was like a time bomb," Melissa says.

Cooper remarried in 1984, to a former Revlon executive, Judith Duncanson. Dorian Leigh, back in America, but still cooking, catered their wedding. Not long afterward Duncanson ran into Eileen Ford in a restaurant. "You should have asked me before you married him," the agent said. Judith called John Warren and asked, "Why didn't you tell me he drinks?" After Bruce beat her with a baseball bat so seriously she was hospitalized, she had him arrested in 1988. He moved out, into a farm near their home in Cooperstown, New York, where he died from a heart attack in 1989. The family had his remains cremated, and the ashes were placed in a plastic urn. At the funeral Melissa kicked it, "for Willie," she says. She also threw a vodka bottle and his favorite glass into his grave.

Bruce Cooper's alcoholism and all the bad behavior that came with it were never acknowledged by modeling folk. But secret sipping, pill popping, and wife beating were as passé as the Ford agency's quaint double standards. As the eighties began, it was in to let it all hang out. "People carried coke in their makeup bags, and they'd load up in the dressing room," says one male model of the time. "If you were at Jim McMullen's," a restaurant owned by a former model, "and saw so-and-so going to the bathroom, you'd go, too."

As the business and the money that came with it grew, "a lot of people wanted the same models and would tolerate anything to get them," says a former model editor. "You couldn't say, 'Your hair's not done? Go home.' You were lucky to get them bathed." It drove some old-timers out of the sittings business. "The last one I remember with any clarity occurred downtown for *Vogue*," says hairdresser Kenneth Battelle. "All this running into the john! They were so high, and it all had to be redone, and I said, 'I'm not going back.'"

One day in the early eighties a Neal Barr shoot was stymied by a model who *couldn't get* drugs. "The poor girl was on the phone with her supplier, he wasn't coming through, and she was panicsville," Barr says. "All I needed was one tight close-up, but she kept moving." Barr finally secured her head with two-by-fours to get his shot. But just as he was ready to shoot, she started crying, destroying two hours of makeup.

Richard Avedon had no time for it. When a model yawned on his set, he threw her out. When hairdresser Harry King smoked a joint in Avedon's bathroom, he was banished. But for every fashion professional who hated the new drug scene, there were five more indulging in it. "Behavior absolutely changed; shoots became insane," King says. "People were on time, and then they weren't. Girls would show up two, three hours late or not at all. Sometimes they'd be in another country. I remember eight of us in the toilet at Albert Watson's studio, and he thought we were doing hair and makeup. Albert was lovely but *very* straight."

Photographers moved in the fast lane, though. Bill King and Barry McKinley were there. "Everybody kissed King's butt because he had so much business," says Dan Deely, "but he was strung out from the very beginning, short-tempered, moody, volatile, brittle. His was the first studio where I heard about drugs." There was also sex. "Stuff I couldn't even dream up!" says a model who worked with him. "Stuff he wanted hairdressers to do to him, and if they didn't, he wouldn't work with them again!"

Hairdresser Harry King stayed close to his friend photographer Bill King even after their romance ended. And he watched as the photographer's craziness spiraled. Bill King would go to the Anvil and dance on the bar in a leather jacket, boots, and nothing else. He got models—male and female—stoned and then took pictures of them—the nastier the better. He gave one model Quaaludes and then took pictures as his assistant and another man performed oral sex on her. "He was kind, sweet, lovely and a great photographer," King says, "but Bill did too many drugs and got off on people's misfortunes."

New Zealand–born Barry McKinley, who died in 1992, was best known in public as a men's fashion photographer. In private, Deely says, McKinley was dealing drugs, got arrested several times, and was threatened with deportation. "We wrote letters supporting him," Deely says. "But he'd turn on you in a minute. He was evil, miserable, bitter, and very talented. You had to deal with arrogant, egotistical assholes."

McKinley got so wild he even attacked a model physically. "I had a half day catalog job booked with him," says Rosie Vela. "But when I got there, he told me he was shooting an ad that would run all over the country." Vela told McKinley she'd have to call Eileen Ford and tell her the job had changed. He started screaming, "You whore! You bitch! You want more money?" Vela thinks McKinley was high on cocaine. "I saw Barry do blow all the time at work," she says.

As the art director and McKinley's assistants joined in the abuse, Vela retreated toward the elevator. "He grabs me just before the door closes and swings me out and starts to slap me and hit me," she says. When she ran from the building, she thinks the photographer and crew threw rocks at her. Finally she was rescued by a friend and went home. "And guess what happened?" she asks. "Eileen Ford called and said, 'You left a booking? You're fired.' And she hung up the phone. I called back and spoke to Jerry, and he calmed her down. The next day Barry sent me flowers, saying he'd love to work with me again."

Peter Strongwater started shooting catalog jobs in the early seventies. "It wasn't so much an art as a mechanical production," he says. "The girls were the worst. You didn't get the stars. It was drudgery. You just did it according to the layouts the client tacked to the wall." Strongwater's first big job was an ad for the Wool Bureau, which sent him to Australia in 1972 with a new model named Lisa Taylor. "By the time we hit Australia, we were *very* good friends," he says, cocking an eyebrow. Not only that, but the pictures turned out well, too, and Strongwater's career took off. "I was very naïve until that point," he says. "I believed in *Reefer Madness*. If you took drugs, you were doomed. Unfortunately I found out that wasn't true."

The years 1978 to 1982 were "a zenith," Strongwater continues. "We couldn't get through a shoot without a major amount of drugs. People dropped coke on the table; they smoked joints. It was accepted. It was heaven. If you were bored, you called for a go-see. We fucked a lot, took a lot of drugs, and worked a lot. I'm sure the agencies knew about it. I was less than circumspect. But I never had one agent say a model couldn't come here because this was an unhealthy place to be." Finally Strongwater "realized drugs were damaging me," he says. "I moved away, went into rehab, and came back in '87. The party was still going on, but I wasn't part of it anymore. People say, 'Are you sad?' No. I had the time of my life."

Matthew Rich came to New York in 1977 and fell in with the Halston crowd at Studio 54. "It was my idea of heaven," says the public relations consultant, who asks to be described as "one of the survivors." Rich longed for a male model he'd seen in *GQ* magazine named Joe Macdonald. They soon met at Studio, "and we ended up necking in the balcony," Rich says. They also sniffed coke, "and my heart was already going a mile a minute. That was it. We became almost live-in lovers."

They hung out with Andy Warhol, Truman Capote, Liza Minnelli, Calvin Klein, and Halston—"all my godheads," Rich says. "Andy drew Joe, drew his penis." Macdonald became interested in art and started collecting photographs. But that and his growing taste for cocaine diverted him from his trade. "He alienated people," says Rich. "He was temperamental."

Macdonald bounced between Zoli and Ford. "Don't call me anymore if you're going to send me on bullshit," he'd yell at his booker. Macdonald was the first male supermodel, and many opportunities were available to him—in play as well as work. "After three years he decided to sleep with every man who ever lived," Rich says. People started whispering to Rich that "Mary," as Macdonald was known, was hanging out at gay bathhouses. Rich and he broke up. Within two years Macdonald was dead of AIDS.

Rich went to work for Studio 54's PR man and got a close-up view of the action there. "The big models were all there with their tops off—male and female—demigods. They were a draw, so they were protected," Rich says. "Steve [Rubell] protected the people he liked. Aspiring models may have gotten a little used."

Everyone was using drugs. "It got to the point where if you wanted to fuck a model, you had to have coke or Quaaludes," says Alex Chatelain. "I'd fuck girls at Studio 54. To have a 'lude made it quite easy. But I wasn't a club person, and I didn't like drugs, so I didn't do it that much." One night Matthew Rich watched a model spy a rolled-up $100 bill between some cushions on a sofa in Studio's celebrities-only basement. "She unrolled it, snorted it, licked it, and then threw it on the ground, having gotten what she wanted," Rich says. "I snapped it up and bought more dust."

The snorting, like the hustling busboys downstairs, who serviced the mostly gay Studio in crowd, were kept an inside secret for many years—even from insiders. *Vogue*'s Polly Mellen saw what was going on in the club's balcony, though. "Two boys going at it, two girls, a girl and a boy. I saw every stage of something going on, and that scared me." It was the same at Halston's house. "*Heavy* drugs," says Mellen. "I came, I saw, I left."

When Kay Mitchell first met freckle-faced sixteen-year-old Patti Hansen at a Wilhelmina party in 1973, "she was very shy," the booker says. "You couldn't get her to talk, but there was something in her pictures." Mitchell sent her to *Seventeen,* and Hansen spent the next two years "leaping and running and jumping" for the young women's magazine. Then *Glamour* booked

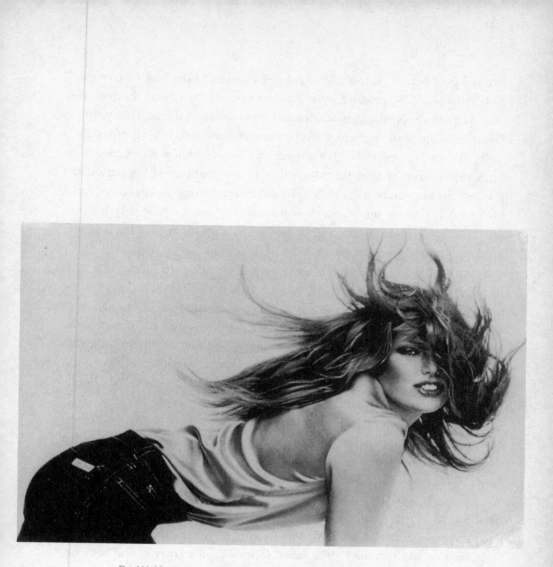
Patti Hansen photographed by Charles Tracy
for Calvin Klein Jeans

her and gave her a new look. "She was the epitome of the healthy teenager," Mitchell says. "The product people all jumped on board and she just took off." Hansen dropped out of school and moved into 300 East Thirty-fourth Street, the same building where Bruce Cooper later stashed his girlfriend.

In the summer of 1974 Hansen went to Europe, where she signed with Elite. "She's basically fearless," Mitchell says, "and that part of her personality gave her the impetus to forge ahead. She did intense, strong pictures there, came back to America, we sent them to *Vogue* and they saw a whole different person." In 1976 Hansen became one of the magazine's stars. In 1978 she appeared on the cover of *Esquire,* representing "The Year of the Lusty Woman."

Hansen's model friend Shaun Casey played ingenue parts longer. She lived in New York with her fiancé, real estate heir Martin Raynes, and caught the last good days of El Morocco and Le Club. It wasn't until 1977 that she went to Paris and grew up. Hairdresser John Sahag cut her hair off and bleached the gamin's cap that remained white. Paris Planning's Gérald Marie took one look at her and decided to make her a star. Helmut Newton put her on the cover of French *Vogue.* Six weeks later she returned to America. "My bookings were off the charts," she says. "I had five a day to choose from."

Casey signed with Estée Lauder and joined the scene at Studio 54. "It was champagne, coke, uppers, downers, poppers, all that," she says. "Everybody was doing drugs at that point." She married Roger Wilson, of New Orleans, whose father had coowned an oil services company. Both his parents had died when he was a teenager, leaving him with a fortune of several million dollars. Though he liked Studio 54, too, "we didn't dive in headfirst," Casey says. "I worked every day. I'd do bookings at night. I was into making money and putting it away."

It went on like that until 1983, when Casey's Lauder contract and her marriage both ended. Lauder, which had always stuck with its faces for years, had grown more fickle. It replaced Casey with Willow Bay, who gave way in a few years to the more international Paulina Porizkova. Casey's husband, Roger Wilson, "didn't want to be married," Casey says. "He wanted to be a playboy." Then, that August, Casey's younger sister, Katie, who was also a model, died of a drug overdose. Overwhelmed, Casey drank, stayed out late, and canceled bookings. "I think I canceled one hundred forty with Lord & Taylor alone," she says. "I wasn't partying. I was an absolute mess. So I changed my life. I married a guy who didn't drink, moved to Florida, got a contract with Burdine's, had a baby, chose my friends wisely, did my work, and went home. If you had money, you could do anything, and if you weren't grounded, you could drown so easily."

Casey's best friend, Patti Hansen, had a wilder reputation. "She didn't really have boyfriends," Kay Mitchell says. "She had hair and makeup guys who liked to hang out and party, and Patti was their star. Gay guys. One of them said to me, 'I'm looking for a man like Hansen.' I said, 'So's everybody.' She was big and strong. A photographer once came on to her, and she flipped him over her shoulder and knocked him out."

Hansen would also "pull her shirt off if no one in the agency was paying attention to her," says a Wilhelmina booker. Ever the athlete, on a shoot with Peter Strongwater at Lake Mohonk, in upstate New York, "Patti dropped acid and went rowing," Strongwater says. Sometime later she went to Mexico City for a catalog shoot with Jerry Hall and photographer Guy Le Baube. "We went to the plane with a bus and a mariachi band to welcome Patti and Jerry and Bryan Ferry," Le Baube recalls. "Patti got off the plane wearing transparent plastic shorts with no underwear and spike heels. She was literally steaming and showing Mexico City she was a real redhead."

Hansen was resilient. "She could drink a bottle of Jack Daniel's and look perfectly normal," says a photographer she got high with. "The key to Patti was her ability to absorb drugs without losing control. What would floor another person wouldn't bother her. She never missed a booking. She was never out of control."

In 1979 Hansen met her match in Rolling Stones guitarist Keith Richard. "He became part of her energy instead of her becoming part of his," says Shaun Casey. "She pulled him up." But not without worrying her friends first. After they were introduced by Jerry Hall, Hansen disappeared for several days. "She got very, very, very skinny," says Kay Mitchell. "Her hours turned around. He stayed up all night and slept all day, and she did, too. But for me that behavior, whether it was cocaine or tossing back drinks, was the aberration. She saved one of the great rock stars of our time. She was goodness personified, and I'm really not putting a pretty face on it. Doing the job and making everyone else look good because she showed up was the norm for Patti Hansen."

Not so for Gia Carangi, a bisexual drug addict whose brief rise, long fall, and final death from AIDS were the subject of a book, *Thing of Beauty,* that infuriated models, who say she was hardly representative. "Gia walked in and walked out," says Mitchell, who booked her as well. "The difference between her and models like Patti or Shaun Casey is that they worked for years. They'd go anywhere and do anything for work."

For a moment Gia was a star, though, working with all the best photographers. She and Joe Macdonald bought their coke from the same Colombian on Fiftieth Street. "Joe would go off to the baths after we scored," Matthew Rich says. "Gia and I would go out. I loved my Gia. She was adorable and sweet and loved to get fucked up the ass with fingers, and that horrified me, so she talked about it more. We loved to spell our names out on a mirror in coke." Gia would get mad because Matthew's name was so much longer than hers.

"Gia was a real mess," says Bill Weinberg. "A trashy little street kid, not unlike Janice Dickinson. If she didn't feel like doing a booking, she didn't show up." Gia hit quickly after arriving in New York. "She was about melancholy and darkness, and that made great pictures," says a fellow model. But it didn't make Gia any happier. At a shoot for *Vogue* she stumbled out of the dressing room in a Galanos gown, collapsed in a chair, and nodded out, blood streaming down her arm, right in front of Polly Mellen. Weinberg told Francesco Scavullo that Gia had become unreliable, but the photographer insisted she'd show up if she knew the booking was with him. Gia always showed up for him. "Frank called up raving and screaming," Weinberg recalls wryly. Gia never arrived. "She would have been a casualty in any life," says John Warren. After several comeback attempts Gia fell out of modeling and died in 1986.

Lisa Taylor never wanted to be a model. She thought the job was prissy and stupid. But the daughter of a J. P. Stevens executive from Oyster Bay, Long Island, did it anyway, to earn extra money while she studied dance. A friend who was a model brought her to Ford. "It was so easy," Taylor says. "I walked in and started working." She won her first cover, on *Mademoiselle,* at nineteen. Three years later, in 1974, she met *Vogue*'s Polly Mellen and became a star.

Eileen Ford introduced Taylor to her off-and-on boyfriend for the next decade, producer Robert Evans. "He was getting divorced, and he saw someone he wanted to meet, and he asked his friend," she says. "I know there was something going on with Eileen and Bob and people like him, but I thought I was more special for Bob."

Unfortunately Evans was often in California. That left a lot of nights free, and soon Taylor filled them with drinking and drugs. "I didn't have too much self-esteem," she says. "I was a prime suspect. I was partying, Studio 54, the whole number. Everyone our age was doing it."

Taylor says she began to hate being touched and prodded by stylists and had paranoid visions of being in the center of a crowd of thousands, all trying

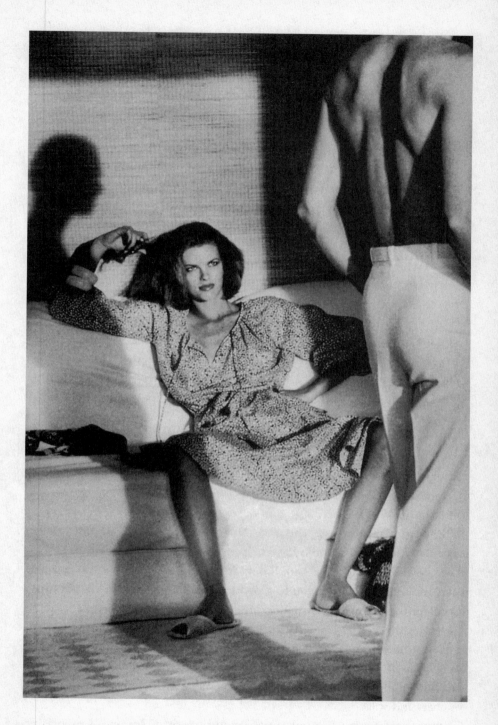

Lisa Taylor photographed by Helmut Newton in 1975

to take her picture. "When you have a certain number of pictures taken of you, you feel robbed," she says. "I felt I was giving, giving, giving and getting nothing back. Drugs made it a lot easier to sit there and look dumb in front of the camera. Modeling isn't the most inspiring, intellectual thing to do. At the beginning the money and traveling were fun, but it gets tired very quickly. Me, me, me. I, I, I."

Unlike some of her peers, Taylor says she kept her fun and games limited to the evening hours. "I was very professional," she says. "And the more weight you lose, the more they love you. It was not a healthy job."

In 1976 Taylor met actor Tommy Lee Jones on the set of a film about a fashion photographer, *The Eyes of Laura Mars.* She abruptly moved to California, informing Ford with a letter. "I wasn't very communicative in those days," Taylor says. A few years later she decided Jones was too possessive and returned to New York. That's when she started seeing Cheryl Tiegs's ex, Stan Dragoti. He didn't make much of an impression either. "He was the next person for me," she says. "Someone I dated. It wasn't a great love affair."

In 1981 the behavior of models and photographers finally started making the papers. *New York* magazine's Anthony Haden-Guest wrote an article, "The Spoiled Supermodels"; the *Daily News* ran a series of profiles subtitled "The Dark Side of Modeling." Taylor was featured in the first installment, "A Top Model's Struggle Back from 'Rock Bottom.'" She admitted her drug problems in often painful detail. "I was finally beginning to see the light," she says. "I was seeing friends on covers whose eyes were dead on drugs. It was the end of modeling and the beginning of my life." She moved back to California, joined Al-Anon, and began doing charity work. She married in 1989 and had twins in 1993.

"I had grown up at last," she says. "Not that it's their job, but the business, particularly the agents, could have helped more. Someone should have said, 'Slow down.' Instead they said, 'Look at the money.' You're innocent and naïve, and they don't want you to grow up. When I realized my life was more important than money, I left the business."

Despite the Ford agency's image, one rival booker says there were drug problems there, too. "Ford is extremely tolerant," said a friend of Taylor's at Wilhelmina. "Nobody ever said to Lisa, 'You moron.' Lisa was screaming for help, but people are afraid to speak up because the girl is going to pack up her vouchers and walk."

Eileen Ford wasn't the only one seeing no evil. A European model hit New York for a *Vogue* booking, collapsed on the set, and was rushed to a doctor who said she was so stoned her gag reflex was suppressed. "*Vogue* wasn't concerned," Wilhelmina's Weinberg says. "All they wanted to know was, Would she be able to work the next day?" Grace Mirabella, *Vogue*'s editor then, sees it differently. "You don't have time to wait," she says. "Long stories don't matter. When push comes to shove, what you care about is whether you have a picture."

Esme Marshall may be the only model whose personal problems ever led to the creation of a new agency. The daughter of a former Chanel model, Marshall was a seventeen-year-old salesgirl in a department store in Cambridge, Massachusetts, when she was discovered by a fashion editor at *Mademoiselle*. That fall Marshall moved to New York, joined Elite, and took up modeling full-time. She fitted Elite's new image precisely. "The style of girls had changed," says booker Gara Morse, who'd left Wilhelmina for Elite's new faces division. "It went from midwestern blondes to darker girls with crooked teeth. They weren't ordinary. The nuttier the girl, the more John liked it." Morse was given a free apartment on the East Side in exchange for playing chaperone to a revolving cast of eight aspirants who were crowded into another apartment next door. "I got what I was paid for," she says. "If a girl wasn't there, I had to go out looking for her."

The night after her first job, Esme was at Studio 54, where she met Calvin Klein, who immediately booked her for an ad for his new line of designer blue jeans. The bushy-browed brunette's career was launched. Soon thereafter she met Alan Finkelstein. The owner of a Madison Avenue boutique called Insport, he was a long-haired New York night bird, ten years her senior. They soon moved into a Greenwich Village duplex together. By 1980 she was one of modeling's superstars, earning $2,000 a day.

Bernadette Marchiano, the then-estranged wife of sportscaster Sal Marchiano, was Esme's booker at Elite. "Esme and I became fast friends," she says. But Finkelstein got in the way. "He told me what Esme should be doing," Marchiano recalls. "She was a child with no self-esteem, and this guy dazzled her."

Finkelstein thought that Elite had gotten too big and that John Casablancas wasn't paying enough attention to Esme. But Monique Pillard says the model wouldn't listen to advice from her agency. "She never wanted to hear anything," Pillard says. "She was telling us what to do. She was mixed up with drugs, everyone knew, but at the time you turned the other way when you had a very big model. I saw a lot. A lot. But I didn't understand. If I'd been in that circle and done it, I might have understood more. It took me a long time to realize." Finally a male model, Jack Scalia, "came in one day and told me all about drugs," Pillard says. "I was so straight, and suddenly I felt very stupid. After that I'd say to girls, 'Do you do drugs?' And I got a lot of 'Will you help me?' But let's face it, when you're seventeen, you fuck around, and you don't tell your mother."

Finkelstein suggested to Bernadette Marchiano that she form a new agency, backed by a friend of his, a record label owner and producer named Jerry Masucci. It would handle just stars, and the first would be Esme. Marchiano liked the idea and spoke to a friend who also worked at Elite, Eleanor Stinson, about joining them. In June 1980 they formed their new agency. They called it Fame Ltd.

"Our approach was to treat models as businesswomen and not as pieces of ass," Marchiano says. "There were no men in the agency. It was women working for women."

The model wars were still raging. That month Ford signed up Lisa Taylor (who'd come back from Elite), Christie Brinkley (from Zoli), and Beverly Johnson (from Wilhelmina). Brinkley was actually suing Elite, as was Opium perfume model Anna Anderson, who'd left the agency and was demanding an accounting of her earnings. But the news wasn't all bad for John Casablancas. Within a month Johnson left Ford for Elite. The same day Wilhelmina's Patti Hansen joined Elite, too.

Almost immediately after Fame Ltd. opened its doors, it was revealed that the new agency had a silent partner: Ford, which owned a third of the agency in exchange for guaranteeing its vouchers. "Alan Finkelstein came to me and said Esme, Eleanor, and Bernadette were unhappy and wanted to start their own agency," says Joey Hunter, a Ford executive.

Born Joe Pantano in Brooklyn, Hunter, a former doo-wop singer and actor, had a successful career as a Ford model throughout the sixties. "He was Mr. *Seventeen,* the cutest clean-cut guy in the world," says Jeff Blynn, who modeled with him. After appearing in an off-Broadway flop in 1969, Hunter asked Jerry Ford for a job. He became Ford's assistant and rose to second-in-command of Ford's men's division. Hunter's involvement in modeling extended to his private life. After his first marriage, to an actress, failed, he married the socialite/Ford model now known as Nina Griscom Baker. They broke up within a year, and Hunter took up with Elite's Debbie Dickinson. Hunter's third wife, Kim Charlton, was also an Elite model.

Hunter and Richard Talmadge, one of the Fords' lawyers and a music business investor, arranged the meeting between Jerry Ford and Masucci. They agreed to do the same thing Elite had done in Paris with its second agency, Viva, and open an independent editorially oriented boutique agency. Stinson and Marchiano got 5 percent each. Talmadge got 10 percent and was named a director. Masucci owned the remainder of the stock. "It was an opportunity for us to get two great bookers who had control of a couple models," Hunter says. They hoped that Kelly Emberg and Nancy Donahue would follow Esme to Fame. It was also a chance to see if John Casablancas could take what he'd been dishing out.

No surprise, Casablancas wasn't happy about this arrangement. Between them Bernadette and Eleanor "had every phone number, contact with every girl. It was the scariest moment I ever had," he says. "So I said to the models, 'If you stay with this agency, there's a bonus. One percent less every year you stay with us.' Some years later I had to write a letter to people like Paulina and Carol Alt saying, 'I can't do this. I can't have you under a certain percentage.' " He'd won the battle, but the war wasn't over. "I will never sleep with both eyes closed as long as that woman is around," he said at the time of Eileen Ford.

Alex Chatelain was one of the first photographers to shoot Esme. "I believed in her," he says. "She was wonderful." But he thought Finkelstein was a bad influence on her. "The drugs were so out in the open," he says. "Finkelstein was friends with everyone who was in. If they were famous, he was with them. Esme was in love with him. He took her everywhere, and you'd see her getting hyper and thinner, and at a certain point I couldn't use her anymore. She was too thin. Finkelstein had destroyed her." Esme dismissed published reports that she and her lover were cocaine users as ridiculous. "A lot of people like to blow things out of proportion," she said.

Fame signed a few more good models, including Terri May and Nancy Decker, but it was short-lived. The first sign of trouble came when Alan Finkelstein called the booking desk, demanding that Marchiano cancel one of Esme's bookings. If she didn't, Finkelstein threatened, he would go to Albert Watson's studio and drag her out. "Watson stopped the shoot and let her go," Marchiano remembers. Then Finkelstein called back. "I was just playing with you," he said.

"Fuck you," Marchiano replied, hanging up. Their relationship went downhill from there. "It was beyond my control," Esme said later. "He used to not let me go to bookings. It was very weird. He tried to run me over once. He was jealous of my booker 'controlling' me." Though Finkelstein had promised he wouldn't try to play agent, "he threw a monkey wrench in for no reason," Marchiano says. "We'd have battles, battles, battles. Boyfriends are the major flaw in the modeling business. I wouldn't talk to boyfriends. Ninety-nine percent of the time it was a problem. My problem was Esme's boyfriend. Someone else had control. Alan didn't want that."

Finally, early in 1981, Finkelstein took Esme from Fame to Ford. According to an $8 million lawsuit Marchiano and Stinson later filed against their partners, Joe Hunter assumed the presidency of Fame at that time. "We stayed around awhile, booking the other models," Marchiano says. But one morning in late May she arrived to find the locks changed and Fame's books, records, furniture, and models all moved to Ford. Hunter told them they'd henceforth be working for the Fords. Less than two weeks later they were fired. Two days after that Fame Ltd. was formally dissolved.

"What happened was, the money went out of control," says Hunter, who claims that Marchiano and Stinson were spending without consulting Masucci. "Jerry got disenchanted," Hunter claims. "We felt we had a runaway ship financially, and we decided enough is enough. We did lock them out, and we bought Masucci out over a period of a couple of years." In response to the bookers' lawsuit (which was prepared by Elite's lawyer, Ira Levinson), Jerry Ford said they'd been dismissed for incompetence and dereliction of duty and claimed that Fame was insolvent.

Marchiano categorically denies that Fame was losing money. In fact, she says, it had just started turning a profit when Ford closed it down. "There was no financial reason to close it," Marchiano says. "I finally decided it was a whim of Alan's." She turned down Hunter's offer to work at Ford and instead went back to work for Casablancas, who was starting a chain of franchised modeling schools with his brother, Fernando. Stinson moved to Miami, where she still works as a modeling agent. Their lawsuit against the Fords, Hunter, and Masucci was eventually abandoned. A suit the Fords subsequently filed against Ira Levinson for defamation was decided in Levinson's favor.

At Ford Esme remained erratic. "She was always out, and you'd never know whether she would get to her booking or not," Joe Hunter later said. In the *Daily News* series published in April 1980, unnamed sources referred to the twenty-year-old as "a burn-out" and "sort of gone." It was said she'd stopped taking location trips, canceled bookings, turned up late, cried on sets, lost weight, and lost her luster. Elite was promoting a new model, Julie Wolfe, who was an Esme look-alike. Chain-smoking Marlboros, Esme denied it all, saying she lost weight because she was hyperactive. "I really don't care what the fashion industry thinks," she said. "They have a warped perspective anyway."

Janice Dickinson later told writer (and ex-model) Lynn Snowden that the problem wasn't drugs. Finkelstein was beating Esme up. "She was covered in bruises and didn't want people to see her like that," Dickinson said. "Esme was getting the shit kicked out of her. She just entered into this Svengali relationship." Once she even showed up at Marchiano's door bleeding. "He abused her," Marchiano confirms. "She was physically abused and controlled."

Finally, Esme told Snowden, she manipulated Finkelstein into throwing her out. Even then he kept victimizing her. "I just signed everything over to him," Esme said, including property she'd bought in Colorado. She ended up owing $350,000 in back taxes. Esme retired from modeling in 1985, married a professional volleyball player, moved to France, had a baby, divorced, and launched a brief comeback in 1990. Friends say she's since moved to California. Finkelstein lives there, too. He resurfaced in 1992, running a supper club called the Monkey Bar, part owned by his best friend, Jack Nicholson.

Nicholson's friend Zoli kept a diary for the last five years of his life. Though there is scarcely anything written in it, a few sketchy passages offer a glimpse of his life and thoughts. On September 8, 1977, he and an "R. H." attended an Irving Penn opening at the Marlborough Gallery and "saw I. Penn, L. Hutton, the Fords, Karen Bjornsen, Tim and Joe Macdonald, Mrs. V." They went on to Julie Britt's birthday party for model Peter Keating, where they saw Patti Hansen, Patti Oja, Janice Dickinson, and Lisa Cooper. "Home with R. H.," the entry concludes. "HANGover."

On September 8 Zoli picked up his mother, who'd been diagnosed with cancer, at the hospital. "She's doing fine." An entry about falling in love with R. H. follows. "It's the only thing that I can't count on like my job, my house, my family, my friends and yet in that uncountability [sic] I feel more stable than in all those other temporary securities." That October Zoli noted his plan to move from the town house to 955 Lexington Avenue. "It'll be fun to live alone and somewhat strange," he wrote. Not long after Zoli and his partner, Bennie Chavez, began to have differences over money.

Chavez says, "There were people in his life who were rather unsavory. A couple of his lovers were great sources of trouble, asking why I should have half the business. The problem was, we had a written agreement." Then Chavez fell in love with an Englishman and decided to marry him. Zoli felt sure she was making a mistake. The next entry in Zoli's diary are notes headed "CHAMELEON." After a scientific description of lizards Zoli added, "also a changeable and fickle person."

Zoli was having a crisis. "I thought the solution would be to move from this house, this beautiful house inhabited by ghosts, namely me, mutti [his mother] & B. C. [Chavez]," he wrote. "The next minute, it was to change professions completely as work seems to be a compote of self-indulgent, greedy, ungrateful, egotistical narcissists. . . . I've arrived somewhere and stayed too long." That Christmas he went to Aspen and saw ex-model and designer Jackie Rogers, François de Menil, and Jack Nicholson. "What a blasé, spoiled man I am," he wrote. "How well I seem to have it, but if I could only get some real enthusiasm for anything I would be most pleased. I am learning to resign myself, to accept reality in people without rose-colored glasses. . . . It's no fireworks for me. I'm probably better off for it. But I yearn for the passions of the moment and also want to pass my life in insanity and recklessness which I repress for the sake of? what I don't know."

There are no more diary entries for six months until Zoli notes a July 1978 sailboat trip to the Virgin Islands with a man named Bob. "Both quit smoking and eating meat, a changing time," Zoli noted. When he got back, it was time to split up with Bennie Chavez. The next few pages were filled with angry ideas on how to separate their business. "A lawyer convinced him he should get tough, and he took me to court," Chavez says.

Zoli's diary picks up again many blank pages later, with the 1981 notation "My dear sweet mama died on April 16 at 1 A.M." Again many pages intervene, and then in the very back of the book are three more entries. The first two are lists of Zoli's stock holdings late in 1980 and in mid-1981, when they totaled almost $145,000. The last entry in the diary appears to be the beginning of a screenplay. Two men meet in a dark gay bar. A young executive type picks up an older man, takes him home, and they have sex. Then the man reveals "he's a vampire," Zoli writes. "Vampire is . . . 30 going on 300. Likes boy and confides that he is tired of being a vampire. . . ."

By all accounts, Zoli was only a voyeur at the party that fascinated him so and was in certain ways quite bourgeois. He was never promiscuous, according to his friends. He had boyfriends and "lived with them," says Barbara Lantz, who now co-owns Zoli with Vickie Pribble. "He was very relationship-oriented. In one case, Zoli's mother lived with them and Zoli moved out and the guy kept living with [Zoli's] mother."

But not long after his mother died, Zoli started feeling ill. "He had the weirdest symptoms," Lantz recalls. "He went to forty doctors all over the country for tests. Joe Macdonald had already been diagnosed with AIDS. Zoli had an AIDS test, and it came back negative." He went to clinics and gurus and even hooked himself up to a biofeedback machine. On one of his trips he visited ex-Wagner model Geraldine Clark in California. "I got very frightened when I saw him," she says. "He was thin as a stick and had a high fever." He cried while they were having dinner. In September 1981, Zoli's sister says, his doctors diagnosed lung cancer. "We thought he was being melancholy," says Lantz. "He had a tendency." He'd lost his case against Chavez, and they'd finally split their holdings. She kept the town house; he got the agency.

In November 1982 Zoli checked into the hospital. He had his doctors tell his employees he had tuberculosis and would be all right. Bennie Chavez knew differently. "I saw him on the street a few days before he went into the hospital," she says. "He was very thin; he had no voice. He had a look of peace in his eyes. It was almost hypnotic, and it disturbed me." Geraldine Clark flew to New York to nurse him. The cancer had spread to his esophagus, and the radiation treatments that doctors prescribed caused his food and air pipes to fuse together. Clark prepared food in a blender for her friend. That was the only way he could eat. Finally, the day before he died, Zoli sent his sister back to her home in Virginia and Clark back to California. "He knew there was the possibility he had AIDS," Clark says. "He had one lover who'd been very promiscuous. He'd become like a pariah. No one wanted to touch him. I was terrified, but before I left, I pushed the pipe away and kissed his lips. It was the first time he'd smiled in days."

Finally Zoli succumbed. He was forty-one. To this day his friends and family aren't sure what really caused his death, though they note that his last boyfriend later died of AIDS. "There are no records saying it was anything but cancer," says Lantz. "It certainly sounds like AIDS. But there was never a diagnosis."

The day Zoli died, the word went out among the models, but they were asked to keep his death a secret. A quiet memorial was scheduled because Zoli wanted no fuss, and indeed, except for a brief notice in a photographic trade newspaper, his death was never publicly acknowledged. Meanwhile, Zoli's lawyer called six key employees together. There were two wills, he told them.

Only one was signed. Both split the agency among the employees, but in different ways. The minority shareholders wanted to sell. But Lantz and Pribble wanted to keep the agency going and did.

If there is such a thing as karma, Zoltan Rendessy's stayed good to the very end. Shortly after Zoli died, John Casablancas and Wilhelmina's Fran Rothschild both called and offered to lend the agency bookers, so the staff could attend the memorial service. Zoli's most fitting epitaph may be what *didn't* happen next.

"We didn't lose a single model," says Barbara Lantz.

BITTEN KNUDSEN *
TARA SHANNON

O f all the models who emerged in the early eighties, Bitten Knudsen had one of the worst reputations. She was a free spirit who one minute would be climbing the walls, and the next, collapsed in a heap on the floor, unconscious on drugs, and uncaring about who knew it. Bitten's fantasy was to open a model agency called the Unprofessionals. Its motto? "Double rate if we show up," Bitten says. "Triple rate if we step on the set."

Tara Shannon's reputation couldn't have been more different. She was known as a consummate professional, a modeling virtuoso. Sitting down for lunch in a restaurant near her Manhattan apartment, Shannon wears studious frameless glasses that almost give her a schoolteacher's look but can't quite obscure the beauty lurking just underneath.

Today both models are in their late thirties and have gone on to other careers. Shannon has appeared on several television shows. Bitten makes films, lives in SoHo with a painter, and still sees lots of her friends from the old days—at least, those who are still alive. "I feel like I'm a warrior who survived the front lines," she says, her voice slinking out from under a thick mane of white blond hair. "There weren't any medals, but we were definitely out there with guns, shooting straight at the enemy."

TARA SHANNON: "I was this flat-chested, skinny, blue-eyed, curly-haired little girl in Denver. I would take *Cosmo* magazines, paint tits on my chest like circles, and copy the poses. I loved *Milly the Model* comic books. I have my collection still. You would draw the hairdos and clothes, and mail them in, and they would give you a little credit in the comic. One of the tragedies in my life is that my mother never mailed the letters. It made me what I am today.

"I dropped out and left home when I was thirteen. I was living on my own in a hippie house. My first modeling job was *Playboy*. I was sixteen, and I was going to be a centerfold, but it was never published because I wasn't girl next door enough. Which turned out to be what made my career. I wasn't the girl next door.

"I really started when I was eighteen. I hustled, hustled, hustled, hustled. I went to the department stores, to the illustrators. I went to restaurants and said that I knew a clothing store that wanted to do tearoom modeling. And then I would go to the clothing store and say I know a restaurant that wants to do clothing modeling.

"I had so much drive to be a model. I would practice in the mirror with makeup, with my hair, with poses. I went to see photographers, and I was teaching them how to light, how to crop. I was getting locations. I would get my contact sheets, and my goal was to go from having ten percent of the shots be good to twenty to thirty to fifty to seventy percent. And I had all my newspaper ads, and I would take my ads and a pencil and I'd retouch them myself."

BITTEN KNUDSEN: "I started in Denmark. I was fresh out of school, and I had a bunch of jobs. One was tutoring an actress who was an ex-model, and one day she sent me to her agency with her book. They said, 'What if we take some shots with you?' The next thing I knew I was flying off to Germany. I went with a photographer to shoot covers for sexy magazines. Dorothy Parker-Sed said I should stay there. She said, 'You're such a kid,' and I became known as the Kid."

SHANNON: "I wanted to get to New York. I got hooked up with this guy— my Svengali—who was a total asshole. I'd organized a troupe of disco-dancing models, and he was my dance partner. He had been in Dallas as a model, and he knew an agent, Kim Dawson. I broke up with him, and I went to Dallas in '77.

"Kim sends me to Neiman Marcus for a go-see for a shoe shot. Whoever fits the shoe gets the job, and the shoe fit me. Cinderella. I am so thrilled. And shaking. Then she asks me to go to the Bahamas for Neiman Marcus. I'd never been out of Denver and Dallas. So I go to the Bahamas, to Mexico, to Thailand. I did shows, too. And I became the top model in Dallas, the highest-paid girl ever, five hundred dollars a day.

"Sometime they would fly in girls like Apollonia, and I would be beside myself. One time I went to Maine for a catalog, and Patti Hansen was com-

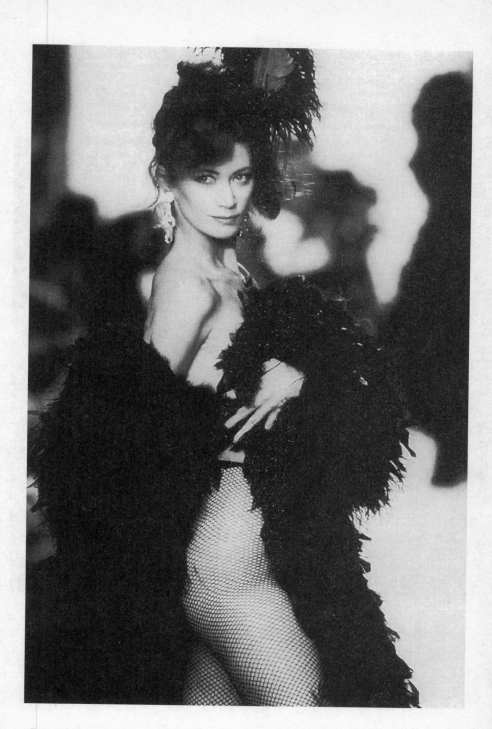

Tara Shannon in Patrick Kelly's autumn 1989 fashion show in Paris, photographed by Dan Lecca

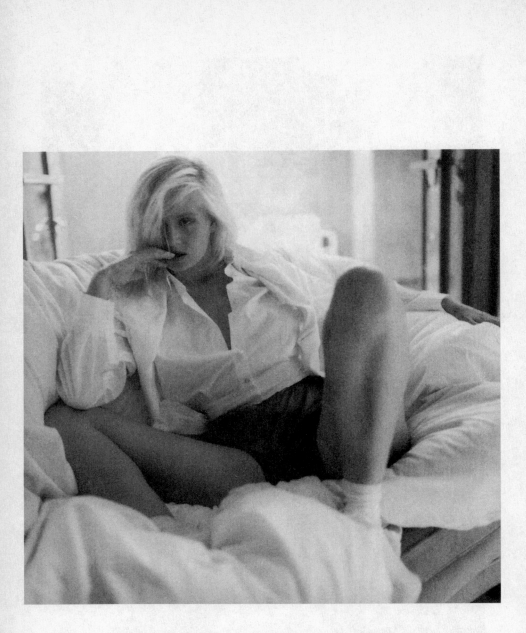

Bitten Knudsen photographed by Robert Graham

ing! I mean, my God! And she got off the plane from Europe with a back-pack, no luggage. And I just followed her wherever she went. We were in a small Maine village and she went to a store and she bought a pack of Haines men's underwear and a pack of men's T-shirts to wear and a big bag of potato chips. I was like Miss Anal Compulsive Professional Model with my little makeup kit, and I had never seen anything like her. I'd be taking notes, you know?"

KNUDSEN: "Giorgio Piazzi heard about me, came to meet me, and I went to Milan for six months. I rented a room in a *pensione* with another Danish girl. We worked all week and went to castles on weekends. It was the beginning of the era of the hustling dinner whores in Milan. The girls were so broke they needed the playboys to buy them meals. I was always in a relationship, so I was never up for grabs. Milan was like organized crime, but the real crime was how naïve American girls are at eighteen! Danish girls have level heads. Playboy behavior got on our nerves. We would go to Nepenta after dinner and make fun of them—greasy Italians disco dancing and working the room.

"But at least Italians are artistic about their approach. The French are true dogs. John Casablancas was a dog. I'd actually met him in Denmark at a trade show where I was working for a designer. He kept following me around, and I was *not* interested. I said, 'Who is that creepy guy? Tell him to stop.' I don't think all men are dogs. But most of them are. Alex Chatelain was a bulldog. I remember him getting tacky on a trip. Peter Beard is into what he calls living sculpture, a girl willing to be flattered into action. He goes for his type, and he's very straightforward about it. He's an honest dog.

"Giorgio Piazzi would protect me, because I was the Kid. He made sure I came to his house to eat. I wanted to come to America to study with Lee Strasberg. So Piazzi introduced me to Eileen Ford in Milan. I met her again in Denmark, and then I came to New York in 1977.

"Eileen arranged everything, and she had me modeling immediately. On my first day I rested a few hours, and then I worked nonstop. I was really pretty lucky; the timing was just right for my look. Some girls work really hard for it. I didn't. In the beginning people said I was too blond, just like they said Janice was too Polynesian. We'd say, 'Forget it. It's not about that. It's about opening up the looks.'

"I met Strasberg and started studying with him, but I wasn't disciplined enough. The classes were so emotional it took me days to calm down, so I quit. I was spoiled already. Now I could kick myself, because he's dead."

SHANNON: "Everybody had come to Dallas and seen my book. Bruce Cooper told me girls made ten thousand dollars a month in New York. I was like, whoa! So finally, after a year, I went to New York. Before I left, I had my eyes done because I had puffy, fat bags. Honey, I tried everything, I knew every makeup trick, lighting trick, everything. I slept with pillow, no pillow, stayed up, slept a lot. Nothing worked. So I got my eyes done, I got my SAG card, I got my AFTRA card before I went to New York. I was a professional. I wasn't going to waste my time when I got there.

"I visited all the agencies in one day. Eileen Ford says, 'I'm going out for a manicure. I'll be back in an hour; wait for me.' I don't think so. I go to Johnny Casablancas. 'Oh, no, no, no, *darrrling, honnnney,* it is about sex with the photographers, you cannot be so businesslike, you know, you must be a woman. . . .'" I don't think so, Johnny. So then I go to Wilhelmina, and she says, 'Honey, here's what we're going to do. We're going to get you an apartment, put your money in the right bank, bang-bang-bang.' She was my kind of girl, so I went with Wilhelmina, and she got me a place to stay, and I immediately started my life with catalog modeling because Wilhelmina cut deals with the catalog houses. If they used all her models, she would give them a much cheaper rate.

"It's 1978. Milan and Paris are beckoning. Gérald Marie from Paris Planning sees me in New York. He tells [photographer] François Lamy about me. Lamy liked redheads, so I get a direct booking to Italy. I'm wearing Valentino, and I have more hair and makeup put on me than I've ever seen in my life, and I'm eating it up, man. I thought this happened to all the girls, getting a direct booking. And then I kept getting direct bookings, and I start doing all the runway shows. This is before you were allowed to be in Italy legally. You'd get chased; they'd stop you at the border; they'd take your money; it was all cash.

"The print girls were pretty, you know, dumb. They were just corn-fed, and I don't mean this in a bad way, but Nancy Donahue, Kim Alexis were not internationally savvy. The show girls were from these incredible countries, and they came from good families. They had rich husbands and clothes and a savvy that you get from working with the top designers around the world and hanging out in Monte Carlo doing benefits for Princess Caroline. Everybody spoke five languages. I was kind of a little pet, the jester, the mascot, in awe of everything.

"So I'm doing shows and photos. I get a thousand a show. I put it in a Swiss account. It was a day trip. They took a bunch of girls to Switzerland; you opened up your account. I asked the other girls. Dalma and Iman, whatever they did, I did. They were smart.

"I met all the playboys. They'd pick you up from the airport and drive you into town so you didn't have to take a taxi. If you had a job in another town, it would be like a convoy taking the girls to the job. You'd go out to dinners with them. It was commerce. All the other big girls were going, so I was going to go, too. 'Cause they were *top* model hounds, those guys. You wouldn't get a ride from the airport unless you were up there. They were into being in our presence. It wasn't sleeping with us, although I'm sure that helped them score extra macho points.

"Nobody got in my pants. I'm an American guy kind of girl. Europeans never held an ounce of attractiveness to me. They tried. Oh, they tried. There was weekends in the country, but nothing happened. That little one—what's his name?—the really little rich one: Umberto Caproni! Oh, Umberto, I loved him. That guy didn't have a broom up his ass; he had a two-by-four.

"Gérald Marie was my agent in Paris. He was with a model named Lisa Rutledge, and they had a baby. I didn't have a boyfriend, and one day Gérald is gone somewhere, and we decided we were going to go out. We go to Champs-Élysées to a photo booth and have our pictures taken. And then we walked down Avenue George V, and who do I see coming out of the Hôtel George V? Jack Nicholson. I've got to do something. So I say, 'Jack, what are you doing in Paris?' I've never met Jack Nicholson in my life. Lisa's from Australia. She doesn't know who he is. So he looks me up and down, he looks Lisa up and down, and he says, 'Uh, ladies, I'm going to a little party if you'd care to join me.'

"So we go around the corner to this apartment, he rings the doorbell, and who answers the door but Roman Polanski. Oh, *shit*. We walk into a room full of fourteen-year-old blondes. We're too old, and we're looking at each other like, we've got to get out of here. Someone brings out a joint. Lisa doesn't smoke pot. She's a mom. But I smoke. I love to smoke. And all of a sudden I have to lie down. I feel really ill. I come out of it in two minutes. But there are other girls passed out, you know? Very nasty. We're out of here. We head to the elevator, and Jack says, 'What are you doing?' So we kidnapped Jack Nicholson."

KNUDSEN: "I did it all. I was at Studio 54 on opening night. You grow up really fast. I was out of control and rebellious right from the first. America has all these taboos about sex that didn't exist in Scandinavia. I was staying at

Eileen Ford's house, and I was invited to my first New York party. I had a see-through pink silk jump suit, and Eileen went, 'Aaaaach! You can't go outside like that.' I was used to topless beaches!"

SHANNON: "Until that time I was very naïve. I was very scared of people. I didn't go out. I wore no makeup, glasses. I had this big secret to hide. I was from the wrong side of the tracks. Then I started noticing something going on in the studios. People kept going to the bathroom in groups. And I wasn't invited. I felt very left out and abandoned, which was plugging into my childhood issues 'cause I came from a one-parent home. So I started putting two and two together, and I finally kind of weaseled my way in at one point, and I saw that this was important. I needed to be a part of it really badly, 'cause my life was about getting to the other side of the tracks.

"So I transformed myself. I took off my glasses, borrowed an outfit from Bill Blass, bought some cocaine, hired a limo, and I went to Studio 54. And this was my coming-out party. Everyone was like, Tara? Wow! I had cocaine, and I was very popular. Suddenly I'm hanging out with the rich and famous. I get the rock star boyfriend, one of the first. Hamish Stuart from the Average White Band. Oh, he was so cool. I'd met him in Denver. And then, when I was in New York, I called him, and we got engaged."

KNUDSEN: "Drugs were a really big part of fashion, especially at the top. I remember a shooting for *Vogue*. People at the studio said, 'Take this powder. It'll be good for the shot.' Cocaine really ruled. It got crazy all over. Dark circles under my eyes became something of a trademark. Your weakness can become your strength once you find it.

"Even though we were all crazed, the work was still the focus. When people are in altered states, it's all about the vision. We were a continuation of the sixties. You had to expand the borders. And you couldn't have that look unless you could walk the plank. Style is perverse, always. Part of the glamour is the decadence, being able to swim in deep water.

"I did lots of jobs with Bill King. He hired me at the beginning and shaped my career. Bill was a bad boy, always waiting for something to break out. He'd turn on his big fans and wait to see what happened. He booked me with Jerry Hall, and she would flip her hair in my face to cover it in every picture. Each time she did it, I threw some confetti in the fan so it would blow right in her face. It stuck to her, and she'd have to run off the set and fix it. Bill liked that."

SHANNON: "I switched to Elite in '79 'cause I wanted more of that editorial work. I liked that. I'd started to wake up a little bit. Monique Pillard called me. She wanted me. But I had signed a contract with Wilhelmina. So how do you get out of the contract? Monique called Johnny in. He says, 'Tara, what you must do is tell her that it is like a love affair, it is over. Don't say that you want more editorial, don't say you want the room painted pink, 'cause they'll say OK. Just say it's time.' And I said those things to Wilhelmina, and she gave me the contract, and I walked out. John wasn't an issue. He likes the younger girls. I had no use for John, really. I wasn't dumb enough to fall prey to his magnificence."

KNUDSEN: "There was a lot of laughing. Everything was fun. Location trips were like going to camp. You could get away with even more. You ran the risk of being sent home on the next plane, but that's what editorial work was about. In St.-Barth we'd open the hotel bars after they'd closed, mix drinks, and wake people up. One time we were on the beach, rolling joints and drinking all night, and the next thing we knew, the sun came up, and we were right in front of the client's room, trying to hide the bottles! On hot days we'd jump in the water with the client's clothes on, and they'd freak out. One time I was doing a photo in a boat, and I rocked it till it sank. The client gave me such hard time! Then he used the picture for a double spread."

SHANNON: "Excuse me—you put a fourteen-year-old on Wall Street, unchaperoned, what do you think they're going to do? This is a bunch of big unchaperoned babies getting away with murder. Nobody put any boundaries up. The fallacy that models are stupid I think comes from their being fifteen years old. It's your job when you're fifteen to be stupid. You're putting these children in these adult situations and then making fun of them? Oh, please don't get me started. I saw a girl faint twice at a booking. She hadn't eaten in days 'cause she was trying to lose the baby fat."

KNUDSEN: "I met Janice Dickinson on a shoot at Mike Reinhardt's house in the Hamptons. She was wild, but it's funny, her reputation was all that people focused on, and there was a very nice, exposed child inside.

"It becomes a duel. As bad as you are, that's how good you can be at your job, and that fascinates people. How can this girl get away with this? We all behaved like superbrats. Sometimes I do things just for shock. People don't get that it's a joke. You just do it to get a reaction. We were all young, and that's how we dealt with our situation. It's a big risk to put yourself out there."

SHANNON: "Oh, Janice. She's like a flame, and you're the moth. You've got to go to her, and you get burned, you can't help it. I would seriously say that she has a chemical imbalance, and that if she got medication, it would really help her. I mean in the most loving way I say that. But she's fucking brilliant. She's a brilliant model, the best ever, I think. She will be talked about for as long as modeling exists. She was good to me. She really would teach the girls, man. Here's how you do it, you just tell those guys to fuck off. *Grrrrrr.*"

KNUDSEN: "Gia was my best girlfriend. She was just beautiful. When she was first starting out, we did a job in the south of France with Helmut Newton. He said, 'Throw on the red lips and the bad eyes!' Helmut had Gia and I be girls, and the two other models were dressed as guys. One of them was Swedish, and she'd been a real bitch to me when I was starting out. So Gia sent roses to her room with lipstick all over the card, and then she called and said, 'Let's have some fun.' The girl broke out in a rash. Gia and I were like lion cubs having fun. We got a reputation because we didn't hide anything. We did a lot of drugs and went to a lot of parties. So many! We were both constantly on trips, which I think saved my life, because you don't do drugs when you travel. Except when I traveled with Gia. We brought a whole medicine kit.

"Gia was the peak. She pushed the borders right to death."

SHANNON: "Men never gave me anything. I made my own money. I never dated a guy for money, I never dated a guy for drugs, I had my own, you know. I always had my own coke. I didn't accept it. It was part of my obscure feminism."

KNUDSEN: "I always knew how to deal with men. I never understood professional affairs, even though photographers have always done that and a few girls work the couch better than they do. But somebody always gets hurt. I mean, who's working who?

"But I didn't know what a hustler was. I was very open and ready to be used. After I got my own apartment, I always had people living with me, tapping my bank accounts, using my drug dealers. You're making thousands and thousands of dollars, and you're constantly working and being flattered, and you're not emotionally mature, and you almost feel that you need to strike a kind of balance.

"When I was eighteen, a guy almost killed me. He called himself Dean Avedon, but that wasn't really his name. He was a bastard. He nearly tore my heart out. It got so crazy the police came to my door and he was behind me with a knife at my back. I said everything was OK, and they believed me. I was winking at them, but they went away, and then the guy tortured me for hours and hours. I started thinking of the scene in *Lawrence of Arabia* where Peter O'Toole is tortured. So I said, 'I know you're going to kill me, but can I have one last wish? Can I watch this movie?'

"He said yes, and it saved my life. Lawrence is riding through the desert and the guy fell asleep. I snuck out. All I had was my coat. I borrowed five dollars from the doorman and went to Bill King. He ran a bath, cleaned my wounds, and called Jerry Ford. The Fords had a house in Connecticut then, and Jerry took me there for a couple of days. A few days later the guy came back. Where do you think he'd been? In Milan, picking up another girl! He ended up working for a model agency. He died a couple years ago.

"After that I didn't want to stay in my apartment anymore, and I moved into a new flat. But I was nowhere! I was definitely on the skids. My career was going a little bit down. I owed drug dealers money. I was surrounded by rock and rollers who were feeding me substances, and my ego was getting out of hand. I was breaking down from too much stress, too much work, too much drugs, too much everything. That Christmas was the first when I didn't go back to Denmark. I called my father, but I kept it real brief."

SHANNON: "I was a real isolator. And when I got into my drug bit, I isolated even more. When I was in Paris, my favorite thing to do was go to the Maison du Caviar on Place de la Madeleine and sit there and write and drink champagne and have different caviars and smoke cigarettes, day after day after day. I was tired, man. I was working thirty shows a week. It was rough. Iman would be vibrating, hung over, coked out. They all were at one point or another. You'd get there on a Monday. Monday, Tuesday, Wednesday you're doing all the shows, you're not eating, you're all right, though. Thursday things start getting a little hairy, you're getting tired, you start bursting into tears. Thursday night, time for the vultures with the cocaine. You're so tired. You're really lonely, and you know—*boom*!

"People would drink, do a hit, and go on the runway. I never would do that. And then sure enough, as the years went by, I started going on the runway a little stoned. Just a glass of champagne to loosen up. And then one time I nearly fell over on the runway, I was so drunk.

"I have a good rep, but I went through a really rough time. At one point I'd been around the world in nineteen days or something. You get off a plane and nobody meets you; you go to a hotel where you don't know anybody; you go to a booking where you don't know anybody. Everybody wants, everyone's got a vested interest, and then while everyone else goes home to sleep, you're on another plane. And you've got a husband who's an asshole on top of it, who's destroying you psychically, and nobody says, 'What would be good for you?' Nobody ever says, 'Take a vacation, you're looking like you could use a little moral support, *something*.' "

KNUDSEN: "I'd been with Ford for three or four years when Jerry and Eileen called me in and said they wanted me to go into detox. When you're doing it, that's the last thing you want to hear, so I said no. I was being an asshole. Then Eileen heard a rumor that I was going to Elite, and she called my parents and started a family feud. She said I was doing a lot of drugs, it was a matter of days before I died, and I needed my family. They didn't know Eileen is cuckoo. My mother had a nervous breakdown! But my father said he'd just spoken to me, that I'd been talking about new management, and he had the feeling this was a trick. She just wanted to send me home because if she couldn't have me, then Johnny couldn't either.

"I was growing up. I wanted to get a grip on my business. And I had to clean up to prove that my parents were right to stand behind me. I went to Elite. At my first meeting with Casablancas, we were talking about my percentage. Monique Pillard was standing behind me, making signs, trying to send him messages. I didn't want them to talk over my head, so I made them turn the lights out. The first thing I did was get totally straight because I didn't want them telling me what to do. I wanted to make it clear who worked for who. I wanted to understand everything that was happening to me."

SHANNON: "I made it to the fucking top, and there was nothing there. Nobody was home. I started going out with Tony Peck after I broke up with Hamish. He'd seen me on *The Merv Griffin Show*. So now Tony starts teaching me how to do cocaine, like I didn't know. And this man can do cocaine, holy moley! I'm going out to dinner with Gregory Peck's friends, Frank Sinatra, Roger Moore, Jimmy Stewart, Billy Wilder. Gregory was a great guy, a very humble guy. I knew that I didn't like Tony, but I was digging hanging out with all these people that all the other girls were wanting to be with. That was the surprising thing for me. I got to the other side of the tracks, and I looked at these people, and they had no values, and it was bizarre. I started seeing stars, rich people, how they treated their wives. I started hearing the gossip.

How this producer's wife was a hooker, and I just got very disillusioned. Everything that I had worked for was all a sham. I was like a deer. I ran away to Paris. And I broke up with Tony on the phone."

KNUDSEN: "It was healthy to make the change. Monique lifted my career back up. A lot was happening. I moved in with a guy in the rock and roll business, and I hired his business manager. He wouldn't allow me to do anything. I stopped doing coke and started a whole new thing. That's when I found out how messed up everything was. For a long time I wouldn't open my mail unless it was from Denmark. I had boxes of official letters from the IRS. I owed them so much money!"

SHANNON: "I lost a lot of money, I don't know where it went. I don't know what I did with it. I remember taking it out, but that's about it. I took a lot of limos for a while, and I did pay for my own cocaine. And I was so generous. I spent a fortune. I was never a big money-maker. But I made millions and I spent millions.

"Luckily I saved a lot. I could have saved a lot more."

KNUDSEN: "Even after I cleaned up, I still had a 'bad reputation.' But really, it was just pranks. When Carol Alt came into the business, she was a real bitch. She changed really fast, and now she's supercool and we're really good friends, but at first, she was very religious. We went on a trip to Barbados together where there were only a certain number of rooms. I didn't want to share, but I had to. So I went out and got stoned, came back and put a sheet over my head and burst into the room going, 'Wooooo, it's the Antichrist!' I wanted them to separate us.

"Elite turned out to be a bit of a dud. You couldn't get away with it anymore. In the mid-eighties the new girls pulled everything back and became more commercial. They showed up on time. They smiled at the client. We'd pumped the rates up, but when the money got to a certain point, they wanted more professionalism, and the creative side was cut back. There were less nervous breakdowns for the editors, I guess.

"I started traveling to Hawaii and California and Australia, and I studied acting for a couple of years. I'd commute to New York for special jobs. Elite just sort of fizzled out for me because I wasn't in New York. I also started learning to shoot films, and that took me to Australia and Bali. Somehow a rumor started in New York that I'd died, and my booker at Elite repeated it!

That didn't seem very good to me, so around 1987 I went back to Ford, speaking only to Jerry, because every time Eileen saw me, she would throw up her hands. My father wasn't happy that I went back with her. But I'd always felt bad about leaving. And I really liked my booker, Rusty Zeddis. She handled all the brats. She really worked with us. She sincerely cared. Talking to her was very grounding. She'd make you feel professional even when you weren't."

SHANNON: "I go to L.A. I'm going to be an actress. I didn't have a clue. And I get out there, and I pretty much hit my bottom, you know, drinking and drugging. And then I get sober, and then everything took on a new priority. I went back to New York, and I started finding another way of living, a whole other way."

KNUDSEN: "I moved to Malibu, California, fell in love, started surfing, started doing ads for More cigarettes, Clairol, Revlon. Before that I'd always been an editorial hound. I liked the creative side of the business. I made plenty of money, but if I'd done more commercial work, I could've made even more.

"In 1993 I was starting to get antsy. Everyone told me to call Bryan Bantry. He was starting to book people from my time for jobs where they wanted more mature models. He says, 'As bad as she was, that's how good she is now.'"

After the Number One scandal singed Rome's playboy scene, the *dolce vita* moved to Milan. For the next decade the northern Italian city became a nursery school for neophyte models. Beginners could spend a few months there and fill their portfolios with tear sheets—precious pages torn from magazines that showed how well they worked. With those they could move on to New York and Paris, where careers were made. No one made money in Milan. "Everybody cheats with money in Milan," says Giorgio Repossi, a photographer's agent. If any was made, the agents kept it. Milan was like the deep end of a swimming pool. The model business threw girls in to see if they'd learn to swim. "Milan never made a girl," says Jacques de Nointel. "Milan ruined girls."

The agents of ruination were a new generation of playboys, who flocked to Riccardo Gay and Giorgio Piazzi. Count Umberto Caproni di Taliedo's father was one of the pioneers of Italian aviation, building medium-range bombers for the Italian Air Force during World War I and then branching out into tanks, submarines, and other armaments.

Born in 1940, Umberto Caproni studied business administration in Paris and worked in Japan before returning to Europe in the late sixties. There he entered Playboy World, the domain of men like John Casablancas's friend Bob Zagury; Gunther Sachs, an ex-husband of Brigitte Bardot's; Rodolfo Parisi, an aristocrat from Trieste who owned Italy's largest transport company and reputedly had an inch-long penis; Franco Rappetti, a Roman "who could speak to a girl in the lobby of the Plaza in Paris and have her in his room half an hour later," says Caproni; and Gigi Rizzi, "who also had a story with Bardot." To a man, they were tan, handsome lady-killers.

"I realized that the majority of beautiful girls were models," Caproni says, and he dedicated his life to their pursuit. "There were only fifty models then. They all knew each other; they stayed at the best hotels, used the best suitcases. But they weren't easy girls. You would introduce yourself to them and send roses for weeks. Eventually you would have an affair."

Caproni kept peacocks and hunted with falcons, and he and his friends had a similarly sporting approach to sexual conquest. "Everybody had his chance," Caproni says, "and we gave the girls the possibility to choose. If things are too easy, you don't enjoy them." But he wasn't above stocking his forest with bait for his fellow Milanese birds of prey. "Models were single and free, and I decided that if I had to live in Milano, which is not the most beautiful place in the world, I'd have some beautiful people around, so I decided to start a modeling agency." In 1970 he opened Model Ring in Milan with Beppe Piroddi, another playboy pal.

A few years later Piroddi and Caproni sold out to Riccardo Gay, but Caproni stayed a presence on the scene. "I knew everybody," says Caproni. "I was very friendly with Eileen Ford, John Casablancas." Indeed, Caproni and his friends came in handy when young American models grew homesick for their families and boyfriends. "Very famous agents in New York used to give Caproni's address to all the new girls coming to Milan and tell them, 'He will take care you,' " says Marcella Galdi, then a Riccardo Gay booker. "He was considered a gentleman."

So there were dinners and dancing and invitations to weekends at Caproni's splendid villa near Lake Como. "We have the largest collection of pre-1920 airplanes in the world," he says. "I would show them the collection, the house, which has some fifty bedrooms, the rare trees we have here, the rare animals. I would try to make them feel like they were getting out a bit. I was not trying to poison them or do anything wrong to their morals. The agents would only benefit from the fact that the girls were going out with me."

Giorgio Repossi, an advertising manager at a magazine called *Linea Italiana,* was part of Caproni's circle. "We were living in a dream come true," he says. "It was really provincial. The dream of every Italian guy is a beautiful American model in your bed. It was total immersion. For ten years I was going to bed at four, five in the morning and waking up at nine." Like Caproni, Repossi says he and his friends were providing a valuable service. "The only way to survive someplace is to go with somebody rich," he says. "It doesn't mean the models are whores. It doesn't mean the agency knows what they do."

But the agencies knew. Indeed, they oiled this mechanism for keeping models happy in Milan. "They used the playboys to hold on to the models," says Jerry Ford. Girls from Paris or New York would find boyfriends and not want to go back to their original agents. "We would spend weekends at the Caproni villa, and we would see who was arriving from New York," Repossi says. "Piazzi or Riccardo would say, 'Why don't you go pick her up?' " Caproni and friends would then drive to the nearby international airport in his Rolls-Royce. "When a girl arrives, she is met by somebody who speaks English and tells her what Milan is like, the money, how to make phone calls, how to take taxis," Caproni says. "And then somebody says, 'Listen, we have organized a party tonight, so that you can meet a lot of people in Milano and not feel like a stranger.' So the agency would be very happy. They would say, 'Can you please organize a dinner, a party?' And of course, it was also interesting for us."

Some of the men merely wanted to be seen with pretty girls. "We'd get them to buy us dinner and dump 'em afterwards," says model Beth Boldt, who'd come from Paris to Milan. "I was a really rotten model," she says. "I missed appointments. My ambition was pretty low: to party and meet cute guys." When there were no cute ones, rich ones would do. "I stayed at the Grand Hotel, and all the old men came every night, and if you were a model, you could have dinner. We were never pressed for sex. There were times I felt we were taking advantage of them."

Massimo Tabak, a young fur manufacturer, was short and plump but also funny and charming; he was in the fashion business, so he didn't mind shopping, and he had both money and free time. "So it was not difficult for me to spoil the girls," he says. "It was a pioneer time, wild and intense. We had girls getting two dozen invitations each night, forty people at a table at dinner, flowers, food sent to their hotel rooms. Once I came into the room of a girlfriend, and I swear to God, I thought it was a jungle."

Prime prey in this jungle were girls who weren't going to make it big. "Milan is a crash course in the shitty part of the business," says Serene Cicora, who modeled there at the time. "These girls come to Milano without a penny," says photographer Fabrizio Ferri. "They're treated terribly; they shoot with terrible assistants; their books are looked at in a rush. They sit in a residence day and night, get very depressed, and then the agency calls and says they're being sent back to New York. That night she returns to her hotel, and there are fifty red roses at the desk and a playboy waiting outside with a Rolls-Royce, saying, 'I'll take care of the hotel bill.' "

"They'd wait until a girl was so frustrated, she'd take the offer," says Bitten Knudsen. "The weak calves in the herd buy into it. But Italian boys can't give up their mothers, so there's no room for real girls; there's only room for mischief. It's primitive. It's like they're angry at women."

"When you're sixteen, you look up to those guys, and they're gods to you," says Gaby Wagner, who joined Fashion Model in the mid-seventies. "I think those people were helping the girls," says Tiziana Casali, who ran the Hotel Arena—known as the Fuck Palace—before becoming an agent. "They were trying to make their lives better. When they came back from their weekends or their evenings, they would never tell me, 'They forced me to take cocaine.' It was 'There was cocaine. We had a great time.' They knew what was going on, and they were happy to have it."

Until the early seventies Italian *Vogue* had been the dominant Italian fashion magazine. Its photographers, particularly Alfa Castaldi and Gianpaolo Barbieri, were considered the best in the country and were tied up with exclusive deals. *Vogue*'s preeminent position was enhanced by the ready-to-wear revolution. "The fabric companies all invested a lot of money," Barbieri says. "The magazines were full of advertising pages. *Vogue* was like a telephone book."

In 1974 Peppone della Schiava bought the right to publish an Italian edition of *Harper's Bazaar* and went into competition. In 1976 Honduran-born Lizette Kattan, a former model, became the magazine's fashion director. Kattan convinced della Schiava that the way to compete with *Vogue* was to open an office in New York, recruit the best models and photographers, and shoot pictures there. Kattan knew Eileen Ford well. Della Schiava forged an alliance with Elite, which gave him first dibs on its models. Kattan "found Iman, Juli Foster, so many girls," della Schiava says. "I would come to New York and look at a thousand girls."

Italian *Bazaar* thrived. Della Schiava offered complete freedom, plane tickets, and endless expense accounts to photographers. These proved to be pretty lures. Soon Arthur Elgort, Patrick Demarchelier, Jacques Malignon, Alex Chatelain, Chris von Wangenheim, François Lamy, and virtually every other top photographer of the day was working for him. Kattan also gave beginners like Herb Ritts and Steven Meisel some of their earliest assignments.

"They could do whatever they wanted," says Kattan. "We treated them like gods; we gave them champagne all night, phone calls all over the world—because we knew it was a way to get things done and fast." It was the same for models. "I had power because I was the editor and the publisher," says della Schiava. "If I saw a girl I liked, I brought her over, and she'd get incredible treatment."

As the competition between the magazines heated up, neophyte models poured into Milan, in a quest for the editorial tear sheets that were their passports to success. "At that time it was very beautiful because the girl arrived in Milano with maybe two Polaroids, and one week later we had her in Italian *Vogue,*" says booker Marcella Galdi. "The American magazines were very conservative then. To shoot for *Vogue, Linea, Bazaar Italia* meant you had total freedom. Italy was the only place where all these photographers had great creativity and light supervision. It was kind of a royal cult, you know?"

As time went on, Milan's playboys split into two not entirely distinct factions, one orbiting Giorgio Piazzi, the other, Riccardo Gay. "Piazzi didn't like the girls going out with bad people," says Giorgio Repossi, who was part of the Fashion Model clique with Count Caproni. "He gave dinners and invited the nicer guys."

Though Simone d'Aillencourt had been run out of Milan, Gay and Piazzi weren't the only agents in town. "Every two weeks there was a new agency open," says Jacques de Nointel. And it was the same from Barcelona to Kyoto. Every booker with a hold on a couple of girls would henceforth be tempted to change agencies or let another backer into the business. "It became like a pyramid," says Servane Cherouat, a booker since 1957 who now heads a models' union that is the bane of Parisian agencies. "Every booker wants an agency, so nobody can trust an agency."

In 1973 Gloria and Valerie Askew, two sisters who'd operated a small agency in London since 1966, took over a troubled Milan agency. Three years later Beatrice Traissac, who'd run Fashion Model for several years, quit to open an agency of her own. Although she'd worked primarily with Fashion before opening her own shop, Gloria Askew had close ties with Riccardo Gay. One of her models, Sue Nadkani, married Gay's friend Pucci Albanese. Gay, too, married an Askew model. Domestic life seemed to agree with the agent. He settled down and had a child and stopped running around. But Gloria Askew says she and Beatrice were thorns in the side of the male-run Gay and Fashion agencies because "we weren't interested in prostituting our girls" with Milan's playboys.

Gay was close with many of them, particularly Carlo Cabassi, who became a partner in Gay's firm in the mid-seventies. "Whenever the agents needed money, they asked a playboy," says Gloria Askew. Cabassi's family had made its fortune in the construction business before the war and moved into real estate afterward. An older brother, Giuseppe, was religious, successful, and tied in with the ruling Christian Democrats. Carlo, who was known as Piccolo—or Little—Carlo, was the family's black sheep. Although he had real estate holdings of his own, he wasn't involved with Gruppo Cabassi. He was far more interested in cover girls. The first time Peter Strongwater went to Milan in the mid-seventies, he went to a party at Cabassi's villa outside Milan. Gloria Askew calls the place Fuckingham Palace. "Each model got a hat check as they arrived," Strongwater recalls. "After lunch they raffled off pages of Italian *Bazaar.*"

In 1977 Gloria Askew flew to England to have a child. When she returned, she found she had a new partner, Piccolo Carlo. Askew Milano had metamorphosed into Askew International at a new address. "Cabassi was thinking, probably, if you own an agency, it's an easy way to get girls," says Giorgio Repossi. Cabassi was hardly the first wealthy man to open a date farm, but he would be—briefly—the most successful. Askew went along at first, taking Cabassi to New York and introducing him to Wilhelmina. But then, Askew says, Cabassi brought in another partner. "They have quite good girls, but for money, they have nothing," says Roberto Lanzotti, who owned a fur company. "I said to my friend Cabassi, 'Let's put money in the business; we'll work for fun.' He's rich, you see. He doesn't care. I take care of the accounting part-time. Six months later we find out it's a complete disaster. We decided to close. We got back our money."

"Cabassi wasn't a bad guy, but he got corrupted," says Gloria Askew. "The model business attracts thieves and robbers and playboys. They wanted to control the agency. If I'd wanted to be a brothel keeper, I would have kept a brothel. I told the models too much. They never felt intimidated when I was around. They felt they could stay home with me and not go to restaurants and weekends. I wouldn't let them go unless I went along. So Cabassi hated me. He said, 'Models don't need mothers.' " Finally Lanzotti told Askew she wasn't welcome anymore and changed the agency's name back to Team.

Askew refused to leave, and finally, she alleges, she was poisoned at a dinner with her partners. "For some reason I was the only one that got very very ill the next day," she says. "My sister flew me back to London, and I was put in hospital. My husband nearly killed Lanzotti. They had a huge fight in the office, and Cabassi and Lanzotti walked out. I never went back to Milan after that. I couldn't condone a business that supplied drugs to girls and girls to playboys who wanted to fuck them. I couldn't fight them. So I moved to Japan."

* * *.

As Askew recovered from salmonella in the summer of 1977, the fashion world converged on Italy's capital for its *alta moda* collections. The model wars followed. Agencies all over Europe were being forced to choose sides.

London's Models One was at the center of the action. It had maintained ties with both Ford and Elite. "When John went to open New York, we didn't even know," says coowner April Ducksbury. "Eileen sent me a furious telex. I just tossed it aside and said, 'God, Eileen is so paranoiac.' Then I got a call. Ford was suing him. Roy Cohn was their lawyer. I felt weak at the knees with fright."

A few weeks later Ducksbury and her partner, Jose Fonseca, headed to Rome. "We used to do that every year," Ducksbury says. "It was the big gathering of all the model agencies, a lovely four or five days to talk and see each other in wonderful weather." The Fords dominated the shows with a huge entourage and a long wine-soaked lunch every day on the terrace of their suite on the twelfth floor of the Parco dei Principi Hotel. "John had his smaller entourage at the Grand Hotel di Roma, and we'd jump from one to the other, trying to be very tactful about it," Ducksbury says.

But tact was passé. On the last night of the shows Riccardo Gay and his counterparts at the Fashion Model agency traditionally gave a big dinner. Attempting to be diplomatic, they'd set things up so that Casablancas could sit with his friend Gay, and the Fords with their allies from Fashion. Ducksbury and Fonseca had been out with the Fords every night, so they'd agreed to join Casablancas.

"But John and his group didn't turn up," says Ducksbury. "We're waiting and waiting and waiting." Casablancas had decided to make an entrance. He'd gone to the studio where *Vogue* was shooting, to bring all the photographers and models with him. "Finally John and his lot walk in," Ducksbury says. They took their table, models spilling onto the floor, laughing and making a scene.

"Eileen was furious," Ducksbury continues. "And John was frightened. It was like the St. Valentine's Day Massacre." When she and Fonseca made their move to join the Elite table, the Fords were "stone-faced, looking at us like death," she says. "We sat down with John, and the Fords walked out, and then it was a wonderful party."

Casablancas was doing everything he could to make life miserable for the Fords. "I'd reserved a room at the Parco dei Principi, which was her hotel," he says. "When I arrived, a manager says, 'I'm sorry, I can't give you a room.

I'll be honest with you. It's because Mrs. Ford has been in this hotel for years.' So I called Riccardo and asked him how many girls we had staying in the Principi. There were about twenty. I told him to cancel everything. The manager had to go to Eileen and say, 'We couldn't do anything. He had a reservation.' "

In 1975 fourteen top Italian design houses, which had previously held their fashion shows in Florence, broke ranks and moved to Milan. Milanese show models booked their own work at first and were a caste apart from photographic models and their agencies. Within a few years that changed and led to Jerry Hall, Iman, Marie Helvin, and Pat Cleveland stalking the runways. In 1976 Tiziana Casali left the Hotel Arena and cofounded Why Not?, the first agency in Milan dedicated to runway modeling. "The designers were paying very little," she says. "For shows and fittings, fifty dollars! We raised the price immediately to two hundred, and the designers freaked out." Little did they know how good they had it.

That same year Guy Héron, a French actor who'd lived with an Elite model, formed a runway models' cooperative in Paris. With tongue planted firmly in cheek, he named it Cosa Nostra—"our thing"—and offered to work for the models who owned it with him. He signed up *cabine* girls from Dior, Saint Laurent, and Givenchy, including many of the black Americans who'd first come to Paris to work at Versailles. He also visited America and offered its agents 5 percent commission instead of the prevailing 2 percent share, "and by God, he paid it," says Gillis MacGil. "The girls who went with him would come back with a lot of money. They actually gave you detailed accountings. Unusual, to say the least."

Héron came along at just the right moment. At the end of the seventies European runway shows blossomed from intimate affairs that attracted several hundred journalists and retailers to full-blown productions staged for an audience of thousands. "It just went like this," says runway agent Ellen Harth, snapping her fingers. "I don't think the designers expected it to happen." But virtually overnight, Italian designers like Mariuccia "Krizia" Mandelli, Missoni, Armani, and Versace became international stars. The public caught up over the next fifteen years, but already models were positioned to share in the bounty.

Héron began organizing group bookings, hiring chauffeur-driven cars to ferry his girls to fittings and shows. Best of all, he paid with tax-free cash. "I took seventy girls to Milan—Mounia, Kirat, Amalia, Jerry Hall, Inès de la

Fressange, Marie Helvin—and I was carrying in a bag hundreds of millions of lire," Héron boasts.

"Cash was standard," affirms a star model who went on Héron's first trips and continued modeling in Milan through the early eighties. "We were paid fifty thousand dollars for twenty shows in ten days, and if that's what they paid us, God knows what the agents were making." Each season the system, and the models, grew more sophisticated. "We started asking for francs because the bills were larger," the model says. "Lire are dinky little notes." Even still, it was a lot of money to carry across borders. So the models sewed the bills into the hems of their clothes or stuffed them in their underwear. "We didn't talk about it," the model says. "We were horrified of audits."

They were also scared of immigration officers. "I remember some Italian girls would get jealous and phone the police, and we'd all have to hide," Jerry Hall says. Most models of the time have stories about running out the back doors of fashion shows while design assistants held the authorities at bay.

Italian agents tried to curtail Héron's activities. "They sent the police," he says, laughing. "The designers had to pay to set me free. Everyone was afraid of me. All the agencies were against me. All of John Casablancas's friends had a meeting." Then they struck back. "The Europeans swooped down and cajoled his models away," says Gillis MacGil. Riccardo Gay and Roberto Lanzotti opened Collections, a fashion show division at Gay's agency. Lanzotti used the same techniques as Héron and took many of his models. He booked a charter to fly them to Milan and had all the designers pool their money and pay a package price. When the designers balked at that, the controls on show model rates were lifted, and "the girls made *so much* money," Lanzotti exclaims.

Not everything was sunshine and cash, though. A lot of business was being done in the shadows. "Girls were offered ten thousand dollars to go to bed with industrialists," recalls Richard di Pietro, then a runway agent at Wilhelmina. "A lot of Arabs were storming Europe looking for beautiful young girls. A lot of girls made a lot of money *not* modeling. *And* making fifty thousand dollars in cash modeling and stuffing it wherever, even in their bodies. It was becoming totally disreputable."

Then came trouble at Beatrice Traissac's agency. Gay poached one of Traissac's bookers, who'd previously worked for Askew. "Then they arranged for Beatrice's backer to pull out," Gloria Askew charges. Beatrice closed briefly, opened again, and then got a taste of Milan's medicine. "Poor Beatrice," says Zoli's Vickie Pribble. "They threw bombs in her agency." Who's they? The word "Mafia" is tossed around in answer to that question. "But you must understand," says Stéphane Lanson. "In France, when we say someone is mafioso, it means they're not clean, not that they're Sicilian." And many believe that the Mafia in Milanese modeling was really just the near monopoly of the two leading agencies. "Riccardo and Fashion," says Dorothy Parker. "They burned Beatrice down. She had just opened. We went out to lunch, came back, and the agency was gone."

In fact, there were rumors that everyone in Italy but the Vatican was involved in modeling. "There were so many crooks in Italy," says Apollonia van Ravenstein. "I don't know [if the agents had] Mafia connections. But we knew there were things going on. I don't doubt the connections. I never saw them working, but I always felt that they were present. How else could all these models work there without permits, come in and out of the country, and never have the Italian IRS on their backs? Someone had to be paid off."

Certainly organized crime has an interest in drugs, sex, cash, and pretty women. But so do government and big business. And there is one compelling argument against the idea that organized crime has infiltrated modeling in Milan. Roberto Lanzotti puts it best. "Mafia?" He snorts. "It's ridiculous. It's too small business for Mafia."

Milan wasn't the only place where the world of models had taken on a troubling aspect. One of the earliest signs that things were turning nasty came in 1977, when three teenage American aspiring models went to Elite in Paris.

"I was having lunch at Fouquet's with these three girls when a very good friend of mine, a backgammon player, went past," recalls Jacques de Nointel. "I went to the bathroom, and when I came back, they said they couldn't have dinner with me on Saturday night because they'd accepted to go to a country house outside Paris with five or six guys they'd never seen before."

What happened next became a legend in the world of models, in large part because the girls involved have never spoken out about what happened. They were taken to a country house about forty-six miles outside Paris that belonged to Serge Varsano, whose father, Maurice, founded Sucres et Denrées, the largest commodities trading firm in France. Serge was "a plump and boring fellow," says an aristocrat who was part of the every-night crowd at Paris clubs like Privé, L'Aventure, and Élysées Matignon, and in St.-Tropez, where Varsano kept a powerful cigarette boat called Brown Sugar. Varsano's friends included Patrick Gilles, a former lover of Brigitte Bardot's, and several other sons of rich fathers with nothing but time and money on their hands.

"We were out every night," the aristocrat recalls. "We were all very friendly with the model agents. They would appear with four girls and seat them at our tables. Every night was a meat market. The girls were like cattle, readily available. The agents made them understand that if they went with this or that guy, they would have work. The girls would fall in your lap. They wanted the bookings. They knew what was going on." Unfortunately at Varsano's that weekend they were in for a surprise.

Early the next morning Jacques de Nointel got a call from a gendarmerie near the country house. The girls were there. De Nointel called their Elite booker, Caroline Duby, at 6:00 A.M., and the two drove to the country to collect the models. "They told me they'd had drinks and dope, hashish or whatever," Duby recalls, "and then the girls got real afraid." They told de Nointel that the trouble started when Varsano joked about beating them up. "They ran to their bedroom and locked the door," de Nointel says, "but they didn't know there was another entrance through a cupboard." When one of the men burst into the room, the girls locked themselves in the bathroom, then jumped out the window, causing one of them to twist her ankle severely. Fleeing, they were "found in the cold and brought to the gendarmerie," de Nointel continues.

Back in Paris, de Nointel took the injured girl to the American Hospital. The next day Nancy Bounds, the owner of a modeling school in Omaha, Nebraska, and an official of a modeling convention the three girls had attended, arrived in Paris and checked into the Méridien Hôtel. "As I was going in, I heard a voice sing out, 'Hi, Nancy Bounds,' " she recalls. The phone was ringing when she got to her room. "It was a crying girl," she recalls. "She said that one of her friends had seen me going into the hotel. Then she told me what had happened. They'd gone to this man's house outside Paris for dinner, played tennis, and gone swimming. Then a drunk gentleman came in their room and jumped on one of the girls, who was in bed. They got into a scuffle, and the guy hit her. Her jaw was knocked out of alignment, and she had a black eye. They ran into the bathroom, tied sheets together, went out the window, and walked through the woods to a small town. They sat outside the police station all night, and then someone came and took them back to Paris."

Bounds decided to call a press conference. "I was calling the wire services," she says. "The girls were calling me every half hour. They said someone showed up at the model apartment they were staying in and tried to scare them out of there. Then at seven P.M. they called again and told me to cancel the press conference because they'd all gotten an assignment in Greece and were leaving that evening on a plane."

In 1981 the Milan and Paris model scenes merged when Paris Planning's Gérald Marie and Jean-Pierre Dollé reached out to put the touch on one of Milan's playboys. "Carlo Cabassi was out to control the modeling business," Gloria Askew charges. "He and Riccardo Gay bought Paris Planning and got rid of François Lano."

In fact, François Lano's good-bye to modeling was long and tortuous, and even the participants can't agree about what happened. Lano says he sold only the agency's name to Cabassi. Pucci Albanese says that Cabassi and Gay bought half the agency "at the international level," in order to get exclusive rights to Paris Planning's models in Italy. Paris Planning model Gaby Wagner says Gay was a partner, too. But Elite booker Francesca Magugliani says Gay didn't have the money to buy anything, and Stéphane Lanson agrees that Gay had nothing to do with Cabassi's investment in the Paris agency. Gérald Marie, who was in the center of the action and ultimately took over Paris Planning's operations, neglects to mention Cabassi at all.

What is clear is that in the late seventies Paris Planning began having serious problems. "I was head of the agency, but I was not controlling the finances," Lano says. Dollé took care of all that.

"François trusted Jean-Pierre," says Servane Cherouat, the veteran booker, who'd come out of retirement to do paper work for Paris Planning's foreign models. "It was a love story and a money story. François and Jean-Pierre began to fight. They fought for a year." Paris Planning had broken in two. "But François Lano did not accept this," says Cherouat.

Stéphane Lanson had gone to work for Jérôme Bonnouvrier, who'd opened his own agency, Glamour, after his aunt closed Catherine Harlé. By 1980, though, Lanson and Bonnouvrier were at odds. So when Lano approached Lanson to return to Paris Planning, he was interested. "So my bookers and I arrived the second time at Paris Planning with about a hundred sixty star male models, but I didn't know that François had a problem with Jean-Pierre," Lanson says. "François was one of the most wonderful men in this business, but he was a huge spender, making parties, playing backgammon, playing gin rummy, and [he was] a drinker, a big drinker. That's why he took me at Paris Planning, to run the agency. He was never there!"

Within weeks Lanson realized there were "two Paris Plannings in the same building," he says. "Paris Planning girls on the second floor with Gérald

Marie and Paris Planning François Lano for men on the fifth floor with me."
Then Lano—who'd never paid attention to his Swiss accounts—took a trip
to Switzerland to see how much money he'd accumulated in the decade since
Models S.A. had opened. "I was told a number," Lano says. "It was very little,
but what could I say? I never received an accounting. I had no way to discover
the truth." Where did the money go? "To Models S.A.," Lano says. "Probably they paid the commissions to Jean-Pierre in cash."

Jean-Marie de Gueldre, the lawyer who'd helped set up Models S.A. in
1970 and later invested in several real estate ventures with Dollé, insists that
the real problem wasn't the location of Paris Planning's profits but rather
Lano's irresponsibility. "François is cultivated, intelligent, and funny," de
Gueldre says, "but he doesn't care about money. He loves to spend it, and
that is a problem. He took Gérald Marie into his agency and Gérald Marie
is a kind of crocodile, and that is a big problem. Gérald Marie was very effi-
cient. He looked after the girls, he fucked the girls, and the problem is that
the girls belong to their bookers. Gérald saw that François was arriving at
noon and leaving at four and taking money from the company. If you are in
the office eight hours every day, seeing that, you'll think, 'I don't need him.'
Gérald was saying to Dollé, 'We should have our own agency.' Dollé was in
the middle."

Models S.A.'s Swiss owners would finance agency vouchers for half the
commission. "When an agency needs money, [Models S.A.] asks for a percentage of the company," explains Jérôme Bonnouvrier's ex-wife Giselle.
"They didn't steal the company. But when François Lano needed money, they
took advantage of him, took the company from him, and fired him."

Dollé and Marie had united against Lano. "Dollé said his time was over,"
reports Jérôme Bonnouvrier. "Dollé felt safe with Gérald Marie," who
replaced Lano as the company's *gérant* (managing director). "Gérald wanted
shares in the company," says Lano. "I refused, and probably at that time Jean-
Pierre and Gérald banded together against me. Jean-Pierre was created by me.
Gérald Marie existed because of me. They threatened to leave. I told them the
door was open. They proposed to pay me for the company, and I refused. I felt
that even if they left, I was still François Lano, and I would have a hundred
people knocking at my door, proposing what I wanted. I was really wrong."

Finally Marie and Dollé brought Lano an offer that he couldn't refuse:
Carlo Cabassi wanted to buy into Paris Planning. Models S.A. helped broker
the deal. "They were all in it together," Lano says. "They said, 'If you don't
agree, Gérald Marie will leave and empty the agency.' "

In September 1981 Marie and Dollé moved the women's division to new space on the fashionable Faubourg St.-Honoré, while Lano, Lanson, and the male models remained in the original Paris Planning offices. Lano's splinter agency struggled along for eighteen months before going bankrupt in fall 1982.

François Lano finally left the modeling business. "I was trusting, and I was disappointed," he says. "I don't know if I regret it, though, because if I was not naïve, I wouldn't have seen the color of the sky and the sun. If the color of money was fantastically beautiful, maybe I would like it, too, but it's not attractive to me. Money in the bank didn't make me happy. I ended up with nothing. But I can say that I've kept my ideas, and no one can steal them."

Back in Milan, their investments in the modeling business were paying off for the playboys—in more ways than money. "The number of girls went to the thousands, and they were no longer just nice, educated girls, but girls from all kinds of backgrounds, mainly discovered in large discotheques," observes Umberto Caproni. Once his generation of playboys had ruled the town. Now a new group of players was taking over Milan's night life. They were known as *figli di papà* (Daddy's boys). "Kids," says Roberto Lanzotti, "so fucking rich."

It had long been a game. Now it was a war. "It became industrial and aggressive," says Massimo Tabak. "You must have a good atmosphere at a table," says Caproni. "Otherwise the girls get bored, and if the girls are bored, nobody wins anything. Who has the most beautiful girls, the happiest people? Whose table was more interesting and more fashionable? In my table I try to always have good-looking people, which was not the same with Cabassi, I must say."

Cabassi's new status as an agency owner had changed the rules. "Having a big share in Riccardo Gay's agency, he could have the girls go to his house without going to the clubs first," says Caproni. And when Cabassi and his friends did go out, things sometimes turned nasty. One night Cabassi arrived at a fashionable club with a blonde on his arm and was greeted by a regular who said to no one in particular, "Some things are reserved for those with money." Cabassi beat the man up and tossed him onto the street.

What caused this radical shift in behavior was an important shift in fashionable society's intoxicant of choice. Champagne was no longer the favored fuel. "Suddenly drugs are fashion," says Giorgio Repossi. "Coke is fashion." And with that, *Milano per bene*—the city's good boys—became known as *Milano per male*. An ignoble spirit was loose in the world of models.

The first casualty was Giorgio Piazzi's reputation. Of all the agents in Milan, his had been the best. But then Piazzi discovered America—and more. "Giorgio discovered too much," says Giuliana Ducret, who'd worked for him since 1972.

Piazzi moved to New York at the end of the seventies. "He went to America because he found this beautiful girl and married her," says his brother, Giuseppe. "He was going back and forth for two years." He bought Hinchingham, a 314-acre 1774 estate on the Chesapeake Bay shore in Maryland and, early in 1982, opened something called the Model Workshop there. For $3,500 (sometimes billed against prospective earnings), girls got to spend a week there, working with flown-in photographers and stylists to develop their looks and their books. He was supposed to be recruiting for Fashion. "An absolute joke," John Casablancas said.

"He had an idea that for whatever reason didn't work out," says Giuseppe. "Maybe it was too early."

"Giorgio was still the owner [of Fashion Model], but he was living [in New York]," says Ducret. He left his second wife, a model named Jan Stephens, and took up with another model, who became his third wife. He'd first seen her four years before when she signed with Ford at age sixteen. They got reacquainted when she came to Hinchingham to gussy up her portfolio. Though he and his second wife were embroiled in a bitter divorce, the younger girl seemed to give Piazzi a new lease on life. He was profiled by *People* magazine. "I am going to be the new starmaker," he vowed.

In spring 1982 Giorgio Piazzi appeared in Milan, scooped up several bookers, and took them to Maryland. That's where Ducret realized that Piazzi had developed a taste for cocaine. "My husband came for two weeks, and one night, he said, 'Giulie, I'm much younger and I'm always tired, and they are always so alive!' I said, 'You never hear when they go behind the tree and go *sniiiiiifff*?' "

On that same trip Ducret came to New York for Piazzi's fortieth birthday party, where Debbie Dickinson jumped out of a cake in a bikini. Beforehand they'd stopped at Piazzi's suite at the Hotel Tudor, a depressing six-hundred-room establishment near the United Nations that rented tiny staff rooms to aspiring models at cut rates. As many as thirty girls as young as fifteen lived there at any time.

Arriving at the Tudor, Ducret "started laughing, and I never stopped," she says. "It was the image of the playboy suite: bad taste, but rich, mirrors all over, huge bathroom and someone poking a spoonful of cocaine under your nose.

It's the first and only time that I had cocaine, and I went HACHOO! and the whole thing went flying."

The Tudor was owned by a friend of Piazzi's, Steven Silverberg, who hoped that Piazzi would help him turn the hotel into a fashion hangout like Milan's Arena or Grand hotels. Briefly it became a sort of New York annex of the Fuck Palace, with unshaved Italians hanging out trying to pick up young girls. In fall 1983 several agents and models familiar with the scene in the hotel gave interviews to a local newspaper, the *East Side Express*. The resulting story, "Terror at the Model Arms," quoted models telling of men entering their rooms with passkeys at all hours; of thefts and a rape; of a model who was beaten so often she earned the nickname Blond and Blue; of cocaine parties in Silverberg's eight-room penthouse suite; and of a whole catalog of mind games played by Piazzi and Silverberg as a prelude to invitations to the Model Workshop.

"They would call you down to see your portfolio and rip you apart verbally," said a twenty-one-year-old Foster-Fell model from the Midwest. "They'd say, 'Don't you know how to dress? Why do you sit with your mouth like that? You're a fat slob. No one will book you.' They were always doing coke down there." And offering it to the girls. "I couldn't believe the whole scene," she concluded. "The hotel is depressing enough without them hassling you."

The director of security at the hotel, an ex-cop, turned a blind eye to what was happening. "Any girl who mentions it is foolish," he said. "If they don't like it, they should leave. I don't think girls should be allowed to be here at that age. They should be home with their parents. A high percentage of them aren't even models. They don't make a pimple on a model's nose."

Silverberg, today a real estate investor, denies that he ever took drugs, saw drugs, or had any business dealings with Piazzi. "I don't have any memories of problems with any guests," he says. "We stopped with models because they invited men and friends to the rooms. It didn't work out." Silverberg admits that some models got mad at Piazzi and adds that he had reason to be angry, too. "We thought we were going to get publicity from Giorgio staying in the hotel. We didn't get any except bad publicity. I said, 'That's it. I don't want you staying in the hotel.'

"Giorgio's like a big kid," says Silverberg. "He's not a bad fellow. Maybe people thought he was drunk. Maybe he told people they couldn't be models. Maybe he was rude. At the time I was single, I went out with girls. Maybe I made a wrong judgment trying to attract fashion people. Maybe you'd assume I was flamboyant, but I was just trying to be a host. They were nice girls. If I spoke to anyone, I was more a concerned father figure."

Hinchingham closed in 1984. The girls Piazzi trained weren't loyal to him and went off to other agencies. He "lost everything," says Giorgio Repossi. The prevailing wisdom was that he'd gone off the deep end too late in life. "He was destroyed," says Repossi. "He lost his mind." Piazzi also lost his agency in Milan. He'd brought in two partners, Paolo Roberti, an accountant, and Lorenzo Pedrini, an ex-model, beginning in 1980. They were backed by a clothing factory owner and real estate investor named Giorgio Sant'Ambrogio. The source of his funds was a mystery to modeling folk. "How he made money I don't want to know, or if I know, I don't want to say, OK?" says Ducret.

"The legend is that Piazzi was out eating and drinking, and he said, 'I want to sell my company,' and Sant'Ambrogio was there," says Giorgio Repossi. Pucci Albanese confirms that. "Giorgio Sant'Ambrogio proposed to help," he says. "He liked to be surrounded by the most beautiful women in the world. It's not hard to understand his preferring them to carpenters and electricians." According to his brother, Giuseppe, Piazzi left New York. "At this point adventure was his dream," his brother says. "He went to the Caribbean and then on to Venezuela, the Amazon, and then he went back to Anguilla again." There, having lost all his money in a failed gold mine, he became the chef in a restaurant owned by Silverberg (who'd sold the Tudor in 1987). The restaurant closed after Piazzi moved away. He now lives on St. Maarten, where he runs a small importing business. "Giorgio Piazzi never touched drugs until he got here," says Jerry Ford. "He made a total mess of himself, but deep down he's decent."

With Piazzi gone, an era ended in Milan and the Cabassi/Gay clique came to dominate its modeling business. "Being a nice guy doesn't make you a winner," says Umberto Caproni. "The bad guys were getting ten times more results, not in quality but in quantity. I was getting nothing, but I don't regret it. I'd had my chances, and I played fair. You cannot win them all."

Naturally Giorgio Sant'Ambrogio had a model girlfriend. Donna Broome, whom he met in London in about 1979, was a full-bodied dark-haired girl who'd started modeling as a child. She moved to Milan in the early eighties. "When I first arrived, I went out with one guy, and soon I was getting calls day and night from people I never heard of," Donna told a reporter years later. But when she hooked up with Sant'Ambrogio, she was protected from that sort of thing. She worked regularly and had what passed for a settled existence.

Broome was one of the five children that Air Force Sergeant Bill Broome and his wife, Alice Thompson, raised on air bases all around America. She had a tough childhood. Her father "expected his kids to obey like his soldiers and not ask why," Donna has said. Her younger sister, Terry, always felt he picked on her more than the others. Finally Terry ran away from their home in Greenville, South Carolina, when she was fifteen and was raped by two bikers. Her parents made clear their belief that she'd brought it on herself. Married at eighteen for less than a year, Terry then moved to New York, trying to follow in Donna's footsteps. Terry joined Ford in 1978 but was mostly interested in cocaine and the bottle of scotch she drank each day. She tried suicide in 1980 and fled home to South Carolina in 1981 but missed the fast lane. Donna Broome meanwhile moved to Milan, and soon gave Terry a plane ticket and the hope she could revive her career in go-go Milano.

At twenty-six, though, she was too old to start over, and she wasn't pretty enough. The day after she arrived at the Principessa Clothilde, she lost a thousand dollars—all her money—to a pickpocket. "From that moment, it was all downhill," Donna said.

Patrizia Piazzi, an ex-model who worked with her husband, Giuseppe, at Fashion Model, says, "Terry had been very unfortunate in life. So Donna asked me if I could help her, if I could use her, and I told Donna that it was very difficult. Terry was basically hanging out in Milan, and then she got caught up in this terrible world." Her brief sojourn in *Milano male* ended about ten weeks later.

Terry later said that before she arrived, she knew about the systematic abuse of striving models in Milan. Agents wouldn't send a girl's portfolio out "until they did whatever these men wanted them to do," she said. "I heard of a couple of cases in which these men threatened to throw acid in the model's face. One time, they threatened to throw a girl in the river."

Yet she immediately got involved with Claudio Caccia, an insurance broker who knew Sant'Ambrogio. Within a few days Caccia took her to an overnight party at Carlo Cabassi's villa in Casorezzo, between Milan and Novara. Model Shaun Casey frequented the place after Riccardo Gay introduced them, and she and Cabassi had a brief affair in 1982. She describes him as wealthy, very important, very funny, and "over my head." She says: "He had bodyguards and huge dogs. Everything else in his house was dead. He was a hunter. There were tusks, skins on the wall, major killings." There was also cocaine, Terry said. "Enough to be offered to everyone."

She and Caccia went to the party with Francesco D'Alessio, a rich kid who'd been abandoned by his mother at age two. He was the son of Carlo D'Alessio, Italy's king of the horses, the owner of a hundred thoroughbreds and the head of the breeders' union. Francesco grew up a rake and a gambler who played bridge with Omar Sharif and went to the races with Alain Delon. D'Alessio had married a model, and they had two daughters before she left him in 1983. He'd already started taking cocaine and became "a zombie," in the words of Giuliana Ducret, doing coke until 11:00 A.M. and sleeping until 7:00 P.M. in the apartment he rented from Cabassi, who lived upstairs on Milan's Corso Magenta.

The night he met Terry Broome, D'Alessio entered her bedroom in Cabassi's villa while she was dressing and asked her to have sex. Her refusal didn't stop him from sharing his coke with her and Cabassi. Later that night he fondled his crotch while watching her. She proceeded to go to bed with both Cabassi and Caccia.

D'Alessio asked to join the ménage but was rebuffed by Cabassi. D'Alessio had a problem Cabassi could recognize. Since his separation D'Alessio had taken to ritually humiliating women. He'd beaten his wife in a nightclub and punched an American model who'd refused to sleep with him. "He was a jerk, terrible with girls," says Giorgio Repossi. He was certainly terrible with Terry. Every time he saw her over the next two months, he would yank his crotch. He told his friends she'd taken on six men, not two, at the weekend orgy *and* that she might be a lesbian. "He would masturbate in front of people, call me a whore and a bitch in public, and tell people he was going to rape me," Terry recalled. "At one party he came up behind me and threw himself on top of me, pinning me to the floor. He was a vicious sadistic type. . . . I would never *think* of going to bed with someone like that."

But Terry wasn't exactly genteel herself. After she got drunk one night and ripped into Caccia with her nails and teeth, she found herself passed off to Giorgio Rotti, a pudgy jewelry store owner who drove around in a Mercedes, stored the cocaine he served at parties in an emptied can of beer, and manufactured the little spoons, vials, and straws that were necessary accoutrements for hip cokeheads.

She'd become a toy to be passed from hand to hand. "I sold my soul to them for drugs, and they treated me like a prostitute," she said. Terry Broome was "fucking everybody," a friend of Rotti's agrees. "She had no work, so she started living the life. She got lost. Rotti gave her a fuck. If you didn't get lucky, you gave her a fuck." Though Rotti told her he'd heard the rumors she was a lesbian, he had her move in with him in June. Within a week he was financing her test pictures, giving her jewelry, and taking her to meet his parents, introducing her as his fiancée. "I understood that she was a girl who needed love," Rotti later said.

Late in June Broome spent several coke-fueled days and nights with Rotti. They used five grams in three sleepless days and nights and showed no signs of letting up. On the third night of their run Terry and Rotti met Donna and Sant'Ambrogio at Caffè Roma, a bar owned by Beppe Piroddi, another playboy. When Francesco D'Alessio walked in, they got up and left for Nepenta.

D'Alessio was in a particularly foul mood. The day before he'd called his wife in Rome, begged her to come back, and been rebuffed. Now he turned up again at Nepenta. After he approached Broome's table and feigned masturbating again, Terry fled to the bathroom. D'Alessio approached Rotti and Sant'Ambrogio. "Why, when the girls go out with Rotti, don't they want to fuck me anymore?" he asked. Rotti and D'Alessio almost came to blows before the party broke around 2:00 A.M.

Back at Rotti's apartment at the Principessa Clitoris, Terry was furious. "I had done some party scenes," she admitted, but never with six men at once. Then Rotti turned on her, demanded the return of an engagement ring and necklace he'd given her. He went to bed. She sat up doing a crossword puzzle, snorting coke, drinking vodka, and brooding. At 5:00 A.M., she went looking for a battery-operated video game in Rotti's closet. She found more coke and a chrome-plated five-shot Smith & Wesson Chief Special .38-caliber pistol. "It was irresponsible of Giorgio to leave a gun and bullets around his house," says Pucci Albanese. "He is the only one to blame for what happened. You cannot get stoned and go to bed with a girl you've only met two or three times and leave a gun around."

But he had. And now Terry decided to "straighten things out" with D'Alessio. "I only wanted to frighten him," she said.

D'Alessio was at home with a model named Laura Royko when his phone rang. It was Terry, but she called herself Diane and asked if she could come over. Stopping along the way to sniff coke from Rotti's fake Vicks inhaler, she reached D'Alessio's apartment and found Royko drunk and her tormentor sniffing coke. Turning some down, she went to the bathroom and did some of her own. When she returned, the suave D'Alessio asked if she'd have sex with him. With that, she pulled out her gun and started shooting the six-foot-three playboy at point-blank range. Two of her five shots hit him—in the head and chest. Royko, hiding in another room, started screaming. After failing to calm her, Terry ran back to Rotti and woke him up. It was 7:30 A.M. Rotti checked his gun, found five empty cartridges, and quickly hustled Terry to the airport, where he put her on a flight to Switzerland.

Upstairs Carlo Cabassi got the news from Laura Royko. He sent a servant, who returned to inform him that D'Alessio was lying on the floor. Rushing to his friend's side, Cabassi heard "the death rattle" and saw "on the table a paper carton with cocaine," he later testified. "I threw the cocaine in the toilet." He said he wanted to protect his friend's memory. Milanese authorities later charged that Cabassi also took D'Alessio's diary.

Later that day Terry Broome was arrested in Zurich's Bahnpost Hotel and immediately confessed that she had shot D'Alessio "because he treated me in a vulgar way." After months of imprisonment and questioning, a court-ordered psychiatric study said that she was impaired on drugs at the time of the shooting. Nonetheless, eleven months later she was indicted for premeditated murder. Cabassi, Rotti, and Caccia were also charged with various offenses, the most serious that Cabassi had obstructed justice by stealing D'Alessio's diary.

Broome's trial was held in June 1986. It was a public sensation, and Milan's newspaper, *Corriere della Sera,* printed daily transcripts. The three playboys were described as "pallid and a little fat." They refused to look at Terry, who was confined in a steel cage throughout the trial. With her mother and sister in court, Broome took the stand and said, "I confirm that it was I who killed Francesco." Cabassi called his friend "a little like Dr. Jekyll and Mr. Hyde." Tennis players at D'Alessio's club said that the gestures he'd made at Terry were a nervous hand twitch. D'Alessio's father called his son "a gentle boy, always lucid, all there, nice." Rotti testified in dark glasses, his shirt open to reveal a chest full of gold chains. "Do you consider this a normal way to live?" the judge snapped at him.

"These are people who use women as objects and display them like trophies," Terry's lawyer said in his plea for mercy. "She is more destroyed than the other person." The jury apparently agreed, finding Broome guilty of voluntary homicide—a lesser charge—after eight hours of deliberation. She was sentenced to fourteen years in prison. "I've met better people in prison than I met outside," she said. Cabassi, acquitted of obstruction of justice, received a suspended sentence of twenty-one months for cocaine possession. Rotti was also convicted on various charges and received a suspended sentence.

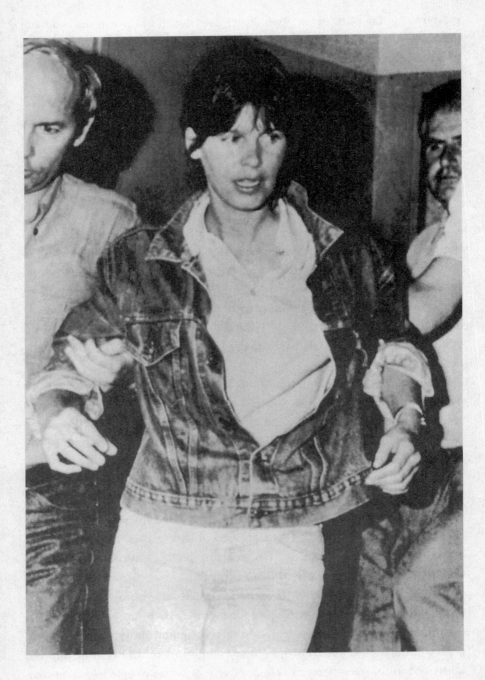

Terry Broome photographed while being extradited
to Italy in 1984

Outside the courtroom Donna Broome proved she'd learned something about agentry in her years as a model. "You want to speak to Terry?" she asked a reporter. "If you really want to, you have to pay. Money. We have lots of expenses. Terry needs things. There are already a pair of offers being considered. Call my boyfriend. Speak to him. . . . Money for the exclusive. Otherwise, nothing."

A year later, in an appeal, Broome's sentence was reduced and Caccia was given amnesty. Terry was released from prison and returned to America in 1992.

Today many modeling professionals dismiss her as a wannabe and a victim. "She was not a model," says Giorgio Sant'Ambrogio. "And this accident changed nothing. The same things happened all over the world, but when it happens in the model business, it's news. Anywhere else nobody gives a shit. Ten years ago drugs were used like cigarettes. If something changed, it's that drugs aren't in anymore. Twenty years ago elite people used drugs. Now drugs are used by my butler and maid."

"It was just a scandal, not a change," says Riccardo Gay.

But in fact, Broome was a watershed. Milan's playboy high life had been laid low. "They were like slobs, they were getting careless and sloppy, and it was not funny anymore," says John Casablancas. "You know how these situations with drugs usually degenerate. It starts as a casual, sexy, trendy thing to do, and it ends up being vulgar. I saw Cabassi go from funny to disgusting. I think they felt they were above the law and above ethics. I avoided these people like hell. But probably this thing saved a lot of lives with those *Milano per bene* boys."

In truth Milan had stood up and said no to the rot. "Public opinion stood on Terry's side against this bourgeoisie type of life," says Giuseppe Piazzi. "Terry became a hero," adds his wife, Patrizia. "The Terry Broome affair pointed a finger at something that had been evolving for a long time."

"Terry paid a price for a lot of victims in Milan," Donna Broome says. "She was the one who exploded. In a way it straightened the whole city out. There was a big difference in the way people looked at models and treated models afterwards."

Carlo Cabassi, for one, never wanted to see another model again. Following the shooting of his tenant and friend D'Alessio, he divested his interests in both the Paris Planning and Riccardo Gay agencies. "The lawyers suggested Cabassi get rid of his shares," says Massimo Tabak. "At this point it's easy for Mr. Gay to get the shares back—probably for nothing." John Casablancas agrees with Tabak's analysis. "Every time I see Riccardo, he's collected a few more hundred million lire to sell his agency. Then I come back six months later, and whoever bought the business is out and he bought them for peanuts. It's his specialty to sell his agency to people, fuck everything up, get the agency back, rebuild it, and then resell it. I think that he's done that four times." With the proceeds he settled down with a new wife and children.

"That was a time of life that hurt Riccardo very much," says Pucci Albanese. "He's very, very Catholic now."

Paris Planning Faubourg St.-Honoré outlived François Lano's Paris Planning agency—but not by much. Its partners were fighting even before Cabassi quit. The ubiquitous lawyer Jean-Marie de Gueldre says Dollé found himself in the middle of a conflict between Marie and Cabassi. The problem? "Cabassi invests and Gérald spends," de Gueldre says. "So after two years they decided to separate."

Cabassi sold his share in Paris Planning for a reported $300,000 to a woman identified as Joan Forbach, about whom little else is known by those few who are even willing to talk about her. "She never got the papers we call a *statut* in France, which proves who the partners are in a firm," says Servane Cherouat. When she realized, she telephoned Jérôme Bonnouvrier, "hysterical," and claiming her money had been stolen, he says. Finally, after six months of fighting with Gérald Marie, she put her stake in the agency up for sale and began writing accusatory letters "to everyone in Paris, even the president of France," says Paris Planning's lawyer, de Gueldre. "I got phone calls from my bank administrators, telling me that she said I was the king of sex and drugs." She also apparently alleged that model agencies in Paris were systematically avoiding taxes through their Swiss agencies.

"It was a very troubled time," says Bonnouvrier. Dollé and Marie "were fighting over everything," he adds. "Gérald was taking more and more power, and he started to do the same thing François Lano did," says Gaby Wagner, then a Paris Planning model. "He started taking the Concorde, went on vacation, had houses on the company, invited people." Finally Dollé "didn't want to work there anymore," says Cherouat. He started yet another agency but kept his share of Paris Planning.

Luckily John Casablancas's old school chum Alan Clore wanted in. He bought into Paris Planning, but it turned out to be an empty shell. "Clore bought an agency that was not worth anything," says Giselle Bonnouvrier.

In summer 1985 rumors were rife that Gérald Marie was about to start his own agency. He came to New York and talked to Monique Pillard and a top booker at Wilhelmina about opening a New York office. Then came a surprising offer. Ever since John Casablancas had moved to New York in 1977, Elite's Paris operation had suffered. "The heart, the soul of Elite had left," says Francesca Magugliani. "By 1983 there was nobody running the place."

Two years later Paris Planning had surpassed Elite in profitability. "Gérald had very few models; but they were very good, and he asked any price he wanted," says Francesca. "He had no expenses. His structure was very good; he had very good bookers who he paid a hell of a lot of money, all young, ambitious. Alain Kittler got drift of this."

Seeking to shore up their Paris operation, John Casablancas's principal partner soon found himself in the surprising position of talking to their sworn enemy. Kittler and Marie first met on Ibiza, an island off Spain where Elite's backer owned property. "We started talking about this business," Kittler says. "I saw that we had the same idea on the management and general direction, and so we met again in Paris, in September, and I officially asked [for] Gérald['s hand] in marriage sometime in October." Kittler offered Marie an equity stake in Elite.

Initially Casablancas was outraged. "I knew too much about the guy that I didn't like," he says. "But he was a good agent. So we had some lengthy conversations, and I told Gérald that there were two things that I would not accept from him as a partner. A lot of girls were complaining that he was rough, that he wasn't nice, that he used his position." Somehow, Casablancas's objections were overcome.

One night during the negotiation Casablancas called Elite's office on the Champs-Élysées from New York to talk with Francesca Magugliani. "At the end of the conversation he said, 'How would you feel about working with Gérald?' I said, 'That's ridiculous. Why?' He said, 'I was just asking.' " Francesca remembered the time that Elite New York's Monique Pillard had received Gérald Marie in her office. "John was furious," says Francesca. "He said, 'If models see Gérald in Monique's office, they could think we have something to do with him. He's a sleaze. He beats up girls. He rapes them. He takes coke.' That was one year before!"

Early in 1986 Gérald Marie became a one-third partner and director of a restructured and recapitalized Elite Paris, relocated in large new offices on the Avenue de l'Opéra. Francesca wasn't the only one upset by Marie's arrival. "We nearly had a nervous breakdown," says April Ducksbury of London's Models One. "Gérald had the most horrible reputation—just a ruthless little barbarian. John had the ideas, the creativity, the charisma. John gave the glamour to the whole thing. Gérald was a poor imitation and not a nice person. We wouldn't want to send our models there. We knew that we couldn't work with him. But John knew that he was another John."

"Clearly, they hired Gérald to replace John, and John was brilliant with that," says Jérôme Bonnouvrier. "He didn't interfere. That was the comeback of Elite in Paris."

There was some sensitivity surrounding Marie's arrival, however. "To mix all the employees, all the models, everything all of a sudden, that might be dangerous," Kittler admits. So Marie was given his own division, dubbed Elite Plus, and quartered in a room of its own. Its assets consisted of all of the models and several bookers from Paris Planning-Faubourg St.-Honoré. To raise the money to buy his stake in Elite, "Gerald sold a shell to Alan Clore: the name Paris Planning and the space," says John Casablancas. "But the company was totally empty, gutted by Gérald," says Olivier Bertrand, a onetime garment executive who briefly tried to resurrect it. In the six months that followed, Clore lost FF 2 million. "Clore wanted girls," Bertrand continues, "and that's part of the reason the girls left. God knows what else was happening." When Bertrand forced the issue, Clore shut the company down.

With a financial settlement, Bertrand opened Success, now the top men's agency in Paris. Indeed, all the children of Paris Planning (and of Elite, Harlé, Models International, and Euro-Planning) were opening agencies of their own. Henceforth they would spring up like mushrooms after a rain. Of the pioneers of modeling, only Eileen and Jerry Ford remained, and more and more they were seen as anachronisms—still powerful but irrelevant. The past was dead. Few models knew or cared who Dorian Leigh or Lisa Fonssagrives were. Says booker Marcella Galdi, who left Riccardo Gay and opened her own agency, too: "Certain moments, when it's finished, it's finished."

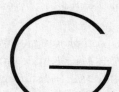érald Marie had conquered
Paris. It was his town now—not John Casablancas's. His reputation as a sexual athlete had, by all accounts, also surpassed the prodigious legend of Elite's founder. By the early eighties Marie was no longer just bouncing from model to model in a manner that stunned even the jaded bed-hoppers of Paris; now he also always had a model to call his own. If before, he'd alluded to work in exchange for sexual favors, by his last days at Paris Planning he'd upped the ante. He promised his girlfriends he'd make them stars. And he did it, too.

Casablancas had long been a proponent of the theory that models were raw stones that needed work to become glittering diamonds. "European men are important abrasives in the finishing process; they tend to be male chauvinists," he'd said. "That attitude . . . gives the model an awareness of her femininity, which is an indispensable quality." But in Casablancas's day that service was provided by the playboys who surrounded the agents. By the time Gérald Marie joined Elite, the sexual polishing process was more often conducted in-house. "He's a good lay, I'm sure of that," says François Lano. "I've heard it from all of them."

Marie says his first serious romance was with the Australian-born model named Lisa Rutledge. They lived together for five years and had a daughter, but domestic life did not domesticate him. "Gérald wanted to fuck the girls," says Jacques Silberstein. "His way was, if you want to work, fuck me." Some models left Paris Planning for Fabienne Martin's agency FAM, claiming that "if they were not having sex with him, he wouldn't take care of them," Martin says. "I don't know whether it was true or not. Some girls could say that because they're not good enough, or they're not doing well, or they just say [it] because he's a flirt."

Two internal Elite memos dated June 3, 1986, indicate that similar rumors quickly became a concern to Marie's new partners at Elite. The first, from Trudi Tapscott, head of Elite's new faces division in New York, to Casablancas, detailed charges leveled against Marie. Carré Otis (who later gained fame when she married and broke up with actor Mickey Rourke) said she was "sick of Gérald and all the drugs and all the women," and charged that he would call her "at all hours of the night [4:00 A.M.]," asking her to come see him.

"It wasn't only Carré Otis; everybody was complaining," says an Elite executive. Casablancas sent Tapscott's memo on to Alain Kittler and Marie. In a cover note he expressed astonishment at this "very disturbing turn of events," "a very nasty business and exactly the type of thing we do not need to have at Elite. . . . This type of rumor must cease at once," he concluded, "and I ask Gérald to be extremely cautious in the future."

But Marie wasn't being careful. Indeed, by American legal standards, he was committing statutory rape on a regular basis at that time. Just before he made the move to Elite, Lisa Rutledge was out of Marie's life—out of Paris altogether, in fact—and Christine Bolster, a California blonde, was in. Rutledge moved to New York in 1985. "I just left," she says. "It was a mutual decision. Our relationship was over."

"Poor Lisa was a fantastic girl," says Servane Cherouat. "Gérald Marie was really a very bad man. I saw Gérald ask a girl to take a line [of cocaine]. All the people at Paris Planning with Gérald smoked joints and laughed at me because I didn't want this. One day I saw a terrible girl, awful, and Gérald said, 'Make a three-year contract at thirty thousand francs a month.' Eight days later he said, 'Cancel it.' I told him to discuss it with her father. Gérald Marie took girls on only to go to bed with them. Christine Bolster was fifteen. *Fifteen!*"

In fact, she was only fourteen when she came to Paris and began sleeping with Gérald Marie. She ended up living with him for six years, before another model, Linda Evangelista, did to her what she'd done to Lisa Rutledge.

"She is very happy!" Marie says when asked about Bolster. "She is very happily married, she has two kids, and she's very balanced, very organized. She's a woman with a lot of charm and a lot of temper. She told me at the time she was modeling because I was a model agent. She was never crazy about modeling. She was only doing the pictures she liked to do with Peter Lindbergh and people like that. I was with Christine for a long time until I

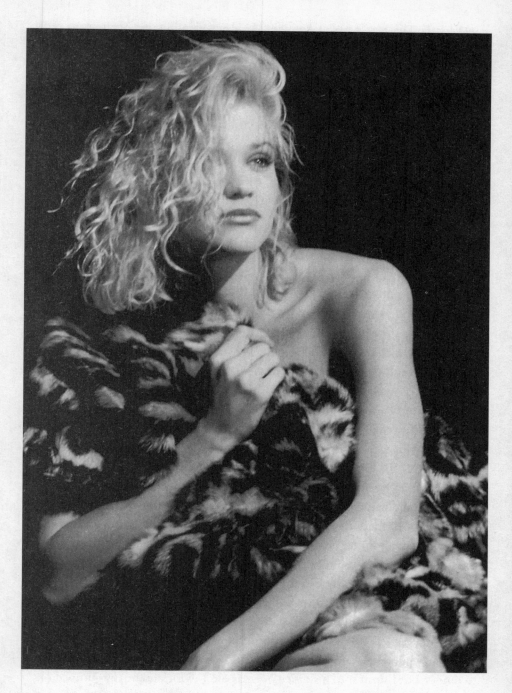

Christine Bolster photographed by Jake Crain

met Linda. That was when it stopped. The day we quit being together she quit the business; she went back to California."

Some of that turns out to be true. Bolster is, indeed, married—to actor Robert Davi, best known for his portrayals of craggy-faced villains in films like *Die Hard* and *License to Kill*—and the mother of two children. They live in a suburban house near Los Angeles. And Christine Davi does indeed seem very happy. At least, until Gérald Marie's name is mentioned. Then her face clouds, and her voluptuous yet stick-thin frame tenses visibly.

"I stick pins into a voodoo doll of him," she whispers, launching into the tale of what can hardly be called their romance.

"I was fourteen and a half when I started modeling. We lived in Palo Alto. I was riding my bicycle one day, and I got pulled over by this white Jaguar. I thought, Oh, God, another schmuck, but this guy was a talent scout at a place called American Models. They were a little shady, but that's nothing that shocks anybody anymore. They were having a contest. The prize was to go to Paris. I ended up winning, and that was the last I heard of them. Five days later I was on the plane to Paris with a list of agencies, by myself. I left California for three months, but I didn't go home again for a year and a half.

"The first agency on my list was Paris Planning, and they took me, right away. François Lano had just exited. It was all just sort of settling itself. Gérald took me. It was like, 'Here's your *Plan de Paris,* and your list of go-sees,' and I still had my luggage. At first I shared an apartment with two other models, one who did OK for herself and another, I forget what her name was, who was there for three weeks and then she was gone. Disappeared.

"I had long hair, and Gérald sent me to cut it. My first job was with Italian *Vogue.* I'd been there three days. I go to Italy, I come back, I have go-sees the following day, a job the next, and it progressed. It was so sudden; it happened so fast. Overnight I was in incredible demand. I was overwhelmed. A few days before, I'd been riding my bicycle to school!

"Then suddenly I found myself moving into an apartment in Les Halles that Gérald Marie paid for. It all started about two weeks after I got there, at the agency actually. I was very surprised. You kind of get a feeling when someone's interested and you're interested. So I was waiting for him to ask me to dinner, but I went into his office one day after work, and he just jumped on me. I was so shocked. There was no way that he was going to get turned down. It was like I had no choice!

"I knew what I was getting myself into. I wasn't like the naïve girl from Podunk that came in and got drugged at a party and sold to the Arabs! I had my reasons, you know? Because things were going so well, and he believed in me, and that's really important when you're young, to have someone really have confidence in you. I was smart. I knew that ultimately I was not going to be with this guy. But I didn't know how powerful he was, and so it was a little more serious and involved than I ever expected it to be. But I walked into it because he was an agent, because he could get me what I wanted.

"At first it was a mistress kind of a thing because he was still living on rue Boissière with Lisa [Rutledge] when I met him. Lisa was working and doing well. It was very sudden. It was like, a decision he made, and then she was just gone. He sent her home. They had already had their daughter. I don't know if they were married. There are some things that I couldn't get ahold of and I didn't care about at that point. Later on I would have been a little more interested in that.

"I stayed in rue Boissière after Lisa left. It was an incredible apartment, but it was costing him forty thousand francs a month, so he decided to get rid of it. Then we found a place on rue du Bac. It was an old apartment, with high ceilings, hardwood floors. He had a bathroom built for me there. It was a bedroom before, and its bathroom became the shower, with shower heads coming down from everywhere. The bathtub was in a box that had trees coming out of it. They built a big vanity out of small pieces of glass that took up the entire wall, all lit up.

"I got a Swiss bank account pretty fast. They wanted to make sure you were going to make money. They avoided taxes. I didn't pay. They filtered all your money up through the agency and cleaned it. They were very careful about the girls they chose. They tried to act like they picked you to have [a Swiss account] because you were intelligent and it would be a wise thing to do. They really played this big game with their heads, which is what the Europeans are famous for anyway.

"I got completely screwed over. I never really had much money because it all went into this bank account. It was siphoned off and invested, and when I wanted to buy a house when I was seventeen, I suddenly couldn't come up with the thirty-thousand-dollar deposit, and I said, 'Well, where's my money? I've supposedly got two hundred thousand dollars in Switzerland. Where is it?' Gérald said it takes six months to get any money out of Switzerland. They were making interest on everybody's money.

"I didn't speak a word of French when I got there, but I picked it up very fast. When it has to do with your life, when it's survival, you really pick it up. I always pretended that I couldn't speak French, but I understood everything, which was great, because at these business dinners they would say things about you. Gérald had dinner with some very shady people, and I understood all the business dealings, and he didn't know that I understood. What Gérald didn't do! He had his fingers in everything you could imagine. Agents aren't supposed to be clean, so it's normal, but they do a lot of really sick things, the good ones.

"At first I felt really strong, and I was passionate for taking pictures. I loved taking photographs. I'd never gotten up at five in the morning before—and I couldn't now if you paid me a million dollars—but I did, every day. I would do anything to get where I had to be. It was my life. I ate, slept, drank, breathed modeling—not to the extent that I was only living on water and lettuce, but I went to every single business dinner, every dinner Gérald had with editors and clients.

"He was like God; he gave birth to me. He decided that I was going to be 'big shit.' That's what he used to call me. Big shit. And he did it. He was so sure of himself. He could sell anything to the client. I was so amazed. He would have the client begging him for a girl. He used to turn down jobs, and I would say, 'But I wanted to do that,' and he'd say, 'Just wait, they'll call back.' And he'd ask them for some ridiculous amount of money, and they would call back and pay. I would tell him, 'I want an Italian *Vogue* cover,' and sure enough, the week after, I had it, which was the biggest thrill of my life. We were sort of helping each other, and we were both aware of that. He's making me a star, and I'm making him a star. It went hand in hand.

"Suddenly there I was in the middle of it all! At a very wild time, too. Everybody was doing drugs. We were going straight from work to the night-clubs. Gérald was thriving. He was starting to build up momentum. He's an incredible agent, one of the best in the world as far as I'm concerned. I have a lot of respect for him—that way. But he was not very discreet. He used to do coke in his office, on his desk, with the windows open, right on the rue du Faubourg St.-Honoré. He'd slide his credit card across his nose, and he'd go right out and meet clients like that. He would laugh, and he'd be wiping his nose. He'd do it on the table in La Coupole; he didn't care. He was untouchable as far as he was concerned.

"It was nonstop. It was night and day and continuous. I would do two jobs a day. He worked me until I was almost dead, and then he would book me out for two weeks and send me somewhere and make me rest. He had to keep his investment sound. I was run-down, and I was doing some drugs. Just cocaine; I never got into anything else.

"My parents came to Paris to meet Gérald. He flew them there, which was awkward, because my father looks like my younger boyfriend and Gérald looked ten times older. It was also very awkward because my father gets feelings about people, and he didn't like Gérald right away! I was at this point still enamored of him. Gérald got them out of there as fast as he could. Gérald had asked me to marry him at one point, and I discussed it with my parents, and my father said, 'No way. You can't marry the guy. He's a sleazebag.' They talked me out of it, thank God. I never met his parents. I didn't know if he even had parents. I never even talked to his mother on the phone, which is odd after five years!

"I would say we were happy and together for about two of the six years I was in Paris. Then it got very cold. We didn't really have sex all that often or really wild sex. He was always too tired from running around, which always made me stop and think. And he did so much blow. There was a point when I stopped. I was still with him, but I'd had it. I liked having control over myself. It started to have control over me. It was there all the time. I don't remember a day that I'd open my eyes that there wasn't a plate on the mantelpiece.

"I was very spoiled in a way. I got the highest-paying jobs, I got the best jobs, and he made sure I got good treatment at the studios. They were all intimidated. All the other girls were having to deal with slimebags, but no one went near me, ever. He put out the word, 'This is mine—don't even think about it.' I was basically his fiancée. I had a ring.

"There was a photographer who was one of the bigger sleazeballs in the business. He and his wife would pick up girls together. He had me cornered once. It was 'If you don't do this, you will never work, you will never model.' I told him to get lost, and I told Gérald, and he disappeared. I think that Gérald had something to do with that. He blackballed him.

"Gérald was like a mini-mafioso boss, but in the modeling world. He would get calls in the middle of the night, and he would hear something that someone said about him, and he would say, 'This one is never going to work again.' His ego couldn't handle anyone saying anything about him that was negative or that he didn't want to hear. He wanted everyone to do what he said. He could say, 'Do this with this person by this day,' and it would happen!

"People were very, very nervous to be around me. Certain hairdressers who were dealing with Gérald on another level were very intimidated by me. The girls felt very threatened, too, I'm sure, because I was the queen mother. It made me feel really strange, because I was nice enough. I was quiet, but I would stand up for something if it wasn't right on a booking or someone was treating a model badly, and I would tell a client to go fuck themselves if I was really unhappy. And Gérald would back me up. He would turn it around so it was the client's fault, but girls were very wary of me.

"So I didn't have any friends, and he wanted it like that. I was isolated from everyone except clients. I always felt like there was a million eyes watching me, because he knew everybody, and he spoke to everybody at every job I went to. I couldn't do anything without him knowing. Even shopping. You know when you're just in a bad mood and you want to buy something? He would know the next day exactly how much I spent, what I got, even if it was hiding in the back of my closet. I felt like I was being followed all the time. Probably was! Who knows? I was sixty-three hours a week in the air, traveling, working, going to Milan and Germany. I was on trips, and he was having a great time! He was always out at the Palace, Les Bains, all those big hangouts, constantly. If I was working or I wasn't in town, he would go.

"He'd changed. I think that drugs had a lot to do with it, and the fact that he had as much power as he did. He was overwhelmed by it. He took advantage of it, and he really became sinister. Eventually I started to get a mind of my own. We had a friend named Jean-Marie Marion who was going out with my girlfriend Elle MacPherson, before she met Gilles Bensimon. Jean-Marie was a male model. He was older, rode a motorcycle, very promiscuous guy. He hung around with Gérald. Gérald started not coming home at night.

"They were so promiscuous it got to the point that our freezer was full of shots, the stuff you take when you've got VD—a box of this in our freezer! I, amazingly enough, didn't get anything because I think he gave himself his own shots! I'd walk in, and they'd be bending over the kitchen table with their pants down, and Gérald would jam them, and they would pay him for these shots! Every now and then something like that would happen that would make me sick to my stomach.

"We ended up with separate bedrooms in rue du Bac because he was seeing other people and I'm not stupid. I would find my clothes walking around Paris. Europeans are very discreet about that stuff. But I knew. I approached him saying, 'How come so-and-so has my Azzedine dress on? I know that's my dress because it's missing!' I spent at least a year and a half trying to catch him. I was just dying to catch him because he was so sneaky. He tried to make me feel stupid. He would say, 'But I spent the night in jail,' or some ridiculous story, and Jean-Marie would call and say, 'Yes, it's true,' and back him up on it. I know they discussed it. He told me at one point, 'You will never leave me; I will leave you.' And I said, 'We'll see.'

"Things finally started to slow down. I couldn't leave. I was literally stuck there because I was doing very well, and I really enjoyed what I was doing, and he told me I couldn't leave him [and if I tried] he would make sure that was the end of me. But I was obviously getting bitter, because I was starting to know, and he was lying to me. I never liked anyone to think I was stupid, so I started to talk back to him. I was speaking French a little bit, and he was surprised. Jean-Marie had little pins that he wanted to stick in Gérald sometimes, but [he did it] through me, so that he wouldn't get in trouble. He would teach me slang that there's no way any American would know, and I would practice and then say it, and Gérald would be like, Where did you learn that? The first thing Jean-Marie taught me how to say was the most disgusting thing I'd heard in my life. 'Blow it out the veins of your ass.' I said it to Gérald at a dinner with the girls from Italian *Vogue,* and he turned red and then white. You didn't do that stuff to him. My nickname, by the way, was *Casse-couille,* which means 'ball breaker.'

"He never laid a finger on me. And I did everything to deserve it, because I couldn't stand looking at him by that point, which was hard, because it's very exhausting to hate someone, you know? You have the same business, the same interests, and I basically had all of his friends like Peter Lindbergh and André Rau, who was Lindbergh's assistant at one point before he started to become a photographer. He was Linda Evangelista's first boyfriend and Gérald's best friend.

"I went on Linda's first trip with her, which I thought was kind of strange because she had longer hair and a long skinny nose and glasses, and I thought she was such a dog and André was the most disgusting person in the world, German, full of pimples, fat and greasy and slimy. I could never understand what she saw in him. But he was a photographer. She knew what she wanted, and she was going to get it, too.

"I'd started to work in America. I didn't have an American agency for a long time, and then I went with Eileen. She got me bookings, a couple of commercials. I was with them for about a year, and then I went with Elite just as the transaction was happening in Europe with Elite Plus and Paris Planning. I remember first meeting John Casablancas at the collections in Rome in 1985 at a dinner. John and Gérald were enemies. They were in competition

for having the reputation for being a womanizer, and they were in competition for having the best agency. Gérald always said that he was going to be bigger and better than John Casablancas.

"I was going to start going back and forth between Paris and New York.
Gérald got me an apartment there. I'd moved most of my stuff there. Unfortunately I had a lot of Erté pieces that he kept. They weren't there when I
came back to get the rest of my stuff. They didn't know I was back in Paris. I
got on a plane myself. I finagled Monique Pillard to give me an advance to get
a ticket back, and there was no way he could find out that I had arrived. I got
in the apartment. Gérald was at work. He didn't know I was there, and I was
digging through the closet, and I found photographs of him and Linda on
vacation with Cookie [Marie's daughter by Lisa Rutledge]. He didn't try to
hide them. They were just in a box in a closet.

"I just thought, *Finally.* It was such a relief that I'd finally caught him. I'd
put up with so many of his stupid alibis because he had three people vouch-
ing for him. I always hated his friends for doing that. I hate it when people kiss
ass and then turn around and they're bad to you. Finally I had proof. And ten
minutes after I found them, Linda walked in, with a key. I couldn't believe it.
I thought, Just the person I want to see.

"I said, 'So, what's going on? And she said, 'Well, I guess it's obvious, isn't
it?' I was so angry. I said, 'I want you to get out until I get the rest of my stuff
packed up.' It was pissing rain, and she said, 'But I don't want to go wait in
the rain.' She was just beside herself. She's very whiny. I can't stand her. She
waited outside for hours, and then she went to the agency and she told him I
was there. I was trying to get everything else that I had there. I ended up staying two days. I'd been there for years!

"When he came home that evening, I had the door locked. He knew I was
leaving because Linda had told him I was packing. He was pounding on the
door. His ego was tremendous. He said no one would ever believe that I left
him. The world would think that he left me. He said, 'You will never get away
with this! In New York you'd better take care, and don't walk past too many
dark alleys.' He basically threatened me. He slept in the hallway that night,
because I wouldn't open the door. I was scared, too. I didn't know if he had a
gun or what he was going to do. I knew a lot of things he did at this point. I'd
sat in on a lot of the dinners that he didn't think I understood.

"I sort of died when I left Paris. I lost all desire to create, and New York
didn't help any, because it was the nine-to-five grind, and it was so cold, and
my apartment there was the dingiest place. I fell in love with someone on the

rebound in New York. A model. He listened to every trouble that I ever had in five years. I sobbed and I wept, and he listened, which is what I really needed, because I had no one to talk to. I was guarded and I felt safe because I moved in with him right away, like after six days.

"I was working, but I wasn't enjoying it at all. Gérald had stolen my *joie de vivre*. I stopped showing up for bookings. I was depressed. I was broke. I had no idea, to tell you the truth, how much money I should have had in my Swiss bank account. I never kept track. I trusted him, you know? And then there was nothing I could do to get the information together. My mom flew to Paris to talk to Jean-Pierre Dollé, and she came home just raging. My money was gone, but I couldn't prove it, because you don't have any records for a Swiss bank account. It's in the agency's name.

"A couple days after I met my boyfriend, I met a lady in New York who was an agent at Zoli, and she believed in me. She was into crystals and that kind of stuff, and she told me that I was a witch, and she got me into this whole voodoo doll thing. She said, 'You can slowly torture Gérald.' I had venom for this guy. It wasn't the things he was into or that he cheated on me. It's because he basically ruined my life.

"I saw Linda once more in the agency in New York. She walked in when I was there, and I turned around and I looked at her, and she started to cry and she ran into Monique Pillard's office, and I never saw her again. Monique said that I was being terrible to her, threatening her. But I didn't say a word. I just looked at her! And she freaked out!

"I didn't trust Elite New York for a second. Gérald obviously had a lot of control over my bookings in New York, because he was now affiliated with Elite New York. Monique was trying to take me to dinner because she could see that my work was suddenly disappearing, and she didn't know if it was because of him or because of me, because I wasn't turning up on bookings and they were having to pay cancellation fees.

"The truth is, I was so depressed that I just couldn't get up in the morning. Everything that I enjoyed he had control over still. I was exhausted, and anything to do with modeling made me think about him, and I just wanted to forget about him. Finally I came out to California to get some sunshine and rest and relaxation. But I started doing drugs again for about a year because I wasn't working and I wanted to work, and I had fucked it up, and clients didn't trust me. Capucine, who is with Elite here, is one of my dearest friends. She broke down my door one day with an ax to get me to a booking for a Vidal Sassoon commercial. She knew what I was going through.

"I suffered a lot, and I still don't trust people, and I don't let a lot of people in. I keep to myself. I go out with my husband. I met Robert Davi in 1989. I was dating a friend of his, Mickey Rourke, who invited me to this guy's house who had a karaoke machine, and we were singing along, and Robert was there. We shook hands, and he told Mickey on their way out the door that he was going to marry me someday. About three weeks later I get this job, which was strange, because I wasn't really modeling anymore, I was doing one job every two weeks. But it was for *GQ,* and it was with Robert, and he had requested me on the shoot. He asked me to marry him on the shoot. I had only known him for twenty minutes! I said, 'Ask me again in a week.' We fell in love right away.

"Modeling was my life for six and a half years, twenty-four hours a day, and I loved every second of it. I have to thank Gérald for that, but that's why I dislike him so much, because he took that away from me. I have a completely different life now. I can't believe it sometimes. I have two children of my own, and Robert has a son from a previous marriage who's thirteen, who breaks my balls! But I feel really clean now.

"I'm just amazed I survived!"

$10,000 A DAY

"I'm not a morning person," Christy Turlington said in apology as she strolled into Superstudio Industria, the fashion photo factory in New York's Greenwich Village just after nine one frigid morning in December 1991. Turlington had been booked for a three-day job, posing for an Anne Klein ad campaign consisting of a dozen studied, glamorous black-and-white pictures by photographer Stephen Klein. Then twenty-three, she was chosen to exemplify classic American beauty. For doing that, she would earn about $60,000 in seventy-two hours. A sum well worth waking up for.

Stripping off a mustard-colored jacket, beige Italian jeans, a white shirt, a scarf, white socks, and black suede Chanel ballet flats, she tried on several outfits over a little lacy bra, white bikini panties, and thousands of goose bumps. Between changes, Garren, a hairstylist, gave her a blunt trim, and makeup whiz Kevyn Aucoin worked on her face, chattering about lipsticks, movies, and models. He did most of the talking. Turlington's task was to sit still while others made her beautiful. Not that she was so bad to begin with. But three hours after she arrived in the studio, she'd blossomed, becoming, as Aucoin cooed in her ear, "the beauty of the earth."

"Thanks, kid," Christy said, brightening.

"I was gonna say the universe," Aucoin went on.

Christy spun around in her chair, her feline eyes widening. "Bigger!" she shouted.

"Bigger!" Aucoin declared. "The most beautiful *anything* there is!"

Christy Turlington was at the top of her profession, one of that small, special band of young women known as the supermodels. Remote confections of cultured image and cherished dreams, she and colleagues like Cindy Crawford, Paulina Porizkova, Linda Evangelista, Naomi Campbell, Elaine Irwin, Tatjana Patitz, Yasmeen Ghauri, Karen Mulder, and Claudia Schiffer had come to epitomize modern beauty and grace. They seemed to be in charge of their lives and their careers.

They'd even remade the ideal of perfection. No longer was it necessary to have a belly like a washboard or skin as white as snow. While Irwin, Patitz, and Mulder all are classic blondes, more than half the supermodels, including Turlington, had dark hair. Some even had dark skin. Crawford has a mole near her lip; Campbell, a scar on her nose. Evangelista is scrawny; Schiffer is strapping.

Supermodels were rich in more than their fortuitous conjunctions of flesh and bone. Like Crawford, who'd become Revlon's principal contract face, and Porizkova, who represented Estée Lauder, Turlington was an "image" model. She'd been the face of Calvin Klein's Eternity fragrance since 1988 and had just signed a new contract to represent Maybelline cosmetics. As that company's symbol Turlington was projected to earn about $800,000 a year for twelve days of work selling makeup. Escalators in her contract, governing geographic areas where her photos could be used, appearances in additional non-makeup assignments, and separate photo usage fees, created the potential for even more income. A million dollars a year was a lipstick trace away.

And that was peanuts compared to what companies had come to believe they could earn by using supermodels. The theory went that image leads to income. "It's like buying a Gucci bag," says Milanese model agent Marcella Galdi. "You show the world you have the money. Especially for an unknown company, you show the world that small as you are, you have the twenty thousand dollars."

Turlington's Maybelline contract was state-of-the-art. Despite the fortune being paid her, she was allowed to continue to work for magazines, for clothing companies like Anne Klein, Michael Kors, and Chanel, for Calvin Klein, who had her under contract as his Eternity fragrance model, and for any designer who could afford to send her stalking the runway in fashion's seasonal selling rituals. Each of the elite young supermodels was regularly raking in anywhere from $3,000 to $10,000 per runway show. Turlington's agents at Ford Models estimated her 1992 income at about $1.7 million. "We completely reinvented the whole money thing, we make a ridiculous amount of money," Christy admits. But it is more than money that sets her apart from the mannequin pack.

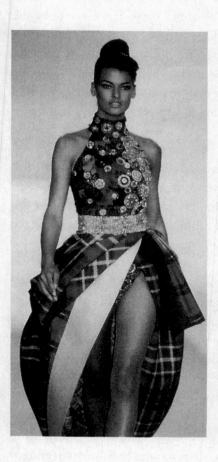

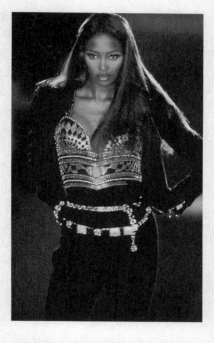

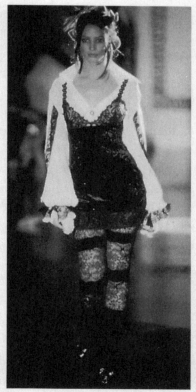

Linda Evangelista
(*above*), Naomi Campbell
(*top right*), and Christy
Turlington (*bottom right*)
in Versace couture,
photographed by Dan
Lecca

"She's a very rare girl," says photographer Bruce Weber, who is best known for his Calvin Klein and Ralph Lauren ads. "She can give herself up totally to the situation, whereas a lot of girls say, 'What'll this picture do for me?' Christy has done more great photos for little money than most models. Most of them are worried about how much they'll make. She wants to be able to look back and say, 'I did great work.' "

As Aucoin penciled and shaped Turlington's pussycat eyes, Stephen Klein came into the dressing room and silently studied her, his basset hound eyes obscured behind blue-tinted sunglasses. Forty-five minutes were spent placing, then re-placing a birthmark, first beside her eye, then higher, then lower.

"Put it in my ear," Christy said.

"I'll put it on the tip of your tongue," Aucoin threatened.

Finally, just before 1:00 P.M., Christy stepped before the camera for the first time. Klein shot a couple of Polaroids, then had Aucoin soften her makeup. Forty-five minutes later Klein finished his first shot and called a break for food. Turning up her nose at the catered health food lunch, Christy ordered from a Chinese menu. "Fried kitten paws?" Aucoin joked.

"Shish-ka-dog," Christy said.

Before her food arrived, the team knocked off another shot, and Anne Klein's then designer Louis Dell'Olio arrived, full of praise for his supermodel. A resolutely regular guy, he explained that Christy was right for all the wrong reasons. In an era when too many models had become as lofty as the Concordes they flew on, Christy was humble and down-to-earth. "She's a real person," Dell'Olio said. "No attitude. With models, when you get 'em in a group, they're not sweet. But not with her. No matter what, she's sweet."

Born in 1969, Turlington grew up in a suburb of Oakland, California, the middle daughter of a Pan Am pilot and an ex-stewardess of Salvadoran extraction. The Turlingtons moved to Coral Gables, Florida, when Christy was ten years old. She never gave a thought to fashion. Her mother had to force her to look at *Seventeen* to spruce up her look. She was more interested in the horse her father bought her. She rode competitively, training every day after school at a local farm.

She was riding the day she was discovered by a local photographer. Dennie Cody was shooting photos of two of her schoolmates, aspiring actresses, when he spotted fourteen-year-old Christy and her older sister, Kelly. "Christy was sitting straight and tall in the saddle," Cody says. "I knew right away. You don't run across many girls you know can make it to the top."

Christy was excited. But she already knew to play hard to get. Cody recalls her as "taken aback . . . reticent . . . skeptical." A family meeting and several phone calls ensued. "I had a long talk with Christy's mother," Cody says. "I told her the only limitation would be her motivation." Finally Elizabeth Turlington agreed and took her girls to Cody's studio.

"He had a couple really sleazy pictures on the wall," Christy says. "Some nudes. I was like, *God*!" But Cody's wife worked with him, so Christy decided to go ahead. "He took ridiculous portraits with a lot of makeup. I was really quiet," she says. "He was really positive I was going to be a star." She wasn't so sure. "I'd watched *Paper Dolls* on TV. I thought this is probably what they all say." She had braces on her teeth and long, curly hair, and she'd always thought her sister was cuter, more outgoing, and more popular than she. Unfortunately Kelly was five feet six inches. Christy was five feet eight inches.

Cody told the Turlingtons about how model agencies worked, the big New York firms using local firms as feeders, the equivalent of baseball's farm team system. "The only one I'd heard of was Ford," Christy says, so she went to see Michele Pommier, an ex-model who was then associated with Ford.

"I said she was going to be a major star," Pommier recalls. "They laughed. She was so shy. She didn't know what was going on." That changed soon enough. "My mom must've gotten excited," Christy says. "She started buying me new clothes for testing. I wouldn't imagine her making the investment just for the fun of it."

Cody never saw the Turlingtons again. After a brief period of testing in 1983—making pictures with various local photographers—Christy put together a portfolio and a composite and began to earn back her mother's investment, modeling after school for $60 a hour. Liz Turlington went everywhere with her daughter, "but she wasn't a stage mom," Pommier says. "I have mothers you could string up. She was just a doll. Always in the background, watching out."

When the head of Karins, Ford's associated agency in Paris, came to Miami, Pommier called Christy in, announced that of course, the big agencies would want her but then decided they couldn't have her. "She's not available," Pommier said. "She's too young. Maybe next summer."

In 1984 Dwain Turlington had a heart attack and moved his family back to the San Francisco suburbs. Christy joined the Grimme agency. She took the BART subway system after school to model for Emporium Capwell, a local store chain. "For a hundred dollars an hour!" she says, laughing. "Which was great."

Mostly she kept her career a secret from her schoolmates. But when she made the cover of the fashion section of the San Francisco *Chronicle,* "somebody passed it around in my French class," she recalls. "The teacher grabbed it, made a big deal, ripped it up, and threw it away. I didn't bring it to school! I never in any way brought it up or bragged about it. But I do remember taking advantage a couple of times when I wasn't prepared for a careers class. 'Shit, what can I use? Oh, I'll use my career.' I must have looked like such an idiot, passing my voucher book around."

Karins invited Christy to go to Paris in 1984. Eileen and Jerry Ford came to San Francisco that spring, met Christy for the first time over breakfast in their hotel suite, and approved the plan. Her San Francisco agent was against it. "I never really liked Jimmy Grimme to begin with," Christy says. "When he said, 'I don't think you're ready to go to Paris, I think you should stay around here for a while,' I was like, 'What do you know? I already have an agent in Paris. I'm going.'"

That summer Christy and her mother went to Paris for a month, partly to test the waters and partly as a summer vacation. "I only worked a couple of times," Christy remembers. "I tested a bit. We were in a little hotel. I remember seeing Linda's pictures in French *Vogue* at that time. They were working, all of them." Cindy Crawford was in Paris, as were Linda Evangelista and a teenage model, Stephanie Seymour. "She was there without her mother, and she was starting to see John Casablancas," Christy says. "That's what my mother was afraid of. I didn't meet any slick people at all 'cause I was with my mom."

There was more than one pair of protective eyes watching the fifteen-year-old. When Eileen Ford arrived for the couture shows in July, she made a point of seeing Turlington and her mother and invited them to stop in New York for a week of testing on their way home to San Francisco. A rude surprise awaited Christy there. Ford didn't remember telling her to come to New York. "I'm thinking, obviously she knows that I didn't work, so she changed her mind," Turlington says. "So my mom goes home, and I stay a week, and in that time I see all the magazines, *Vogue, Mademoiselle,* but then my grandmother passed away, so I went home."

Turlington soon left her San Francisco agency. Like many top models who emerged in the eighties, she realized early on that she would have to run her own career. "I always thought Jimmy Grimme was small-time," she says. "I mean, they have classes in his office to show how to do runway walking, and he used to say, 'Walk as if you had a coin between your buns,' and he'd do the old walk that was so ridiculously dramatic. He acted like he knew it all, and I knew that being in San Francisco, which isn't the fashion capital of the world, he couldn't."

She'd met Gary Loftus, an American who'd worked at London's Models One and Askew agencies before returning to San Francisco to open one of his own. "All the girls were with him," Christy says, "and he was a really nice guy." So she switched agencies; under her sweetness was steel. "I did it mostly to piss Jimmy Grimme off," she says. "I hardly worked in San Francisco, so it really didn't make a difference. And he was such a little snot. He complained to Eileen, but it was out of her hands."

After modeling her way through her sophomore year in high school, Christy, sixteen, arrived in New York in summer 1985, moved into the Ford town house, and began making the rounds of magazines and photographers. On her last day in New York the model editor at *Vogue* saw her, liked her, and sent her to Arthur Elgort.

"It was July," Kevyn Aucoin recalls. "A zillion degrees and no air conditioning. Girls sweating their makeup off before I could get it on. Christy was a real trouper. Excited, into it, and very sweet. I get very concerned about girls that young doing this shit. This business is full of people who'll blow wind up your skirts and two weeks later don't know you. But I could tell instantly—I mean, I hoped—she'd keep her sanity and get whatever she wanted."

"It was very glamorous," Christy says. "Arthur was shooting Cheryl Tiegs in this big, beautiful studio. They were drinking champagne, opera music was on, and he took a roll of film on me. I went downstairs and called my booker. She said I was already booked for a week. I was so excited. *Vogue* was a big deal. That made it legitimate."

Christy went back to school in August, but *Vogue* kept calling. In October she was back in France to shoot the collections. She arrived at the Hôtel Crillon in Paris, where Polly Mellen, who was doubling as editor and chaperone, was staying, only to learn she'd arrived a week too early. "So I sat around for about five days," she recalls. The fashion editor of French *Vogue* took her shopping. "And then we flew to Cannes to shoot with Dennis Piel, but I basically sat in a hotel room eating the whole time" because the team on the shoot seemed to prefer the two other models. Finally, on her last day in the south of France, Turlington got a chance to work. "And they were the two great pictures of the whole series," she says.

The photographs appeared in December. Her school friends were blasé. "I hung around with punk rock kids at home, wore black all the time, this totally antifashion thing," she says. "What I was doing was totally ridiculous to my friends." But it was incredibly exciting to her. "I was so naïve." Christy moans. "I sent family Christmas cards to the editors I'd worked with. Like they were my new friends."

It would be another year before Christy's parents allowed her to move to New York on her own, but she was already a working model. She transferred to a professional school that would accommodate her frequent absences as she became a regular commuter between San Francisco and New York, always staying at Eileen Ford's notoriously strict house-cum-model-dormitory. Ford insisted that Turlington stay until she turned eighteen. She still promoted herself as a paragon of virtue. "Who's to teach these children values if we don't?" she asked.

Christy sneaked out. "I was wired in that house," she boasts. "I'd go out all the time, to Palladium, Area. I'd hide a T-shirt downstairs so that if Eileen woke up, I'd be able to say I couldn't sleep and I'd gone downstairs to get a glass of milk. I knew every stair that creaked. I used to smoke and drink beer and champagne in my room."

In December 1986 she quit school and moved into a loft in New York's SoHo. It shared an entrance with one occupied by Eileen Ford's daughter, Katie. "I had a suitcase of clothes, I got a little kitten, and Katie put a bed in my room," Christy says. "That was all I had." A few weeks later her parents arrived with sheets and a TV.

As Turlington was getting started as a model, the unprofessionals of Bitten Knudsen's day were on their way out. "The girls are getting rich, so rich," says fashion editor Polly Mellen, who recalls Kim Alexis casually saying that she was buying an $800,000 apartment. "Yeee gods!" says Mellen. "We're getting into real stardom."

In many ways Paulina Porizkova set the stage for Christy's success. Paulina was born in 1965 in Prostejov, Czechoslovakia. Growing up, she never gave fashion a thought. "Are you kidding?" She laughs. "In Czechoslovakia?" But there was one fashion she wanted desperately: a Communist insignia. "I was dying to be a Pioneer," she says. "Those are the ones wearing the little red scarves. You can't become a Pioneer until fourth grade. I was in a pregroup. I was brainwashed. I was Red from my toes to my head."

Her mother, a teenage secretary, and her father, a truck driver (who says Paulina was actually "kind of an anti-Communist, but a little punk, really"), split for Sweden on a motorbike during the 1968 Russian invasion of Czechoslovakia, leaving Paulina with a grandmother. When the Czechs

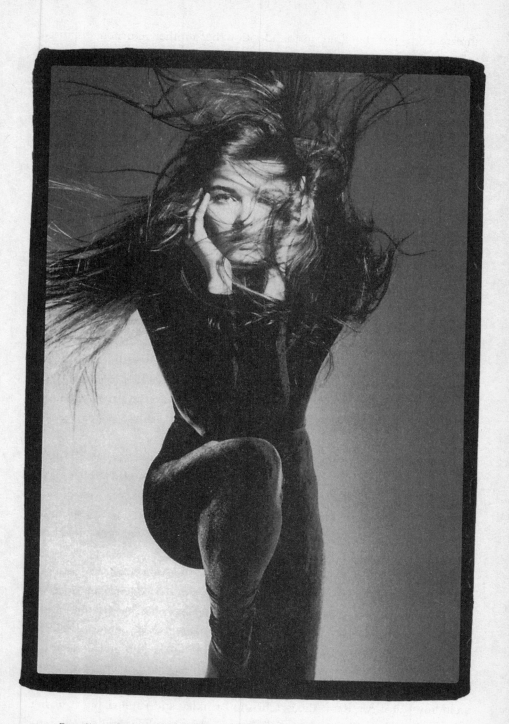

Paulina Porizkova photographed by Marco Glaviano

threatened to put the child up for adoption, her mother returned, disguised, to rescue her. But on her way to rescue Paulina, she was arrested for speeding, and her true identity was uncovered. Paulina's mother spent the next six years in jail and under house arrest. Meanwhile in Sweden Paulina became a Cold War symbol. "Poor political little baby," she says. "Pictures of me hugging my teddy bears saying, 'I want to see my mummy and daddy.' "

Finally the Porizkovas were expelled from Czechoslovakia. "We were too famous to just bump off," Paulina believes. "Our aunt and her husband took us to the border of Austria. There was this long, tall figure: my father, who I basically didn't know. Unbelievable, you know?" Paulina's voice quavers as her story continues. Her father no longer comes up. "I had an awful time because I was a famous political refugee," she says. "I felt terribly sad and everybody told me how ugly I was and my mother was having a nervous breakdown."

Together with a friend who dreamed of being a photographer, Paulina escaped into fantasy. "We copied Estée Lauder ads. We would put me in the foreground and a vase with some old flowers in it and shoot it with a Kodak Instamatic." Her girlfriend sent their photos to a modeling school owner who took Paulina to Copenhagen to see John Casablancas. A month later, in 1980, she was an Elite model in Paris. "It was the biggest whack of freedom I ever got," she says. She wore her TOO DRUNK TO FUCK T-shirt out dancing at night and got up every morning and worked. "When you're fifteen, that's not a problem," she says.

Neither were the other perks that come to teenage models. "You're going to have these old guys knocking down your door and offering you coke. I never . . . it just wasn't my part of life." Being a sex symbol was, though. "I didn't care whether I was known as a face or a body or both," she says. "I couldn't care less as long as it gave me more work and more money. That was just fine with me."

Janice Dickinson had broken the mold. Now Paulina became the first non-blond supermodel. She arrived on the scene just as *Elle* magazine—newly published in America—began regularly running spreads that featured a multiethnic cast. Advertisers like Benetton were starting to do the same. In 1986 Monique Pillard proposed to Paulina that she pose for a pinup calendar.

The Paulina calendar grew out of Pillard's frustration with *Sports Illustrated*'s bathing suit issue. Editor Jule Campbell used a lot of Elite models, including Carol Alt, Kim Alexis, Christie Brinkley, and Paulina, but it wasn't enough for Pillard. "I was always a little annoyed when Jule didn't see potential and I did," the agent says. In 1986 her close friend Marco Glaviano shot a

Paulina calendar. It sold 250,000 copies. The next year the pair released a second Paulina calendar and the first Elite Superstars Swimsuit Calendar. Pillard also started booking her models for tasteful nude spreads in *Playboy* shot by trusted photographers like Glaviano and Herb Ritts. The pictures they produced were far more comprehensible than the images of Patou pouf skirts then prevalent in fashion magazines. "Monique understands what the public wants," says John Casablancas. "And so she produced this kind of populist, sexy, nonfashiony image. And she just touched the right chord. She absolutely deserves credit." Supermodels were here to stay.

The next year—1987—Christy's career went into overdrive. Though she worked with top names like Herb Ritts, Patrick Demarchelier, and Irving Penn, the real source of her new power was her collaboration with the photographer of the moment: Steven Meisel. Meisel looks like a Jewish Cherokee, with thick, straight hair cascading to his shoulders past dark eyes that seem to have been kohled. He has worn only black since leaving high school: black boots, jeans, turtleneck, trench coat, and a do-rag bandanna under a black rabbit hat with flying fur earflaps.

Meisel and a pack of powerful fashion friends have tried to resurrect the cult of the fashion photographer of the sixties, with Steven, Naomi, Christy, and Linda playing updates of Bailey, Twiggy, the Shrimp, and Penelope Tree. Meisel has also been compared to the earlier avatar Avedon, whom he's worshiped since grade school. At first Meisel's work was slavishly imitative of and less intellectual than Avedon's. But Meisel's ambitions have always been different. And his vision is more in tune with this mass-media era than with Avedon's *temps perdu* of an image aristocracy.

"I am a reflection of my times," Meisel has said. More precisely he reflects the paucity of originality in a fashion culture that now slavishly celebrates the past. Meisel plunders and adapts from fashion's memory, not from its collective unconscious. He copies everyone from Horst to Bourdin and poses his models as actresses and mannequins of earlier times. His postmodern samplings are all of a piece with the fin de siècle rag picking that has given humanity the AT&T Building and rap music.

Meisel's unoriginality is an open industry secret. He's considered a sort of rephotographer. "He does a very good job of systematically making a story out of other photographers' styles," says Bert Stern, who once threatened legal action over photographs of Madonna that Meisel copied from Stern's famous 1962 "last sitting" with Marilyn Monroe. In France Jacques

Bergaud, the owner of Pin-Up Studios, dismisses Meisel with the nickname Xerox.

Until he was about twenty-five, Meisel lived at home with his parents in Fresh Meadows, Queens—three blocks south of the Long Island Expressway. He was an indulged child who went with his mother to watch her get her hair done by Kenneth, and he started reading her fashion magazines in the fourth grade. They were his "escape mechanism," he's said. He even cut school—with his mother's permission—to read them the day they were published. "I was obsessed with the magazines, absolutely," Meisel says. "I was totally insane with it." Cheerfully he admits that his interest was "a little peculiar."

In the sixth grade he began using the names of known photographers to pester model agencies for composites. He had friends pose as messengers to get them. He collected them like baseball cards and recalls them with uncanny accuracy. "I had to know who the girls were. What their genius was," he remembers. He lurked outside Richard Avedon's studio in hopes of seeing models arrive. He cut school and hung out at boutiques. When Twiggy came to New York, he called her agency, put on a phony accent, said he had to change a lunch date with her and asked where she was. "Like fools, they [told me]," he says, smirking. Arriving at Melvin Sokolsky's studio, he talked his way past Ali MacGraw and watched as Bert Stern filmed Sokolsky shooting the skinny cockney.

At the High School of Art and Design, Stevan (as he spelled his name) studied fashion illustration and was a member of the Chorus and the Senior Council of the class of 1971. He went on to Parsons School of Art but never graduated. "It was boring," he says. After brief stints sketching for Halston and writing about fashion for *New York Rocker,* Meisel was hired as an illustrator by *Women's Wear Daily.* "I adored him," says his boss, James Spina. Meisel lived at home, "just like the Beaver in a garden apartment," Spina, a neighbor, recalls. Meisel would drive Spina home in a Buick Scamp his father bought him to keep him off the subway. They went to concerts together and would pore through Meisel's collection of old fashion magazines under the gaze of posters of Veruschka and Mott the Hoople.

Meisel was friends with two designers, Anna Sui, who went to Parsons with him, and Stephen Sprouse, whom Meisel met at a drag bar, the 82 Club, in 1974. Soft-spoken Sprouse, thirty-one, first drew clothes as an Indiana nine-year-old, met Norell and Geoffrey Beene at twelve, apprenticed with Blass, and dropped out of design school to work for Halston.

New York's clubland years had begun and were to shape fashion, photography, and modeling for the next two decades. "The scene was very flamboyant," says Deborah Marquit, a Parsons classmate who also got a job at *WWD*. "Everyone came to work crazy from the night before. All they talked about was sex with men." Gabriel Rotello, a musician and night life impresario, met Meisel and Company at the Ninth Circle, a Village gay bar. Rotello, who went on to share a summer house with Richard Sohl, Meisel's best friend from grade school, followed the group's exploits for a decade. At first Sohl was the star. He was the beautiful piano player in the Patti Smith Group. Smith would introduce him onstage as "Richard D.N.V. Sohl." The initials stood for Death in Venice.

"The whole thing was gay," Rotello says. "Richard would entertain us with stories of them coming into the city from Queens in junior high and going to gay bars. They both had real wild streaks, wanting to be where the action was. You'd hear peals of laughter; that was Richard. Steven was very reticent, obviously very talented, very enigmatic. I thought he manufactured his eccentricities as he might an illustration. For effect."

Meisel and Sohl shared a conspiratorial streak. They would whisper in a private language and call each other names—Sissy Meisel and Tanta Ricky. "If you didn't know the codes, you wouldn't know what they were talking about," Rotello says. "Together I found them a little scary." Teri Toye was scarier. Meisel met her at a party at Rotello's loft, jumping on his old sofa and breaking it. "Teri Toye was totally fabulously insane, screamingly funny, and out of control," Rotello says. "Holly Golightly in drag." Born in Hollywood on an early sixties New Year's Eve ("No one ever believes me," she grouses), Teri was adopted and spent a spoiled, sheltered youth in Des Moines, Iowa. Her pale, freckled face is still open as the plains, when it's not closed behind shades. "I was never *really* a boy," she insists, "except for the one obvious thing, and that's the only thing I ever changed. I didn't change my sex. My sex changed me."

In 1979 Teri moved to New York to study fashion design. The first year she registered as a boy, the second as a girl. "I think they were a little confused," she says. Soon she visited school only to model for illustration classes taught two nights a week by Meisel. The pair made quite a statement. Teri's lank blond image complemented Meisel's smoldering Cleopatra pose. They made a pretty Odd Squad.

"We would get together at Sprouse's for four or five days," Teri recalls, "design clothes, have them made, put them on, and take pictures of ourselves. Then we'd wear them out at night with our friends." They became fixtures on the after-hours scene, often in club bathrooms. "We *love* bathrooms," Teri laughs. They would go to the Mudd Club in their pajamas and bragged of flooding the bathroom, "riding" the toilets in a motorcycle fantasy. They began sporting long, lank Dynel wigs and all-black clothes and dressed their friends in Day-Glo neon to stand out from their own in crowd.

The times were wilder than Meisel. Though many people around him were drinking and drugging and having sex obliviously, says Rotello, "Meisel always seemed a little too dignified to be caught with his pants down." He had the same boyfriend for years and studiously kept his private life private, while all about him were flaunting theirs. More recently, with his safe sex posters and an interview in the *Advocate,* Meisel opened up a bit. He said he's always photographed "more effeminate-looking men, more masculine-looking women, and drag queens" in hopes of "teaching that there's a wide variety of people. . . . There's absolutely a queer sensibility to my work . . . but there's also a sense of humor . . . a sarcasm and a fuck you attitude as well as a serious beauty."

Meisel's photographic career began inauspiciously. One night Spina took him to a party for Bette Midler. Meisel borrowed an old Exakta camera and took a picture of the singer that ran in *WWD.* He then took a class in photography. His parents bought him a camera.

Meisel met Valerie "Joe" Cates, an aspiring model from Park Avenue, in a vintage clothing store in 1979. He followed her, asked to photograph her, then asked the same of her sister, Phoebe, a top teenage model at *Seventeen.* "He was the first man we'd met with really long hair who was into dressing us up," Phoebe recalls. "He was different and really playful. Our first grown-up friend." Through the Cates sisters Meisel got work shooting test photographs of young models and an assignment from *Seventeen.* He also worked for the *SoHo Weekly News.* Fashion editor Annie Flanders gave him his first cover assignment and a story on plastic clothes. Joe and Phoebe Cates modeled.

Flanders knew that her friend Frances Grill, a photographer's agent, was looking for new blood. Meisel went to see her. She was impressed. "He knew every single bit of information about every photographer, every model." She sent a carousel of his slides to Kezia Keeble, an ambitious stylist who'd once worked for Diana Vreeland and was looking for a way into fashion's pantheon. Keeble had just been hired to create covers for Condé Nast's *Self* magazine. Meisel had never worked in a studio, and he didn't want to leave his *WWD* job. "He was really insecure," Grill says.

He had reason. An assistant—who was "promised tons of work by Kezia Keeble to show Steven how to do it"—would set the lights and the camera, says someone who watched them work. "Kezia didn't know the front of the camera from the back. She wanted a photographer she could mold. He was her boy. He would tape Avedon spreads to the floor of the studio and say, 'Light it this way,' and, 'Pose that way.' All he would do was push the button." Christopher Baker, another assistant, says that all Meisel owned was one Nikon and one 105 mm lens. "He didn't care. It was weird," Baker says. "He was, like, chosen."

Meisel shot half a dozen *Self* covers, helping turn the new magazine into a million-selling success. He was also working regularly for *Mademoiselle* and its Italian equivalent, *Lei,* and, every once in a while, for *Vogue.* He fitted into his new milieu well. Models loved him; he'd have his makeup done before theirs. "He would speak to the models in sign language, put his hand a certain way, throw his neck, and expect her to imitate him," says Andrea Robinson, who worked at *Vogue.* He wore kohl makeup and a little dirndl skirt over his pants.

John Duka—then Kezia Keeble's summer housemate and soon to be her husband and partner in a PR firm—dubbed Meisel a new Avedon in his influential fashion column, "Notes on Fashion," in *The New York Times.* Meisel quit his *WWD* job. The next step was to make a splash, and he did with a little help from his friends. In January 1983 Sprouse asked him to photograph some clothes he'd been making for a fashion show Keeble was doing. Though they were still sewing on the edge of the runway, the show was a success. "I knew I was looking at a gold mine," Keeble declared. Bendel, Bloomingdale's, and Bergdorf Goodman bought. Odd was in.

The first time Kezia Keeble ever saw Teri Toye, dressed in a demure Black Watch plaid jumper, turtleneck and stockings, ponytail, and flats ("indeed, an odd way for a transsexual to dress"), she knew she'd encountered someone extraordinary. Toye had become a model that fall, when Sprouse held his first fashion show. Frances Grill, who'd stopped repping and opened an idiosyncratic model agency called Click, soon signed Toye up. When the Fashion Group—an organization of women in fashion—asked Keeble and Duka to produce its spring 1984 showing of American fashion, Keeble recalled the group's show of ten years before, starring socialite Baby Jane Holzer—Tom Wolfe's Girl of the Year—and decided it was Teri Toye's time. "Outrage makes Teri *the* person," Keeble said, because "people love to buy what they hate. They resist, but resistance causes persistence. What's most amusing is she's becoming Girl of the Year just because I said so."

A press blitz followed. But when it got to be too much, Toye failed her Svengali and escaped to Key West with Way Bandy, the made-up make-up man who

could have been the Odd Squad's godfather. One friend referred to what followed as "their little *Peyton Place*." Another called it "a lover's spat." Meisel's
odd little squad fell apart. His agent called Toye "boring and sad." Toye put it all
down to a "high school girls' fight." Frances Grill, who lost touch with Meisel
at the time, put it down to boredom. "Steven is fashion," she says. "As fast as you
think you've got it, it changes. That's how Steven is. He moves on."

Following the breakup of the Odd Squad, Meisel was seen far less in public, but his career took off. He quickly left *Mademoiselle* behind. Briefly he
championed a Dutch-Japanese model named Ariane, who was dating a musician who lived in his building. He shot her in an influential makeup spread
for Italian *Vogue*. "I didn't look like a girl," she says. "I didn't look like a boy.
I looked like this rock and roll thing."

Then came Christy Turlington. "I always wanted to work with Steven," she
says. But *Vogue's* editors told her he liked only big, strong girls. "I kept asking,"
she says, "becoming a little baby," and finally a go-see was arranged. "So I met
him one day, and he was very nice but didn't seem to pay much attention." It
wasn't until six months later, in 1986, that she finally worked with him for
British *Vogue*. "I came an hour late, by subway, got off at the wrong stop—a disaster story," she says. "But I worked with him for four days, and we had so much
fun." It was the first sitting where the team of Meisel, hairdresser Oribe Canales,
and makeup man François Nars came together. Henceforth they worked
together all the time. And over the course of the next several years they created
a three-headed monster known as the Trinity: Turlington, Naomi Campbell,
and Linda Evangelista, the three models who came to epitomize fashion.

The second figure in the Trinity was hardly *haute* when she arrived in New
York that April to do her very first shoot—for British *Elle*. Naomi Campbell
was discovered in 1985 by former model Beth Boldt, who'd opened an
agency called Synchro in London. She spotted the fourteen-year-old Campbell buying tap shoes near her office in London's Covent Garden. "She was
wearing a little school uniform," Boldt recalls. "I took her first tests, and she
was *sooo* sweet, like sugar. Everyone who met her wanted to hug her." Some
might say they hugged the sweetness right out of her.

A theater and dance student from Streatham, England, and daughter of a
dancer who'd traveled the world in sequins and plumes, Campbell was already
show biz bound when she signed up for a modeling course at Boldt's instigation. A few short months later she was on her way to America for *Elle,* where
a pretty new black face was always welcome. "A girl from New York let them
down, and Naomi got the booking," says Boldt.

That summer Ford "traded" Turlington to London for a week in exchange for a Synchro model. "I met Naomi the day I got there," Christy says. "We had lunch, and she was in high school uniform, hanging out at the agency. She was really cute. She's still sweet, but she's a completely different human being now."

They hung out together and saw each other again a few months later, when they both landed at the Paris nightclub Les Bains at 4 A.M. Campbell had been taken up by Azzedine Alaïa, a diminutive Tunisian-born designer in Paris. Models loved his sexy clothes as much as he loved models. "He was way ahead of all of them," says John Casablancas. "He created the fashion show as a social event, and he got every single superstar in the business to come for free." He also let them stay in his house and referred to them as his daughters. "Naomi says I am like her mother," he explains. "I keep an eye on her. Cities are dangerous for young girls. There is too much temptation. Everything is easy, and at that age they never think anything can happen to them. For models it goes very fast."

It did for Campbell. Christy recalls, "I kind of felt protective over her, and I was only a year older. I also wanted the company. So she moved in with me." Christy soon introduced Campbell to Meisel. "Because Naomi lived with me, we all hung out a lot," Christy says. "So Naomi got in really quickly."

The final member of the Trinity, the most dedicated model of the three, is Linda Evangelista. Though she's been dubbed Evilangelista by wags at Elite, she's also the most accomplished model of her time. "I know what and where I would be if I wasn't modeling," she once said. "I thank God every day for my looks."

Born in 1965 to an Italian Roman Catholic family in St. Catharines, Ontario, she was the daughter, niece, and sister of General Motors auto plant workers. Her mother enrolled her in dance and self-improvement classes starting at age seven. She became a model as a teenager, working in local stores for $8 an hour. "Even when she was thirteen, I knew she'd be good at it," her mother said.

Like Steven Meisel, Linda "was always obsessed with fashion—with the magazines, the models and the poses," she's said. She signed with an agency in Toronto and in 1981, at sixteen, entered a Miss Teen Niagara contest in Niagara Falls. An Elite scout was in the audience. Not long afterward she arrived in New York to test. But not much happened.

Determined to succeed, or at least not to return to Ontario, Evangelista packed her bags for Paris in 1984. Her father gave her a year to make it. "I thought I was good," she's said, but she was "doing mediocre jobs for $650."

She was her own harshest critic. "I didn't really have myself so together," she's recalled. "I still had baby fat and the hair was a problem."

"Actually, she worked very well," says Francesca Magugliani, who watched her progress at Elite Paris. "She was doing covers right away for *Figaro Madame* and *Dépêche Mode*." Then, Francesca recalls, Evangelista had a booking in Spain with Gérald Marie's photographer friend André Rau. "She did a lot of jobs with Rau," Francesca says. Upon her return Elite got a letter saying she was switching agencies. "André took her to Paris Planning," Francesca says. "I called John, and he said, 'Don't give her her book.' So she leaves, never calls for her book, never calls for her money. And that's when she started her super-star career."

Evangelista had been having an affair with Rau. "She was the only girl he ever loved," a friend of Rau's says. "He was two years with her. Gérald Marie stole this girl from him. After her he never recovered."

Marie met Evangelista at his apartment in Paris. "She came with a friend, and we looked at each other, and in the same moment, boom!" he recalls. "She was with Elite. She was not an important model. I was still at Paris Planning, and she came to work there." Christine Bolster was at Paris Planning, too. And she wasn't Marie's only girlfriend. "Gérald was going out with Linda, with one of my models, with a top booker, *and* with Christine," said a competing agency owner. "There were at least four, and he said to each of them, 'I love you, I'm going to marry you.' "

The next month, when Marie opened Elite Plus, Evangelista switched back, and Marie began making her a star. "Gérald made her career," says Francesca. "Linda was madly in love with him." He introduced her to his close friend photographer Peter Lindbergh. "I brought Peter to my place for dinner, and I told him, 'I bet you when you start working with her, you're not gonna stop,' " Marie remembers. "One month after, he booked Linda, and for one year and a half he never stopped booking Linda. He was the king of Italian *Vogue,* of *Marie Claire;* he was putting her everywhere."

Their new alliance proved a boon to both Linda and Gérald. "Elite was never that hot," says a Paris competitor. "With Linda it got really, really hot. Gérald was using Linda to meet all the photographers, imposing himself in the studios, all the luncheons. I think she's really a cold fish. But she's really clever at keeping relationships with photographers." After a few months Marie and Evangelista came to New York. "We did a list of who we should see, and the first day she went to see Steven [Meisel]," Marie says. Evangelista was the perfect appurtenance for the peculiar photographer. Her desire to make great pictures transcended all else, and as time went by, she proved willing to be bent and shaped to Meisel's every whim. "She had a tremendous desire for success," says Marie. "And she is somebody who knew really quickly to correct what imperfections she had by moving differently, finding the angle for the light. She is no more or less beautiful than many other women, but she wants it really bad."

By the end of 1986 Gérald Marie had "started speaking about marriage," Linda said. "I never ever thought he would get married. So I said, 'Well, put the ring on my finger and then we'll talk about it.' And he did. When I was on my way back here for Christmas, we had a dinner. He put the ring on my finger and I went into shock."

In spring 1987 Christy Turlington returned from a location trip in Russia and went straight into a session with Evangelista and Meisel. "I was helping him," Christy says. "He'd be looking for girls all the time. I got him to work with Naomi. Now Linda arrived. She was a little bit wary of me, because she knew we were all a team and good friends. I never had anything in common with her in the beginning. We were around her a few times, and she was nice; but I found she was a little competitive." As it happened, the only pictures that ran from their first shoot together were of Evangelista. Her success with Meisel proved a perfect wedding present. Marie and Evangelista were married in July 1987 at St. Alfred's Catholic Church, in Evangelista's hometown.

Things began to happen fast for the Trinity after that. Their success was due, in no small part, to a shakeup at Condé Nast. *Vogue* was in a crisis, a result of the success of the upstart *Elle,* just launched in America. In June 1988 S. I. Newhouse, Jr., and creative director Alex Liberman decided they had to do something. In a stunning coup they fired *Vogue*'s editor, Grace Mirabella, and replaced her with Anna Wintour.

Wintour's career in fashion began in her hometown of London in 1970, when she went to work for Hearst's British *Harper's Bazaar* (now called *Harper's & Queen*). Moving to New York in 1975, she joined American *Bazaar* under Anthony Mazzola but didn't last long. "Tony felt the sittings I was doing weren't right for the American market," Wintour says. "And he was probably right." She went on to *Penthouse* publisher Bob Guccione's women's magazine, *Viva,* and *New York* magazine. She spurned Condé Nast's early approaches, although she met with Mirabella. "Grace asked what job she wanted," says an editor who heard of their encounter.

"Grace, of course I want your job," Wintour replied.

Finally, in 1983, Liberman lured Wintour to *Vogue* with the new—and purposefully vague—title of Creative Director and a mandate to use her elbows. Liberman says he felt "an absolute certitude I needed this presence. In my innocence I thought she could collaborate with Grace and enrich the magazine. I'm not sure the relationship was the way it should have been."

Both Wintour and Mirabella felt frustrated. "Things worked differently then," Wintour says diplomatically. "Grace picked the clothes. There was one point of view. It's not how we do it now." Wintour got out in January 1986, when Beatrix Miller, the longtime editor of British *Vogue,* decided to retire. Her new appointment was controversial. Under Miller, British *Vogue* was a whimsical, eccentric magazine, much admired by the fashion crowd, but not terribly realistic. "It was a rare animal," says Liz Tilberis, who started at the magazine after placing second in a 1969 *Vogue* talent contest. Wintour changed it, trading idiosyncrasy for rational uniformity, quirkiness for speed, the strangely erotic for the straightforwardly sexy. Suddenly the magazine looked just like Wintour, in her short skirts, high heels, bobbed hair, and dark glasses.

During Wintour's first months on the job, unhappiness spilled into the pages of the feisty British press. For a supposedly civil people the British gave Wintour an extraordinarily hard time. They nicknamed her Nuclear Wintour, the Wintour of Our Discontent, and Desperate Dan, for, as the *Evening Standard* put it, "her habit of crashing through editorships as though they were brick walls, leaving behind a ragged hole and a whiff of Chanel." By April 1987 speculation was fierce that Wintour's chill reception in London was about to send her scurrying back to America. Pregnant again and often alone in a long-distance marriage, she began discussions with American *Elle.*

"I was having a hard time," she admits. "It wasn't a secret."

Si Newhouse flew to London to see her—and keep her—by offering the editorship of another Condé Nast magazine, *House & Garden.* But Wintour's eight-month attempt to remake the magazine (renamed *HG*) into a cross-disciplinary journal of style quickly ran into trouble. Things got so bad it was widely believed that Condé Nast operators were fielding an avalanche of subscription cancellations. "It was a horrible time," Wintour says. "I thought I was doing an interesting magazine." Meanwhile events outside Condé Nast were conspiring to take it away from her.

As Wintour crossed the Atlantic, *Vogue* still ruled the roost, but things were changing. It was the year of *Elle.* The slick, gorgeously printed Paris-born magazine was growing fast, and suddenly people were noticing it. In 1987

Vogue's advertising revenues hit $79.5 million. *Bazaar*—still in a holding pattern under editor Anthony Mazzola—earned $32.5 million. *Elle,* at $39 million, was gaining fast and outselling *Bazaar.* Hearst seemed not to notice, but Condé Nast did. "There was a slight tremor," Liberman says. "People looked at *Elle* carefully. There was something unconventional and a little new about its approach. It's quite possible we learned certain lessons."

Lesson number one? "It seemed a change at the top was necessary," Newhouse says. "We had a magazine that needed attention."

As far back as 1986 Liberman had let Grace Mirabella know that something was amiss. But he did it with "words I didn't quite understand," she says. "I'm the first to see nothing coming. Even a bus." Si Newhouse admits that Mirabella's firing two years later was badly handled. "Alex and I made the decision to change," he says, and somehow it leaked to Liz Smith, who promptly broadcast the news. "The way it was handled was graceless—without making a pun," Newhouse continues. "So, fine. But it wasn't a spur-of-the-moment decision." Within two days Rupert Murdoch got in touch with Mirabella. A few months later he made her an offer she couldn't refuse: a new magazine bearing her name.

Wintour's first revamped issue of *Vogue* appeared that fall. Linda Evangelista got a makeover at precisely the same moment. In October 1988 Peter Lindbergh convinced her to let Parisian hairstylist Julian D'Is cut off her hair—just as Gérald Marie's previous charges Shaun Casey and Christine Bolster had done before her. "I was terrified," Evangelista said. "I cried through the whole thing." She was canceled from more than a dozen runway shows as a result, but she had the last laugh. "Between December and March I appeared on every *Vogue* cover—British, French, Italian, and American," she later boasted.

Christy Turlington chose that moment to make herself scarce. In fall 1987 she met Roger Wilson—Shaun Casey's ex-husband—at a party in Los Angeles. Before his marriage to Casey broke up, Wilson had decided to become an actor and debuted in *Porky's,* a witless 1982 teen sex comedy that made a fortune. It kick-started his new career but also spelled the end of his marriage to Casey. "He says things didn't work out because he had other things to do and she was used to having this young kid with a lot of money who was home all the time," Turlington says. Wilson got a job on a television series. He dated model Kelly LeBrock. "Most of this stuff I found out afterwards," Turlington says. "I thought he was a cute, sweet, normal guy when I met him."

Around the same time Turlington did her first big-money job—for Calvin Klein. Bruce Weber was in the midst of shooting Klein's faux-orgiastic Obsession perfume ads when Turlington flew in for two days. "The shoot was wild," she recalls. "Tons of people. Guys and girls. The clothes would come off. I was like, 'What's going on?' " As the ladylike ads that resulted attest, Turlington kept her clothes on. She didn't like the pictures. But Klein liked her. And during the fittings for his fashion show in spring 1988, he started questioning her closely about her ambition. Later that day Klein called her. "I have this really crazy idea," he said. "I love you so much I would marry you, but I already got married. So I want you to be the girl for my new fragrance. Just do me a favor, don't break me."

Turlington starts hyperventilating remembering the moment. Eileen Ford tried to talk her out of it. But Turlington wanted to spend more time with her new beau, and being a contract model would allow her that. "I signed very quickly," she says. "I didn't have a lawyer. When I got home, Roger read the contract."

"You're screwed," he said.

Though she was to be paid $3 million for eighty days' work a year over four years, she was locked up. She couldn't do interviews, editorial spreads, or any other advertising. At first that didn't matter. The first month of her contract was a busy one. She shot photos with Irving Penn, began work with Richard Avedon on Eternity's television commercials, and then headed to Martha's Vineyard to shoot magazine ads with Weber. That's when the problems started. Weber hadn't been consulted on Klein's choice of Turlington. "I think he should have had a voice in who the contract girl was," she says.

Their first shoot together—inspired by Toni Frissell's photos of Elizabeth Taylor, Mike Todd, and their daughter—went well. At least Weber thought so. Surrounded by children, Turlington "let her ego go completely," he says. "Most girls are afraid of not being the star." By giving up center stage to the children, he concludes, "she was the star of the shooting." Unfortunately few of the photos ever appeared. "Calvin never ran that many pictures," Weber says. "You know how it is: You shoot eight dresses, but they really only plan to run two. Christy was used to seeing a lot of pictures of herself. She really felt frustrated, and through that frustration she lost interest."

Between shoots Turlington moved in with Wilson in West Hollywood, enrolled in literature and writing classes at UCLA, and went stir-crazy. By fall she was ready for a change in her relationship with Calvin Klein. Reports at the time said she'd angered Klein by getting her hair cut without his permission, but the real situation was considerably more complex. "I felt Bruce didn't like me," she says. "It would get real uncomfortable on the set. We'd be butting heads without speaking to each other. It was awkward. So I felt, fine, I'll do my couple days work a year. But I did miss working—a lot."

Watching from the sidelines while other models worked didn't help her mood. She'd kept in touch through Naomi Campbell and Linda Evangelista, whose rapid rise coincided with Christy's departure from the scene. Evangelista had even taken Turlington's place on jobs she'd been barred from doing. "The year that I disappeared is when a lot happened for Linda," Christy says. "She did Barneys after I left. I was supposed to go on a trip for Blooming-dale's to China with Cindy [Crawford], and Linda got my spot." Despite their initial wariness, they'd become friends. And by mid-1989 Christy was staying in Linda's New York apartment in the same building where Naomi lived. Visiting them on sets, Christy grew green with envy. "*Then* I got a haircut."

Christy had just finished a long Calvin Klein job and was taking a few days off in Woodstock with Oribe. As she drove in an open jeep, her hair got tangled in the wind. "I figured they wouldn't need me for a month or two, so I said, 'Just cut it,' " she recalls. They made a video of the shearing, laughing and joking about how they were going to get sued. Then Klein's minions called with a photo assignment. "Uh-oh," Christy said.

She'd already hired a lawyer to try to loosen the ties that bound her to Calvin Klein. Everyone knew it wasn't working out. But suddenly the designer agreed, and her contract was renegotiated. Her agency was delighted. "You don't want to stop the momentum of building a star," says Katie Ford. But it took some time for her to get back up to speed. She visited Evangelista and Meisel on an Italian *Vogue* shoot, "one of their most beautiful series with lingerie and corsets," she says. "They stuck me in a picture, and I was so uncomfortable. I was so unused to being photographed. My steam was very low, photographically."

In Christy's absence, Evangelista had become Meisel's muse. "They worked together all the time, and he did beautiful pictures of her," Turlington says. "I think Linda had been really monumental in his career, changing him as a photographer and being an inspiration. They did a really incredible variety of things that year when they started working together a lot."

But now Turlington was back. And just as she'd helped Evangelista, says Gérald Marie, his wife returned the favor. "The relationship they had together was like two fingers, the same hand," he says. "Linda took Christy by the hand to all the designers. Linda engaged her with Peter Lindbergh at

the time, put her back together with Steven Meisel. To all these [people],
Linda was very hot."

So was Naomi Campbell. After arriving in New York under Turlington's
tutelage, she and Evangelista had become friends, often meeting at Meisel's
studio. Naomi also became a darling on the city's scene—stage-managed by
Meisel. "Yes, there was a strategy that had to do with getting noticed," he said.
"It was simply a question of publicity." It started coming after December
1987, when she met heavyweight champion Mike Tyson at a party at designer
Fernando Sanchez's apartment. Various versions of their meeting have the
sexually hypercharged Tyson virtually molesting her before guests pulled him
away. Told she was only a baby, he replied, "I'm a baby, too." Around then,
Campbell approached a reporter at Azzedine Alaïa's house in Paris, rubbed
against him, and asked, "When you gonna write a story about me?"

By the time Turlington was freed from her bondage at Calvin Klein,
Campbell had emerged as a star, with covers of both French and British *Vogue*
behind her. So suddenly, instead of one muse, Meisel had three in residence at
the all-white Park Avenue studio he dubbed the Clinic. "We re-make people," he once said of the place. "We make them beautiful." In 1988 he began
photographing Turlington, Campbell, and Evangelista together because "he
thought it would be a neat look," says a stylist. "Steven made them the Trinity by booking them together. He does such great work, and he's so charismatic he kind of possessed them. Being in Steven's studio is like being with
the cool kids in the lunchroom in high school. Christy got into it for a while,
but it never suited her. She was like Cinderella with her two stepsisters. It was
a phase. A naughty phase."

Just as he had with Teri Toye and Stephen Sprouse, Meisel turned the models, his stylists, and friendly editors like *Vogue*'s Carlene Cerf into the in-est in
crowd in fashion. His power shed light on how fragile a grasp most fashion
editors had on their trade. "That guy could say a piece of crap was fashionable, and we'd all go *Yes!*" says an editor at *Vogue*.

Meisel's control was absolute. "I don't think he liked any of our
boyfriends," Christy says. "Linda he couldn't help because she got married
before we met her. But as far as what I did and Naomi did, he was very protective." All-consuming is more like it. "They became a cult," says Polly
Mellen. "They moved together, went out together." They even began to be
booked together.

In 1988, when Ford Models abruptly ended its relationship with Karins,
Turlington signed up with Elite in Paris, at Evangelista's instigation. Naomi

Campbell had been with Elite Paris ever since Beth Boldt discovered her. Now Gérald Marie began aggressively packaging Christy and Naomi with his wife. "It started just because they were girlfriends," Marie says. "But it was really nice to promote them together, sell them together, put in the client's brains some ideas about them being together. If you want those two, why not take number three? They gained three hundred percent out of this pact."

"That first season after I went back to work, he booked us for all the shows," Turlington says. "We'd never done shows before in Paris, so he somehow built some hype around Linda and I. There's not that many girls who look good together. We complement each other. Naomi's a very good friend of mine and Linda's, so somehow that all happened."

Watching Gérald Marie from the sidelines, John Casablancas felt a new respect for his former enemy. "Gérald positions a girl, makes her understand what her star quality is all about, maintains the prices, the pressure; he does not get intimidated; he'll lose a big booking; he'll select photographers really intelligently; he does a tremendous job," Casablancas says. "There was also the social scene. He not only had the talent and the understanding, but he was married to Linda, so he was a player. I'm an agent, but I don't go behind the scenes the way he did. So I think this gave him an extraordinary position."

Graciously Marie says it was his photographer friends who sent the supermodels into orbit. "The photographers who pushed the most and created the models are Steven Meisel and Peter Lindbergh," he says. "But the models got so enormous in answer to the sudden need of the time. Actresses started to hide themselves, and people needed something else in their mouths. So, next story came the models. We were right there at that moment."

Naomi Campbell's affair with Mike Tyson survived his marriage and divorce from actress Robin Givens. When she appeared at ringside at one of his fights in February 1989, their semisecret relationship went public and increased her renown immeasurably. That September she became the first black woman ever to grace the cover of the all-important September *Vogue*. Three months later she and Tyson finally admitted their affair in the same magazine. "She has a great body and she's scared of nothing," the boxer said. "That's why I like her."

In January 1990 the cover of British *Vogue* featured Turlington, Campbell, Evangelista, Cindy Crawford, and Tatjana Patitz. So impressed was pop singer George Michael that he cast them all in his next music video, "Freedom." It was filmed in August 1990. Evangelista had just bleached her hair almost white. "I spend all my free time coloring my hair," she said later. Her constantly changing coif became big news.

Publicity seemed to come naturally to the Trinity. Campbell got more when, hard on the heels of her breakup with Mike Tyson, she began seeing Robert De Niro and Sylvester Stallone. Christy and Linda got into the swing of things in April 1990, when they went to the Roxy, a New York disco, and were photographed straddling each other in a giant swing suspended over the dance floor. Needless to say, rumors they were lovers followed.

All the action didn't do much for Evangelista's marriage to Marie. They saw each other only five to ten days a month, "and that is a good month," Marie said. But there were compensations. "I like the traveling," Linda said, "the money . . . seeing myself in magazines. And I *love* clothes." Marie was having a good time, too. He convinced designers, beginning with Gianni Versace in Milan, that it was worth paying double, triple, even ten times more than ever before, to put gaggles of top editorial models on their runways. They were paid back in international publicity. Versace, whose design antennae are particularly attuned to the new, "liked what he saw," says Polly Mellen. "They affected his designing. Then they moved from Versace to Chanel."

Finally, they were everywhere—or at least seemed to be. Versace's exclusive bookings—paying extra to be the only designer a girl worked for in Milan— started it. "Then all the other designers said, 'I'll match that. I'll pay you the same thing, and you don't have to be exclusive,' " Turlington recalls. "The designers said, 'You can do ten shows if we all approve of the other designers, and you can all be paid the same amount of money.' It got bigger and bigger because they were outbidding themselves. Every year I thought, I can't make more than this, but every year I almost doubled my income. It's supply and demand, like sports. The best of the sports people will be paid any amount."

Runway by runway, atelier by atelier, magazine by magazine, the Trinity conquered. Whole issues of the various *Vogues* seemed to be dedicated to their worship. "I *never* thought that models could take so much space in the world and in people's impressions," Marie avers. "But we followed the movement when we started to smell and feel that people were asking more about the girls. We saw that if you put a photographic model on the runway, they started to get really famous right away, because they get photographed by three hundred people at the same time, and some designers understood right away. Then we started to ask the magazines to name the girls. Then we worked to make the models a little more famous, to introduce them a better way, to produce their careers, to insist on certain things to do, certain things to avoid. I was not the only one. People catch on fast. If I ask the magazines to put the name of the girl on the cover, the agent next door, he's not stupid, he's going to ask for the same thing. That helped."

From her privileged perch at *Vogue,* Polly Mellen saw the Trinity blossom—and then watched fame go to their heads. "They were always together," she says. "It was a clique and a tight one, believe me. Occasionally they would talk to other people, but basically they talked to themselves. They'd consult on bookings. One would say to the other, 'You're past working with *him.*' They were able to pick and choose what they wanted to do. The more they asked for, the more they got." First a short list of supermodel-ready lensmen: Demarchelier, Meisel, Elgort, Lindbergh. Then the Concorde, then cars and drivers, personal chefs, and the best suites at the best hotels.

"They could write their own tickets," says Mellen. "And they knew it."

Back at the Anne Klein shoot, late in 1991, Turlington is eating rice and broccoli from an aluminum tin while simultaneously getting a pedicure and leafing through a pile of old magazine clippings. Right on top are two stories about her famous friendship with Evangelista and Campbell. Those pieces caused Christy endless grief, thanks to tactless comments, mostly made by Evangelista, about the unprecedented sums the three models earned and their feelings about the world of fashion. "We don't vogue—we are vogue," Linda told *People.* To *Vogue,* she revealed, "We have this expression, Christy and I: We don't wake up for less than $10,000 a day."

"I'd *never* say that," Christy gripes, dropping her fork into the Chinese food. And though she truly believes Evangelista didn't mean to appear crass, after those stories came out, Christy had a nightmare about them. "I was on the Arsenio show," she says, "covering Linda and Naomi's mouths with my hand!"

That $10,000 quote, more than anything, began the backlash against the Trinity. Soon everyone was taking shots at them. Even *ArtForum* described supermodels as "totally packaged commodities," "live cash," and "professional surrogates for the frustrated emulative instincts of the mass pecuniarily deprived." It was later said that Evangelista's words had been taken out of context. But insensitivity was a leitmotif of the Trinity. Not long afterward Linda was approached by France's *Nouvel Observateur* for an interview on modeling and asked $10,000 plus a 20 percent service fee. The paper replied by telling readers how many Somalis could be fed for that sum.

On another occasion Evangelista defended the price of her services. "Before supermodels, there was one price for everyone. I don't think a new girl should get the same," she said. "That's why Gérald introduced the new price. If you wanted me, there was no way 'round." In another interview she announced that "I have become bigger than the product." Campbell's antics at fashion shows, including refusals to share the runway with other black models, didn't win her many friends either. The shows had always run behind schedule, but when "the late" Naomi Campbell was added to the mix, editors and buyers could count on an extra half hour's delay. "I won't use her," said designer Todd Oldham. "We have a No-Assholes clause."

The Trinity's disdain worked as a pose on the runway, but when the girls were quoted in cold type, they came off like spoiled little snots. "The girls you speak of," says one of America's most renowned fashion editors, "are rude because everybody coddles them. We do what we need to get what we want, but it's *beyond*. I was at a party where a waiter grazed Linda's arm, and she screamed, 'You *burned* me!' "

"They became very powerful and not nice about it," another top model says. "They were very snobby and cold and shut people out. We had to deal with the disgusting influx of negative attention to models that they generated."

"I have to beg, borrow, lie, and steal to get them," says a top model editor. "You have to have the right photographer, the right makeup, and a ninety-nine percent cover guarantee. And we booked them all when they were starting, when they were no good." Besides disenchanting their old friends, the Trinity was also courting overexposure. Fickle fashion people were already tiring of this latter-day Terrible Trio when a *People* article appeared, chronicling a bitchy night on the town with Meisel and the models. "Naomi and Linda really wanted to do it," Christy says. "I didn't at all. But they made me do it. It was really tacky and horrible, and I was so embarrassed. It pissed my mom off. And they didn't even quote the worst things that were said that night."

Turlington knows that a model's public image is a fragile thing. "People don't want to like you," she says. "You're young and beautiful and successful. They think you don't have a skill. So when things go well for you, they aren't happy. That's just human nature." She knew not to rub people's faces in her success. But her friends didn't. And now, Christy was seeing the downside of her in-crowd.

"I've never thrown any kind of fit; I've never refused to wear anything; I've never refused to do a picture," she says. "But girls do that all the time. Naomi can be a little difficult. I love her dearly, but people know she can be difficult. 'Difficult' meaning, 'she needs to be entertained.' Then she'll do her job very well. Linda is difficult, on the other hand, because she knows herself very well.

She knows all of her imperfections. She does not want to look stupid. That's her job, really. She's doing the best that she can for them. And it's to their advantage that she does that. Linda knows what's best."

Despite their continuing mutual-admiration society, the Trinity disbanded in 1991. The more time they spent together, the more their differences became apparent. Evangelista, the most malleable of the three models, became Meisel's clear favorite. "Christy does the job," an insider says, "but she can turn it off, go home, and live a life. That became a problem."

Christy agrees: "I love fashion, but I'm not obsessed with it." Linda's obsession and plasticity clearly appealed more to fashion's most plastic photographer. "Women today are striving to be perfect, to be the ultimate Barbie doll," Meisel has said. "I can't think back in history where women have been so plastic. I mean, how many women are going out to have face lifts and are having their teeth done and are dying their hair? Sociologically, it's definitely a modern thing."

In September 1991 Linda dyed her hair red and won thirty pages and the cover of *Vogue*. "Meisel used Linda much more than Naomi and Christy, and it really hurt Naomi, but that's what photographers do," Polly Mellen observes. "His eye never tired of Linda. It was about manipulations and jealousies and a real craving to work with the best, and Linda was, and they wished they were."

"I think it blew up because girlfriends have their ups and their downs and sometimes don't get along," says Gérald Marie. "There were certain jealousies and little things between makeup artists, girl stories. Everything was so big it started to be ridiculous."

Christy got lonely in the in crowd. "I was successful before I knew any of them," she says. "I'd always been an individual, and I started feeling like part of a package deal. When I was younger, I wanted to be talked about because of me, not because of what I wore or who I was hanging around with. And I was always that way, until we were together. At first I didn't pay much attention to what things looked like. And then all of the sudden people starting thinking that Linda was a ringleader. I've been around longer than she has, and people are thinking that she's controlling me! I hated the idea of people thinking that. I wanted to distance myself, not work with anybody else. Be myself again."

They all knew it had gone too far. "Of course, people got bored with us," Christy says. "We were bored with each other. We even thought about staging a fight on the runway." (They didn't.) But Naomi and Linda *were* fighting ("They always fight," says Turlington. "And always have. It's love-hate. Not even love, just me, me, me. They're like sisters"). And Turlington was having arguments over money with Elite in Paris. "They were very slow in paying, and I wasn't used to that," she says. "Ford paid me immediately. So it was always uncomfortable because it's my good friend's husband that's my agent, and I can't call him up and scream like I can to my normal agent."

In spring 1991, after Ford opened a Paris branch, Turlington and Campbell both signed up. When Elite's lawyers sent her a threatening letter in response, Christy got mad. "Linda knows everything that goes on with that agency," Christy says. "She tries to stay on the outside, but she is in the middle. It's her husband. Nothing was ever mentioned. If there is some kind of problem, they don't have to make it a legal situation, they can call me. I will do my best to make it right. I felt hurt because of that."

A close friend of Christy's thinks the breach was inevitable: "The infatuation boiled down to real people. They were a neat look, but that doesn't make you best friends." For months afterward they hardly saw one another. Later Marie said that his feelings had been hurt. "Christy was staying home with us, going to weekends," Marie says. "We are really close friends, and when you help set her back into the market and [she] leaves you for whichever money deal she could have, you feel like someone shot you, bang [in] your head, and your wife's, too."

For two days during Turlington's shoot for Anne Klein late in 1991, Linda Evangelista was working in a studio next door with Steven Meisel, shooting ads for Barneys New York. On the first overlapping afternoon Meisel's set was still humming when Christy's shut down. Christy stuck her head in. "Turlie!" Evangelista cried when she saw her friend. "I didn't see you for so long!"

Catching up for several minutes, Evangelista told Turlington about her recent operation to repair a collapsed lung. She'd had to decide whether to recuperate with her husband or her mother, she confided, and she'd chosen her mother. It was a sign. By the next July, when French *Glamour* ran a spread on their villa in Ibiza, Gérald and Linda had already separated. "We are still married but we are no longer lovers," Marie told an interviewer. "We decided one day to lead separate lives. . . . Linda is not a bird that you can keep in a cage. . . . We both needed more space and freedom. . . . She was only spending four or five days a month with me. . . . If you stay away from the person you love for three weeks . . . you get independent. You exist . . . as a single person. . . . Linda is one of the most beautiful women in the world but there are lots of others." He was obviously quite pleased that she, like Christine

Bolster, was staying with Elite. "I have loved Linda and kept her," he concluded. "I haven't lost her."

But he had. "Something happened," says the head of a competing agency in Paris. "Linda didn't believe the rumors. Then she walked out on him. He was destroyed." The story went around that he'd hooked up with a booker at a third agency. "Maybe he needed a mother at that point," the agency head snickers.

The separation wasn't made public for months, while gossip raged in fashion circles that Evangelista had taken up with actor Kyle MacLachlan, whom she met on Meisel's set at another Barneys shoot. The talk was fed by Evangelista's disappearance from fashion runways for several months. She finally reemerged in March 1993 at the Paris shows. That season she gave an interview in her suite at the Hôtel Ritz. "We separated in August and I started seeing Kyle after Thanksgiving," she said. "I liked him. He was sweet, but I wasn't looking then. . . . What went wrong? I haven't got the words."

Christy got a famous boyfriend, too, dropping Roger Wilson and picking up with actor Christian Slater, then dropping him for Jason Patric. Turlington also became best buddies and something of a modeling mother to Kate Moss, the leading member of the post–Trinity generation.

Naomi Campbell hasn't been so lucky in love. After being linked to Eric Clapton, she hooked up with U2's Adam Clayton for a long engagement that finally led them to alter their plans. Then, in November 1993, Monique Pillard and John Casablancas faxed a letter around the world about her. "To Whom It May Concern," it read. "Please be informed that we do not wish to represent Naomi Campbell any longer. No amount of money or prestige could further justify the abuse that has been imposed on our staff and clients. All who have experienced this will understand."

Those in the know said Campbell had at last made one demand too many—for a room at the sold-out Four Seasons Hotel in Milan during collection week. "Buy a first class hotel? *Fuck you,*" said Roberto Lanzotti, who works closely with Elite. "I don't need that. I get rid of Naomi in the middle of the collections. I don't want to represent her anymore. She was a pain in the ass. Forget it. It's too much."

The members of the Trinity all continued to have healthy careers, but their modeling moment was over.

On the last day of Christy's shoot for Anne Klein, she headed next door to Meisel's studio to say good-bye to Linda before flying to her next job.

There she spied Lauren Hutton, the original contract girl, and the photographer quickly shot a roll of pictures of the three women. Christy pinched Linda. Lauren screamed and mugged. Then Turlington ran for the door, her floor-length pea coat cradled in her arms.

"Bye," she called to Evangelista. "I'll call you."

"Really?" Evangelista answered. "Turlie? Aren't you going to be cold?"

"Thanks, Mom," Christy replied, throwing her coat around her shoulders.

"It feels like Paris used to feel," Linda said wistfully as Christy turned to leave.

Outside, a silver town car was purring at the curb. Christy glanced up to the windows of Meisel's studio. A strobe light flashed once, and again, behind the dirty glass. And then Christy Turlington clambered into her car and was gone.

Veronica Webb's favorite model
is the artist William Wegman's weimaraner, Fay Wray. Webb's reverence for her profession is but one of the things that sets her apart. Her verbal skills (displayed in *Paper* and other magazines and on various Fox television shows) also make her an uncommon mannequin. It is a mark of her accomplishment, and of the changing condition of models, that those things come before these: She is black in a white woman's world; nonetheless, she's scored a contract with Revlon.

Veronica is waiting backstage at a Todd Oldham fashion show, shopping a Sotheby's catalog. There's a Picasso drawing she wants. She can afford it. Christy Turlington and Naomi Campbell come by, followed by Lifetime cable and *Good Morning America*. "Clash of the camera crews!" Veronica exults. Hers is just behind—but of course—led by Albert Maysles for HBO.

She eyes a man standing next to her critically. "I wish you were a movie star," she tells him. "That way I'd have a full model's accessory kit."

She sets herself apart from modeling's top cat pack. "Because it's a youth-driven industry, it's at once fantastic and terrible," she says. "It's intimidating—like going to the bathroom in high school with popular girls—only you're not one of them." She smirks. "You grow out of that."

She has been reading Joseph Campbell's *The Power of Myth*. "He says a monster is whatever throws off your ideas of harmony, scale, and reality." A hairdresser approaches, comb at the ready. "We now begin to prepare the monster."

"I was born in Detroit in the blizzard of 1965. The first nickname I ever had was Snowflake because my mother was trapped in her car and a police car got stuck trying to get her out and another police car had to come and push the first police car out so she could get to the hospital. And that's how little Veronica came to be.

"I grew up in a working-class neighborhood. Most of the people had emigrated from the South in the thirties, forties, and fifties to work in factories. My father was an electrician at the tank division at Chrysler, and my mother was a nurse at Detroit General Hospital. They'd both done twenty years in the Army.

"I thought about fashion all the time. I remember looking at magazines when I was very young. They showed women doing whatever they wanted. Nobody was telling them to wash the dishes, mow the lawn, don't say this, don't do that. It was soothing looking at women who had freedom. That's what fashion represents to me: freedom. I didn't intellectualize it then. I was seven. But eventually I figured out what it was that appealed to me.

"I wanted to be an animator. I loved comic books. That's another thing that appeals to me about being a model. My job, when I'm being photographed, is to fill up a frame, which is exactly what you do with an animated character. And comic books are about the sort of person who comes from a mundane place, someone who doesn't know they have any extra ability but they're very curious, nerdy, disenfranchised, have a heavy fantasy life and then suddenly they're put into a fantastic situation, and they discover they have superpower.

"Models have control over their looks, and most women don't. It's very hard to get yourself together, to get the appearance we're conditioned to want and have fantasized about having. Imagine waking up in the morning and having someone there to do your hair, your makeup, sewing you a brand-new outfit all night, giving you music to get you into the mood as you go from child to supervixen. So modeling is sort of a dream come true, even though it only lasts for thirty seconds.

"I went to art school. It was an excuse to get to a big city. I came to New York because it looks so good in the movies. All the opportunities, they're all here, all the doors, all the offices, all the avenues. I knew I was pretty, but I didn't think I was glamorous or beautiful. It's like a creek and the Rio Grande. There's a big difference.

"I was working as a cashier in a store in SoHo in the early eighties, and all these people came in, makeup artists, agents, hairdressers, and they all said I should be a model. At that time, though, no models looked like I did, so I didn't really think it was possible. I certainly don't look like Kelly LeBrock.

"I didn't know that the market was opening up. But I went to an agency called Click, and I started working. I did six or seven jobs, for Bruce Weber,

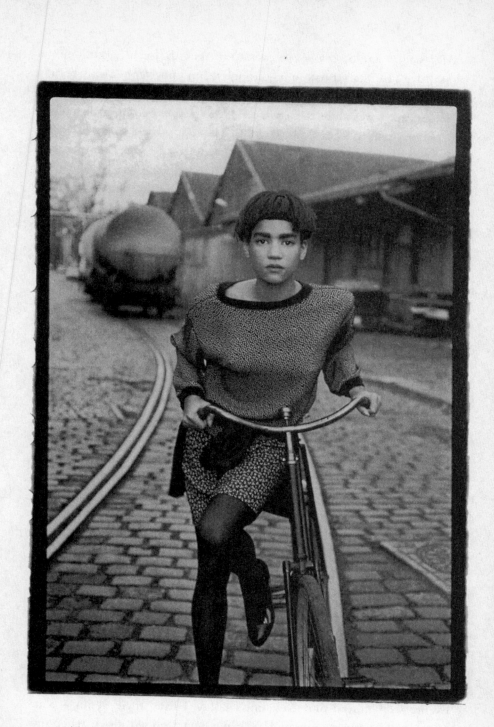

Veronica Webb photographed by Peter Lindbergh

for *Mademoiselle* and *Seventeen*, a press kit for Agnès B. I made a little money. I didn't have a bad start. But you go through that money very quickly because you're setting up a business and it takes awhile to turn a profit.

"Every time I went into the agency, I'd hear people on the phone, talking to Paris, girls calling from Paris, and I had always wanted to go to Paris. I didn't know how long this would last. If it would just be like a summer job, I didn't want to lose the opportunity. So I arranged for Click to get me an agency there, and I went off to Paris with a hundred dollars, three shirts, three sweaters, two pairs of shoes, three pairs of pants, and two skirts. I thought I'd stay at least long enough to make the money to buy a ticket home.

"Paris was frustrating and beautiful. I used to sit on the curb and cry at the end of the day because I couldn't speak any French. I'm very dependent on language, and I stepped off the plane and I was rendered an imbecile. But Paris opened my eyes. I learned so many things about aesthetics and craftsmanship and dedication. France looks good; it feels good; it smells good; it tastes good. French people make two-thousand-dollar cashmere bathrobes. They don't mess around.

"I sort of invented this look for myself. I cut my hair really short, in a bowl cut, and I drew on these really big, long, thick eyebrows, and I went to see Peter Lindbergh, and he got really turned on. He started booking this little character I had created. We were doing Italian *Vogue,* French *Vogue,* and *Marie Claire,* going to Arabia and Brittany and doing all these amazing pictures. And when they came out, Azzedine Alaïa came looking for me.

"I couldn't speak French and he can't speak English, but I met him, and he had this rack of dresses and he had me try them on. He was holding my wrist like he was taking my pulse, having this whole conversation with me, very slowly, and I couldn't understand. The only thing I got out of this initial conversation with Azzedine was to put my hands in my pockets.

"Azzedine is very paternal. I started to spend a lot of time with him. Azzedine always works. He is constantly working, drawing, sewing, cutting, creating, fitting, thinking. We'd watch TV and he would fit things on me and he would teach me words in French. I got a little blank book and I would write down words every day, and then I started putting words together into sentences, and when I didn't have the words, I would make them up by putting *ez* or *ique* on the end and making it sound French.

"Eventually I moved into Azzedine's house. I lived there about a year. Azzedine was like my second father. When a boyfriend left me or when my father died, or when I was trying to do something artistically and it didn't work, he was one of the people I called and cried to.

"I love to understand an outfit and to bring it to life. That's what my job really is. Designers make these clothes, but they can't wear them, in the street anyway. You get there, you see what they're proud of, what they're afraid of, and they're looking at you to put that thing on and bring it to life. It must be the same for a playwright, hearing his words for the first time. Will it play in Kansas?

"I spent two years in Paris, and then I came back to New York. I felt deeply dissatisfied because for the most part models don't create anything. You don't have a product you can hold up and say, 'I did this.' You're in a collaboration that isn't driven by your intelligence or your imagination.

"I took a month off, and I thought about what I wanted to do. I decided to try acting. The fantasy of being in a movie or on the stage is interesting to most people. I spent two years in acting class. While I studied acting, I also produced theater for children uptown at the Harlem YMCA. It centered me. It gave me somewhere I had to be every day. And I couldn't just smile and get by. You couldn't fool people with makeup and lights. You had to do it every day without anyone there to prop you up.

"Then I met Spike Lee, and I did the movie *Jungle Fever*. That was sort of a turning point in my career. It affirmed that I could do something else. Because it's a very scary thing, modeling, you can get hooked on this life. Very, very hooked on this life. It's hard to imagine working in a store or going to an office every day again. But I realized that acting wasn't for me. The work isn't right for me. I didn't want to assume someone else's personality.

"[Gossip column items about a romance with Spike Lee] really upset me, but then I realized the lion was out of the cage. Either I can run from it, or I can stick my head in its mouth. And it's become a very nice pet. I got famous, and fame is currency. It's not hard currency, but you can trade that shit on the open market like nobody's business.

"I came back in 1991. While I was gone, the whole business changed. The whole world's imagination [was] captured by models. It was planned. Of course it was a plan. I wasn't in the war room. I don't know exactly whose plan it was. And I really didn't think it was going to work. But none of those girls are stupid. You would never catch them not looking fabulous, not dressed, not up-to-the-minute, not being that thing. And we all have to thank them, because they did raise rates and the profile of the job.

"I'd never imagined that people could become so interested in models. It was very eighties. There was such a rush of attention and excitement. A lot of the other models felt: Oh, my God, can I compete? Can I be shiny enough? Will anyone notice me? My feeling was, Versailles was occupied by different kings and queens, but Switzerland was always Switzerland. It's quiet and works well.

"I was still frightened when I came back. I didn't know what would happen. This business has been really, really, really good to me. It was like I'd never been away. Nobody punished me, or stuck me in the corner, or pretended they didn't know me. It was grace. Not my personal grace. The grace of God. Major concept.

"Karl Lagerfeld really helped me a lot. A lot. I spent a lot of time in the studio with Karl, and he really paid attention to my ideas and who I was as a person. *And* Karl put me in his advertising. Before that there was no advertising, 'cause advertising did not exist for blacks. At least not until maybe two or three years ago, when miraculously, Revlon happened. There was a *Time* magazine cover, after the 1990 census, on the browning of America. You must serve your consumer! You must serve your market! That census made a lot of companies respond.

"The great thing is, it's just given to you. I have no credentials except for having shown up and lived the life. But the catch is, you can wake up and not be able to do it anymore. The problem is, you don't own it. You can never own it, and it can be taken away from you at any moment. Someone could throw hot coffee in my face. Some designer can say he doesn't like the way I look. Some magazine can decide that's horrible. Every four years a new generation comes up. And another generation is getting ready to happen right now. It's just very, very, very fragile. There's no sense of security.

"Beauty is a fleeting thing; fashion is a changing thing. It makes the world go 'round. But you have to protect your soul. So at the end of the day I'm not defined by modeling. I'm not going to go home and cry because I didn't get the outfit I wanted or because someone was in the makeup line ahead of me and I didn't feel like I got the attention I deserved.

"I'm at the top of my game now. The question is, Where do I go from here? I'm twenty-eight. I'd like to model for as long as the check is there, because let's be serious, my sister is an oncologist who went to school for fourteen years and her income does not compete with mine. So I'm not going to say I'm above that check.

"Let's face it, I hit the jackpot. But you only hear success stories. So the problem is, all those little girls in Iowa and Kansas think they're going to become millionaires: You're better off buying a lottery ticket."

$25,000 A DAY

Shortly after Elite Models opened in New York in 1977, Jeanette Christjansen arrived to join her boyfriend, John Casablancas. "It was a critical period for me," she says. "I was turning thirty. In America nobody knew me. My career was over." A new generation of models—Esme, Nancy Donahue, Kim Alexis, Kelly Emberg, Carol Alt—had arrived via an Elite recruitment blitz in America's small local agencies and model schools. Though she worked here successfully for six months, that fall Christjansen got pregnant. "It was a very nice way for me to quit," she says.

Julian Casablancas was born the next summer, and John and Jeanette finally got married late that year at New York's City Hall. But his first wife—Elite—was demanding all his time. "America just took us over," Christjansen says. "The business became his life, and there was nothing left." Casablancas was doing one-nighters in cities around the world. "I was so happy being a mother," says Jeanette. "It was no fun to join him, so I didn't. When I look back, maybe I should have." Until that time Casablancas had been relatively discreet about his extramarital activities. "He was unfaithful to poor Jeanette from the word go, but she had no idea," says April Ducksbury. It was an open secret in his agencies, though. "I knew he was sleeping with underage girls, but not big models," says Elite booker Monique Corey. "John always screwed around, always, the younger the better. I worried that he'd get in trouble with a mother, but it never fazed me. I'm French."

"Take the whole Elite head sheet," says Francesca Magugliani. "There were three nos and five yeses." The affairs never lasted long. "When you reach eighteen, you start thinking and become intelligent," says Francesca. "The day the girl matured and had a mind of her own, it was finished. John wants adulation.

They'd start talking back to him. In my opinion, John was afraid they'd find out he's a terribly insecure man, loyal only to himself, born to have fun. When a girl starts questioning what you're doing, it becomes itchy. He's afraid of a woman. So he withdrew from them and made the affairs end. John has never left; he makes the girl leave."

Nearing forty, Casablancas was still a magnetic charmer. "I've seen girls scratch at his door," says photographer Guy Le Baube. "Modeling brings out the worst in girls. But John was very careful. He's not mercantile." Many found no fault in his behavior. "OK, he goes out with young girls, but it's not dirty," says a woman who owns one of the larger agencies in Paris. "Young girls say yes. I never heard he forced a girl." And unlike many other men in modeling, Casablancas, by all accounts, never took drugs or offered them.

But then Casablancas made what many perceive as the biggest mistake of his life. He began getting serious about the girls he was sleeping with. And where once they were the children of sophisticated Europeans, now they were Americans, descendants of Puritans. In 1982 Casablancas was thirty-nine when he began courting a barely postpubescent girl from the South. "She was thirteen or fourteen, a baby when she met John," says Francesca.

Casablancas had dinner one night with photographer John Stember and Gunilla Lindblad's husband, Jean-Pierre Zachariasen. Stember was just back from a trip for *Vogue* in Florida. "John had been selling him a new girl who was about thirteen," Zachariasen says. "He was extremely involved in this girl for some reason." Stember was telling Casablancas about the horrors of the trip—lost luggage, bad weather, bad moods—when Casablancas interrupted. "What about my young girl?" he demanded.

Finally, Stember admitted that he'd never even shot her. "John was banging his fist on the table," Zachariasen says. " 'Why didn't you use this girl?' Stember said, 'Because she was brand-new and she was stiff, and the others were broken in.' John said, 'My God, what did this poor girl do the whole time?' " "Don't worry," Stember replied. "She went to the beach every day. She bought a pail and a spade, and she made sand castles!"

By 1985 the southern girl was gone. "She was very intelligent," says Francesca. "Then she grew up. She looked at John, and he wasn't an idol anymore." The brown-haired, brown-eyed woman—who remained with Elite for many years and is now married and a mother—confirms her affair with Casablancas. "It happened," she says. "It was a nice part of my life, but I'd prefer it to be unpublished."

She was gone, but Casablancas had a new source of temptation. That year Elite launched an international competition modeled after Steward Cowley's failed Model of the Year pageant and the Ford agency's Face of the '80s contest, which quickly became an internationally televised event.

Promotional literature for the Look of the Year contest boasted that Elite models had been featured on 60 percent of major magazine covers in the preceding eighteen months, more than all the other New York agencies combined, and that the Elite Group of ten agencies had booked $22 million in business the preceding year. The John Casablancas Career Centers—franchised modeling schools coowned by Kittler and the Casablancas brothers—had also taken off after a rocky start that cost Casablancas and Kittler at least a million dollars. Now fourteen schools had opened, and thirteen more were planned.

Stephanie Seymour, who'd just turned fifteen, was an entrant from San Diego in California's semifinal for the first Look of the Year. Casablancas chose her as the local winner. But he really preferred her mother. "Stephanie was a charmer, a puppy dog, a pony with long legs," Casablancas says. "But she was such a baby that there was no way. If I looked at anybody with interest, it was her mom! I was not having any affair with the mother, but she would not have had to ask me twice for me to say yes."

In November one hundred aspiring models from America and thirty from other countries competed for Elite contracts guaranteeing as much as $200,000 a year at the finals in Acapulco, Mexico. Up against Cindy Crawford, among others, Seymour appeared in a tank T-shirt, suspenders, and a Farrah Fawcett-Majors hairdo. She placed in the top fifteen but didn't win a contract and returned to school. Throughout her freshman year in high school, she wrote to Casablancas. "The kid was delightful," he says. "She charmed everybody. She would send little letters to everyone at the agency, and when you'd open the letter, little silver stars fell out." He responded, urging her to come to New York and join Elite. Seymour's mother finally convinced her husband in June 1984. "The mother of this model should have kept her daughter out of the way," says April Ducksbury. "But she wanted her daughter to be a model."

After testing in New York, Stephanie went to Europe and was booked to shoot the *alta moda* in Rome for Italian *Bazaar*. "I sent her a note saying, 'We'll go to the ball, save a dance for me,'" Casablancas says. At the Rome shows Casablancas posed for a picture with her. As she leaned against him, she told him it was her sixteenth birthday. He was thunderstruck by the change in her. "By that time her physique had changed. She was not anymore a little girl; she was this young woman. Her body was extraordinary—she was long and thin, and the shapes were where they had to be—and her face was gorgeous, with this innocent little-child voice."

The next fall the child's body was back in school, but her mind was on modeling. Then she and her mother went to Acapulco as Casablancas's guest at the second Look of the Year contest. Casablancas's attentions had the desired effect. Stephanie transferred to professional school in New York and moved into a model apartment—next door to John, Jeanette, and Julian Casablancas.

The next January at the collections in Rome, Stephanie was booked into one of Italian *Harper's Bazaar*'s model rooms, but she didn't sleep there. "I saw Stephanie Seymour take her suitcases and move them into John's bedroom," says Francesca, whose room was across the hall from John's. "And that I will never forget. I'm not saying John didn't entice her. But he'd never slept with her. And then Peppone made a stink because he didn't want to pay for Stephanie's room." Casablancas insisted that she had to keep the room for the sake of appearances.

After Rome Seymour went to Paris, where she worked for the rest of the summer. Back in New York the affair continued. "Stephanie would come over and play with Julian; they were about the same age anyway," says Francesca, only half-jokingly. "Jeanette would cook dinner for them." Some of Elite's bookers were outraged. "She was living with John, and her mother thought it was the greatest thing in the world," says one. "Stephanie was a little kid. I found it shameful."

Casablancas was walking a fine line. "He was crazy, madly in love," Francesca says. He says his marriage was failing. "We were beginning to have problems. I was losing interest. I'm dating Stephanie on the side. Jeanette knew about it because I'd spoken with her. Obviously she could see it; she's not a dummy."

Jeanette Casablancas says she *was* in the dark, but she wasn't for long. Seymour shared an apartment with another contestant from the 1983 Look of the Year contest, Hunter Reno, whose aunt Janet later became the attorney general of the United States. In midsummer Hunter Reno busted John and Stephanie.

Reno "was living at the model apartment with Stephanie and two other girls," Francesca recalls. Casablancas was at Alain Kittler's house in Ibiza with Seymour when he got a call from Elite's lawyer. "The night before, Hunter

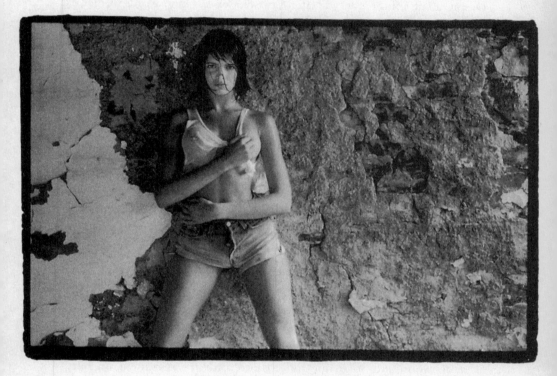

Stephanie Seymour photographed by Marco Glaviano

Reno had come over and told Jeanette everything," Francesca says. "Details, dates, everything." Though she'd had her suspicions, Seymour was the first girl Jeanette ever *knew* about. She sent Casablancas a telegram and told him their marriage was over. He wanted to come back to New York and talk about it. She said no. "I think I would have strangled him," she says. They didn't see each other again for months. Then Jeanette asked for a divorce.

Despite it all, almost a decade later Christjansen has kind words for her ex. "I don't feel he left me for a young girl," she says. "Maybe he went through his menopause. Men get funny at forty, and girls were serving themselves up on silver platters to him. He didn't want to leave; but he did things, and when I found out, I just went crazy. I didn't even let him explain. I told him, 'If you want to do this, do it a hundred percent.' Sometimes I wonder, Should I have reacted differently? I care a lot about John. I couldn't accept him as a husband, but as a person, I still respect him very much. In a way it's courageous. John lives the moment. He's always had a good heart."

Though Stephanie's mother knew about the relationship, her father didn't. So at Thanksgiving Casablancas flew to San Diego to meet him. "After dinner, he said, 'OK, ladies, you go to sleep,' and him and I, we got drunk together," Casablancas recalls. "We talked all night, and by the end of the night he said, 'I think that you really love my daughter. I think that you're taking a lot of risks, but if you want to see her and she wants to see you, I'm not gonna stand in the middle.' "

"[John] is a brainwasher," Seymour later told an interviewer. "He convinced my father that he loved me more than anybody in this world, and my father gave his consent. . . . My dad just didn't even want him to leave." On their return John and Stephanie moved into a luxury apartment on Fifty-seventh Street.

The next summer—just after the breakup of his marriage and his affair with Stephanie, now seventeen, made gossip columns—Casablancas arrived at a party in St.-Tropez, at the villa of Régine, the nightclub owner. Lauren Hutton, in the south of France filming a miniseries, was at a table with several other Americans when the tanned, beaming Casablancas strolled past, Seymour under one arm and an equally young girl under the other. "Who's she, the mother's helper?" Hutton cracked.

Apparently unaware that she wasn't a fan, Casablancas later approached Hutton. She sneeringly addressed him as "Jimmy Morocco" and told Stephanie and the other model, "Run for your lives." Casablancas says that only Bob Zagury's intervention kept him from punching Hutton. "I thought

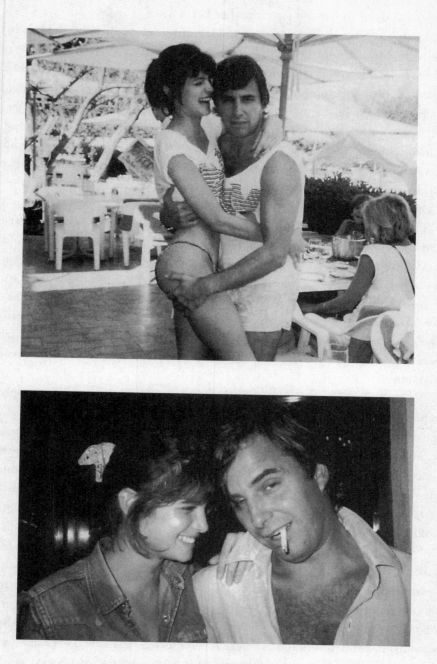

John Casablancas in Rome *(top)* and New York
with Stephanie Seymour in 1985

she was a dyke, so I felt like treating her like a man," Casablancas says. "Bob said, 'She's not worth it, just leave,' and I left. But I was ready to break her rabbit teeth, I was so angry."

Stephanie Seymour chose to walk—not run—about six months later, just after she made the jump from Model Management, the agency's second tier, to Elite, its star board. At Christmastime Casablancas felt a change in her. They'd planned a trip to St.-Barth, but he ended up going alone. Jeanette and Julian were on the island with Patrick Demarchelier, but John's ex-wife refused to see him. Then, in a matter of days, Casablancas developed a toothache and almost broke his ankle, swimming in rough surf. "I was so fucking miserable," he says. "It was like God was punishing me."

Francesca Magugliani realized John's love affair was over at the January 1987 couture shows in Paris. They'd had dinner with Jacques de Nointel and Casablancas was driving down the Champs-Élysées, when suddenly he U-turned and began racing back to his hotel. "I'd never seen John so desperate in my life," Francesca says. Arriving at the hotel, he called Seymour at a studio. "She said she couldn't come over because she wanted to look at slides," Francesca continues. "John tore the phone out of the socket." Then he headed to Les Bains, where he sat until 4 A.M. praising Seymour to a photographer.

"I don't think he was conscious that it was finished, but he was extremely depressed," Francesca says. "She was the only girl he didn't want to leave. He must have sensed she was pulling out. The roles reversed. I'd never seen him so in love. She pulled a John Casablancas on him." To this day Casablancas finds it hard to admit that he was dumped. "When I broke up with Stephanie," he says, it was her father who "made her have the guts to tell me."

"I just needed freedom, period," Seymour said, after moving into a loft with another model. Eventually she would leave Elite as well.

"It was the first time in my life that I found myself alone, really alone," Casablancas said.

Stephanie Seymour wasn't alone. She briefly got married and had a son she named Dylan in 1990. By 1991 she could be seen on the cover of *Sports Illustrated*'s swimwear issue *and* on the arm of Warren Beatty. A year later she was linked with Guns N'Roses singer Axl Rose, who gave her a 4.5 carat diamond and ruby engagement ring and, that July, used a Paris concert as an occasion to abuse Beatty from the stage as "an old man who loves to live vicariously through young people and suck up all their life because he has none of his own."

This latest relationship was high-profile and highly volatile. Seymour appeared in Guns N'Roses videos and had a ring of roses tattooed around her ankle. But things took a bad turn at their Christmas party in Malibu in 1992. They'd been bickering when Rose asked everyone to leave. During the forty-five-minute fight that followed, Seymour swung at him with a chair and punched him in the crotch. Stephanie, said the singer's sister, "wants to push things to the edge."

By February 1993 they were broken up. Seymour, twenty-four, had contracts with L'Oréal and Victoria's Secret, and she'd become Richard Avedon's favorite model. She was also pregnant again. And the father of the child was married, but not to her. He was Peter M. Brant, forty-seven, an entrepreneur, horse breeder, polo player, publisher, and newsprint manufacturer, who already had five children by his wife of almost twenty-three years, Sandra. He also had a criminal record. In 1990 he paid a $200,000 fine and served eighty-four days in federal prison for failure to keep proper tax records after pleading guilty to billing $1.5 million in personal expenses—including silk sheets and massages—to two of his companies.

Within weeks Rose sued Seymour in Los Angeles Supreme Court for assault and battery at the Christmas party, emotional abuse, and the return of $100,000 in jewelry, including her engagement ring. Rose said he hoped to sell the jewels and donate the proceeds to a child abuse charity.

Seymour countersued. She said Rose punched and slapped her, gave her a bloody nose and black eye, and kicked her down a flight of stairs after their party. "I was never engaged to Mr. Rose," she said. "I have gone on with my life, and I hope he can do so as well." Her second baby was born late in 1993. Sandra and Peter Brandt were still married late in 1994.

The facts about Casablancas's affairs with the underage models became known in January 1988, when *New York* magazine ran a profile on him under the title "Girl Crazy." The cover showed Casablancas framed by models Andie MacDowell, Iman, and Carol Alt. The article painted him as a champagne-guzzling pasha of pleasure, ogling the breasts of his charges. The article shocked Casablancas. He called Francesca in Paris, "totally hysterical about it," she recalls. "I said, 'John, everything is true.' He said, 'Yes, but it's very bad for me. Find out what people think about it.'" Francesca duly polled all his contacts, some of whom had received copies in the mail from Eileen Ford. One suggested dryly that the next time Casablancas was photographed, he should try drinking milk.

He's still angry six years later. "In Europe no one gives a shit if someone is older," he says. "There's something that Europeans have understood that Americans don't want to admit to. A young girl will fall in love with a guy who's famous and who's done things and who's got power. She's not being a whore; it's just that it's intoxicating. [Americans are] programmed to say that it's disgusting."

At a party in the Rainbow Room of Rockefeller Center, celebrating Paulina Porizkova's contract with Estée Lauder that week, Casablancas joked darkly about throwing *New York*'s editor, Edward Kosner, out a window. Casablancas admits he can be childish. "The personal drama of my life is that I have lacked maturity to really build a relationship that overcomes the erosion of time," he says. "I get along great with younger girls. I *really* get along well with them, you know? I've always been a little bit of a Pygmalion. I love the way they're natural about everything, about their bodies, about relationships; they're frank; they don't carry with them the burden of past relationships and problems. I really understand their mind very well, and they understand mine."

He thinks he's always been a gentleman. "Have I taken advantage of my position? Probably yes," he admits. "Where I feel that someone is being easy with me because she wants something from me, then I might take advantage. Why not? If she is ready to do that, why should I be shy? But it doesn't happen very much. Have I ever taken advantage of a young girl's innocence? I categorically say no. All my ex-girlfriends are friends of mine. I got [a few] days ago a thank-you note from Stephanie Seymour, because I sent her a little present for her kid. This was a girl who could have said, 'When I was sixteen, this guy took advantage of me.' She stayed with Elite for years after that happened!"

Nonetheless, Casablancas was labeled a libertine. Trudi Tapscott had to deal with the fallout. She worked on the new faces board at Elite. "People in this business use their power to manipulate people in ways that are unfair," Tapscott says. But she told the many parents who were concerned about Casablancas that he wasn't a manipulator. "My answer was always that no one ever did anything that they didn't want to," Tapscott says. "I'm amazed how these girls act in certain situations. They know more about making passes than I ever knew. It *is* part of taking good pictures."

"One day I'll take him by the balls," Gérald Marie once said about John Casablancas. Their rivalry didn't end when Marie joined Elite. If anything, it

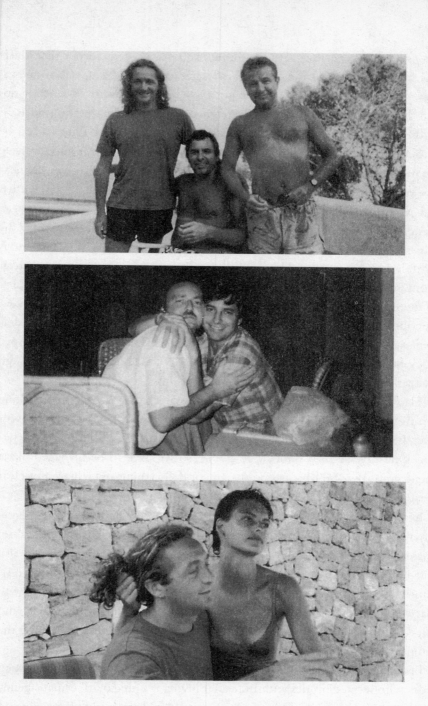

Top to bottom: Elite's Gérald Marie *(left)*, John Casablancas *(seated)*, and Alain Kittler in Ibiza in 1988; John Casablancas and Riccardo Gay in Mauritius in 1985; Gérald Marie and his then wife Linda Evangelista, in Ibiza

intensified. Top executives at Elite think that it was no coincidence that Marie was brought into the fold in Ibiza the same summer that Casablancas was there with Stephanie Seymour. He lost his wife that summer of 1985. It was also the beginning of the end of his reign as the European king of models.

By 1979 Casablancas and Alain Kittler had decided that Elite had to be autonomous, free of dependence on other agents. "John was trying to create the most powerful network in the world," Trudi Tapscott says. Over the next few years they created it. A holding company owned by Casablancas, Kittler, and Monique Pillard controlled Elite New York and the other American agencies. Another holding company, based in Switzerland and owned by Casablancas, Kittler, and Gérald Marie, controlled the European operations. A third holding company, Hong Kong Global, is something of a mystery. Monique Pillard first learned of its existence from a reporter. Kittler brushes off questions about its purpose. But a Swiss company, Elite International, S.A., functions much as Models S.A. does, helping Elite's owners skirt France's draconian tax laws. "There's a lot of cash booking through Elite," says April Ducksbury. "Hundreds of thousands of dollars. All the bookings went through Switzerland. The girls all had Swiss bank accounts."

Alain Kittler is the manager of Elite in Switzerland. "I have my working permit in Switzerland, my home in Switzerland," he says. "We pay the Swiss taxes. It's perfectly legal. After a while I thought that we should have a structure. One day we may want to go public, so we have to be managed like a public company. We have passed the age of doing things which are not clear because we are too rich and too exposed to do anything illegal."

Elite's expansion sputtered in the mid-eighties. "We had a big head," Kittler says. "We wanted to create agencies in Copenhagen, Brussels, London, Miami. And we lost a lot of money by going too fast." The company was also roiled by the power struggle between Casablancas and Marie. "Gérald is on a maniac ego trip," says Francesca Magugliani, who found herself at odds with Marie after Elite Plus opened. "Gérald wanted to get rid of all the people who helped John make Elite in Europe." Francesca was one of them, leaving the company in September 1988.

In a treatment for an as-yet-unproduced film called *Model Mafia,* Sebastien Sed—who severed his ties with Elite after giving it a precious German agency license—writes that Gérald Marie "swore he would make Elite Paris equal to New York and at the same time take control of Europe by destroying John Casablancas's relationships with his associates in Milan, London and Hamburg." Nobody was betting against him. "He saved Elite," says Jerry Ford.

Adds Monique Pillard: "Maybe his morals are not to my speed, but he knows how to develop and sell a girl."

After stabilizing Elite in Paris, Marie went hunting for Casablancas's friends. For years Casablancas had protected Riccardo Gay's position, even though he admits that his friend played fast and loose with Elite. Gay billed his clients from Lugano, Switzerland, and pocketed the Italian taxes he deducted from his models' checks, says Sed's wife and partner, Dorothy Parker. At first Elite ignored what was seen as a common practice in Italy. "All Riccardo wants is money," says Casablancas. "So when I sent my girls to Milano, I couldn't care less if they were making money or if I was being paid my commission. You sent a girl with the hope that she'd come back with a great book."

But now Gérald Marie began agitating for a change in the relationship with Gay. Kittler, too, began pressuring Casablancas. "How long is this guy going to call on the fact that he sent you a booker fifteen years ago?" he demanded. Responding to the pressure, Gay vowed to change his ways. But "his accounts were always late, inexact, incorrect, incomplete," says Casablancas. "He sent checks for partial payments. His computers never worked. It was a *commedia Italiana,* a big farce. His accounting was all in pencil! He enjoyed swimming in troubled waters." Finally Kittler confronted Gay himself. "He took the accounting of one year from Riccardo and threw it into the wastepaper basket," Casablancas says. "He took a check for ten million lire and tore it up."

In fall 1987 Casablancas's growing irritation with Gay burst out in an internal Elite memo. Casablancas wrote that Gay's methods of vouchering through Switzerland were compromising the agency. "We are becoming more Italian than Riccardo!" Getting out in front of Marie, Casablancas suggested opening a branch of Elite in Milan and asking Gay to be a partner. "In front of the world he would be the king of Milano," Casablancas says. "It was his chance to be number one. I was his savior. He accepted the deal."

Then Gay changed his mind. He called a meeting of all the agents in Milan and demanded they all sign a document promising never to deal with Elite. "It was like a Mafia film," says Sebastien Sed. "Riccardo put pepper in his eye, crying, playing *Rigoletto,* making a big opera." But no one signed, and Elite opened in Milan.

In response Gay "went to every ally I ever had and told them that I had betrayed him," Casablancas says. One of them was José Fonseca at Models One in London, who soon decided it was time her agency opened a branch in Paris. Alain Kittler considered this a betrayal. Among other considerations, Elite had never taken commissions from Models One. Marie was unhappy, too. "Gérald was jealous," Casablancas says. "The relationship between Models One and Elite was a relationship between April and José and me. So what does he do? He goes around saying, 'I'm thinking of opening in London.'"

Through the summer of 1988 London's agents were in an uproar. Finally Marie talked three of them, including Models One and Synchro—Beth Boldt's nearly bankrupt agency—into opening a desk within Elite Paris instead. But before the deal was finalized, Models One pulled out. "We weren't getting [Elite's] top models," April Ducksbury says. "We were getting the beginners. We sent a fax to John saying it's about time we had a rest from each other. The minute we said that, they went in with Beth Boldt."

Then came a tragedy. Late that August fifty people died when a party boat called the *Marchioness* sank in London's Thames River after being hit by a barge. Among the dead—all guests at a party hosted by a former Synchro booker—were bookers, agents, photographers, hairdressers, and models. Soon afterward Elite "announced that they were closing Synchro down and taking over its accounts receivable," Boldt says. She blames Marie. "Gérald came to London and wanted to rule. Everything had to be his way. Gérald once called me 'a worse bitch than my wife.' There were too many drugs, too much craziness."

In 1991 Elite merged with yet another London agency, Premier. The next year Elite severed its ties with Parker-Sed and opened in Hamburg and Munich. It now has fourteen separate companies, "all making profit," according to Kittler. By handing the reins of power to Gérald Marie, says Ducksbury, "John finally got the empire he always wanted."

Elite wasn't the only agency with image problems at the end of the eighties. Indeed, just a few months after the story of John Casablancas and Stephanie Seymour was made public, another scandal made Elite's problems yesterday's news.

In April 1988 Craig Pyes, an investigative reporter under contract to *60 Minutes,* met two models at a party in Paris and, through their friends, heard of models who'd been drugged, raped, or sexually pressured by two agency owners, Claude Haddad of Euro-Planning and Jean-Luc Brunel, who'd taken over the Paris agency of Eileen Ford's friend Karin Mossberg after her banker husband was transferred out of town.

Haddad's reputation had spread since the days of Antonio Lopez and Jerry Hall. For a time his star had been on the rise. He started exchanging models with Elite in 1978. He also worked with the Fords, who sent him one of their Face of the 80s winners, Suzy Amis, in the summer of 1980. Amis, seventeen, became Haddad's girlfriend before returning to New York in 1982. Haddad called her John Wayne, because he thought she walked like the western movie star. Amis won't discuss her relationship with Haddad, but Jacques de Nointel says it ended badly. "She doesn't like him anymore," de Nointel says. "He took advantage."

When Ford stopped working with Haddad, he formed Prestige, a joint venture with Elite. "Claude wanted an interest in a U.S. agency," says Doug Asch, a tennis partner of Casablancas's who went to work for the new agency. "It's not fashionable to say you like Claude," Asch says, "but in his time he had one of the best eyes in the business. He was very perceptive about character. It's often not the most beautiful girl who makes it. Did she have that killer thing? If a girl had it, he went with it."

The Elite-Prestige partnership ended two years later, in 1984. "Claude Haddad has a devious way of trying to get into girls' pants," John Casablancas told a journalist in an unpublished interview. "It's pathetic. I stopped my relationship with him after I sent him a girl, he had her in his apartment, he never even made a *pass* at her. He never tried to sweet-talk her or hold her hand. He just got into bed with her. It was embarrassing for me as a man. Certain moments he doesn't think with his head; he thinks with his cock."

By that time it seemed that everyone in the modeling business had a story to tell about Haddad, and few of them were good. After the breakup with Elite, Haddad seemed to lose control. Nobody stopped him. "We were guilty of neglect, but we weren't conspirators," says Doug Asch. "We weren't pimping for him."

They were an audience, however. "Claude would go in his office and lock the door, and we'd all laugh," says an ex-employee. "It was done up like a Moroccan nightclub, dark red, with a big couch and an armchair for two, but a tight two. Everything was scaled to make people two. And he had a scale to weigh girls. We never scaled girls. But he would say, 'Undress, I have to weigh you.'" After his closed-door weighing sessions, Haddad would emerge, hair askew, and announce that he'd taken on a girl who, as often as not, was "a monster who could never be a model," the ex-employee continues. "So we knew of course something must have happened."

On one occasion, says a regular on the agency circuit, a young model burst out of Haddad's office, screaming, "He told me to give him a blow job!" The action wasn't confined to Haddad's office. He bunked aspiring models in his apartment. Their bedroom and his connected through a bathroom, and he was in the habit of walking into the models' room unannounced. A Parker-Sed model once threw a bottle of wine at him as he came through the door.

"Claude would take out ten girls and find the one who wanted to be with him," says Asch. "But instead of saying, 'Let's go out and get crazy,' he'd get her trust and do something rude in the house. What killed him was 'Stay in my house, and everything will be fine.' " Asch thinks Haddad was addicted to sex with young girls. "He was like any other addict in the world. I don't think he'd hurt a fly, but you create messes with an addiction, and you change everything else to cover up your problem. Claude's addiction affected his business, his friendships, everything. I always thought he was an asshole not to admit it. People would've been sympathetic."

But he didn't admit it. He just kept going. And after six months of investigation, *60 Minutes* aired his problems for all America to hear in late 1988. "Every once in a while he'd catch a girl who wasn't pleased," says Asch. And one of them, identified only as Lorraine, told the newsmagazine show how Haddad had tried to corner her in the apartment and finally crawled into her bed. Most of the girls who stayed with him had the same stories to tell, she said.

Confronted with her accusations in an on-air interview, Haddad not only was unapologetic but even seemed proud of himself. Correspondent Diane Sawyer laid her trap well. How did he feel, she asked Haddad, waking up in his apartment full of models each morning? Like a gardener in a flower shop, he replied. "They are flowers. Just smell them, that's it. Just smell the perfume." Sawyer pressed: Had he tried to pluck any of the flowers in his shop? "When people say something, it's always a little truth," he allowed. "I hugged them. . . . I tried to flirt with them . . . never more." No rapes, no sexual blackmail? "I don't remember," Haddad replied. "Maybe. It's possible. I don't know," he continued weakly.

Five years later Claude Haddad is still angry about what he considers a sneak attack in which he was singled out for crimes many others had committed, too. His bitterness over the *60 Minutes* report is evident in his response to a request for his first interview since the show. "I don't like the American way," he says. "They picked the weakest one, and I did [the show] and I'm stupid. I work with beautiful girls. OK, I try to fuck them. It's not a crime. In France you can fuck all the girls you want to."

Six months, and several phone calls and letters later, Haddad arrives at the Café Flore on Boulevard St.-Germain looking like a professor of poetry, glasses hanging around his neck on a cord. "I'm out of the business now," he says. "I cannot survive." His long, center-parted brown hair parts to reveal deeply circled eyes and skin pale as paper. He shut Euro-Planning in 1992. Though he tried to stay in business, fax attacks flew anywhere he went scouting. "From Elite," he says. "They still do it."

As he sits, a pink-cheeked teenager from the Baltics chucks him on his bottom. He introduces her as Goda and sends her to sit at another table out of earshot of his conversation. "I came from the street, and I want to take people from the street," he says, glancing over at Goda every few seconds. "That's the only reason why I did this business. Now I go to Eastern Europe and find girls who are hungry and don't like to hear scandal shit." Many agencies still use him as a scout, he claims. "All the bookers are kissing my ass, they are giving me blow jobs to find girls. I can still find beautiful girls." But he doesn't take money when he does, he insists. "They pay me travel expenses. Nobody can buy me. Bookers are like hookers. They all get bought by people with money."

Haddad's attitude toward bookers is benign compared to how he feels about the agents *60 Minutes* inexplicably ignored. "There are people who are killers who are still in the business," he says. "You should investigate the life of Gérald Marie. Investigate Paris Planning. Models died when they were with Paris Planning. Every girl that came to his agency, they had to fuck with him! If not, they don't work, and he scare them to death. I know a girl who cannot come back to Paris because she's scared to death."

Haddad goes on, building up steam as the topic turns to the focus of his life—young girls. "I have been with some girls, but I never forced them. You manipulate them, but with . . . words, with . . . charm, with my power"— not drugs, like other agents, he says. He draws the line at fifteen-year-olds, he says. "Above sixteen is not bad, because they're a woman and they know what they do."

Why was he singled out? Haddad thanks his enemies: Casablancas and Ford. "They couldn't accept that I could establish myself in New York," he says. "I would rather marry and fuck with Yasir Arafat than be friends with these people! They are disgusting. John is a pig, and Ford is a witch. I don't buy girls like John does. Half of his models, they fuck with him. He force them psychologically, with money: 'You fuck me, you get what you want.' In Ibiza Gérald Marie has girls for his guests. I have never in my life done that. What do you call that? I call that a kind of prostitution."

Marie denies Haddad's charge. "I have never done things like that for my friends," he says. Haddad says he never played that way either. "The girls who fucked me, they fucked me maybe expecting something would happen," he says, but "maybe they love me. You never hear a big model complaining of being in bed with me." He calls the *60 Minutes* interviews "the revenge of mediocre girls" who never made it big. "They are saying, 'He tried, he tried!' In France a man is allowed to try, and a girl is allowed to refuse. [To] every girl, I say, 'I like you. I would like to make love with you. If you don't want to, fine.' "

That's why he can't understand Diane Sawyer. "This girl who interviewed me, could she swear that she never fucked people to succeed?" he asks. "I hate American people. I want to kick the American girls out of the business, because they are prostitutes, sex cash machines, whores. You are the most dirty people I met in my life. I'm not bitter. It's a fact."

After dispatching Claude Haddad, *60 Minutes* shone its light on Jean-Luc Brunel, a diminutive party boy who could always be counted upon to be at Les Bains, the most durable nightclub in Paris, at a table full of models and friends.

Brunel says he grew up among the haute bourgeoisie in Paris. He started out in the public relations business, specializing in restaurants and tourism, and got into fashion, by arranging locations trips for magazines. He married a Swedish model, Helen Högberg, who was with Élysées 3.

"We played gin together," says Paris Planning's François Lano, who appreciated Brunel's taste, education, and gambler's outlook on life. "Helen came with him to my flat, and we played all night long, with John Casablancas, too." Brunel organized dinners where celebrities like Johnny Halliday and Omar Sharif met models. "One day he told me he wanted to work with me on public relations, just to be there," Lano says. Helen Högberg came along as part of the deal. But when Gérald Marie arrived at Paris Planning, Brunel left. "He said, 'It's Gérald or me.' "

Jean-Luc and Helen moved to Ibiza, where he opened a bar and restaurant called El Mono Desnudo—The Naked Monkey—with a few partners. "He had no money or at least not enough to support his tastes," says someone who knew him well there. "If not for Helen, he would have starved."

Ibiza had long been a destination on the hippie trail. In the mid-seventies it turned into a refuge of decadent chic. Young British lords and ladies with heroin habits mixed with dethroned royals and Paris models. They all went to El Mono Desnudo. There were lots of women. "He had them all," says Brunel's friend.

Gaby Wagner, the onetime Paris Planning model, was Helen Högberg's friend. "I knew he was taking coke," Wagner says. "I knew he was cheating on Helen. I traveled with her to Ibiza, and I went out with the crew at night, and I saw all these girls sitting on his lap." But then Brunel ran afoul of some powerful people who gave him twenty-four hours to get off the island. "Whatever it was that he did, it was real bad," the friend says. Borrowing money from one of his partner's parents, Brunel ran.

Divorced, he was looking for something to do in 1979, when another of his ex-wife's friends, Karin Mossberg, asked him to work for her model agency. She needed a man around "because Claude Haddad had scouts like Dominique Galas and they were cleaning Karins out completely," Brunel says. "Karin called me up and said, 'As you're going out a lot, and you know everybody, can you come and help in the agency?' " He says he agreed to give it six months and buy half the agency if things worked out. Two years later he owned the place.

When Brunel arrived, Karins "was an empty shell," he says. "Slowly the agency started to pick up. We developed the girls that nobody wanted! And I then got back all the girls that Karin loved who went to other agencies." Brunel did know everybody, including some of the more interesting characters around modeling in Paris. And though he denies it, many modeling folk say that after he took over Karins, he started sharing his models with his friends. Where Gérald Marie operated "for himself," says Jacques Silberstein, Brunel "operated for other people."

"Jean-Luc is considered a danger," says Jérôme Bonnouvrier. "Owning Karins was a dream for a playboy. His problem is that he knows exactly what girls in trouble are looking for. He's always been on the edge of the system. John Casablancas gets girls the healthy way. Girls would be with him if he was the butcher. They're with Jean-Luc because he's the boss. Jean-Luc likes drugs and silent rape. It excites him."

"I really despise Jean-Luc as a human being for the way he's cheapened the business," says John Casablancas. "There is no justice. This is a guy who should be behind bars. There was a little group, Jean-Luc, Patrick Gilles, and Varsano. He was the guy flying all the girls from Karins for the weekend to St.-Tropez. They were very well known in Paris for roaming the clubs. They would invite girls and put drugs in their drinks. Everybody knew that they were creeps."

"Jean-Luc is a pimp and was a pimp," says Dorothy Parker. "Before Karins, he took girls and sold them to agencies in Paris. I was in Ibiza with the daughter of a friend, fifteen years old, and he came to the table and wanted this girl."

Despite his bad behavior, Brunel led a charmed life. It couldn't have been otherwise with Eileen Ford as his guardian angel. "Eileen took Jean-Luc as her son," says Jacques Silberstein. "She let him become very powerful. Jean-Luc's education impressed Eileen. He played the game well. He could be charming." Some saw a flirtation between them. "Jean-Luc made her feel girlish and desirable," a model school owner says.

"Not with my girls" was the motto of most agents who sent models to Europe in the days when that meant dropping them like raw meat into a tank of piranhas. Brunel seemed to honor that pact with Ford. "I love Jean-Luc. I think Jean-Luc's great," says Christy Turlington. "I stayed at his apartment all the time, and never once did I ever see anything wrong, never once did he treat me wrong."

Finally, though, people began warning Eileen Ford that her partner in Paris was up to no good. Bonnouvrier told Ford how Brunel was thrown out of a modeling convention in Las Vegas after a drug party in his room. "She started screaming, 'You're jealous, he's successful!' " Bonnouvrier recalls. "I said, 'I'm not sure jealous describes my feeling. I'm talking about drugs.' She refused the evidence. She said, 'He makes me laugh.' "

After leaving Brunel's employ, Gaby Wagner set up her own boutique agency, Zoom, with the help of her friend, the lawyer Jean-Marie de Gueldre. One of her models soon left her for Karins. Not long afterward, the model called Wagner, "and she said, 'Gaby, you have to pick me up here. I'm in this apartment and I'm scared and I took drugs.' At eleven at night I got her out of the apartment of Karins." Though Wagner wanted her to go to the police, the girl left for America. "I picked up the phone and called Eileen Ford and told her what was going on in Karins," Wagner says. "I said, 'This is something I've seen, and I can tell you this is absolutely true.' She would not believe me."

The seven-month CBS investigation changed that. "Nobody in the industry wanted to talk," says reporter Craig Pyes. "They were protecting their own interests. Nobody was protecting the girls." John Casablancas told Pyes it was a major scandal, "a conspiracy of silence, greed, and fear," and then declined to go on camera. But Eileen Ford agreed to an interview at the Hôtel Ritz in Paris during the October fashion shows and, by all accounts, walked into a sneak attack.

Pyes had found two models called Courtney and Shari. On the show they called Brunel's parties a "meat market . . . for the purpose of somebody wanting to take you home to bed." Brunel was "the matchmaker . . . he's got the girls." And if a girl said no, she got no work. "I was personally proposed to . . . by Jean-Luc," one said. "I laughed in his face, and I had no more appointments and I never worked." Courtney and Shari were followed by another model, who was not identified. She said Jean-Luc had given her cocaine and taken it himself. "He'd always give me a little vial of cocaine," she said. "He did that with all the girls." Finally another unidentified model said Brunel gave her a drink at his house that made her pass out. She awoke the next morning in his bed, positive she had been raped.

Before she showed the tapes of the girls to Eileen Ford, Sawyer asked her what she'd do if someone made those accusations. Ford said she wouldn't believe it but would dump Jean-Luc if she did. Then Sawyer played the tapes. "That's horrible," Ford said. It was the first time she'd ever heard such accusations, she said. Sawyer told her the show had interviewed five models who said they'd been drugged by Jean-Luc. "For his sake, I hope you're wrong," Ford said. "I have certainly asked him never to have drugs around in front of my models."

Ford looked as if she'd seen a ghost. Unfortunately Jean-Luc Brunel was alive. "She was very concerned," says Pyes. "She put on an incredible amount of pressure. She called with all kinds of stories, seeking to discredit us. She put all kinds of pressure on the girls who appeared through their agents, trying to get them to pull out."

"American Models in Paris" aired in December 1988. Within weeks screenings of bootleg copies of the show were held in Paris, and transcripts were circulated. Within months Ford cut off its relationship with Karins. Brunel's scouting sources dried up—for a year. But unlike Haddad, Brunel survived and remains a power in modeling, the owner of Karins and a partner in an agency in New York.

Jean-Luc Brunel receives a visitor warmly in an office he shares with Karins's director, Ruth Malka, whose power grew after the *60 Minutes* broadcast. "After CBS Ruth stood up and said, 'I'm in charge,' " reports Jérôme Bonnouvrier. "She's now a partner."

Brunel is, as advertised, a charmer, small, with hollow, Gallic features, a broken nose, long, wavy brown hair, and a slightly dangerous air, softened by a blue cashmere sweater and a pair of tortoise-framed glasses. "I'm no saint," he says by way of introduction. "But I never messed with the girls of the agency, and not one girl left me. That's the big difference between Claude and I."

He readily allows for another difference: that he had a problem with cocaine for half a decade. "I admit it," he says. "So, big deal! I never did it in the day. I was not mixing it; it never happened in the agency. I did it as an experiment. Fine, it lasted maybe a bit longer than it should. I started to do it for a few years, and then I stopped it; it was ruining my life."

Brunel says he's lived the night life in Paris since he was a teenager and admits that models have passed through his bed. "You get laid tonight with a model, is that a crime?" he asks. "I don't understand why people go into your personal life, what you do yourself, and to yourself, and they don't look at things that are really important!" What's important? Brunel believes that teenage girls shouldn't be allowed to go to Paris by themselves to model. "I'm against it, it's crazy, it's nuts," he says. "I don't like having girls who are fifteen, sixteen. The only thing they give you is trouble. You just have to mother them; you just have to look that they're fine. When that image of big super-models started, it gave hope. But it doesn't work that way. And what happened was a lot of agencies took too many people that weren't the right people. There were so many girls with nothing to do."

Like Haddad, Brunel feels the *60 Minutes* report was unfair for singling out Paris agents. "It was exactly the same in America," he says. "If I'd had a daughter, I wouldn't have sent her to New York. It was a hundred times worse at Studio 54 than at Les Bains."

Brunel has heard all the stories that go around about him and brings them up to deny them. "You're going to hear I bring girls to St.-Tropez," he says. "I never took girls to parties, to dinner, never, never." But he admits he does invite girls to dinners with his friends. "If I have a dinner, I don't pay any attention," he says. "I've dined with many girls from my agency, and then it becomes like twelve, twenty people, but the girls they can go whenever they want, nobody's going to bug them."

Karins is "a business," he goes on. "Otherwise it would not last this long. Then you have my life. My life is not a story as long as I don't take young girls to serve either my own, or . . . I mean, I don't need those doors to open," he says, referring to the sorts of men who would invite him places because he might bring models along. "I know tons and tons and tons, and I don't want to see them," he says. "I don't want to be invited for a girl. How many times have I been invited on a boat and this and that; I never said yes, never, never, never."

He found out about the *60 Minutes* investigation after Diane Sawyer had interviewed Eileen Ford, who called him. "She was horrified," he says, "and then they called me to see me, [but] when I heard how they were doing it, I refused to see them." Brunel says he tried, but failed, to stop the show from airing. Afterward, he says, he was treated like a pariah.

Brunel married model Roberta Chirko the day before *60 Minutes* aired. Though the timing was curious, they'd been together for two years, he says. Others add that she was so in love with him she'd stop girls on the street and recruit them for Karins. Nonetheless, people talked. "Jean-Luc married Roberta right after *60 Minutes* to clean up his image," says an American model who worked in Paris. But he hadn't cleaned up his act, she adds. "He'd call her from other girls' beds and say, 'I'm so lonely.' " Though they've since broken up, Chirko is still with Brunel's agency in New York.

Despite his outraged innocence, Brunel thinks *60 Minutes* did a good job. "*60 Minutes* is *60 Minutes* because they're good," he says. "A good journalist knows what people want. You just have to catch the moment. It came at the right time." He knows things had gotten out of hand. "*60 Minutes,* it was like the end of something," he says.

Craig Pyes of *60 Minutes* brushes off Brunel's and Haddad's denials, even though French authorities apparently never pursued the matter. "Hundreds of girls were not only harassed but molested," Pyes says. "We're talking about a conveyor belt, not a casting couch." Nearly two dozen models talked to CBS, repeating the sexual allegations about Haddad and Brunel. Five others claimed they'd been drugged by Brunel or his friends. Independent witnesses also confirmed key details of the stories told by the models who appeared on the air. Pyes adds that two of the models he investigated ended up hospitalized with ongoing, severe psychological problems. One claimed she'd been drugged by Brunel's friends, and the other was involved "in a sordid party scene," Pyes says. "I spoke to the parents of both girls."

It was natural to wonder—and many did—why Eileen Ford hadn't done the same. "Didn't you know?" Ford employee Iris Minier asked her boss shortly thereafter.

"Girls always say things," Ford replied with a sigh.

"She really did have a heart," Minier insists five years later. "She'd heard. She just didn't believe it. If she had, she would've cut his balls off." Indeed, she'd already cut off Claude Haddad, as she told Sawyer on the air. She wouldn't deal with him anymore, and "he knows why," she said righteously. "I don't think he behaved properly. I know he didn't. It's just so reprehensible, just so appalling that some old sleazebag would come along and touch a girl." Unless it was her sleazebag, that is.

Even after *60 Minutes* aired, Ford didn't believe what had been said about Jean-Luc. That November Minier moved to Paris to be Eileen Ford's "eyes and ears," she says. Her brief was to handle scouting throughout Europe—and to ask questions about Brunel. "I told Eileen it was serious," she says. "She went to the girls and heard for herself. She couldn't deny it anymore. She pulled her girls out of Karins."

"We knew Jean-Luc was on coke, and I knew he liked young girls," says Jerry Ford, but Brunel had sworn he'd stopped taking drugs in 1987. Ford says that only once did they hear of an attempted rape, and the girl involved "absolutely denied it." But after she returned to New York, Eileen Ford called one of the girls who appeared on *60 Minutes* and asked her why she'd kept the story to herself. The girl replied that she was afraid.

"That," Eileen says, "was the end of us and Jean-Luc."

The Fords had ended up at odds with Dorian Leigh, Simone and José Benazaref, John Casablancas, and now Jean-Luc Brunel. The obvious solution was to open Ford in Paris, but Eileen and Jerry didn't want to own foreign agencies. "It was the last thing in the world I wanted to do," Jerry says. "A little out of laziness, a little out of an appreciation of how difficult it is to run a remote office." And the Fords seemed to think that they could rest on their laurels. "We were strong enough to survive a real assault—John Casablancas and all the outriders," Jerry says.

The Fords hadn't sat still in the years since the model wars. They and their children had traveled the world, vigorously promoting their Face of the 80s contest. Renee Simonson, the contest's 1981 winner, earned more covers than any model except child star Brooke Shields. In 1983 Ford started boards for older models, meant to appeal to aging baby boomers. It was a pioneering move and a bit ahead of prevailing attitudes, even Eileen's. "I don't want to look at a magazine and see an old trout like me," she said. In 1984 they launched a venture to open Ford Model Schools, only to dissolve it three years later. But their move into the runway arena that same year was a hit.

It was around this time of expansion that a question arose: Who would run Ford after Eileen and Jerry retired? Though all the children had worked at the agency, "there was an outspoken desire on their part not to be involved," says Jerry. Eldest child, Jamie, and youngest, Lacey, had bailed out of the dynasty. Easygoing Billy Ford took charge of publicity and promotion. But only daughter Katie seemed to have the interest and drive required to move Ford into the future. "I was really pleased when she decided to come into the company," says her father. "She's tough, calm, and almost unforgiving in her decision making."

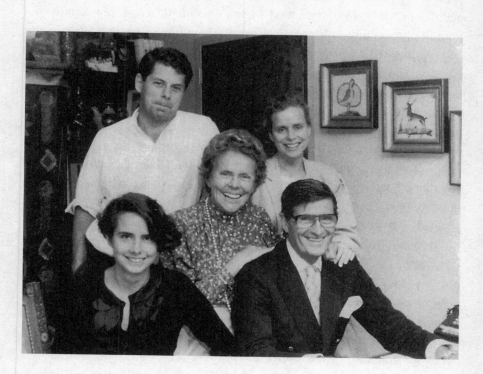

Eileen and Jerry Ford with their children Katie (*left*), Bill,
and Lacey Ford in 1984

Katie had earned an M.B.A. and worked for a television syndicator and a management consultant before deciding that Ford Models "looked pretty good to her," her father says. But she was far younger and less experienced than Joe Hunter and Marion Smith, the agency's two top executives. After marrying André Balazs, a wealthy young entrepreneur in 1985, Katie Ford proved her mettle by opening branches of her family's business in the late eighties in São Paolo, Brazil, and Miami's South Beach, a new frontier for fashion photography. It became clear that "the future of representation is that you will have to service people all over the world," Jerry Ford says. "Katie is going to be one of the key figures in that process." In 1989 she took a brief break to have a daughter. Early in 1991 she was back in the trenches.

The agencies the Fords had allied themselves with in Paris were not working out. "We were not getting cooperation," says Jerry Ford. "They're concerned with their own market, and they know models [want to] come to America, so they were afraid." They were also afraid that Ford was using them as stalking horses for a Ford office in Paris. "Rumors were flying that we were going to open," says Iris Minier. "I told Eileen we had no choice. They finally decided to do it."

"Billy was always after us to open in France," says Eileen, but finally Paris was Katie's idea. "We'd lost one model too many," she says. "It was time to get on a plane." So Katie left her husband in America, where he was building a hotel empire, flew to France with their baby daughter, and spent two months living in Minier's apartment, plotting and planning. "Word got out," says Minier. "People were panicked." One night Minier's phone rang. "Look over your shoulder," a voice warned.

The day Ford opened on the rue Rivoli in March 1991, Christy Turlington and Naomi Campbell joined up. Elle MacPherson, Rachel Williams, Shalom Harlow, Basia, and Amber Valletta followed. Finally, Ford seemed to have entered the modern age. From Paris the agency began sending scouts into Eastern Europe. By 1992 Ford was even holding semifinals for its model search contest (renamed Supermodel of the World) in Croatia. That same year Ford released a hard-cover promotional book as lavish as any Elite had ever produced. More astonishing, it included photographs by Giovanni Gastel of bare-breasted Ford models. Why did they do it? In an interview at the time Gastel said he wanted to portray the women of the millennium, "fractionalized and magnificently different." Eileen Ford's explanation was somewhat less poetic. "Honey, there's a recession out there," she said at the time. Later she admitted that Katie did the book without telling her.

Elite had long been the financial innovator in modeling, raising both commissions and service fees from 10 to 20 percent. Now Elite seemed hidebound as it insisted it would pay only 5 percent commissions to schools and small agencies that discovered new models, while Ford raised the bounty to as much as 25 percent.

The most visible symbol of the newest-fangled spirit of competition were scooters or castors—free-lance scouts who scour the world for pretty girls. They ply a thriving trade—particularly in Paris, selling models back and forth between agencies, like so much meat. Paid scouts had scoured Scandinavia for years, working for the Fords, Elite, and also magazines like *Playboy* and its French offshoot, *Lui*. "That's how it started," says Jean-Luc Brunel. "Then Claude Haddad sent guys in discos, trying to bring those girls. Dominique Galas was one of them. They go in the streets; they bug every single girl in town." Every agency, too. "You see them downstairs," says Ford's Iris Minier. "They stand near magazines and castings. They'd sell their grandmothers for a buck. They say, 'Show me your book. This is shit. We can do better.' "

The most aggressive such company, competitors say, is Paris-based Metropolitan Models, formed in 1986 by the trio of ex-model and Euro-Planning *rabatteur* Dominique Galas, a clothing manufacturer named Michel Levaton, and a booker, Aileen Souliers. The next year Metropolitan got its big break when Galas and Levaton spotted Claudia Schiffer, seventeen, a high school student from Rheinberg, Germany, dancing with friends in a Düsseldorf disco. "You look really good," Levaton told her. "Do you want to be a model?" Schiffer brushed him off. "You know how the French are," she says with a little giggle. "I kept dancing. He kept trying to speak to me. I told him to stop bothering me. So he went to talk with my friends."

Finally, hoping to scare him off, she gave Levaton her parents' phone number. He called the next day, invited them for lunch, and they had "a long, long, long talk," Schiffer recalls. With their blessing she began spending weekends and school holidays in Paris. Before she finished school, she'd won a Revlon ad and a cover of *Elle*. "I was convinced," Schiffer says.

Her stardom was cinched when she met a model turned photographer, Ellen von Unwerth, who saw in her clean, healthy German face an echo of Brigitte Bardot. After shooting Schiffer as Bardot for *Lei,* an Italian magazine, she offered the model to a big client, Guess, the giant jeans maker. Von Unwerth's Guess ads starring Schiffer gave modeling its newest superstar. In 1990 Souliers and Levaton moved to New York and opened a branch of Metropolitan there. In 1993, when Schiffer inked a $6 million contract with

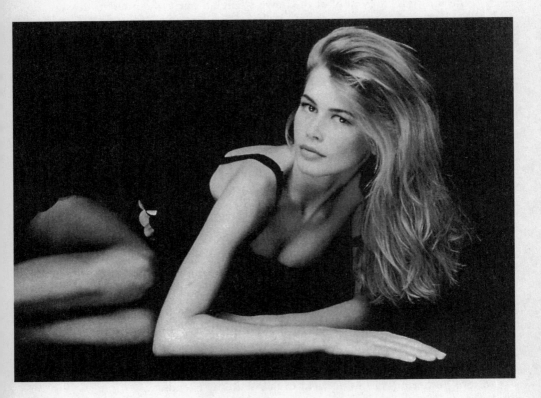

Claudia Schiffer, Metropolitan's ornament, in the early 1990s

Revlon *and* became the latest favorite of her countryman Chanel designer Karl Lagerfeld, Metropolitan's hood ornament was the world's highest-paid model, earning about $10 million a year. In effect, Schiffer *is* Metropolitan.

The upstart Metropolitan's success with Schiffer didn't make the agency many friends in modeling. "If Claudia quits tomorrow, what do they have?" one competitor snipes. But Metropolitan has been aggressive in recruiting models from other agencies. In 1988, competitors charge, it was Levaton who circulated copies of the *60 Minutes* show throughout the modeling business. Levaton says he wasn't the only aggressor. "I was not the one who started this thing," he snaps. "When we went to New York, the competition was very rude, trying to steal our girls, calling them and saying I was not going to come back to Paris." So in 1993 Levaton returned and "hired scouts all over," he growls. "We have to protect ourselves."

Bill Weinberg and Fran Rothschild had run Wilhelmina jointly since its namesake's death in 1980. But by 1988 they'd come to loathe each other. Rothschild didn't get along with Weinberg's wife, who'd begun to play a role in the agency. "Fran's hatred was disproportionate," says men's division head Dan Deely. "But Bill had a very lazy attitude." At first that was fine for the staff, which could do what it wanted in the absence of leadership. Then Deely left, and Weinberg had a quarrel with the women's division head, Faith Kates. Soon after, Deely saw her out to dinner one night with a distinctive-looking Italian—Fashion Model's owner, Giorgio Sant'Ambrogio.

Early in 1989 the Next agency was opened by Kates, with three other Wilhelmina staffers, and thirteen of its models. A friendly client had called in the books of all the models Kates wanted, so they would be out of Wilhelmina's hands when she opened. "She called me up one day and said she'd been offered a business," says Jan Kaplan Planit, who worked with her at Wilhelmina and became vice-president of Next. "She said she had backers. She wouldn't say who."

For public consumption Next belonged to Kates. Behind the scenes people knew better. It simply wasn't a good time to reveal who her backers were. "After the *60 Minutes* thing, Faith opened," says Jean-Luc Brunel. "When she opened, I took an option to buy. I didn't know what I wanted to do." He was still trading models with Ford when one model threatened to leave the agency. Brunel claims, "Eileen said, 'If she goes to Next, then I will never speak with you in my life.' I was not going to give up my business because it suited her. I switched twenty-six girls in one day, and that really made Next."

A few months after Next opened, Brunel exercised his option to buy a piece of it through the holding company that owns Karins. At the same time the company that owns Milan's Fashion Model invested in Next as well. Fashion Model kept working with Ford for several years. That may explain why Fashion's owner, Giorgio Sant'Ambrogio, denies his interest in Next.

But with agencies in New York, Miami, Milan, and Paris, the Next-Karins-Fashion axis took third place in world modeling, after Elite and Ford.

Suddenly networks were chic. Everybody had to have one. Indeed, as Kates, Brunel, and Sant'Ambrogio formed theirs, Wilhelmina also began to expand around the world. Back in March 1989 Fran Rothschild had tried to sell the agency to an investment group. Weinberg refused. Then he showed up with a buyer, a German businessman named Dieter Esch. Rothschild was inclined to hate him on sight. But "the more I spent time with him the more I liked him," Rothschild said. "He was exciting. He had wild ideas." In September 1989 Esch bought 95 percent of Willie's stock.

The son of a welder from Weingarten, Germany, Esch was a newcomer to modeling. As a young man he sold heavy construction equipment in Canada. In the seventies he returned to Germany, where he founded IBH, a conglomerate that gobbled up troubled machine makers until it was stymied by recession in 1982. The next year IBH's debts led to an investigation of a private bank in Frankfurt, Germany, which had lent IBH about $245 million—$200 million more than the bank had. Esch was blamed for setting off the second worst banking crisis in Germany since World War II and sending half a dozen bankers and executives—himself among them—to jail. Convicted of negligence and making false declarations to the government, he was sentenced to three and a half years in prison. After he admitted he'd defrauded an investor of about $50 million and delayed the announcement of IBH's bankruptcy, his sentence was increased to six and a half years.

Jeremy Foster-Fell first met Dieter Esch through a mutual friend. "He said a very close colleague was looking to buy an agency, and would I meet with him?" Foster-Fell recalls. Learning Esch's plan, he introduced the ex-convict to the owners of agencies big and small, including Wilhelmina. Esch had nerve. He immediately offered to buy Ford and Wilhelmina. But it was no sale—at least not yet.

Esch soon lowered his sights and began approaching the owners of small agencies. He disarmed them by introducing himself with an article about the time he'd spent in jail. Some of them, lured by the scent of big money, went so far as to open their books for him. Esch thinks they didn't know what they were giving him. "P and Ls, trial balances, statements, accounts receivable," he says. "When I went through my learning phase, I realized I was probably the only person with an overview of the entire situation. I know exactly what the salary structure is, what the commission structure is, what volume is."

Finally Esch found a live one: Sue Charney, the former Ford VP. Charney had opened a small agency called Faces, backed by the well-known financier Asher Edelman's brother, John. He wanted out. "Dieter sold me a bill of goods," says Charney. "I gave him credibility in this business." Esch closed his deal to buy Faces in June 1989, paying for little more than accounts receivable. Before the final contracts were prepared, he was hunting for more agencies to buy, and within a few months he landed Wilhelmina.

In 1990 Esch bought Jérôme Bonnouvrier's bankrupt agency in Paris and changed its name to Wilhelmina-Glamour. He also bought Oz, a hair, makeup, photography, and styling agency, and Trouble, a "body" agency in Los Angeles that booked well-developed models for neocheesecake jobs. But his biggest deal was yet to come. Working with an international mergers and acquisitions firm, Esch entered new negotiations to buy Ford for a reported price of about $15 million *and* the much larger Elite network for about $25 million up front and $5 million later. He had a plan to create a holding company to own and operate all three companies and rule the world of modeling.

In 1989 Ford executive Joe Hunter brought Dieter Esch to meet Jerry Ford. Ford admits that the price he asked—$20 million—was "far beyond what our earnings should command on a multiple basis." Then, late in 1992, Esch returned. A condition of Esch's new offer "was us and the children out," Jerry Ford says. "I thought that was OK." Eileen and Jerry Ford expressed their willingness to sell to him despite his past and the fact that their daughter Katie actually wanted to stay.

Esch's intelligence-gathering operation had served him well. He'd learned that Katie and Bill Ford's inevitable progress to the agency's throne was a bone in Hunter's throat and and that of the women's division head, Marion Smith. It couldn't have been easy for Katie either. She couldn't make deals on her own. When she tried to hire Beth Boldt to run a board at Ford New York while she was in Paris, "Joe and Marion were threatened," says Boldt. "They flipped."

Clever Esch insisted on dealing with each of Ford's shareholders separately. Hunter and Smith met him in mid-November. Esch said his deal with the family was set and he wanted the duo to stay and run the company. "I was a little bit surprised, knowing his background, that he'd gotten as far as he did with the Ford family," says Smith. She was also unnerved by Esch's hard sell. "Dieter needs to rule the world," she says. "I wondered what would happen to anyone who got in his way."

Hunter found Esch's ideas interesting. "Taking the model business global is the ultimate concept," he says. "Really expanding and being every place was what I always wanted to do. We thought about it. Then we sat down with Jerry and talked alternatives. It forced the issue." When it emerged that none of them trusted Esch, says Katie, "we discussed it, and we all liked the idea of running Ford together." With that, they spurned Esch's offer.

In May 1993 Ford announced a restructuring. Jerry and Eileen would no longer run the business. Smith, Hunter, and Katie Ford were named to a three-headed presidency. They soon absorbed Clip, one of the best small agencies in Paris, and its director, Jean-Michel Pradwilov, after Clip's backer, Jean-Pierre Dollé of Paris Planning, died late in 1994.

"Dieter Esch made us sit down and outline our future," says Katie Ford. "Ford is a very strong name. We've opened offices in Arizona and Argentina. We feel those are emerging markets. We also want to expand based on what a strong name Ford is. We've talked about licensing the name on all kinds of products, about opening a beauty division for hair and makeup. There are ways to expand when a business matures, which this business is doing. In hindsight it's amazing we hadn't sat down and discussed it."

John Casablancas, too, was initially taken with Esch's offer for his agency. "It's a very simple story," he said at the time. "We are service providers. We don't have solid assets or inventory. The fact is, we have a business that is very fragile. Look at the Fords. Their business was worth much more ten years ago than it is now. That will happen to us, too, unless we become a more structured corporation. So the dream is to sell."

The deal was to work like this: A new Swiss company was to be formed. Esch would contribute Wilhelmina. Investors he had gathered would pay for Ford and Elite. Esch would run the holding company while the model managers managed the models. "We figured he would probably make a good profit by overvaluing Wilhelmina, but that's normal," Casablancas added, laughing.

The Esch juggernaut first faltered in March 1993, when the Ford deal fell through. Elite stayed interested through the spring, but once the Fords dropped out, it was less inviting to potential investors. Other factors also worked against Esch—among them his reputation and the fact that his holding company would be a Swiss entity controlled by a foreign national.

Finally, on June 4, Casablancas sent a fax to all his partners, clients, models, and friends, acknowledging the talks with Esch but reporting that the deal was dead.

As with Ford, the end of the deal proved to be a boon to Elite. "It was a very amusing exercise," says Casablancas. "It caused an extraordinary soul-searching and introspection. We scrutinized every element of the company. There are lots of possibilities. After twenty-five years it rekindled my interest. And I'm sure Alain Kittler, who loves deals, has acquired a taste for mergers and acquisitions and sales and so on."

Just as Esch was forming his master plan, his inspiration, Mark McCormack, was having a similar idea. The sports agent had owned two model agencies for more than a dozen years, but he'd never made anything of them. Indeed, they were the only stain on his reputation for keen business acumen.

McCormack had retained his interest in modeling even after his brief representation of Jean Shrimpton ended. He'd met Veruschka through Shrimpton and tried to set up endorsement deals for her, including the ill-fated Veruschka Vodka. Then he picked up an English model named Maudie James. "She was still an active model," McCormack recalls, "and she wanted traditional bookings." McCormack's International Management Group had more than thirty agents, but they were "totally indifferent to modeling," he says. So he backed a London agency.

McCormack also attempted to start a New York agency, Legends, with partners who were ex-models and agency executives, but after a promising start in 1981 it foundered. Nonetheless, it limped on for years, until McCormack installed Chuck Bennett, an IMG agent, early in 1992. Bennett believed the model agency was being wasted. "Instead of being an eight-hundred-pound gorilla who wasn't sitting anywhere, we needed to become a credible player, and that required a credible reorganization," he says. Bennett changed the staff, divested all the agency's models, hired scouts around the world, and started rebuilding from scratch. He also dropped the name Legends and made the agency part of IMG. The London office that had operated for years under the name of its founder, ex-model Laraine Ashton, was similarly renamed.

Top models began signing up. Niki Taylor was one of the first. Liv Tyler arrived not long after her agency, Spectrum, blew up. In September 1993 Lauren Hutton walked in the door, followed by Carol Alt. They'd smelled the promise in IMG's pitch. "The structure we already have is such that if you're Lauren Hutton, you'll be able to exploit what you are throughout the world,"

Bennett says. "Arnold Palmer, Rod Laver, and Jackie Stewart are all still with IMG," he adds, referring to three aging sports stalwarts in the agency's stable. "I don't think that happens in the modeling business. We have seventy-five people in an office in Tokyo, not some booker in blue jeans in New York, wondering how to find the right guy at Dentsu advertising. Dieter and John can open modeling agencies. We have sixty-two offices dedicated to helping models make money beyond modeling—in publishing, events, television. They don't have the money or the expertise to do that. We can exploit their names, reputations, and excellence around the world." Bennett plans to open IMG Models offices in major markets, buying existing agencies when possible. "We really believe models have arrived," he says.

Looking around, you'd have to agree. The early nineties have seen Aaron Spelling's *Models, Inc.* join such nonfiction shows as *Fashion Television, House of Style,* and *Style with Elsa Klensch* on television; Australian swimsuit star Elle MacPherson's appearance in the film *Sirens;* the publication of *Top Model,* a new magazine from the publishers of *Elle;* the release of calendars by Kathy Ireland, MacPherson, Claudia Schiffer, and Niki Taylor; and near-daily round-the-world coverage of such important news as the status of Cindy Crawford's thing with Richard Gere (terminal), Elaine Irwin and John Mellencamp (holding steady), and Claudia Schiffer and David Copperfield (heading for the altar).

Strangely, just as the modeling business was poised to get bigger, models got smaller. The waifs, as the new generation was called, seemed like both a reaction to the excesses of the supermodels and a perfect reflection of a time of diminished expectations—in fashion and life. "The movement happened because we needed a change," says Polly Mellen, who'd moved from *Vogue* to a new beauty magazine, *Allure.* And just as in the sixties the signs of changing times first appeared in England.

Sarah Doukas was a teenager, working in an antiques market on London's King's Road in 1972, when someone took her picture and sent her to an agency. For three years she modeled and sold antiques in London and Paris, before changing careers and managing a punk rock band, The Criminals, at the end of the seventies, when punk rock swept England. A few years later she met and married an American musician, the lead singer of a band called Earthquake. They moved to San Francisco, where they had a child and lived until 1982.

Earthquake had disbanded, and Doukas needed a job. A photographer friend sent her to Laraine Ashton. In six years there she rose from junior assistant to running the place, booking models like Jerry Hall and David Bailey's then wife Marie Helvin. Then, with the help of the rock band U2's lawyer, she put together a business plan for her own agency and began seeking backers, including Virgin Records tycoon Richard Branson, whose brother was one of her friends. In 1987 he agreed to give her interest-free loans until the agency, which she called Storm, got on its feet.

Working out of her bedroom, she recruited two bookers and began searching for girls. She found many of them on the street. "Wherever I was going, I was looking," she says. "I found a great girl outside a garage in Battersby, in her school uniform." Another discovery had pink and green hair. Clearly Doukas had a different kind of eye.

Once she'd gathered seven girls, she took their test photographs on a trip to Paris, Milan, and Japan. "So things progressed," says her younger brother, Simon Chambers, who joined the company, computerized its accounts, and acted—he laughs—as "a reluctant babe magnet." Fashion editors soon came sniffing around. Harriet Jagger of British *Elle* lived a street away, "and she would walk by on her way to work and come in and see who I had new, nearly every day," Sarah says.

Sarah and Simon were on their way home from a scouting trip to Los Angeles and New York in 1988 when Sarah spotted a scrawny fourteen-year-old at Kennedy Airport. Kate Moss, a schoolgirl from Croydon, and her travel agent father had been waiting three days for standby seats back to England, where they were expected at a wedding. Kate's father was arguing with people at the counter when Doukas spotted them. Luckily they made the flight. "As soon as the seat belt sign switched off, we rushed over," Sarah says.

Kate's father had seen Doukas on television and knew she was legitimate. The next day Kate's skeptical mother agreed to accompany her to Storm. "She thought it was major con," Kate recalled.

"I didn't think I was going to change the face of modeling," Doukas says. "But I'd found this amazing-looking girl. She came into the office, and she did a job immediately." Doukas called all the magazines and faxed photographs of Moss to everyone she knew. "Nobody was interested," she says. Moss was only five feet seven inches. Her career started slowly. "She was in school, and I don't ever agree with taking anybody out of school," Doukas says. "We worked on the holidays and stuttered along for a year. But she wasn't greatly interested in

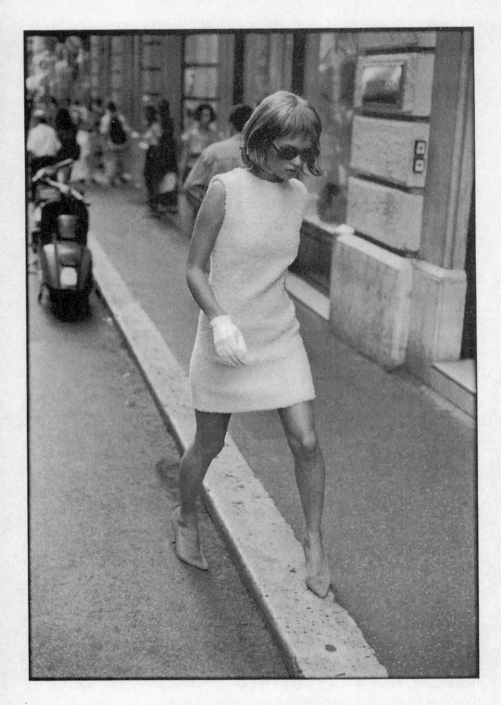

Kate Moss photographed (as Anna Wintour?) by
Peter Lindbergh for *Harper's Bazaar*

school, and then she left, and then we started. Every day I said, 'I'm going to make you a star.' I didn't know I was going to make her a superstar."

Late in 1989 a young photographer named Corinne Day spotted a Polaroid of Moss and booked her for a shoot for the trend-setting English youth-cult magazine *The Face*. It was looking for a face to represent the magazine, and Kate's clicked. Her first appearance was in March. Her first cover was in May.

Though she worked successfully for the next two years, Moss's real break came in 1992, when she returned to America to shoot a cover for *Harper's Bazaar*. Earlier that year Hearst Magazines in New York had poached Elizabeth Tilberis, who'd succeeded Anna Wintour as editor of British *Vogue,* and installed her as the American fashion magazine's new editor in chief. For a quarter century Condé Nast had been the American magazine king of fashion, and its longtime rival, Hearst, had seemed rudderless. Hiring Tilberis was a bold move in Hearst's quest to restore itself to glossy glory.

It would be an uphill battle. Through the early eighties *Bazaar* had registered consistent gains, more than doubling ad pages between 1977 and 1984. But in 1985 ad pages started falling, and revenue was flat. The downward trend continued, and by decade's end there were constant rumors in bitchy fashion circles that *Bazaar* editor Anthony Mazzola's days were numbered.

Elizabeth Tilberis had joined British *Vogue* during the reign of Wintour's predecessor, Bea Miller. When Miller retired, Wintour "made changes, of course," Tilberis says. "Excellent changes. It wasn't the same as Bea's magazine. We did less whimsy. We did a lot of running on the street." Much as she approved, Tilberis almost went to work for Ralph Lauren in 1987, saying she was tired of traveling. She stayed in London after Wintour quit, she says, because "you don't get offered the editorship of *Vogue* too often in life."

Tilberis started talking to Hearst in October 1991. "It took awhile," she says. "I wanted to find out how committed they were. They are totally committed to do the magazine I would like to see done." That December Mazzola "announced his plan to retire early next year or as soon as a successor is found," according to a press statement. Assurances in hand, Tilberis signed up in January 1992.

Her first issue, published that September, threw down a gauntlet. After a fierce bidding war with *Vogue* for the services of several top photographers, Tilberis had signed Patrick Demarchelier (who'd worked extensively for her at British *Vogue*) and Peter Lindbergh to exclusive contracts. She and her new team, notably art director Fabien Baron, then concocted a magazine that would stand apart and offer a clear alternative to Wintour's cacophonous *Vogue* and its trendish chief photographer, Steven Meisel. The clean, airy, elegant publication she produced harkened back to the glory days of Alexey Brodovitch without seeming like a reproduction and quickly won acclaim, awards, newsstand sales, and attention from upscale advertisers.

While Tilberis was still planning, Kate Moss was on her way to America, where she signed with Woman, another new boutique agency. It quickly sent her on a go-see with Steven Meisel, who'd been shooting the Barbie-esque Shana Zadrick. Moss was something completely different, and Meisel used her for a Dolce e Gabbana catalog and an Italian *Glamour* cover. Woman also sent Moss to see Sara Foley-Anderson, who'd just been hired away from Wilhelmina's exclusive W2 division to be *Bazaar*'s model editor. She and *Bazaar*'s editors "fell in love with Kate," Foley-Anderson recalls. "We believed that models and fashion needed to be less hard-edged, more pared-down and accessible, less complicated and more open and real than they were in the eighties. Kate was the original herald of this movement, which, in its extreme, became 'waif.'" The magazine immediately sent Moss to Patrick Demarchelier, who apparently agreed. A nine-page spread in Tilberis's first issue that September, "Wild: Fashion that breaks the rules," broke the rules concerning who could make it as a supermodel. Every month Moss gathered more *Bazaar* pages.

Demarchelier had also won the job of shooting launch ads for CK, a new, youth-oriented line by designer Calvin Klein. Marky Mark, the pop star, had already agreed to appear in the ads, but Demarchelier and Klein needed a girl. The photographer introduced Moss to the designer, says Doukas, "and before we knew it, we had a contract on our hands."

A nod from Calvin Klein was a star-making moment in any model's career. But Moss's first ads were more than that. Demarchelier's photographs of a topless Moss, straddling the buff body of Marky Mark, started a furor that continued long afterward. They also posed a challenge to the supermodels, several of whom criticized the ads in public. Claudia Schiffer's comments about unnecessary nudity won her a blistering reply from Moss. "That's how she made her fortune," cried the waif. "She's got an amazing body and big tits. She sold her body like I sold mine."

With the Calvin Klein seal of approval, Moss was launched. "Calvin has intuition," says Doukas's brother, Simon. "He knew that this wasn't just a modeling thing; this was a whole new generation. In the eighties young people, whether fifteen or forty, liked the same music, wore the same fashion, and da-da-da-da-da. But then the baby boomers got a little bit older, and their children came in behind them. Calvin knew that they had to have their own representative. The young want an icon like Kate, and the rest of us want our own. So there is also, simultaneously, a new realism in advertising, thanks to women out there spending money who want models to look realistic."

Klein took the lead there, too, working both sides of the generation gap. The first indication that postpubescence had surged into fashion's bloodstream came from Barneys New York. The store had just done an ad campaign using supermodels Christy Turlington, Naomi Campbell, Linda Evangelista, and Rachel Williams. Afterward Barneys' ad crew—baby boomers all—were sitting around talking about the disparity between the teens in the ads and their customers. Lauren Hutton ended up starring in a Barneys campaign that fall and again the following spring.

Then Calvin Klein booked his old friend Lisa Taylor. She'd found herself, early in the 1990s, in the office of a friend, contemplating turning forty.

"What should I do?" she asked Bryan Bantry, Patrick Demarchelier's agent.

"You look incredible," he told her. "Call Calvin."

Soon afterward several misty ads were created for Klein's collection. When they appeared in March 1992 magazines, they had an extraordinary impact. Clairol launched an ad campaign featuring twenty models over thirty years old. In April 1993 Klein began alternating waif models like Moss with five women who'd worked for him fifteen years before: Hutton, Rosie Vela, Jane Hitchcock (who'd started her career as a fourteen-year-old waif), Patti Hansen, and Donna Jordan. "They look just as right in my clothes now as they did then," Klein said. "I have to be honest. I really don't focus on age. I focus on the beauty of women."

But the message *was* all about age. Kate Moss appeals to kids who buy jeans, Lauren Hutton to grown-ups who buy $2,000 dresses. Klein—ever the cultural barometer—had cottoned on to something important. Baby boomers—the protagonists of the last youthquake—had seen their elders make fools of themselves at the time trying to act young, and they had no intention of doing the same.

"We're like crusaders, pitching this idea and trying to get people to change what they think about women and age and advertising," says agent Bantry. He's signed up Haddon, Vela, Hansen, Marisa Berenson, Shaun Casey, Debbie and Janice Dickinson, Kim Alexis, Lois Chiles, Lisa Cooper, Ann Turkel, Donna Mitchell, Shelly Smith, Margaux Hemingway, and more as members of what he describes as an informal support group aimed at reinventing and reestablishing models of the 1960s and 1970s.

"This generation is healthier, living longer, spending more money; they're much younger at forty than any previous generation," Bantry says. "Clint Eastwood said he never dates women under forty. What would they talk about? The weather? I have that kind of respect for these women. They're grown-ups. They've gotten through very difficult times in the seventies and the eighties and they're better for it. At first people said we were nuts, but each month there are more bookings. Our girls are showing the rest of the world." A pause. "I mean, our women."

Still, by fall 1992 the waif look had conquered fashion. Corinne Day and Mario Sorrenti, Kate Moss's model-turned-photographer boyfriend, began snatching up jobs that would have once automatically gone to Demarchelier or Meisel. That season Moss walked the runway in fashion shows for the first time, wearing grunge, gamin, and bohemian fashions that seemed inspired by the new wave of models. That December she made her first appearance on the cover of *Bazaar*. Early the next year she appeared in a campaign shot by Helmut Newton for Yves Saint Laurent.

In her wake came a wave of waifs. Another of the new breed photographers, Andrew Macpherson, called their look "elegantly wasted." Storm signed up Emma Balfour, Louise Gander, and Patricia Hartmann. Lucie de la Falaise, Kristin McEnemy, Cecilia Chancellor, Kati Tastet, Amber Valetta, Beri Smithers, Janine Giddings, Benedicte Loyen, Simone Bowkett, and Shalom Harlow all signed with other agencies, which hurried to catch up. By March 1993 the waif take-over seemed complete. "Something had to give," opined London's *Time Out*. "Christy, Cindy, Claudia, Naomi et al. had to get their comeuppance."

Ultimately, though, the waifs proved uncommercial. Moss's scrawny form, seen the world over in advertisements and on billboards and telephone kiosks, inspired protests. "Feed me" was scrawled across her bare belly in a spontaneous graffiti protest. In June 1993 New York's *Daily News* inveighed against *Harper's Bazaar*'s "page after sickening page of skin-and-bones model Kate Moss who looks like she should be tied down and intravenously fed." It wasn't only *Bazaar*. "Every magazine got threatening letters," says a fashion editor in a position to know. "There was enormous reader mail, and then all of a sudden you didn't see waifs anymore. The best got absorbed, and the rest disappeared." And 1994's next wave of hot models was led by the taller, more traditional Nadja Auermann. "We are already seeing the pendulum swing back," says *Bazaar*'s Sara Foley-Anderson, "but not all the way." Bald and tattooed Eve Salail and pierced Stella Tennant symbolize modeling's latest stage of diversification.

Kate Moss survived. She started hanging out with Christy Turlington and Naomi Campbell, was regularly referred to as a supermodel, and even acquired the requisite hotel-room-smashing actor boyfriend, Johnny Depp.

The pendulum swung back in the modeling business, too. Finally a trend that began in the late seventies seemed to take hold in the early nineties, giving hope that modeling wouldn't always remain a treacherous minefield for young girls.

There are now many women running their own agencies in all four of the world's fashion centers, but the most forthright seem to be in Paris. Marilyn Gaulthier, a boisterous, buxom woman, was an English student when a friend suggested she become a booker at a model agency. "I thought being a booker meant taking care of books in the library," she says, laughing. After six months with Guy Héron's Cosa Nostra agency, Gaulthier went to work for Claude Haddad at Prestige. Though she says she never had a serious problem with Haddad, she still didn't like his style. The worst thing was the way Haddad and his friends spoke about women. "I couldn't believe it," Gaulthier says. "I would not tell my mother to come and pick me up, even for lunch."

In the early eighties Gaulthier left Prestige with several other bookers to start Delphine, an agency backed by Paul de Senville, a music business millionaire. When it fell apart, in 1985, Gaulthier opened her own agency, where she books stars like Helena Christensen and Storm's Kate Moss and Carla Bruni. "After I left Claude," she says, "I decided this is a woman business, definitely. So when I started Delphine, there was not a man in the agency. Not to put a nail in the wall. I was totally disgusted."

Onetime Paris Planning model Gaby Wagner spent a year at her agency, Zoom, before anyone took notice. But Wagner offered a real alternative. "I didn't want to be part of all the crap," she says. "I didn't have a man in the agency. It was 1987. Problems had started in Paris with the men, with the owners of the agencies screwing around with young girls. The models were running away at night to the airport, no money, no suitcase, crying over the phone to their mothers. I was coming in against macho agencies as a woman, an ex-model. I got girls very easily, because they were afraid to send them to Jean-Luc or Claude Haddad or Gérald. I was safe, no men, only girls."

Ironically Elite gave birth to the prototype sisterly agency, Fabienne Martin's FAM. Martin worked for Viva when John Casablancas and the boutique agency's founder, Christine Lindgren, went off to open Elite New York in 1977. "Christine came with me to New York," Casablancas says.

"But she did not at all adapt. She was crushed by New York, and so she went back to Viva."

Martin soon quit Viva; Casablancas had promised her shares in it and hadn't delivered, she says. But she found she missed working with Lindgren. "We had a wonderful understanding," Martin says. "I was really a radical. Every time a girl [was booked for] an advertisement, I would ask to see the rough of the campaign, the text, how she was going to be positioned. I would lose a lot of money, and girls would leave me. In the end I could get them where I wanted them to go, so I was proud of my position."

Martin founded FAM, and in 1988 Lindgren joined her there. "I was wanting to do something more personal," she says. FAM acts like an artistic matchmaker. "I always try to create a concept," says Martin. "I always go back to personalities." Martin isn't a fan of supermodels. "Creativity doesn't really work with this supermodel story," she continues. "I don't want to criticize what's going on now. I think it's wonderful for these young women. But my line is to be creative, to work with intelligent women, and it's working out very well."

Martin and Lindgren screen their models for ones they want to work with. "I cannot work with a dummy," Martin says. "I get so bored, and it's so uncontrollable because they can do the most stupid things. She may not understand why she has to work with this creative photographer, why she has to do this campaign rather than another, why I turned down the big money job because I think it's kind of uninteresting. In the beginning I had a lot of girls leaving FAM because I would say, 'No, you're not going to do this.' I realized that was a bit too much. Why should I choose for her? They have to choose."

Martin prizes a model who can think for herself. "Now, when I interview people, I see what the potential is, what the creativity is, how the mind is functioning," she says. "If she gives me a certain confidence and trust, I'm going to do everything to raise her image as much as I can."

FAM begat City. Its founder, Louise Despointes, was a FAM model at the end of her career. Though she has since left the business, she casts a long shadow. "Louise Despointes deserves the award for modernizing the image of models," says David Brown, the director of Riccardo Gay. Despointes opened City in Paris in 1979. "She was following what I had created, but she did it better," Fabienne Martin admits.

· Despointes felt that agencies were factories. Hers was an artist's atelier. "I did everything wrong when I started City," she says. "I had a small office, no backer. They all laughed. But Gérald Marie knew. He came to my first party. He was smart. He said, 'She's dangerous.' " John Casablancas said City would last three weeks. "Nobody wanted to see a model taking over," says Despointes' then boyfriend, the guitarist-photographer Steve Hiett. "She knew too much. It would blow the whole thing of guys in charge. This was a girl with balls who wasn't scared of anybody. Fabienne Martin started using poetic, soulful sorts of girls. Louise took it to its conclusion, and now every girl you see is a City-style model."

The image of City was set by its first star, Juliette. "The way she looked was so different," Despointes says. "She had a profile like Elvis Presley, but she was blond and had fine bones. And she didn't want to be a model. She didn't give a damn. She had a lot of character. She wouldn't sell herself. She'd do the opposite, and it made people want her even more." Next came Felicitas, a girl photographer David Hamilton found on a nudist beach. "She's weird enough to be your type," he told Despointes.

"I was concerned about them," she says, "and not just as models. Who would they *be*?" Over the years she launched the careers of Cecilia Chancellor, Laeticia, Claudia, Carla Bruni, Lara Harris, Suzanne Lanza, Kristin McEnemey, Marie-Sophie, and Vanessa Duve. "I put out a type of girl that didn't exist," she says. "It was my taste, and it became the standard. Most agents don't work as an artist. They go with the flow or their dicks, not the sensibility of the street."

City was established by the early eighties. "I felt like I was on a big spiral," Despointes says. "Every girl was knocking on our door, but we didn't want them. We wanted to find our own. I didn't realize I was successful. But then all the photographers started coming to the agency. We got Christie Brinkley and Kim Alexis, girls from big agencies, because I felt I had nothing to lose."

Like Martin, Despointes's gods were creativity and personality. Unfortunately she treated business as a lesser deity, so there were problems. "Everyone was attacking me," Despointes says. "Eileen Ford and John Casablancas were trying to take my models. I had to go everywhere with them. It was that bad." Clients thought City's girls had an attitude problem. "They fought with everyone," Despointes says. "My girls were threatening, smart. People thought they were impossible and didn't know how to handle them. I told my girls, 'Make them respect you. Don't be a phony or an asshole. If they pull a switch on you, fuck it, walk out.' Then I'd raise hell, and they'd get mad at *me*!"

Happy models gave great word of mouth. "I would defend the girl," says Despointes. "I wasn't selling a carpet." When Despointes pulled a model off a set in Italy because she'd been lied to about money, the client told the girl Despointes was crazy. "They said my girls were impossible and I was spoiling the business," she says. "They wanted me out, dead. I told them *they* were going nowhere. At the time they didn't want to hear what I had to say. Now they all want smart girls."

In 1983 Despointes opened a City desk at Wilhelmina in New York. "I thought it would be interesting to have a base there," she says. "But they couldn't understand our concept, and things turned sour." In March 1984 Despointes disappeared from Wilhelmina and resurfaced with a new agency. Its name was Name.

"We knocked everyone's socks off," says Sara Foley-Anderson, who quit her job at Wilhelmina to join. "What was so amazing about Louise was that she encouraged girls to be more than models. They weren't just something to mold."

But after an abortive attempt to open City in Miami, Despointes veered off course. "I didn't want more, but I was caught in a spiral. More models. More employees." The employees she'd left in charge in Paris resented the time she spent in New York. "It became uncontrollable," she says. "It didn't suit my personality anymore, but I couldn't detach." Instead she started taking drugs. "I took a lot of drugs," she says. "I was a heroin addict for three years when I had Name. I wanted out, but I didn't know it yet." Modeling had claimed another victim.

Despointes's account of how she lost City and Name is a confusing swirl. Sometime in the late eighties, she says, she got a call from one of her employees in Paris telling her City was bankrupt. She believes money was stolen—a lot of money—but she was "totally confused," she admits.

Finally, in 1991, her financiers at Models S.A. in Switzerland took over, and Despointes left the business. "I was so caught up with money and lawyers." She sighs. "It was suicide. Name was stolen from me. It's a very long story, like a soap opera. I'd quit drugs, but I was dying, trying to work and run a lawsuit with five lawyers, and nobody could make any sense out of what was going on. All I could do was quit, good-bye. I left all my money in the company. Every girl was paid. I walked away, abandoned everything I owned. But I wanted to get out." She smiles. "And anyway, everything I had to do was done."

Besides Eileen Ford, the only agent Despointes says she respects is Frances Grill, the founder of Click. The daughter of a longshoreman, Brooklynite Grill worked in the coat room of the Village Gate nightclub in New York's Greenwich Village before becoming an agent for photographers Jeanloup Sieff, Frank Horvath, Oliviero Toscani, Fabrizio Ferri, and Barry McKinley. In

1980, when her marriage to a Swedish menswear designer broke up, she went to work for an agency called Ten. A year later, when it went out of business, Grill inherited several of its male models and opened a place of her own with $30,000 raised mortgaging her house. She named it Click in tribute to "my photographers," she says.

Grill had spotted a void in the model market. "Eileen Ford had given dignity to modeling," Grill said at the time, "but after all these years in the business, she represents a stereotype of what beauty is about." Wilhelmina had just died, Zoli was dying, and Elite "has grown so large, models feel a bit at loose ends," Grill observed. "Photographers crave new images. The images on the market, though beautiful, didn't reflect where fashion was going." Grill thought men were where fashion was going and determined to sell them, not as props, but as "beings in their own right."

Bruce Weber, who'd just emerged as the greatest photographer of men since Hoyningen-Huene, shot Click's first head sheet. In the age of AIDS Weber's homoerotic fascination with heterosexual athletes changed men's fashion photography forever, banishing the rugged, often gay male models of the old school to the sidelines in favor of fresh faces found by Weber on beaches and college playing fields. One of those discoveries, surfer Buzzy Kerbox, put Click on the map when the agency negotiated an exclusive contract for him with designer and advertising innovator Ralph Lauren. Click really took off in 1982, though, when Isabella Rossellini, the half-Swedish daughter of director Roberto Rossellini and actress Ingrid Bergman, asked Grill for a home-cooked Swedish Christmas dinner. That night Grill suggested to the twenty-nine-year-old Italian television interviewer that she could make a fortune as a model. A $2 million contract with Lancôme and six magazine covers followed in a few months.

Grill had a knack for publicity. As *Vanity Fair* later put it, Click's specialty was "quirky models who didn't exactly fit." Her models were the wrong sex, the wrong age, the wrong weight, the wrong color. Wrong was right. After Attila, a long-haired hunk who was part of the Steven Meisel-Teri Toye clique, got a Calvin Klein ad, he insured his hair with Lloyd's of London. Grill also signed up transsexual Toye and bald Jenny O.

Rossellini was the first of a series of all-star models to join Click. By mid-1983 Grill had signed the bullfighter Dominguin's daughter Paola, Isabelle (daughter of Group Captain Peter) Townshend, Linn (daughter of Liv) Ullman, Tahnee (daughter of Raquel) Welch, Robbie (daughter of Tommy) Chong, Chris (son of Peter) Lawford, and Cecelia (daughter of Gregory)

Peck. She'd also proved that unlike the huge Elite and Ford battleships, her modeling speedboat could turn on a dime. That same year she rode the cutting edge with eccentric models like the wan midwesterner Bonnie Berman, Elisabetta Ramella, who refused to cut her long, thick, curly hair, and Talisa Soto, one of the first Hispanic modeling stars. "I wanted to expand the conception of what was beautiful," she said. "America is not only made up of blond-haired, blue-eyed girls." Of course, if you wanted classic looks, Click had them, too. Grill booked Elle MacPherson, the Australian beauty who went on to marry Gilles Bensimon, finally injecting some sex into the image of the droll French photographer with coke-bottle eyeglasses. And every week there was a new Bruce Weber discovery, carpenters, farm boys, clammers, volleyball players, swimmers. With Weber's help, Click gave birth to buff.

Grill was turned down the first few times she tried to join IMMA, New York's society of model managers, formed at the time that the agents returned their employment agency contracts. After those rebuffs Grill refused to join, cementing her status as a renegade. Dedicated to the idea of maintaining a model boutique for contrarian tastes, she carved out a niche for herself where she would reign, essentially unchallenged for years. Only in the nineties would more American boutiques pop up, and only a few matched Click's sophistication.

The model business remains, as it has always been, a seething morass of beauty and money, grace and envy, sensuality and lust, yearning and backstabbing, glamour, greed, and glory beyond measure. Models are richer and more independent. Elite and Ford are still fighting each other. New agencies come and go, and the story is always the same. A booker has left another agency with a couple of models. The booker's backer is—surprise!—a rich man. "I know a billion rich, powerful men who'd give me money to open an agency and let me stay in the red just to have the chance to be a nebbish with a tall, beautiful woman sitting next to him," says ex-model Serene Cicora, now a booker with Mary Webb Davis in Los Angeles.

The latest topic of conversation in modeling is the resurgence of drugs—particularly heroin—among a clique of models who, in macabre homage, reportedly call themselves Gia's Girls, in honor of Gia Carangi, the bisexual addict who had a brief career in modeling and then died of AIDS. But self-hatred and destructive behavior, too, are nothing new in modeling.

The models of the moment are Elite's Nadja Auermann, a German with a pneumatic body and white-blond hair, and Ford's Bridget Hall, a sixteen-year-old Texan whose childhood has already ended in photographic studios and on fashion runways, where she'll be admired, inspected, and—most likely—tossed aside as soon as the next hot face comes along. "Except for rare smart ones like Lauren Hutton, they still feel totally unempowered," says a former *Vogue* editor. "It's a very aimless existence. What do they do all day except stand around and do what other people tell them? They come in and complain, 'Nobody likes me for anything except my pretty face.' You have to bite your tongue."

There are people in the business who truly love models for themselves and not just for the money they earn. And at the head of the class are Eileen Ford, the Last Mother of Modeling, and the First Boyfriend, John Casablancas. One of them can't wait to get out of the business. The other can't imagine ever leaving. But don't make any bets on which is which. In modeling, nothing is what it seems.

When he is in New York City (as opposed to his other homes, Southampton, Paris, and Ibiza), John Casablancas lives in a country house in the city, a duplex penthouse apartment on the roof of a building with a long reputation for housing models and other young transients. The apartment has an open kitchen and living room, off which is a carpeted "pillow room," stocked with a huge television and several teddy bears. Books are everywhere, shelved, stacked, and stuck in corners, They include worn and well-read classics, bestsellers, books on fashion photography, and an *Encyclopaedia Britannica*. There are also several antique globes, a stand-up piano, several bar trays, dozens of framed family photos, and two walls covered with photographs, mostly of beautiful women, some of them nude. One of them, wearing only a garter belt, is caught kissing Casablancas on the street.

It is midmorning, and Casablancas is having breakfast. He is dressed in black slacks and a blue cashmere polo. He sits on a turquoise suede sofa, where his third wife, Aline, delivers a cup of herbal tea, some toast, and a piece of tinfoil with John's drugs for the day, an assortment of vitamins that he swallows, one at a time, over the course of the next half hour.

Casablancas, now fifty, met Aline Wermelinger (a virgin, a junior in high school) in 1992, at that year's Look of the Year semifinals in her native Brazil. Discovered by an Elite scout in Brazil, the sixteen-year-old had traveled the hundred miles from her hometown, Cordeiro, to Rio de Janiero for the contest, and made it to the finals in New York despite the small flaw Casablancas spotted on her nose. She told the judges her favorite book was the Bible and God was her idol.

Casablancas says he didn't really notice her at first. "And she didn't pay the slightest attention to me," he adds. "She had cute boyfriends. We were absolutely not attracted. I was older than her father by eleven months. She is a Baptist, she's very observant of the rules of her church, and I'm the opposite." They went out for dinner one night in New York nonetheless. "It was her birthday, and we toasted, and I gave her a little innocent kiss," he says. "I think it kind of had an effect." But after kissing him, Aline went back to flirting with younger men at the table. "So I left, and she went back to Brazil," Casablancas says.

Not long afterward, though, he found himself talking about Aline on the phone with one of the directors of Elite in Brazil. "He said, 'I think she would be happy to hear from you.' I said, 'You've got to be kidding,' but I gave her a call, and we started this thing by telephone, and then we arranged to meet."

Casablancas, who counts Portuguese among the half dozen languages he speaks, arranged a booking for Aline in Miami, equidistant between New York and Rio. They started seeing each other there, "but we were not having an affair," he points out. "We were just dating." That December Casablancas went to Cordeiro and met Aline's accountant father and her seamstress mother. "I saw her family and her house, and I asked for permission to marry her, and her father and mother looked at her and said, 'You want to marry this old man?' " But her mother decided her suitor was a gentleman, and three months later a wedding ensued, one day after Rio's renowned Carnival.

In what must be a first for him, Casablancas says that he and Aline didn't go to bed together until after they married. "It's the first time I got married in church," he adds. "We decided to go the traditional route. It was a big gamble. But I loved the values that she brought." Casablancas knew he was asking for trouble, marrying another teenager. Alain Kittler, for example, declined to attend, telling a mutual friend, "I went to number one and number two; why go to number three when there will probably be a number four?"

"I'm surprised I didn't get more hell than I got," Casablancas admits.

A year later Casablancas and Aline still seem to be honeymooning. She quit modeling to tend to his needs full-time. And her attentions to him border on worship. She can usually be found wedged into his side, their fingers entwined, curled on his lap like a voluptuous kitten, or nibbling at his ear. But she menaces him with a butter knife when he talks about Stephanie Seymour. And when he makes the mistake of referring to Jeanette Casablancas as his wife, she bristles.

"Ex-wife," she says.

"Yeah, you're right, you're right, madame," Casablancas says by way of apology. "This one, she picks up everything." A few minutes later she fetches a glass of water, so he can swallow the rest of his vitamins. "My geisha," he says, leaning back with his usual satisfied smile.

Casablancas seems entirely too happy. "I'm very comfortable with who I am," he says. But others say different. "He's sick and tired of the business and wants to get out," says his old friend Francesca Magugliani. Why? The answer is simple. Gérald Marie now runs Elite in Paris with a firm hand; Monique Pillard does the same in New York, where her motherly style has vastly improved the agency's image. The chairman of the board has little to do except indulge himself in what appears to be his ongoing world championship midlife crisis.

Perhaps Casablancas will again fall out of love with his latest Eliza Doolittle—and back in love with Elite. But for the moment he will only admit to a different worry, and it's one that will likely hound him the rest of his life. "I really believe I have a very romantic relationship," he says. "Aline and I get along beautifully. But will it last forever? Will she one day wake up and find out that I'm very old and not want me? It's possible."

He pauses, and his voice turns querulous and almost vulnerable. "I'm the one who's taking the biggest risk, in fact, you know?"

In March 1993, just as their deal with Dieter Esch fell apart, a fire destroyed the country house Eileen and Jerry Ford had built for their retirement. The emotional toll it took on the couple was plainly evident. "We can't afford not to work," Eileen Ford said not long afterward in a heartbroken voice.

A year later the Fords are ensconced in a rental—a neo-Georgian pile on a big property in Bernardsville, New Jersey—as they rebuild their ruined dream house. Wearing sweaters, chinos, and moccasins, the couple lunches on borscht with creme fraiche, chicken salad with bacon, and green salad in the large but featureless house. "I'd be having a peppermint schnapps if you weren't here," Eileen tells a visitor, quaffing a big glass of iced tea.

After lunch Jerry takes his Audi full of family jumble—tapes, maps, crushed gloves, and wrapped red-and-white-striped peppermints—on the long drive to their fire-gutted house on a hill. It boasts an incredible view across the Jersey countryside's rolling hills from the master bedroom, a sprawl of family rooms, three maids' rooms, and an extra floor for more expansion. Not for models, but for grandchildren. A library with a seventeenth-century mantel and matching carved wooden walls and Jerry's two-thousand-bottle wine cellar directly beneath it were the only rooms that survived the fire. That means they still have their two cases of 1961 Pétrus, but Jerry doesn't like to drink the $600-a-bottle wine. "It's obscene," he says. So it sits, unappreciated.

Jerry has to do this whirlwind inspection because he and Eileen are rarely at home anymore. Trips are what they do now that they've been eased upstairs to figurehead roles in the agency they founded. Trips for work. And lots of vacations, although Eileen will tell you that a model agent never stops working, as long as there are pretty people around. So Jerry and Eileen, just back from Anguilla, are off in two days to Snowmass and then Paris for the collections and so on and so on.

Back at the house, Eileen is ensconced in front of the TV, intently watching the Olympics. Though she never once looks at the screen while a visitor is in the room, it's abundantly clear what she'd rather be doing. After seventy years of living, self-analysis still doesn't come easily to Eileen Ford. Neither is it easy for her to contemplate, let alone talk about, the possibility of her retirement.

The Fords profess to be happy about their situation, but a discordant undertone sounds. "Every company that has a second generation in management has tension," Jerry says about Ford's new leadership. "We have three presidents. A strange phenomenon. I don't care as long as they're happy."

Though others say they're being kept as far as possible from the office, Ford says he and his wife are delighted to still be hopping around the globe, promoting the Supermodel of the World contest. "Everybody wants Eileen," he says proudly. "She is a unique figure. Who can replace that?" He pauses a moment and then adds, "But if the three of them feel we should go, we'll go."

Eileen Ford looks up angrily. She has no intention of going anywhere. "There is so much work at the Ford agency that if Jerry and I left, who on earth would take our place?" she demands. "Nobody could do what we're doing. Who will answer the mail? Who will send the Christmas gifts? Who has the time? Who has time to make all those phone calls? Who'll travel for Supermodel? They all have too much to do. As long as I can walk across a room and remember a name, I'll keep going."

She is quivering, outraged at the thought of a Ford agency minus Eileen Ford. Then, as suddenly as she blew up, she deflates, and the mother of modeling, the last pioneer, looks like nothing so much as another victim of the never-ending quest for beauty and youth. She can't imagine stopping. Like so many models, she has nothing else. "There must be golden years, but I'm just too damn busy to find them," Eileen Ford says angrily. "Paradise is when you're dead."

"MODELS SUCK" reads the tiny T-shirt on the drop-dead blonde squirming past table 44 at Bowery Bar. She's doing her best not to give away her purpose—but it just may be checking out who's sitting at 1995's celebrity bullseye, the bar's prime booth.

It's models (of course), about six of them. As one talks on a cell phone, another tries to grab it, a third fiercely vectors for someone more famous than she, and another stares down glumly into a glass of wine. Contemplating Hegel's *Phenomenology of Mind,* no doubt.

The passing T-shirt notwithstanding, Modelmania shows no sign of abating. Cindy Crawford made a movie so troubled it wasn't released until long after it had been advertised and publicized, but Cindy nonetheless made more magazine covers that summer than any politician, warrior or movie star. *Top Model* magazine has been joined on the stands by *Supermodel* magazine. A New York *Daily News* columnist has made a career of dispensing a diet of 95 percent model dish.

Helena and Naomi have a catfight over a dress? *Hard Copy* comes to attention. Janice Dickinson marries a guy after three dates and soon announces her divorce? Christie Brinkley's ski-slope marriage falls apart? Cheryl Tiegs gets suddenly single, too? *Entertainment Tonight, Extra!* and *Inside Edition* have all the scoops.

The world at large is even more supermodel saturated than it was at the height of the Trinity's reign in 1992. The same stars who ruled before are ruling still. While by all known standards they should have reached the end of their run (modeling generations typically last about seven years), Christy, Linda,

Naomi, Cindy, and Claudia have yet to cede their places in the public's appetites. And only Kate Moss has joined them, another rare angel dancing on the head of modeling's pin. Karen Mulder, Meghan Douglas, Claudia Mason, and Shalom Harlow are great models, but they'll never be as famous as the supermodels—short of skirting a scandal.

In the image-hungry enclave of fashion the bell may be tolling for the cult of the skinny six-foot celebrity. Its devotees have always been addicted to novelty; the supermodel with staying power is the exception to their rule. The most immediately vulnerable, the models now hovering just below superstar level—the Meghans and Shaloms—are in danger of being superseded by fresh faces. Jodie Kidd, Irina, Navia, Danielle, Farrah, Ingrid, Kirsty, Trisha, and Chandra are already gaining on Helena, Nikki, Amber, and Stella. But they are flying below the general public's radar. And for the moment at least that's where they're likely to stay. Even the supermodels are at risk of falling from favor.

Consider some evidence. In April, *Women's Wear Daily* reported a survey that showed that women in the fashion profession—who, not surprisingly, are among the biggest buyers of designer clothes—were no longer responding to ads featuring supermodels. Only 17.5 percent of them considered top models to be effective selling tools. Only violence scored worse.

In early fall, *Fashions of the Times,* the New York *Times's* twice-yearly fashion supplement, abandoned models altogether, stating in a manifesto that only "real women" posed for the pages that followed. And then, the always surefooted Calvin Klein proved anew his uncanny ability to connect with his moment when he hired Steven Meisel to parody a chicken hawk's fantasy and half-undress a bunch of street kids—male and female innocents hovering around the age of legal consent, none of them known by name—in a series of ads for his CK line that flaunted glimpses of underwear at the apex of akimbo lower limbs, set against a backdrop of cheesy wood paneling. The ads stirred up a scandal and were quickly abandoned. But prescient Calvin knew that in 1995, a model's greatest asset may well be anonymity. CK-logo clothes started flying off the shelves and Calvin, as always, emerged smelling even better than any of his notorious perfumes.

As in photography, the antimodel mood emerges on fashion runways, too. At the fall 1995 ready-to-wear shows in New York, supermodels were conspicuously absent, at least partly in protest over a designer decision to draw a line on the runway over ever-rising model fees. The city's designer trade group, the Council of Fashion Designers of America (CFDA), had briefly attempted to set a market rate for fashion shows in the tents they'd begun erecting for that purpose in Bryant Park. After a Federal Trade Commission investigation into price fixing, the threat of legal action led the designers to agree not to take such a step in concert again. But now it seemed they'd instead taken action independently (if simultaneously).

Why were New York's designers declaring war on models? With saturation coverage of fashion a fact of modern life, ever-savvier consumers were balking at designer price tags that reflect such costs of doing business as $250,000 fashion shows starring models who won't get out of bed for less than $10,000. Indeed, in celebrating what the model industry considered a victory, runway agent Ellen Harth let it slip that superstar models now regularly receive $18,000 per fashion show.

Not for long, perhaps. Hints of incipient revolt were everywhere. At the 1996 resort shows, the big-name models were absent again, replaced by young, new fresh faces. "It's so refreshing," murmured veteran fashion critic Mary Lou Luther.

Indeed, the latest crop of dream babies are a breath of fresh air, meant to captivate a new generation of consumers, and not the so-called Baby Boomers, now lumbering into middle age. *Their* aging taste in models has dominated the fashion culture ever since Jean Shrimpton. But Kate Moss, whose skinniness offends so many thickening old hippies, is really no more than a new generation's Twiggy. Just as the Neasden girl annoyed one generation's parents, the Croydon girl offends a new gang, who've apparently forgotten the enthusiasms of their not-so-distant youth.

It's ironic that Kate Moss and the other pierced, tattooed, and strangely shaven models of the moment are posing in the service of another claque of aging postwar babies—only in this case it's one that *won't* give up the ghosts of youth. Fashion pros like Patrick Demarchelier, Calvin Klein, Steven Meisel, and Anna Wintour ballyhoo their models' independence but brand them with a handful of momentarily hip labels. The new models are being used to push products to a new generation of consumers at the very moment when the last "fashion" generation has turned away from clothes and begun investing its money and time in everything but. Generation X must replace them in fashion's ever-renewable audience. So now, Kate and grunge models like Stella Tennant and Jenny Shimuzu are selling material representations of a new "rebellion." The last youthquake, however misguidedly, sold peace and love. But this one is sans content, sans message, concerned with images of insurrection only. The well-constructed facade is all (even if it's extraordinarily ugly). The Potemkin Village of fashion passes for home. There's nothing behind it but commerce.

As the apotheosis of the "Top"-heavy Top Model syndrome, the opening of the Fashion Cafe, latest of the crop of theme park–like eateries that have popped up in midtown Manhattan as often as pimples appear on the faces of their just-pubescent patrons, was the most visible event in modeldom last year. It may well have been a defining moment, the moment at which the model phenomenon peaked. Ever since its launch in April, the Cafe's cadre of PR people has relentlessly flacked the notion that Naomi Campbell, Claudia Schiffer, Elle MacPherson, and (late addition) Christy Turlington are the Cafe's "owners" and "partners." The press bought that hook, line, and sinker and repeated it ad nauseum, like hostages suffering a fashion version of the Stockholm Syndrome, parroting the lies of their captors. "We make all the decisions," Claudia told *Time*.

Like so many fashion pictures, this one was a sham. And not just because the glitterati, who eagerly appeared on opening night, abandoned the place to the Calvin-clad masses immediately thereafter.

A few weeks after the Cafe's opening, Daniel Green and Frank DiGiacomo, reporters for the New York *Observer,* unearthed a public record of its ownership—its State Liquor Authority license. According to New York State law, any owners or partners would be listed there. But the only names that appeared were those of minority owners Tomasso Buti, husband of *Sports Illustrated* swimsuit model Daniela Pestova, his accountant brother Francesco, and their backer, a Los Angeles oral surgeon named Guido Bracetti. A lawyer for the partnership, Warren Pesetsky, told *USA Today* that the filings would be amended within a week. Five months later he issues the same assurance. "It's still in the works," he says. "It will be done." But the Butis and Bracetti remain the only listed owners.

Don't think for a moment the supermodels were superchumps, though. The word on the modeling scene had each of the pseudo-owners getting $500,000 for the use of their supernames. Unfortunately, that also earned three of them a lawsuit after Buti sued Giorgio Sant'Ambrogio, co-owner of Milan's Fashion Model, over the rights to the name Fashion Cafe. Sant'Ambrogio, who has owned a Fashion Cafe in Milan for more than eight years and has trademarked the name in Europe, countersued Buti and all the models except decision-maker Schiffer, because "she is a good friend," he said.

None of this, not even Turlington's description of the place as "a tacky theme restaurant for tourists," has kept away those tourists or the much-derided "bridge and tunnel" crowd from New York's suburbs. They come hoping (typically in vain) for a glimpse of one of their idols in the flesh. Instead they have to settle for lank dresses, perfume bottles, and backpacks glassed-in like artworks, with plaques proclaiming they were "worn by" the likes of Nicole Kidman (once, in a photograph for a magazine). Those sealed vitrines are perfect symbols of the insular, airless little world the supermodels inhabit, out of reach of the hoi polloi who buy the burgers, the blouses, and the blue jeans that are the real bottom line of the fashion equation.

Naomi, Claudia, Elle, and the rest may indeed be helping to seal their fate by pushing their fame past the boundaries of fashion. For the greed and snotty *hauteur* that were initially part of the supermodel appeal—and worked particularly well in the often greedy and snotty world of fashion—have all worn thinner than John Casablancas's skin. And hubristic extracurricular efforts like the Fashion Cafe and the well-intentioned but nonetheless unfortunately named DISHES (Determined, Involved Supermodels Helping Erase Starvation) have done little to correct the impression that Supermodels have overstayed their welcome and come to believe their own hype.

Amber Valletta saw the writing on the wall as early as 1993 and railed against her inevitable fate. On the brink of supermodel superstardom, she launched a tirade at a Reuters reporter who asked about the possibility that model fees might start falling for the first time in two decades. "Look at my face!" Valletta whined, "I have red eyes, my skin looks like crap and I'm losing weight. I'm not going to look this way and feel this way for nothing and I don't want anyone telling me I don't deserve the money."

Why shouldn't she make out as well as Linda, Cindy, and Naomi, Valetta demanded. "They made their money, now are we going to be denied ours? We're doing the magazine layouts and we're selling the clothes. If the money is such an important issue, then the designers should think twice about buying their expensive luxury homes. If they don't want to pay us, then they should give it to charity."

To DISHES, presumably.

It isn't only models who are having adjustment problems. The mid-'90s are a time of retrenchment and redefinition for the big model agencies. Elite, says a well-placed source in Paris, has recently reorganized its Swiss operations. Why? Jerome Bonnouvrier, now running an agency called DNA in America and fighting his most recent backer in court for possession of his Paris firm

Partners, says that in spring 1995 French tax authorities published a confidential pamphlet warning its employees to be aware of how Swiss offices are used to shelter money from taxes, setting off a flurry of such reorganizations.

In America, things were changing, too. Both Ford and Elite opened Arizona branches, chasing business that was fleeing the crime and sameness of South Florida locations. In an attempt at diversification, the two leading agencies also started licensing the names of models for clothing and accessory collections and opened celebrity divisions. Elite's—booking "stars" like Nastasia Kinski and Drew Barrymore—was headed by Monique Pillard; but someone quite close to her said she'd actually been pushed aside by John Casablancas, who was determined to assert his authority in New York now that his Paris agency had been taken over by Gérald Marie. Early in fall 1995, reports even circulated that Pillard was set to leave Elite with several of its models. But although Pillard's complaints were heard outside the agency, she stayed within, where her small equity interest kept her subject to the will of Elite's chief model-monger.

Ford's top earners Christy Turlington, Vendela, Veronica Webb, and Bridget Hall joined its star board. But in July 1995, Hall left Ford for IMG. She rejoined Ivan Bart, her old Ford booker, there. Bart had left Ford the year before, as did Jeni Rose, director of Ford's Paris office, who resigned upon news that the agency was reorganizing in France, merging with Clip, the last of Jean-Pierre Dollé's agencies. In a move that solidified Ford's until-then precarious position in Paris, Clip's Jean-Michel Pradwilov was named to head its French operation. A decent young man married to the model Ilonka, Pradwilov had one of the best reputations in Paris modeling.

Though things in Paris soon settled down, the Ford flagship in New York continued to be rocked by comings and goings. In April, Jerry Ford gave his chief executive officer title to his daughter Katie, ending what, in retrospect, seems the inevitable-to-fail three-headed presidency with Ford's longtime executives, shareholders and board members Joe Hunter and Marion Smith. Katie soon announced that she was relocating the women's divisions from Ford's famous 59th Street townhouse to a loft in SoHo, near where she lives. Smith, who'd been at Ford when Katie was a young girl, soon left, joing the up-and-coming Company Models, which had survived financial difficulties to become a major player in American modeling. Smith also sued Ford and was countersued in a replay of the same sort of litigation that entangled the Fords and Elite for years. Hunter, demoted to head of Ford's men's division, was considered likely to follow Smith out the door. Ironically, Company, run by an Elite-trained booker named Michael Flutie and his family, is one of the agencies that has up-held the Ford tradition of trying—at least—to be responsible towards it models and treating them like people as opposed to blow-up dolls or packaged goods.

It wasn't all bad news for Ford. They'd snagged Elite's Kristin McMenamy, the face of 1995. Fashion's *Pulp Fiction* (in contrast to its *Forrest Gump,* Claudia Schif-fer), McMenamy had blossomed from oddity to great beauty after briefly taking off work to have a child. The newly multicultural Ford also attracted Irina Pan-taeva from Women, Beverly Peele from Elite, Laeticia Herrera and Fabienne from IMG, and signed former MTV VJ and Revlon model, Duff. Ford also got rid of the prima donna Naomi Campbell, who'd joined the agency amidst great hoopla in 1993. At the time, Elite's Casablancas spat at her back, saying she was "a spoiled selfish brat and a mercenary" who "needs a slap." Now, with Camp-bell back in the fold, a newly charming Casablancas cooed, "She's matured."

Simultaneous with Marion Smith's departure, there were a few defections from Ford. Several bookers and models Jerry Hall (Mrs. Mick Jagger) and Rachel Hunter (Mrs. Rod Stewart) left, although as Katie Ford pointed out, neither was exactly a working model. "I'm getting the agency in tune with the times," an unbowed Ford told me. "Several employees were unable to adjust. It's a whole new Ford." Ford probably also got some pleasure from the news a few days later that Naomi Campbell had left Elite—again—for Women, the agency of Kate Moss and Elle Macpherson.

Other models made news, too, and not just for changing agencies. Rachel Williams, for instance, did it by changing her sexual preferences. Again and again. The model who once made a shimmery silver dress into an object of teenage lust in an Absolut vodka ad made headlines, announcing her preg-nancy by her former boyfriend, model-loving restaurateur Eric Goode (owner of the Bowery Bar) not long after declaring her love for a woman, British mu-sician Alice Temple. Further confusing matters, Williams posed naked for *Penthouse.* Which—when you think about it—was really no stranger than MAC Cosmetics choosing the black transvestite RuPaul as their spokesmodel. Modeling is finally getting more diverse, and in so doing, helping encourage more tolerance of diversity in society. But this is only the latest manifestation of the process begun by the mad-bad Beylorussian brunette Janice Dickinson almost a quarter century ago.

As she has throughout her career, "model" model Christy Turlington stands head and shoulders above the pack, an example of how much better the rest of her business can be. And not just in pictures. Right from the start, when she arrived in Paris with her mother, while the similarly teenaged Stephanie Seymour was there in the company of John Casablancas, Turlington has had her head screwed on right. And in a display of loyalty rare in the modern modeling world, she has never left Ford since the day she started modeling in New York.

In April 1995, however, Christy did shock the modeling and fashion worlds by announcing she was quitting the international catwalks that helped propel her into the supermodel pantheon. After several weeks of speculation as to her reasons for leaving—the most publicized one had it that she'd gotten fat—Turlington finally issued an explanation. Describing the shows as overhyped, the still-thin supermodel said she'd had enough of an atmosphere that "encourages fashion people to become critical, mean, and vicious."

Christy has even taken out the belly button ring she had implanted a few seasons back. She's hardly given up modeling. In fall 1995, Turlington appeared in ads for Max Mara, renewed and expanded her contracts with Calvin Klein and Maybelline, and signed a new deal with Japan's Shisheido Cosmetics. But she seems to be that rare model who can discern a difference between real life and that rare, glittery two-dimensional facsimile called fashion.

"I have chosen to remove myself from all that," Christy Turlington said. "You have to try and maintain some mystery, or people get bored."

EPILOGUE

May 1989: Marie Anderson Boyd, the vice president of the Chicago office of fashion modeling's largest agency, Elite, is sunbathing, listening to Springsteen on her Walkman during a break in a meeting of the company's corporate elite in Ibiza, where the firm's owners—Alain Kittler, Gérald Marie, and John Casablancas—all have summer homes. When the tape ends, the vacuum fills with the sound of Marie, Casablancas, and two of the company's top women executives, Lisa Herzog and Trudi Tapscott, having a vicious argument.

"We are men," snaps Marie. "We have our needs."

"C'mon Trudi, Lisa, relax," says an unruffled Casablancas.

This is disgusting. I'm outta here, thinks Anderson Boyd, who knows they are talking about sex with young girls. She will soon quit the agency.

January 2000: John Casablancas sat in his office, surrounded by raw wood, brown leather, and Southwestern textiles, a tape recorder running by his side. He didn't entirely trust me. He was still a little angry over this book. But something had changed. Casablancas, now nearly sixty, who initiated this chat, said he agreed with a lot of what I'd said on television a few nights earlier, during an interview about a BBC documentary that had just rocked the modeling business: hidden-camera footage of a drug sale to a teenager by a staffer at another agency; pimping of models in Milan; agency executives expressing racist views and pedophilic desires.

I had been cast as an enemy of Elite even before I wrote *Model.* "I am Linda Evangelista's husband, Paris is my town. If you write another word about me or my wife, you'll never take another step here," Gérald Marie said to me the night we first met at a party in Paris. Bob Zagury, an Elite investor, invited me for lunch at Brasserie Lipp, but showed up only for coffee and to say, "If you harm Elite, Elite will harm you." Casablancas threatened to sue to stop the book when it was first published.

But that is not what this meeting with Casablancas was about.

During the next half hour, he tacitly admitted to bad behavior (before his second marriage and the birth of his third and fourth children); called on Elite—and his industry—to clean itself up with strict, sensible standards; and distanced himself from his partners. He even vowed that if Elite did not shape up, he would sell his shares in the company he founded in 1971.

Hearing this unlikely hero break the fashion world's code of *omertà* took my breath away. Sure, it was a pre-emptive strike against the airing of the BBC program in America (though, in fact, it never was shown, after Elite argued—both in court and in the media—that it was selectively edited). But it is nonetheless fact that there is a fashion cabal that promotes itself and protects its members, especially those with big advertising budgets and those (such as model managers) deemed essential to the fashion process. When *Model* was published in France, an editor of a fashion magazine there told my publisher she would not mention it in her pages because Elite models were more important to her than acknowledging what was in the book. (After the BBC program aired, the same magazine ran an editorial professing to be shocked at the goings-on and demanding that things change.)

But now Casablancas wanted to speak out. He told me he thought it was time to clean up, and that he had sent a fax to his competitors the previous month, challenging everyone to do it together lest they each sink alone in the mire.

His proposed code of ethics was simple, though he admitted that some ideas would be hard to implement. The code would ban models from working regularly until they were sixteen; ban international travel without parental chaperones until age seventeen; institute a listing system for agencies "known for lenient attitudes toward drugs, drinking, and sexual promiscuity"; mandate the immediate termination of any agency employee who had sex with underage models or was involved in the use or sale of drugs; and require the immediate assignment of models with drug problems to rehabilitation programs, backed up by an agreement among agencies not to take on models who would rather switch managers than fight their addictions. "I find that repulsive, and I've done it; I've taken advantage of that type of situation," Casablancas admitted. "Because if you don't, someone else will."

Casablancas fit in. "It's a question of time in life," he said. "I'm not seeking re-
demption. I'm proud of the story of my life. I enjoyed it. I had a lot of fun. I
made money. I had prestige. I'm comfortable with what it was—with its
weaknesses."

Yet Casablancas had decided to go out a crusader.

"It's about time," said Marie Anderson Boyd, when I told her of his manifesto. She chuckled before asking: "Is he still with that wife? Good for him."

Nothing changed, of course, and John Casablancas did sell his shares in
Elite and retire from the model business a few weeks after giving that interview.
Then, in December 2000, Katie Ford, who'd effectively assumed control of
Ford Models in the mid-'90s, slowly inching her parents to the sidelines, sold
their business to Magnum Sports and Entertainment, Inc., a sports marketing
agency that was trying to become an IMG-like entity, combining sports, entertainment, and fashion. Corporate IMG had become the newly dominant force
in the modeling business, and in the wake of the retirements of the founding
mother and fathers of modern modeling, Ford and Elite became just two more
agencies, no longer the twin pillars of posing they once had been.

As always, agents and agencies came and went. Jerome Bonnouvrier formed
a new one in New York, DNA, which quickly established itself as a quirky,
Zoli-like boutique shop, run by his son David. Marilyn Gaulthier threw in her
lot with Dieter Esch at Wilhelmina, working out of his offices. Donald Trump,
the mogul and serial model-seducer, became the latest rich man to open his
own model shop, hiring one of Elite's top bookers away to run it. With the
playing field leveled, Trump's T Management and other little agencies like
Woman seemed more important than they actually were. And although owners and bookers of Company, 1 Management, and NY Models made the papers, their every movement tracked by a new batch of model-centric gossip
columns and Web sites, none of them attained the larger-than-life quality of
the Fords, Wilhelmina, and Casablancas in their heyday.

In fact, a sea change had hit modeling in 1996, and a shrunken model business seemed to remain the same for the next seven years—which, appropriately
enough, is the approximate length of a modeling "generation." Though new
faces still were dubbed supermodels before their test photographs were dry, in
that time only one true new supermodel emerged, Brazil's Gisele Bundchen,
whose bodacious body and odd, long-nosed visage made her heir to the lucrative Cindy Crawford/Claudia Schiffer franchise, appealing to both men and

women, to both the commercial and the high-fashion markets. At the start of the millennium, she stood at the pinnacle of modeling—alone.

In fall 2002, at the New York fashion shows, other putative modeling "stars" like Sophie Dahl, Caroline Murphy, Carmen Kass, Karolina Kurkova, and the compelling Jacquetta Wheeler walked the runways but gave off none of the excitement that a short time before had attended every twitch of a supermodel hip. Indeed, the few runway walks taken that season by Naomi Campbell and Amber Valletta were palpably thrilling, a reminder of the days not so long past when Crawford (now married and having children with her pre–Richard Gere beau, bar owner Rande Gerber), Linda Evangelista (whose comeback attempt a year earlier fizzled), Schiffer, Stella Tennant and Kate Moss (both sidelined by pregnancy), and Christy Turlington (who still sometimes models but seems far more focused on a new career as a purveyor of yoga-inspired clothes and ayurvedic skin-care products) seemed to rule the fashion world.

Like Gloria Swanson in *Sunset Boulevard,* those supermodels still seem big. It's modeling that's gotten smaller. But as with hemlines, which rise and fall like the tides, that's an almost certain sign that the next supermodel era is almost at hand.

—Michael Gross
New York City, October 2002

ACKNOWLEDGMENTS

I covered models, fashion, and fashion photography for a decade beginning in 1983 for *Photo District News,* the *East Side Express, Manhattan, inc., Vanity Fair, The New York Times,* and *New York.* Like the editors of each of those publications, William Morrow's Paul Bresnick saw that there are dramatic depths to these most superficial of subjects, and made it possible for me to plumb them.

Modeling owes Richard Avedon a great debt. So do I. He pointed out to me that no one had ever told the story of the trade in pretty people and suggested I write this book.

Thanks, too, are due to the biggest names in modeling. Eileen, Jerry, and Katie Ford endured long interview sessions that I'm sure they would have preferred to avoid *and* gave me private rundowns on everyone in the industry. John Casablancas talked a blue streak through several morning-long conversations and was more open than I had any right to expect. François Lano was gracious enough to spend several hours with me on two separate trips to Paris. Dorian Leigh Parker was a wonderful hostess for the three days I spent with her—and far-and-away the most interesting, complex person I met in the modeling world.

Many people sat for interviews with me in the ten years I wrote about models and the year when I wrote about little else. Some have not been mentioned in the book. A few preferred it that way, and a few made it a condition of cooperation. I thank them in their anonymity. For the record, most are currently active in the fashion business and are justifiably concerned about remaining so. The rest were left out inadvertently or because there simply wasn't space. Of those, I would particularly like to thank Susan Moncur and

Marie Helvin, whose careers are given short shrift here. That's because each of them has written her own book. Moncur's spare, impressionistic *They Still Shoot Models My Age* and Helvin's *Catwalk* are two of the best books by models on modeling. Naomi Sims's *How to Be a Top Model* is the best of many guidebooks available and was the source of most of the information on her pioneering career.

Some special people gave me special courtesy. Helen Rogers was my entrée to the world of modeling, her conventions a story I stumbled upon in 1982. She introduced me to Jérôme Bonnouvrier. His willingness to share memories of his family's thirty-five years in the modeling business was a gift. Suzy Parker Dillman is as delightful as she is different from her sister, Dorian. Polly Mellen is an inspiration always. Wilhelmina Cooper's family, particularly Melissa Cooper, and her stepmother, Judith Duncanson Cooper, allowed me into an attic full of Wilhelmina's belongings. More important was their desire to air the truth behind her legend. Judith Cooper also introduced me to Hannah Lee Sherman, who agreed to talk about her career for the first time since it ended almost sixty years ago.

Almost all my sources are cited in the text in a way that makes clear where information came from. Any quotations in the present tense (i.e., followed by "she says") were spoken directly to me. Quotations from previously published sources are attributed in the past tense (i.e., "she said"). In general, newspaper and magazine clippings are not cited in the text. Most of the clippings came from two newspaper morgues, at the New York *Post* and at the Harry Ranson Humanities Research Center at the University of Texas in Austin, where the morgue of the defunct New York *Journal-American* remains a living resource. The Ranson Center's Ken Craven deserves a special thanks. As the clippings often present or repeat unsourced information, I have tried to indicate in the text what may be exaggerated, one-sided, or apocryphal.

Only a few of the living key figures in the history of modeling refused to give interviews, or to update old ones. Bettina Graziani, Irving Penn, David Bailey, Twiggy Lawson, Jean Shrimpton, Bob Williamson, Arthur Elgort, Naomi Campbell, Linda Evangelista, Steven Meisel, Donna Broome, Terry Broome, Stephanie Seymour, Peter Brant, Jean-Pierre Dollé, Jacques Buchi and Claude Grangier of Models S.A. in Switzerland, Alan Finkelstein, Thierry Roussel, Penelope Tree, Alan Clore, Carlo Cabassi, and Patti Hansen all declined or didn't respond to requests for interviews. Riccardo Gay began one and then never completed it. China Machado, Giorgio Piazzi, Karl Lagerfeld, Bill Helburn, Justin de Villeneuve, Kelly Emberg, Ann Turkel, Tony

Spinelli, Susan Train, Peter Lindbergh, and Beverly Johnson all agreed to interviews that were never successfully arranged. Dorothea McGowan, Esme Marshall, Brian Duffy, Eileen Green, Cherry Marshall, Claudio Caccia, Giorgio Rotti, Pier Luigi Torri, Laura Royko, Joan Furboch, Lisa Vale, John Stember, Evelyn Tripp, and survivors of Walter Thornton and Sunny Harnett are believed to be living but could not be located.

However, hundreds of people in the world's four modeling centers—New York, Paris, London, and Milan—and beyond took time to see me, talk to me on the telephone, or, at the least, confirm facts about themselves. I'd like to thank Azzedine Alaïa, Pucci Albanese, Suzy Amis, Marie Anderson, Sara Foley-Anderson, Ruth Ansel, Jeff Aquilon, Douglas Asch, Laraine Ashton, Gloria and Valerie Askew, Kevyn Aucoin, Lisa Baker, Judy Baldwin, Mark Balet, Bryan Bantry, Gianpaolo Barbieri, Neal Barr, Lillian Bassman, Kenneth Battelle, Peter Beard, Simone d'Aillencourt Benezeraf, Chuck Bennett, Gilles Bensimon, Marisa Berenson, Nancy Berg, Jacques Bergaud, Pauline Bernatchez, Olivier Bertrand, Bernadette Reinhardt Bishop, Bernard Blanceneaux, Nina Blanchard, Bill Blass, Anthony Bloomfield, Jeff Blynn, Gillian Bobroff, Beth Boldt, Christine Bolster, Eric Boman, Ulla Bomser, David Bonnouvrier, Giselle Bonnouvrier, Tina Bossidy, Ingrid Boulting, Nancy Bounds and Mark Sconce, Patti Boyd, Mark Bozek, Dan Brennan, Bob Brenner, Christie Brinkley (and her assistant, Margot McNabb), Dana Brockman, Emerick Bronson, Barbara Brown, David Brown, Jean-Luc Brunel, Rose Bruner, Nan Bush, Jule Campbell, Umberto Caproni, Paul Caranicas, Christieve Carothers, Joyce Caruso, Tiziana Casali, Patrice Casanova, Shaun Casey, Oleg Cassini, Michel Castellano, Cindy Cathcart, Simon Chambers, Sue Charney, Jade Hobson Charnin, Alex Chatelain, Bennie Chavez, Servane Cherouat, Cheyenne, Jeanette Christjansen.

Willy Christy, Serene Cicora, Geraldine Frank Clark, Dennie Cody, Carol Conover, Harry Conover, Jr., Monique Corey, Bernie Cornfeld, Francine Counihan Okie, Stewart Cowley, Cindy Crawford, Mary Webb Davis, Kim Dawson, Jean-Marie de Gueldre, Inès de la Fressange, Jacques de Nointel, Barbara deWolf, Gerald Dearing, Dan Deely, Carmen Dell'Orefice, Patrick Demarchelier, Micki Denhoff, Louise Despointes, Cathy di Montezemolo, Richard di Pietro, Martine Diacenco, Debbie Dickinson, Janice Dickinson, Lorraine Dillon, Clay Deering Dilworth, Guido Dolce, Terence Donovan, Betty McLauchlen Dorso, Sarah Doukas, April Ducksbury, Giuliana Ducret, Mary Duffy, Diana Edkins at the Condé Nast Archive, Bernadette Marciano Ellinger, Dieter and Natasha Esch, Jinx Falkenburg, Ed Feldman, Fabrizio

Ferri, Bob Fertig, Christa Fiedler, Michael Flutie, José Fonseca, Fernand Fonssagrives, Susan Forristal, Juli Foster, Jeremy Foster-Fell, Judith Foster-Fell, Bob Frame, Dottie Franco, Edward Gainsley, Marcella Galdi, Colette Gambier.

Marilyn Gaulthier, Diane Gérald, Marco Glaviano, Richard Golub, Jan Gonet, Wynne Gordine-Dalley, Sunny Griffin, Frances Grill, Brigitte Grosjean, Lisa Gubernick, Lucy Angle Guercio, Jean-François Guille, Sean Gunson, Claude Haddad, Anthony Haden-Guest, Paul Hagnauer, Maarit Halinen, Chad Hall, Jerry Hall (and her assistant, Jane Hayes), Jane Halleran, Shirley Hamilton, Celia Hammond, Beth Ann Hardison, Huntington Hartford, Juliet Hartford, Ellen Harth, Bonnie Haydon, Charles Haydon, Will Helburn, Guy Héron, Astrid Herrene, Steve Hiett, Jane Hitchcock, Horst P. Horst, Jane Hsiang, Marion Hume, Joe Hunter, Lauren Hutton (and her assistant, Dee Galucci), Pippa Imrie, Just Jaeckin, Stanley Juba, Leslie Kark, Faith Kates, Lizette Kattan, Harry King, Sally Kirkland, Alain Kittler, William Klein, Polly Ferguson Knaster, Bitten Knudsen, Paul Kopp, Lee Kraft, Ewing Krainin, Gene Krell, Karin Mossberg LaMotte, Judy Lane, Stéphane Lanson, Barbara Lantz, Roberto Lanzotti, Barry Lategan, Estée Lauder, Leonard Lauder, Guy Le Baube, Kim LeManton.

Michel Levaton, Angie Lewis, Alexander Liberman, Freddie Lieba, Gunilla Lindblad, Christine Lindgren, Jean Louis, Gene Loyd, Peter Hope Lumley, Gillis MacGil, Robert MacLeod, Francesca Magugliani, Jacques Malignon, Nikki Maniscalco, Gérald Marie, Irene Marie, Fabienne Martin, Jo Matthews, Mark McCormack, Tex McCrary, Eric McGrath, Bob McKeon, Peggy McKinley, Nando Miglio, Iris Minier, Grace Mirabella, Donna Mitchell, Kay Mitchell, Robbie Montgomery, Linda Morand, Barbara Mullen Morel, Daniel Moriarty, Gara Morse, Kate Moss, Jean-Jacques Naudet, Ruth Neumann Derujinsky, S. I. Newhouse, Jr., Bruce Oldfield, Livia Rendessy Oliver, Natálie Nickerson Paine, Sir Mark Palmer, Tom Palumbo, Dorothy Parker and Sebastien Sed, Norman Parkinson, Jean Patchett, Lorenzo Pedrini, Giuseppe and Patrizia Piazzi.

Hervé Picard, Betsy Pickering Kaiser, Monique Pillard, Aldo Pinto, Jan Kaplan Planit, Giorgio Poli, Michele Pommier, Paulina Porizkova, Jean-Michel Pradwilov, Vickie Pribble, Roger Prigent, Craig Pyes, Karen Radkai, Charles Rainey, Juan Ramos, Abel Rapp, Mike Reinhardt, Giorgio Repossi, Matthew Rich, Bob Richardson, Herb Ritts, Jeni Rose, David Rosenzweig, Isabella Rossellini, Fran Rothschild, Chris Royer, Edward and Mary Jane Russell, D. D. Ryan, Giorgio Sant'Ambrogio, Odile Sarron, Percy Savage, Francesco Scavullo, Jerry Schatzberg, Giuseppe della Schiava, Claudia Schiffer,

Barbara Schlager, Mark Sconce, Chelita Secunda, Tara Shannon, Jacques Silberstein, Steven Silverberg, Babs Simpson, Victor Skrebneski, Sarah Slavin, Marion Smith.

Shelley Smith, Jerrold Smockler, Lynn Snowden, Evelyn Kuhn Sokolsky, Melvin Sokolsky, Mia Fonssagrives Solow, Franca Sozzani, Richard Stein, Norma Stephens, Bert Stern, Eleanor Stinson, Don Stogo, Dick and Barbara Thorbahn Stone, Peter Strongwater, Constance Stumin, Geraldine Stutz, Massimo Tabak, Richard Talmadge, Trudi Tapscott, Dick Tarlow, Lisa Taylor, Ingo Thouret, Alberta Tiburzi, Tichka, Cheryl Tiegs (and her assistant, Barbara Shapiro), Elizabeth Tilberis, Reeshe Tivnan, Beatrice Traissac, Sarah Trimble, Christy Turlington, Barbara Tyler, Apollonia van Ravenstein, Mary Anne van Sickle, Auro Varani, Rosie Vela, Vera "Veruschka" von Lehndoff, Edward von Saher, Ellen von Unwerth, Gaby Wagner, Paul Wagner, John Warren, Ben Washington, Veronica Webb, Bruce Weber, Bill Weinberg, John Weitz, Lenno Wells, Preston Westenburg, Anna Wintour, Marysia Woronieka, Dan Wynn, Jean-Pierre Zachariasen, and Rusty Zeddis.

Finally, thanks to my agent, Ellen Levine, and Ann Dubuisson and Diana Finch of her office; my fashion rabbi, Bernadine Morris; Fabien Baron, who designed a cover with both impact and grace; picture editor Philip Gefter; photographer's agent Pamela Reed; Bill Tonelli of *Esquire* magazine, who helped wrestle the manuscript into shape; my assistant, Stephanie Frank; transcriber Jean Brown; researchers Emma Beal in London (and Miles Chapman, who found her), Cecile Bloc-Rodot in Paris (and Alexis DuClos), Chris Lynch in Milan (and Richard Buckley); and interns Dorian May, Tim Kitchen, Vanessa Richardson, and Allegra Abramo.

And for care, feeding, and otherwise tending to my needs, thanks to Jerry Simon Chasen, Kee and Lee Neidringhaus, Zoe Beresford, Peter Waldman, Thom O'Dwyer, Jane Proctor, Gene Gutowski, and Lisa Eveleigh; Lyssa Horn, Claude Roland, Jim Haynes, Pamela Hanson and George Klarsfeld, Katell Le Bourhis, and Christy and J. P. Sadron; Fabrizio Ferri, Lisa Immordino, and Kim Clyde of Industria; Gerlinde and Eduardo Guelfenbein, Marpessa Hennink, Giorgio Guidotti, Giulio Viggi, Giorgio and Lavinia Cesana, Noona Smith-Peterson, Gabriella Forte, Romeo Gigli, Grazia d'Annunzio, Nando Miglio, Tom Ford and Karla Otto; Andre Balazs, Janis Kaye French, Peter Herbst, Eric Pooley, Mary Michele Rutherfurd, Christine Biddle and Michael Millius, Holly Solomon, Margery Goldberg, Maury Rogoff, Scott Manning, Ted Savaglio, and Susan Wiggins.

BIBLIOGRAPHY

Aitken, Jonathan. *The Young Meteors*. New York: Atheneum, 1967.

Anderson, Marie P. *Model: The Complete Guide to Becoming a Professional Model*. New York: Doubleday, 1989.

Avedon, Richard. *Photographs 1947–1977*. New York: Farrar, Straus & Giroux, 1978.

———. *An Autobiography*. New York: Random House, Eastman Kodak, 1993.

———. *Evidence 1944–1994*. New York: Random House, Eastman Kodak, 1994.

Bailey, David, and Peter Evans. *Goodbye Baby & Amen: A Saraband for the Sixties*. New York: Coward-McCann, 1969.

Bain, Donald. *The Control of Candy Jones*. Chicago: Playboy Press, 1976.

Balhorn, Linda A. *The Professional Model's Handbook*. New York: Milady, 1990.

Batterberry, Michael and Ariane. *Fashion: The Mirror of History*. New York: Greenwich House, 1977.

Boucher, Françoise. *20,000 Years of Fashion*. New York: Harry N. Abrams, 1965.

Carmen. *Staying Beautiful*. New York: Harper & Row, 1985.

Cassini, Oleg. *In My Own Fashion: An Autobiography*. New York: Pocket, 1987.

Castle, Charles. *Model Girl*. London: David & Charles, 1977.

Coleridge, Nicholas. *The Fashion Conspiracy*. New York: Harper & Row, 1988.

Condé Nast Publications. *On the Edge, Images from 100 Years of Vogue*. New York: Random House, 1992.

Conover, Carole. *Cover Girls: The Story of Harry Conover*. New York: Prentice-Hall, 1978.

Cooper, Wilhelmina. *The New You*. New York: Simon & Schuster, 1978.

Demarchelier, Patrick. *Fashion Photography*. New York: Little, Brown, 1989.

Dessner, Clyde Matthew. *So You Want to Be a Model!* Garden City, N.Y.: Halcyon House, 1948.

Devlin, Polly. Vogue *Book of Fashion Photography: The First Sixty Years.* New York: Quill, 1979.

Di Grapp, Carol, ed. *Fashion: Theory.* New York: Lustrum, 1980.

Ewing, Wiliam A. *The Photographic Art of Hoyningen-Huene.* New York: Rizzoli, 1986.

Farber, Robert. *The Fashion Photographer.* New York: Amphoto, 1981.

Fried, Stephen. *Thing of Beauty: The Tragedy of Supermodel Gia.* New York: Pocket Books, 1993.

Das Gewissen Steht Auf (Conscience on the Rise). Mainz: V. Haise & Koehler, 1984.

Graziani, Bettina. *Bettina by Bettina.* London: Michael Joseph, 1963.

Grundberg, Andy. *Brodovitch.* New York: Harry N. Abrams, 1989.

Gubernick, Lisa Rebecca. *Squandered Fortune: The Life and Times of Huntington Hartford.* New York: Putnam, 1991.

Hall-Duncan, Nancy. *The History of Fashion Photography.* New York: Alpine, 1979.

Harrison, Martin. *Shots of Style.* London: Victoria and Albert Museum, 1985.

————. *Appearances.* New York: Rizzoli, 1991.

Hearst Corporation. *125 Great Moments of* Harper's Bazaar. New York: Hearst, 1993.

Helvin, Marie. *Catwalk: The Art of Model Style.* London: Pavilion Michael Joseph, 1985.

Jones, Lesley-Ann. *Naomi: The Rise and Rise of the Girl from Nowhere.* London: Vermilion, 1993.

Keenan, Brigid. *The Women We Wanted to Look Like.* London: Macmillan, 1977.

Kenmore, Carolyn. *Mannequin: My Life as a Model.* New York: Bartholomew, 1969.

Klein, William. *In and out of Fashion.* London: Jonathan Cape, 1994.

Koch, H. W. *Volksgerichthof (People's Court).* Munich: Universitas Press, 1988.

Lawford, Valentine. *Horst: His Work and His World.* New York: Knopf, 1984.

Lehndorff, Vera, and Holger Trülsch. *Veruschka, Trans-figurations.* New York: New York Graphic Society, 1986.

Leigh, Dorian, with Laura Hobe. *The Girl Who Had Everything.* New York: Doubleday, 1980.

Leproux, Beatrice. *Mannequins à Contre-jour.* Paris: Balland, 1990.

Liaut, Jean-Noël. *Modèles & Mannequins, 1945–1965.* Paris: Filipacchi, 1994.

Lloyd, Valerie. *The Art of* Vogue *Photographic Covers.* New York: Harmony, 1986.

McDowell, Colin. *McDowell's Directory of Twentieth Century Fashion.* London: Frederick Muller, 1984.

Mellor, Dr. David, ed. *Cecil Beaton: A Retrospective.* New York: New York Graphic Society, 1986.

Milbank, Caroline Rennolds. *Couture: The Great Designers.* New York: Stewart, Tabori & Chang, 1985.

Moffitt, Peggy, and William Claxton. *The Rudi Gernreich Book.* New York: Rizzoli International, 1991.

Moncur, Susan. *They Still Shoot Models My Age.* London: Serpent's Tail, 1991.

O'Hara, Georgina. *The Encyclopedia of Fashion.* New York: Harry N. Abrams, 1986.

Parkinson, Norman. *Fifty Years of Style and Fashion.* New York: Vendome, 1983.

Penn, Irving. *Passages.* New York: Knopf/Callaway, 1991.

Penrose, Antony. *The Lives of Lee Miller.* London: Thames and Hudson, 1985.

Perutz, Kathrin. *Beyond the Looking Glass: America's Beauty Culture.* New York: William Morrow, 1970.

Powers, John Robert. *The Powers Girls.* New York: E. P. Dutton, 1941.
————. *How to Have Model Beauty, Poise and Personality:* Englewood Cliffs, N.J.: Prentice Hall, 1960.

Ray, Man. *In Fashion.* New York: International Center of Photography, 1990.
————. *Self-Portrait.* Boston: New York Graphic Society, 1988.
————. *Bazaar Years.* New York: Rizzoli, 1988.

Ross, Josephine. *Beaton in Vogue.* New York: Clarkson Potter, 1986.

Scavullo, Francesco. *Scavullo.* New York: Harper & Row, 1984.

Seebohm, Caroline. *The Man Who Was* Vogue: *The Life and Times of Condé Nast.* New York: Viking, 1982.

Shirer, William L. *The Rise and Fall of the Third Reich.* New York: Simon & Schuster, 1960.

Shrimpton, Jean. *The Truth About Modeling.* London: W. H. Allen, 1964.
————. *An Autobiography.* London: Sphere, 1991.

Sims, Naomi. *How to Be a Top Model.* New York: Doubleday, 1989.

Stegemeyer, Anne. *Who's Who in Fashion.* New York: Fairchild, 1988.

Steichen, Edward. *A Life in Photography.* Garden City: Doubleday, 1963.

Thurlow, Valerie. *Model in Paris.* London: Robert Hale, 1975.

Tobias, Andrew. *Fire and Ice.* New York: Warner, 1975.

Twiggy. *Twiggy, an Autobiography.* London: Hart–Davis, MacGibben, 1975.

Vreeland, Diana. *D. V.* New York: Knopf, 1984.

Weitz, John. *Hitler's Diplomat.* New York: Ticknor & Fields, 1992.

Wolfe, Tom. *The Kandy-Kolored Tangerine-Flake Streamline Baby.* New York: Noonday, 1973.

PHOTO CREDITS

INDEX

Palumbo, Tom, 226–228
Paola, 493
Paolozzi, Christina, 250
Papadakis, Jovanna, 196, 197, 198
Paper, 443
Parents, 318
Paris Match, 109, 137, 204
Paris Planning, 202–204, 207, 208, 246, 259, 266, 267, 279, 282, 283, 286, 287, 291, 292, 300, 302, 306, 384–386, 395–398, 399, 402, 407, 428, 465
Parker, Dorothy, 307, 360, 382, 461–462, 467
Parker, Elizabeth Dorian Leigh, *see* Leigh, Dorian
Parker, Suzy, 75, 86, 108, 114–122, *115*, 137, 196, 206, 332
    Avedon and, 102, 107, 114, 118, 119–120, 121
    in car accident, 113, 120
    fees and income of, 105, 109
    first name of, 114–116
    Ford Models and, 101, 105–106
    Georgia, daughter of, 118, 121
    Leigh and, 101–102, 103, 105, 111, 119–120
    as photographer, 109–110, 118
    Pitou and, 109–113, 117–118, 120–121
Parkinson, Norman, 78, 91, 103, *148*, 153, 154, 156, 157, 165, 167, *299*
    career of, 163–164
Parsons, Louella, 112
Passport, 279
Patcévitch, Iva, 223
Patchett, Jean, 85, 86, 87–91, *89*, 92, 95, 96, 107
Patitz, Tatjana, *150*, 412, 435
Patou, Jean, 40, 44–46, 141
Patrini, Maximiliano, 285
Paul, Sondra, *201*
Paul Wagner, 197, 248
Peck, Cecilia, 493–494
Peck, Tony, 335, 370
Pedrini, Lorenzo, 389
Penn, Irving, 78, 86, 88–90, 102, 103, 110, 132, 153, 172, 189, 199, 223, 230, 238, 255, 294, 298, 324, 355, 421, 432
    Fonssagrives and, 84–85
    Leigh and, 82–83, 107
People, 26, 313, 387, 437, 438
Peterson, Gösta, 235
Peterson, Pat, 235
Peterson, Sondra, *201*
Petrie, Milton, 111
Photo, 299
Piazzi, Giorgio, 277, 363, 373, 375, 377, 387–389
Piazzi, Giuseppe, 387, 389, 390–391, 393, 395, 396
Piazzi, Patrizia, 390, 395
Picasso, Paloma, 294
Pickering, Betsy, 128–129, 146
Piel, Dennis, 417
Pillard, Monique, 14, 17, 21, 24, 308, 309–312, 322, 323, 328–329, 351–352, 367, 370, 371, 396, 397, 408, 409, 420, 421, 441, 460–461, 497
Piroddi, Beppe, 374, 392
Pitou (Pierre De La Salle), 109–113
Planit, Jan Kaplan, 477
Playboy, 10, 23, 25, 192, 360, 421, 475
Plaza Five, 128, 131, 136, 149, 197, 217, 276
Poiret, Denise, 39

Poiret, Paul, 39
Poitier, Suki, 175
Polanski, Roman, 287, 365
Pollack, Alice, 176
Pommier, Michele, 415
Porizkova, Paulina, 12, 346, 412, 418–421, *419*, 458
Portago, Carroll de, *see* McDaniel, Carroll
Portago, Marquis de "Fon," 111–112
Portfolio, 107
Power, Tyrone, 37, 112
Power of Myth, The (Campbell), 443
Powers, John Robert, 2, 10, *33*, 38, 54, 59, 62, 95, 97, 103, 123, 128, 132
    agency of, *see* John Robert Powers
    death of, 61
    Dorso and, 35–36
    head book issued by, 34
    modeling "invented" by, 31–34, 36
    radio show of, 60
Powers Girls, The (Power), 60
Pradwilov, Jean Michel, 480, 504
Prebble, Dorothy, 242
Premier (agency), 462
Prestige (agency), 463
Pribble, Vickie, 249, 250, 356, 358, 381–382
Prigent, Roger, 105, 228, 282
Privilege, 172
Prouvost, Jean, 139
Prue, Edwina, 40
Pucci, Emilio, 109, 233
Pugh, Bronwen, 138–139
Punderford, James C., Jr., 123, 126, 127
Puzzle of a Downfall Child, 230
Pyes, Craig, 462, 468–469, 471

Quant, Mary, 166, 173
Queen, 153, 156, 167, 179
Qui Étes-Vous, Polly Magoo, 29, 151

Radkai, Karen, 228
Radziwill, Lee, 333
Rainey, Charles, 34–35, 59, 60, 61
Ramella, Elisabetta, 494
Ramos, Juan, 293–294, 297, 300
Randolph, Gwen, 231
Rappetti, Franco, 373
Rau, André, 407, 428
Ravenstein, Apollonia van, 256, *257*, 261, 264, 267–268, 314, 360, 382
Rawlings, John, *71*, 78, 82, 87, 102, 163
Ray, Man, 39, 41, 42, 77
Raymond, Edith, 128
Raynes, Martin, 346
"Rayographs," 39
ready-to-wear clothing, 96, 376
Rees, Tom, 123
Reinhardt, Mike, 255, 265, 279, 281–282, 283, 313, 314, 317, 318, 319, 328, 329, 367
Reinhardt, Tammi, 317
Rendessy, Zoltan, *see* Zoli
Rendlesham, Clare, 170
Reno, Hunter, 452–453
Repossi, Giorgio, 373, 374–375, 377, 378, 386, 389, 391